Yale and Slavery

Yale and Slavery

A HISTORY

David W. Blight
with the Yale and Slavery Research Project

Foreword by Peter Salovey

Yale UNIVERSITY PRESS
New Haven & London

Published with assistance from the Office of the President, Yale University.

Published with assistance from the income of the
Frederick John Kingsbury Memorial Fund.

Published with assistance from the foundation established in
memory of Calvin Chapin of the Class of 1788, Yale College.

Foreword by Peter Salovey.
Introduction; Chapters 1, 2, 3, 4, 5, 7, 8, 9, and 12; "Birth of a Nation in New Haven, 1915"; Epilogue; and Acknowledgments by David W. Blight.
Chapter 6 by Michael Morand.
Chapters 10 and 11 and "Gradual Emancipation," "A Yale Family," and "Black Employees" by Hope McGrath.

Yale University Press books may be purchased in quantity for educational, business, or promotional use. For information, please e-mail sales.press@yale.edu (U.S. office) or sales@yaleup.co.uk (U.K. office).

Set in Garamond Premier type by Westchester Publishing Services.
Printed in the United States of America.

Library of Congress Control Number: 2023946263

ISBN 978-0-300-27384-7 (hardcover : alk. paper)

A catalogue record for this book is available from the British Library.
This paper meets the requirements of ANSI/NISO Z39.48-1992 (Permanence of Paper).

10 9 8 7 6 5 4 3 2 1

To Jethro, Ruth, Mindwell, Gad, Rose, and Ame Luke,
builders of Yale

(Open your eyes and ears to every fact connected with the actual condition of slavery everywhere—but do not talk about it—hear and see everything but say little).

—BENJAMIN SILLIMAN SR.,
professor of chemistry and natural history at Yale, to his research collaborator Charles Upham Shepard, giving instructions on how to conduct their study of the sugar industry in Louisiana in 1833

Contents

Foreword

Yale's history, from its founding in 1701, in many ways mirrors the broad and complex history of the United States. Five U.S. presidents graduated from Yale's undergraduate or graduate schools, and eighteen U.S. Supreme Court justices studied at the university. Others who attended Yale have become leading scientists, scholars, artists, educators, clinicians, business executives, and policymakers. Yet Yale's deep participation in the U.S. narrative also means that—from its beginnings until well into the twenty-first century—Yale has been part of an uglier side of the American story.

That more painful part of U.S. history came to the fore yet again in 2020, following repeated acts of intentional or thoughtless brutality against Black Americans, which in turn spurred a national reckoning over pervasive racism in U.S. society. We at Yale had been grappling with some of these issues and knew that our university, as an American institution more than three centuries old, had a past that included associations, many of them formative, with individuals who actively promoted slavery, anti-Black racism, and other forms of exploitation. As an academic community devoted to truth and knowledge, we also knew that we had a responsibility to explore this history more deeply.

With that in mind, I reached out to Pulitzer Prize–winning Yale historian David W. Blight, one of the world's experts on the history of slavery, abolition, and their memorialization. I asked Professor Blight to organize and lead a team to explore our institution's ties to slavery and racism, and to research, understand, analyze, and communicate that history. I was pleased that he not only accepted the proposal but fully embraced it: he asked to research and write not a scholarly report for a narrow audience but a narrative account that would engage readers across a broad spectrum of backgrounds and interests.

Professor Blight was joined in this work by members of the Yale and Slavery Working Group, which includes other distinguished Yale professors, staff members, archivists, student researchers, and community members. They in turn learned much from the broader New Haven community; from generations of previous scholars on Yale, New Haven, slavery, and national history; and perhaps foremost from the work of many individuals who, since the university's earliest days, retained and managed Yale's voluminous archives, ensuring that certain knowledge, while neglected, was not extinguished. To all of those who helped, I am grateful.

You have in your hands the result of those efforts. As you read the pages that follow, you will learn about the enslaved individuals who contributed to the building of Yale both directly and indirectly. Most of Yale's Puritan founders owned enslaved people, as did a significant number of Yale's early leaders and other prominent members of the university community, and we have identified over two hundred of these enslaved people. Some of the enslaved were vital in the construction of Connecticut Hall, the oldest building on campus. Others were forced to endure grueling labor—in sugar factories, rum refineries, cotton fields, and countless other unimaginably harsh places—to benefit businesspeople who helped fund Yale's growth.

Other aspects of Yale's history are also illuminated in this account, from the failed attempt to build a college in New Haven for Black youth in 1831, to the Yale Civil War memorial that equally honors those who fought for the North and the South—without any mention of slavery. Even celebratory stories from this era reveal deep suffering. Edward Bouchet, the first African American ever to obtain a PhD in the United States, earned that honor at Yale in 1876. He was the sixth person of any background or race to earn a doctorate in physics from an American university. In addition, he had been a distinguished undergraduate at Yale. However, when he later applied to teach at Yale in 1905—with an enthusiastic reference from Arthur W. Wright, an eminent Yale professor of experimental physics—he was denied that opportunity. Bouchet died in New Haven and was buried in a grave that remained unmarked until 1998.

Few historians are better suited to take on the task of telling this upsetting, enlightening narrative than Professor Blight, Sterling Professor of History and director of the Gilder Lehrman Center for the Study of Slavery, Resistance, and

Abolition at Yale. Professor Blight is the author or editor of a dozen books, including *American Oracle: The Civil War in the Civil Rights Era*; *Race and Reunion: The Civil War in American Memory*; and *A Slave No More: Two Men Who Escaped to Freedom, Including Their Own Narratives of Emancipation*. He has been awarded the Bancroft Prize, the Lincoln Prize, and the Frederick Douglass Book Prize, among others. And he won a Pulitzer Prize for his monumental biography, *Frederick Douglass: Prophet of Freedom*, about that great American born into slavery who escaped to become the country's foremost Black abolitionist.

The unsettling narrative Professor Blight and his team have produced can be read simply as a story about Yale. It can also be understood as a story that has commonalities with those of countless other American institutions, including more than ninety universities across the country that have undertaken similar efforts as part of the Universities Studying Slavery consortium. Former Brown University president Ruth Simmons deserves particular praise and appreciation, as she led the way by commissioning a 2006 report on Brown's ties to slavery. Together, these studies are part of even wider efforts to uncover and address the deep history of racism and its ongoing repercussions across the United States.

This vital work is far from done; there remains much to be accomplished in the years ahead, both in revealing and coming to terms with injustices of the past and in confronting current wrongs. But the Yale team has provided us with a deeper, more honest understanding of who we are and how we got here—a necessary foundation from which to build a stronger, more knowledgeable, and more vibrant university and society.

—PETER SALOVEY, President of Yale University, August 1, 2023

Introduction

To summon the presences of, or recollect the absences of slaves . . .

—TONI MORRISON, 1988

A multitude of Yale University's founders, rectors, early presidents, faculty, donors, and graduates played roles in sustaining slavery, its ideological underpinnings, and its power. Yale also nurtured some in its first two centuries who opposed, strove to destroy, and even fought against slavery and its power. Along with Connecticut and New England generally, Yale developed a decidedly conservative to moderate approach to national contradictions, to reform, and to the maintenance of the social order. As did the nation, so did Yale grow in prestige and power as it relied on the unrecognized labor of Black people, enslaved and free, to create and sustain this most American institution in the heart of New Haven. Black and Native American peoples who were displaced by war and conquest, enslaved and free, have been active agents in making and sustaining the institution in New Haven. They played increasingly important historical roles in the making of Yale as employees, as neighbors, and eventually as students. Yale's entanglements with racialized chattel slavery leave haunting shadows on its campus, in its hometown, and in its archives.

With this book, we seek to bring these shadows into the light, to face them, and to expose a past the university has been all too willing to avoid. Above all, we wish to write a history of documented memory, a history that humbly makes an offering to knowledge, which is an essential mission of a university. We make no righteous claims except to seek truth and tell a story that may both inform and motivate readers to know more and do better. Benjamin Silliman's counsel to his research partner, which forms the book's epigraph, has been our guiding counterexample: we have endeavored to open our "eyes and ears to every fact connected with the actual condition of slavery" and its aftermaths on campus and in the New Haven community, and to communicate honestly about what we have discovered.

Avishai Margalit, a philosopher of the ethics of memory, concludes that "even the project of remembering the gloomiest of memories is a hopeful project." Probing the genuine tragedies in the past, the slow unfolding of our species' inhumanity as well as its humane counteractions and stories, says Margalit, "rejects the pessimist thought that all will be forgotten." So much of the past is irretrievable, just beyond the grasp of the most up-to-date research tools; it can be terrifying to contemplate what in experience has been lost. But much is also waiting for us in plain sight when we ask the right questions and doggedly search for the threads that can be woven into a coherent fabric. Yale's association with slavery is a case, decidedly, where the archives are not silent. And stories have moral meanings as well as mere plots or narrative turns. "Why ought humanity remember moral nightmares rather than moments of human triumph—moments in which human beings behaved nobly?" asks Margalit. Because, he contends, "the issue for us to sort out is what humanity ought to remember rather than what is good for humanity to remember."[1] Human impulse often draws us to the good, the pleasing or uplifting tale, especially as institutions tell their story to successive generations who feel an irresistible need to venerate family, country, religion, university, hometown, or simply a narrative within which they wish to live. The *ought* takes hard work, acts of will, of conscience, and of imagination. The good might yet flow from the ought if openly faced.

In September 2020, in the depths of the COVID-19 pandemic and at the end of a summer of protests and the resurgence of the Black Lives Matter movement, established first in 2013 and growing internationally after the killing of George Floyd in Minneapolis by a police officer in May 2020, President Peter Salovey called me to ask if I would lead a research project and write a report on Yale's historical roles in and associations with slavery over time. Throughout the project, President Salovey and his office have offered strong institutional and public support. Among many other questions, President Salovey wanted to learn "who built Yale." In the fall of 2020, I immediately began pulling together a working group of faculty, library and other staff, New Haven community members, student researchers, and key staff at the Gilder Lehrman Center for the Study of Slavery, Resistance, and Abolition, the oldest such research center dedicated to the subject in the world, founded in 1998. Over the next year, amid all manner of pandemic obstacles, we hosted at least a half dozen webinars with faculty at other universities conducting similar studies, students, alumni, and Black descendants of early Yale graduates. We convened a prominent panel of scholarly and political experts on the subject of comparative reparations in recent modern history. As chair of the working group, I conducted online conversations about the project with various alumni, student, New Haven community, and faculty emeriti groups. Then we organized an online conference, introduced by President Salovey and keynoted by Elizabeth Alexander, president of the Mellon Foundation, and Jonathan Holloway, president of Rutgers University, both with deep ties to Yale and its history. That conference garnered one of the largest online audiences for a scholarly and public history conference ever held at Yale; it tackled all manner of subjects, from the arts and iconography to the West Indian trade in the eighteenth century and to the leadership and theology of eighteenth-century Puritans and New Haven Black churches. The 2021 gathering exposed some key events and people, such as the near but failed creation of America's first Black college in New Haven in 1831 and connections between Benjamin Silliman's scientific work and slavery. The conference also featured student presentations about the history of science and its entanglements with race and slavery. Finally, the meeting included a valuable panel with researchers and librarians on "finding slavery in the archives."[2] The conference left many people hungering for more information and for the book we announced we were writing. It left those of us in the Yale and Slavery Working Group daunted but inspired.

President Salovey's impetus in 2020 was a response, in part, to America's latest racial reckoning. These issues were not new to him, nor were they to Yale. At the end of the summer of 2015, he and then-dean of Yale College Jonathan Holloway both addressed the new first-year students in their opening assembly by discussing at length the June massacre in Charleston, South Carolina, of nine African Americans at Emanuel African Methodist Episcopal Church during a prayer meeting. The victims included that church's revered head pastor, Clementa Pinckney, who was also a South Carolina state senator in his native state. The murderer was a young avowed neo-Confederate and white supremacist who posted his racist beliefs and intentions on the internet. President Salovey announced that during the coming academic year, 2015–16, Yale would conduct a campus conversation about the eighty-two-year-old use of the name on one of its residential colleges—John C. Calhoun. The Charleston murders, in the wake of the well-publicized shootings of Trayvon Martin, Tamir Rice, and others, shocked the country. A grieving President Barack Obama tried to understand their meaning, as did thousands of others in local, difficult discussions, including a public panel held at Yale that September, sponsored by the Gilder Lehrman Center.[3] The unspeakable violence and the vivid realities of white supremacy burst into American consciousness once again. History never stands still, and it always holds the capacity to shock us.

President Salovey's decision to launch the Yale and Slavery Research Project in 2020 had longer lineages in the Yale community. In 2001, three Yale graduate students, Antony Dugdale, J. J. Fueser, and J. Celso de Castro Alves, wrote a report, *Yale, Slavery and Abolition*, published by the New Haven–based Amistad Committee, as a response to the celebratory commemoration of the university's three hundredth anniversary that year. As an effective counter to the claims made about Yale's modest antislavery heritage, the three students' research demonstrated with detail that eight of the original ten residential colleges established in the early 1930s and one in the 1960s were named for slaveholders. Written respectfully, but also in the midst of a bitter labor dispute between the graduate assistants' union and the university, the report used sources from Yale's own libraries. It garnered a great deal of publicity nationally and consternation locally within a largely unknowing Yale community.[4]

In 2002, Yale president Richard Levin, in conjunction with dean of the Yale Law School Anthony Kronman and the Gilder Lehrman Center, sponsored a conference that took on the questions of slavery in New England and the North, its legal foundations, and its role at Yale and other universities. At that point research on these subjects was relatively nascent. That conference avoided fundamental confrontations with Yale's own history. The Gilder Lehrman Center continued in the ensuing years to host hundreds of research fellows, sponsor the annual Frederick Douglass Book Prize, organize dozens of lectures and an annual major conference, and conduct outreach to schools and secondary school teachers in a myriad of summer institutes and monthly gatherings.[5] Down to that time the Gilder Lehrman Center had rarely focused inwardly on its home institution. The center's purpose had always been to study the problem of slavery and its legacies across all borders and all time, and to take any such knowledge and teaching outside its institutional and national boundaries to the wider world. The internal Yale history awaited later imperatives and events.

Near the end of the 2016 academic year, Yale announced the much-anticipated names of two new residential colleges, one for Pauli Murray, celebrated Black lawyer, Episcopal priest, and author, and the other for American founder Benjamin Franklin. At the same time, causing enormous controversy, President Salovey and the Yale Corporation, the university's board of trustees, announced the retention of the Calhoun name on Calhoun College. They argued that it was best to retain and use Calhoun's legacy on issues of race and slavery for the purpose of teaching and learning, an argument that did not hold up well in an environment of roiling conflict over all things related to proslavery thought, white supremacy, and Confederate memorialization. Yale students especially organized creative and concerted protests in response to these decisions. President Salovey soon appointed a committee of faculty, alumni, staff, and both undergraduate and graduate students, chaired by professor of law and history John Fabian Witt, to study and propose "principles" by which a university might justly and effectively rename existing buildings, sites, or institutions. President Salovey and the trustees sought a deliberative process, in line with the meaning of a university, through which to make sensitive decisions about naming and other powerful symbols. Some in the Yale community were impatient with this process and advocated for a prompter resolution to the decades-old issue of Calhoun's troubling legacies.[6]

After four months of deliberation and public conversation, the "Report of the Committee to Establish Principles on Renaming" announced a method of application and of administrative action, as well as three essential principles through which any proposed name change must pass. First, renaming on account of institutional values should happen only under the presumption of a rare, exceptional event. Two, renaming is sometimes warranted and can proceed based on the stated values and the "mission" of the university. The authority making the decision must seek through research the "principal legacy" of the person under review. And third, any renaming entails the obligation of nonerasure, contextualization, and careful process. Based on the methodology of the renaming report, the university officially renamed Calhoun College on February 11, 2017, for Grace Murray Hopper, famed computer scientist, software pioneer, inventor of technical languages, and longtime U.S. Navy officer who retired at the rank of rear admiral. Hopper earned an MA in mathematics in 1930 and a PhD in mathematics in 1934, both from Yale. The choice of Hopper was, by and large, popular and surprising in a variety of Yale communities.[7]

Many universities over the past twenty years have taken on the task in one form or another to uncover and commemorate their relationships to slavery and the slave trade. This movement began initially with Oxford University in the United Kingdom and the College of William & Mary. But in 2001, with the succession of Ruth Simmons as president of Brown University, the first African American ever to hold such a position at any Ivy League institution, a right-wing provocateur, David Horowitz, placed a paid advertisement in several university newspapers entitled "Ten Reasons Why Reparations for Slavery Is a Bad Idea—and Racist Too." His targets included the *Brown Daily Herald*, and it touched off a bitter controversy over free speech. After her inauguration, Simmons responded by challenging the Brown incoming freshmen in the fall of 2001 to face hard questions from the past. "If you come to this place for comfort," she announced, "I urge you to walk to yon gate, pass through the portal and never look back." With such a challenge, she also established the Brown University Steering Committee on Slavery and Justice, chaired by professor of history James T. Campbell. The Brown committee hosted workshops on reparations, historical memory, and the history of the slave trade over the next five years. Indeed, Brown and Yale, through the Gilder Lehrman Center, collaborated on a major international conference in 2005 entitled "Repairing the Past: Confronting the Legacies of Slavery, Genocide, and Caste." The keynote speaker at that conference was historian Mary Frances Berry, author of the just-published *My Face Is Black Is True: Callie House and the Struggle for Ex-Slave Reparations*.[8] The conference was full of roiling discussions, civil confrontations between scholarly and public audiences, and a thoroughly international sense of the necessity of transnational comparison in approaching the problem of repair for past wrongs.

Brown produced its report in 2006 with numerous recommendations for institutional repair, creating among other measures its own Center for the Study of Slavery and Justice. Increasingly, more universities and colleges, particularly in the American South, began to join in devoting time and resources to exploring their own pasts with enslavement and slave trading, as well as the ideologies that supported these powerful systems. Prominent scholars also began to devote their energies to studying this new kind of history of education—the role of universities in the forging of an American slave society. First, Craig Steven Wilder of the Massachusetts Institute of Technology came out in 2013 with the marvelous book *Ebony and Ivy: Race, Slavery, and the Troubled History of America's Universities*. Wilder looked deep in the archives of Ivy League universities as well as other Northern colleges and brought forth the stunning origin stories of many institutions, as well as deep ties to anti-abolitionism, the American colonization movement, and the growth of the racial sciences. Yale featured prominently in Wilder's careful but withering revelations. Then historian Alfred L. Brophy of the University of North Carolina looked south and to ideology, publishing, in 2016, *University, Court, and Slave: Pro-Slavery Thought in Southern Colleges and Courts and the Coming of Civil War*. Even before the Brown report, spurred by Brophy's work, the University of Alabama faculty senate voted a resolution of apology in 2004. Historians had for decades demonstrated how deeply slavery had gripped the American mind, economy, and polity throughout the early republic and antebellum eras. From the early 1970s the study of slavery in many dimensions had been one of the most influential fields in the entire history profession, and some of the most significant works were written by scholars at Yale.[9]

By 2014, a growing number of universities and colleges in Virginia began to coalesce around the University of Virginia, which established the organization Universities Studying Slavery. At last count in summer 2023, this consortium had over ninety members nationwide. In 2016, they were famously joined by Georgetown University, where a massive sale in 1838 of some 272 enslaved people by its founding Jesuit priests, in order first to save the college and later to thrive through expansion, was the subject of explosive reporting by Rachel L. Swarns in the *New York Times*. The high-profile exposé of Georgetown's past with plantations and outright sale of hundreds of people westward to Louisiana and elsewhere supplied concrete times, names, and locations and highlighted deep institutional complicity in the worst of slavery's heart of darkness: the rendering of humans as chattel property, their sale and conversion into financial assets upon which a growing university, one dedicated to Catholic teachings, was founded. Georgetown's working group on slavery quickly became yet another model of how to dig for and tell the story of institutions choking on slavery's legacies. The Georgetown case has now resulted in the moving book by Swarns, *The 272: The Families Who Were Enslaved and Sold to Build the American Catholic Church*.[10]

Many universities, including Princeton, Harvard, Rutgers, Sewanee, the University of Texas at Austin, and a host of others too numerous to report, have now produced studies, created committees, issued findings, or promised financial recompense in some form in the future. The Princeton and Slavery Project produced a compelling story of how steeped that university was in slaveholding and slave-grown wealth in the eighteenth century. The Princeton study showed, as Martha A. Sandweiss and coauthor Craig B. Hollander wrote, that the first nine presidents of the university down to 1854 held slaves. During the entire antebellum period, nearly 40 percent of Princeton students were from the slave states; the New Jersey institution owed its successful rise to these multigenerational connections to slaveholding and proslavery thought. Similarly, Harvard faculty and researchers demonstrated in 2019, before its major report was released in 2022, that the oldest university in America was deeply "complicit with slavery, benefitting both directly and indirectly from slave labor."

Historian Sven Beckert and his colleagues discovered a pervasive donor history linking slavery and slave trading to Harvard's growth. Intriguingly they also demonstrated, as U.S. president and Harvard graduate John Adams said, that slaveholding in eighteenth-century Massachusetts was very common and considered "not disgraceful" or "inconsistent with their character" among the "best men" of the colony. Harvard's efforts are a model of how a university can devote resources to this kind of study and signal its history through and not against its own evidence.[11]

The West Indian trade in the Caribbean fueled the growth of the economies and colleges in the Northern colonies, including Connecticut and Yale. The ownership and selling of slaves, both African and Native American, was not taboo among Puritan clergy; it was quite normative. Part of the challenge in our research and writing is to educate the surprise out of this reality. The Yale and Slavery Research Project has been late to this scholarly scramble by universities investigating their complicity with American slavery, but there are advantages to joining now. We have been able to learn a great deal from our colleagues at other institutions, and we have engaged a national and international conversation already accustomed to controversy and difficult truths, even as we face our own.

Why has this public and scholarly course of study emerged now, in the early twenty-first century? The answers, as in most historical phenomena, are both long and short term. Memory "studies" and the philosophical concern with memory are as old in Western culture as when Moses told the Israelites to place stones of remembrance on high ground after they had crossed the Jordan River in their search for a way home to a promised land. All peoples and cultures through time in varying ways have left remnants, objects, sites, and above all stories of who they were in the worlds they occupied. Irresistibly, we search for those stories even as we fashion our own, often with no less attention to mythmaking and fable than our ancient ancestors. In the *Confessions*, in the fifth century, Saint Augustine was awed by memory in one of the most remarkable meditations on the subject ever written. "Great is the power of memory," he wrote, "a fearful thing, O my God, a deep and boundless manifoldness, and this thing is the mind, and this am I myself."[12] In effect, argued Augustine, we are our memories, both individual and collective; we cannot function as humans without them, but that is also the eternal human burden—to live with our memories, those that please and those that terrify our consciousness.

Often considered the "father" of modern memory studies, the French sociologist Maurice Halbwachs, in his classic study *The Collective Memory*, demonstrated how humans remember in groups, associations, frameworks, communities, and institutions. It is in the ritual practices and historical evolution of identities rooted in such groups that we find the inherent workings of memory across time and cultures. Everyone does it, including universities with their traditions, high ideals, aspirations both for the liberation of the mind and spirit and for power and dominion over law, society, polity, and economy. Indeed, universities are by definition collective intergenerational memory communities rooted in alumni associations and rituals that, inevitably, tell stories of cohesion, nostalgia, and sometimes glory. The idea of a liberal education has been one of modern humankind's greatest inventions even as it has lived deeply within human nature and ambition. Hence, universities over time have been great laboratories of innovation, learning, and discovery as well as avenues to power and the furtherance of practices that violate their missions. As living architectural and human vessels of memory, they have always lived in the worlds they make and interpret.[13]

Augustine's awe was rooted in his humility. In the face of something so infinite as memory and the history that forges it, we ought to stop every day and declare our weakness, our tiny place in the quest to harness the infinity of knowledge. As the historian John Lukacs wrote in 1968, a year of many turning points, "What historians ought to consider are not only increasing varieties of records but a deepening consciousness of the functions of human memory." He suggested both humility and engagement in the face of public memory, which seemed so vast. "The remembered past," warned Lukacs, "is a much larger category than the recorded past . . . and this is especially important in the democratic age in which we live."[14] The public is engaged every day, knowingly or not, in remembrance. There is far more public memory than there is scholarly history in the daily lives of most people. Such a premise may be hard to contemplate while gazing at the magnificent interior of the Beinecke Library at Yale or the reading room at the Library of Congress with their vast holdings. But history has perennially been weak in its fealty to the mythos of memory yoked to power, its beguiling tales of progress and triumph. Projects like this book on Yale's own developing memory over time help us to better understand this weakness and the narrow, privileged histories such memories created. We need to enter the fray; what is at stake is a better future.

In the past thirty years and more, many scholars have come to see a "memory boom" across world cultures. Why such a boom and why now? many of us have asked. So often, it seems, it is in the starkest and most brutal of historical contradictions that we find our deepest understanding of the obligation to remember. In the early 1990s, when a tourist arrived at the Bahnhof in Weimar, in eastern Germany, they were confronted with a rare orientation. A large sign read, "Yes, this is the city where so much great art was created. It is also the city next to Buchenwald. Weimar is both, and we want you to be aware of this awful contradiction while you are here." I saw that sign in 1993, and ever since, through huge transitions in our own confrontations with historical memory, I have wondered how many American cities would confront visitors at airports or train stations with similar memorial honesty. How many universities might alter their welcome tours with stories of contradiction, with narratives that do more than exalt founders, donors, and leaders who have merited statues? Such gestures are not easy in the United States, a land that still demands, collectively, a progress narrative at its core, and universities, justifiably, represent the aspirations of mobility, equality, and freedom.[15] Americans are, however, capable of confronting and facing their pasts, even in the places where many spent the best years of their youth.

Toni Morrison wrote *Beloved*, published in 1987, because, as she explained, "there is no place you or I can go, to think about or not think about, to summon the presences of, or recollect the absences of slaves. . . . There is no suitable memorial or plaque or wreath or wall or park or skyscraper lobby. There's no 300-foot tower. There's no small bench by the road. There is not even a tree scored, an initial that I can visit or you can visit in Charleston or Savannah or New York or Providence, or better still, on the banks of the Mississippi. And because such a place doesn't exist . . . the book had to." In the United States, the memory boom came about in no small part because the entry of Black scholars made manifest the myriad ways Black lives and histories had been forcibly repressed from the American memory of the American experience. There are now places one can go to summon the presence of enslaved ancestors.[16]

Such a visible marking of the American landscape, as Morrison suggested, calls to the truth that the attention to the relationship of memory and history has enlightened us, even as critics sometimes claim that Western cultures have created a consumerist memory culture, rooted in tourism and commerce. As we look deeper, though, many historical causes emerge for so many courses, conferences, books, and public programs about memory or commemoration over the past three decades and more. Writing in the long wake of the attacks of September 11, 2001, the cultural historian Daniel T. Rodgers brilliantly analyzed in *Age of Fracture* how, during the quarter century since the 1980s and the influence of

Reaganism and its liberal discontents, American society became a place in which institutions began to fray and "history gave way to conceptions of human nature that stressed choice, agency, performance, and desire." Certain kinds of social consensus born of the massive experience of World War II and the Cold War eroded. "Imagined collectivities shrank; notions of structure and power thinned out," argued Rodgers. "Viewed by its acts of mind, the last quarter of the [twentieth] century was an era of disaggregation, a great age of fracture." Anyone seeking to understand the roots of the "polarization" we live under in the 2020s, and why universities are confronting their pasts as well as providing one of the primary battlegrounds in the nation's culture wars over identity, could do no better than to start with Rodgers's astute study, which includes a remarkable chapter on "Race and Social Memory."[17]

If attention to the full complexity of America's racial history has fractured a particular postwar narrative of progress, it offers a way to confront and face troubled pasts and help us locate the universities' role in searching for their own stories. Hence in these contexts universities have looked inward as they learned from the outside world how to imagine self-examination about the past and some sort of repair in the present. We know we now live in an age of apologies, and a rich literature has arisen around such actions and their meanings. At Yale, we have put our heads down in the archives, accomplished mountains of research, built on the labors and memory-keeping of previous generations, and attempted to write a narrative history covering more than the first two centuries of Yale's saga in New Haven and far beyond. Many people contributed to this project (a fuller accounting of which is given in the acknowledgments). I worked closely with a talented team of researchers, especially my two primary coworkers, Hope McGrath and Michael Morand. Michael is the primary author of chapter 6, and Hope is the primary author of chapters 10 and 11 and the first four interludes. Together, our team has developed a more detailed understanding of the intertwined history that New Haven and Yale have shared.

We tell a story that begins in the seventeenth century when Puritan immigrants from England drove Native Americans largely out of Connecticut in two bloody wars of conquest. We take it all the way into the early twentieth century, to Yale's two hundredth anniversary in 1901, and then to the creation of its Civil War Memorial in 1915, which stands today as a stunning symbol of the university's willful blindness to its active participation in shaping the American story of slavery. Along the way we have kept a keen eye out for the ways Yale University represented itself, told its own stories, and shaped its own memory. In the dozens of histories of Yale, on all subjects from its roots in theology and the ministry, to its architecture, to its leaders who attained national and worldwide fame, there are very few mentions of the issue of slavery or the people enslaved in and around the university.[18] We have uncovered the names of more than two hundred enslaved people who were the property of Yale presidents, rectors, trustees, founders, donors, and famous graduates. And we have told the stories of many extraordinary African Americans who dreamed, survived, worked, and studied at the college, and then the university, near the New Haven Green. We have endeavored with great care to be fair to the humanity of all the people we have encountered, those whose humanity was stolen, abused, or destroyed and those who enacted, perpetuated, or justified the practice of enslavement. All were all too human, like the rest of us.

We organized the chapters in chronological order, with many themes addressed in most parts of the book. The reader will, hopefully, gain a sense of context: how different the past is from any present, how change over time is the lifeblood of historical understanding, and how the legacies of the experiences we portray are all around us today. Yale possesses an antislavery as well as a proslavery history, beginning in the late eighteenth century in its own halls of learning and around the edges of campus among former slaves, Revolutionary War soldiers who petitioned for their freedom, and community leaders, and extending into the nineteenth century when the abolition movement gained a tenuous but visible presence in New Haven. The beginnings of Yale's own antislavery impulse on its campus and in the worlds it influenced receive, we hope, fair and robust treatment.

As President Salovey contemplated a broad study of Yale's past in 2020, he drew on the reports, national and local contexts, pivotal events, and experiences discussed here. When we met to contemplate the direction of the Yale project, I told him I did not want to produce a report, like many universities had before. I suggested we write a narrative history that people beyond our boundaries would read. As universities and representatives of the universe of letters and ideas, our aim should be to never give up faith in the power of history, well researched and written, to capture, inform, and motivate the imagination. This book, with its flaws, is that result. We have not sought to root out evil from the soul or the history of a great university. No single book, nor even a room full of them, could do that for any institution, organization, or government. This is a history, and history can instruct, inspire, and sometimes give us truths with which to make a better day.

CHAPTER 1

War, Slavery, and Christianity

Should not Christians have more mercy and compassion . . . but we will not dispute it now. We had sufficient light from the word of God for our proceedings.

—CAPTAIN JOHN UNDERHILL,
officer in command of English soldiers at the massacre of Pequots,
Fort Mystic, Connecticut, May 26, 1637

In the fall of 1676, during the brutal and destructive conflict that came to be known as King Philip's War, James Noyes wrote to John Allyn, a colonial military and political official, pleading for Native captives. Noyes, a Harvard-educated minister, was serving as chaplain to a company of colonial settlers led by Captain George Dennison. Feeling wronged and overburdened, he reminded Allyn he had "been 3 times in your war service," and on each occasion he was cheated out of the wages and captives rightfully due him. Noyes was sure that colonial leaders "will never know the hundreth part of what service I have done by my interest with the English & indians, & am willing not to particularize." Yet over the course of a lengthy letter, Noyes did particularize, especially when it came to the human property he sought. Already in possession of four captives—a fourteen-year-old girl, a five-year-old girl, their sick mother, and "a Gentleman never used to work, [who] had been sick & lame in his limbs"—Noyes wanted Allyn to send him a young, healthy captive. The minister had sent the sick man away, presumably to die, but, regrettably, he returned to him, and Noyes had been nursing him with food and medicine for three weeks. Noyes seemed well informed about the other available captives and was not interested in any of them; "I know of none I like lately come in," he said. Still others, he knew, had been sent to Barbados—a reminder of this war's global reverberations in the West Indies and throughout the Atlantic. Noyes was willing to keep the girl, her mother "if she live," and the five-year-old, but he hoped to receive "a young man a fourth when I can light of one that maye be worth having." *Worth* having; the Reverend Noyes wanted a laborer to own in body and perhaps soul. Moreover, he implored Allyn to give the settlers greater freedom regarding their property: "I hope the . . . Honrd. Court will give us leave if a pest to us to sell [them] to English or someway to rid our hands of them."[1]

In this wartime emergency as well as in more stable times, the Reverend Noyes viewed enslaved Native Americans and eventually Africans as saleable property, commodities at his disposal as a Christian Englishman in a colonial frontier society. In their ambitions, their theological certainties, and their material quests, the Puritans at war in seventeenth-century Connecticut were also the drivers of an early form of commercial expansion and conquest. As the theologian Willie James Jennings writes, the Christian "imagination" of the English colonists in New England produced a "breathtaking hubris" demanding that "the natives, black, red, and everyone not white, must be brought from chaos to faith. The land, wetlands, fields, and forests must be cleared, organized, and brought into productive civilization." In this lethal mixture of historical circumstances forged by mercantile empire, religious migration, displacement into new worlds, and war for survival and dominance, the Christian imagination, writes Jennings, fell into a "diseased form" increasingly linked to slavery and conquest, to a concept of property in man that demanded ever more creative justifications. Some of the best minds of Puritan New England became the creators as well as, eventually, critics of those justifications. And herein lay the authentic "tragedy," argues Jennings, of the epic collisions of race, religion, and land in colonial America.[2]

Twenty-five years after writing his letter to Allyn, in 1701, Noyes was one of the ten trustees who established the Collegiate School, the forerunner to Yale College, in Saybrook, on the shoreline of Long Island Sound. When Noyes and his contemporaries set out to found their school, they did so within a political, cultural, and demographic landscape that had been transformed by decades of warfare—by the blood shed—between settlers and Indigenous peoples. Yale's New England origins lie in these seventeenth-century stories of destruction, migration, and enslavement, both Indigenous and African. Native groups with differing languages did not, of course, call this region "New England" like their new neighbors. They may have called it *ndakinna*, an Abenaki word meaning "our land" or "the place 'to which we belong.'" Others called the region Wôpanâak or Wabanaki, for "the land where the sun is born every day."[3] The sun was born in the same place every day, but nothing was ever the same for these Native peoples after the wars of the seventeenth century. They shattered one history and began a new one. And they opened territory for the creation of a small theology school in southern Connecticut.

The Pequots of the Narragansett Bay region and what is now eastern and middle Connecticut numbered approximately thirteen thousand people at the time of contact with the first Dutch sailors in 1613 and English settlers in the 1630s. Pequots were hunters, gatherers, and good fishermen, but they also lived in small, semipermanent villages. They were one of the three river tribes along the Connecticut River with the Mohegan and the Niantic. The Pequots had achieved relative power in relation to their neighbors, including the rival Narragansett and Wampanoag peoples just to the east in what is today Rhode Island and lower Massachusetts. They had even gained authority over and drew tribute from the Montauks across the sound on Long Island. They were a people of the forests, which stood dense with tall white pines, cedars, and spruces; of agriculture; and of the marshes and estuaries along Long Island Sound. They were landbound and maritime people. They grew corn and squash but also tobacco, and they fished for everything, including Atlantic sturgeon on a large scale. They harvested lobster long before it became a part of New England lore and high cuisine. Trade with their neighbors was economic lifeblood as well as a source of rivalry for the Pequots and the other Native peoples of lower New England, including the Pocumtuck, Nipmuck, Massachusett, Pennacook, Mahican, and Wabanaki to the north. All spoke various dialects of the Algonquin language. When Europeans in their large ships arrived along their coasts, their lives and livelihoods changed forever.[4]

Northeastern Native peoples were fiercely independent, living in polities ruled variously by sachems, men and women of special status and authority, often by descent, with power to make trade arrangements, treaties, and war. Some sachems were of greater or lesser power depending on the size and territorial domain of the tribe. They tended to rule by networks of relationships, obligations, and alliances, as well as by rituals of gifting and paying tribute. From the very beginning of contact and the development of increasing trade, Native Americans fought to sustain what later would be called their *sovereignty*, their sense of land possession, of self-rule, and of demands for equality with rivals and would-be conquerors. The Europeans had to learn these systems of exchange and leadership in order to coexist. Indigenous societies and their leaders approached the Dutch, French, and English, at least at first, with these centuries-old systems of power and prestige in mind. Both the Native peoples and the Europeans, in the beginning, sought relationships of mutual exchange.[5]

Like most Native peoples in the region, the Pequots developed a significant mode of trade and a currency called wampum, consisting of shell beads and other precious and decorative items, assembled with skilled craftsmanship into elaborate belts and jewelry by women, which the Dutch first and then the English learned to adopt and desire as a means of trade. Wampum belts became symbols of beauty but especially of social, political, and spiritual power, and they became the means by which European cloth, metals, and guns were infused into Native cultures. Wampum belts had long been part of rituals and epics among some peoples, but now in the seventeenth century they became an essential element fueling the lucrative fur trade.[6]

Mutual dependence between the English and the Native Americans came first; soon after came epidemics, conflict, and war. European diseases devastated the Pequot population and most other Native groups in rapid order even before war laid waste to their society. The English settlement of New England was a demographic disaster for Native Americans. In 1600, an estimated 70,000 to 150,000 Native people lived in the Northeast, and they had dwelt there for ten thousand years. By 1700, on the eve of Yale's founding, only 10 percent remained. The vast majority had succumbed to European-borne diseases, especially smallpox. The first epidemic to sweep through northern and middle New England came in 1616–19. Whole Native villages ceased to exist as thousands died in a single growing season or two. Especially after 1630, and the huge Puritan migration, pressures on Native peoples intensified from a combination of deadly pathogens, mounting conflict, and spreading English settlement. Before the end of the 1630s, writes historian Ned Blackhawk, "Puritan colonization" became an "engine of Indigenous dispossession." Native sachems increasingly sought alliances with the English in some areas as their people died of disease. In 1634 an epidemic hit Pequot-dominated villages in Connecticut, killing several thousand. Ritual mourning and remembrance emerged quickly in these cultures after so sudden a devastation of family and identity.[7]

In some Native communities the destruction was so profound that those spared turned to the settlers' God, sought solace and meaning in a new faith, and became what the English called "praying Indians." Puritan histories of this early period of settlement, written late in the seventeenth century, are replete with stories of the Indian mass death from disease. Some English writers were especially fond of the stories of smallpox-induced conversions to Christianity. The famous Puritan divine Cotton Mather described New Haven, Connecticut, as one of those towns where, despite "kindnesses passed between them [English and Natives]," "nevertheless there are few of those towns but what have seen their body of Indians utterly extirpated by nothing but mortality wasting them." The English also struggled to understand the epidemics, often relying on Christian, providential explanations to justify the Native liquidation as God's plan for the Puritan mission. Or sometimes they just practiced denial as a means of advancing religious and imperial expansion. What became all too obvious was that Native mass death from disease made English settlement all the more swift. The lethal combination of epidemics and eventual warfare led the historian Francis Jennings, in 1975, to describe New England by the late 1830s as "a widowed land."[8]

When the Pequot War broke out in April 1637 with an attack and mass killing by Natives in the English village of Wethersfield, Connecticut, as well as murders of Natives by the English on land and water, the Pequot population already had declined by roughly 77 percent to only around three thousand people. With their culture and security under great pressure from English settlers, they now faced a war aimed at their extermination. In May, with some Native allies, English troops surrounded and massacred an entire village of four hundred Pequots in their fort on the Mystic River. Most of the victims were women and children. A captain among the English force left a description of the killing that combined sentiments of Christian virtue and a biblical justification for the beginnings of a genocide. "The fires . . . in the centre of the fort, blazed most terribly," wrote the officer, "and burnt all in the space of half an hour." The captain wished for better of his men but concluded, "Great and doleful was the bloody sight to the view of young soldiers that never had been in war, to see so many souls lie gasping on the ground, so thick, in some places, that you could hardly pass along. . . . Should not Christians have more mercy and compassion?" Then he remembered King David's war and how scripture had declared that some peoples, by their "sin against God," merited the "most terriblest death."[9] Such are the arguments through the ages of soldiers who must reach for justification for their worst deeds—slaughter in the name of some ordained cause. This kind of colonial war was violence without mercy.

Remnants of the surviving Pequots moved westward to the region around New Haven Harbor, seeking refuge among a small group of Native people called the Quinnipiac. The English made chase in the summer of 1637, and when they captured a Pequot sachem they beheaded him. Pequots who were captured in the wake of the Mystic fort massacre were enslaved, some by the Mohegan or Narragansett allies of the settlers, and some were dispatched by the English to Bermuda. Others remained in the region, enslaved by Puritan families. The war devastated the Pequots, and in September 1638, the Treaty of Hartford was forced upon them, designed to both humiliate and liquidate them as a people. The very

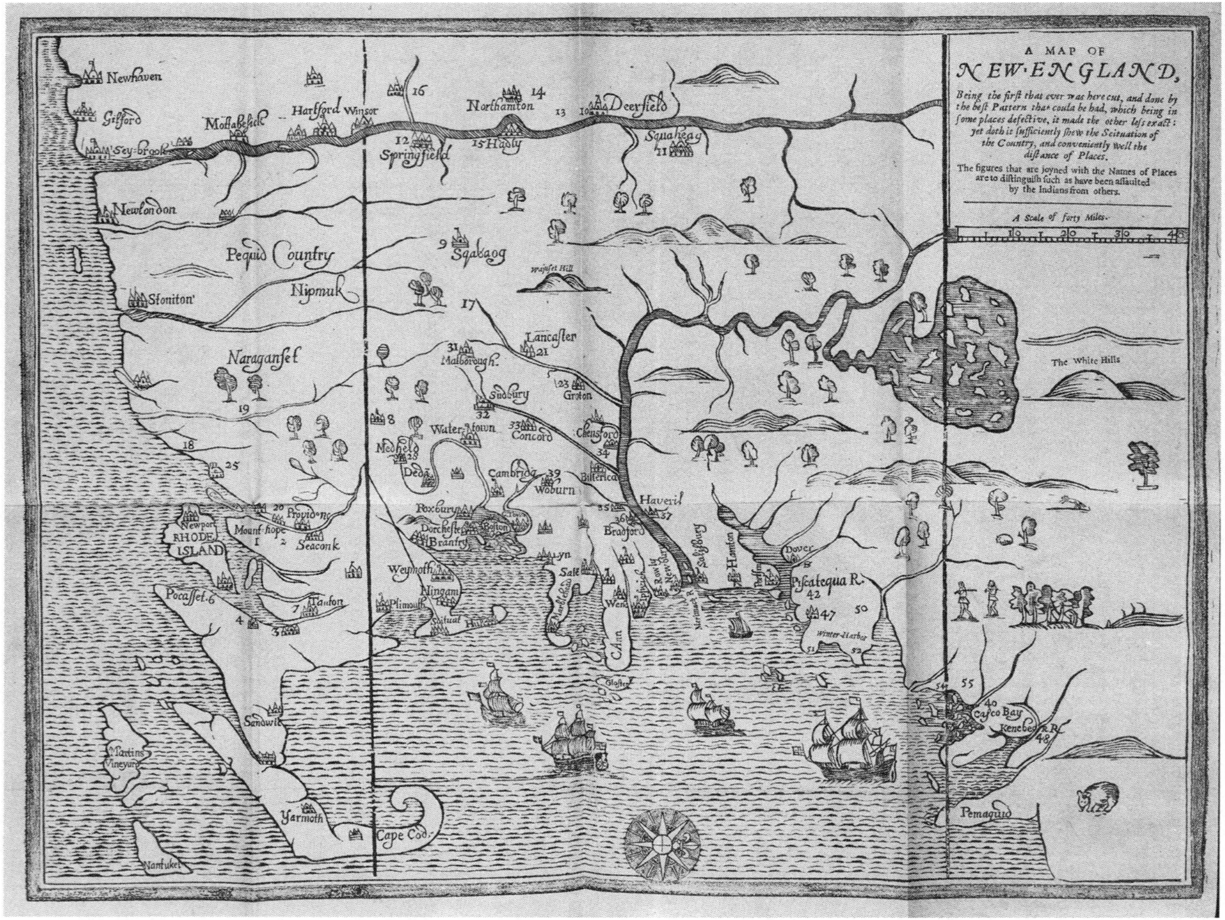

Printed in Boston in 1677, this map—considered one of the first made by English colonists—appeared in William Hubbard's term "Pequot" was outlawed, and they were declared extinct.[10] Despite these claims, the Pequots of Connecticut would revive over a long period of time in small numbers, and they still live in twenty-first-century New England. However, their near extermination in the seventeenth century left a hideous legacy and opened the territory of both eastern and southern Connecticut to further English settlement.

More than three decades after the Pequot War, what came to be called King Philip's War broke out in 1675 from a complex web of conflicts and rivalries over land and waterways between the English and the Native groups of coastal Massachusetts, Rhode Island, and parts of Connecticut. Yale College emerged in the long wake of this colonial struggle over the conquest of land and resources, which engulfed all the major groups of Algonquin-speaking peoples in the Northeast region: the Massachusetts, Wampanoags, Narragansetts, Niantics, Quinnipiacs, Mohegans, Pequots, Schagticokes, Pocumtucks, Pennacooks, Nipmucs, Penobscots, Abenakis, and others. Lest there be any ambiguity about English claims to Native land, the Puritan minister Increase Mather, later president of Harvard and one of the key people who persuaded Elihu Yale to make his gift to the Collegiate School in Connecticut, made the story explicit. "The Heathen people amongst whom we live," he declared, "and whose Land the Lord God of our Fathers hath given to us for a rightfull possession, have at sundry times been plotting mischievous devices against that part of the English Israel which is seated in these goings down of the Sun." The war also stemmed from hatred and fear among the English that, in living so near to what they considered heathen and barbarous peoples, they were losing their faith and purpose on their errand into the wilderness. And the Natives, too, had come to loathe the English for their greed, arrogance, and conquest; many sachems now feared, rather than welcomed, the process of conversion to Christianity of some of their rival neighbors. These were two civilizations in lethal collision, both dreading that they had no future in each other's presence. Mather preached a sermon in 1674, "The Day of Trouble Is Near." Tragically, he was altogether prescient. Mather warned of "great decay as to the power of godliness amongst us." He preached from the famous text in Matthew 24:6: "Ye shall hear of wars, and rumours of war."[11] In Puritan theological reasoning, sin sometimes might be countered with greater sin on the way to virtue, redemption, and power. But we also see here the fruition of Willie James Jennings's notion of tragedy and a diseased Christian imagination put to the service of all-out war.

Once the pretext for war exploded in June 1675, after three Wampanoags were executed for murder near Plymouth, Massachusetts, both sides waged unrelenting violence for nearly two years. Native warriors, sometimes under unified commands and often not, attacked and burned dozens of English towns, slaughtering women and children. The English, utterly militarized by this point and amply supplied with firearms, swarmed over Native villages, burning wigwams, killing families, and selling captives into foreign and domestic slavery. Both sides practiced torture and mutilation in a vicious bloodletting without quarter. The name "King Philip's War" is an odd product of postwar English narratives about the conflict. King Philip's real name was Metacom; he was sachem of the Wampanoag of southeastern Massachusetts, and for some time conspiratorial rumors had swirled around him as the most dangerous of Indigenous leaders. The suspicion was that Metacom forged a plot to create an all-Native alliance with the French and the Dutch to wipe out the English.[12] When war broke out, Metacom strove for an Indigenous coalition and, indeed, he tried to drive the English and their God back into the sea. Likewise, the war became for the English an existential struggle to maintain and spread their colonial foothold deep into the New England landscapes. All sides fought a seventeenth-century version of a regional total war, a struggle to determine whether the Puritan Israel or various Native homelands would survive at all.

Some Indigenous peoples divided and supported the English, such as an offshoot of the Narragansett. But the larger portion of that tribe's warriors and civilians were trapped in the late fall of 1675 in and around a fort in what colonists called the Great Swamp, a wetland west of Narragansett Bay. Hundreds were killed or captured and enslaved by an English force a thousand men strong. Refugees who survived trekked northward to try to connect with Metacom's coalition of fighters. His warriors made many raids and took the war to the English, but starvation forced men, women, and children to seek food and safety back toward the eastern shores of Massachusetts. Some were captured and sent to internment camps on Deer Island and Long Island in Boston Harbor, where a frightful number died of disease and winter cold in 1676. Metacom's coalition ran out of time and supplies. The leader was shot in August 1676 by a Native marksman serving the English, his body dismembered and decapitated; his body parts, whose whereabouts were unknown, became mythic objects in the lore of the war for many years to come.[13]

The refugee crisis launched by the war fueled the growth of slavery and exile for significant swaths of the Native population. In the summer of 1675, approximately 150 Wampanoags surrendered at Plymouth Plantation, seeking shelter and food. But the English, according to one account published that year, said the victors "sold all but about six of them for slaves, to be carried out of the country."

Despite opposition from some (but not all) clergy, kidnapping and a regional slave trade of Native refugees intensified as a profitable business in the wake of the war. Jamaican and Barbadian officials considered Algonquin captives dangerous and disgruntled products of war and dispossession and sometimes refused to buy or trade for them, although genealogies done much later demonstrate that many ended up on those islands. Hence, many Native refugees were scattered in an "Algonquin diaspora," to far-flung places from the Caribbean to Cádiz, Málaga, Calais, Tangier, London, and Amsterdam.

In the wake of this destructive war, some among the English looked for opportunities to profit from Native enslavement, but far more often, the conquerors' interest was simply to be rid of their Indigenous neighbors. As one historian of the Native peoples of the coastal Northeast has shown, the real meaning in King Philip's War was "political." In this war without limits, "both sides of the conflict," writes Andrew Lipman, "had attempted to utterly terrify and demoralize their opposition, but only the English truly succeeded." Metacom's wife, Wootonekanuske, and a nine-year-old son were captured after the sachem's killing. The boy was sold away into slavery; the fate of his mother is unknown. The English debated the morality of enslaving their conquered enemies, and New England did not quite yet have a fully developed race-based system of slavery, but in the end, the trade thrived; commerce prevailed. In 1676, a merchant named Thomas Smith was given permission by Plymouth and Massachusetts colonies to round up and transport the "heathen Malefactors men women and children" on board a ship called the *Sea-Flower* and sell them, their destiny being "Perpetuall servitude & slavery." The historian Christine DeLucia has shown that dozens of "New England Indians" appear in records of an "Algonquin diaspora" among the galley slaves in the ports of Tangier, Constantinople, Tunis, and Tripoli. "The conditions of existence," writes DeLucia, "in that sun-baked, multi-lingual milieu of onerous forced labor can only be imagined."[14] Enslavement and slave trading of Native Americans by the English and other Europeans left deep legacies from the seventeenth century, sometimes culturally explosive and sometimes suppressed or silent. In the occasional stirrings of conscience about selling and buying Africans in the early eighteenth century among some Puritan divines, this slaving without mercy against Native Americans lay restlessly in fetid memories of wars of the 1670s and their long aftermath.

King Philip's War, in its savage destructiveness and its social consequences, was a kind of civil war. In memory it had to be rendered somehow a safe past, a necessary cataclysm on the way to English destiny and to a growing array of biblical commonwealths. The violence needed justification and narrative harmony. So, in a Connecticut historian's account written a century after the war in 1767, Indigenous people are rendered a "Stubborn and desperate" lot prone to wanton "Cruelty." Their captured warriors deserved no respect, wrote the Yale-educated Benjamin Trumbull, because they "Sat in Heaps like a Company of Sullen Doggs too Self willed to ask for Life, the most of them, and choosing to be shot in heaps." To kill or enslave other humans, dominant groups have always sought to dehumanize their victims. Trumbull provided a religious lesson and a morality tale in the final lines of his narrative. "Yea while we read these barbarous Things," he declared, "How fervently and affectionately should we Pity and Pray for the Savage Nations of this American Wilderness that God would Send the Gospel among them and Pour out another Spirit upon them so that none may hurt or Destroy or Exercise Cruelty any more."[15] On any side of any armed conflict, a perverted hubris may be necessary to sustain the violence; but Trumbull's logic is as clear as it gets.

The first Africans in the Connecticut colony likely arrived during the years of the Pequot War, perhaps as a result of trade in Native men who were taken prisoner and enslaved. In fact, the first known Africans in neighboring Massachusetts were bought from the proceeds of selling Pequot captives; they arrived in 1638, on a ship with cotton and tobacco. This trade continued, and in 1646, the New England Confederation codified that Native captives should "be shipped out and exchanged for Negroes." Although it is uncertain exactly when the first Africans arrived in Connecticut, their presence was initially recorded in 1639, when an enslaved Black boy named Louis Berbice, from Dutch Guiana, was killed by his owner in Hartford. And Africans may have been present in New Haven even earlier, likely from its founding. Lucretia, a Black woman, belonged to the colony's founder and governor, Theophilus Eaton, and may have arrived with him.[16]

Africans came to New England generally via British colonies in the West Indies, although some were transported directly from Africa. They hailed from the Senegambia basin of West Africa, the Grain Coast, the Windward Coast, Benin, Biafra, Dahomey, West Central Africa, and once in a while even as far east as Madagascar. But after 1700, the majority had been swept from the coastal and inland regions of modern-day Ghana, known by the eighteenth century as the Gold Coast or the "slave coast" to European slave traders. They departed African shores from the Anomabu slaving fort, east of Cape Coast Castle, the administrative center of British slaving, and Elmina Castle, the first major trading fortress built by Europeans in sub-Saharan Africa, erected by the Portuguese in the late fifteenth century and later under Dutch rule.[17] Their horrible experience began inland, generally by capture in war, but also as the fateful necessity on the part of African leaders to sustain trade between their polities and European ships and agents at the coast. The ghastly business of the slave trade was a three-to-four-century-long commercial enterprise in which Africa provided the one product Europeans most wanted—people—in exchange for firearms, textiles, and other manufactured goods. Its scale, methods, and consequences have defined the meaning of inhumanity, as well as forged humane mass movements against oppression, ever since the emergence of a modern world. New Haven, home of Yale College, was an integral node, especially because of increasing reliance on trade with the West Indies, in the vast worldwide network of commerce in human beings and cultural transformations.

The twentieth-century African American poet Robert Hayden, in his spectacular "Middle Passage," attempted to capture the terror and wretched irony in some of the slave ships' names: "*Desire, Adventure, Tartar, Ann*," and especially the good ship "*Jesús*." Then he took the measure of English and Puritan complicity in a mass crime:

> Middle Passage:
> voyage through death
> to life upon these shores. . . .
>
> Standing to America, bringing home
> black gold, black ivory, black seed.

Then Hayden froze and tortured the Puritan souls in their places of worship.

> *Deep in the festering hold thy father lies,*
> *of his bones New England pews are made,*
> *those are altar lights that were his eyes.*

As if taking the pulpit himself, Hayden made the flock gaze at what they would refuse to see:

> *Deep in the festering hold thy father lies,*
> *the corpse of mercy rots with him,*
> *rats eat love's rotten gelid eyes.*
>
> *But, oh, the living look at you*
> *with human eyes whose suffering accuses you,*
> *whose hatred reaches through the swill of dark*
> *to strike you like a leper's claw.*
>
> *You cannot stare that hatred down.*[18]

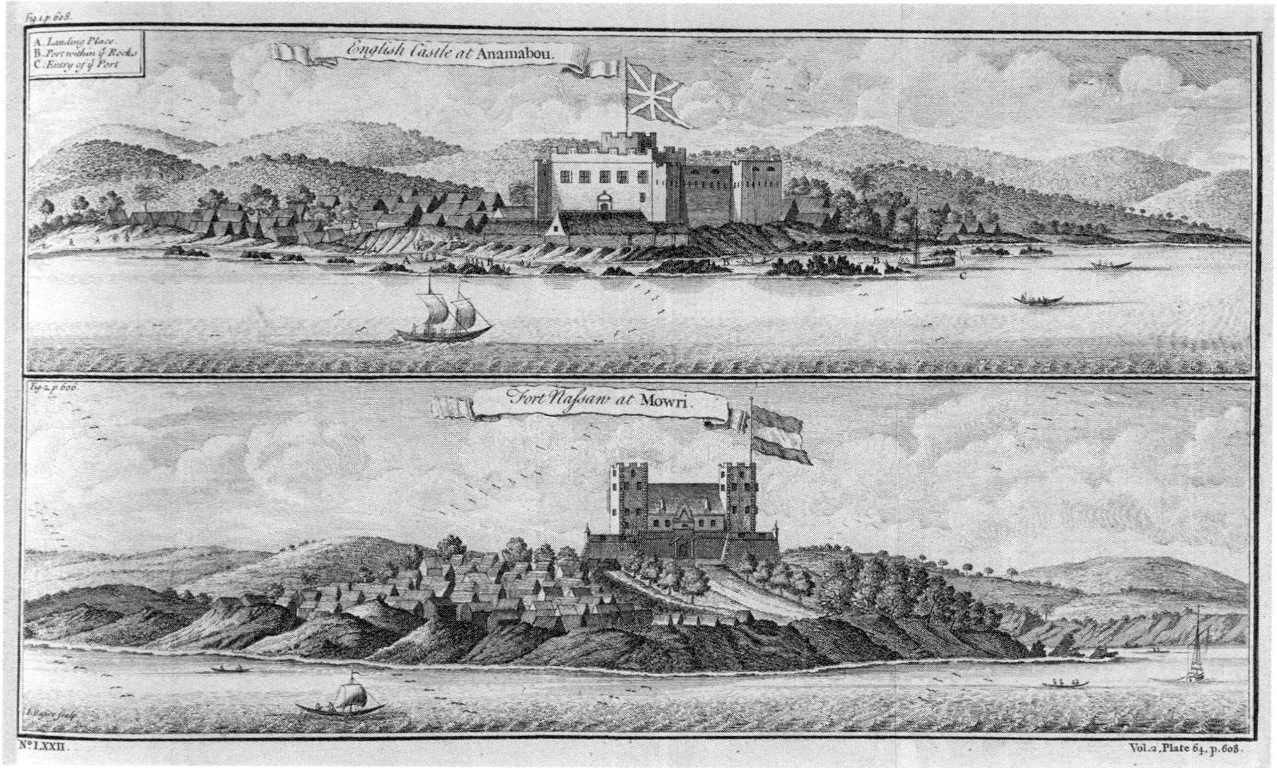

English fortress at Anomabu (present-day Ghana), mid-eighteenth century.
Beinecke Rare Book and Manuscript Library, Yale University.

Hayden's poem reminds us of the terrifying distance between horror over the reality of the slave trade and the everyday circumstances of Africans and Englishmen, living in small towns and on farms in bucolic and dangerous New England, drawing water from the same wells, praying to different, but sometimes the same, gods for mercy and sustenance in a world they were trying, under terrible strain, to make together. Hayden reminds us that historically profound events, results, and legacies often lay only half-hidden in the mundane circumstances of life, around the corners of our movements where we do not look, in the heavy doors we open, and even in the bricks of buildings we occupy. The perils of remembering might be anywhere, and they will surprise us.

Most of the Africans who survived the cruel filter of the slave trade and landed in New England spoke Akan languages, and their spiritual and cultural heritages were Asante and Fante, among other ethnic backgrounds. They carried many skills in agriculture and the arts of trade.[19] They brought their gods, their imaginations, their music, their languages, their domestic creative arts, and their stories. African cultures were ruptured from their moorings, but they both survived and were transformed in this new Native, English, and African world. Some of the earliest Africans likely came as indentured servants or were at least treated as such. Regardless of their status, some form of bonded labor defined their lives; they were denied nearly all rights enjoyed by Englishmen, although they forged ways to push back at these rigid barriers.

Africans were considered in law dangerous to the social order, especially if they became free—as sometimes happened through manumission, self-purchase, fulfilling the terms of an indenture, or even escape. The General Assembly of Connecticut, based in Hartford and in New Haven, drew up numerous laws restricting the lives of both free and enslaved Black people in their midst, showing a concern that trouble lay ahead in a society guided by a strained combination of the teachings of Jesus, the conquest of land, the collision of cultures, and the claim to the right of property in man. In 1660, Africans were prohibited from serving in the military, and by 1690, the colony banned Black and Indigenous people from occupying public roadways after 9:00 p.m. In 1717, New London went so far as to petition the colony for an exclusion law denying Black people the right to live in the town or own land in the colony. The assembly rejected the petition but immediately seized upon the idea and banned free Black and mixed-race people from living in any town in the colony. It also prohibited free Black people from purchasing land or opening businesses without the town's consent. And in 1730, the colony passed a law stating that Black, Indigenous, or mixed-race people would be "whipped with forty lashes" if they "uttered or published . . .

words" about a White person that were deemed "actionable" under law.[20] Stymied by their impossible quest for racial purity, these laws were ambiguously enforced by the Puritan elders; their purpose was social control and intimidation. Above all, these laws increasingly drew rigid lines defining people by race and status in their Bible commonwealth.

In 1700, on the eve of the creation of the Collegiate School that would soon become Yale, one in ten property inventories in the colony of Connecticut included enslaved people. The prominent property-holding families in the principal towns of New London, New Haven, Norwich, and Hartford were slaveholders. Fully half of all ministers, doctors, and public officials in the colony owned at least one or two enslaved Africans. Indeed, merchants, sea captains, military officers, and some small farmers held Africans in bondage for labor of all kinds, in fields, on water, and in domestic settings. One could not live and work in or near a Connecticut town without seeing enslaved Black people. Although the numbers were small at first, they and their bondage were a commonplace of life on farms, in taverns, on waterways, and in all manner of physical labor.[21]

The Black population in the colony of Connecticut grew decisively in the first six decades of the eighteenth century, down to the American Revolution. In 1730, Africans numbered approximately 700 out of a total of 38,000, or 1.8 percent of the population. By 1749, the Black population reached 1,000, and in 1756, it was 3,587. On the eve of independence, a 1774 census counted 6,464 Black people in Connecticut, the largest number of any New England colony, and 3.2 percent of the population. They were, of course, *people*—with identities, although too often recorded only by first names. In Farmington, an Isaac Miller owned Phebe, Cuff, and their son, Peter. Cuff was sold to a Joseph Coe in 1744, and Phebe to the same slaveholder ten years later. A notation in Coe's deed of sale demonstrates the enslaved man's demand for a last name that he himself chose: "Cuff desires to have the Sir Name Freeman annexed to his Name."[22] Dignity for Cuff Freeman, as for all the enslaved, came at an extraordinarily high price in colonial Connecticut. Cuff and his son both served in the American Continental Army during the Revolution.

In the fall of 1701, the Colony of Connecticut passed legislation allowing for the establishment of a college, and soon after a group of ministers met to devise plans for what they called the Collegiate School. (It would later be renamed Yale College.) In 1716, the trustees voted to move the college to New Haven, but before that, students and tutors met in various nearby colonial settlements, all part of a landscape shaped by nearly a century of warfare, migration, slave trading, and enslavement. So it was that a thirteen-year-old Jonathan Edwards began his studies in Wethersfield, Connecticut, just south of Hartford, one site where Collegiate School students were educated. The principal commodity produced in Edwards's colonial town was onions, shipped to the Caribbean from New Haven Harbor to feed enslaved people. It is not clear whether the young Edwards was aware that the town of Wethersfield was the scene of the opening battle of the Pequot War some eighty-five years earlier. But he must have known people whose lives had been altered by those events: a Native American woman and her children, Ambo and Desire, enslaved and belonging to Edwards's tutor, shared a house with Edwards and his classmates.[23]

Edwards had been born in the small village of East Windsor, near Hartford, Connecticut, in 1703, a place on the far western frontier of the British Empire. He and his college came of age in the midst of tremendous religious, political, and colonial turmoil. As Edwards's modern biographer George Marsden puts it, the theologian-pastor lived in a dangerous conflict zone between three overlapping and warring political entities: "British Protestant, French Catholic, and Indian." Edwards became deeply aware of, and influenced by, the Native American cultures and heritage all around him; he showed concern for the lives and souls of Native peoples with whom he worked, although he remained ambivalent about their place in the family of man.[24]

Some of Edwards's earliest childhood memories involved the terror and impact of the Deerfield raid of 1704, a devastating attack on the English settlement in the town in western Massachusetts where close family relatives were killed and captured. In a defining event of the first decade of the eighteenth century in the region, Native warriors from the North, aided by French officers, slaughtered 39 of the 300 residents of Deerfield and seized another 112, carrying them off in the winter snow to Canada. Among the captives were one of Edwards's uncles and three cousins. As a child Edwards learned quickly that these frontier towns lived in fear of three great threats: Satan, Roman Catholics, and Native Americans. As soon as he could read, he would have been intrigued by the famous book by his uncle, the Reverend John Williams, *The Redeemed Captive, Returning to Zion*, a compelling account of the murderous Deerfield attack and captivity in Canada.[25]

In 1720, Edwards, an extraordinarily well-read teenager, completed his baccalaureate degree in New Haven at what had become Yale College. Over the next nearly four decades he became America's greatest theologian. Tutored in Greek and Latin and a student of Enlightenment thinkers such as Isaac Newton and John Locke, but especially committed to a Calvinist theological vision of the world and the place of humans in it, Edwards, like his college, believed society should operate by the strictures of God's word in biblical scripture. As a theological thinker Edwards came to see human history as a drama between good and evil played out before the "moral government" of an all-sovereign God; he believed fully in a heaven and a hell—especially hell.[26]

By the mid-1730s, in his pastorship in Northampton, Massachusetts, Edwards increasingly examined the growing phenomenon of Native American missions. Here, another close relative, Edwards's uncle Colonel John Stoddard, helped forge a treaty with Mahican and Housatonic groups to create what became a flourishing mission in Stockbridge, in far western Massachusetts. Edwards himself would end his life and career there, with his family living among Indigenous peoples experiencing varying degrees of Christian sympathy or conversion. The theologian viewed all races of people as descendants of Adam and Eve, and therefore of the same original sin and human possibility. He saw Africans and Native Americans as equal to Europeans in their potential for godliness and evil. In 1739, he surmised that when the millennium arrived in a few hundred years, "Negroes and Indians will be divines." They would write "excellent books," become "learned men," and "shall then be very knowing in religion." Edwards contended that a slaveholder should not abuse his servant because "we are made of the same human race."[27] Although he would condemn slave trading in the Atlantic, he never opposed the ownership of enslaved Africans in his community and his household. Indeed, Edwards, perhaps Yale's most prominent graduate in its first century, was a willing and representative slaveholder, a famed model for so many other Yale leaders and graduates.

In a sermon to a large group of Mohawks in 1751, Edwards made it clear he viewed the Natives and the English as equal in degeneracy and equal in their capacity for redemption by God. He greatly admired the Mohawk leader Chief Hendrick, who had converted to Christianity. Edwards and his fellow Puritan missionaries would have comprehended no paternalism or imperial bombast in his entreaty to the Mohawks: "We are no better than you in no respect, only as God has made us to differ and has been pleased to give us more light. And now we are willing to give it to you." With twenty-first-century sensibilities, and of whatever faith, it may be hard to grasp Edwards's equal-opportunity Calvinism. But grasp it we must if we are to understand the moral and intellectual environment from which Yale College emerged. Edwards believed Natives, Africans, and the English capable of the same "stupid paganism." His favorite target was always his own degenerate English flock, some of whom drove the stern and scolding minister out of his Northampton pulpit. "To what a prodigious height," he exhorted in his treatise *Original Sin*, "has a deluge of infidelity, profaneness, luxury, debauchery and wickedness of every kind arisen! The poor savage Americans are mere babes and fools (if I may so speak) as to proficiency in wickedness, in comparison of multitudes that the Christian world throngs with."[28] In his essential calling, Edwards found it hard to write and speak about the pitiful souls of his own people without thinking of those Indigenous people who never vanished around him.

With his unmatched revivalist spirit and fierce logic, Edwards spared no one the fear of death and eternal agony if they did not find faith. In a sermon to rapt children in 1740, Edwards declared, "If you love Christ, you will be safe from the devil, that roaring lion that goes about seeking whom he may devour. . . . Christ will bring down that dreadful giant and cause all holy children that love him to come and set their feet upon his neck." And in his most famous sermon, "Sinners in the Hands of an Angry God," delivered in Enfield, Massachusetts, in 1741, Edwards forced his sin-soaked listeners into the unforgettable vision of themselves, irreparably loathed by God, being held hanging in the air by him "over the pit of hell, much as one holds a spider . . . over the fire." He warned his terrorized parishioners, "Consider the fearful danger you are in." In a fragment of notes he prepared for repeated use in this sermon, Edwards may have revealed not only his rhetorical strategy but larger fears that dominated his frontier society, always threatened from without and within. "They have those Hellish principles in that if G. [God] should take off his Restraints," Edwards schemed. Then he reminded himself of "Their own care & prudence to preserve their own lives. The schemes they Lay out for Escaping Damnation. There is no promise."[29] With these notes on the sin and tragic propensities lurking in the hearts of his listeners, was the Awakener preparing to puncture the declension and perfidy of his flock? Or were they evidence of the contradictions in Edwards's own faith, his colony's, or that of all humankind? Many hopes, schemes, and dreadful giants were at large in colonial Connecticut and at Edwards's fledgling college. The demands of white supremacy and Calvinism itself stalked Edwards's New England; they tortured the free will of this minister's flocks with aims unattainable.

A genius with rhetoric and the most probing founder of American theological and philosophical literature, Edwards embodied multiple contradictions or "Puritan dilemmas." Piety and oppression, deep personal religious faith and a fully hierarchical view of human society, marched together in the Puritan worldview. The Puritan approach to slavery has been called by some scholars a "middle way." To comprehend slaveholding, they drew not on the Gospels of the New Testament but on the law books of the Old Testament: Exodus, Deuteronomy, and Leviticus. In the first legal code adopted by the Colony of New Haven in 1639, called *Moses His Judicials*, "Man-stealing," as in the Atlantic slave trade, was deemed a crime punishable by death. Yet in time the Puritans drew distinctions between unlawful and lawful slave ownership. Those enslaved people somehow already captive by some legitimate historical action could indeed be purchased and owned, especially if treated well. Here, like so many after them across the American South and in New England, they strove to square the impossible contradiction of "humane" slavery, as they participated in the nearly century-long process by which the system of indentured servitude (serving a term of labor, generally seven years) transformed by the early eighteenth century into hereditary, racial slavery.[30] Edwards would in some respects lead the way in guiltless Puritan slaveholding.

The Reverend Edwards purchased and held in slavery several people over the course of his adult life. In 1731, he traveled to Newport, Rhode Island, a major slave-trading port, and bought a fourteen-year-old girl named Venus. The minister did not keep full records on his slaveholding, but in 1736, he and his wife, Sarah, enslaved a woman named Leah. And in 1740, Jonathan and Sarah cosigned to support a "Jethro Negro and his wife Ruth," whom Sarah's mother, Mary Hooker Pierpont, had manumitted in her will. When they moved to Stockbridge they brought another enslaved woman, Rose. In the 1750s, Sarah corresponded with various family members about her efforts to purchase yet another enslaved person. After her death, two other enslaved members of their household, a married couple named Joseph and Sue, were sold on the open market in 1759. Another boy, Titus, who may have been the son of Joseph and Sue, remained enslaved, but he was later freed by Edwards's oldest son, Timothy.[31] The Edwardses, like so many other New England ministers' families who held prominent status in every town, appear to have enslaved a woman for domestic work and a man for labor in the garden and fields. Clergy in and around New Haven, as well as most of the founding trustees and first rectors and presidents of the Collegiate School and Yale, were slaveholders.

The Puritans came to accept the existence of slavery, while endeavoring to control and condemn the abuses of slaveholders. They tried to infuse the inhumanity of slavery with ethical guards against the tyranny of the slave owner. As Kenneth Minkema has shown, Edwards was a prototype of this particular Puritan conundrum. As he contemplated slavery, the theologian, always in search of divine logic, found his in a passage from Job 31:13: "If I despise the cause of my man or maidservant when they plead with me, and when they stand before me to be judged by me, what then shall I do when I come to stand before God to be judged by Him? . . . I am God's servant as they are mine, and much more inferior to God than my servant is to me."[32] Be careful how we judge, Edwards wisely admonished. But he also betrayed this essential paradox of an early modern religious world increasingly under great duress by Enlightenment ideals. Servitude was somehow natural, including chattel slavery, but the slaveholder must not abuse his terrible power, an ethically untenable proposition. Such a complex paradox in the life of Edwards informs much of the evolving early history of Yale College as well.

During his undergraduate years at Yale, the young Edwards kept a spiritual diary, attempting to record the nature and growth of his faith. Intensely intellectual, antisocial, and constantly questing to embrace an elusive "holiness," Edwards struggled with inner "wicked inclinations," as "God would not suffer [him] to go on with any quietness." And there is little surprise that Edwards's inward "violent struggles" did not concern the fate of the Black and Native people he saw around him, free or enslaved.[33] Their fate, though, walked within and without his life and that of Yale College.

Whereas Edwards and many Yale undergraduates in the eighteenth and nineteenth centuries kept written diaries, the Native peoples of southern New England possessed spiritual diaries, but they took many forms other than written texts. Their diaries, it might be said, were located in memories of ancestral land, in their habits of mind and agricultural practice, in their coastal fisheries and their maritime skills as boatmen, in their worldviews born of centuries of cultivating and navigating the region we call New England, in their quite different conceptions of political organization, and in their stories of heroism, defeat, and displacement during and after the devastations of the Pequot War in 1637–38 and King Philip's War in 1675–77.

The founders of Yale College a quarter century after King Philip's War would have been amply aware that they could bring the highest measure of English civilization and Christian mission to the trading port of New Haven because the wars of the 1630s and 1670s had rendered the region relatively peaceful. And they were fully aware that they now lived in an Atlantic world in which the African slave trade was peopling the Americas at a scale not seen before the eighteenth century, a trade now dominated by British slave traders who seemed the agents of a permanent, lucrative industry in human flesh. Some, like Yale founder and trustee James Noyes, had fought in and profited from the wars of conquest. Later students, like Jonathan Edwards, inherited a world shaped by violent and bloody conflagrations that had enveloped the region in slaughter, starvation, migration, and enslavement. Yet from its earliest founding as a fledgling school to its emergence as Yale College after the gifts from Elihu Yale and into the 1730s, the school grew in stability because of donations of land in various parts of Connecticut. An initial gift of 637 acres from James Fitch in Killingly in 1701 transferred into 628 acres in Salisbury in 1730 in northwest Connecticut. In 1732, the general assembly of the colony gave 300 acres to the college in each of the towns of Norfolk, Canaan, Goshen, Cornwall, and Kent.[34] The wars against Native Americans in the previous century made possible these land acquisitions and the beginnings of Yale College's wealth and stability in Connecticut.

The New England Puritans had never really found any "middle way" with their Native American neighbors, unless it was one achieved through blood as an arrangement somewhere between wars of conquest and Christian conversion. The college they planted took root in a landscape shaped by decades of war, as well as trade in Native captives and Africans that connected Connecticut to an Atlantic and West Indian English empire. The college was also founded to save these same Puritans from themselves. Quite a "grand errand" it was, perhaps, as the historian of Yale's ministers, Roland Bainton, has written. "Yale was conservative before it was born," declared Bainton, in the classic first line of his book published in 1957. "The reason for its founding was to conserve and revive the ways of the fathers." Quoting from Samuel 4:21, "The glory is departed from Israel," Bainton declared the degeneracy of the Puritan flock as the principal purpose for a new college to train a growing clergy for the New England commonwealths. "Prophets are notoriously prone to chide their own generation," said Bainton, "by the example of some other idealized time or clime."[35] How true. But in its founding, and surely with time, Yale also had to account for its legacies of war, captivity, and slaveholding, lying in waiting in its past, around the corner, and in its archives. Those altar lights will never spur the congregation to faith or attainment until they know from whence they came.

CHAPTER 2

Founders

Let us now praise famous men,
and our fathers in their generations. . . .
There are some of them who have left a name,
so that men declare their praise.
And there are some who have no memorial,
who have perished as though they had not lived. . . .
But these were men of mercy,
whose righteous deeds have not been forgotten.

—Ecclesiasticus 44:1, 8–10

In the decades following the establishment of Yale College, numerous advertisements for slave sales appeared nearby in the New England press. They might announce "choice Gold Coast Negroes," as one did in 1726, or "lately imported from the West Indies" and "fit for town or country service," as ads read in 1741 and 1718. This brutal merchandising language often included physical descriptions such as "likely," "well-limbed," "stout," or "lusty strong"—indications of the physical labor these people would be forced to do. The enslaved were sometimes identified as having "agreeable" or "honest" personalities. Occasionally they were labeled "born in the country" or speaking "good English," to imply a certain comfort or safety for the purchaser. Such market language bespoke the ugly truth: slaves were humans made commodities, people with a price. Native Americans were still thrust into this commercialized horror. "A Lusty Indian Man-Servant, aged about 20 years," was offered up in a 1717 notice.[1] Each person offered for sale who landed in a domestic or agricultural setting was forced into labor relationships with English settlers. They planted and harvested the summer corn, cleaned the tankards and tables at a tavern, dug latrines, nursed other women's babies, laundered preachers' robes, sawed wood, made bricks, and loaded goods on ships at the docks. They arrived in such circumstances through the system of transport, sale, and resale in the ports of Boston, Massachusetts; Newport and Bristol, Rhode Island; Portsmouth, New Hampshire; or New London, Hartford, Middletown, and New Haven in Connecticut.

The Africans who landed in New England, whether directly from Africa or via the Caribbean, were forged by the system of the slave trade into precious human commodities. In the second half of the seventeenth century, warfare among African kingdoms along the Gold Coast (present-day Ghana), particularly the Denkyira, Akwamu, and Asante peoples, prompted in part by the infusion of European firearms and a robust trade at the seaports, provided the majority of the enslaved people who would eventually make up the Black population of New England. African polities derived their power increasingly from their engagement with the Atlantic economy, especially from their ability to provide captives for sale. Slavery and slave trading were well established across West Africa before European contact. But from roughly 1650 to 1700, as the British entered the slaving business with enormous zeal and capital, the Gold Coast joined the "slave coast" as the productive engine of this trade. The average annual export of enslaved people, just from the numerous commercial trading posts of the Gold Coast, rose nearly every decade from 1670 for the next half century. The number of enslaved people leaving these entrepôts increased by roughly a thousand each decade, growing from 888 people between 1662 and 1670 to 4,708 people transported between 1720 and 1729. Most Africans were shipped to Cuba, Brazil, and other Dutch, British, and Spanish colonies in the Caribbean, where large sugar-producing plantation complexes were expanding, but a share reached the shores of New England. In total, from 1676 to 1802, an estimated 10,000 Africans arrived in New England on ships directly from Africa. Far more arrived in the Northeast via the Caribbean trade. Most Africans disembarking in New England experienced the Middle Passage in the holds of ships owned by investors in Boston, Newport, Bristol, and Middletown.[2]

In the first years of the Collegiate School, and then of Yale College, down to the 1730s and beyond, the identities of Black enslaved laborers in Connecticut were embedded in these commercial statistics. Some would have been born into slavery in Barbados or Jamaica or Saint Kitts, but the majority were African born and survivors of the journeys to a new existence on American shores, experiencing varying degrees of dehumanization, shackled limbs, terrible sickness, nakedness, despair, and death. For African women, their bodies and their wombs provided a target of this commerce, its source of profits and its future growth. Turning people into the objects of market transactions and "exchangeability," as historian Stephanie Smallwood puts it, required great violence, incarceration, and ever-new forms of iron shackling, forts, dungeons, and prison facilities on the African coast. And then there were the ships, from some as small as two hundred tons to over one thousand tons. They carried "cargoes" of many hundreds of human beings chained in the holds in spaces barely three and a half feet high. The Middle Passage across the Atlantic aboard these floating prisons constituted a disease and death machine and an intercontinental crossroads for pathogens. Staggering mortality rates—between an average of 12 and 29 percent during the Atlantic crossings, which lasted from six weeks to sometimes two and three months—reside in accounting tables on a page as mere numbers. But over the long, nearly four-century course of the slave trade, the bones of more than two million Africans dissolved in the saltwater of the Atlantic Ocean.[3]

The world has never quite devised a satisfactory way to mourn this mass death, except to try to grasp the victims' fear, sacrifice, and unbearable pain in memorials, in art, and in the silence of recognition at the scope of both human evil and human endurance. The slave trade has challenged modern memory and traditions of mourning as few other human endeavors have. And part of that mourning is to keep telling the stories of those who walked off the ships in the Western Hemisphere and became the "founding fathers and mothers," as historian Nathan Huggins once wrote, of a new African American people.[4]

The vast majority of enslaved Africans, like other laboring peoples, did not have the opportunity to record the events of their lives, and their final resting places are unmarked. Yet traces of their lives survive through deeds, through baptismal records, and most of all through wills and probate inventories; they were valuable property, their lives and bodies bequeathed as intergenerational wealth. In such records are over two hundred people bought, sold, and owned by Yale's founders, early leaders, trustees, and donors. Their names compel us to recognize the humanity and the labor of the "many thousands gone" into this crucible through which Yale College was, in part, founded. For many, their lives were an epic tragedy: from war captives to chained humans in coastal African forts, to saltwater slaves desperate to survive inhuman conditions, to wilted bodies and souls sold in American ports, to laborers transplanted into an ever-growing Atlantic economy, doing every manner of work a colonial society demanded. Yet for so many, their brains and their skills survived and transcended the damage to their bodies.[5]

The story of how African and Indigenous people came to be the property of Anglo-American settlers, including many Yale leaders and trustees, begins across an ocean, with the wars and convulsions of seventeenth-century Europe. John Davenport, founder of the colony of New Haven, was born in Coventry, England, in 1597 and lived through the regicide of Charles I, the bloody English Civil War, and a Puritan revolution by which he was greatly inspired. Popular learning was growing to a degree when Davenport went to Oxford University in 1613 to prepare for the ministry. Soon he would be resisting King James I and his attempt to forge a new established church and thwart, if not wipe out, the separatist Puritans and their Calvinist theology. England shook with embittered religious and political turmoil as Davenport emerged as a brilliant and popular preacher in London. Religious nonconformity became a dangerous vocation, and in response, some embraced a Puritan migration, first to Holland and soon to the newly founded colonies in North America. Davenport spent three distressed years in exile in Holland. In 1637, he sneaked back into England and joined several other Puritan divines as well as the prosperous businessman Theophilus Eaton and his stepson David Yale, the future father of Elihu Yale, to embark for the Massachusetts Bay Colony.[6] God and mammon joined hands in this errand to a new continent, and in the roots of a college.

Thus began Davenport's quest to establish a separatist church-state, a holy commonwealth, and indeed an independent Calvinist society. Davenport did not stay long in Massachusetts, and by April 1638, with the Pequot War ending, he and a party of people led by Eaton sailed down the coast into the Long Island Sound and came to the land of the Quinnipiac people. And so "Newhaven," as the new settlers named it, gained a foothold as a Puritan community, a "Civil Government in a New Plantation whose Design is Religion," as Davenport declared. All "planters" had to agree that they would be governed only by "rules held forth in Scripture." But Davenport and Eaton also stressed the commercial and material quest of their colony. They called for "the better trayning upp of youth in this towne, that, through God's blessing they may be fitted for publique service hereafter, in church or commonweale." Among Davenport's highest priorities was education, the creation of schools, and from the beginning, a new college in which to train ministers in the principles of Calvinism. Davenport would not live to see such a college in New Haven, but through many trials and fits and starts over the next half century, the idea never died. At the heart of this quest was the need for an educated ministry and good governance in towns. But even more central to Davenport's dream was the desire for an institution that would train the clergy in a true Puritan faith against all the growing heresies, such as Arminianism (the liberal, anti-predestinarian belief that Christians do have free will in seeking salvation) and the Half-Way Covenant (adopted in 1662 in Massachusetts, allowing the second and third generations of Puritans to be baptized whether they had experienced true conversion or not). Before he died in 1670—and before he delivered his last sermon in 1668 in the meetinghouse on what is today the New Haven Green—Davenport amassed one of the best book collections in North America, intending for it to be the basis of a new college.[7]

A straight line is often drawn between Davenport's quest for a college for learned ministers and leaders and the creation of Yale in 1701. But in fact a rather crooked path winds through the dark, transforming, and tragic history of the English Civil War, the rise of Oliver Cromwell, Davenport's strong support of nearly all aspects of international Puritanism, and his eventual sheltering and defense in New Haven of some of the regicides who signed the death warrant for King Charles I in 1649. Yet by the time the monarchy was restored in 1660 and New Haven Colony was incorporated into the larger colony of Connecticut in 1665, Davenport's dream of a New Jerusalem on Long Island Sound was already beginning to fade. Ecclesiastical bloodletting and religious war, as well as the precipitous decline of Puritan theological rigor and church discipline, meant that the erection of a college was left for future generations to imagine. Davenport also was among the first slaveholders in New Haven, establishing a legacy that would continue with many of the future founders of Yale and leaders of the city. In his will, he listed at least one slave, recorded as "one servant boy, £10."[8] In its early years, Yale College, in small but growing ways, incorporated Davenport's quest for piety and power, and it relied on far more than £10 of human property.

Uncompromising to the end, Davenport is distinguished by his ferocious faith, his embrace of essential Calvinist doctrine, and his theocratic state-making vision. He and his cofounder, Eaton, left a story of economic enterprise that would animate New Haven as well as Yale. These principles became formative values at the college's founding thirty years after his death. For Davenport and his successors, God and holiness were utterly real, profound presences in their minds and lives. Prayer could be visceral nourishment as well as terrifying revelation. To watch churches decline into indifference or irrelevance, to see piety collapse in the gutter outside tippling houses, to see ministers who could not inspire shuddering confrontations with God, to compromise with what one understood as the devil, was to watch society and God's creation die. God's rule over the universe was the hand of Providence; it was mysterious and beyond human understanding. But there were signs laced throughout scripture, and a trained ministry devoted to deep study, commentary, and sermonic explication stood between believers and their certain doom. The faithful and the saved, who were few, had to live among the godless; therefore worship, teaching, admonition, and godly discipline were crucial in daily life. It was an offense to God to try to know his intentions, but in the classic Puritan paradox, one had to strive for deeper personal faith in order to ever hope to build a holy commonwealth of all people. A well-ordered state was a high temporal achievement, and Davenport and his associates laid out New Haven in "nine squares," designed, they believed, after the encampments of the Israelites in their exile. And exile—its necessity, its travails, its overcoming, and its power as a story—remained central to these dissenting, nonconformist, monarchy-hating pilgrims in a foreign land. A predestinarian doctrine about grace alone made the Puritan "errand" a fraught and nearly impossible challenge, yet they pursued it with unbounded zeal. Their hierarchical view of human society and their largely unthinking defenses of slavery were commonplace elements of Puritanism in Davenport's time.[9]

On October 9, 1701, the general assembly in New Haven authorized the creation of a college and named ten clergymen as trustees of the new school. The next month, seven of these ministers, all but one trained at Harvard, gathered in Saybrook, Connecticut, on the shores of the Long Island Sound, for their first meeting. In attendance were Samuel Andrew of Milford, Thomas Buckingham of Saybrook, Israel Chauncey of Stratford, James Pierpont of New Haven, Abraham Pierson of Kenilworth (later Killingworth, now Clinton), Noadiah Russell of Middletown, and Joseph Webb of Fairfield. They likely met at Buckingham's house. Three others of the founding trustees were ill and missed their first meeting: Samuel Mather of Windsor, Timothy Woodbridge of Hartford, and James Noyes of Stonington. Together, what they established was essentially the *idea* of a college, with a few rules about how degrees were to be administered and a stipulation that its leader would be called "rector." Fledgling to say the least, this school had been authorized by the colonial assembly, which began with a grant of £120 as well as the assembly's approval to spend an additional £500 per annum. A wealthy landowner, James Fitch, also donated a farm the college might use for rental revenue. And so instruction of a sort began, with one undergraduate degree given in 1702, along with a handful of master's degrees.[10]

Some slaves were likely present at the first trustees' meeting. An early twentieth-century history of Yale describes the journey to Buckingham's house, picturing the clergymen "followed on horseback by their men-servants or slaves, into old Killingworth Street." In early eighteenth-century Connecticut, laborers of all sorts, particularly those who served the clergy class, were frequently

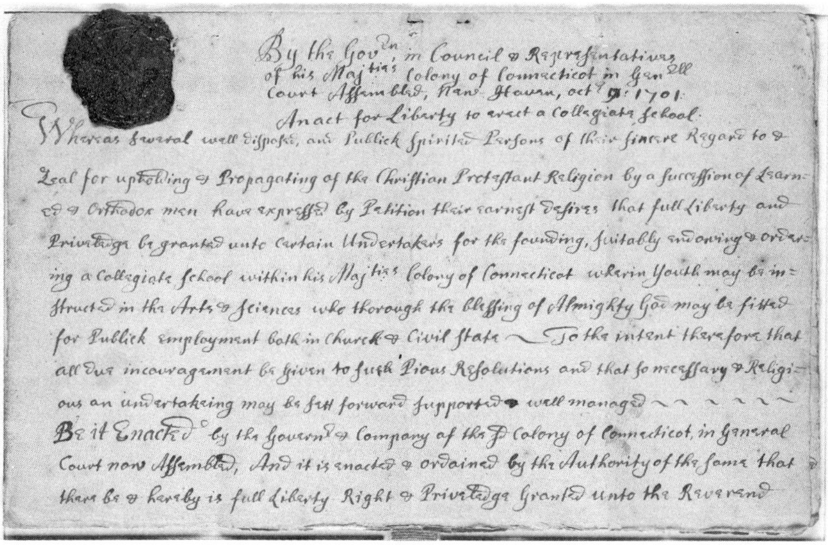
By the Gov^n in Council & Representatives of his Maj^ties Colony of Connecticot in Gen^ll Court Assembled, New Haven, oct^r 9: 1701.

An act for Liberty to erect a Collegiate School.

Whereas severall well disposed, and Publick spirited Persons of their sincere Regard to & Zeal for upholding & Propagating of the Christian Protestant Religion by a succession of Learned & Orthodox men have expressed by Petition their earnest desires that full Liberty and Priviledge be granted unto Certain Undertakers for the founding, suitably endowing & ordering a Collegiate School within his Maj^ties Colony of Connecticot wherein Youth may be instructed in the Arts & Sciences who through the blessing of Almighty God may be fitted for Publick employment both in Church & Civil State. To the intent therefore that all due incouragement be given to such Pious Resolutions and that so necessary & Religious an undertaking may be sett forward supported & well managed

Be it Enacted by the Governo^r & Company of the s^d Colony of Connecticot, in General Court now Assembled, And it is enacted & ordained by the Authority of the same that there be & hereby is full Liberty Right & Priviledge Granted unto the Reverend

"An Act for Liberty to Erect a Collegiate School," 1701. Early Yale Documents Collection (RU 1154). Manuscripts and Archives, Yale University Library.

enslaved or indentured servants. Indeed, of the first ten trustees of what became Yale College, at least seven, and possibly others, owned one or more slaves.[11]

The Reverend Buckingham, in his will, left to his son, Hezekia Buckingham, "my negro boy called Peter to be his Slave Servant," and to his "son-in-law John Kirtland of Saybrook my negro boy called Philip to be his Slave Servant." The Reverend Chauncey, in the inventory of his estate, listed "A Negro girl" valued at £40, below "An horse" and "eight sheep" and above "a Great Brass kettle." Most ministers trained in the seventeenth century and involved in the creation of Yale left such calculations and matter-of-fact statements of human chattel property in their estates and inventories. The will of the Reverend James Noyes II, dated 1719, did not include any human property, but years earlier he had held several Native Americans in captivity. The Reverend James Pierpont, along with his two brothers, Benjamin and John, owned two men named Tom and Pung. Benjamin, also a graduate of Harvard, moved to pastor a church in Charleston, South Carolina, where he acquired a plantation along the Ashley River, enslaved workers, and other property. James Pierpont took the pulpit of First Church, New Haven in 1685, where he later baptized Thomas and another man he owned named Benjamin. Eventually Reverend Pierpont inherited his brother's South Carolina plantation and the enslaved people living there. The Reverend Pierson followed his father's group of dissenters from New Haven Colony to found Newark, New Jersey, in 1668. According to historian Craig Steven Wilder, Pierson inherited from his father a large farm in New Jersey and became a slaveholder before moving back to Connecticut in 1692.[12]

The Reverend Russell owned three enslaved people, a woman named Jane, a girl named Libs, and a baby, Sampson, at his death in 1714. In 1720, a Black woman valued at £40 was listed as part of a "Lost Estate Spent in the family." Distribution to his son John included "7-15-10 in the negro boy Sampson"—that is, the child was by then valued at 7 pounds, 15 shillings, 10 pence. The girl Libs, who had been valued at £35, was not mentioned again. The Reverend Webb left a Black girl named Phillis, valued at £80, in his estate at the time of his death.[13] Enslaved men, women, and children in the archives of Yale's founders have remained nearly invisible for three centuries, but to a degree they have been hiding in plain sight.

Of the founding trustees, the Reverend Woodbridge—namesake of Woodbridge Hall—was the largest slaveholder. Church records show that he and his wife owned and baptized Black individuals named Isabella and Cesar Diego, Thomas, and a thirteen-year-old boy named Thorn, whom he sold "in plain and open market." Furthermore, Abigail Woodbridge, his wife, inherited from her first husband a man named Andrew, who eventually married Tamar, a slave owned by the Reverend Woodbridge. Tamar and Andrew had children named Lydia, Isabella, and Daniel. Parents, children, and siblings were often separated, sometimes as gifts or when an estate was broken up. It appears the Woodbridges gave Tamar, Andrew, and their son Daniel to Abigail's son. In his will, Timothy Woodbridge left Lydia to his own daughter *if* she would pay his wife for her, stating that he was giving his "Negro girll named Lydia" to his wife or his "Davghter Susannah Treat may haue sd Negro girll paying a Reasonable price for her." Other arrangements were nominally temporary but in reality long lasting. Woodbridge baptized "John Waubin my Indian servant" on August 10, 1711. Over twenty years later, in his will dated 1732, he gave to his "loving wife Abigaill Woodbridge . . . the Improvement of John Waubin during the Time he is bound to serve me." A Black man, Cato Sessions, was also indentured to Woodbridge. After her second husband's death, Abigail used the proceeds of her husband's estate to purchase at least four additional people, Dinah, Jacob, Candace, and Sam. Jacob and Sam were included in the list of valuables in her will when she died. In all, a Hartford-based history project led by Kathryn Hermes estimates that Abigail Woodbridge and her two husbands, including Timothy Woodbridge, held a total of thirty-one people in bondage in addition to one indentured Native American person and one indentured Black man—a remarkably large number for the time and place.[14] Such a blizzard of names, transactions, and bequests serves to illustrate how normative and unchallenged slaveholding, even at this relatively small scale, was in Connecticut.

These founders all came from the top echelon of Connecticut society and possessed close ties to the colonial assembly and the governor's council. They were linked to one another by family, marriage, and many other shared experiences. All but one of the Collegiate School's founders had educational roots at Harvard and had come of age to one degree or another committed to preserving Calvinist purity and orthodoxy against a liberalism that many perceived as ascendant in Massachusetts. Yet the Connecticut founders took many cues from their associates in Massachusetts, especially the Reverend Cotton Mather, Secretary of the Massachusetts Bay Colony Isaac Addington, and Samuel Sewall, a member of the governor's council and later chief justice of the superior court. Addington and Sewall provided the ministers valued advice as orthodox Puritan laymen, recommending many measures in a draft charter they wrote in October 1701 and sent to Buckingham. Sewall and Addington gave the ministers a modest blueprint but firmly expressed their "sorrow" at the liberal "decay" at Harvard.[15]

Sewall in particular offered a complex legacy, should the founding ministers have chosen to follow it. In 1700, he published the first-ever Puritan denunciation of slavery in America. Sewall had emigrated from England as a child in 1661 and had become a justice on the Massachusetts Superior Court as well as a successful merchant. He had participated as a judge in the Salem witchcraft trials in 1692, condemning women to the gallows, acts for which he had recently publicly repented (the only judge to do so). *The Selling of Joseph* is a unique text for its time, both a lament and an appeal in pamphlet form, an altar call to the Puritan faithful to save their own souls and those of the enslaved as well. It is a work of Christian conscience. In the sermonic tradition, the essay is laced with scriptural references such as Acts 17:26–27 ("God . . . hath made of One Blood, all Nations of Men, for to dwell on all the face of the Earth"); the Golden Rule, Matthew 7:12 ("All things whatsoever ye would that men should do to you, do ye even so unto them"); and Paul's Epistle to the Ephesians, imagining that humanity might live under a unified "law of love." Invoking Exodus 21:16, Sewall condemned the capture and sale of human beings, writing, "He that Stealeth a Man and Selleth him . . . he shall surely be put to Death." The judge's essay practiced the tradition of the Puritan jeremiad, condemning especially the commerce in human cargo, as well as the breakup of families, White and Black, and warning, "It is too well known what Temptations Masters are under, to connive at the Fornication of their Slaves."[16]

Sewall's *The Selling of Joseph* was a radical document for its time, even for the eighteenth century as a whole. Sewall knew New England slavery well; his diary is full of casual and explicit references to enslaved people, to the West Indian trade, and to his deep disquiet about the pernicious effects of racial slavery at the heart of the Puritan experiment. He remarkably employed many arguments that would survive and grow in American antislavery activism for a century and a half. But racism then disrupted the judge's moral case. It was the buying and selling of people that Sewall condemned, even as he also worried about "a disparity in their Conditions, Colour & Hair" and that "they can never embody with us, and grow up into orderly Families." Sewall viewed African peoples as possessed of a different "blood," rendering them naturally inferior in capacity. These racial views were completely normative in 1700 among his fellow English colonists. *The Selling of Joseph*, however, prompted counterattacks immediately for its condemnation of the slave trade. John Saffin, a prosperous Massachusetts merchant and fellow judge on the court with Sewall, published in the same year *A Brief and Candid Answer to a Late Published Sheet, Entitled "The Selling of Joseph."* In this first-ever American point-counterpoint over slavery, Saffin tried to match Sewall scripture for scripture and called him blasphemous for his effort to "invert the Order that God hath set in the world." The "degrees and orders of men" (the races) must be held sacred, Saffin argued. Many Puritan divines, at Yale and beyond, including Jonathan Edwards, employed this troublesome distinction to oppose slave trading and selling ("manstealing") but support slaveholding, usually without the tortured conscience of a Samuel Sewall. Ultimately, *The Selling of Joseph* fell into obscurity, although it was reprinted in 1737, and then again much later in the midst of the American Civil War in 1863.[17]

As a kind of justification for his pamphlet, Sewall quoted from the most often used verse in the entire African American Christian tradition, Psalm 68:31: "Princes shall come out of Egypt; Ethiopia shall soon stretch out her hands unto God." Well before virtually all his contemporaries, Sewall was absolutely clear on the meaning of at least one part of this great passage. "Under which Names [Ethiopia]," he wrote, "all *Africa* may be comprehended; and their Promised Conversion ought to be prayed for." Over the next three centuries, Black Christians in America would again and again return to Psalm 68 to fashion hope and identity in a hostile world. Yale's founders either chose not to or did not comprehend what Sewall glimpsed in 1700, and tragically, they seem to have been unaware of the judge's moving prescriptions against slavery, even though, according to historian Mark A. Peterson, Sewall likely distributed the essay to the Collegiate School founders.[18] But religious orthodoxy overwhelmed the lonely conscience of Sewell in 1700, as did the otherwise unchallenged economic and moral habit of procuring enslaved labor. The vaunted conservatism of the Yale founding ministers, targeted so sternly at the liberalism and religious backsliding of their neighbors to the north, may also have been rooted in a fierce refusal to countenance Sewell's bold antislavery treatise.

The small Collegiate School foundered for the next decade and more, with instruction conducted in Saybrook, Wethersfield, and other Connecticut towns until it moved permanently to New Haven in 1716. During this period the college found a major benefactor from abroad and a namesake. Elihu Yale was a wealthy man, born in Boston, who had moved to England as a child and grown up as landed aristocracy in Wales. Yale spent many years in Madras, India, first as a clerk, then as a writer, eventually becoming governor of the East India Company in that lucrative outpost of the British Empire. In accepting Yale's largesse, those pious, dissenting ministers—who kept one pecuniary eye on the main chance—were forced to avert their eyes and accept books, cash, and other goods from an Anglican donor who shared none of their orthodox Calvinist heritage.[19]

Yale arrived in India in 1672 and moved up the ranks in the colonial council until 1687, when he was appointed governor of Madras and agent in charge of Fort St. George. The East India Company conducted enormous commerce out of Madras, on India's southeast coast, and it sanctioned and regulated part of the Indian slave trade from Yale's post. An English traveler in 1675 described an earlier Madras governor's "personal guard of three or four hundred blacks" and said he traveled with "fifes, drums, trumpets, and a flag" and was hoisted up and "carried in a gorgeous palankeen, and shaded by an ostrich-feather fan." The Indian Ocean slave trade, which eventually matched the Atlantic in size and scope, did not become so extensive until the nineteenth century. But on the Indian subcontinent, the trade in human beings along its coasts as well as inland and to islands was very old.[20]

Whatever level of ostentatiousness Yale demanded, he oversaw many sales, adjudications, and accountings of enslaved people for the East India Company. In 1680, while only a bookkeeper, Yale was assigned a "peon," a person in the Southeast Asian context who was bound to servitude as an attendant or an orderly, a common practice. "Yale and Sayon [another factor]," records indicate, "having acquainted the Councell, that unless they have Servants allowed them to summon People before them, and to Imprison if occasion bee, they cannot performe their Offices. It is thought fit each of them have one of the Hono$^{ble.}$ Companies Peons appointed to attend that Business." When Yale was governor, the "Consultation Books" frequently would report such decisions, as in 1687, when he and his agents, over Yale's signature, "Order'd that ten Slaves be sent upon each of the Europe ships for St. Helena, to supply that Island." Because of a famine in 1687, enslaved people were frequently sold off to Indian Ocean coastal ports and islands. That same year, the governor's office reported "that one hundred Slaves bee sent them [unnamed Indian port] on both Ships they being by the famine, extreamly cheap, and also many by us, & that as many handicrafts, & Peons do go." In 1689, Yale reported that the frigate *Pearle* returned from Vizagapatam. Part of the cargo was shackles "for well secureing the slaves." Sometimes Yale and his fellow agents dealt out enslavement as punishment for crimes, as on September 24, 1687, when "Three people were punished for a crime by being sentenced to life slavery for the company." A 1688 decision found two Black men guilty of robbery, with one sentenced to death and the other "branded and banished" to Saint Helena (in the South Atlantic Ocean). And in 1689, an enslaved man named Francisco ("alias Chico") was convicted of theft, even though the only evidence was a confession given under "punishment before his tryall." Rather than sentencing him to death, the officers ordered Francisco publicly whipped, branded, and banished to the west coast of India as a slave to the company in order to serve as an example to others. Dozens more of these kinds of reports exist in records of Fort St. George.[21]

The matter of Elihu Yale's ownership of enslaved people or his involvement in slave trading has long been a subject of speculation, but the East India Company kept records of Yale's key leadership role in the business of human trafficking. "In the 1680s," writes historian Joseph Yannielli, "when Yale served on the governing council at Fort St. George on the Madras coast, a devastating famine led to an uptick in the local slave trade. As more and more bodies became available on the open market, Yale and other company officials took advantage of the labor surplus, buying hundreds of slaves and shipping them to the English colony on Saint Helena." Yannielli continues, "Yale participated in a meeting that ordered a minimum of ten slaves sent on every outbound European ship. In just one month in 1687, Fort St. George exported at least 665 individuals. As governor . . . Yale enforced the ten-slaves-per-vessel rule." Precisely whether or how many people Yale personally may have owned is not yet discernable, nor perhaps even a key question. Much of his growing wealth derived from the lucrative trade in cloth, silks, precious jewels, and other commodities. Yet this commerce was inseparable from the slave trade. There can be no question that some portion of

Yale's considerable fortune, amassed while British governor-president in Madras, derived from his myriad entanglements with the purchase and sale of human beings. The records further demonstrate that in this busy and valuable port of the British Empire, varying practices of slavery were ubiquitous.[22]

Yale was dismissed from the governorship in 1692 and for a while placed under house arrest because of embezzlement charges that embroiled him in legal proceedings that lasted seven years. He returned to England in 1699. On board the *Martha* with him was an enslaved woman named Ellea, her destination unknown but her presence another indication of how movements between England and India were enmeshed in flows of enslaved people as well as the profits derived from their sale. Yale also brought with him five tons of personal cargo, which would allow him to live in high style both in London and at his Wales estate, with most of his fortune intact. In a highly favorable history of Yale College's origins written in 1918, Franklin Bowditch Dexter admits that Yale's fortune

Elihu Yale with Members of His Family and an Enslaved Child, attributed to John Verelst, circa 1719. Yale Center for British Art, Gift of Andrew Cavendish, eleventh Duke of Devonshire.

stemmed from "profits of private trade" but dismisses the embezzlement charges as committed by others. Dexter does leave a remarkable statement about the governor's character, however, saying he left a "record of arrogance, cruelty, sensuality, and greed," and compares him to the biblical king Nebuchadnezzar. In London, an agent for the Collegiate College, Jeremiah Dummer, with the help of other Puritan correspondents such as Cotton Mather, courted the wealthy Yale as a donor. The former East India Company official was now a merchant grandee, a collector of art, jewels, Chinese porcelain, textiles, fine furniture, and books, and the subject of numerous portraits in his lifetime. His book collection was estimated at his death in 1721 to contain upwards of two thousand volumes, including many works of science and a large portion in Greek and Latin.[23]

Yale had three daughters but no male heir. In 1689, his wife, Catherine, and the daughters left Madras, ten years before Elihu, and moved back to England; their son David had died at age four the previous year. In his family's absence, Yale took up with a housekeeper-mistress, Hieronima, the widow of a Portuguese diamond dealer. They had a son named Charles, who did not take his father's last name, and who died in 1712 back in England.[24] Yale's legal and personal-political dramas within the East India Company did not seem to burden him after his return to London. He knew he had strong family ties to Connecticut, even to New Haven, and he responded to the college's solicitations. Between 1713 and 1721, Yale sent hundreds of books, a portrait of King George I, and "sundry goods and merchandizes" to support the Collegiate School of Connecticut. As per Yale's instructions, the goods were sold, and the proceeds went to the building of the college house. In Boston, the goods and merchandise sold for a total of £562 12s. colonial currency, well above the £300 Yale believed they were worth. Along with the books and the portrait, which were not sold but were valued at an additional £600, the total value of Elihu Yale's gift to the college was roughly £1,162. It was not an insignificant donation, but in the context of Yale's enormous wealth, the college was hoping for more. As Dummer wrote to James Pierpont, "Mr. Yale has done something, tho very little considering his Estate and particular relation to your Collony."[25]

The imperial and Indian origins of Yale's wealth are inscribed in his donation to the college. At least ten types of fine cloth, most of it likely Indian and produced by weavers recruited to the coastal areas near Madras and exploited by the East India Company, were listed in the inventory of Yale's donation. This inventory document remains in the Yale archives; yellowed, folded eight times, it appears to have been rarely opened in more than three hundred years. The textiles—garlix, muslin, calico, stufe, Spanish poplins, black and white silk crape, camlet, Madras chintz, cloth flowered with inlaid silver, and satin—were the product of hand spinning and an intricate process of dying, painting, printing, and other aesthetic practices; they were the most sought-after commodities in Europe of the vast East Asia trade.[26] From the donation of such valued goods and luxury commodities was a college's name derived.

In honor of Elihu Yale's contributions, and to entice him into additional donations, the Collegiate School constructed a building called Yale College. From that day forward, the third-oldest institution of higher learning in America would be known by that name. The house, the first school building for instruction in New Haven, was finished in October 1718 and stood three stories high, 170 feet long, and 22 feet wide. Built at a cost of approximately £1,000, it contained some fifty studies for students. On September 12, 1718, Yale College held a "splendid Commencement" ceremony. Connecticut's governor Gurdon Saltonstall delivered a Latin oration after the degrees were awarded, thus reinforcing Yale's evolving public and private identity. The name of the donor, Elihu Yale, rose very prominently from pronouncements. In naming the college, the trustees paid tribute to their "Munificent Patron" and declared their gratitude for the "lasting Monument of such a Generous Gentleman." Saltonstall honored Yale as "a Gentleman, who greatly abounded in good Humour and Generosity, as well as in Wealth," and thus a long tradition was born. Whatever his "humour," over time, as a writer on philanthropy said in 1999, "surely, never has so much immortality been purchased for so paltry an eleemosynary sum."[27]

From its founding to its renaming in 1718, and in the years to come, Yale College would steadily benefit from significant support from funds provided by the Connecticut colonial assembly. Throughout the eighteenth century the college received many gifts of land, goods of many kinds, cash derived from rents on its lands, and outright donations in British sterling. Yale College and New Haven also gained in wealth and power due to their close economic ties to the West Indian trade in many commodities, not least of which were sugar and rum, linked inextricably to Caribbean slavery. Over the following decades, as Yale College collected ever more books, hired rectors to teach, constructed buildings, probed the fluent and contested intellectual universe of Reformed theology, and imagined its future, enslaved labor remained as integral to the growth of the college as it was at its beginning.

INTERLUDE

Names of the Enslaved

Enslaved people were part of New Haven and Connecticut from the beginning days of European settlement and of the extended community of Yale University from its founding as the Collegiate School in 1701. The people whose names are recorded here were enslaved by the founding and successor trustees, rectors and presidents, and major early donors in Yale's first century. Most lived in Connecticut, but some were in nearby places such as New York or Rhode Island. The vast majority of the people listed here were identified as Black, but in some cases they were identified as Indigenous. Records of inheritances, sales, baptisms, and other events provide some details, such as family relationships and ages, but in many cases their names are all that the surviving evidence provides. However they attained their names, they all lived in a highly stratified society in which the idea of equality had very little grounding.

This list, although it contains the names of over two hundred human beings, is incomplete. Research has focused on wills, estate papers, church records, and the federal census. Estate documents present an accounting of a household only at the time of a person's death. Yale's leaders, like fellow elites of church and society in Connecticut, often enslaved other people earlier in their lives whose names were not recorded in their wills (because they died, were sold, escaped, or were manumitted). For this and other reasons, further research would likely show evidence of additional enslaved people connected to Yale.

The names listed are those given, in most cases, to these people by their slaveholders. Individual names listed may thus differ from names given at birth by their parents. Many names were drawn from the Bible—Leah, Hagar, Sampson, Jacob, Job, Joab, Isaac, and Luke. Others seem to have been adopted from classical times or characters, such as Venus, Titus, Nero, and Hector, while still others had African or Hebrew origins, like Juba and Kedar. And a few are place-names, such as Newport, York, and Devonshire. In some instances, the available records note a person without including any name, and these people are included as well. The absence of a name in the records does not constitute the absence of a life.[1]

Flora
Ishmael
Ishmael
James
Phillis
Polag
Sylvanus
Unnamed man
York
Ziba
Unnamed person
Bristo
Agnes
Anthony
Philip
Peter
Philip
Devonshire
Jethro
Unnamed girl
George
Phillis
Pompey
Sylva
Tamar
Cloe
Dick
Dinah
Ann
Moll
Primus
Aaron
Lettice
Ollive
Sue
Maria
Naomi
Unnamed "next youngest"
York
Joab Binney
Joseph
Leah
Rose
Sue
Titus
Venus
Coke
Hager
Lilly
Peg
Samson
Kate
Kedar
Unnamed person

Dauphin
Toney
Jenny
Phillis
Unnamed person
Unnamed person
Benjamin
Cesar
Daniel
Hannibal
Jack
Joe the Miller
Mary
Piet
Pietvlek
Saar
Son of Joe the Miller
Tom
Jenne
Cato
Chiman
Chloe
Daphnis
Dina
Dinah
Elus
Eolus
Exeter
Fortune
Pero
Pero
Rubie
Scipio
Sylve
Unnamed fourteenth child of Dinah
Unnamed fifteenth child of Dinah
Unnamed sixteenth child of Dinah
Unnamed seventeenth child of Dinah
Unnamed eighteenth child of Dinah
Unnamed nineteenth child of Dinah
Unnamed twentieth child of Dinah
Cesar
Juba
Nero
Rose
Betty
Dolle
Linus
Michael
Ceaser
York
Dinah
Unnamed girl
Unnamed girl
Unnamed man
Unnamed woman
Ashor
Cloe
Jack
Luke
Sabina
Arabella
Benjamin
Pung
Thomas
Elle
Unnamed man
Cuff
Jane

Libs
Sampson
Don
Lettice
Sampson
Andrew
Pompey
Presey
Amos
Annise
Clary
Cloe
Ely
Iago
Jerusha
Job
Job
Levi
Lowes
Peter
Rachel
Rhoda
Rose
Sue
Tego
Newport
Hagar
Jenny
Zylpha
Easter Williams
London
Unnamed person
Cate
Grigg
Hagar
Lemmon
Mabel
Peg
Bristol
Grace
Hector
Isaac
Rose
Phillis
Cloe
Flora
Isabel
Phillis
Rhoda
Dick
Jenny
Tully
Unnamed boy
Unnamed woman
Unnamed man
Unnamed woman
Ambo
Cass
Desire
Flora
Jude
Merea
Newport
Peter
Pitt
David
Unnamed woman
Cash
Dinah
Pero
Pompey
Cato
Prince
Sarah
Silvi
Tony

Andrew
Candace
Cesar Diego
Isabella
Daniel
Dinah
Isabella
Jacob
John Waubin
Lydia
Sam
Tamar
Thomas
Thorn

CHAPTER 3

West Indian Trade, Connecticut, and the College

> The trade with the West Indies is therefore hardly to be considered as external trade, but more resembles the traffic between town and country.
>
> —JOHN STUART MILL, *Principles of Political Economy* (1848)

In 1700, the Barbadian planter Thomas Tryon complained of his travail in operating the boiling house on his sugar plantation, a delicately timed, loud, factorylike production system and an early illustration of the industrial revolution rooted in enslaved labor. He described the "perpetual Noise and Hurry" and the "Tyrannical" demands on both himself, the English owner, and his African bondmen. "Climate is so hot," moaned Tryon, "and the labor so constant that the Servants night and day stand in great Boyling Houses, where there are Six or Seven large Coppers or Furnaces kept perpetually Boyling." The weary planter stood nearly in awe of his besieged laborers before claiming most of the woe for himself. "With heavy Ladles and Scummers they Skim off the excrementitious parts of the Canes, till it comes to its perfection and cleanness, while other Stoakers, Broil as it were, alive, in managing the Fires; and one part is constantly at the Mill, to supply it with Canes, night and day, during the whole Season of making Sugar, which is about six Months of the year." With any luck, and if he did not lose too many workers in this dangerous labor, Tryon might make a large profit in selling the crushed cane, turned into molasses, to old England or New England, where it would be distilled into rum or converted into savory sweeteners for the Atlantic world's new palate. But he did not leave this moment without grumbling that "a Master Planter has no . . . easy life."[1]

Yale's leafy campus may seem a long way from the boiling houses of Barbados, but by the late seventeenth century and through the eighteenth, colonial

Connecticut and its New England neighbors were deeply intertwined with commerce and slavery in the Caribbean. Cities like New Haven became "Atlantic" cities, connected through trade to the commodity-producing plantations of the West Indies as well as to England, the center of colonial banking, insurance, and great wealth. The horses that turned the wheels and rollers of the sugar mills, the food that fed enslaved and free people alike, many kinds of wood products and building materials, tools and farming implements, and even the dung that fertilized the cane fields were shipped directly from Connecticut, as well as other New England colonies, into Barbados, Jamaica, and other islands. In return, the northern colonies received ever-increasing supplies of sugar, molasses, rum, salt, and cotton, all produced by the labor of enslaved people in the vast Caribbean plantation complex.[2] Because of their economic interconnections, New England and the West Indies were, as John Stuart Mill put it, like town was to country, a constant, mutually dependent commerce. The wealth generated from this trade not only helped finance the earliest plans for the Collegiate School—the forerunner to Yale College—but also underwrote the construction of its buildings well into the eighteenth century.[3]

The "sugar revolution," as scholars have come to call it, swept over Atlantic commerce for more than a century after the 1660s. In the early years of sugar production, the commodity was still a symbol of status, consumed and enjoyed largely by the upper classes. But by the second quarter of the eighteenth century, a woman on a small farm in New England or in the heather fields of Yorkshire sweetened her morning tea with sugar, and her husband might take a dram or two of rum by evening. Indeed, rum was the elixir of the sugar revolution and its most powerful commodity. Replacing gin and other potent spirits, this product of rolling cane into molasses and then distilling it became a fuel of psychological survival for countless sailors, dock workers, farmers, planters, and others, as well as the engine of a massive growth of distilleries and commerce from Massachusetts and Connecticut to Amsterdam and London. Rum consumption exploded around the British Atlantic empire from the 1690s to the 1770s. In 1698, approximately 207 gallons of rum were imported into England itself, but by 1771 to 1775, the annual average was over *2 million* gallons, and that does not include smuggling figures. The drink even became a regular ration in the British navy. Rum emerged as a kind of barter currency, used to trade for every manner of foodstuff and livestock needed in the plantation societies of the West Indies. On most Caribbean sugar islands, enslaved workers themselves consumed on average three and a half gallons of rum per year. One early critic of the rum trade said in 1648 that the drink was a "beverage fit only for slaves and donkeys." But by the early eighteenth century, "demon rum" flowed in the fanciest "punch bowls" of the aristocracy in England and the wealthiest merchants in New England towns.[4]

The greatest trading partners for Barbadian and Jamaican rum were the northern colonies in British North America. And all over early and mid-eighteenth-century New England, particularly in Connecticut, economic production of many kinds depended on sugar as it provided for the West Indian trade flowing in and out of its two primary ports, New London and New Haven. By 1774, some 180 seafaring ships had been built in those two ports, and more than a thousand oceangoing sailors made a living aboard these ships. In the period from 1715 to 1765—the key years of Yale's growth—forty-six ships built in Connecticut entered North American ports, transporting enslaved people for sale. Farmers raising cattle, sheep, poultry, and horses; unpaid women known as "dairywomen," who generated cheese and butter; carpenters and sawyers who cut pine boards and made staves and hoops; oarsmen on flatboats and ferry operators along the many rivers; workers who cured, bunched, and weighed onions; and shipbuilders and seafarers all labored to produce and deliver the dozens of commodities to the booming market of the Caribbean plantation complex. Connecticut colonial customs records indicate that in one five-year period from 1768 to 1772, 444 ships cleared New Haven, 43 percent of which sailed to the West Indies. Of the 1,870 vessels that departed from New London, the bigger harbor, 42 percent headed to the Caribbean. Of 993 ships arriving in New Haven in this same time period, 407 came from the West Indies; in New London, roughly one-third of inbound ships were arriving from there. Sugar, molasses, and rum production—indeed the entire plantation system—relied indispensably on Connecticut commerce. Given the commercial entanglements between Connecticut and the Caribbean in the early eighteenth century, students at Yale most likely enjoyed meals conjured from the same foodstuffs, derived from the same fields and barnyards and carried along the same ferryboat routes, as the enslaved workers of Jamaican plantations.[5]

The dangerous and unhealthy conditions of sugar production, from the fields to the boiling rooms, required a constant flow of laborers to sustain it. By the 1660s, approximately eighteen thousand enslaved Africans arrived in all of the Americas each year. But with the sugar revolution and the British embrace of the human-trafficking business, eventually more than one million enslaved people landed in Jamaica, and a half million on the smaller island of Barbados.[6] And although very few English colonists in New England ever saw a maimed or crippled watchman from a sugar mill, unknowingly or not they carried some part of that person's soul within their own. The sounds, smells, blood, and agonies of the West Indian sugar mill may not have been sensed in churches on New England town greens, but their lethal combination built the pews and the high pulpits. Unknowingly, the crushing of the cane rollers a thousand miles away poured forth in Old Testament sermons about sin and all but impossible redemption.

Rum became the fuel of economic growth in the New England colonies, used by civil society to build new institutions. In 1721, the Connecticut General Assembly passed "An Act for the better Regulating the Duty of Impost upon Rhum," which included the provision "that what shall be gained by the impost on rum for two years next coming shall be applied to the building of a rectors house for Yale College."[7] In its first century, Yale College was thus a public as well as a private institution. In addition to these public funds, private donations derived from the Caribbean trade underwrote professorships and other expenses. The early rectors, tutors, and students practiced their Latin and Greek morning recitations in comforts provided by trade in sugar, molasses, and rum produced by enslaved people. As in nearly all places of learning, a well-turned Latin phrase could be performed in a quietude purchased from afar.

From its founding, Yale received financial and political support from some of the most influential and prominent families in Connecticut and beyond. These same families were often involved, personally and through their business interests, in slaveholding. As governor, Gurdon Saltonstall actively supported Yale in its early days. He persuaded the founding trustees to move the Collegiate School from Saybrook to New Haven and consulted in the building of the college and the rector's house. And it was Saltonstall who signed the 1721 act directing taxes from West Indian rum to fund the college. In his will, he left one hundred pounds to Yale College, and to his wife an enslaved person named Pompey. But the governor owned many more people whose names he did not record. According to historian Robert Forbes, he engaged in an "ostentatious display of command over his slaves." When he died, the Reverend Eliphalet Adams, a fellow slaveholder and a college trustee, eulogized him as Yale's "*best Friend under God*."[8]

Saltonstall used his position as a prominent politician to strengthen the institution of racial slavery in the colony. In 1704, arguing against the freedom suit of a mixed-race person named Abda, Saltonstall presented a passionate defense of slavery on political and religious grounds. Rejecting Abda's claim that he was free because his father was English, Saltonstall argued, "According to the laws and constant practice of this Colony, and all other plantations, (as well as the civil law) such persons as are born of negro bondwomen are themselves in like condition, that is born in servitude." And by using an estate inventory where Abda's mother was included along with other "chattel," Yale's "*best Friend under God*" helped reinforce the inherited status of bondage in Connecticut's Black and mixed-race population. In solidifying slavery in law, Saltonstall acted, as one would expect of a person in power, in his own and the colony's economic interests.[9]

Saltonstall's children inherited great wealth from their father—thousands of acres of land, luxury items, cash, and several enslaved people—which they reinvested in the West Indies trade. His son, Colonel Gurdon Saltonstall Jr. (Yale 1725), himself became a successful merchant. In 1755, his ship, the *Betsey*, sailed to the Caribbean laden with horses, barrels of fish, and empty hogsheads for molasses. Just one year later, he sent another vessel, the *Lyon*, to Saint Eustatius again with horses and barrels of fish, barrels of pork and beef, fifty-two empty barrels, and thousands of hoops, staves, and shingles, as well as twenty-two thousand feet of boards.[10] All of these goods were the valuable Connecticut necessities for plantation production in the Caribbean. Those empty barrels came back full of rum. In civil, ecclesiastical, commercial, and educational life, slavery was entangled with the "best" Connecticut families. Closer to home, Cush, Duba, Garrick, and Mehitable—all enslaved to the younger Gurdon Saltonstall—tended to the family's needs and were willed to his family members when he died.[11]

Other merchant families gave significant support to Yale. The multigenerational Munson family—successful traders, physicians, and builders—contributed prominently to Yale's future. Captain Theophilus Munson donated eleven pounds to the college and left two enslaved men, Dick and Peter, to his heirs when he died. Munson's son Benjamin worked building Connecticut Hall in the early 1750s, alongside Dick, who by then was enslaved by another Munson son. And Eneas Munson (Yale 1753), a student at the time of Connecticut Hall's construction, later in his life came to own at least two enslaved people. He became one of the most distinguished physicians in New Haven and was given an honorary position at the Yale medical school when it was founded. His son, Aeneas Munson, graduated from Yale in 1780 and also owned slaves in the early years of the nineteenth century. Trained as a physician like his father, Aeneas prospered as a merchant, underwriting a number of incoming voyages from the West Indies to New Haven in the 1790s.[12] Many of the successful professionals and businesspeople who supported Yale in its early years enjoyed wealth derived from their connections to West Indian trade, slavery, and the commercial growth it fostered.

Such was also the case with churchmen of differing persuasions. Enos Alling (Yale 1746) was the grandson of John Alling, treasurer of the college from 1702 to 1717. Enos Alling joined the Church of England and was one of the founders of Trinity Church in New Haven. In addition to his benefaction of Trinity Church, Enos Alling donated £15 to Yale College and records show him as the owner of several incoming voyages to Connecticut and New Haven containing rum, sugar, and molasses from Anguilla, Turks and Caicos, and the Leeward Islands. When he died in 1779, Alling left an estate valued at over £3,000, which included many parcels of land, furniture, luxury household goods, forty-two gallons of rum, "1 negro woman" (valued at £35), and a "negro child Ann" (valued at £10). Some of Alling's slaves escaped, and he pursued them tenaciously. An advertisement for Jack, "a Spanish Indian Servant" who escaped from Alling, appeared in the September 13, 1760, issue of the *Connecticut Gazette*. Although the term used here was "servant," it is likely Jack was an enslaved Native American. The lines between slavery and indentured servitude were often rigid after the adoption of racial, African enslavement, but also sometimes fluid even into the late colonial period. Alling was buried in New Haven. His tombstone, now in the Grove Street Cemetery, reads, "In memory of Enos Alling, Esq., Merchant who Received a liberal Education in Yale College, Became an industrious and useful member of Civil Society, and in a course of an extensive and successful commerce, He proved himself the man of Integrity, Virtue, and Honor. He was a Member of the Episcopal Society for Propagating the Gospel In Foreign Parts, and died universally respected."[13] In a through line of the history of early Yale, men attained honor both despite and because of their slaveholding, in a legal structure that fully supported their endeavors.

One of the wealthiest and most significant family benefactors of Yale were the Livingstons of New York, a dynasty of three generations of human traffickers and merchants. In 1690, New Yorker Robert C. Livingston first invested in a slave voyage to the west coast of Africa. Until the late seventeenth century, the family had built their wealth in the fur trade from the interior and as merchants to the Atlantic world. But as the fur trade declined, they entered the Caribbean business in foodstuffs and rum. Robert Livingston married the widow Alida Schuyler Van Rensselaer, and the couple's wealth skyrocketed as they gained ownership of some 160,000 acres along the Hudson River and made investments in the slave trade. Robert's son, Philip Livingston Sr. (1686–1749), patriarch of the eighteenth-century extended family, sent four of his six sons to Yale College, including Philip Livingston Jr., who later signed the Declaration of Independence. For the senior Livingston, an education at Yale for most of his sons represented the kind of learning as well as prestige he sought for his family's ascendance into the world of the New York mercantile elite.[14]

By the 1730s, Philip Livingston Sr., with his own sons attending Yale, owned shares in at least four slave ships operating out of New York Harbor; all told, he and his sons invested in at least fifteen slave voyages to and from Africa. The family's trade routes reached all the way to Madagascar off the eastern coast of Africa in the Indian Ocean. The Livingstons imported enslaved Africans directly from the continent; records exist for at least seven ships that disembarked 549 slaves in New York. Their wealth also stemmed from a steady trade of grain, flour, and meat to the islands. Many in the family, moreover, were significant slaveholders. A Columbia University study found that, by the 1790 federal census, a tally of all branches of the family tree came to some 170 people enslaved by the Livingstons. Philip Sr. inherited eight enslaved people in 1728, including "Joe the miller," his son Hannibal, Cesar and his son Jack, Piet, Pietvlek, and Saar. When the patriarch of the family died in 1749, his will named "my Negro man Tom and his wife Mary and my Negro man Benjamin." To his wife, Philip Sr. left "three Negro men and three Negro women her choice." Of the sons with Yale degrees, John's estate inventory listed three enslaved people, but only two named, Cato and Robin; and Philip Jr. left four: Scipio, Plato, Mary, and John (who was blind). A runaway ad placed in the *New York Gazette* in November 1752 by Philip Jr. indicates the flow of Africans into the Livingston universe of property. The fugitive is not named but is described as "lately imported from Africa . . . his Hair or wool is curled in locks in a very remarkable manner," and he "cannot speak a word of English." The Livingston sons engaged in essentially every element of slave trading and Caribbean commerce. At least three of them, not long after their time at Yale, went to the islands to work as business managers of the sugar, rum, and slave interests.[15] The daily entanglements of the Livingstons in slavery and slave trading were even more "remarkable" for their commonness.

Their Yale degrees no doubt served all the Livingstons in their rising civic and social prestige. Philip Jr. was a deacon of New York's Dutch Reformed Church, a founder of New York's Society Library as well as New York Hospital, a trustee of Queen's College (now Rutgers University), and a patron of King's College (now Columbia University). Philip Jr. clearly considered his family fortune at stake in the conflict with Great Britain. In July 1776, he represented his state in Philadelphia and etched his name into history as a signer of the Declaration of Independence. The Livingstons of New York needed no crowned head three thousand miles away to protect their financial and mercantile interests, and certainly not to tax them. And Philip Jr. joined the many other American founders who considered the combination of slaveholding and republicanism no contradiction at all.[16]

The Livingstons were keepers of a civic flame and major donors to Yale, their motives richly mixed. In the 1750s, William Livingston, Philip Sr.'s son, became a frequent contributor to the *Independent Reflector*, a prominent journal in New York. Among his brothers, he embraced more of a literary career than a mercantile one. In one of his essays William wrote with poignant irony and honesty that, "Tis true, every Man ought to promote the Prosperity of his Country, from a sublimer Motive than his private Advantage: But it is extremely difficult, for the best of Men, to divest themselves of Self-Interest." Rarely has the "paradox" at the root of the American Revolution for slaveholders been so concisely stated. Belief in individual liberty, in the necessity of a dependent labor force, and in the right of slave ownership all combined in a lethal package for some of America's most distinguished founders.[17]

In 1745, William's father, Philip Livingston Sr., donated the considerable sum of £28 10s. to Yale College "as a small acknowledgment of the sence [*sic*] I have for the favour and Education my sons have had there." Livingston's gift, one of the largest in the middle of the eighteenth century, was originally intended to finance building projects. However, the ambitious president of Yale, Thomas Clap, asked that the money instead be used to create an endowment for the college's first professorship. Combined with other funds, Livingston's gift became the basis for the Livingstonian Professorship in Divinity in 1756, one of the most prestigious at Yale for many years. The New York clan remains well commemorated at the university: at the Memorial Quadrangle, the Livingston Gateway was dedicated in 1921. Such a gate reminds us that memory surrounds us at universities, both visible and unknown.[18]

Without these merchant families, the college would not have prospered into the leading American institution of higher learning that it became by the time of the American Revolution. The West Indian trade, rooted so deeply in slavery, was an indispensable element in Yale College's birth, growth, and eventual prosperity. Craig Steven Wilder, a historian of America's early universities and slavery, puts it simply: "The American college was an extension of merchant wealth."[19]

If the labor of enslaved people on distant Caribbean plantations enriched Yale, so too did that of unfree Black workers on its grounds. In 1732, George Berkeley, an Irish-born Anglican bishop and prominent philosopher and poet, donated his large Rhode Island farm and house, Whitehall, to the college. Berkeley's gift also included funds to establish graduate study at Yale. In 1733, he donated nearly one thousand volumes, which Yale's first president, Thomas Clap, later deemed "the finest Collection of Books that ever came together at one Time into *America*." Disheartened with what he saw as the corruption and lack of religious faith in England, in 1723 Berkeley began to look toward the Americas. He planned to establish a college in Bermuda that would train the sons of colonists for the ministry and convert and educate Native American youth. Berkeley wrote that "the children of savage Americans, brought up in such a seminary, and well instructed in religion and learning, might make the ablest and properest missionaries for spreading the gospel among their countrymen." He suggested that if "peaceable methods" failed to attract Indigenous children to the school, it would be necessary to "tak[e] captive the children of our enemies." Berkeley insisted that such kidnapped children be no older than ten, young enough that they had not fully learned the "evil habits" of their people and better able to embrace Christian civilization. These Native youth would be trained in the ministry and become missionaries to their former communities, and thus would begin in America the tragic history of forced education in so-called Indian schools.[20]

Berkeley spent five years garnering support and funding for his Bermuda college, ultimately securing a charter from King George I as well as a contingent grant of £20,000 from Parliament. While awaiting the grant, Berkeley and his wife sailed to Newport, Rhode Island, arriving in 1729. He bought his farm of initially about one hundred acres and built a house. While in Newport, Berkeley wrote, occasionally preached, and founded the philosophical society that developed into the Redwood Library and Athenaeum, still a prominent institution in that city today. Berkeley's Bermuda educational and missionary dream, however, never came to fruition. In late 1731, he returned to England with his family. While in Newport, Berkeley had developed a friendship with Samuel Johnson (Yale 1714), a former Yale tutor who became an Anglican priest and would in 1754 found King's College, later renamed Columbia University. At the prompting of Johnson and Jared Eliot (Yale 1706), Berkeley gave his Newport estate to Yale College. The purpose, he stated, was to promote "Charity, Learning and Piety in this part of the World."[21]

During the ensuing decades, Yale College benefited substantially from renting Whitehall farm and from the enslaved laborers who worked it. Berkeley himself bought at least three enslaved people at a market while living in Newport, which was emerging as a significant slave-trading seaport. He baptized them and likely gave them their names: Philip, Anthony, and Agnes. Beyond his own household and property, Berkeley's views on slavery had a sweeping influence. He advocated for the baptism of enslaved people, and he condemned what he called "an irrational Contempt for the Blacks, as Creatures of another

Species." Such preaching elicited protest from West Indian slaveholders, but his views on baptism did not challenge the sanctity of slavery itself. On the contrary, Berkeley argued that slaveholders would benefit from the conversion of their enslaved workers. "Gospel Liberty consists with temporal Servitude," he wrote, trying to assuage the fears of slaveholders. "Slaves would only become better Slaves by being Christians." Berkeley's arguments may have even shaped legal doctrine that temporarily put slavery on a more secure footing in England. In a 1735 tract Berkeley suggested that temporary enslavement may be used to eradicate poverty in Ireland. He argued that "the most indolent" people should be "seized and made slaves to the public for a certain term of years." Berkeley insisted that such a proposal would benefit the poor while discouraging "idleness and all idle folk." During the following century and more, American proslavery writers would use these kinds of conventional paternalistic arguments in favor of slavery; by the antebellum era a vast literature emerged defending racial slavery as the best—even utopian—means of sustaining a natural, organic, hierarchical social order.[22]

Whitehall, before and after Berkeley gifted the farm to Yale, was worked by enslaved laborers who helped make it profitable. Joseph and Sarah Whipple, who sold the estate to Berkeley, owned and traded in people in Newport. Records show that at least three lessees paying rent to Yale in the ensuing decades were slaveholders on some scale. Charles Handy, a merchant and shipowner, owned four slaves by 1772. A tavern keeper, John McWhorter, also rented Whitehall and owned at least one enslaved person. Silas Cooke Sr. held both Africans and Native Americans in slavery, claiming a total of seven people in bondage by 1772, when he was a prominent rum trader. Over the years, Silas Cooke worked assiduously to retrieve runaways, and especially an enslaved man named Sharpe Cooke in 1781, who worked in his rum distillery. The slaveholder Cooke experienced great difficulty maintaining the Whitehall operation during the American Revolutionary War and could not meet the rent, a problem Yale experienced with all of its lands and farms. The Yale farms in the northwest corner of Connecticut fell into disrepair, as did Whitehall for parts of the late eighteenth century. But a treasurer's report from 1795 still listed annual income from Yale lands higher than any other source of funds except student tuition. One of the most enduring legacies of Berkeley's gift, however, were fellowships created for the best students in Greek and Latin, which over time many famous graduates held, including Yale's first president, Thomas Clap. Yale never forgot George Berkeley; by the 1930s, the university had named one of its modern residential colleges for the philosopher-benefactor.[23]

Berkeley's gift of his Rhode Island estate was just one example of the college's entanglement in a wider web of buying, selling, and holding people in bondage. Enslaved people were close to the teaching and learning at the heart of Yale College, at times living and laboring alongside students and their instructors. The Reverend Elisha Williams of Wethersfield served as rector at Yale, the early equivalent of president, in the pivotal years of 1726 to 1739. Williams held at least eleven people, Black and Indigenous, as slaves over the course of his lifetime. For at least three years before his appointment, Yale had muddled along without stable leadership, and the colonial general assembly demanded action. Minister, scholar, Harvard graduate, member of a prominent New England family, and onetime member of the general assembly, Williams accepted the position after a series of other ministers turned it down. By many accounts, he was an effective manager as the college grew in enrollments and prestige. By 1735, the college had enrolled eighty-two students and graduated twenty-four. Williams and two tutors did all the teaching, and a new administrative person, called a butler, managed accounts as well as monitored the studies and behavior of students. For funding, the college still relied heavily on the general assembly, especially for the salaries of the rector and other employees.[24]

The earliest records of Williams's slaveholding are from the period when he served as a tutor and Collegiate School students lived and studied with him at his home in Wethersfield, providing a glimpse into the way domestic slavery coexisted alongside students' academic and ecclesiastical training. At the time, Williams owned a Native American woman who gave birth to a son named Ambo on June 5, 1715, the year before some Collegiate School students went to Wethersfield to study with their tutor. On February 17, 1717, a daughter named Desire was born to the same woman. Years later, Ambo served in the military and "march[ed] against the French in Eliphalet Whittlesey's company with seven others of his kind," according to the historian Edwin Oviatt. Although Ambo's mother was described as "Indian," when Ambo was listed in the muster roll for the company, he was described as "negro." Ambo died on June 1, 1801, well into his eighties. The records of the First Congregational Church in West Hartford, which list his death, also describe him as a "negro," but as none of their other records mention whether Black individuals were enslaved, it is difficult to know whether Ambo died as a free Black man.[25] His longevity, however, gives us a glimpse into the kinds of sagas that African and Native peoples lived from the colonial through the revolutionary eras. Ambo's life of eighty-six years spanned all of the epic events of the eighteenth century.

After his tenure at Yale and over the remaining sixteen years of his life, Williams became a significant landowner in Connecticut and the proprietor of an ironworks in the northeast corner of the colony, as well as of other retail businesses. He also engaged in a mercantile business partnership with Jonathan Trumbull between the colony and London. And he continued to buy and enslave human beings. In 1744, he recorded days worked by Peter and David, whom he enslaved, on behalf of other leading men of Wethersfield; Williams would have received payment for this work done by others. Records show he later bought shoes for Peter as well as for his "Indian woman." A draft of a codicil to Williams's will and his last will and testament describe the disposition of several people as property, including Peter and another Black man named Newport; a Black woman named Merea (also called Marea); a Native American woman named Jude; and Jude's three children, Flora, Cass, and Pitt. At the time of his death in 1755, Williams's household also included two servants, Thomas and Anna, left to his wife; but they were most likely White and not enslaved, as distinct from Merea, who was "to be at [his wife's] absolute disposal." This distinction between temporary servant and property for life had a long-lasting effect: Merea was included in the estate of Williams's widow, Elizabeth, when she died twenty-one years after him. In fact, Merea was the first "item" Elizabeth listed in her estate. "My faithful Marea I give, with also twenty pounds to Elisha Williams Esqr. or to any of the sons or daughters of the Rev Doctr Solomon Williams who shall chuse to take her, she freely consenting thereto, not in the least doubting or questioning their tender care of her, both in Soul & Body while she continues in life. . . . I desire also she may be well clad in all my common winter apparrel & one good Linnen Gown over & above." In addition to her person, the executor of Elizabeth's estate allotted twenty pounds to himself and to "Colonel William" (likely Colonel William Williams, a son of Solomon Williams, later a signer of the Declaration of Independence and a delegate to the Constitutional Convention) for the "support" of Marea.[26] These records for Elisha Williams, his wife, and his descendants demonstrate the depth of propertied entanglements between White, Black, and Native Americans in the social hierarchy of colonial Connecticut. Would that history had given us a narrative recorded by the "faithful Marea," who died in the year of American independence, of her long labor for this leading Yale family. What tales she might have told.

Whether working in the homes of Yale rectors and students or laboring in sugar fields that created benefactors' largesse, enslaved people were present throughout Yale's first decades. And although the West Indies trade must have seemed far removed from campus, slave-produced merchant wealth resides in the bricks and mortar and certainly in the nearly lost and invisible labor that built the earliest structures of Yale College. *Nearly*, but not completely, lost: some individuals did leave traces in the written and visual records of Yale and New Haven.

Born somewhere around the turn of the eighteenth century, an African- or perhaps American-born Black man named Jethro Luke worked at Yale College. He was free by the 1740s but had been earlier the slave of Mary Hooker Pierpont, the granddaughter of Thomas Hooker, one of the principal founders of the

Mary Hooker Pierpont (1673–1740), Pierpont Limner, 1711. Bequest of Allen Evarts Foster, B.A. 1906. Yale University Art Gallery.

Connecticut colony, and the widow of James Pierpont, minister of the First Church in New Haven and a founding trustee of the Collegiate School in 1701, which became Yale. Mary Pierpont was also the mother-in-law of Jonathan Edwards, who married Sarah Pierpont in 1727. Familial connections in this relatively closed and intermarried Puritan society were widespread. Luke and his first wife, Ruth, were manumitted on Mary Pierpont's death in 1740.[27]

On the earliest known surviving map of New Haven, made by an eighteen-year-old student named James Wadsworth (Yale 1748), in the upper left, at what is today the intersection of Grove, Ashmun, and York Streets, is a small, rectangular piece of land labeled "Jethro a blackman farmer." Luke, his second wife, Mindwell, and his son Gad owned and worked that land; in the mid-nineteenth century, it would come to be known as "Jethro's Corner." Hand-drawn dwellings appear all over the map, and the drawing of the Lukes' house abuts the location of the park that sits at that corner today, immediately adjacent to Grove Street Cemetery. Luke appears vividly in account records kept by Yale's first president, the Reverend Thomas Clap, in 1752. Jethro and Gad Luke worked for many months, walking across what is today the heart of the Yale campus for approximately a quarter mile every morning for at least 191 days. They specialized in mixing mortar for the bricks in the building of Connecticut Hall, and they may have labored on the foundation of the now-historic structure. Making mortar entailed a careful process of mixing sand, water, lime, and sometimes crushed oyster shells into a putty that could hold bricks together. Luke became a member of the First Church on the Green on May 15, 1728, died in 1761, and was presumably buried in the land immediately behind the church, which was set aside as the town burial ground.[28]

Jethro Luke and his family intersected frequently with Clap, a 1722 Harvard graduate who was appointed rector of Yale in 1740. Five years later, the trustees named Clap the first president of the college. Over the course of his long term of leadership (1740–66), Clap reshaped many aspects of the college, helping it grow and expand with merchant and colonial assembly support and guiding its curricular reform. Like many New England divines of his generation, Clap was a slaveholder. He was a Calvinist, always fighting the onslaughts of liberal religion as well as the excesses of the many revivalists spurred on by the Great Awakening in the 1740s, and he tried his best, unsuccessfully, to keep Anglicanism—the Church of England—from getting a foothold in New Haven or anywhere near Yale's campus. At the same time, he became a major proponent of Newtonian science at Yale. Clap fundamentally reformed Yale's curriculum, especially in mathematics and science, as well as its administrative structure and rules of

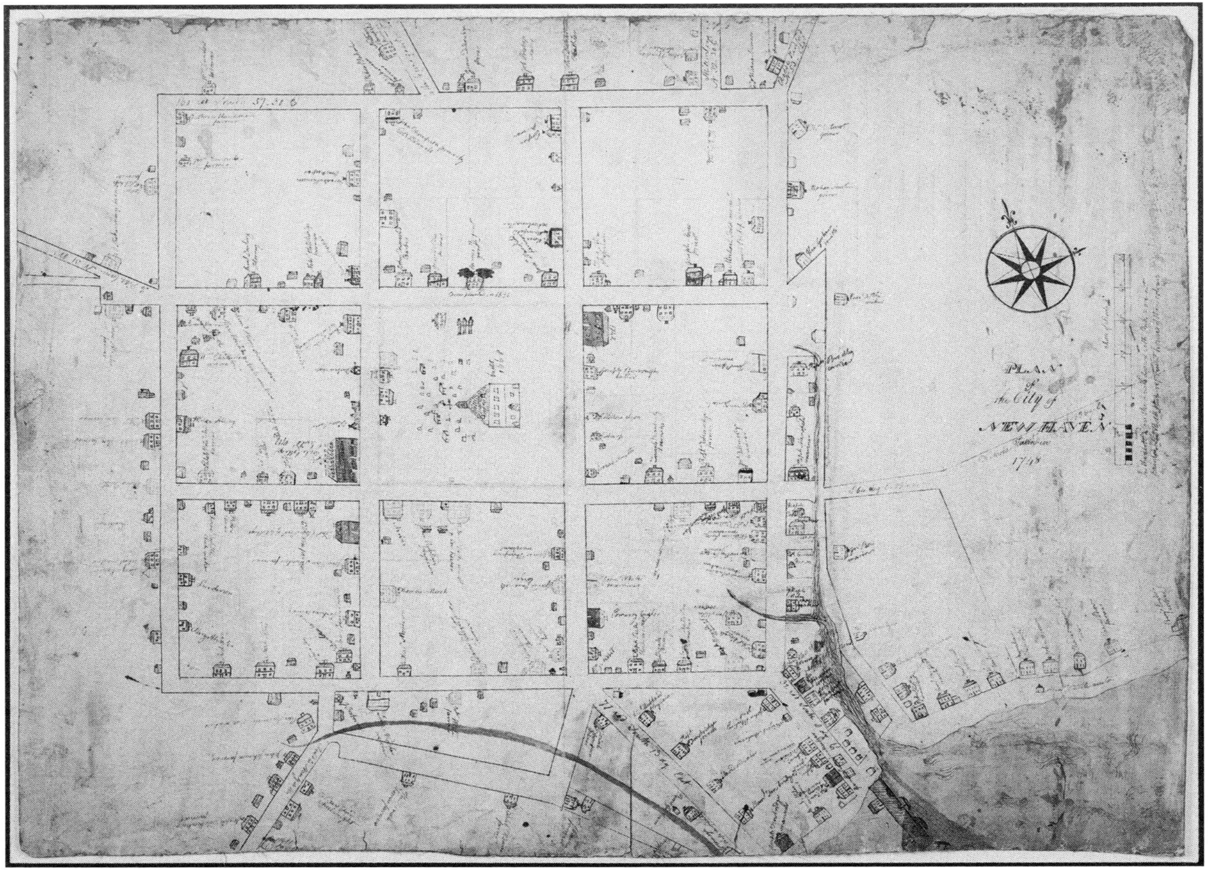

Plan of the city of New Haven, 1748, James Wadsworth. Beinecke Rare Book and Manuscript Library, Yale University.

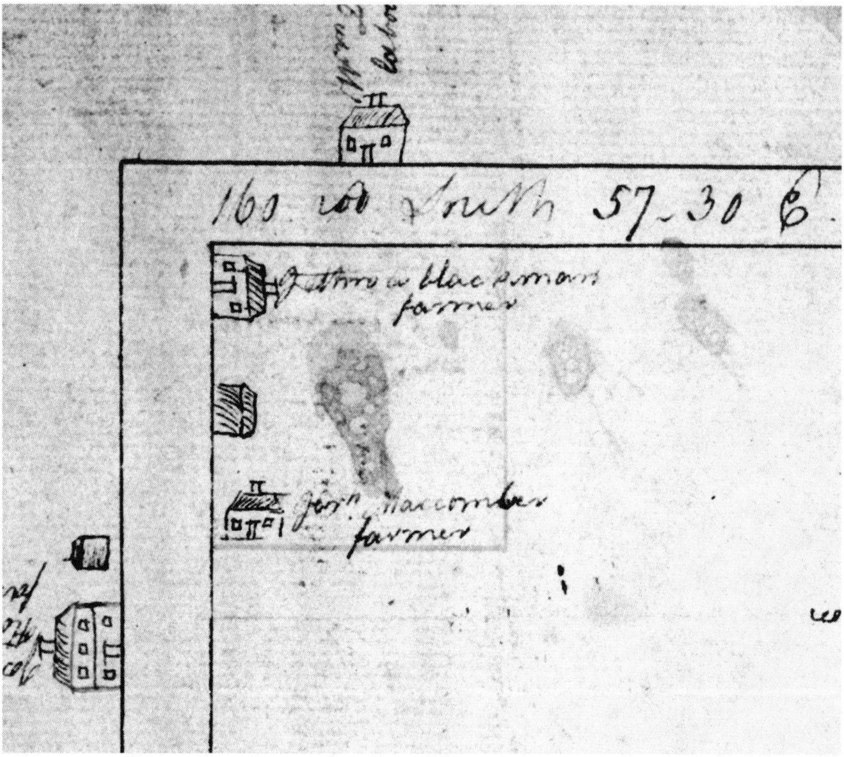

Detail of Wadsworth map noting "Jethro a blackman farmer."
Beinecke Rare Book and Manuscript Library, Yale University.

governance. Seeking advice from the best minds he could engage, he corresponded a good deal with Benjamin Franklin, through whom Clap procured a fair number of electrical and other scientific instruments. In 1753, Yale bestowed an honorary MA degree on the learned doctor from Philadelphia, and when Franklin visited campus, Clap urged him to bring a printing press to the city. Franklin agreed to the proposition, which also led to the establishment of New Haven's first newspaper, the *Connecticut Gazette*, in 1755. Clap continued to build the college's scientific collections, and by the latter part of his presidency, Yale possessed an array of the most modern scientific instruments, especially for astronomy. Clap carried out endless astronomical measurements, published them in the *Gazette*, and cultivated his personal fascination with meteors and comets with great zeal. He brought order and structure to the Yale library and greatly increased its holdings by more than 1,400 volumes over his tenure, even as he practiced censorship, especially of Baptist tracks, among other books. As the institution expanded, Clap and his small staff grew; more tutors were hired and the president himself, with donor support, became a builder.[29]

Moralist and Calvinist, Clap never seems to have troubled his conscience about the racial slavery he himself practiced and from which the college and the town benefited. A great list maker, Clap recorded the names and birth years of his children and other household members in 1737, including the enslaved Pompey, born "About 1713"; Phillis, born "about 1717"; and Tamar, recently born on December 18, 1736. Clap continued to purchase or acquire enslaved people, baptizing "Sylva, negro child," in 1738. And in 1758, he placed an ad in the *Connecticut Gazette* for George, a man he enslaved who had escaped from the New Haven jail, accused of stealing hundreds of dollars in lottery tickets and currency from the New Haven post office.[30] Like so many other founders of the college, Yale's first president practiced slaveholding as an essentially unthinking part of everyday life.

Hierarchy was central to the structure and functioning of Yale College, from the ranking of the students (freshmen were emotionally abused and ruled by upperclassmen) to the status of the educated clergy and the merchant class. Labor was no different, and it is hardly surprising that such a hierarchy operated in the construction of Connecticut Hall from 1750 to 1753. The hall is a prized work of architecture at Yale, the oldest building on campus, and the oldest surviving brick structure in the state. Today, this still-beautiful edifice in the Old Campus area remains an important university building, recently home to the Philosophy Department. Its large meeting room on the second floor, lined with portraits of Yale deans, long served as the site of Yale faculty meetings. The building is well marked with commemorative dates on plaques, but nowhere does it record how and by whom it was constructed. Connecticut Hall was built, in part, by Black workers who were enslaved by Yale luminaries.

Clap's first task was to secure donors to pay the bills and provide the construction materials. He was remarkably assiduous in pursuing both aims. Among eight particular donors Clap recorded who specifically made gifts to the building of the "new college," at least three were slaveholders. They included the Reverends Jared Eliot of Killingworth, Solomon Williams of Lebanon (brother of Elisha Williams), and Jonathan Todd of East Guilford, Connecticut. Slaveholders Simon Tuttle and Joseph Tuttle, residents of New Haven, may also have been contributors to the construction of Connecticut Hall. Other donors in Clap's records for this period include Mr. Ingersoll of Ridgefield, Mr. Stiles (father of future Yale president Ezra Stiles) of New Haven, and a Mr. Woodbridge of

Wm Stanton

April 12. 1755. NUMB. I.

NEW-HAVEN, THE

Connecticut GAZETTE,

With the Freshest Advices Foreign and Domestick.

BROKE Out of His Majesty's Goal in New-Haven, *last Thursday Night two Prisoners, viz,* Charles Roberts, *alias* German, *a Molatto about 25 Years of Age, pitted pretty much with the Small-pox, well set, talks good* English, *and is a smooth tongued Fellow, committed on Suspicion of robbing the Printing-Office in this Town some Time since: The other a Negro Fellow, named* George, *about 19 Years old, of a middling Stature, a Slave, lately belonging to the Rev'd Mr.* Clap *of this Place. Whoever shall take up said Fellows, and return them to the aforesaid Goal, will be well rewarded for their Trouble, and all necessary Charges paid.*

New-Haven, October 7.

come speedily and settle their Accounts with Jared Ingersoll, *Esq; or with said* Hotchkiss, *as they would avoid Trouble.*

T*Hese are to give Notice, that there is now in the Custody of* Samuel Gillet, *of* Lebanon; *a sorrel Horse, white Mane and Tail, a Star in his Forehead, branded with 9 on the right Shoulder, five Years old, goes well on the Pace, and can Trot; he was taken* Damage Feasant, *about one Month ago; shod only before: Whether he had been in the Service of the Government, is uncertain; — The Owner may have him, on paying reasonable Costs.*

SAMUEL GILLET,

To be SOLD in Waterbury,

A *Strong healthy and active Negro Wench, in the 13th Year of her Age; born in the Country: Enquire of*

M. LEAVENWORTH.

N*OW in the Keeping of Mr.* Stephen Ball, *of* New-Haven; *a black trotting Horse, about 13 Hands high, thick set, has a small Star in his Forehead, something like a Brand on the near Thigh, but is not plain: The Mark out of his Mouth.*

NEW-HAVEN,

Printed by *James Parker,* near the *Hay-Market.*

Masthead from the first printing of the *Connecticut Gazette* on April 12, 1755; notice offering a reward for the recapture of Charles Roberts and George, "lately belonging to the Rev'd Mr. Clap"; advertisements of horses and a Black woman for sale, December 6, 1755. Beinecke Rare Book and Manuscript Library, Yale University.

Amity, Connecticut. In 1748, Clap's construction team, under the direction of Thomas Bills and Francis Letort, began to purchase and amass the materials, which included door locks, shingles, masonry of all kinds, hay, thousands of bricks, kilns, lime, stones, carts for hauling, long beams, joiners, pine boards, nails, "oyl," "White Lead," "41 Squares of Glass for Round Windows," and various tools.[31] Clap's detailed records tell a remarkable human, as well as material, story.

The first stone was laid on April 17, 1750, and the brickwork finished in July 1752. Clap was extraordinarily meticulous in his recordkeeping, assembling notes on the approximately twenty-two laborers who worked over two to three years. They did all types of construction labor: laying stone foundation; making bricks in three kilns; carting, by Clap's accounting, 230,000 bricks to the site; hauling beams and pulling them into place with ropes; carpentering with boards planed from timber brought from the countryside and the wharf; mixing lime with other substances, likely oyster shells, to make the mortar; and crafting the 122 windows in the four-story structure, all perfectly aligned, including the dormers across the top. The laborers plastered and painted interiors, fashioned the stairways, which still exist, and perhaps made the small stage that stands at the front of the second-floor faculty room. Clap recorded the days of work for almost every worker; some were paid, and some were not. "Jethro's Gad," a free person of color, and the son of Jethro Luke, worked 161½ days. "Mr. Noyes's Negro" (named Jack) put in 172¾ days. "Theophilus Munson's Negro" (named Dick) labored 68 days. "Mr. Bonticou's Negro" (his name as yet unknown) spent 96 days on the job. "Mingo," enslaved by Archibald McNeil, worked 92¾ days. Finally, "Mr. President's Negro"—that is, one of the people enslaved to Clap himself, possibly George—gave 83 days of strength, sweat, and skill to the job. Foreman Francis Letort was employed for 165 days, according to Clap's accounts. Many of the White workers, though perhaps not all, are named with their days of labor as well in the president's "Account of the Cost of New College." They include Letort and Bills, Samuel Tharp, Samuel Griffin, Daniel Sperry, Joseph Stacey, Nicolas Wood, Abel Wood, John Osborn, Daniel McConnelly, and Richard Cutler.[32]

This record demonstrates that Black workers (almost all unpaid), including Gad Luke, who was free, worked a total of at least 672 days in building this prominent Yale structure. Those who walk its reinforced stairs and attend meetings and visit faculty offices every day may not know this eighteenth-century story of design, imagination, donations, labor, and human exploitation. One can only wonder whether Clap and the trustees of Yale College ever arranged any recognition

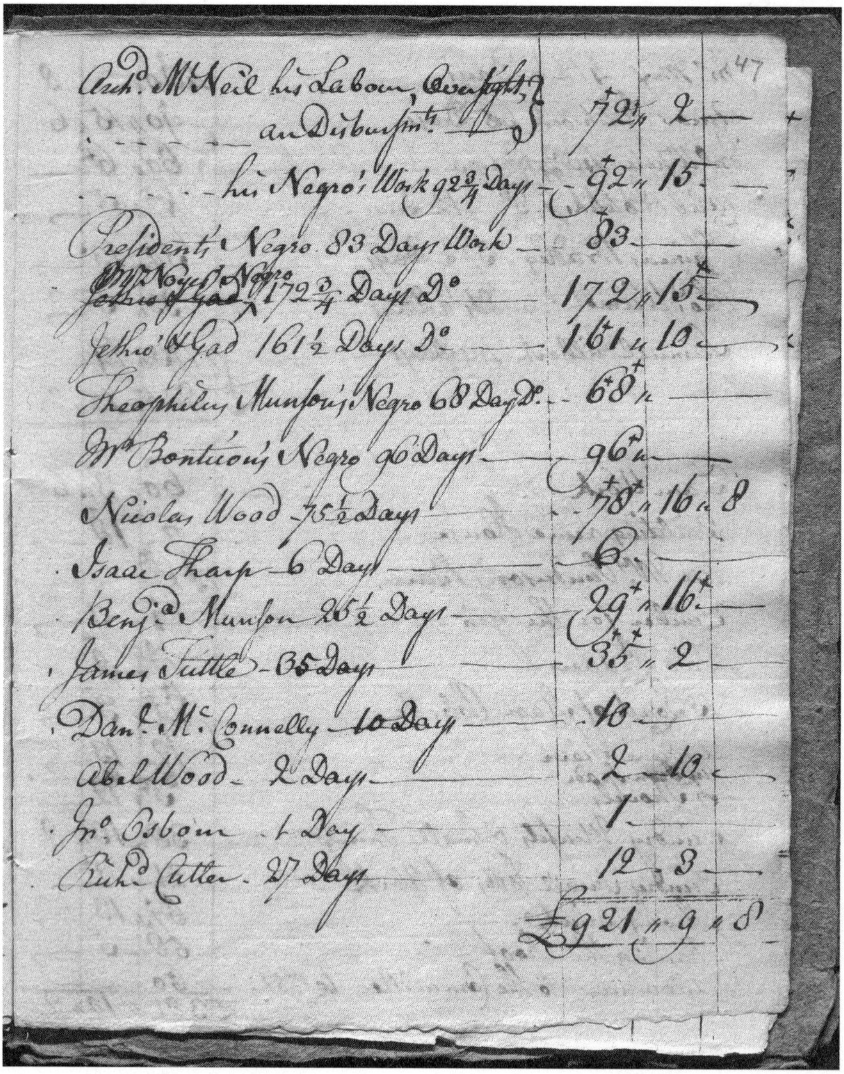

Archd. McNeil his Labour, Oversight & an Disbursmts.	72	2	
his Negro's Work 92 3/4 Days	92	15	
President's Negro 83 Days Work	83		
~~Jethro & Gad~~ Mr Noyes's Negro 172 3/4 Days Do	172	15	
Jethro & Gad 161 1/2 Days Do	161	10	
Theophilus Munson's Negro 68 Days Do	68		
Mr Bontecou's Negro 96 Days	96		
Nicolas Wood 75 1/2 Days	78	16	8
Isaac Tharp 6 Days	6		
Benja Munson 26 1/2 Days	29	16	
James Tuttle 35 Days	35	2	
Danl McConnelly 10 Days	10		
Abel Wood 2 Days	2	10	
Jno Osborn 1 Day	1		
Richd Cutter 27 Days	12	3	
	£921	9	8

Yale president Thomas Clap kept detailed records of laborers, supplies, and costs associated with building Connecticut Hall. Thomas Clap, President of Yale College, Records (RU 130). Manuscripts and Archives, Yale University Library.

of the many people, enslaved and free, Black and White, who built this edifice in the heart of the educational enterprise at the corner of Chapel and College Streets. Gad Luke worked elbow to elbow with Samuel Tharp and Joseph Stacey, and they may have spent days mixing mortar together. Mingo must have carted bricks and lifted beams with Daniel Sperry. Dick and Abel Wood likely

A view of Old Brick Row, including Connecticut Hall, 1807.
Yale University Buildings and Grounds Photographs (RU 703).
Manuscripts and Archives, Yale University Library.

dug the cellar or fired up a kiln on numerous mornings. On several pages of Clap's accounts, he describes payments for "team work," a term with no irony in the listing of people and numbers at that time. It took a team to raise beams or install a window or large door. Some days Gad broke from the "team" on the construction site and worked "culling tobacco" personally for Clap.[33]

The students, rectors, teachers, and anyone who lived or worked around Yale College as it grew from the 1730s to 1760s would have known Jethro Luke and his family, and perhaps Jack, Dick, Mingo, and other enslaved workers, just as, in earlier decades, the Yale students at Wethersfield must have known the enslaved Native woman and her children, Ambo and Desire, who lived with them in their tutor's house. The Wadsworth map and other records show us that Jethro and Gad Luke and their family lived on the edge and in the center of things; their labor took many forms, physical and domestic. It takes only a little imagination to see that thousands of Luke's laboring descendants may have worked at Yale over the next two and a half centuries among the grounds staff, in the dining halls, in security, as clerical workers, and in the building trades. Do these early workers who laid the foundations of Yale also deserve the title "founders"? How might we break the silence about their vivid visibility in the university's archives?

Account books are a narrative. They can tell a story both utterly banal and richly revealing of the economic, moral, and social worlds from which they emerge. They can record both simple, inert facts and larger truths. Thomas Clap left a story of labor and enslavement, as well as an architectural and construction history that has been hidden in plain sight in the Yale archives for more than two and a half centuries. At every magnificent Yale commencement ceremony, students and their residential college heads and deans march to, near, or around Connecticut Hall on their way into Old Campus, the band playing grandly, flags and banners waving with impressive pomp. Perhaps one day that march will include robust public awareness of the racial and class origin story of Yale's eighteenth-century founding. Perhaps there will be new banners honoring Gad Luke or commemorating "Mr. President's Negro." Maybe even a huge banner will be unfurled down one side of Connecticut Hall, on which Yale student artists will depict the construction of that edifice to help us see and feel the past from which this university came. Then the rolling sounds of ovations on Commencement Day will provide a truly new feeling in the spring air. Might we even imagine a posthumous honorary degree for the formerly enslaved Jethro Luke, who walked and labored on these very grounds?

CHAPTER 4

Slavery and the American Revolution

Whether enslaving Negroes be right? Negative.

—DIARY OF EZRA STILES,
president of Yale College, December 7, 1779

In 1779, when the British invaded New Haven, Sarah Lloyd Hillhouse was twenty-six years old and pregnant with her first child. Her husband, James Hillhouse, a Yale graduate and future college treasurer, was off commanding a company of volunteers—including many Yale students—as they attempted to defend the city. Sarah described her ordeal to a relative: "You who have gone through a like scene can easily imagine the consternation this town must be in on the occasion," she wrote. "However we fared much better than we feared as we expected nothing but to see the town reduced to ashes . . . the rest of the inhabitants were plundered & abused without regard to friend or foe." Fortunately for young Hillhouse, she was not alone: an enslaved Black man named Jupiter Hammon was with her at the time of the invasion. "I am happily reassured & have abundant reason to rejoice in the merciful protection of a kind providence—Our old faithful Jupiter happened to be here & was a great comfort to me in my flight."[1] In the years to come, "faithful Jupiter" would decry slavery in verse and claim his place as America's first published Black poet. Hammon remained an integral part of the Hillhouse family history as he wrote his way quietly into literary history.

That same year, two men, Prime and Prince, submitted a petition to the state general assembly on behalf of "the Negroes in the Towns of Stratford and Fairfield . . . Who are held in a State of Slavery." Demanding their freedom in the name of both Enlightenment doctrine and Christian virtue, they called slavery "this detestable Practice." The petitioners argued, "Altho our Skins are different in Colour, from those who we serve, yet Reason & Revelation join to declare, that we are the Creatures of that God who made of one Blood, and Kindred, all the Nations of the Earth." Prime and Prince considered their fellow Black people "endowed, with the same Faculties" as their slaveholders and claimed that nothing obliged them to serve White people more "than they us, and the more we Consider of this Matter, the more we are Convinced, of our Right (by the Laws of Nature and by the whole Tenor, of the Christian Religion, so far as we have been taught) to be free." The current revolutionary crisis rendered them "impatient under the grievous Yoke." They preferred reason over violence and reminded the legislature of its historical responsibility in its war against tyranny. "Your Honours," they appealed, how could the "united States to hold so many Thousands . . . in perpetual Slavery. Can human Nature endure the Shocking Idea? can your Honours any longer Suffer, this great Evil to prevail, under your Government?" Drawing on the great drama of their historical moment as well as close reading of the scriptures, they had stated the meanings of the American Revolution as clearly as anyone. Prime and Prince, perhaps speaking for others in their community, drew from the same ideologies, the same sacred texts and philosophical traditions, especially the natural rights tradition, as the famed founders of American independence. Like them, and like better-known petitioners of the era, they made their claims before and from "the Laws of Nature and of Nature's God."[2]

The question of slavery, a metaphor that many White American revolutionaries applied to themselves in their struggle against what they deemed British monarchical "tyranny," underwent transformation. Many Africans and African Americans, some born in Connecticut or Pennsylvania or Virginia, some fighting as soldiers in the Continental army or the British Army, demanded their "rights" to the various "liberties" at stake in this inspiring, if bloody, new age. In one of dozens of petitions from this period, a large group of Black writers in Massachusetts declared on May 25, 1774, "We have in common with all other men a naturel [*sic*] right to our freedoms." Two years later, Thomas Jefferson enshrined this natural rights tradition for all time in the first principles of the Declaration of Independence. As the historian J. Franklin Jameson wrote, "The stream of revolution, once started, could not be confined within narrow banks, but spread abroad upon the land." Indeed, a debate ensued over the future of slavery in New England, the United States as a whole, and beyond. A small number of those African Americans became immediately free by law and by their service in New England states, and a larger number by escaping to the British and into exile.

Others, like Jupiter Hammon, expressed their own humanity and courage in word and in deed. Many would liberate themselves and make an indelible mark in the emerging republic. Most Black Americans, however, found themselves riveted to enslavement more rigidly even as the nation quarreled over how to define them or liberate them.[3]

Connecticut was but one stage in a larger arena during the Age of Revolution. Beginning in 1756, the Seven Years' War—a global, maritime, and imperial war between Britain and France—was waged in part for possession of the precious lands of North America. In that long conflict, Native Americans fought largely, but not exclusively, on the side of the French, and they tried to sustain control of as much of their territory, resources, and sovereignty as distinct peoples as possible against the expansionist British. Enslaved people across the Caribbean and the northern rim of South America organized and led a number of major insurrections that demonstrated the dangerous and unstable nature of plantation slave regimes. Revolutions for human liberty, in the name of popular sovereignty, republicanism, and even equality, raged in America, France, and the Caribbean in the 1790s, reaching a crescendo with the establishment of the world's first independent, free Black republic—Haiti—in place of what was once France's most valuable sugar colony. Of all the great issues at stake in these revolutionary struggles, none was more pivotal than the spectacular contradiction of slavery and freedom—two great competing impulses—in these nascent, emerging republics.[4]

At times the Revolutionary War resembled a civil war, or an imperial colonial war, as much as a formal revolution. Americans divided and had to choose sides. What patriots called their "sons of liberty," British officials considered "sons of anarchy." Native Americans sought both land and sovereignty, and, as in earlier wars, they allied with whomever might help them defend their territory in the interior. Real revolutionaries likely amounted to no more than two-fifths of the White American population. But many colonists preferred reform of British policy rather than rebellion and war. Between one-fifth and one-third opposed independence and considered their best interests within the British Empire and as subjects of the English sovereign. The revolution reverberated throughout Britain's empire, with profound significance in Canada and the West Indies; British farmers and merchants in Nova Scotia as well as the slaveholding planters in Jamaica were staunch loyalists. And perhaps as many as one-third of American colonists did their best to remain neutral, sometimes being condemned by patriots as "flexibles," amid the bloodletting.[5] In the South after 1779, the struggle was an intense civil war, in part because of the region's significant enslaved population and their importance to such a racialized labor system.

The American Revolution "would change everything" about Yale College, and the history of the country surrounding it, wrote the Yale historian Edmund Morgan. The British invaded the town of New Haven, scattering the students and faculty into both hiding and resistance, and the colonial militia into a bloody pitched battle. The college not only survived but sustained its student population relatively well due to the fact that the Connecticut assembly, not always the institution's friend, exempted the students from militia service. An educated elite was considered too important to risk to the perils of cannon shot and disease. Scarcity of food and other goods, currency confusion, and existential political fear took over wartime consciousness in and around New Haven. The old Puritan ideals, long in decline religiously, faced numerous other revolutions in thought, religion, science, and the very definition of an education. Some of what Morgan called the "Puritan ethic" would survive as values, habits of mind, and temperament for generations. But Calvinism in the pews and in the statutes of a modernizing society had waned.[6]

Despite the rhetoric of freedom so prevalent in these years, the purchase and sale of enslaved people continued across Connecticut. In his exhaustive study of slavery in the state, historian Guocun Yang found that from 1764 to 1816, Connecticut newspapers carried 139 sale notices, and from 1771 to 1792, there were 23 purchase announcements for enslaved people (162 announcements in total). These notices involved 231 different enslaved people advertised mostly in the *Connecticut Courant* (Hartford), the *Connecticut Journal* (New Haven), and the *New London Gazette*. These inert numbers do not tell us much about the people offered in the Connecticut economy. In 1763, the *Gazette* announced, "A Likely *Negro Wench* and *Child* to be sold.—Inquire of the Printer. To be sold by the Subscriber of Branford, a likely Negro Wench, 18 years of age, is acquainted with all sorts of House Work; is sold for no fault." Less than a year later, in January 1764, the New Haven paper reported from the harbor, "*Just Imported from Dublin, in the brig Darby*, A parcel of Irish Servants both Men and Women, to be sold cheap, by Israel Boardman." Another New Havener declared in 1779 that he needed a "second-hand *Sulkey*," a small horse-drawn carriage, and "*Wanted to purchase immediately*, Two Negro or Mulatto Boys or men, from 14 to 24 years of age." In 1769, Bernard Linnot of New Haven seemed pleased to get thirty pounds for his human property and offered to postpone payment, "as he is not young." In 1774, and presumably through the war years, "Captain Beecher's Tavern" in New Haven remained a place for human sales. The printers of the newspapers became not only middlemen in sales but in fact traders themselves. "Inquire with the printer" became a common refrain in such advertisements. Bondmen's values manifested in many forms; an owner touted an enslaved man from New Haven named Bill because "he plays well on the flute and fife." Slavery and the use of other unfree labor were still common practice in revolutionary New England, even as human bondage legally came under attack.[7]

Slavery died a slow and fitful death during the ensuing Revolutionary War. In 1774, the Connecticut colony outlawed further importation of enslaved people into its borders, a statute not easily enforced. The external slave trade increasingly had little or no public defense. Connecticut's long history of slaveholding and trading made its actions more conservative than any other New England state. By 1776, the year of American political independence, almost one-quarter of wills probated in Connecticut included enslaved property. In the sales that continued through the revolution, a variety of reasons were expressed by owners for their taking human cargo to the market: "want of employ," the need of cash, a sixteen-year-old girl for being "with suckling child," "for no other fault but her breeding," and for various modes of behavior such as "too great fondness" of a young male for a local Black girl. Some slaveholders bartered their human property as part of sales for livestock and other goods, and some demanded "hard money only." One combined his "Negro boy" with the sale of a plow, a yoke, and a "three cattle team." Some just used their human property to settle debts, attached them to land sales, gave them as personal gifts, or left them to heirs in their wills. And slaveholders routinely and explicitly sought to get rid of children under ten years of age.[8] They were bad investments in a society eventually planning to free them beyond chattel status.

Benjamin Huntington (Yale 1761) provides a noteworthy illustration of the persistence of slaveholding during this time of upheaval. Huntington, a clerk of the state house of representatives, wrote in a letter on March 19, 1777, to his cousin Jabez Huntington, begging that he "make my excuse to his Honor the Governor for being absent a day or two." (The governor was Jonathan Trumbull, a Harvard graduate and himself a slaveholder, for whom Trumbull College at Yale is named.) With the British Army occupying New York, the Continental Congress was about to institute conscription to fill the depleted American army ranks. Yet Huntington was preoccupied with the purchase of a "fine boy," and he told his cousin he "must attend to the appendages of the bargain." Wartime state business and defense of the state from foreign invasion could wait for an important purchase. The good clerk ascended Connecticut politics steadily, serving in

Connecticut's house of representatives (1771–80), as a delegate to the Continental Congress (1780–84, 1787–88), as a member of the state senate (1781–90, 1791–93), and as mayor of Norwich, Connecticut (1784–96). Banality and inhumanity marched together on Connecticut's path to independence and slavery's road to transformation and slow extinction.[9]

Contracts of indenture are yet further windows into the nature and persistence of slaveholding in Connecticut and in Yale's vicinity during the revolutionary period. In 1771, in a bill of indenture in Hartford County, a nine-year-old "Negro Girl" named Silpah was to serve William Jearom for sixteen years. The indenture bound Silpah to "faithfully Serve her Master & mistress in all their Lawfull Commands not absenting from their business by night or by Day their Secrets keep their Commands obey & behave in all points faithfully as a good servant aught." In return Jearom was to "provide for her in Sickness and health according to her Dignity & at the End of the above—sd Term her sd master is to give her two good Sutes of apparel fiting to all parts of her Body."[10] We do not know whether Silpah made it to her twenty-fifth birthday, to womanhood, through and beyond the revolution, nor her fate in sickness and health. She would have reached the end of her indenture three years after Connecticut's gradual emancipation law went into effect and in the year the U.S. Constitution was drafted. The "ordered liberty" that James Madison's constitutional structures sought to create did not address situations like Silpah's in Connecticut.

Although Yale's own community saw a decline in its enslaved population, people of African descent, enslaved and free, were visible everywhere. In 1774, 854 enslaved people lived in New Haven County; by 1790, 433 did. The town of New Haven recorded 262 people held in bondage in 1774, and 76 remained enslaved in 1790. Amid this demographic change, people in the state fled from slavery in search of their natural rights. By one accounting of advertisements in Connecticut newspapers, between 1763 and 1820, some 620 slaves or indentured servants fled their owners for sufficient time to merit the public notice. Of those advertised, 564 were male and 85 female. Such a legal and business matter was commonplace in counties like New Haven, where 69 of the total Connecticut escapes took place.[11] Slavery was in decline in these years, but many who were enslaved could not wait for a future they could only control by flight.

Advertisements offer limited information, but most contained names and amounts or forms of rewards for the return of people considered valuable property. Pharaoh in Groton seems to have escaped twice during the period. A fourteen-year-old, Jube, in Hartford ran away in 1784. The eighteen-year-old Chloe in Stonington sought her freedom in 1795, and the seventeen-year-old

Alexander in New Haven in 1794. Humpton and Gad fled together from New Haven in 1781. A fourteen-year-old named Pitchford ran away in Middletown in 1774. When Sy ran away in New London in 1776, the owner, James Rogers, offered a twenty-dollar reward. John Fenner in Rhode Island offered thirty dollars for the return of Jock Why in 1777. The twenty-year-old Tamar left John Foot in Cheshire in 1777. Quam, Moses, Primus, Bilhah, Nero, Sampson, Sambo, and dozens of other enslaved men, women, and children emancipated themselves—some temporarily and some for all time.[12] Their resistance, their willingness to risk extreme punishment for the promise of freedom, gave the lie to the claim that slavery in Connecticut was "mild" or "benign."

Religious awakenings were a recurring phenomenon in early America, and revivalism swept into and through Connecticut, including New Haven, in 1740, with aftershocks for years to follow.[13] By the opening of the revolution, the ironies of "Christian" slaveholding animated the private, and soon the public, declamations of Africans in New England. No one used the contradiction of a brewing revolution for liberty against monarchy by a Christian people reliant on the enslavement of another people as much as Black people themselves. The same organized group of Black writers who submitted their petition in May 1774, mentioned earlier, proclaimed to the Massachusetts governor and general court that they were "held in a state of Slavery within the bowels of a free and Christian Country." Just five months later, a "*humble Petition of a Number of poor Africans*," addressed to the "Sons of Liberty in Connecticut," declared the case even more boldly. This extraordinary document appealed to the consciences of White elites on several levels. Signed by Bristol Lambee on behalf of many others, the petition considered the radical Sons of Liberty the "most zealous assertors of the *natural* rights and liberties of mankind" and asked for help in their own "deliverance from a state of *unnatural* servitude and bondage." The petitioners further asserted "that LIBERTY, being founded upon the law of *nature*, is as necessary to the happiness of an African, as it is to the happiness of an Englishman." They claimed, "in common with other men, *a natural right to be free*." Their "services" could only be exerted by "voluntary compact," they maintained, stating in clear language the doctrine of consent. They had been captured and taken to "this distant land to be enslaved . . . to serve like a horse in a mill," and they established, in light of such dehumanization, a right to resist in self-defense. Their deepest sense of family, of "endearing ties," had been sundered; they were "strangers" in their new land. They felt blocked from properly serving God because they were chattel, under "absolute controul" of a "master." And finally, Lambee and his friends knew the religious teachings of slaveholders. "So contrary is slavery to the very genius of *Christianity*," they argued in a reversal of the platform of the revivalists they may have seen, that the good men of Connecticut risked their own eternal damnation. The Connecticut petitioners begged those with the revolutionary spirit against Great Britain to "hear our prayers." As the revolutionaries of the colony protested those who "would subject you to slavery," the petitioners demanded they reflect on their own "unnatural custom" of holding property in man.[14] All of Jefferson's four first principles in the later Declaration of Independence are addressed in Lambee's eloquent petition: natural rights and consent explicitly; equality and the right of revolution more implicitly. There were many declarations of independence in revolutionary America.

This appeal emerged in 1774, coming on the heels of the Tea Act, the Coercive Acts, and the convening in September of the First Continental Congress. Resistance to tyranny, with its inspirations and its potential consequences, was in the air. As the Connecticut colonists took their stand against the British Parliament's oppression of their rights, Lambee and company asked for an equal awareness of their fellow people "groaning under the insupportable burthen" of injustice. They broached the subject of reparation for slavery, to "recover pay for past services," but stopped short, saying they would not demand a "rigid justice," only to be "released" to exercise the "free use" of their "natural rights."[15] Thus did enslaved Black inhabitants of Connecticut ingest, express, and even anticipate every element of the emerging American revolutionary ideology. They even gestured to the issue of repair and recompense that would reemerge in the ensuing centuries. Lambee and his fellow petitioners seemed amply aware that they too were laying down principles for future use and remembrance.

Better known than such petitions are the sermons and arguments of White, Yale-trained ministers who laid the foundations for biblically grounded abolitionism in the nineteenth century. One of the most prominent among them was Samuel Hopkins (Yale 1741). Born in Waterbury, Connecticut, the Reverend Hopkins came under the profound influence of the New Light revivalists while at Yale, including George Whitefield, Gilbert Tennent, and especially Jonathan Edwards himself. Hopkins studied personally with Edwards in Northampton, Massachusetts, in 1741 and indeed lived with the famed theologian's family. From about 1743 to 1769, he was the minister at the First Congregational Church in Great Barrington, Massachusetts. Hopkins's theology was strict Calvinism; he was a staunch advocate of Edwards's "New Divinity," the attempt to keep alive the vision of the "visible saints," that only the truly demonstrated converts to Christ (always a small number) should be admitted to church membership, to communion, and certainly to the ministry. But he also imbibed deeply Edwards's idea of "disinterested benevolence," a profound assertion of the Golden Rule, a renunciation of self-love, and the demand that caring about the fate and the good of all humanity was the obligation of every Christian. But Hopkins did not merely adopt Edwards's teachings; he undertook, according to scholars Kenneth Minkema and Harry Stout, a "major revision" of Edwards's theology. A selfless vision of human responsibility emanated from Edwards's notion of "true virtue," but for Edwards this did not translate into antislavery. The mentor, Edwards, never liberated his own slaves; he turned an all but blind eye to his own slaveholding. Hopkins, however, converted disinterested benevolence into radical antislavery activism. To Hopkins, slaveholding was a mortal personal and social sin. He was a staunch supporter of American independence but converted republican ideology into a rationale for abolitionism as well as for resistance to Britain. He became Edwards's "most renowned intellectual heir."[16]

Hopkins wore out his welcome in Great Barrington; his parishioners found him impossibly strict and a dull preacher. From 1770 to 1803, he lived in Newport, Rhode Island, where, except for the three years of British occupation during the war, he pastored the First Congregational Church. Hopkins had enslaved one person and sold him for one hundred dollars; he later donated the money to support sending Africans back to their home continent as Christian missionaries. Newport also greatly affected the minister as the largest slave-trading port in the northeast. He witnessed its terrible, daily reality at the wharves. In his own congregation sat some wealthy shipowners and slave traders. Hopkins was physically awkward; he spoke without grace in a "drawling and monotonous" voice that one contemporary described as "sound[ing] like a cracked bell." He bitterly confronted his congregants with the guilt for what he called the "30,000 murdered every year" in the slave trade and scenes of Africans "herded together, examined as to soundness, branded with a hot iron, manacled in the holds of ships, and transported to the West Indies."[17] Yet Hopkins trained his criticism on slavery itself, not merely the trade.

In a sermon Hopkins delivered in 1776, he appealed, as firmly as the latter-day radical abolitionists of the early nineteenth century, to the consciences of American patriots. "Rouse up then my brethren and assert the Right of universal liberty," he pronounced. "You assert your Right to be free in opposition to the Tyrant of Britain; come be honest men and assert the Right of the Africans to be free in opposition to the Tyrants of America." Hopkins drew directly from the Declaration of Independence, just recently released in Philadelphia, to drive his point even further. "Tis self Evident," he said, "as the Honorable

Continental Congress ob[served]: '*that all men are created equal, and ali*ke endowed by their *Creator with certain unali*enable rights, as *Life, Liberty the persute of hap[p]i*ness &c' That Slavery is an open violation of the Great Eternal Law of nature." Hopkins may have been dull in the pulpit, but with his pen he penetrated to the heart of the matter: "We cry up Liberty but know it the Negros have as good a Right to be free as we can pretend to."[18] Hopkins may rightly be said to have been present at the creation of *moral suasion* in American abolitionism. He and Lambee's petitioners wrote and spoke from the same script.

Hopkins also wrote imaginatively about slavery in a dialogue he constructed in 1776. Responding to common defenses of slavery and the slave trade, he insisted it was "impossible to vindicate" these practices based on "the holy scripture." And to those who argued immediate emancipation would be unsafe, he responded, "While there is no insurmountable difficulty, but that which lies in your own heart." Hopkins did not let the dialogue fade until he delivered a forthright denunciation of racism itself, the "strong prejudices" that White people hold so as not to consider Black people their "brethren," but "another species of animals."[19] This was a brand of abolitionism rarely heard or read during the 1770s, but one that Hopkins had cultivated well before the struggle for American independence. This Yale-trained theologian has never received the attention he deserves as a forerunner of the nineteenth-century abolitionist movement, which his writings nurtured.

Another disciple of Edwards forged his own approach to abolitionism in these years. Jonathan Edwards Jr., the theologian's own son, was born in 1745—a full generation younger than Hopkins, although very much his protégé. Always in the shadow of his famous father, Edwards Jr. was orphaned by age thirteen. While a boy living in Stockbridge at the Indian School, he studied Indigenous languages and was sent to live with the Iroquois near Albany, New York, in preparation for future missionary endeavors. Graduating from the College of New Jersey in 1765, Edwards Jr. eventually moved to New Haven, where he pastored the White Haven Church for most of the rest of his life (1769–95). He developed many associations at Yale and delivered examinations to students, although it appears President Ezra Stiles passed him over for a professorship of divinity in 1781. Stiles and the Edwardseans had never been on the best of terms. In 1773, Edwards Jr. published a series of five articles anonymously in the *Connecticut Journal and the New Haven Post-Boy*, entitled "Some Observations upon the Slavery of Negroes." The articles established a New Divinity theological basis for the antislavery cause. They challenged slavery and the slave trade as Christian hypocrisy. They drew directly on scripture (the Golden Rule, Matthew 7:12). Edwards Jr.

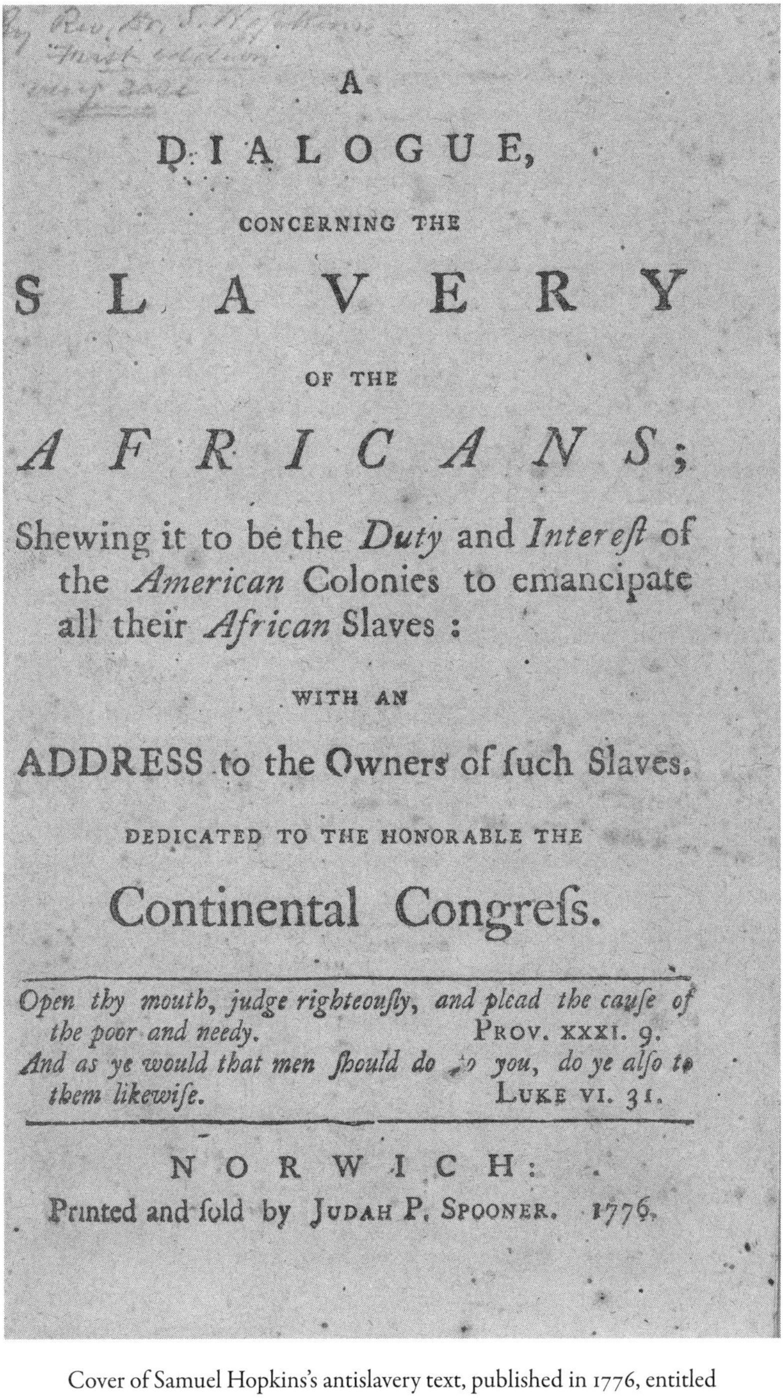

A

DIALOGUE,

CONCERNING THE

SLAVERY

OF THE

AFRICANS;

Shewing it to be the *Duty* and *Intereſt* of the *American* Colonies to emancipate all their *African* Slaves:

WITH AN

ADDRESS to the Owners of ſuch Slaves.

DEDICATED TO THE HONORABLE THE

Continental Congreſs.

Open thy mouth, judge righteouſly, and plead the cauſe of the poor and needy. PROV. XXXI. 9.

And as ye would that men ſhould do to you, do ye alſo to them likewiſe. LUKE VI. 31.

NORWICH:

Printed and ſold by JUDAH P. SPOONER. 1776.

Cover of Samuel Hopkins's antislavery text, published in 1776, entitled *A dialogue, concerning the slavery of the Africans . . . .* Beinecke Rare Book and Manuscript Library, Yale University.

countered specific proslavery arguments, rejecting all biblical justifications for slavery. He noted that although God had permitted the ancient Israelites to invade Canaan and enslave the Canaanites, that did not give Europeans and Americans the right to do the same thing to Africans. He also condemned the idea that slavery benefited Africans by making Christians out of heathens—an idea that would take generations to weaken and die—asserting that religion had nothing to do with why Africans were enslaved. By repudiating the argument that war captives were fair game for enslavement, he took on one of his father's own weakest justifications for slavery.[20] These early antislavery writings would have been relatively well known around Yale College in a year of increased resistance to British authority, although the younger Edwards's parishioners frequently found him too radical and theologically rigid.

Beyond the pulpit, slavery was an animating issue for colonial governments as they waged war with Britain. Many northern and middle colonies passed bans on the foreign slave trade by 1774–75. Indeed, Connecticut adopted "An Act for Prohibiting the Importation of Indian, Negro or Molatto Slaves" in 1774. Even Rhode Island, with its previously thriving slave trade in Newport and Bristol, enacted at least a partial ban on the foreign traffic in the face of the revolutionary fervor over resistance to British imperial rule. New England's enslaved and free Black people sensed their opening and crafted ever more impatient and aggressive petitions for freedom. By 1779, a group of enslaved Connecticut residents demanded liberty because of the "miserable Condition of Our Children, who are training up, and kept in Preparation, for a like State of Bondage and Servitude." In October of the same year, Pomp of Norwalk, enslaved by a Tory who had fled to the British, petitioned the state legislature for his freedom. And the next month from Salem, Connecticut, came a petition from eight slaves belonging to William Browne. "Great Prince, Little Prince, Luke, Caesar, and Prue and her three children" announced themselves "all friends to America." They trusted that "our good mistress, the free State of Connecticut, engaged in a war with tyranny, will not sell good honest . . . friends of freedom and independence."[21] Resistance to taxation without representation, boycotts, and mob action by White colonists had opened larger paths to liberty. Leaders of Connecticut's enslaved people quickly adopted the language of revolution.

In June 1778, Ezra Stiles, the minister, intellectual polymath, and Yale graduate who was serving as pastor of a church in Newport, Rhode Island, prepared to move to Connecticut to take up the reins as president of Yale College. He took over an institution in financial crisis and in chaos due to the war raging all around.

Stiles had felt torn over the decision; in March, he recorded in his diary that he had finally determined to wear Yale's "crown of thorns." Before leaving Newport after many years, Stiles took care of business, including the liberation on June 9 of a Black man named Newport, whom he had purchased twenty-two years earlier. In 1756, the young Ezra, following the practice of his slave-owning minister father, Isaac, had arranged to buy a slave. Stiles paid a ship captain, William Pinnegar, a hogshead of rum (106 gallons) to bring back a boy, ten years old, from his voyage to West Africa. Stiles named the boy "Newport," and the youth grew up to be the enslaved jack-of-all trades for the minister's family.[22]

At that point in time Stiles did not stop to weigh his actions; he neither opposed nor thought much about the Atlantic slave trade, which he would later morally condemn. But by the time of the crisis of the revolution, and as an ardent believer in the quest for independence and liberty from Britain, Stiles suddenly needed to give Newport his liberty as well. Since we live in the fallen world and not only in our minds, moral growth for most humans is a response to external events. In his diary, Stiles wrote matter-of-factly, "I freed or liberated my Negro Man Newport, about [age] 30. Settled all my Affairs, & myself & seven children set out in two Carriages for New Haven." Stiles's biographer, Edmund Morgan, declared it "astonishing" that the learned and discreet minister "still owned a member of the human species in 1778."[23] But looking at Stiles's long history among the slaveholders of Connecticut, it may no longer be so startling. In fact, it was a common practice, and many of his religious and professional models, including Jonathan Edwards, owned and trafficked in human beings.

Ten years after writing his biography of Stiles, Morgan began writing *American Slavery, American Freedom*, an original analysis of the generation of Virginians who led the way among American revolutionaries who "bought their independence with slave labor." Morgan subtly omitted the astonishment he had felt at the slaveholding by staunch republicans and believers in liberty and equality. He demonstrated how White Virginia planters had long distrusted and feared an "idle poor," or a dangerous, propertyless class of unmarried indentured or formerly indentured White male servants who might and did rebel against colonial authorities. New England slavery, of course, was a much smaller cog in the economic wheels of production and commerce. Nonetheless, old and former Puritans cared about nothing quite so much as social order, regulated by their preferred theocratic vision of politics. They, too, like their future countrymen from Virginia, relied on a dependent, either poor or bound, labor force. Freedom and independence meant, in both the North and South, the ability to protect individual natural rights to property. In New England the "contradiction" or "paradox" of slavery and freedom manifested in deep reliance on the West Indian trade, on hierarchical social strata, and on racism.[24] The practice of resistance to British interference in their economic and political lives forged an experience with powerful ideas that would make slavery less and less tenable north of Long Island Sound for intellectuals such as Stiles, but also for members of the merchant and farming classes alike. In Connecticut and at Yale, this great American paradox of slavery and freedom would play out in a long, contradictory process, with Stiles at the institution's helm.

In a diary entry for December 7, 1779, Stiles wrote, "Whether enslaving Negroes be right? Negative." This may have been a random comment, although it is more likely a description of a student debate question, a possible demonstration of how the revolution had thrown the matter of slavery into full relief on the Yale campus in the midst of unprecedented turmoil over republicanism and natural rights. In his voluminous diary, Stiles discussed his slave, Newport, many times. He referred to him variously as "my negro man," "my negro servant," or "manservant." Stiles baptized Newport and admitted him to full church membership and communion in his Rhode Island congregation. During these years, the minister conducted prayer meetings both in his own home with Black congregants and in the homes of other Black residents of that city. Newport married a woman named Violet, with whom he had two sons named Jacob and Abraham, likely illustrating his biblical learning. Sometime after his manumission, perhaps unable to make a living, Newport and Violet moved to New Haven and were employed by the Yale president. According to Leonard Bacon, the long-time minister of the First Church, Newport was a church member who received "alms" from the deacons in his later days. Newport and Violet's son Jacob was further "indentured" to Stiles until he reached his twenty-fourth birthday.[25]

As early as 1776, but especially during his presidency, Stiles worked with Samuel Hopkins on an African missionary project. The scheme involved two African men, called "Guineans," John Quamino and Bristol Yamma, who were to be trained in Congregational theology and English literacy, and then sent to West Africa, with some kind of Yale College support, to work among, as Stiles wrote, their "poor, ignorant, perishing, heathen brethren." In keeping with their support of colonization schemes, Stiles and Hopkins believed that Black missionaries would not only help spread the Gospel but also encourage Black people to emigrate, leaving America. The mission never came to fruition, partly because Quamino died in 1779, and perhaps because of inept planning and insufficient resources. Stiles took a personal interest in the emergence of a Connecticut antislavery group, called the Connecticut Society for the Promotion of Freedom and the Relief of Persons Unlawfully Holden in Bondage (founded in 1790), which counted among its members Simeon Baldwin, Elizur Goodrich, and other Yale people. Several important sermons against slavery and the slave trade were delivered before this society, but according to historian David Brion Davis, "in New Haven the organizational activity was weak and short-lived." Like Hopkins, Stiles also gave his support to colonization schemes for removing Black people from the United States.[26] Befitting the role of a college president, Stiles was a consummate gradualist and his actions in the antislavery society, which seems to have quickly ceased to exist, remained only temporary.

Stiles's leadership of Yale started as the war came to Connecticut. After the end of Thomas Clap's unsettled presidency, Naphtali Daggett (Yale 1748) served as president pro tempore for eleven years until Stiles arrived. A more moderate minister than the doctrinaire Clap, Daggett had to manage the college in crisis and in the early war years, beginning in 1766. He was the first to hold the Livingston Chair of Divinity and the first Yale graduate to hold the presidency, albeit always on a temporary basis. He was described as "slow in his gait," a bit "corpulent," and sometimes "dull" in his preaching. But the colonial general assembly looked fondly on the new leader and decided to pay off the college's deficit with a £160 impost on rum. The staple drink, produced by enslaved labor in the Caribbean, was still a kind of currency in the colony. So were enslaved people for Daggett. At the time of his death in 1780, his will reported approximately £100 in human property, roughly a quarter of the estate's value: a woman named Sue, a boy named Aaron, and two young girls named Lettice and Ollive. It appears that this nearly one-quarter of his valued goods was bequeathed to his children.[27] The presidency of Yale, republicanism, and slaveholding in the Daggett family remained joined at the hip.

The college was no haven for Tories as the revolution broke out. In 1767, when the Townshend Acts came down from Parliament on the American colonies, demanding they buy taxed goods only from Britain, the senior class announced that they would be "wholly dressed in the Manufactures of our own Country." As the first Continental Congress convened in Philadelphia in 1774, a dialogue between MA students at commencement engaged the topic, "The Rights of America and the Unconstitutional Measures of the British Parliament." And by 1775, Yale students drilled and practiced with muskets in the college yard and on the Green, while some loyalists left the institution never to return. During the war years, 1775–81, Yale held no public commencements and periodically sent students to other towns in order to attend safe remote classes in Wethersfield,

Hartford, and Glastonbury. One angry loyalist alumnus, Thomas Jones (Yale 1750), complained that, in his view, the college had become a "nursery of sedition, of faction, and republicanism." Revolutions force people to take sides. Jones claimed that Yale now manifested a "persecuting spirit" and "utter aversion to Bishops and all Earthly Kings."[28]

Yale was indeed a stronghold for the revolutionary cause. It could boast of four signers of the Declaration of Independence—Philip Livingston Jr. (New York), Lewis Morris (New York), Oliver Wolcott (Connecticut), and Lyman Hall (Georgia)—all of whom were slaveholders. And Yale sent twenty-five sons to the Continental Congress. The famous captured and martyred spy Nathan Hale, remembered with a statue in front of Connecticut Hall today, graduated from Yale in 1773. And Roger Sherman, the treasurer of Yale from 1765 to 1776, was the only person to sign all four founding documents: the Articles of Association, the Declaration of Independence, the Articles of Confederation, and the Constitution of the United States. But the war was a serious threat to the college, and when the British invaded Connecticut, Yale and New Haven took up arms to resist.[29]

Many hardships of war, and a change in college leadership, disrupted education at Yale. After changes to curriculum, stabilization of student enrollments, and growing tension over the coming of the revolution, Daggett resigned under pressure from both the trustees and students in 1777 but remained as professor of divinity. Stiles was only several months on the job when the institution essentially ran out of food; bread and flour were scarce when the new president had to send the students home two weeks early in late 1778. In the public press, Stiles wrote an appeal for help: "It is only a delusion," he said, "that scholars can study nearly as well at home as at college," a notion that all who have experienced "remote learning" understand in any century. Someone heard the call, food arrived, and classes resumed in July 1779, with the British Army headquartered in New York and their navy threatening the coastlines.[30]

Late in the evening of July 5, 1779, startling news arrived that dozens of British ships had been sighted off the coast in the sound near Bridgeport. By two o'clock that morning, they were anchored off West Haven and threatening New Haven itself. The British fleet was estimated at between thirty-eight and forty-eight vessels, manned by some two thousand sailors and perhaps three thousand soldiers, an overwhelming number for the small militias of New Haven County and its environs. President Stiles climbed to the top of a church steeple, peered through a telescope, and could see the ships by dawn. Alarm spread. Many people in New Haven fled north and west, and Stiles packed up the college files, his personal papers, and his diaries and sent them with his family to Cheshire. "But all was confusion," Stiles remembered later. When the British attacked, New Haven's badly outmanned militia, including many Yale students with limited, if any, training, stood and fought. "Perhaps one Third of the Adult male Inhab.," Stiles said, "flew to Arms and went out to meet them."[31]

The British troops came ashore in boats as the American militia fired on them throughout the days of July 5–6. The Redcoats plundered parts of the town, used their bayonets indiscriminately, and insulted and abused women. According to Stiles, British soldiers invaded some homes and bayoneted two older men in their own dwellings. Both sides took prisoners, and the fighting became desperate and bloody, especially in East Haven. British soldiers camped on the town green for one night, most of them too drunk to continue any organized raid. On the final day of the forty-eight-hour battle, the British dead were carted down to the wharf in wagons. The Americans had many dead to bury as well. The incursion, the military strategy for which was unclear, ended with, according to one report, dozens of casualties: some twenty-seven Americans killed and nineteen wounded, and ten British dead and forty-nine wounded. The commander of one of the British regiments was Edmund Fanning (Yale 1757), and Ezra Stiles Jr., the president's son, commanded a unit of volunteer militia.[32]

Among the fighters in the Yale contingent of the militia was former president Naphtali Daggett. Whatever his shortcomings, Daggett was a patriot and no reclusive scholar. He took up arms with his fowling musket during the battle for New Haven. Daggett fought with a volunteer company that included many Yale students. "Dr. Daggett Professor of Divinity," Stiles reported, "was captivated [captured]. He discharged his piece and then submitted as Prisoner—they after this pierced & beat him with Bayonets & otherwise abused him." In Daggett's own dramatic account, he was dragged by British soldiers some five miles to the town green, bloodied and unable to stand. He recuperated in a widow's home near the college, proud that the "Enemy" had called him a "damned old rebel." But his injuries were so severe that his health deteriorated; Daggett died the next year in 1780 at only fifty-one years old.[33]

The British did not burn the town proper, nor any Yale buildings, but they did destroy many houses, shops, and vessels at Long Wharf. Stiles, in his diary, reported the death of an MA student as well as others associated with the college. When the president returned to the town, he "visited the Desolations, dead Corpses, & Conflagrations." He also reported with alarm that the British general had "read on the Long Wharf a Proclamation of Freedom to the Negroes which should joyn them; but few, & I think none of the Negroes went off with them."[34] Stiles could not make such a statement with certainty; the flight of Black men, women, and children seeking the British promise of freedom was already well underway.

Later in 1779, the Revolutionary War moved south. New Haven and Yale College slowly recovered from the battle. But the questions of Black freedom and enlistments only grew in intensity. African Americans' paths to military service were riddled with obstacles—racist, historical, and legal. But serve they did, especially as General George Washington's struggling army sought their service out of military necessity. Yet allegiance on the part of soldiers, Black or White, to the patriot cause was anything but assured. Before the war ran its course, and as the British military evacuation took place in 1782–83, some sixty thousand Americans chose exile to many far-flung parts of the empire. This exodus included between eight thousand and ten thousand escaped slaves who had followed the British promise of "freedom" in exchange for their allegiance (issued famously by John Murray, or Lord Dunmore, governor of Virginia, in 1775). Most tellingly for the conflict's impact on New World slavery, an estimated fifteen thousand enslaved African Americans were carried abroad by slave-owning loyalists. In this historical open door, those Black people with a choice opted for paths they believed would lead to their personal freedom, even as many were thrilled by revolutionary and natural rights rhetoric, that of the founders and their own. Some historians have called the Black quest for freedom in this war a "mass movement" in many directions.[35] Black allegiance became an important element in American victory and British defeat, as well as in the longer-term consequences of the Age of Revolution.

White observers understood how American slaveholding undercut the patriots' appeal to would-be Black enlistees. When Josiah Atkins, a Connecticut soldier marching with the Continental army into Virginia, saw George Washington's plantation at Mount Vernon, he wrote, "Alas! That persons who pretend to stand for the rights of mankind for the liberties of society, can delight in oppression, & that even of the worst kind!" Atkins scratched out these remarks in a private journal his commander, of course, never saw. Some of General Washington's slaves escaped to the British, never to return, joining what some have called a "global loyalist diaspora." In New England, however, where Black populations were smaller than in the South and slavery was now more vulnerable, African Americans joined the patriot cause in significant numbers. Nearly every town in Connecticut reported at least some enlistments of Black soldiers in the Continental army, including New Haven. For example, ten Black men enlisted in Stratford and thirteen came from the town of Wallingford. In these relatively

The Battle of Bunker's Hill, June 17, 1775, John Trumbull, 1786.
Trumbull Collection, Yale University Art Gallery.

small Black communities, free and enslaved, such numbers had profound effects for Black families and their futures. Approximately 5,000 Black soldiers served in the American forces during the war, making up roughly 2 percent of the total force; they mostly served alongside White soldiers. Black soldiers and camp aides appear in numerous noted paintings of the war's events, such as John Trumbull's famous work *The Battle of Bunker's Hill, June 17, 1775*, displayed prominently at the Yale University Art Gallery, and Emanuel Leutze's *Washington Crossing the Delaware*.[36] But the Black presence in the American armies appeared in far more ways than legendary artistic depiction. They also left their indelible mark in wartime documentation.

An official report by an adjutant general in the Continental army from late summer 1778 counted 755 Black soldiers spread across fourteen brigades. The majority of the 148 Black soldiers in General Samuel Holden Parsons's brigade, the unit with the highest percentage of Black soldiers, were from Connecticut. Born in Lyme, Connecticut, Parsons had been a leader of the rebel cause in New London before the war, and likely had a hand in recruiting so many Black soldiers. In the Sixth Connecticut Regiment's muster roll, 34 Black soldiers appear; all enlisted in 1777 or 1778. They hailed from towns in the corridor from Middletown south to Fairfield and eastward up the coastline to Saybrook. Six were from

New Haven: Andrew Jack, Jack Little, Lewis Martin, Sharper Rogers, Jeffrey Sill, and Hector Williams. All 34 were listed now with first and last names, as though this act of soldiering, which led to the advent of their liberation from slavery, had given them new identities. Eleven chose new surnames to demonstrate their redefined futures: one chose Freedom, seven Freeman, and three Liberty. Dick Freedom, Cuff Freeman, and Pomp Liberty were telling a story. Nearly all in the Sixth Regiment enlisted for the "War," meaning its duration, while a few were recorded as three-year recruits. Their experiences are at least partially represented by the notations in the records that three were "transferred to invalid corps," two died in service, one was taken "prisoner," and one "deserted."[37]

Some of these Black soldiers had ties to Yale College. The Black man depicted with musket in hand in Trumbull's painting of Bunker Hill, long thought to be named Peter Salem, now is believed to be a man named Asaba, enslaved by Lieutenant Thomas Grosvenor (1744–1825), a 1765 graduate of Yale College. Grosvenor served a full eight years in the Continental army, then four years in the Connecticut General Assembly, seven more years on the governor's council until 1801, and as a judge until 1815. Asaba may have accompanied Grosvenor through most of his military career at war; he appears as a free man in his household in the 1790 census, along with his enslaved son, James Peter, later freed on his twenty-fifth birthday in 1794. An enslaved man named Jeffrey Sill enlisted with the approval of his owner in New Haven, Samuel Hemingway, who was a direct descendant of Yale's first official student at the Collegiate School, Jacob Hemingway. Samuel Hemingway and Sill supposedly made a deal that Sill would remain Hemingway's slave at war's end. Sill apparently had other ideas, and he reenlisted after three years. According to historian David White, Hemingway petitioned the general assembly, offering to manumit Sill under the condition that the state compensate him for the loss of his property. The assembly denied Hemingway's request, and it appears service did indeed mean freedom for Sill. Hemingway, however, still owned four enslaved people in the 1790 census.[38]

Another Black Revolutionary War soldier established deep ties to New Haven through his children, who became active in religious and educational work in the city. Prince Duplex Sr. was born into slavery, but he was free and a "basket maker" by the time he enlisted in 1777 in Colonel Isaac Sherman's Connecticut Regiment; he served three full years. Duplex fought at the Battle of Germantown on October 4, 1777, and survived the winter at Valley Forge with George Washington's army in 1778. After his discharge, the state paid Duplex a final amount of eleven pounds, two shillings, and three farthings. Some three months later the soldier turned over his wages for his entire war service (over forty-four pounds) to a Jonathan Barnes, who was either Duplex's owner or the man for whom he had agreed to be a substitute. The cost of Duplex's freedom was three years at war, suffering and nearly freezing to death at Valley Forge, and forty-four pounds. As a free man, Duplex married Lement Parker at a Congregational church in Wolcott, Connecticut, and together they raised seven children who survived into adulthood: George, Sylvia, Arena, Craty, Prince Jr., Vashti, and Mark; several of these children became notable leaders of New Haven's Black community. In 1819, the senior Duplex claimed a pension for his wartime service and began receiving eight dollars per month, listing the following modest possessions and responsibilities: two drawing knives, one ax, one hoe, four jackknives, two wooden plates, two iron teaspoons, one desk, and a debt owed of two notes for twenty dollars. In time, however, he acquired substantial farmland in Connecticut and, later, in New York, which he passed to his children.[39]

Prince Duplex's son Prince Duplex Jr. was the first clerk of the African Ecclesiastical Society, organized in 1820, and was active in establishing the Temple Street Church in New Haven. A daughter, Vashti Duplex Creed, became the first Black schoolteacher in New Haven. Vashti's son was Cortlandt Van Rensselaer Creed, who graduated from the Yale medical school in 1857—the first Black person to do so. When the American Civil War broke out, Creed sought to serve as a surgeon but was rejected because of his race. Not until January 1864 did he receive his appointment as the physician for the Thirtieth Connecticut Volunteers, the second Black regiment organized in the state.[40] Military traditions ran deep among Prince Duplex's extended family through more than fourscore years. In their inventories of possessions, their careers and academic degrees, and especially their intergenerational memories, the Duplexes and Creeds linked the freedoms attained in the revolution to those reborn in the Civil War as much as any American family.

A final fascinating link to New Haven and Yale is the case of Jack Arabas. In 1777, Arabas, an enslaved man, entered the Continental army as a replacement for the son of his owner, Thomas Ivers. After Arabas fled upon his honorable discharge from the army at the end of the war, Ivers sought to reclaim his "property": he found and seized his former slave and brought him to New Haven, where the soldier was jailed. While incarcerated, Arabas appealed to the superior court for a writ of habeas corpus. The court granted the writ and proclaimed Arabas to be "a freeman, absolutely manumitted from his master by enlisting and serving in the army." An intrepid scholar, Mark David Hall, uncovered the original manuscript in the case, *Arabas v. Ivers*, long considered lost. Samuel Huntington, Eliphalet Dyer, Roger Sherman, and William Pitkin presided over the case. The judges decided that "none but freemen Could by the Regulations of Congress be Enlisted in the Continental army," and therefore, since Ivers must have allowed Arabas to enlist, it follows that he freed him as well. The legal logic was strained, but the conclusion clear. Hall argues that, along with his colleagues, Sherman "consciously pushed the boundaries of the law," and reaped the egalitarian meanings of the revolution, in order to liberate Arabas. *Arabas v. Ivers* was a significant case. It was not uncommon for courts to follow suit and find enslaved people to be free; but this was not always the case. The decision, however, clearly said in part, "Said Negro Jack cannot be any longer held as a Slave for life and therefore Order and Decree that he be no longer held in Custody but Set at Liberty."[41]

When Jack Arabas walked out of that New Haven court a free man on December 7, 1784, we are not certain where he went; did anyone across the Green at Yale College give him aid and comfort? This Black veteran surely could hope, at least, that he had helped to create a new history for his race. He was one of the thousands of the formerly enslaved who, as historian Benjamin Quarles puts it, declared their own independence—by their actions, by their bravery, and now by law. Arabas was among those African Americans who, writes Quarles, "clothed the War for Independence with a meaning and a significance transcending their own day and time and not confined to the shores of the new republic."[42]

The same year Arabas won his freedom, the state of Connecticut enacted its gradual abolition plan. Called "An Act Concerning Indian, Molatto, and Negro Servants and Slaves," the law provided that anyone born after March 1, 1784, to enslaved parents was to become free on their twenty-fifth birthday for males; an addition to the act in 1797 freed women born after this date on their twenty-first birthday. *Gradual* indeed. Of the Northern states that adopted gradual emancipation (the others being Rhode Island, New York, and Pennsylvania), Connecticut enacted the most conservative. The proponents of the law, including Noah Webster (Yale 1778), author of the famous *American Dictionary of the English Language* (1828), condemned slavery but stressed stability, advocating for a slow and gradual end to the institution. The law also included incentives for slaveholders to remove the formerly enslaved from the United States. No ringing statements of "natural rights" graced the pages of this law; it led, as one legal scholar has written, to "slavery's atrophy" but not to genuine "emancipation." Real abolition in Connecticut would be an agonizingly long process: in 1790 the state still counted 2,764 people enslaved; in 1800, there were 951; by 1820, fewer than 100 lived in legal bondage; and by 1840, only 17 remained. Slavery was not finally officially abolished in Connecticut until 1848, seventy-four years after the gradual emancipation act became law.[43] The tradition of moderation and conservatism ran deep in Connecticut.

Black people, enslaved and free, did not stop articulating their hopes that the country would make good on the promises of the revolution. In the 1780s, a group of Black New Haveners, living not far from Yale College, produced yet another extraordinary petition for freedom. It likely found its spirit in resistance to the nature of the long-term gradual emancipation scheme. The petition was crafted with verve and passion for the same natural rights and Christian religious inclusion as earlier documents. The words were visceral and grew from sensibilities and yearnings rooted in experience. These people considered themselves "Africas Blacks," declared themselves still in "Chaine Bondage" and "Cruil Slavirre." They wanted their "human Bodys" recognized as such. They had "fought the grandest Battles . . . in this War," the petition maintained, demanding "Rite and justes" if America was ever to become a "free contry." They felt the power of natural rights in their bones and their souls. The New Haveners, in the shadow of the famous college at Yale, declared their right to "Pubblick woship," and to "larning . . . our C A B or to reed the holy BiBle."[44] Simple justice, born of a revolution for human liberty, had rarely been stated so directly.

In 1791, Jonathan Edwards Jr., the Yale-trained abolitionist minister, delivered a sermon before the Connecticut Society for the Promotion of Freedom. Confrontational with his audience in the wake of the gradual abolition plan, which he opposed, Edwards condemned prejudice based on skin color and argued that the curse of Ham in the Bible applied only to the Canaanites and not to Africans. He asserted that the slave trade caused endless, unjustified war, and enslavement in the United States hardened the hearts and poisoned the laws of the new nation. And in the classic form of the jeremiad that his father had pioneered, he denounced the idea of "political slavery" to the king, alleged during the revolution, which he considered "inconceivably preferable to the slavery of the Negroes." The American republic was in peril due to slavery, argued Edwards the younger, saying, "We cannot sin at so cheap a rate as our fathers," a telling phrase considering his lineage.[45]

Both Samuel Hopkins and Edwards supported colonization schemes promoting the removal of African Americans from the country when feasible; they were precursors of the early nineteenth-century leaders, slaveholders and nonslaveholders, Northerners and Southerners alike, who could not conceive of the future United States as a society of biracial equality. At the end of his 1791 sermon, though, Edwards contended forcibly that White Americans should stop worrying about the release of formerly enslaved Black people into the larger society. Those frightened that former bondmen would "cut our throats" were fools, he believed. Rather ahead of his time, he claimed the races would mix and blend in future generations. Both Hopkins and Edwards left an important legacy of antislavery ideas with which New England and their Yale community could grapple if it so chose. They were a bridge to future abolitionist ideas and strategies. Other Yale luminaries joined them in a slowly growing antislavery impulse in the expanding networks of Yale College, including the professor of divinity and future president Timothy Dwight, who, despite his conservativism, even opposed colonization schemes.[46] These thinkers demonstrate not only that abolition had old if troubled roots at Yale but also how slavery died so hard in Connecticut and New England, despite the profound transformations of the American Revolution.

In the wake of the Revolutionary War, Americans discovered readily that they needed government. They also knew, from many different perspectives, that the conflagration had left deep and unresolved legacies. Slavery was now both under attack and in decline in some regions, while it would soon thrive and expand as never before in others. The fledgling nation teetered, on the brink of extinction, with a collapsed economy and a very uncertain future. Thousands were dead or homeless; farms were destroyed, food scarce, some towns completely burned. The new republic based on powerful but abstract creeds might or might not survive in a hostile world of empires and monarchies. Its own society had a budding aristocracy of slaveholders and urban merchants, as well as a turbulent egalitarian spirit—if it could sustain it under law. Many Native Americans were ambivalent at best about just who and what had won the war, and African Americans had fought and suffered on both sides. Liberty had won, but how much and for whom?[47] Surely this new beginning had taken history forward into a new dispensation and not into division and chaos.

That is certainly what President Ezra Stiles of Yale believed. With his customary boundless curiosity, and his research into various scientific, literary, and historical subjects, Stiles emerged from the American Revolution as one of its most hopeful advocates. No radical abolitionist, Stiles nevertheless supported Connecticut's 1784 Gradual Abolition Act, even organizing an effort to count the enslaved people in the state, and served as president of the short-lived Society for the Promotion of Freedom and for the Relief of Persons Holden in Bondage in 1790. Stiles rejoiced that monarchy had been defeated and he wholeheartedly praised the French revolutionary movement when it commenced.

Ezra Stiles (1727–1795), B.A. 1746, M.A. 1749, Samuel King, 1771.
Bequest of Dr. Charles Jenkins Foote, B.A. 1883, M.D. 1890. Yale University Art Gallery.

Indeed, as historian Edmund Morgan demonstrated, it is hard to find by the 1790s a more fulsome enthusiast for *democracy*, a term the Yale leader avoided, than Stiles. In 1793, Stiles appended a 130-page manifesto for human rights and representative government to a disorganized document exalting the regicides who had overthrown and killed King Charles I of Britain in 1649. Political "emancipation," Stiles argued, "cannot be made but by the people." Stiles combined his visceral faith in education with the broadening horizon of democracy and maintained that common people "will generally judge right, when duly informed. The general liberty is safe and secure in their hands." This child of Puritanism and republicanism, as calm and thoughtful a product of the Age of Revolution as one might find, had come to believe that democracy was not the opposite of human nature but its learned and practiced creation. Stiles even signed some letters late in life, "Ezra Stiles, an unchanged Son of Liberty."[48]

Stiles's story is one of remarkable growth in response to events. He had managed to steer Yale College through the brutal disruptions of the revolution and, by 1792, after long and arduous conflict with the Connecticut State Assembly, finally reached a deal for new public funding that helped to secure the institution's future and make possible the eventual building of a true university. Stiles was not a highly astute administrator; he preferred to read and think, an intellectual debate to a legislative negotiation. Rather than labor to find a proper professor of Hebrew, he famously learned the language on his own and taught it himself.[49] But in the wake of the revolution, he attracted a number of significant donors to Yale, many of them wealthy merchants.

In 1786, Jupiter Hammon, the enslaved man who had protected and comforted James Hillhouse's young wife as the British attacked New Haven, wrote a poem, "An Essay on Slavery," a revelatory work of Christian devotion and moral condemnation of slavery. Hammon was a devout Christian, and much of the poem reads like an expression of faith, a prayer for deliverance for all the enslaved, and a praise song for Jesus, an all-powerful and liberating God. The manuscript was a working draft, including revisions by Hammon himself.[50] This rare find from the depths of the Yale archives can leave one breathless at the brown paper, the slightly faded ink, and the careful writing. Here as well is tactile evidence of the paradox of slavery and freedom in the Age of Revolution.

Hammon was born enslaved in 1711, the property of a wealthy family on Long Island.[51] Yet well into his seventies, he used his considerable literary gifts to envision an end to slavery and the suffering that African and African American people had experienced at the hands of their fellow Christians. Hammon gave keen attention to his rhyme and meter; his handwriting was strong. He repeatedly references both salvation and America through the metaphor of a "distant shore" and the "Christian shore." He names the Middle Passage with fatefulness and controlled emotion:

> Our forefathers came from africa
> tost over the raging main
> to a Christian shore there for to stay
> and not return again.

Exuding Christian humility and supplication in the face of the awesome power of God, Hammon demands that the enslaved and free pray together for "Liberty."

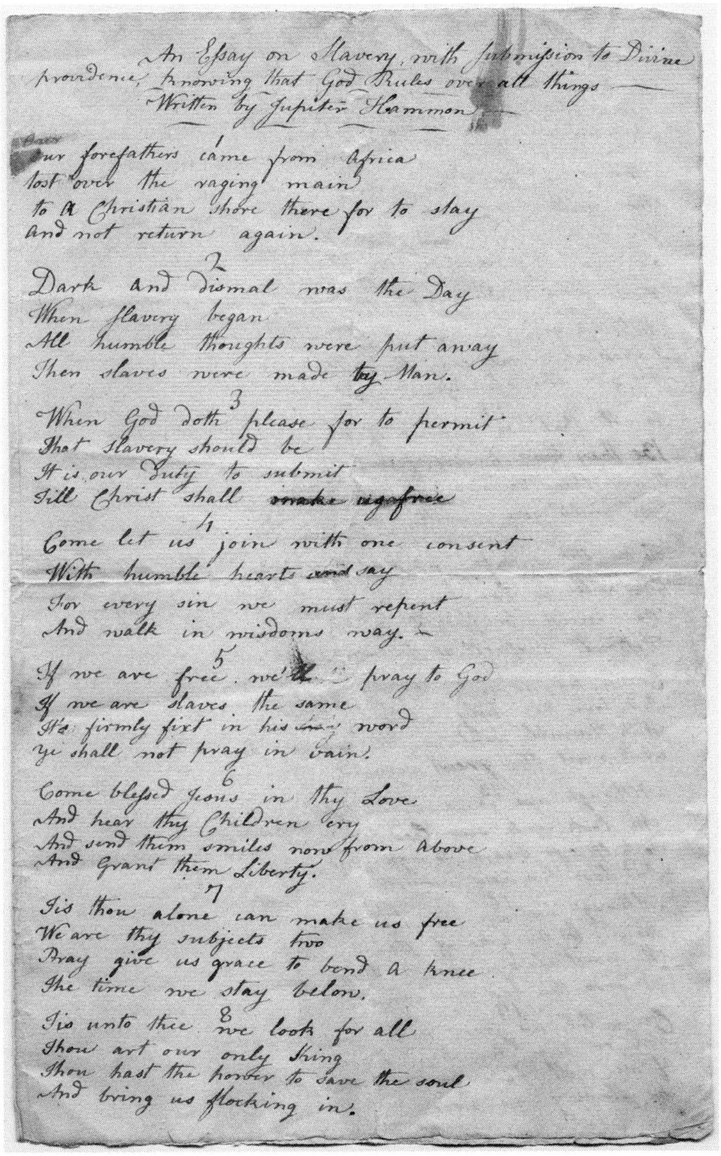

An Essay on Slavery, with submission to Divine providence, knowing that God Rules over all things —
Written by Jupiter Hammon

1
Our forefathers came from Africa
tost over the raging main
to a Christian shore there for to stay
And not return again.

2
Dark and dismal was the Day
When slavery began
All humble thoughts were put away
Then slaves were made by Man.

3
When God doth please for to permit
That slavery should be
It is our Duty to submit
Till Christ shall ~~make us free~~

4
Come let us join with one consent
With humble hearts ~~and~~ say
For every sin we must repent
And walk in wisdoms way.

5
If we are free we'll pray to God
If we are slaves the same
It's firmly fixt in his ~~[illegible]~~ word
Ye shall not pray in vain.

6
Come blessed Jesus in thy Love
And hear thy Children cry
And send them smiles now from Above
And Grant them Liberty.

7
Tis thou alone can make us free
We are thy subjects two
Pray give us grace to bend a knee
The time we stay below.

8
Tis unto thee we look for all
Thou art our only King
Thou hast the power to save the soul
And bring us flocking in.

First page of "An Essay on Slavery," Jupiter Hammon, November 10, 1786. Hillhouse Family Papers (MS 282). Manuscripts and Archives, Yale University Library.

Hammon's language is King James in style and tone; many a "thee," "thou," and "ye" give beauty to the verse. "Tis thou alone can make us free," the poet declares. In stanzas 11 and 12, Hammon enters briefly the actual voice of God: "Come unto me ye humble souls . . . bond or free." After freedom itself, the poem insists on human equality. As he moves the poem with refrain toward crescendo, Hammon returns to the idea of the "shore":

Come let us join with humble voice
Now on the christian shore
If we will have our only choice
Tis slavery no more . . .

When shall we hear the joyfull sound
Echo the christian shore
Each humble voice with songs resound
That Slavery is no more.[52]

Hammon and Stiles were both men of the eighteenth century, witnesses to epochal historical change, both realized and merely anticipated. With vastly different beginnings, they were both in their own ways Christian men of the Enlightenment imagining a future for their new, shared country.

INTERLUDE

Gradual Emancipation in Connecticut

Believe me now my Christian friends,
Believe your friend call'd HAMMON:
You cannot to your God attend,
And serve the God of Mammon.

—JUPITER HAMMON,
"A Dialogue, intitled, The Kind Master and the Dutiful Servant" (ca. 1778)

The name of James Hillhouse, perhaps the town's most prominent citizen of the early republic, is inscribed across the city of New Haven, including on the city's oldest public high school and one of its famous avenues. Born in Connecticut in 1754, he graduated from Yale in 1773. Only a few years later, in 1779, he was called on to command a company of volunteers, including college students, in the battle against the British Army as they invaded the city. He survived that ordeal and trained as a lawyer. In 1782, Hillhouse was appointed treasurer of Yale College—a position he held until his death fifty years later. An astute money manager and a builder, Hillhouse left an enduring mark on the college and the city, helping design Yale's famed Old Brick Row, draining and beautifying the New Haven Green, and organizing Grove Street Cemetery, the first cemetery of its kind in the country. He hired and worked with the African American entrepreneur William Lanson, who was responsible for the crucial Long Wharf extension, allowing ships to unload directly to the docks in the shallow harbor. Hillhouse also was instrumental in constructing the Farmington Canal, which connected the New Haven Harbor to the inland. Hillhouse took over as commissioner of the Connecticut School Fund in

1810, reviving it by investments and fundraising from a deficit to an institution worth $1.7 million.[1]

Hillhouse became a powerful politician, holding office in the state legislature, U.S. Congress (1791–96), and U.S. Senate (1796–1810). Like his friend, Yale president Timothy Dwight, he was a staunch Federalist, critical of Thomas Jefferson, and in 1808, he proposed a series of constitutional amendments that would have curbed Southern influence in the federal government. While serving in the U.S. Senate, Hillhouse introduced a number of amendments that would have restricted slavery, particularly in the new lands added to the United States through the Louisiana Purchase. Some of these legislative efforts were successful initially, including one that prohibited the transportation of enslaved people into Louisiana by anyone other than the owner for his own use. The historian Don Fehrenbacher describes Hillhouse's proposed legislation as "the strongest antislavery restriction imposed on any portion of the lower South between 1733 and 1865." In 1805, however, Congress passed new legislation that, in Fehrenbacher's words, "wiped out the Hillhouse ban on domestic slaveholding." Thus lower Louisiana joined the rest of the slaveholding South.[2]

In the same years that Hillhouse built an illustrious career as a public servant, he enslaved other people, including children, and a number of enslaved people were part of his daily life. His first wife, Sarah Lloyd, came from the large landowning and slaveholding Lloyd family on Long Island, New York. She died along with her infant child in 1779. The poet Jupiter Hammon had been held in slavery by the Lloyd family and was living with the Hillhouses at the time of the Revolutionary War battle and Sarah's travails. Hillhouse soon remarried, this time to Rebecca Woolsey, a double first cousin of his first wife. Rebecca's grandfather, the Reverend Benjamin Woolsey, a member of the Yale class of 1707, left five enslaved people in his will when he died, specifying that these people—Primus, Hagar, Ishmael, Judith, and Candace—were to "be Sold and the Money Thence Arising to be . . . for the Use of my said Wife." When Rebecca's father, Colonel Melancthon Taylor Woolsey, died, the inventory of his estate in 1758 included enslaved Black men, women, and children named Ishmael, Saul, Prissila, Jack, and Patience. Both of Hillhouse's wives, Rebecca and Sarah, served together as witnesses to the sale of human beings. According to a 1773 bill of sale, the young cousins witnessed their father and uncle purchasing a six-year-old girl named Phebe for "Twenty five pounds Current money." In James Hillhouse's private worlds, his own and those into which he married, wealth, status, and New England racial slavery were central features of daily life, even as he sought higher aims in his political work. Both Sarah and Rebecca knew Jupiter Hammon well, since he lived for long periods in their home in New Haven. And Hillhouse knew Hammon, calling him, on one occasion, "our good old respected Jupiter."[3]

Despite the affection the Hillhouses expressed for some enslaved people in letters, slavery as practiced in their family lasted a long time, and its effects were far from benign. Rebecca Hillhouse wrote many letters to her husband during the extended months each year that he spent in his official duties in Philadelphia and Washington, DC, frequently reporting on various household laborers, free and enslaved, White and Black.[4] Hillhouse himself held people in bondage, and still others, enslaved by family members, lived under his roof. In 1790, for example, the first federal census recorded the presence of two "other free persons" (meaning free persons of color) and one slave. We know some of these people belonged to his wives' relatives. Rebecca Hillhouse's mother, Rebecca Woolsey, and her unmarried sister Theodosia moved from Long Island to live with Rebecca and James in New Haven after they married. Jack, one of these enslaved people, accompanied the Woolseys to New Haven. (This may have been the same Jack who, as a boy, appeared in her husband's will some thirty years earlier.) In 1784, Mrs. Woolsey, James's mother-in-law, wrote of her great distress that Jack had to endure a major, costly medical surgery and lamented her son's financial woes. She declared herself "as poor as a church mous" and complained of having to pay for Jack's operation—this, after listing her supply of satin bed linens and many other fine items of clothing. Jack recovered and continued to wait on Mrs. Woolsey.[5]

Hillhouse enslaved other people himself. According to New Haven vital records, he recorded in front of the justice of the peace his ownership of two enslaved children: a girl named Hagar, born on March 17, 1786, and a boy named Jupiter, born on June 22, 1789. Hillhouse further swore that these "children will by Law be free at ye age of Twenty-five years." The names of these children, Hagar and Jupiter, strongly suggest ties to James's wives. In addition to Jupiter Hammon, enslaved by the Lloyds, his wives' grandfather, Benjamin Woolsey, owned a woman named Hagar at the time of his death in 1755. Slaveholding was a broad family affair in the Hillhouse extended network.[6]

The children Hagar and Jupiter were born enslaved, and their world and lives were shaped by the institution. They also grew up in the shadow of Connecticut's Gradual Abolition Act, which gave them only the nebulous future hope of freedom and autonomy. Following the revolution, a number of Northern states, beginning with Pennsylvania in 1780, passed laws providing for gradual emancipation. But the process was uneven and far from speedy—what one historian calls "protracted and idiosyncratic." New York and New Jersey, with significant enslaved populations, did not pass such laws until 1799 and 1804, respectively. And Connecticut's Gradual Abolition Act did not actually free a single person, and it did not fully end slavery in the state; the institution lasted in Connecticut until 1848. Instead, this legislation placed a limit on the lengths of enslavement for those *yet* to be born. Passed in 1784, the act stipulated that children born to enslaved mothers after March 1, 1784, would be free on their twenty-fifth birthday, for boys, and their twenty-first birthday, for girls. Another act, in 1788, required Connecticut slaveholders to register the birth of enslaved children, which explains why Hillhouse recorded his ownership of young Hagar and Jupiter when he did. Older people, born into slavery before March 2, 1784, remained enslaved for life. And despite prohibitions on transporting enslaved people out of state, slaveholders continued to do so, in defiance of the law. Slavery declined in Connecticut over the first decades of the nineteenth century, but it died a fitful death, to the detriment of children like Hagar and Jupiter. Indeed, Hagar would not live to experience freedom. Hillhouse, a member of the First Congregational Church in New Haven, had the young girl baptized "in private" on July 21, 1794. Hagar died two days later at the age of nine, and like her biblical namesake, one of Abraham's wives, she died a slave.[7]

Her brother, the little boy named Jupiter, outlived Hagar, but only to endure other trials of slavery, separation, and hardship. In 1795, the boy's mother, Judith Cocks, wrote Hillhouse, bereft and confused. Cocks and her son had been taken to Marietta, Ohio, by Hillhouse's first cousin, Lucy Backus Woodbridge and her husband, Dudley Woodbridge (Yale 1766). (This fact alone suggests a disregard for the law, since it was illegal to transport enslaved people outside the state.) Cocks told Hillhouse that Mrs. Woodbridge and her sons "thump and beat [Jupiter] as if he was a Dog" and begged for clarity about Jupiter's status. Telling Hillhouse she was living in a "strange country without one friend," she asked him to "be so kind as to write me how Long Jupiter is to remain with them." Woodbridge had told Cocks that Jupiter "is to live with her untill he is twenty five years of age this is something that I had no idea of I all ways thought that he was to return with me to new England." Cocks further implored Hillhouse not to sell her boy to Mrs. Woodbridge.[8] Even more wrenching, she mentions her daughter Hagar, apparently unaware that the girl had died the year before.

In this rare document, an enslaved mother speaks directly to one of the most powerful men in the country about her fears and, in doing so, articulates the grief, frustration, and sense of powerlessness many enslaved parents must have felt. Unable to navigate the gradual abolition law with any certainty or genuine hope, Cocks was trying as best she could to protect her children from the violence and cruelty of slavery, appealing to Hillhouse's sense of humanity to spare her son. In the starkest terms, her letter dramatizes the painfully slow and extended process of abolition in Connecticut, which made children property and subject to the violence and whims of their owners through early adulthood. Young Jupiter's fate is unknown, but slavery continued in the Woodbridge household. For although since 1787 the Northwest Ordinance had prohibited both slavery and indentured servitude in the territory, which included Ohio, Lucy Woodbridge declared in a letter to a friend a few years later, in November 1802, "I have bought a good natured Negro boy who has five Years to serve."[9]

The American Revolution forever changed Yale and New Haven, but slavery itself was far from dead in Connecticut. The state was one of only three that had not ratified the Bill of Rights in 1791. And many moderate, Yale-educated leaders viewed their gradual abolition law as sensible and benevolent. Because of this legislation, the last enslaved person in Connecticut was not legally freed until 1848. Even forward-looking Yale alumni like James Hillhouse were unwilling to dismantle the systems of bondage and oppression that robbed other people of autonomy over their lives, bodies, and futures. Hillhouse, like other Yale leaders, including Timothy Dwight, continued to enslave young children at the dawn of the nineteenth century. While protecting his city from the British, serving in the U.S. Congress and Senate, serving Yale as its treasurer, establishing Grove Street Cemetery, orchestrating the planting of New Haven's signature elm trees, and doing countless other works of civic improvement, Hillhouse, his wives, and his children benefited from the labor of enslaved people. Beginning with Jupiter Hammon's companionship and protection of his first wife in 1779, James Hillhouse and his extended family relied on and benefited from the labor of enslaved people. Slavery intruded into the most private and intimate aspects of Yale leaders' daily lives, and it underwrote their most striking accomplishments.

CHAPTER 5

Yale in the Early Republic

> If it were not for the stripes on my back which were made while I was a slave, I would in my will leave my skin as a legacy to the government, desiring that it might be taken off and made into parchment, and then bind the constitution of glorious, happy and *free* America. Let the skin of an American slave bind the charter of American liberty!
>
> —WILLIAM GRIMES, *Life of William Grimes, the Runaway Slave, Written by Himself* (1855)

What happened to the Black soldiers and their families who had hoped, prayed, and fought for freedom from chattel slavery and the rights of citizens in the late Revolutionary War? Many former Black soldiers from Connecticut lived long enough to seek and receive pensions, recording some of the details of their lives early in the next century in return for the promise of reward for their years of military service in the nation's cause. Pomp Liberty, enslaved when he enlisted in 1776, served in three Connecticut regiments, the Second, Fourth, and Sixth, for a full eight years during the entire war. Chatham Freeman, a farmer, served three years in the Fourth Connecticut Regiment, and after the war married a woman named Maria, with whom he set up a life in freedom. Dan Mallory was born in Africa, captured, and transported to New England at age five, landing in Saybrook, Connecticut. He was sold three times and experienced as many enslavers before enlisting in Colonel Lemuel Canfield's Connecticut Regiment. When they died, Black soldiers left lists of modest but respectable possessions. Cato Treadwell, of Stratford, Connecticut, served three years in the war in the Fourth Connecticut Regiment; when he died, he passed on one table, one plain chest, six old chairs, one porridge pot, an old chest, spoons, one ax, a cider barrel, one umbrella, a silver watch, an iron bake kettle, and an "old log house belonging to an Israel Hawley."[1]

Perhaps these American revolutionaries also bequeathed to their children their stories of valor and their memories of Yorktown or Valley Forge or the battle of White Plains or Princeton. They may have been bitterly frustrated when the state of Connecticut formalized their exclusion from suffrage in 1814. Some may have had to watch their children wait until they were twenty-five years old to become free under the state's gradual abolition law. None ever marched in a parade for the unveiling of a monument in their honor. In old age their daily lives may have been surrounded by old chairs, tables, and porridge pots, not public tributes. But theirs was a legacy, along with thousands of other American soldier-patriots, to which the Yale College community owed its continued development, and to which the United States owed its existence.

One or more of the Black war veterans may have witnessed a singular incident on the New Haven Green on October 20, 1790: an execution that sent a very public message about the lives of Black people in the community. Joseph Mountain, a thirty-two-year-old Black man, was convicted and hanged for rape. A reported crowd of ten thousand people, more than twice the size of the town's population and rivaling some of the largest revivals of the Great Awakening, gathered in New Haven on the day of the spectacle to watch the execution. Mountain's notoriety traveled broadly thanks to a purportedly autobiographical account of the crime, *Sketches of the Life of Joseph Mountain*, published by prominent New Haven printers Thomas and Samuel Green. *Sketches* was printed and sold to the crowds who came to watch Mountain's execution. Historian Brian Baaki has identified nine subsequent editions for a total of ten printings of the sensational story. Mountain's case was decided by Judge Eliphalet Dyer (Yale 1740), and *Sketches* was in all likelihood ghostwritten by David Daggett (Yale 1783), one of the future founders of the Yale Law School. Daggett claimed to have only taken dictation, but he was the magistrate who took the confession and saw that it was published. The popular text widely disseminated ideas of Black criminality, threats to social order, and propensities to sexual violence.[2]

The Mountain hanging on the Green, only steps from Yale College, provided an eighteenth-century precursor to many such incidents, both judicial and brutally illegal, that would follow over the next century and a half in American history. The massive crowd that the hanging of Joseph Mountain attracted may demonstrate how resolved Connecticut citizens were about their long, slow gradual abolition plan enacted just six years earlier—or how *unresolved* the future of Black Americans would be in the new republic. Public executions were not uncommon in this period, but some people were beginning to question the morality and utility of capital punishment and its spectacle. However, in Connecticut, African Americans were convicted and sentenced to death for crimes such as rape and homicide far out of proportion to their share of the population. Mountain's was not the only execution of a Black man to draw a large crowd of spectators in the state; in 1817, fifteen thousand people came to see Amos Adams, who was African American, hanged in Danbury. Like Mountain, Adams was convicted of raping a White woman.[3]

Not long after Mountain's execution, on a day in late 1793, Ezra Stiles recorded in his diary a visit from a Yale graduate who had just returned from a journey to Georgia. "Mr Whitney brot to my house and shewed us his Machine, by him invented for cleaning Cotton of its seeds," Stiles wrote. The president thought the small boxlike structure "a curious & very ingenious piece of Mechanism." Eli Whitney had only recently graduated from Yale in 1792. Stiles could not know at that moment how Whitney's cotton gin would influence the expansion of cotton production and therefore slavery across the South in future decades. Stiles saw slavery as a relic that the "contagion of liberty" would with time sweep away in this new American experiment. As Yale historian Edmund Morgan astutely wrote, in political and religious terms, Stiles had, by the time of his death in April 1795, "grown to a faith surpassing knowledge."[4] This founder of Yale and the United States did not have to suffer seeing slavery's reach greatly expand in his beloved republic.

In 1795, Timothy Dwight succeeded Ezra Stiles as president of Yale College. In that year New Haven had a population of approximately four thousand; its roads were still all dirt and there were no streetlights. The city remained the joint capital of the state along with Hartford. By 1811, the town had grown to over five thousand, with all manner of stores and trades in the bustling port, and a growing Yale College nestled among a multitude of elm trees—part of a beautification project spearheaded by another Yale graduate and leader of the revolutionary generation, James Hillhouse—that gave New Haven an additional name, the "Elm City." Dwight, too, was part of the Revolutionary War generation—he briefly served in the Continental army as a chaplain—but his legacy is part of a broader conservative turn against the egalitarian principles of the revolution. A 1769 graduate of Yale, Dwight was a member of the theological and political elite, Jonathan Edwards's grandson and first cousin of Aaron Burr, who was elected vice president of the United States in 1800. If Stiles had left Yale a place of prorevolutionary and at least some antislavery sentiments, Dwight took the college into the nineteenth century as a bastion of tradition and authority.[5]

Dwight's influence went far beyond Yale. As a major voice of New England's "Standing Order," through his published writings, poems, speeches, and sermons, he urged the nation to follow his vision of Protestant moral and religious precepts. An ardent Federalist and opponent of Thomas Jefferson, Dwight told his friend and treasurer of Yale, James Hillhouse, that Jefferson's election in 1800 would "ruin the Republic."[6] And most definitely, Dwight did not accept the new creed of separation of church and state. He favored the public payment of ministers by the state, and he helped lead the evangelical and religious revivals that swept over Yale in the early decades of the nineteenth century. As a staunch partisan, he was never shy of mixing politics and religion, sometimes banishing those who did not adhere to his brand of "evangelical orthodoxy" and hardened anti-Jeffersonianism. All these positions led his critics to call him the "Federalist Pope."[7]

Dwight was a devoted builder of Yale as America's premier institution of higher learning, but he molded it, the faculty and curriculum, on a rigidly conservative model. He delivered sermons that openly attacked the prophets of the French Revolution, such as Voltaire, whom he deemed threats to all things sacred, and he criticized parts of the American Bill of Rights, especially the religion clause in the First Amendment. Openly Francophobic, he believed in and propagated conspiracy theories about "Jacobins," a label for all manner of radicalism, irreligion, or potential violence. The French Revolution remained a moral threat in his view, especially the Illuminati, a bizarre theory of a secret society, originally based in Bavarian freemasonry, swept up by the French in the 1790s, and allegedly spreading internationally as a shadowy means of undermining the stability of church, state, and social norms. According to one historian of Dwight's rule, Ralph Gabriel, the Yale president "never transcended the Federalist's contemptuous attitude toward the common man." In a letter to his son, Dwight expressed his view of working-class people and the revolution's regrettable influence on them: "You must have a house keeper and I think you will be put to some trouble to get a good one in this age of liberty and equality."[8]

Indeed, Dwight seems to have been driven by the notion that the Age of Revolution had fomented too many excesses in democracy and in human behavior, and one element of that was the socially disruptive potential of an antislavery movement. When it came to slavery and democracy itself, Dwight was openly counterrevolutionary. In 1788, Dwight bought a Black woman named Naomi. Although he claimed that she would be allowed to pay for her freedom, Naomi's fate is still unknown. The minister enslaved three other people. Vital records from Fairfield, Connecticut, tell us that he registered "a negro Maria b. Oct. 14,

1789; York b. May 31, 1794; next youngest born June 1, 1797." The 1784 Gradual Abolition Act in Connecticut required slaveholders to "register" the births of any enslaved children born after that date. Dwight lived in Fairfield County before moving to Yale, and that region had long contained the state's largest enslaved population; it is possible that most registrations were done there. The possibility exists that Naomi, still enslaved by Dwight, was the mother of the three children he registered; the father has not been identified. These are hardly shocking revelations, given that slaveholding was practiced well into the nineteenth century.[9]

During his twenty-two years at the helm of Yale, Dwight emerged as a significant voice of anti-abolition activism in this era of gradual emancipation. Nothing charts Dwight's equivocal path from American revolutionary to reactionary counterrevolutionary quite as clearly as his changing positions on slavery. Before moving to Yale, Dwight had lived in and pastored a church in Greenfield Hill, Connecticut, near Fairfield. In 1794, he published a famous epic poem, *Greenfield Hill*, that reveals some of his conservative attitudes toward slavery. He celebrates the small-town virtues of Connecticut village life, while infantilizing people of African descent and romanticizing their degraded social position. Dwight admitted that slavery deprived Black people of "liberty," and devoted much space to condemning the cruelties of the West Indian plantation world as much worse than the bondage practiced in Connecticut.[10] In contrast, New England slavery, to Dwight, remained benign and part of a culture of religious obligation, and he did not acknowledge Connecticut's deep economic interdependence with Southern and Caribbean slavery. To attack it threatened the social order.

At Yale Dwight sent a couple of generations of an educated elite of clergy, teachers, merchants, and politicians into American society steeped in his theocratic and racial vision. As president, Dwight delivered many sermons that fleshed out his authoritative worldview. He constantly warned that social change could usher in anarchy, that challenges to the social and religious order could ruin the New England ideal as he fancied it from his Congregational Yale pulpit. A historian of proslavery thought, Larry Tise, identifies Dwight as the anchor of an early American, New England style of anti-abolitionism, sympathetic with efforts to secure the future of slavery. Not unlike the conservative, organic proslavery thinkers of the South of this period and later, Dwight believed that nothing should change before its time, and not even likely then. In a 1798 Fourth of July sermon, "The Duty of Americans, at the Present Crisis," the Yale leader tilted at fears and plots of all kinds, usually French inspired, that endangered piety and especially the sanctity of "property." "Without religion," Dwight declared, "we may possibly retain the freedom of savages, bears, and wolves; but not the freedom of New-England."[11]

Dwight was a mercurial millennialist; he believed God entered history with periodic shocks, predicted a timing for the Second Coming, and then changed it more than once in relation to circumstances. As America went to war with Britain in 1812, he seemed quite assured of this apocalyptic warning: "At no time, since the deluge, has the situation of the human race been so extraordinary; the world so shaken; or its changes so numerous, sudden, extensive, and ominous." Like a bird of prey, Satan had the country, and especially New England, in his talons. Doom awaited an unworthy people steeped in sin and a polity poisoned by radical ideas. Although Yale College grew into the beginnings of a major university under Dwight, and the minister-president warmly supported the establishment of science in the curriculum, his deep conservativism prompted one modern Yale historian, Brooks Mather Kelley, to characterize his teachings as "at heart anti-intellectual." And Vernon Louis Parrington, an early twentieth-century scholar, quipped that Dwight's mind "was closed as tight as his study windows in January."[12]

Dwight, like Jefferson and many others of that generation, loved numbers as a way of discerning the social order. In 1811, he produced a *Statistical Account of the City of New-Haven*, a compendium from which we learn more of his racial views. He counted the number of free Black people as only 150 but had much to say about their habits, capacities, and appearance. "Their vices are of all kinds," he wrote. They lacked "habits of industry and economy," and they "acquire" and "expend" only to "gratify gross and vulgar appetite." As freed people, many became "thieves, liars, profane, drunkards, sabbath-breakers, quarrelsome, idle, and prodigal." Their "ruling passion," observed Dwight, was to be "fashionable." They did not merely "dance" but engaged in "frolic." White people of the same class as these lower sorts were at least "decent," said the minister, whereas free Black people only seemed satisfied to "ape those who are above them." Here and there some attained "property," and some of the women, he had observed, were better "behaved."[13] These observations represented the iron curtain of racist ideas through which an antislavery movement would strive for African American dignity, much less freedom and equality, in the coming decades. They may also be evidence, in spite of Dwight's intentions, of a vibrant, creative cultural life among free Black people in the Elm City.

In significant ways, Dwight was an embodiment of a lost cause, but in other ways he presaged proslavery, anti-Black currents that would become even more powerful in the years ahead. The Federalist Party was in decline and indeed effectively died by 1816. Dwight still thought religion could save New England, and in the Second Great Awakening's revivals he took new hope. Back in 1802, as a revival swept through Yale's campus, stoked by the president, allegedly one-third of the students converted to Christ and orthodox Congregationalism. But slavery now expanded with the country in leaps and bounds, in part due to the invention of a world-changing mechanical instrument by another Yale graduate, Eli Whitney. Dwight approved of the boom it fomented, and he defended Southern slaveholding planters. "The Southern Planter," argued Dwight in 1815, "who receives slaves from his parents by inheritance, certainly deserves no censure for holding them." And especially if the planter treated his slaves "with humanity, and faithfully endeavours to Christianize them, he fulfills his duty, so long as his present situation continues."[14] Here was no gradualist lament from southern New England about slavery's future in America, but a full embrace of its perpetuity at the very moment of the system's rise as the prime mover of the national economy.

In 1792, a twenty-seven-year-old Eli Whitney arrived at the Mulberry Grove plantation, some ten miles north of the city of Savannah, Georgia. Like Dwight years later, the young mechanical wizard seemed untroubled by the large number of enslaved Black men, women, and children on the rice operation. The Yale graduate had first gone to South Carolina in search of a tutor's position on a plantation but failed to land the job. Through connections, Catherine Greene, widow of the Revolutionary War hero Nathaniel Greene and mistress at Mulberry Grove, invited Whitney to take up residence at the bend in the Savannah River. There he would tutor and begin to study for the law. After overhearing conversations among local planters lamenting that they could not grow short-staple cotton to any profit because of enormous difficulty in extracting the green seeds, Whitney did what he had always done—he found some tools and wire and experimented. He had grown up on a farm in Massachusetts and from an early age loved making, fixing, and imagining new things. His family scratched together money and sent the promising lad to Yale College in 1789 at the age of twenty-three, older than most students.[15]

At the Mulberry Grove plantation, Whitney constructed a small box with two cylinders rotating in opposite directions and wire teeth in the middle. It worked; after demonstrating it to the locals and showing that the seeds in the cotton could be removed mechanically, all around him he saw the potential for "ginning" (an engine) the crop at ever-increasing scale. Whitney returned to New

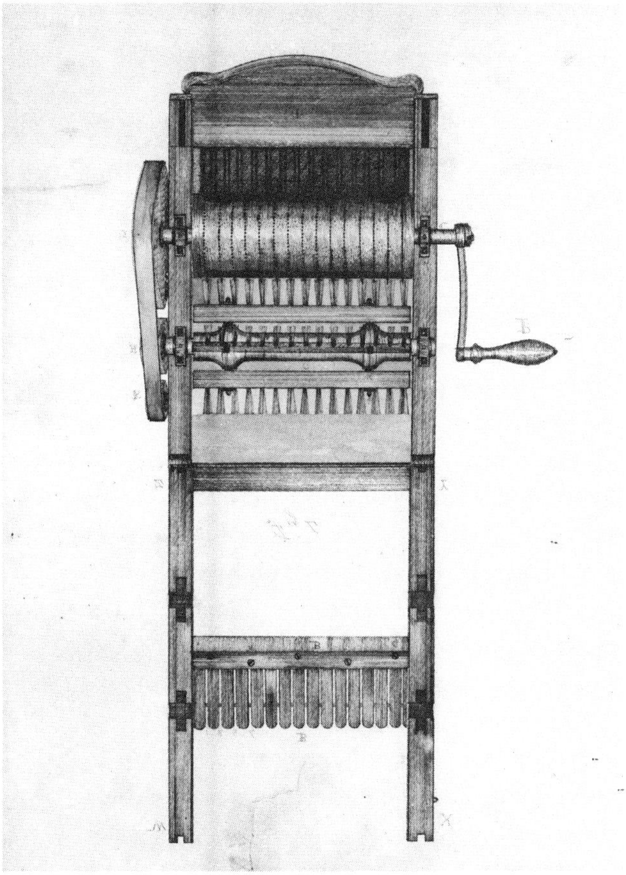

Undated drawing of a mechanical cotton gin.
Eli Whitney Papers (MS 554). Manuscripts and Archives,
Yale University Library.

Haven. With excitement and vigor, he began to make the cotton gins in his own shop and quickly tried to achieve a patent. But he was too late; his idea and model were duplicated that same year in Georgia and soon other Southern states. He eventually obtained a patent in 1794, but the machine was out of the bag. Through some sixty or more lawsuits over several years, Whitney strove to control his invention as it revolutionized cotton production, the explosion of the textile manufacturing business in the North, and indeed slavery's expansion in the South.[16] Although many other factors in the world economy and in technological change fueled the growth of slavery, the cotton boom would not have happened without the gin, which within two to three decades grew from small hand-cranked devices into huge shed- and even house-like structures driven by droves of enslaved people and, eventually, by steam power.

Contrary to legend, Whitney was hardly the first to invent cotton-ginning technology; he is merely the most famous. From as early as the fourteenth century, ginning processes had been used in Europe and India for various products; in time these devices were foot driven. In America the cotton trade to the Caribbean and to Britain long predated the boom of the early nineteenth century. In 1788, a Bahamas-born Philadelphian, Joseph Eve, invented a self-feeding roller gin that eliminated the need for a ginner risking injury. He did not achieve a patent until 1803 for a drawing of his loom-like machine with fly wheel and pulleys that drove the device. By his own self-promotion and that of others, Whitney's role in this story grew as a formative myth in the development of American slavery and technology. As his cotton gin proved commercially unsuccessful in competition with many producers, Whitney turned to the manufacture of firearms in 1798, through a process of "interchangeable parts" in his growing factory complex on the north edge of New Haven along the Mill River. Whitney did achieve great success with guns over time. His fame, though, is forever tied, not without reason, to the massive expansion of cotton production in the United States. In 1790, the United States produced 1.5 million pounds of cotton but exported far less. In 1800, after Whitney's invention, the United States produced 36.5 million pounds, and then, in 1820, 167.5 million pounds.[17]

Cotton production boomed in the American South exponentially in the coming decades, especially in the wake of the War of 1812 and the nation's military-backed conquest of Native Americans' land. The number of African Americans enslaved grew in proportion with the cotton revolution. In 1790, there were approximately 700,000 people enslaved in the new United States; by 1800, 908,000; in 1810, 1.19 million; in 1820, 1.55 million; in 1830, 2.02 million; in 1840, 2.53 million; in 1850, 3.2 million people were enslaved. On the eve of the Civil War in 1860, when the South produced its largest cotton crop ever and dominated the nation's exports, almost 4 million people lived and labored in bondage. Each of these increases was, roughly, a demographically astonishing 25 to 30 percent per decade.[18] Such growth, with the significance slavery assumed in the American political economy, produced the most divisive issues in U.S. history and led, by the late 1850s, to a tragic house divided in the country between a proslavery and an antislavery future.

Dwight's Yale-educated contemporaries could hardly have anticipated how the college president's rigid conservatism would, with time, contribute to this growing slavery crisis in America. One important action by Dwight that changed Yale and its approaches to race and slavery was the appointment of a science professor, Benjamin Silliman. Silliman entered Yale as an undergraduate in 1792, graduated in 1796, was named a tutor in 1799, and remained on the faculty (with brief interruptions) until 1855. In that time, Silliman became Yale's first professor of chemistry and natural history (1802) and helped found the Yale School of Medicine (1810) as well as the Sheffield Scientific School (1847). Silliman was also a key figure in professionalizing and popularizing antebellum American science. In 1818, Silliman founded the *American Journal of Science and Arts*, one of the nation's first and most prestigious scientific publications.[19] Silliman gave frequent, high-profile lectures on chemistry and natural history across the country and worked as a consultant for the federal government in the antebellum era, especially in Louisiana, involved in the science of improving the production of slave-grown sugarcane.

Born in 1779 in Trumbull, Connecticut, in Fairfield County, Silliman was part of one of the largest slaveholding families in the state. The Sillimans owned enslaved house workers and farm laborers, at least twelve in total. Indeed, Benjamin's widowed mother, Mary, sold two people to pay tuition for her two sons to attend Yale College. For his commencement, Silliman composed a poem, "The Negroe," a depiction of slavery as unrelenting evil: "the uncur'd gangrene of the unreasoning mind." Yet after graduation, he took charge of the family farm, Holland Hill, and its enslaved laborers. Silliman's years as a slaveholder coincided with the implementation of Connecticut's gradual emancipation plan. In addition to the 1784 law, the state legislature passed, in 1792, a law forbidding Connecticut slaveholders from selling their slaves outside the state. The Silliman family worked within—and sometimes against—these laws in order to preserve control over their enslaved people. When Silliman's brother moved to Rhode Island, he tried to take an enslaved woman named Cloe with him. Cloe resisted, claiming (correctly) that by law she could not be removed from Connecticut. In the early 1800s, the Silliman family leased out several so-called statutory slaves (enslaved people born after the passage of gradual emancipation in 1784) as a way of generating cash. By law, these leases should have lasted only until the enslaved people they covered turned the requisite ages (twenty-five years of age for men and twenty-one for women) and gained legal freedom. In one case, however, the Silliman family leased out a nineteen-year-old enslaved man named Ely for a term of seven years—that is, until he was twenty-six. Silliman initially hesitated about keeping Ely beyond the legal age limit but later wrote his brother that he "was convinced that it would be quite as well for him."[20]

Later in life, Silliman reflected on these experiences. His statements are often contradictory. At times he seems to have been eager to excuse his family's slave owning. "Our northern country was not then fully enlightened as now regarding human freedom," he said in an unpublished memoir; "there were house-slaves in the most respectable families, even in those of clergymen in the now free States; and those who fought for their country, of whom our father was one, did not appear to have felt their own inconsistency." Nonetheless, he portrayed New England slavery as mild and benevolent. "The in-door servants were often favorites with the family, and especially with the children," he contended. "In the North, slaves rarely became fugitives, and were never hunted by the gun and the blood-hound, and were never loaded with the ball and chain, or with the iron collar." Similarly, Silliman seems to have drawn a distinction, common at the time, between the *slave trade* (an unmitigated evil) and *slavery* (a contingent evil, depending on particular circumstances). In 1805, during a trip to Great Britain, Silliman observed a slave ship in Liverpool. Afterward, he penned the following reflection: "Liverpool is *deep*, very *deep* in the guilt of this abominable traffic. It is now pursued with more zeal than ever & multitudes in this town are at this moment rioting on the wealth which has been gained by the tears, groans & the stripes of Africans."[21] Rhetorically at least, Silliman seemed to support the British crusade to end the slave trade.

However, the defense of his family's slaveholding is somewhat belied by a letter Silliman wrote in 1863, in which he recalled, "Although my father . . . was an owner of slaves, and although I was brought up among them, I do not remember the time when slavery was not detestable even to my juvenile mind." Finally, in another part of the memoir, Silliman offered a veritable mea culpa, blending the sense of personal shame he felt as a former slaveholder with the sense of national shame he felt as an American. "A sense of integrity alone induces me to record these painful facts regarding the participation of our family in the sin and shame of slavery," he wrote in the midst of the Civil War. "I trust that we have been for many years cleared of these injuries to our fellow-men, and our nation is now settling an awful account with heaven for the accumulated guilt of more than two centuries, for which we are paying the heavy penalty of our blood."[22] By the time Silliman wrote these words, he had lived through every postrevolutionary stage of both American slavery and abolition; he had also become adept at the art of selective family and collective memory. Silliman was trapped in a memory he could neither silence nor control.

The reminiscences left out a crucial part of Silliman's story—how his assiduous work as a famed scientist at Yale entangled him with international scholars and with Southern slaveholders and slavery. In 1805, Silliman spent extended time in Europe, especially at the University of Edinburgh. There he encountered and eventually purchased a "cabinet" with two thousand minerals from Benjamin Perkins, Yale class of 1794. The Yale treasury repeatedly opened its resources to Silliman, who paid $1,000 for the "Perkins Cabinet." More importantly, Silliman struck up a courtship with George Gibbs, a wealthy slaveholder in Newport, Rhode Island, who had amassed an even larger mineral and geological collection. The "Gibbs Cabinet" contained roughly twelve thousand mineral objects, obtained by a family steeped in the slave trade and in commerce with the West Indies, Brazil, and many parts of the American South. The Gibbs family had been investors in many slave ships and their produce. Silliman found the Gibbs collection astounding and, in 1825, persuaded Dwight and Yale to purchase it for $20,000, approximately two-thirds of the college's annual revenue. Gibbs drove a hard bargain and insisted that Yale build a permanent home for the cabinet, thus planting the earliest seeds of what would become the Peabody Museum of Natural History. Many Southern graduates of Yale made significant gifts in order to enable this purchase and to establish the university as the leading institution of science education in the country. Yale alumni of South Carolina gave $800 for the project, with the young John Caldwell Calhoun of South Carolina, class of 1804, contributing $100. Citizens of New Haven donated $10,000; another group of New Yorkers gave $3,500; a Thomas Day of Hartford put in $2,000; and the Reverend John Elliot of East Guilford—a Yale trustee and, at one point, a slaveholder—sold some land for $360, which he gifted to Yale.[23]

Silliman's work with Southern planters and Yale's ties to the region's slave economies had only begun. Calhoun, who had entered Yale as a junior in 1802, spending two years as an undergraduate, became a prominent politician in South Carolina and the ur-father of both proslavery ideology and states' rights doctrines in the coming decades. Early in his career, however, he was more of a nationalist than a sectionalist. As secretary of war under President James Monroe, Calhoun took a serious interest in building the nation's scientific institutions. Silliman and Calhoun became good friends and correspondents. In 1822, the secretary of war asked the professor to visit the West Point Military Academy and examine the science and engineering curriculum. Silliman produced a careful report, and Calhoun financially supported the new science journal as well as the Gibbs cabinet initiative.[24]

As Calhoun forged his state's nullification policy against a federal tariff in the late 1820s, a scheme as much in defense of slavery and cotton production as it was a theory of federalism, Silliman struck up a relationship with the Carolinian's nemesis, Andrew Jackson. The friendship began back in 1821 when Jackson sought Silliman's help in bailing his foster child and Yale student, Anthony Butler, out of trouble on campus. The hero of the Battle of New Orleans swallowed honor and asked the chemistry professor to "erase the sentence" of expulsion for bad behavior from Butler's record. Ten years later, as president, Jackson's treasury department extended Silliman a major federal grant of money to study the sugar industry in Louisiana. Sugar was booming in the state; from 1827 to 1831, plantations producing cane increased from 308 to 691. The government wanted to stimulate "modern improvements" and new technologies to vastly increase the American share of the world's sugar market. Silliman enlisted his colleague at

Portrait of Benjamin Silliman Sr., by Samuel F. B. Morse. On display in Silliman College, Yale University. Medical Historical Library, Cushing/Whitney Medical Library.

Yale, natural history professor Charles Upham Shepard, as well as a member of the chemistry faculty, to join him in the two-year investigation. Together, Silliman and Shepard traveled extensively in 1832–33 to plantations across the South, and in particular in Louisiana. Yale president Jeremiah Day promised Silliman all the money he needed, and the federal government paid the professor a generous personal fee of $1,200.[25]

Silliman embraced the science of the sugar study and met many Southern planters who became collaborators and supporters of his work. But he also expressed moral reservations about his experience at the heart of plantation slavery. In addition to all manner of scientific observations that Silliman asked Shepard to record, he also queried, "The slaves on the sugar estates—do they appear hard worked, dispirited, and oppressed?" Then in one of the most telling comments of all by a Yale leader in this period of the early American republic, Silliman gave an instruction to his research partner: "(Open your eyes and ears to every fact connected with the actual condition of slavery everywhere—but do not talk about it—hear and see everything but say little)." This parenthetical statement provides a perfect illustration of an antislavery moderate's tepid, sometimes pathetic, approach to slavery. The point was to not offend any slaveholders, to use them for valuable information, and not to tarnish the relationship with potential donors and with the system of human exploitation they were funded to study. Although Silliman never employed the word "slavery" in his 126-page government report, *Manual on the Cultivation of Sugar Cane*, published in 1833, he made concerted arguments that use of modern technologies and techniques such as steam, vacuum, and juice-evaporation processes could reduce the need for "considerable labor."[26] Steam power, the report implied, might erode if not defeat slavery; the opposite, of course, became the ultimate reality throughout the cotton and sugar kingdoms.

Silliman is honored today for his contributions to establishing and promoting scientific education both at Yale and in the United States more broadly. More recently, historians have explored Silliman's status as a slaveholder and his views on the institution of slavery. Few if any, however, have noticed his close relationship with his longtime assistant, a free Black man named Robert M. Park. In the census and city directories, Park was described as a "custodian" and "sexton." Yet Silliman's own accounts suggest Park's duties extended far beyond cleaning or janitorial tasks; he participated in and contributed to the professor's scientific work. In fact, the elder Silliman came to rely on and credit Park with some of his own success.[27]

In 1835, the celebrated professor was invited to give a series of lectures to the Society for the Diffusion of Useful Knowledge at the Masonic Temple on Tremont Street in Boston. Already well known as a scientist, textbook author, and founder of a leading scientific journal, Silliman was keen to further bolster his reputation and attract funding. The opportunity in Boston was well paying and promised to connect him with even larger audiences.[28] Park accompanied Silliman to Boston, staying for over a month while Silliman delivered his lectures. In his journal Silliman noted several occasions when they worked together to get ready for the demonstrations: "The morning of March 3d was passed with Robert in the Temple in arranging the specimens into groups, and in preparing for the first lecture." On another day, he "made gases with Robert for the afternoon lecture." Park's role was not only behind the scenes but out front during the lectures. On March 9, Silliman wrote, "I am well, and all goes well—charmingly indeed,—cordiality and interest and numbers far beyond my expectations. Robert is well and does exceedingly well; he is much admired in his station, and is regarded by the audience as a sub-professor!" Perhaps the audience was able to see what Silliman could not.[29]

The great scientist may have thought it was amusing to consider his "faithful Robert" a "sub-professor." But he acknowledged Park's contributions. On their return home to New Haven several weeks later, Silliman decided to sit with his assistant in the second-class car since, he wrote, "objections might be made to the admission of a colored man into the passenger cars of the first class." Silliman continued, explaining that he accompanied him in part because he had been "unwilling to disturb the feelings of one who had served me so well, and contributed materially to my success."[30] Park may have been contributing to Silliman's success for years. Historian of science Margaret W. Rossiter notes that even before the Boston lectures, Silliman had been giving talks at lyceums in New Haven and Hartford. He "was reputed to be a good lecturer whose many demonstrations always 'worked.'" We may wonder if Park's assistance was key to those successful demonstrations as well, and if perhaps that is why Silliman made sure to take him on his extended trip to Boston. Certainly Silliman himself profited "materially" from the Boston lectures. In addition to his fee, reported to be $2,000, he received an invitation to return the following year and give a series of lectures on chemistry. After all expenses were paid, Silliman earned an additional $2,200 from the following year's lectures. Afterward, he gave a substantial gift of $1,000 to his daughter; it is unknown what, if any, additional pay he gave Park. And the fact that Park also worked for the younger Benjamin Silliman Jr., who was appointed to the Yale faculty in 1853, speaks volumes about the family's enduring reliance on Park and his abilities.[31]

In 1884, at the unveiling of Silliman's statue on the Yale campus, Andrew Dickson White—a former Silliman student and by then president of Cornell University—told the story of his old professor choosing to sit in the second-class car. To White, an erstwhile abolitionist, the anecdote illustrated Silliman's humanity and humility. But he also told another story that perhaps better illuminates the place of Robert M. Park—and no doubt others like him—in Yale's history: "Professor Silliman says to a student. 'How would I test sulphuric [*sic*] acid?' The student answers: 'You would taste it.' Silliman, indignantly, 'Taste it, sir; it would burn my tongue out. Tell me, how would I test sulphuric acid?' Student: 'You would make Robert taste it.'" White called Park the "faithful servant whom all old Yalensians must remember with honor." Indeed, the joke "works" because those hearing it would have known Park and would have recognized him as a "faithful" associate who stood by Silliman's side and did what he was asked to do—whether to further the cause of science or because his job depended on it. Silliman had been dead twenty years when White recounted those stories, but Park was there, on hand to do a job both dignified and menial: drawing aside the veil covering the statue of his late employer. Although Park was never officially recognized as a "sub-professor" or anything like it, he earned a reputation for his learning and knowledge. When his daughter Eliza Park Bassett died shortly before he did in 1895, her lengthy obituary in the *New Haven Evening Register* included details about her respected father as well: "Mr. Park was for more than 30 years in the service of the elder Prof. Silliman, who was wont to speak of him to the college folk as 'my friend and assistant.' It was currently said on the college campus that he knew all the learned professor's lectures by heart." And Park lived a life that went well beyond his job. In the 1820s, he was one of the four men who, with twenty-one women, founded the Temple Street congregation in New Haven, a center of Black community and antislavery organizing; he later served as clerk at the church. In 1849, he was a delegate to the Connecticut State Convention of Colored Men, held at the Temple Street Church, "to consider our Political condition, and to devise measures for our elevation and advancement." Black suffrage and increased educational opportunities "for our children" were on the agenda. Park's commitment to antislavery and social and political movements for Black rights paid some dividends: he lived to see one of his grandchildren graduate from Yale only months before he died.[32]

When Calhoun was a student at Yale, Silliman served as his tutor. Despite growing differences over slavery, they remained friends for a long time. In the era of the early republic, as Yale became more of a national institution, it welcomed increasing numbers of students from the South. In the period from 1805 to 1815, for example, an average of 25 percent of all graduates were from outside New England. Ten percent in that same period were planters' sons from the slave states: forty young men came from South Carolina, ten from Georgia, nine from North Carolina, and six from Virginia. When Silliman paid his first visit to Charleston, South Carolina, in 1815, he met numerous Yale alumni from famous Lowcountry families such as the Grimkes, Legares, and Gadsdens. And these close connections to the South evidently colored his response to the coming of the Civil War, even when many of his Northern peers and fellow Yale faculty members strongly condemned the "Slave Power." Many years after the war, his former student Andrew Dickson White remarked, "There are those here to-day who, young and ardent when the irrepressible conflict between freedom and slavery drew on, lamented that [Silliman] still struggled for peace. . . . On the other hand there are doubtless those present who lamented even more bitterly, that when the day of compromise and peace was clearly past, he entered so earnestly into the great contest." Silliman's ambivalence had to be explained, and his affection for the White South, rather than his sympathy with slavery, was the preferable explanation. "To him the South was as dear as the North," White said. "He had, indeed, from his childhood abhorred slavery, but he recognized the fact that the sin of its origin and development was shared by the entire nation North and South. The currents of sympathy always vibrated between his heart and the hearts of thousands of old pupils on southern plantations."[33]

Calhoun's relationship with Dwight was more troubled. The young Calhoun connected well with President Dwight's conservatism, if not his Calvinism, but they followed different political paths, at least in party loyalty. Calhoun was a solid Jeffersonian Republican as a student who found himself in a sea of Federalists at Yale. Indeed, his most recent biographer, Robert Elder, suggests that Calhoun likely first encountered serious ideas about states' rights or even secessionist constitutional thinking at Yale, where Dwight helped a coalition of Connecticut and New York Federalists at least contemplate a "Northern Confederacy" that would combine to thwart Jeffersonian expansion (symbolized by the Louisiana Purchase of 1803) and Southern dominance in the federal government. After Yale, Calhoun's law teacher, Tapping Reeve, with whom he studied for one year in 1805 in Litchfield, Connecticut, was closely involved in what some called the Northern "conspiracy." Any secession at this juncture did not come to fruition, but it served as a trial run for the Hartford Convention, which had similar aims, in 1814. The serious, studious, and ambitious Calhoun soaked in these ideas about union, liberty, and separation. As a later political philosopher, the Carolinian famously argued for a contractual form of government in which each state reserved its veto over federal legislation (known as nullification) in what he conceived as a "concurrent majority"—every state had agreed to form the central authority and could therefore choose to reject its laws.[34] That this philosophy, which had much influence by the two decades leading to the Civil War, might have taken early form while he devoured the reading lists and sat in the lectures of Timothy Dwight at Yale is not an irony we often include in remembrances of John C. Calhoun.

Yale College produced no more influential political actor or thinker in the half century after the revolution than Calhoun. He studied law for one year, and after practicing as a lawyer back in the town of his roots, Abbeville, in the South Carolina upcountry, as the cotton boom and slavery surged, he entered politics to stay by 1810. The brilliant and ambitious politician would become congressman, senator, secretary of war, secretary of state, presidential candidate, and vice president. In his path he would leave a trail of awe, loathing, failure, and collective tragedy. He was revered and feared for his genius, but also obsessed with duty and zeal in protection of the "liberty" and the "minority rights" of slaveholders. He strove most of his career for the failed dream of a unified South. He believed liberty had to be earned and checked by power, and that democratic virtues were no match for the darkness of human nature. The former Yale historian David Potter once called Calhoun "the most majestic champion of error since Milton's Satan."[35]

Above all, through his arguments first honed in the nullification crisis of 1828–33, Calhoun became the principal voice of the compact theory of government, an increasingly rigid states' rights doctrine first rooted in his Jeffersonianism and with time transforming into secessionism. Similar to the counterrevolutionary Dwight, Calhoun advanced a theory of the natural *inequality* of humankind, based in the widespread claim that humans are divided by nature into laborers and property holders. Finally, and most lastingly, he defended slavery as an eternal "positive good," rooted in part in the historical claim that African peoples had never created a civilized polity and never could do so in the Americas. In his time, these ideas were anything but fringe constitutionalism or lonely historical theories; tragically, they served as the intellectual fuel of what many Northerners came to call the "Slave Power," a radical proslavery persuasion satisfied only by vigorous expansion and then by withdrawal from the federal union. With singular force of mind and logic, Calhoun advanced this cluster of constitutional and moral positions to such a powerful extent that some abolitionists by the 1840s and 1850s referred to the South itself as "Calhoundom." As his biographer Elder writes, "We do not have to honor John C. Calhoun, nor should we. But he has not left us the luxury of forgetting him." Nor has our history forgotten him, before and during the twenty-first century.[36]

Most Yale leaders and teachers settled on a much more modest approach to slavery in the early nineteenth century than Calhoun. Colonization, the movement to remove free Black Americans and some slaves from the United States, driven always by a complex mixture of motives, both humane and racist, took firm hold in the country in the wake of the War of 1812. Even as early as the 1780s, some residents of New England towns and states had sought the removal of Black people and other "strangers" deemed deviant, disorderly, or without property. "Warning out" had a long history in eighteenth-century Puritan New England. More and more in this era of gradual abolition and the rise of free Black communities, organized efforts for their removal—almost always suggested as voluntary—took hold. The American Colonization Society (ACS), born in Washington, DC, in 1816, with prominent clergy, members of Congress, and border state slaveholders as leaders, grew rapidly with state affiliations, fundraising, and an emerging array of rationales. Some rhetoric of the ACS, especially as it spread its influence in New England, stressed Christian mission to improve the lives of uneducated and poor Black people by removing them from fierce competition with White neighbors. The argument easily followed that they were destined to inferior political and economic status due to insoluble White prejudice. The ACS also created the grand scheme of founding the new colony of Liberia on the west coast of Africa and sending willing Black people there to establish an American-style republic and thus redeem the supposedly heathen, underdeveloped continent. Some colonizationists across New England and in the border regions also saw removal on even a small scale as a first step in an eventual gradual abolition of slavery in the upper South states.[37]

The colonization movement became very popular, indeed beguiling, to Americans of all political persuasions in the early republic. No less than James Madison and, succeeding him, Henry Clay served as presidents of the ACS. Andrew Jackson and James Monroe also supported colonization. They held meetings in the U.S. Capitol to plot what they convinced themselves was the humane removal of Black Americans from their native land. Racism and benevolence often marched in the same paragraphs in colonization publications and sermons. And colonization came to define much of what "race" meant in the second and third decades of the nineteenth century, even in early reform circles in New England. As historian Joanne Melish writes of the movement's leaders, they became "fixed" on a "'racialized' perception of free people of color as permanently estranged and inherently unequal noncitizens."[38] Abolitionists, Black and White, would fight these core ideas, which only persisted with remarkable consistency down through the Civil War.

Fever dreams of Native American removal always lay beneath or in tandem with ideas about African American removal in the minds of White Americans. By the 1830s, though, many radical abolitionists condemned Indian Removal policies of the Jackson administration, a fight they would soundly lose. Jedidiah Morse (Yale 1783), the Connecticut-born geographer and gradual abolitionist of a kind, who took his divinity MA at Yale in 1786, became intensely involved after 1815 in colonizing, assimilating, and Christianizing Native Americans of the Great Lakes region. In 1820, Morse embarked from his home in New Haven on a two-year, 1,500-mile journey to observe and study Native Americans all over the Old Northwest. John C. Calhoun, then secretary of war, commissioned Morse to conduct the study to determine policies toward Native Americans in this new expansionist era. Ohio, Indiana, and Illinois had already reached statehood in the region. Morse had a keen interest in the welfare of Native peoples, but he advocated strongest for the Christianizing and "civilizing" of the survivors of the Iroquois federation and many other groups. As a classic "civilizationist," Morse believed, as did most Americans, in a spectrum of developmental "progress" for human cultures, races, and ethnicities from primitive up a scale to advanced and civilized. He fully believed in the improvability of Indigenous people, claiming that they had the same origins and nature as White people and were "of one blood, with ourselves." But they had suffered and been "degraded" by living so close for generations to "enterprizing whites," an argument considered sweet reason in 1820s reform circles. Morse especially wanted to protect Native peoples from greedy, land-hungry frontiersmen; and the solution, just as for colonizationists advocating expatriation for Black Americans, was their removal farther into the hinterland, giving them time and space to evolve as assimilated Christian Americans. Morse recommended to Calhoun that the federal government relocate Native communities and then place a White agent with them as a missionary of civilization. And when he returned to Washington to write his thorough report, he solicited Calhoun's support in launching an advocacy project for Indian Removal called the American Society for Promoting the Civilization and General Improvement of the Indian Tribes of the United States.[39] Morse saw his organization as benevolent and providential, but he died in New Haven in 1826, not living to see the violent and racist character that removal would attain over the following decade.

Some staunch colonizationists were well aware of their "absurd inconsistencies," as one said in 1827, espousing natural rights and republicanism while putting free Black people on a "footing with ourselves" with "equal rights," a result "utterly out of the question." Others were more direct about their racist motives. The ACS existed, wrote a Vermont leader, "to relieve our nation from an onerous burden, the free coloured population." Many followed the Presbyterian minister, Yale graduate, and leader of the ACS by the mid-1820s, Ralph Gurley (Yale 1818), in a holy crusade to enact colonization as a dictate of "Providence," the working out of both racial and national destinies for Americans and Africans. Gurley made colonization into a kind of religious nationalism; the movement raised money and saved souls, while the United States might one day be "liberated from her black population." One of Connecticut's strongest disciples of Gurley, and one of Yale's most prominent colonizationists, was Leonard Bacon, a Congregational minister and an 1820 graduate of Yale. Born in Detroit, then part of the Northwest Territory, Bacon moved to Connecticut, his father's home state, as a child. With zeal, Bacon threw himself into organizational and fundraising efforts on behalf of the colonization movement. In the 1820s, he attended national meetings of the ACS in Washington, DC, where he argued for

Reverend Leonard Bacon. Images of Yale Individuals (RU 684). Manuscripts and Archives, Yale University Library.

the creation of a system of traveling agents and auxiliaries to raise money. Bacon was offered a full-time position with the ACS but declined it in order to assume the pulpit of the First Church of New Haven, also known as Center Church, a post he held for forty-one years. In 1827, Bacon joined Benjamin Silliman in founding the Connecticut branch of the ACS.[40]

Silliman was drawn to colonizationism for many of the same reasons as the younger Bacon. Like Silliman, Bacon believed that Black people were "degraded" (a term Bacon repeatedly used) and questioned whether they could build viable communities. A return to Africa thus offered African Americans, they believed, as Yale historian David Brion Davis puts it, "a genuine emancipation . . . a rebirth into a world in which the yearning for freedom was not nullified by white mockery and prejudice." Silliman and Bacon feared that immediate emancipation would spark a race war in the South, and they worried that radical antislavery agitation threatened national unity. Colonization, according to Bacon's modern biographer, gave him ways to find "a middle ground between the radicals and the conservatives." Silliman too identified agitation over slavery as a profound threat to the nation. "Between these two extremes," Silliman explained in public addresses, "it appears indispensable to find a golden mean, which shall at once preserve the public peace and in the end bestow freedom and improvement upon the African race." This "golden mean" was removal of Black people from the country. Additionally, Silliman deeply worried about—indeed, fixated on—what he saw as the inexorable growth of the Black population in the United States, which he deemed "an incessant source of anxiety." As the devoted statistician explained to a fellow colonizationist in 1832, "There are two million now, and there will be three millions by the next census, and five by the time the children are men and women." Unless it was arrested, this "appalling tide of population" could only mean racial violence and civil conflict.[41]

By the 1820s the colonization movement adopted the common practice of holding meetings and fundraisers on July 4. Clergymen used their churches as money mills and gave colonization sermons on the Sunday closest to the holiday. In a sermon on July 4, 1825, in New Haven, entitled "A Plea for Africa," Bacon delivered perhaps his most fulsome embrace of colonization. He described free Black people as hopelessly alien from society. "In short," Bacon declared, "are they not, in the estimation of the community and in their own consciousness, aliens and outcasts in the midst of the people?" With such exclusionary and racist language, removal could seem logical, especially when the destination was an allegedly African "native" land. Bacon employed not quite the ugliest rhetoric among colonizationist orators, but he was close. Africans, in his estimation, including those in America, "combine all that is degrading in human imbecility, and all that is horrible in human depravity, unrefined by civilization and unrestrained by the influence of Christian truth. . . . Whereever they are found they are partakers in the misery of one common degradation." Such ignorance of Africa and its history, not to mention the penchant to speak for Black people's own "consciousness," makes Bacon a pariah in retrospect, but in the heyday of colonization, he represented its solid mainstream. By 1834 he still built the movement for removal with the oldest stones he knew. He "had read of a colonization society," he announced, "that undertook three thousand years ago, to colonize in the land of their fathers, three millions of slaves. The President of that Society was one Moses," and the anti-colonizationist president was "one Pharaoh."[42] White supremacy took many cunning forms in these years on either side of the growing debates over the future of both slavery and abolition, and some of the best minds educated at Yale took center stage. Colonization became a long-standing, multipronged way of harnessing racism to the social end of ridding the United States of Black people, wrapped in the American flag and comfortable notions of Christian mission.

While Bacon and Silliman were busy leading colonization efforts in New Haven, the city's Black residents had other ideas. On August 7, 1831, a group calling themselves the Peace and Benevolent Society of Afric-Americans met in New Haven and unanimously passed a set of resolutions condemning colonization. Their resolutions represented both condemnations and collective resistance:

> Resolved, That we consider those christians and philanthropists, who are boasting of their liberty and equality, saying, that all men are born free and equal, and yet are endeavoring to remove us from our native land, to be inhuman in their proceedings, defective in their principles, and unworthy of our confidence.
>
> Resolved, That we consider those colonizationists and ministers of the gospel who are advocating our transportation to an unknown clime, because our skin is a little darker than theirs, (notwithstanding God has made of one blood all nations of men, and has no respect of persons,) as violators of the commandments of God and the laws of the bible. . . .
>
> Resolved, That we will resist all attempts made for our removal to the torrid shores of Africa, and will sooner suffer every drop of blood

to be taken from our veins than submit to such unrighteous treatment.

Resolved, That we know of no other place that we can call our true and appropriate home, excepting these United States, into which our fathers were brought, who enriched the country by their toils, and fought, bled and died in its defence, and left us in its possession—and here we will live and die.[43]

Free African Americans in the shadows of Yale College knew religious and secular hypocrisy when they saw it, and their responses were nothing short of a counter-revolution against this existential plan for their elimination couched in benevolence. They sent out these resolutions as shots across the bow of the good minister of the Center Church and the famous scientist on the Yale campus. Bacon was certainly aware of African Americans' overwhelming opposition to colonization. However, it is not clear that he cared. As David Brion Davis notes, Bacon's writing on the subject "wastes no words on this vital question of black consent."[44]

New Haven's Black society also reserved scorn for their own community members who might flirt with the romance of colonization. "We are Americans," they declared, "and any of us who goes to colonization is either weak in mind or a traitor." Since the 1790s, and especially after the founding of the ACS, some Black leaders did take interest in voluntary removal, especially as it might combine with serious efforts for racial equality for the majority who would stay in the United States. No less than Richard Allen, the founder of the African Methodist Episcopal Church; James Forten, the successful sailmaker and businessman in Philadelphia; and Samuel Cornish and John Russwurm, the cofounders of *Freedom's Journal* in 1827, the first significant Black newspaper, were courted largely without success by colonizationists. Paul Cuffe, the New England mariner, whaler, and ship captain (son of an enslaved African-born father and an Indigenous Wampanoag mother), most fully embraced immigration to Africa before he died in 1817. Cuffe made two voyages and transported some African Americans to Sierra Leone, but not on behalf of the ACS.[45]

Most Black abolitionists despised colonization as the antithesis of their dreams of freedom and equality. No one leveled a more withering ridicule of colonization than the former fugitive Frederick Douglass in his early career. Advocates of colonization, wishing Black people away from America, surpassed even the "vast cartloads of sophistry piled up by Mr. Calhoun and others in favor of perpetual slavery," said Douglass in a speech in 1849. To him the ACS was simply "the old enemy of colored people in this country." Their "piety" was just so much "cant" to Douglass, their aims "diabolical" at their core. And in an 1851 speech, he lampooned the notion that Black people should give their "consent" to be removed to Africa or anywhere else. "If a highway-robber should at the *pistol's mouth* demand my purse," Douglass announced at his satirical best, "it is possible that I should *'consent'* to give it up. If a midnight incendiary should fire my dwelling, I doubt not I should readily *'consent'* to leave it." Douglass spoke for many African Americans in his hatred of colonization schemes. "The highway robber has his method," he declared, "the torturous and wily politician has his." To Douglass colonization denied everything free antebellum Black people strove for; he compared it to Satan "transform[ed] . . . into an angel of light." It was a plan to maintain white supremacy, Douglass argued, a "plot" steeped in "barbarous villainy." Colonizationists' objectives were simple, he said: "*to get rid of us*."[46]

Under the radar of all these roiling debates about abolition (gradual or otherwise), colonization, and the future of slavery in America, a man named William Grimes lived and labored in New Haven, along Chapel Street and across the Yale College campus. Although Grimes shared many experiences in common with other Black New Haveners, free and enslaved, his saga is unique; he became, by 1825, the author of the first published narrative by an American-born slave. He was born in 1784 not far from Fredericksburg, in King George County, Virginia, son of his owner, Benjamin Grymes Jr., a Revolutionary War veteran. His mother was enslaved to a Dr. Steward; her name is unknown. Grimes was sold the first of five times when he was ten years old, separated forever from his mother. He experienced numerous violent owners; one woman had him beaten mercilessly as a child when he did not make the morning coffee quite right. He attempted his first escape at the age of fourteen in 1799, without success. In 1811, Grimes was sold for the final time to a Georgia slaveholder from Savannah. In a long overland journey, the twenty-seven-year-old man, scarred and desperate, despaired of his fate and tried unsuccessfully to take an ax to his own leg, thus rendering himself no use to his new owner. Being sold south to Georgia had always been the worst threat held over Virginia slaves, and in these years the domestic slave trade had exploded in scale. Grimes later implied that God intervened and he resolved "no more to destroy myself." The year after his arrival in Savannah, the War of 1812 broke out, and by 1814, he was working among seamen and dockworkers, as well as aboard a captured British man-of-war and an American ship, the *James Monroe*, in the harbor.[47]

This experience among sailors and on ships paid off for Grimes as he plotted his maritime escape in 1815. After being shunted from one owner to another, doing all manner of urban labor, including handling and driving horses and a carriage, Grimes resolved on a plot of flight. Some "Yankee sailors" were his allies. His final owner, a Bermuda native and merchant named Francis Harvey Welman, had traveled to the Atlantic island for a visit. A Massachusetts ship, the *Casket*, came up the Savannah River and docked at the great cotton warehouses. Grimes performed as part of a crew loading bales of cotton and other goods. Some of the sailors, including one who was Black, took a liking to Grimes and helped him prepare a hiding place among the bales on deck. In this manner the stowaway made his escape to freedom, which he captured in his narrative in dramatic form. He would come out of his hiding place at night and mingle with the sailors, the captain and mate never detecting him because many of the hands on board were of "different complexions." When they arrived in New York, the "quarantine ground" was on Staten Island. Grimes described his moment of "greatest fear" as when his group entered the packet boat to be rowed into the main city of Manhattan. Upon his arrival, a friendly sailor took him to his lodgings and protected him. "I being a stranger there, was afraid of being lost," he recollected. Soon, after purchasing a loaf of bread and some meat, Grimes set out by foot to walk northeast to New Haven. After the long trek—eighty miles or more—a woman proprietor of a boarding house took him in on his first night in New Haven because she assumed he was White. Grimes, a survivor and a hustler, exploited every advantage he could find, always looking over his shoulder to sense where danger lurked.[48]

In his first months in New Haven, Grimes worked a variety of jobs, including for Abel and William Lanson, two Black businessmen and entrepreneurs. His labor included for a while pounding rocks in a quarry to prepare stones for building materials. Remarkably, Grimes encountered a White person who had known him in Savannah, evidence of how many Southerners came to the port city of New Haven. For safety he traveled out of town, first to Southington, where he worked on a farm and experienced a terrible accident that temporarily crippled him. Soon he was back in New Haven and found work "about the Colleges," cutting wood for the students at a wage of about one dollar per day. Grimes moved wherever he heard of a prospect; in 1816, he went to New Bedford, Massachusetts, and opened a short-lived barber shop. By August 1817, Grimes was back in New Haven, where he married Clarissa Caesar. In 1819, the couple moved to Litchfield, Connecticut, where Grimes again started a barber shop and bought some real estate that he rented. The year 1820 found the peripatetic Grimes and Clarissa back in New Haven, where the barber did many odd jobs around Yale College. He drove horses and gigs for people, and he delivered meals to Yale students. To one group he took large quantities of wine and food, and the Yale boys invited him to indulge with them; they got him "making speeches" and "as drunk as a fool," Grimes reported.[49]

Grimes rented lodging from David Daggett, a lawyer, a graduate of Yale, and a founder of its law school. Daggett was also a colonizationist and no abolitionist. Grimes ran what he called a "huckster shop" near the campus (one among many lining the college property) where he sold furniture and wood to students and faculty. He developed rivalries with other shop owners and engaged in lawsuits and was himself sued. Students became Grimes's clients, and when he needed favors he could call them in; he told of disputes and even physical scuffles with some of the young Yalies who likely both respected and lampooned the older, scrambling businessman. Grimes was a jack-of-all-trades, survival his stock in trade. He also proudly declared that he "knew a great many of the students." One even gave him a room in the house where he boarded. Grimes claimed to be so close to some students that he was part of their blustering conversations about "Yankee girls" and their various traits. "I have seen so much behind the curtain," the middle-aged Grimes boasted, that he knew much he did "not want told."[50] Grimes's observations show how much a part of campus life enslaved and free African Americans were in the 1820s.

In 1824, after considerable correspondence and lawyering, Grimes's final owner, Welman, found Grimes and demanded payment for his continued freedom. In the settlement, Grimes had no choice but to pay $500, which broke him and his family financially. The following year, 1825, Grimes finished and published, in New York City, the first edition of *Life of William Grimes, the Runaway Slave, Written by Himself.* The text of this early slave narrative is extraordinary in its sui generis character, since the author wrote in an environment without precedents, genres, or conventions on which he might model his writing. Large gaps emerge in Grimes's life as he tells it, but the book is stunning in its bluntness, its anger, and its despairing tones. Grimes's is not a redemption story, nor a tale of progressive striving or providential intervention; it is a saga of woe and suffering, obstacles, brutalities, blood, and sacrifice. It is an unrelenting catalog of pain, especially psychological, in the life of this literate witness to the barbarity of racism and slavery. Grimes's embittered sense of injury flows throughout the document; he tells over and again of his poverty, living hand to mouth, going about New Haven in search of "cold bits and happiness," and, on communion Sundays, to churches to get some leftover wine.[51] Profound injustice is Grimes's subject; he wears its scars on body and soul.

Grimes's book had no White sponsors as did the later, more famous slave narratives of Frederick Douglass, William Wells Brown, Harriet Jacobs, and others, and it was not a spiritual autobiography seeking to demonstrate the rise of a person from the depths of evil to Christian conversion and salvation. Grimes does not seem to trust his reader to believe him as he tells of many floggings and other violence in Southern slavery; in one instance he describes the back of one victim looking like "nothing but a field lately ploughed." He makes his reader feel the extremes of hunger among slaves as well as the pain of humiliation. His chamber of horrors is anything but conventional nineteenth-century sentimentality. Grimes was unaware and uncaring of the tender sensibilities of his audience. He spared nothing in depicting his eating of "hog's entrails" when especially hungry, nor the savagery of the brawling he engaged in with foes in the South "in old Virginia style (which generally consists in gouging, biting, and butting)." Grimes expressed no forgiveness for those who harmed him; he wrote, argues his best critic, William Andrews, "more like a prosecutor than an analyst."[52]

Most of the later narratives—part of what Andrews calls the "Frederick Douglass school" of such texts—were ascension stories: their trajectories followed paths from slavery to freedom and self-realization. Grimes tended to write in the opposite direction, telling of his personal descent into loss and unending grievance. This solitary man, a product of slavery and an anguished freedom in the unholy North, was a good ironist. His ending remains one of the most powerful expressions about America itself anywhere in antislavery literature: "If it were not for the stripes on my back," he wrote, "which were made while I was a slave, I would in my will leave my skin as a legacy to the government, desiring that it might be taken off and made into parchment, and then bind the constitution of glorious, happy and *free* America. Let the skin of an American slave bind the charter of American liberty!"[53]

Thirty years later in 1855, Grimes published a second edition of his narrative, softening the contents only slightly. For the later edition, he crafted a new "conclusion," in which he portrayed himself as "Old Grimes," as a "fixed institution" in New Haven, and "pretty generally known." He also made the spectacular claim that he fathered "eighteen lovely and beautiful children, of whom only twelve, I believe, are living." Grimes waxed proud of his "barber shop and clothes cleaning establishment in Chapel Street," and he repeatedly reminded readers of his famous "old friends" at Yale College. He placed an advertisement in the local paper, he recalled, in verse and wit:

Old Grimes is not dead,
But you may see him more,
Cleaning coats and shaving heads,
Just as before.

Though long old Grimes has slept,
He only sleeps to wake;
And those who thought him dead and gone,
Now laugh at their mistake.

With working-class scorn and humor, Grimes always reached for the last laugh. Jailed twice, mired in many lawsuits, forever looking for the next deal, Grimes, he wrote, "did almost everything to get an honest living," while for more than thirty years he "worked at the Colleges."[54] As in twenty-first-century New Haven, Grimes's working-class life and that of Yale College students and faculty were both separated by no space at all and a world apart.

Grimes died in New Haven in August 1865, at age eighty-one, just months after the Civil War ended. We do not know his thoughts on the massive war waged to end slavery, nor did he live to see the second U.S. Constitution written on the new parchment of the Thirteenth, Fourteenth, and Fifteenth Amendments. He was buried in Grove Street Cemetery, also the final resting place of many Yale luminaries from the past century and a half; his wife, Clarissa, had moved to California but would later be interred in the same plot in 1869. The 1860 census listed Grimes as head of an eight-person household in New Haven, and his occupation as "Lottery Policy Dealer." An obituary said of Grimes, "All New Haven knew him, he was always on the corners of the streets, basket in hand." He "sold lottery tickets and was versed in theological lore," the remembrance continued. "He was the head of a prosperous barber shop opposite the colleges. All Yale patronized him and thousands of Yale graduates knew him."[55]

In 1825, the same year the first edition of Grimes's narrative was published, the last sale of enslaved people in New Haven took place on the Green, but this exchange did not end in further bondage. The local abolitionist Anthony P. Sanford bought Lois and Lucy Tritton, a mother and daughter, and immediately freed them. Lois Tritton went on to live a long life until her death in 1894. She was a faithful member of Trinity Church on the Green and a founder of St. Luke's

Cover of 1855 edition of *Life of William Grimes, the Runaway Slave.* Photograph by Tubyez Cropper. Beinecke Rare Book and Manuscript Library, Yale University.

Engraving of the New Haven Green from John Warner Barber's *Views in New Haven and Its Vicinity*, published in 1825.
Beinecke Rare Book and Manuscript Library, Yale University.

Episcopal Church, a Black congregation.[56] Although significant, the end of human sales and the trend toward emancipation did not come close to settling the questions concerning Black freedom and opportunity in the United States, or even just in New Haven.

In July 1827, journalist John B. Russwurm, cofounder with Samuel Cornish of the nation's first Black newspaper, *Freedom's Journal*, visited New Haven, Middletown, and Hartford, Connecticut. The purpose of the visit was to convey the importance of this new venture and seek subscribers and financial support. In four letters to Cornish, Russwurm wrote about meeting various members of these communities, with special attention to institutions and the lives of free Black people. Russwurm was born in 1799 in Jamaica. He graduated from Bowdoin College in 1826, one of the first Black people to graduate from an American college. Russwurm's scorn for the colonization movement is evident throughout these letters. However, he had a change of heart. In 1829, after *Freedom's Journal* closed down, he moved to Liberia, becoming superintendent of the schools and editor of a newspaper there, the *Liberia Herald*. He served as governor of the Maryland Colony at Cape Palmas from 1836 until his death in 1851.[57]

While touring New Haven, Russwurm engaged in many conversations with Yale's top officials, all prominent colonizationists, as well as with Simeon Jocelyn, the distinguished minister and abolitionist who had studied at Yale. Russwurm considered Jocelyn, who was the first minister of the Black Temple Street Church, "so great a philanthropist, and so warm a friend to the improvement of our brethren." Russwurm met Yale's newest president, Jeremiah Day, whom he admired as a great mathematician, but Day's eager work for the ACS seems to have curtailed their conversation. Russwurm favorably reported on two Black schools in New Haven and applauded the newly formed community organization, the African Improvement Society, for its work in forging a respectable class of leaders. He lamented, however, that "some of our New-Haven brethren, have acquired; we cannot help mourning," the habits of "vagabonds and outcasts—a nuisance to society, and a disgrace to us all." Russwurm's observations were hardly uncommon among many Northern free Black community leaders trying to convince all around them that they were effective citizens.[58] Russwurm's view of the Black working class might seem harsh, but self-reliance, and all the demands and disputes that come with it, was a necessary burden of free Black communities in early nineteenth-century America. They were in some ways a prescribed caste, expected to earn their way to respect, dignity, and citizenship rights.

Russwurm visited the Yale campus and met a rector, Theodore Dwight Woolsey, a nephew of Timothy Dwight who would himself serve as president of Yale from 1846 to 1871. Woolsey was at the time also a colonizationist; no wonder Russwurm departed from his immersion at Yale disappointed on that score. "The Colonization Society," Russwurm wryly wrote, "appears to have some friends in New-Haven. Almost everywhere I called, the views of the Society were immediately introduced for conversation." The genteel gradualists were all learned but seemed to have little interest in the development of educated Black people, much less citizens. Their elitism conditioned them to admire an exceptional Black person, but to hold the vast majority in contempt for their allegedly natural, and inferior, tendencies. Russwurm also saw and examined the Gibbs cabinet of minerals and came away astounded by its scope and brilliance. He further admired the four-story brick buildings at Yale, as well as its library with so many volumes. As for those Black schools he noted in New Haven, Russwurm wished for much more. And as he ended his public letters, he left a warning. "Me-thinks, slaveholders must be somewhat lacking in their crania," said the wily editor, "to dream even of being able to keep in the nineteenth century, nearly two millions of their fellow beings enslaved! Knowledge must spread. It cannot be kept from them. Did all other methods fail, I verily believe, like heaven's fury lightnings, it would descend upon them. Can the justice of God tolerate so much iniquity and injustice?"[59] New Haven and Yale's next great challenge would be just how much knowledge—the purpose of Yale College—would be allowed to spread. The challenge did not arrive by an apocalypse, but by the simple idea of a new college.

CHAPTER 6

The 1831 Black College

The Convention would remind our brethren that knowledge is power.

—Delegates to the First Annual Convention of the People of Colour, Philadelphia, 1831

September 10, 1831, was a day when hope unborn was killed in New Haven.

Earlier that year, an impressive new State House opened on New Haven's upper green, just behind the First (or Center) Church and immediately across College Street from the Yale campus. New Haven had been the co-capital of Connecticut with Hartford since 1701, as it would remain until 1875. Designed by Ithiel Town and modeled after the Parthenon, the three-story building housed meeting rooms for the state general assembly on its upper floor, committee and court rooms on the second level, and a town hall space for New Haven on the north side of the ground floor. The relationship between the state's government and its preeminent institution of higher learning—Yale—had always been close. Among the early acts by the colonial general assembly meeting in New Haven was "An act for Liberty to erect a Collegiate School" on October 9, 1701, authorizing the establishment of the institution that would come to be called Yale some years later.[1]

Located at the very center of the community, part of the upper green behind the First Church had served as New Haven's burial ground until 1797, when the Grove Street Cemetery opened. The last interment occurred there in 1812. The new 1831 State House had its east side "built over the graves of a number of persons," a later historian would note. "The workmen in digging for a foundation came across numerous bones," it was reported in 1889, "and instead of exposing them to view, pounded them down into the earth."[2]

Only months after the State House opened, New Haven's freemen—the White male property owners, many affiliated with Yale—gathered for an extraordinary town hall meeting that would obliterate, like those bones pounded down into the earth, bold hopes for the nation's first Black college. The college would have been America's inaugural Black college or university and would have been known today as an HBCU (historically Black college or university). It was an idea brought to life by a coalition, both local and national, of free Black leaders and White allies. They considered New Haven a prime location in part because it was vibrant and urbane, had ties to the Caribbean, and was a noted center of higher education as home to Yale.[3]

For White business and civic leaders, New Haven in the early 1830s was a city on the rise. It was a major center of education and publishing. Noah Webster had just completed the epic *American Dictionary of the English Language* in 1828. Connecticut boasted the highest college matriculation rate in the nation and the highest literacy rate. As of 1830, New Haven was the nation's twenty-third-largest city, with a population of over ten thousand. White elites were accumulating great wealth, manufacturing was growing, and immigration from Europe was on the rise. The first steamboat service between New Haven and New York City had started in 1815. The Farmington Canal opened in 1828. Signs of prosperity included the Hillhouse mansion, originally known as Highwood and later called Sachem's Wood, built just north of the town center in 1829. On the Green, local congressman and Yale graduate Ralph Ingersoll built his impressive red-brick house in 1829 at the corner of Temple and Elm Streets. The town and its famous college were thriving.[4]

Slavery, though not widespread, remained legal at the time. Connecticut would not formally abolish slavery until 1848, making it the last state in New England to do so. New Haven was home to nearly six hundred free Black people and four enslaved people in 1830, accounting for 7.5 percent of the city's populace in 1820—the largest share on record in the nineteenth century. (By comparison, by 1920–30, as the Great Migration out of the South began to transform Northern and Midwestern cities, Black people made up around 3 percent of New Haven's population.) In New Haven in 1831, free Black people still faced severe restrictions on their liberty, and Black citizenship was both heavily contested and often aggressively resisted. In 1814, the general assembly passed legislation that formally prohibited Black men from voting. Despite eloquent petitions from William Lanson and Bias Stanley, both prominent Black figures in New Haven, the restrictions were incorporated into the Connecticut constitution of 1818. Economic and educational opportunities for Black people were extremely limited.

At the same time, Black women and men were beginning to organize churches and build community institutions, creating their own spaces of liberation. These New Haveners were also active in the growing network of free Black leaders nationally.[5]

In the 1830s, Yale was the nation's largest college. With an enrollment of 496 in 1830, the students were all male, Protestant, and of European descent. Not only a leading light for New Haven and Connecticut, the institution had broad influence nationally. Its *Reports on the Course of Instruction in Yale College of 1828* would later be considered "one of the most important documents in American higher education" and establish "the parameters of liberal education for much of the nineteenth century." Yale's impact in this era would later earn it the appellation "mother of colleges" in recognition of its alumni being the founding presidents of institutions including Georgia University (1801), Hamilton College (1812), Kenyon College (1825), Illinois College (1830), Wabash College (1833), the University of Missouri (1840), the University of Mississippi (1848), and the University of Wisconsin (1849). This generative role for other White colleges makes Yale's involvement in aborting a Black college proposal even more notable.[6]

This was the setting in New Haven at the time a bold proposal was made to create the nation's first college for Black men. The year 1831 was a crucial milestone in the origins of the abolition movement. The previous year, in September, Black leaders from throughout the antebellum North had gathered at Mother Bethel African Methodist Episcopal Church in Philadelphia. Delegates included New Haven's Scipio Augustus. That convention was "the meeting that launched a movement," an evolving crusade for Black freedom, which emerged from within African American communities as well as among White allies across the North. Bishop Richard Allen gave the main address at his church at that 1830 convention, and its success led to the decision to hold annual meetings beginning the following year.[7]

These productive years of social and political organizing gave birth to the dream of a Black college in New Haven. White allies of the project included New Haven's Simeon Jocelyn and his Boston friend William Lloyd Garrison, who began publishing the abolitionist newspaper the *Liberator* in January 1831. That same year, New Haven Black leaders John Creed and J. L. Cross became agents for the *Liberator*. But the seeds of the abolition movement in the Elm City had been planted years before, and they could be found in a newly formed Black church. Beginning in 1820, Black parishioners had gathered for services with Jocelyn, a White pastor and abolitionist, in his home. In 1824, early free Black leaders in New Haven including Prince Cooper, Prince Duplex Jr., William Lanson, and Bias Stanley joined with Jocelyn to establish the African Ecclesiastical Society, which would soon come to be known as the Temple Street Congregational Church, the first officially recognized Black Congregational church in the country. From early on, the church had a school, with Vashti Duplex Creed, wife of John Creed and sister of Duplex, as its first teacher. In 1829, eighty children attended the church's Sabbath School, while sixty learned reading, writing, and arithmetic in the day school, which was funded in part by the city. An evening school offered women perhaps their first chance at formal education, and thirty women, many domestic laborers, attended. This community knew the paramount importance of education.[8]

A college education remained out of reach for most Americans, White or Black, in the antebellum period. Just over 1 percent of White men in New England attended college in 1830. Yet as new colleges opened, expanding opportunity for at least some rural and middle-class White young men, the options for Black students remained virtually nonexistent, although a number of "firsts" had taken place. In the decade before the college was proposed in New Haven, Alexander Twilight had graduated from Middlebury College; Edward Jones from Amherst College; John Russwurm from Bowdoin College; and Edward Mitchell from Dartmouth College—all the first African Americans to do so at their respective institutions and in the country as a whole. And a few training schools that accepted Black men aimed to prepare them for mission work in Africa, with the ultimate goal of emigration. A few decades before, the Reverends Ezra Stiles and Samuel Hopkins had hoped that, by educating John Quamino and Bristol Yamma, they might not only spread the Gospel in Africa but also inspire other Black Americans to repatriate. Such a plan did not appeal to the majority of Black Americans in 1830, however, who simply sought greater educational opportunities or vocational training in their native country of the United States.[9]

Expanding access to education was widely seen as essential to Black people's social and economic mobility, and it was integral to the abolitionist agenda as well. On May 28, 1831, Jocelyn wrote to Garrison about an idea to establish a college for young Black men. Jocelyn told Garrison that he had met with the Reverend Peter Williams, a Black leader in New York, about a mutual interest in education. Williams and Jocelyn decided to merge their interest in a new college, which would combine "the Mechanics arts & some degree of agriculture and horticulture." Jocelyn described to Garrison the visionary idea of an institution "connected with many useful pursuits, and with the advantages of domestic & social life as would prepare the young men for active life and to aid their brethren in other places in all those things which make men happy and which give them as individuals [and] as communities influence in the world." Their ambitions for this college were both specific and broad, based on a hope that education would provide a path forward for individual students while also enabling them to contribute to the larger society.[10]

Jocelyn asked Garrison to accompany him and Arthur Tappan, the noted White New York philanthropist and abolitionist who had a second home in New Haven, to present the whole plan "at the convention of the people of color who meet the week after next in Philadelphia." The financial backing of Tappan was considered key to the effort. Jocelyn revealed that Tappan had committed $1,000, and he wrote that a site had been chosen in the southern section of New Haven. A newspaper notice later in 1831 reported "the extensive establishment at New Haven formerly known as the 'steamboat hotel,' and laterally as Dwight's gymnasium for boys, has been purchased by a Mr. Jocelyn, and is to be converted into a college for blacks."[11] The site for the college would have been on Water Street between East and Wallace Streets, land that sits now below the busy juncture of two major highways, Interstate 91 and Interstate 95.

These visionaries had done their homework, as planners, as educators, and as national and local organizers. And they sought support from a burgeoning national movement that was grounded in grassroots communities like the Temple Street Church. Historian Kabria Baumgartner notes that delegates to the Colored Conventions had "established 'education, temperance, and economy' as the three pillars of progress" at the first five national conventions held between 1830 and 1835, and that education "was a recurring subject at national Colored Conventions in the pre–Civil War era."[12] With great hope, Jocelyn, Tappan, and Garrison journeyed to the first annual convention to seek the support of these leaders of the Black community in the antebellum North.

The convention met June 6 to 11, 1831, with delegates hailing from Pennsylvania, New York, Maryland, Delaware, and Virginia, including James W. C. Pennington of Long Island, who would later study at Yale and serve at the Temple Street Church and in Hartford. Jocelyn, Garrison, and Tappan were invited to speak on June 8. The delegates endorsed the proposed college and identified agents to lead the fundraising with the Reverend Samuel Cornish, a Black man, as general agent and Tappan as treasurer. Several provisional committees were established with free Black leaders in fourteen communities, including Bias Stanley, John Creed, and Alexander C. Luca in New Haven. The reasons Jocelyn, Tappan, and Garrison offered for locating the proposed college in New Haven,

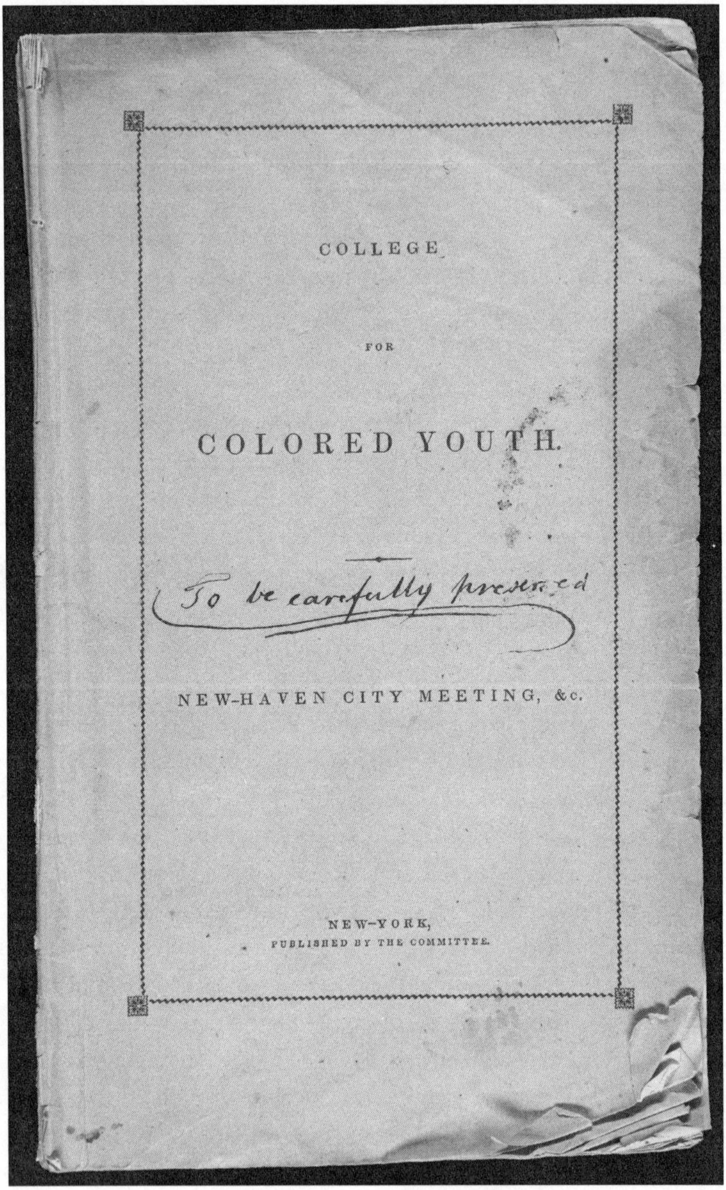

College for Colored Youth: An Account of the New-Haven City Meeting and Resolutions: With Recommendations of the College, and Strictures upon the Doings of New-Haven, 1831.
Beinecke Rare Book and Manuscript Library, Yale University.

recorded in the convention proceedings, underscore their optimism and faith in the city and its people. "1st. The site is healthy and beautiful. 2d. Its inhabitants are friendly, pious, generous, and humane. 3d. Its laws are salutary and protecting to all without regard to complexion. 4th. Boarding is cheap and provisions are good. 5th. The situation is as central as any other that can be obtained with the same advantages." A sixth reason they cited was that New Haven had extensive trade ties with the West Indies. With the abolition of the slave trade and growing free Black communities in the Caribbean, "many of the wealthy coloured residents in the Islands, would, no doubt, send their sons there to be educated, and thus a fresh tie of friendship would be formed, which might be productive of much real good in the end. And last, though not the least, the literary and scientific character of New Haven, renders it a very desirable place for the location of the College." In fact, Tappan believed Yale professors might visit the Black college and lecture to the students.[13] Out of all the possible locations to establish such a pioneering institution of higher learning for Black students, New Haven—home to Yale—seemed the most promising and welcoming. Thus a dream was born at a Black convention.

This alliance in 1831 between Black leaders and White allies to establish the first HBCU was, according to historian James Brewer Stewart, "a truly revolutionary turn in the history of race relations in the United States." Black organizers had real power and direction. The proceedings announced that "the Convention would wish it to be distinctly understood, that the Trustees of the contemplated Institution, shall a majority of them be coloured persons; the number proposed is seven, three white, and four coloured." The still-youthful Garrison said at the time, "Great things are in embryo" that "will command the attention of the whole country, and operate upon the colored population with the power of electricity."[14]

Garrison visited New Haven not long after the convention in late June and gave two public addresses. He would speak and write about the college proposal in the following weeks and months, including in pieces circulated through the *Liberator*. The proposal was noted in the July 30, 1831, edition of the *New York Evangelist* newspaper, which described the work of Black leaders and philanthropic White allies to establish a college at New Haven, with $10,000 to be raised among White donors and $10,000 from Black donors. "The idea is a good one. We wish success to the undertaking with all our heart." On September 5, the provisional committee of Philadelphia published an "Appeal to the Benevolent" in the *Philadelphia Chronicle*, outlining plans for the Black college. Back in New Haven, Simeon Jocelyn gave an address on Wednesday, September 7, at the Third Congregational Church on "the subject of the moral, intellectual and civil improvement of the people of color in the United States."[15] No doubt he promoted plans for the new Black college as he discussed abolition and antislavery efforts.

At the same time, in the same newspaper that took note of Jocelyn's address on September 6, the first New Haven mention appeared of the insurrection in Virginia known as Nat Turner's Rebellion. The *Connecticut Journal* reported, "The insurrection in Virginia appears to have been very easily suppressed." Some historians cite the news of Nat Turner's Rebellion as a factor in the vituperative reaction by New Haven's White leaders and residents against the Black college in New Haven in the following days and beyond.[16] The direct influence of Nat Turner's Rebellion in Virginia, which was tremendous news all across the nation, on the Black college dispute in New Haven is difficult to measure, but it surely was on the minds of White residents at the time.

The day after Jocelyn's address, on Thursday, September 8, New Haven mayor Dennis Kimberly, an 1812 graduate of Yale, gave notice of an "extraordinary meeting" of the freemen—that is, the White property owners—that would be held two days later on September 10, "to take into consideration a scheme (said to be in progress) for the establishment, in this City, of 'a College for the education of *Colored Youth*,' and to adopt such measures as may be deemed expedient relative to the same." Just underneath this notice was one announcing the preliminary meeting of the alumni of Yale College to be held on Tuesday, September 13.[17]

The September 10 meeting was held in the State House, the co-capital building that had opened earlier in the year, which had a town hall space. A contemporary account describes that intense afternoon: "So great was the interest to hear the discussion," declared the *New Haven Advertiser*, "that, notwithstanding the excessive heat and the almost irrespirable atmosphere of the room, the hall was crowded throughout the afternoon."[18] Many hundreds of White men packed into a 2,940-square-foot room on that hot Saturday afternoon. At question was whether New Haven would make history as home to the first college dedicated to the education and advancement of the Black race—or whether it would gain notoriety as a city where those dreams died.

The White male voters of New Haven spoke with a near-unanimous voice: seven hundred stood opposed to the college and only four in favor. Accounts from the time indicate that the four supporters were Jocelyn; the engraver and printer John Warner Barber; Roger Sherman Baldwin (Yale 1811), the future governor of Connecticut and U.S. senator; and the Virginia-born James Donaghe.

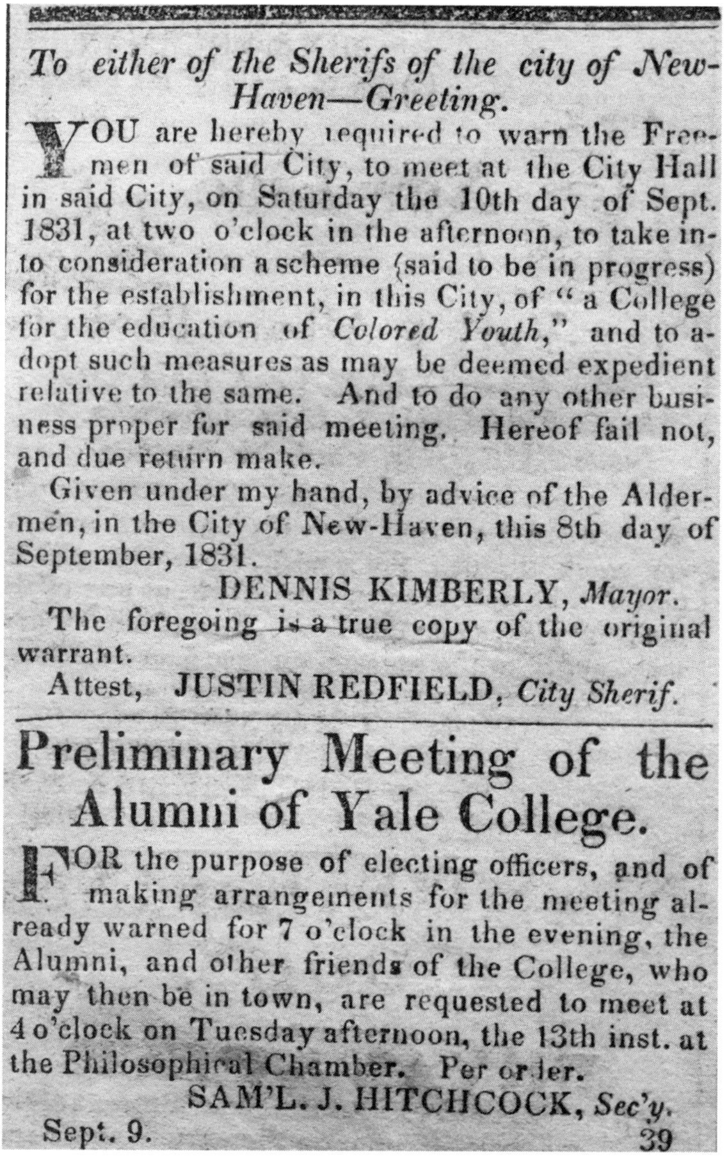
To either of the Sherifs of the city of New-Haven—Greeting.

YOU are hereby required to warn the Freemen of said City, to meet at the City Hall in said City, on Saturday the 10th day of Sept. 1831, at two o'clock in the afternoon, to take into consideration a scheme (said to be in progress) for the establishment, in this City, of "a College for the education of *Colored Youth*," and to adopt such measures as may be deemed expedient relative to the same. And to do any other business proper for said meeting. Hereof fail not, and due return make.

Given under my hand, by advice of the Aldermen, in the City of New-Haven, this 8th day of September, 1831.

DENNIS KIMBERLY, *Mayor.*

The foregoing is a true copy of the original warrant.

Attest, JUSTIN REDFIELD, *City Sherif.*

Preliminary Meeting of the Alumni of Yale College.

FOR the purpose of electing officers, and of making arrangements for the meeting already warned for 7 o'clock in the evening, the Alumni, and other friends of the College, who may then be in town, are requested to meet at 4 o'clock on Tuesday afternoon, the 13th inst. at the Philosophical Chamber. Per order.

SAM'L. J. HITCHCOCK, *Sec'y.*

Sept. 9. 39

On September 9, 1831, the *New Haven Daily Advertiser* announced two upcoming meetings—one to discuss the proposed Black college and another of Yale alumni. Photograph by Tubyez Cropper. Beinecke Rare Book and Manuscript Library, Yale University.

Contemporary newspapers reported that five people addressed the meeting. The speakers against it—Isaac Townsend, Ralph Ingersoll, Nathan Smith, and David Daggett—included three Yale alumni. Only the Reverend Simeon Jocelyn spoke in favor. On the table were resolutions put forward by a committee that Mayor Kimberly had appointed. The committee included ten people, at least six of whom were Yale alumni: Simeon Baldwin (father of Roger, who supported the college), William Bristol, Samuel Hitchcock, Ralph Ingersoll, Augustus Street, and Isaac Townsend. These men were top figures of civic, legal, and political leadership. Ingersoll was a congressman, Baldwin had been mayor of New Haven, and Hitchcock was a leading lawyer. Street, an 1812 graduate, became a major donor to Yale; his gifts helped establish the School of Fine Arts, and Street Hall is named in his honor. Of the four who spoke against the college, Yale graduate David Daggett was at the time associate justice of the Superior Court of Connecticut. The next year, he would be chief justice of the state's supreme court. He was, along with Hitchcock, a founder of the Yale Law School.[19]

Opposition to the proposal stemmed from several quarters, but the committee members began by expressing their disapproval of—even horror at—the abolitionist impulses latent in the scheme to educate Black Americans. The committee's resolutions had two parts. The first part read, "The immediate emancipation of slaves in disregard of the civil institutions of the States in which they belong, and as auxiliary thereto the contemporaneous founding of Colleges for educating colored people, is an unwarrantable and dangerous interference with the internal concerns of other States, and ought to be discouraged."[20] Although at a comfortable, safe distance from the recent bloody uprising in Virginia, these Yale graduates and their neighbors viewed the Black college as an "auxiliary" to emancipation. Thus the entire abolition movement, along with plans to open educational and other opportunities to *free* Black people, was depicted as an "unwarrantable and dangerous interference" in Southern institutions—that is, slavery. In voting to support this resolution, seven hundred to four, New Haven's leading citizens went on record. These Northern gentlemen of standing, in opposing the college proposal, stood together in defense of the South's proslavery regime.

Other objections hit closer to home, particularly concerns about the potential damage to Yale's reputation. The second part of the resolution stated, "Yale College, the institutions for the education of females, and the other schools already existing in this city are important to the community and the general interests of science, and as such, have been deservedly patronized by the public and the establishment of a College in the same place to educate the colored population is incompatible with the prosperity, if not the existence of the present institutions of learning, and will be destructive of the best interests of the city. . . . We will resist the establishment of the proposed College in this place, by every lawful means." New Haven's White freemen, including the elites of "town and gown," were clear: they felt a Black college would be a threat to Yale and other schools in town.[21]

A few weeks after the vote, the newspaper in nearby Middletown commented on "the feelings evinced" at the town meeting. "The support of Yale College," the correspondent wrote, "depends in no inconsiderable degree, on the character of the inhabitants." That character would be threatened if "the students of Yale are to be met by [Black college students] in all the pride of supposed equality," a threat also worrisome to the majority culture fearful that "young ladies are to be elbowed at every corner by black collegians." The sentiment of many Yale students was confirmed that fall in a November 9, 1831, campus debate by the Society of Brothers in Unity on the topic, "Ought a college for free blacks to be opened in this country?" The resolution: negative.[22]

White supremacist sentiments in New Haven are well documented in contemporary newspaper accounts, as were the city's ties to the South. One paper wrote, "Here we have Yale College, among the highest ornaments of which, are sons of southern planters. We have several most respectable institutions for the instruction of young ladies, some of whom are from the south. There is no other town or city in the United States, where a Liberian College would be as fatal to all the prospects of the inhabitants." Another New Haven paper said, "The establishment of a College here would at once give an eclat to our college population, that would ring through the land a summons, that would hurry in the blacks, as bees to a hive. It would communicate to the world the impression, that New-Haven was overrun with a vicious population; for throughout the United States vice is uniformly associated with a large colored population." It is more than a little ironic that a proposal to establish an institution of higher education—one that its organizers hoped would teach "many useful pursuits" and impart "the advantages of domestic and social life" as well as valuable economic skills—would have been opposed for attracting "a vicious population." Yet such virulent racism had been expressed for decades in newspapers and by Yale leaders like President Timothy Dwight; Black people were associated with crime and poor character while being denied access to the education, skills, and opportunities that would lead to greater affluence and respectability.[23]

The Creeds, the Stanleys, Jocelyn, and other advocates no doubt felt disheartened by the proposal's resounding defeat. They had chosen New Haven in part because they imagined it as welcoming to such an institution of Black advancement. They even believed that Yale's proximity would be a point in its favor, rather than yet another reason to oppose the plan. Just a few days after the town meeting against the Black college, New Haven and the Yale campus were full of celebrations, with commencement held that year on Wednesday, September 14. Newspaper accounts of the time report that the graduation exercises were "attended by a large concourse of people, not only from the immediate neighborhood of that ancient seat of learning, but of distinguished gentlemen from other States. It is said that the number of visitors was greater than was ever assembled at New Haven on any previous anniversary of the College." Perhaps some had been in town from the weekend before, and surely nearly all in the crowds learned of the New Haven town meeting vote. So large were the crowds that "every hotel was crowded to overflowing, and had not the citizens thrown open their doors to the throngs of attending strangers, much inconvenience, if not actual suffering, would have been experienced."[24] The very same White Christians who had been overwhelmingly inhospitable to their Black neighbors' hopes and plans for education welcomed strangers visiting to celebrate Yale's strength and glory.

The commencement exercises, in keeping with long-standing tradition, took place in the Center Church on the Green, next door to the State House where the college proposal was voted down. Moreover, that week marked the launch of Yale's first formal fundraising campaign, with the plans for what would become known as the Centum Milia fund kicked off at the annual meeting of alumni on September 13. "On Tuesday evening, at a large meeting of the Alumni," a New York paper reported, "a plan previously formed for raising the sum of one hundred thousand dollars, was unanimously adopted. It is understood that about thirty thousand dollars are already pledged. The principal object of the effort is to erect additional buildings, of which the College is in great need."[25] No doubt many local Yale alumni who joined to launch the campaign to boost Yale that Tuesday had been among those who gathered to block the Black college just the Saturday before. These Yale alumni and officials, as well as local town leaders, may not have consciously faced the bitter contradiction they had enacted on their community. Such is the nature of hypocrisy. Somehow, if they needed it, they found justification in the hardened core of their racial beliefs, as well as in their fears of the educational liberation of their Black neighbors. Indeed, Yale's ethos at this time was colonizationist at best on the slavery issue, and the idea of a Black college in their own neighborhood violated such aims. Nothing in the law, despite the moral philosophy and biblical teachings they imbibed at their beloved college, forced them to share the educational opportunities they financed for their own sons.

Abolitionists, however, saw the irony. The *Liberator* noted the juxtaposition of these two events—the town meeting against the Black college and Yale's commencement and fundraising. Yale evinced a "spirit of monopoly" as its "upholders" refused "to establish a colored College beside it," read a story by Stonington Phenix. "Such inconsistencies and acts of injustice as these, affix a shame on our Literati, which the 'glory' of a thousand such Commencements; yea, which 'all the chemistry in the world' can never wash away." In a similar vein, Garrison responded in poetry about "the disgraceful proceedings" and said, "New Haven, thou hast rashly done a deed, / Which shrouds thy glory in a black eclipse."[26]

The town meeting to thwart the Black college fueled White rage against local Black residents that continued in the weeks afterward. Riotous spirit and action were documented in the papers of the time. The next month, a New Haven paper reported that "a negro hut," home to several families, was torn down early in the night on a Saturday. "Every body rejoices that the building is gone," the paper claimed. In October, the *Liberator* had an article titled "Riots at New Haven!," reporting that the summer home of Arthur Tappan in New Haven had been "rudely assailed by some vile fellows who gave utterance to their malice in words the most obscene and blasphemous," and that a house owned by a Black person on Mount Pleasant in New Haven had been "leveled to the ground." A Philadelphia newspaper reported of New Haven, "A Black man was knocked down in the streets, and on Friday evening, the house of the most respectable gentlemen was assailed with shouts, indecent songs, and a shower of stones." There were many reports of such activity, and in a letter to Garrison on October 18, Tappan noted conjecture that Southern medical students at Yale were among the protagonists in the riots.[27]

Beyond New Haven, the defeat of the Black college was the talk of the nation, and even the toast of White Southerners. Many voices in the slaveholding South took note of the seven-hundred-to-four decision and celebrated it. A Georgia newspaper said, "We are glad to find that the good sense of the people of New Haven has induced them to act promptly and vigorously in opposition to the ill-judged and unjustifiable enthusiasm of misguided zealots." A Richmond newspaper described what New Haven had done as an "admirable lesson." In October, a Natchez, Mississippi, newspaper spoke glowingly of their Northern neighbors: "The attempt made by a Convention in Philadelphia, to establish a college at New Haven for the education of the blacks, has been met by the citizens of the latter city in a spirit that will be duly appreciated by the people of the South."[28] The significance of New Haven's decision to oppose the college was reflected in such widespread press coverage. At a time of increasingly heated national conversations about race, slavery, and abolition—still only months after the Nat Turner uprising and its bloody suppression—here was another turning point. For a city like New Haven—a bastion of New England values, and inextricably associated with Yale—to resoundingly oppose the idea of a Black college seemed to speak broadly about the country's attitudes. In an immediate sense, it foreclosed possibilities for Black education and uplift. But it also sent a clear message about the place of Black people, free and enslaved, in the nation, thwarting plans to promote education and liberation and reinforcing the status quo of slavery and racial oppression.

The defeat of the 1831 Black college would play a meaningful, if underappreciated, role in the coming decades leading up to the Civil War. Two years later, the New Haven experience was cited by opponents of Prudence Crandall, who had opened her all-White Canterbury Female Boarding Academy to one Black student in 1832 and faced strong pushback from her neighbors. In response, she decided to run the school exclusively for "Young Ladies and Little Misses of Color," advertising to Black families in Boston, New York, and Philadelphia seeking an education for their daughters. Faced with violent physical attacks on the school by the White citizens of Canterbury, she finally closed the school for the safety of her pupils. A newspaper in Norwich proclaimed, "We believe that this effort [Crandall's school], as well as that at New Haven, were links in the chain which would bind upon us the blacks, and create an amalgamation, by affording precedents for bolder efforts." In bald language, the writers expressed their fears that "amalgamation" would lead to greater social and political power for Black people. "If they have their seminaries of instruction, why shall they be debarred from the ballot-box? The next step in the progress of fanatacism [*sic*] will be, that we shall be a parti-colored race, ranging from the purest white down to utter darkness. Even the contemplation of such a possibility is shocking to common delicacy." Such reactions demonstrate that the oldest mixtures of ideas about race, sexuality, and gender formed the core of resistance to Black education. And as in the case of the New Haven college, Southern observers took note of Connecticut's actions. A Baltimore newspaper wrote, "If the people of Connecticut are so incensed at the establishment of a public school among themselves for the instruction of blacks . . . we take it for granted that they are willing to show all charity to the prejudices of the Southern people in similar matters."[29] Here again was another Northern vote in favor of the South's "peculiar institution."

Back in Connecticut, both the proposed Black college and Crandall's school were followed by severe reaction at the state legislature. On May 24, 1833, Connecticut lawmakers passed what became known as the Black Law, preventing the education of Black people from out of state. Crandall was arrested and placed on trial. When her case came to trial, the judge was David Daggett, Yale alumnus and former faculty member who had led the opposition to the Black college in 1831. Daggett was a jurist and legal scholar who had enjoyed a brilliant and influential career. In addressing the jury before their deliberations, Daggett spoke for over an hour, providing direction to the jurors regarding what he considered the pertinent law. In the course of his lengthy remarks, Daggett told them, "To my mind, it would be a perversion of terms, and of the well known rule of construction, to say that slaves, free blacks, or *Indians*, were citizens, within the meaning of that term, as used in the constitution." He went on, "God forbid that I should add to the degradation of this race of men; but I am bound, by my duty to say, they are not citizens."[30]

The influence of that ruling far outlived Daggett and Crandall, reaching even to the eve of the sectional crisis. In his infamous 1857 ruling in *Dred Scott*, Chief Justice Roger Taney drew support from Daggett's decision in *Crandall*. Again, it mattered to Taney, a Marylander, that the case had taken place in Connecticut. Taney wrote, "We may expect to find the laws of that State as lenient and favorable to the subject race as those of any other State in the Union, and if we find that, at the time the Constitution was adopted, they were not even there raised to the rank of citizens, but were still held and treated as property, and the laws relating to them passed with reference altogether to the interest and convenience of the white race, we shall hardly find them elevated to a higher rank anywhere else." If the rights and personhood of Black people could be so thoroughly rejected by Judge Daggett, spokesperson for Connecticut's legal and political establishment, surely it was a lesson for the rest of the country. Thus Taney found justification in the words of a Yale alumnus, a founder of its law school, for his assertion in *Dred Scott* that Black people were "so far inferior that they had no rights which the White man was bound to respect." The direct line of legal thinking from Daggett in 1833 to Taney in 1857, however, only inspired an emergent antislavery interpretation of the Constitution among both moralistic and political abolitionists.[31]

The defeat of the Black college was a setback for the Black people of New Haven and their White allies. The Black leaders who gathered at the first Colored Convention in 1831 had declared "knowledge is power," underscoring the importance a college would have in building the movement for liberation, equality, and citizenship. They published their proceedings so that future generations would know of their efforts. It was true that their hopes and aspirations that year were decisively blocked by White New Haven leaders, many of them Yale men who sought again to maintain a standing order of white supremacy in society. The White leaders also knew that knowledge was power and that education and citizenship were inexplicably intertwined. That is why this fight mattered so much to both sides; two diametrically opposed dreams were in conflict in this story. Power won out. As historian Hilary Moss notes, "It was no coincidence that Connecticut was both the only New England state to fully disenfranchise African Americans and to formally proscribe their right to an education."[32] New Haven and Yale helped make it so.

Black leaders persisted and the dream of Black colleges did take root, beginning with Cheyney University of Pennsylvania in 1837. Yale, however, which long has prided itself as a progenitor of many universities, helped thwart the opportunity to help Black higher education find its first fertile ground in New Haven. In 1831, Yale's people refused to shed its light on the truth of Black education. Dedicated to preserving their own standing order, the leadership of New Haven and Yale blocked an institution that would have illuminated Black knowledge, citizenship, and power.

CHAPTER 7

La Amistad

The spirit of the Lord God is upon me; because the Lord hath anointed me to preach good tidings unto the meek; he hath sent me to bind up the brokenhearted, to proclaim liberty to the captives, and the opening of the prison to them that are bound.

—Isaiah 61:1

The African survivors of a rebellion aboard *La Amistad*, a coastal schooner from Cuba, were the talk of New Haven and of the nation in 1839–40. Hailing from the Gallinas coast and Sierra Leone region of West Africa, these people had been captured in Africa, enslaved, and transported across the Atlantic. Then, bought and sold like chattel in Cuba, they had—through an unfathomable combination of daring, courage, and luck—overthrown their captors and seized a kind of tentative, uncertain freedom. Yet in 1839, forty-three of the original captives were imprisoned and put on trial just steps from Yale's campus. Their ordeal—years of incarceration and complex legal battles—attracted thousands of onlookers, gawkers, and what might be called slavery "tourists" from all over the northeastern United States. The famous White New York abolitionist Lewis Tappan came to New Haven to help organize the defense and publicity of the survivors, and a cast of Yale characters became involved in the unfolding legal and cultural drama, including the Yale-trained lawyer Roger Sherman Baldwin; the Yale-educated minister and abolitionist editor, the Reverend Joshua Leavitt; the Yale divinity professor George E. Day; a Yale senior, Sherman Booth; and the Yale linguistics professor Josiah Willard Gibbs. Over the next two years, the African people of the *Amistad* would leave their mark on the city of New Haven, on Yale, and on the American abolition movement.[1]

No one in Connecticut, or elsewhere in the nation, had ever seen a mass sensation quite like that of the *Amistad* Africans. Their principal leader, Sengbe

Pieh—better known as Joseph Cinqué in America—whether he sought it or not, quickly emerged as a romantic hero to the antislavery cause and a dangerous, bloodthirsty villain to proslavery interests. The story of the *Amistad* Africans galvanized American abolitionists in a decade when they had grown in numbers and notoriety but faced violent resistance. No less than former president John Quincy Adams, now a congressman from Massachusetts, came to the New Haven jail to meet with the captives in preparation to take their case to the U.S. Supreme Court. On any given day of the trials in the New Haven courthouse, Yale students swarmed the cramped judicial quarters as eager spectators. The appearance of these Africans seemed to many Americans a sudden providential visit, exposing the country's most vexing problem, and their fate became a test of American law, politics, and conscience like no other before it. At Yale, the *Amistad* story left a lasting, if ambivalent, legacy. No enslaved rebel in history, with the possible exception of Toussaint Louverture in Haiti, was ever celebrated in art and verse as was Cinqué.[2]

The fifty-three West Africans aboard the *Amistad* when the uprising occurred had all been swept up in the twin terrors of nearly endemic war between rival African ethnic or tribal groups and the surging slave trade along the Gallinas coast. Most were from an inland people known as the Mende, themselves an expanding kingdom of warriors, farmers, traders, and urban dwellers, some from towns as large as early nineteenth-century New Haven. Slave trading in Sierra Leone was many generations old; villages raided other villages, which were often well fortified, in order to produce captives for the European and Creole merchants and their customers—the ships and the Atlantic trade—at huge slaving forts. By this point in the nineteenth century, unlike the eighteenth, such transatlantic slaving voyages were outlawed by treaties among most of the European powers, but the violent trade persisted.[3]

In April 1839, as many as five hundred Africans were assembled, placed in leg irons and neck chains, and taken in long boats aboard a Spanish ship, the *Teçora*. Some of the group who became the *Amistad* rebels may have been captives in war, while others were seized while traveling about "on the road." By one account, the holds of the *Teçora* included "plenty of children." These ships packed hundreds of enslaved people into utterly inhumane, cramped, disease-ridden lower decks of the ship on a voyage of nearly two months across the Atlantic to Havana, Cuba. An American abolitionist, George Thompson, later a participant in the *Amistad* story, boarded and made drawings of a Brazilian slave ship of roughly the same size and vintage as the *Teçora*. He described the decks "literally covered with men, women, and children *in a state of nudity . . . crowded between each other's*

Cinque: The Chief of the Amistad Captives, John Sartain, after Nathaniel Jocelyn, circa 1840. Yale University Art Gallery.

legs," in a space "not sufficient for a person to sit up straight!" And Cinqué, who established his leadership of the eventual rebels during the *Teçora*'s journey, later sat on the floor in a federal courtroom in Connecticut, demonstrating for a judge his manacled and shackled condition.[4]

According to the captives' testimonies, "many" aboard the *Teçora* died at sea, and it became a daily ritual for the dead and dying to be carried out of the holds in the morning and thrown overboard. Upon arrival in Havana in June 1839, the

Africans were housed with oxen, sheep, and cattle as they awaited sale. José Ruiz purchased a group of forty-nine men for transport elsewhere in the plantation system of Cuba, and a second trader, Pedro Montes, purchased four children, three little girls and a boy, named Margru, Kagne, Teme, and Kale, separately at a shop in Havana.[5] Although it was legal to transport enslaved cargo between Cuban ports, the *Teçora*'s voyage from Africa had been in violation of international treaties effectively outlawing the transatlantic slave trade. And since British vessels roamed the Atlantic in their own national attempt to suppress the slave trade, Ruiz and Montes disguised their lot of captives in sailors' clothing as best they could and, under cover of darkness, quietly boarded them on a low, seventy-ton schooner built in Cuba as a coastal trading vessel. On its square stern it read *La Amistad* (friendship). The ship's captain and owner, Ramón Ferrer, had only four crew members—two sailors, a cabin boy named Antonio, and a cook, Celestino. Down below through a large hatch in the middle of the deck was a 6,600-cubic-foot hold, and this is where the captive Africans were forced to assemble, chained to each other, amid many bales and boxes of goods. Among all these items was an assortment of national flags, since this was an illegal voyage and the captain might need to claim various identities, depending on who challenged him. There also were dozens of knives and machetes.[6]

The *Amistad* was a fast ship once it found good wind, but the challenge emerged quickly on the second night out, and it came from below after a mighty rainstorm. As the winds subsided and the sounds of the creaking masts were again audible, the small crew was asleep on June 30. One of the Africans, Cinqué, found a nail with which he and others managed to pick the padlock of the neck chains. With cane machetes and other iron weapons they seized, the former warriors among the captives rose out of the hold and attacked first Celestino, the cook, killing him in the small boat where he slept. A considerable fight followed, with Ferrer ordering Ruiz and Montes to attack the Africans. Eventually, the captain was killed in the struggle. The two crewmen seem to have leapt overboard and swum for it, likely dying in their desperation. Ruiz and Montes were both attacked and wounded, but some among the rebels cautioned Cinqué that they needed someone to sail and steer the ship in their quest to turn it toward the rising sun and return to Sierra Leone. Much older than Ruiz, bloodied and in shock, Montes had previously been a ship captain; he was forced to take the helm.[7] What ensued was a meandering two-month, deceptive, and deadly journey up the coast of North America.

The African rebels washed and cleaned the blood-stained deck, carried Montes up to the forecastle, nursed him to strength, and ordered him to chart an

Death of Capt. Ferrer, the Captain of the Amistad, July, 1839, John Warner Barber. Yale University Art Gallery.

eastern course. The captives had to rely on an untrustworthy captain, never fully sure if Montes was steering them back to Cuba and to slavery. They wished to return home to Sierra Leone, but eventually they agreed to head to the United States. Running out of water and food—ten captives died at sea—the wounded ship with tattered sails and its sickened passengers continued northward. After 1,400 miles and eight weeks, following the Gulf Stream up the coast, Cinqué and his companions spied the Montauk Point Lighthouse at the far eastern extension of Long Island in late August. Four or five men went ashore in a boat and encountered a group of White men. They learned that this was not "slavery country," and that there were no Spanish on the land. At Culloden Point they parlayed with three men who had been sea captains and were out hunting, one of whom, Henry Green, quickly began to try to claim the *Amistad* as a prize ship for his financial benefit. Cinqué did not allow the captain to come on board the schooner, although they learned even more about their location in a "free country" called America. Soon a U.S. naval survey ship, the USS *Washington*, appeared on the horizon of the Long Island Sound and brought the *Amistad* and its rebels to the New London Harbor.[8]

News spread rapidly throughout New England and down to New York about the "ghost ship" with its suffering group of Africans, many in bad condition. Huge crowds gathered in the harbor to get glimpses of a spectacle blown in from the sea. A correspondent of the *New York Sun* also joined the onlookers on board the *Washington* for the initial interrogations, with U.S. District Court judge

Andrew T. Judson presiding. Cinqué stood at the hearing in manacles, with a cord tied around his neck. He was quickly portrayed as a romantic, heroic leader. The *Sun* exploited the story immediately; a lithograph drawing of Cinqué was published as early as August 31 and prints offered for sale. The newspaper's long article, "The Long, Low Black Schooner," parts of which were reprinted as far away as Charleston, South Carolina, portrayed the Mende leader as a "son of an African chief" and "one of those spirits which appear but seldom."[9] Here first emerged the endless depictions, for numerous racial, legal, and political purposes, of Cinqué as exotic; as a benevolent killer; as a noble, natural leader; and even as a dangerous if praiseworthy pirate. Heroic stories of the often lawless sea were wildly popular in this age of sail.

Immediately, numerous legal questions arose about just who and what the *Amistad* Africans were. Were they slaves and murderers, and the property of their Cuban owners, or were they free people exercising their natural rights to liberty and the right of revolution? Were they Spanish property, seized on the high seas by the United States in violation of Pinckney's Treaty of 1795? Would this ship's story and the fate of its passengers grow into an international crisis between the United States and Spain that might itself stoke the flames of the slavery issue in American politics? And as abolitionists quickly seized on the *Amistad* survivors' legal case, if a Northern state like Connecticut could "free" captive Africans, what might it mean for enslaved African Americans in the South?

On September 1, 1839, the *Amistad* captives, except for Cinqué, were taken on a sloop to New Haven and housed in six separate rooms in the county jail on Church Street, on the town green, where city hall is located today. Cinqué was kept in forced isolation to prevent the charismatic leader from inciting any further rebellion. Many of the others were still sick or injured; some began to recover as they became local incarcerated celebrities, while others never recovered and died in an infirmary. Six men who died between September and December—Fa, Tua, Weluwa, Kapeli, Yammoni, and Kaba—were buried in Grove Street Cemetery near the Yale campus. The four children were housed in their own room, although the New Haven jailer, Stanton Pendleton, a brutal and abusive man, took the three girls into his own home as domestic servants. In their continuing fear and bewilderment, the Africans expected they would soon be executed and struggled to gather by windows to find air.[10]

In the first two weeks that the *Amistad* Africans occupied the New Haven jail, huge crowds flocked to the town to gawk at them. As estimated four thousand visitors from all over the northeast paid a "York shilling" (twelve and a half cents) to see the prisoners. Pendleton took in approximately $500 in these first days, profiting from what historian Marcus Rediker calls the "carnival curiosity" of the scene. And according to another historian of the event, Joseph Yannielli, a "lurid peep show" had been opened in downtown New Haven and the populace flocked to the late-summer entertainment. The Africans slept on straw, desperately wished for privacy, and stared back at the ladies dressed in finery and other tourists. Some visitors, though, were abolitionists seeking to defend and aid the captives, to tell their story and liberate them. They were led by Lewis Tappan and a team of lawyers and activists who constituted themselves "the Amistad Committee," which eventually included the Yale College and theology school graduate Joshua Leavitt, editor of the antislavery *Emancipator*; the lawyer Roger Sherman Baldwin; and a variety of other Yale luminaries such as linguist Josiah Willard Gibbs, physicist and astronomer Denison Olmsted, and the longtime New Haven minister and Yale graduate Leonard Bacon. Even the famous scientist and Yale professor Benjamin Silliman visited and took a keen interest in the *Amistad* captives.[11]

Among the visitors to the jail was a seventeen-year-old New Haven resident, William H. Townsend, who sketched extraordinary portraits of twenty-two of the captives. The portraits are both frontal and in profile. Townsend did not draw Cinqué, possibly because he was housed separately. But he sketched Grabeau and Kimbo, two leaders of the rebellion, as well as two of the children, including Margru, the lone girl, and an especially unforgettable profile of Kale in his stocking hat. On some of the sketches Townsend wrote their names, such as "Little Kale." The intimacy of these images, their power, and their originality are like nothing else in the documentation of the Atlantic slave trade or of the abolition movement itself. They are quite small, ranging from four inches square to as large as five by seven inches. Townsend's sketches are among the collections of the Beinecke Rare Book and Manuscript Library at Yale, centerpieces of this deeply documented episode in the history of self-emancipation and antislavery in America.[12]

Other unsung heroes of the case made the abolitionist cause viable and effective. As soon as the *Amistad* arrived in New London Harbor, a local grocer of antislavery sentiments who knew the maritime situation well, Dwight Janes, went aboard the *Washington*, took detailed notes, and, in a series of letters, laid out a strategy to follow without delay. He stressed the need to find translators and legal representation. Janes declared the *Amistad* survivors "Citizens of Africa," illegal slaves from the first day of their horrible experience, and he saw a golden opportunity for American abolitionists to strike blows for freedom before the nation. This is exactly what Tappan, Baldwin, and others immediately

Sketches of Margru and Kale. Beinecke Rare Book and Manuscript Library, Yale University.

undertook to do. But language presented a major barrier, which is where James Ferry, a Kissi man from West Africa who spoke Vai, a language of the Gallinas region, came in. The roughly thirty-year-old Ferry had been kidnapped as a boy, survived the Middle Passage to South America, and, by a largely unknown saga, ended up in New Haven. He could communicate with Bau, one of the captives, who also spoke Vai, and it was in this circumstance that the captives were able to provide, in their own language, the first full description of their ordeal. Soon thereafter, Professor Gibbs went to New York, having learned how to count in Mende, and there along the docks he found yet other interpreters, two African sailors, James Covey and Charles Pratt, who worked aboard the British brig the *Buzzard*, an anti–slave trade patrol ship. Covey in particular played a vital role; he was both Kono and Kissi but grew up in Mende country and spoke the language. With intense commitment to the case, Gibbs brought Covey to the jail in New Haven, and the *Amistad* captives were jubilant to hear and engage in their own tongue. Soon Gibbs had Yale students come to the jail and help in English language instruction for the captives.[13]

The African translators Covey and Pratt were crucial now to the abolitionists' preparation of the case; their translations made possible the reconstruction of the facts of the story, and indeed the legal status of the rebels captured off Long Island. Their assistance led to lawsuits filed against Montes and Ruiz as well as suits on behalf of all the *Amistad* Africans. By September 14, many of the captives were transported north to Hartford for their first of several trials. Slavery was legal in Cuba, but the *Amistad* Africans had been kidnapped into the illegal Atlantic slave trade, and their sale and transport along the coast of Cuba was, therefore, illegal, according to their American defenders. Led by Roger Sherman Baldwin, one of the few prominent White New Haveners who had supported the Black college in 1831, the abolitionists built their strategy on aggressive publicity—keeping the case before the public's attention—and on the natural rights tradition. They filed in the Hartford court for a writ of habeas corpus, freeing the Africans, arguing that they were not slaves when taken into custody on New York soil. "All beings, who have the form of our nature, are free," said Baldwin in court. "It is only when men come here with a black skin, that we look upon them in a condition in which they may by any means be made slaves. But, when we find them here from the coast of Africa, the same rule must apply to the black as to the white man." On this basis, from start to finish a year and a half later, the case for freedom was made not on Spanish or U.S. law but, as Baldwin declared, on "the laws of nature." On the other side of the aisle, Yale graduates Ralph Ingersoll—instrumental in the defeat of the Black college a handful of years earlier—and William Hungerford represented Ruiz and Montes, arguing the *Amistad* captives were the enslaved property of their clients and not entitled to a writ of habeas corpus, according to the laws of the United States.[14]

Numerous other legal issues and lawsuits were yet to be adjudicated. Quickly, in Washington, DC, President Martin Van Buren, a Jacksonian Democrat beholden to proslavery interests, and Secretary of State John Forsyth, himself a slaveholder, took serious notice of the international implications of the case. The administration saw that the legal outcomes for the *Amistad* Africans might cause a dangerous rift in U.S.-Spanish relations, as well as potential consequences for American slavery. If these people could sue in U.S. courts for their freedom, what about those enslaved in America? The Spanish minister in Washington, Pedro Alcantara de Argaiz, had already demanded the return of the *Amistad* and all its cargo as "property" under a treaty of 1795. Forsyth hoped for a quick court decision declaring the captives "slaves" so he could comply with the Spanish demand and usher the story out of the news.[15]

But this was no ordinary case. Judge Smith Thompson ruled on September 23, in a packed courtroom, that he would not release the Africans or offer bail. He declared his personal "feelings" against slavery but claimed, in a move of legal avoidance, that the "LIBERTY" of the captives was not the issue before the court. He did dismiss the charges of mutiny, murder, and piracy against the Africans, but remanded the case back to a federal district court for future consideration. The captives would remain in the New Haven jail and be permitted visitors, teachers giving language and religious instruction, and exercise on the Green. The case did not return to court until November, and during the two ensuing months, the *Amistad* captives became an obsession of both the abolitionist and proslavery, racist press. Cinqué was the object of rumors and caricatures, a kind of blank canvas on which all could imagine either the noble warrior-chieftain or the murderous heathen who had himself, allegedly, been a slave trader. A proslavery New York paper, the *Morning Herald*, ran stories and an engraving of Cinqué in jail kissing the White child of a visitor, with other Africans leaping and somersaulting in the background. Meanwhile, Ruiz and Montes told their stories in Spanish, translated into English and published in October in the *New Haven Daily Palladium*. New Haven artist John Warner Barber serialized sketches and capsule biographies of the *Amistad* Africans in the *New Haven Daily Herald*. Abolitionists, aided by Yale students, wrote letters for many of the captives, humanizing them, making their identities known, and allowing them to skewer the jailer, Pendleton, for his brutality and racism. And George E. Day, a teacher at Yale as well as at the New York Institution for the Deaf and Dumb, came to the New Haven jail, established some manner of sign communication, and then wrote two long published letters that developed the Africans' stories with sympathy and sentimentalism.[16] In the court of public opinion, the *Amistad* people were winning, and that fact greatly concerned the Van Buren administration, which sought to keep this story out of national politics before the president's run for reelection in 1840. That desperate mystery ship had now plunged into American politics.

Back in court in November, this time before district judge Andrew T. Judson, an avowed anti-abolitionist, the captives' case faced long odds. The history of racism in early America, the surging spirit of colonization, and the lack of clear law about the rights of citizenship all augured badly for the captives. Moreover, in 1833 the state assembly had passed the Connecticut Black Law, which explicitly denied residents of the state the right to "set up any school, academy, or literary institution for the instruction or education of colored persons who are not inhabitants of this state." That law had been prompted by the proposal in 1831 for a Black college in New Haven and the case of Prudence Crandall, the young White woman who opened her school to Black girls and set off a firestorm. Leading the effort to convict Crandall had been none other than Judson, Canterbury politician and member of the American Colonization Society. In his arguments in the Crandall trial in 1833, he had declared the United States a "nation of *white men*" and claimed the young teacher's "*professed object*" had been the "universal amalgamation of the two races."[17]

By the time the *Amistad* captives came to trial in 1839, Judson was a federal district judge. In the proceedings in November, he made the work of Baldwin and defense attorneys difficult; he did not at first look kindly on their request for a delay so they could have their chief translator, James Covey, testify in order to establish that the *Amistad* rebels were all native-born Africans and not Cuban slaves. Covey had fallen ill, however, and could not travel to Hartford, so the judge reluctantly granted a postponement and resumption of the trial in January in New Haven. Judson, too, had political ambitions, and he may have sensed the winds of public admiration for the imprisoned Africans.[18]

By January 7, 1840, when the trial resumed in New Haven, the Van Buren administration had become intensely engaged. It sought to keep the *Amistad* case from affecting American politics, especially in the South, where Van Buren's Democratic Party needed to fully protect slavery. Argaiz, the Spanish minister in Washington, DC, had protested vehemently from the beginning that the United States must return the *Amistad* captives as "slaves" to Cuba. But now, in early 1840, he called the rebels "assassins" and threatened a major breakdown in U.S.-Spanish relations. Anticipating a judgment from the court that the captives would be returned to Cuba, the Van Buren White House overstepped the lines of checks and balances between executive and judicial authority by sending an American naval ship, the USS *Grampus*, to New Haven Harbor in readiness to spirit the prisoners away southward the moment the trial ended, thwarting, they hoped, any abolitionists' attempts to violently free them.[19] Van Buren and Forsyth were perfectly willing to violate due process and constitutional ethics to prevent this case from affecting both the laws and the politics of slavery.

After Covey and Pratt, the two African translators, and Professor Gibbs testified about the origins and language of the captives, Judson declared himself "fully convinced that the men were recently from Africa and it was idle to deny it." This claim itself made it clear that the trial would not be fixed by political allegiance and racism alone. Then, in a hushed and overcrowded courtroom, Cinqué took the stand and told his story of capture and sale and his ordeal during the Middle Passage across the Atlantic to Havana. Cinqué further described, through Covey as interpreter, how Ruiz had physically inspected their bodies before their purchase at the Havana barracoon, as well as the brutal treatments aboard the *Amistad*. He also recounted the captives' arrival on the Long Island shore. Later the same day, two other *Amistad* captives, Grabeau and Fuliwa, told of their seizures and enslavement in Africa. Defense attorneys for the Spaniards tried to counter with witnesses who claimed to have heard contrary statements by the Africans at the jail. So Baldwin brought in Yale professor George Day, who attended many of the interrogations and denounced the defense witnesses.[20]

After a week, the trial ended on January 13, as Judson announced the *Amistad* Africans "not slaves" because they had been "born free" under Spanish law. He dismissed the murder charge since they had rebelled out of "desire of winning their liberty," thereby acknowledging their right of revolution. Judson then freed the captives not into American society by U.S. law but to the custody of the president of the United States, who would arrange for their return to Africa. The judge hoped to give Van Buren a way to save face, end the crisis, and come out on high ground.[21] The abolitionists were delighted thus far but had not fully won the case. Judson's decision had no effect on the issue of Black people and citizenship; it did not test the legality of American slavery. The Van Buren administration quickly appealed the case to the Supreme Court.

The decision, however, was momentous for the *Amistad* survivors. Throughout the rest of 1840 and into 1841, the *Amistad* captives remained in New Haven, but most were moved from the downtown jail to Westville, some three miles away and in a more open, and it was hoped, healthier setting. In their continued imprisonment, many of the Africans continued their zealous study of the English language and of the Christian religion. Bonding together several ethnicities in their collective travail, the captives increasingly referred to themselves as the "Mendi People." As historian Marcus Rediker has observed, this identity was an American creation, as well as a collective invention by the Africans themselves. The "Mendi People" was a multiethnic label, combining at least Mende, Temne, Kono, Gbandi, Loma, and Gola people into one category. Willing teachers, including those from Yale, stepped forward to help. Everyone who worked with the *Amistad* captives in jail and beyond raved about their zeal for education, language, and human connections. They took especially to maps, almanacs, grammar books, and the Bible. For days on end, the *Amistad* captives sat in groups with books and slates and practiced their English. Cinqué, Kinna, and Fuli were often leaders of these study sessions, and the best pupils were the youngest, especially Kale. In their own letters, many of the Africans clearly felt the need not only to describe their conditions but to make appeals to be returned to their home continent, as Cinqué did on behalf of the group. They also seemed compelled to defend themselves against the various accusations they had endured. "Mendi people," contended Kinna, "no lie, not steal, no swear, no drink rum, no fight." And Kale, one of the young boys, complained with a sense of humor. "Some people say Mendi people crazy dolts," he wrote, "because we no talk American language. Americans no talk Mendi. American people crazy dolts?"[22]

As the star student at eleven years old, Kale embraced English and Bible reading with a child's delight. He wrote a letter directly to John Quincy Adams as the Supreme Court case underwent preparation. "Dear friend," wrote Kale to the former president of the United States, "We want you to ask the Court what we have done wrong. What for Americans keep us in prison." Kale's youthful logic and emotional appeal affected Adams. The boy demanded, "We want you to tell court that Mendi people no want to go back to Havana, we no want to be killed. . . . All we want is make us free, not send us to Havana." Kale recited details of the rebellion on the ship and of their long incarceration. He stressed the Africans' joy in their studies: "We love books very much." Kale recited the Golden Rule from the book of Matthew and gave a child's unforgettable definition of natural rights to the former president: "Dear friend Mr. Adams, you have children, you have friends, you love them, you feel very sorry if Mendi people come and take all to Africa."[23]

Now two years into their epic ordeal, the *Amistad* Africans were caught between the international interests of two governments and an American judicial system they could not trust. But their abolitionist defenders remained steadfast in their cause. Ample evidence shows that Tappan and some on the Amistad Committee seriously considered a violent jailbreak, or some sort of extralegal effort to free the captives, if the Supreme Court decision sent them back into slavery in Cuba.[24] The defense team fully expected even further White House interference in the case as it moved to the drama of argument. The case was first heard by the Supreme Court on January 25, 1841. None of the captives were allowed to attend in Washington, but spectators gathered at the U.S. Capitol to observe the *Amistad* case. In an ornate chamber on the first floor of the Capitol, the justices sat on a high bench. Lawyers and their associates sat or stood at tables in the middle of the room; members of the public and press gathered in a horseshoe gallery space around the exterior; senators such as Henry Clay attended. The *Amistad* rebels, according to the U.S. administration's argument, were "pirates or robbers on the high seas" and therefore "enemies of all mankind." To support the contention that the *Amistad* Africans were "slaves" and "property," Attorney General Henry D. Gilpin cited resolutions sponsored in 1840 by John C. Calhoun, and passed unanimously by the U.S. Senate, declaring that slaves, though freed as people, still remained enslaved if the country in which their owner resided condoned slavery.[25] In this now internationally famous case, the full force of the United States was marshaled in defense of slavery.

Roger Sherman Baldwin spoke first for the Africans' position, declaring that Ruiz, Montes, and the shipowner Captain Ferrer, not the rebels, were the true "pirates." The captives aboard the *Amistad* had a perfect right to "revolt" and seek "their deliverance from slavery, on the high seas." They were indeed the "victims of piracy," not their Cuban and Spanish enslavers. Baldwin also made the key claim that if the court ruled in favor of the Spaniards, it meant that the U.S. government would have to "re-enslave" the Africans "for the benefit of Spanish negro-dealers." He invoked James Madison in the original debates over the Constitution, condemning "*property in men*." Baldwin also condemned the repeated presidential intrusion into the case, thus forcing the other side into a dual constitutional quandary: an illegal federal enslavement of foreigners in an Atlantic world where the slave trade had been outlawed, and executive misuse of power to satisfy domestic political ends as well as diplomatic relations with Spain, a nation still clinging to empire and sugar-based slavery in Cuba.[26] If the justices were listening, Baldwin had shoved the government into an uncomfortable legal corner.

Adams followed Baldwin's brilliant presentation with his own playful and astute performance of more than seven hours over two separate days. He attacked the "absurdity" of the other side, saying that the government's argument would make the Africans as human beings into both "robbers" and "merchandise." Adams pointed vividly to a copy of the Declaration of Independence on a courtroom pillar and used its language to assert, "I know of no other law that reaches the case of my clients, but the law of Nature, and of Nature's God on which our fathers placed our own national existence." The former president called for "JUSTICE" and accused the Van Buren administration (now a lame duck) of unconstitutional misuse of executive power. Adams thus illuminated how the *Amistad* story had been infused with sectional, international, and racial politics from the beginning. But the abolitionists, the Amistad Committee, and all their allies greatly feared that neither legal logic nor moral arguments would carry the day before this proslavery court, presided over by Chief Justice Roger Taney, a Maryland slaveholder. The Africans themselves, back in Westville on the edge of New Haven, waited in agony for news as they underwent considerable humiliation and bad treatment in the jail.[27]

On March 9, Justice Joseph Story of Massachusetts rose in the court chamber and announced the ruling, a vote of seven to one to deny all the Spaniards' claims, free the *Amistad* captives, and asserted their *legal*, if not their natural, rights. Story, who was antislavery but contemptuous of abolitionists, wrote for the majority that the *Amistad* captives were free-born, were illegally enslaved even under Spanish law, and had struck for freedom by the right of "self-defense." Story's opinion adhered carefully to the law and did not acknowledge Baldwin's or Adams's arguments about any moral dimensions of natural liberty. The ruling also did not touch any of the claims made about the Van Buren administration's political or constitutional malfeasance. Morally, as historian Howard Jones remarks, the *Amistad* decision was a "Pyrrhic victory," since it clung to the notion that the slavery question only hinged on positive law, not natural law.[28] The Supreme Court, therefore, made certain that this decision would in no way threaten American slavery where it was lawful. The abolitionists who had spent more than a year and a half fighting for the captives celebrated for the moment; they had won the Africans' freedom and their liberty to return to Africa if they chose, but they had not won a victory over any legal underpinnings of slavery in their own country.

The years of the *Amistad* controversy, 1839–41, were full of ferment for the American antislavery movement. All manner of anti-abolition violence and resistance had erupted during the 1830s. William Lloyd Garrison had been dragged through the streets of Boston and nearly killed by a mob in 1835, and the New England–born abolitionist editor Elijah Lovejoy had been assassinated, his printing press destroyed, by proslavery riflemen and arsonists in Alton, Illinois, in 1837. By the same token, Frederick Douglass had escaped from slavery on Maryland's Eastern Shore in 1838 and was living and working in New Bedford, Massachusetts, when the schooner *Amistad* came ashore on Long Island a year later; he would deliver his first major public abolitionist speech on Nantucket in August 1841, as the liberated African captives toured to raise money for their return to Sierra Leone. Moreover, on November 7, 1841, Madison Washington, a slave from Virginia, led a revolt aboard a brig, the *Creole*, sailing toward the slave markets of New Orleans and commandeered the ship to Nassau and British custody. The slaves' eventual liberation by an admiralty court in the Bahamas, and Washington's heroic leadership, was later immortalized in a novella by Douglass as well as in other works of poetry and art. The Colored Convention movement, begun at the beginning of the previous decade, and which led directly to efforts for the Black college in New Haven, picked up steam again by the 1840s.[29]

By 1840, the antislavery movement had reached one of its crossroads. Schisms emerged between evangelical abolitionists, led by the Tappans in New York, and Garrison, whose Boston organization demanded strict adherence to a kind of religious perfectionism, aggressive nonpolitical action, pacifism, women's rights, and strict moral suasion. Radicals on both sides of these debates had more in common than these disputes sometimes implied, and they both drew the allegiances of Black abolitionists such as Henry Highland Garnet, James W. C. Pennington, Douglass, Sojourner Truth, and many others, especially former fugitive slaves, who tended to prefer a pragmatic radicalism that brought the greatest possible pressure on slavery and advanced free Black rights in the North. At the 1840 annual meeting of the American Antislavery Society, attended by more than a thousand delegates in New York, warring factions divided, with a strong minority joining Amistad Committee leader Lewis Tappan's newly formed American and Foreign Antislavery Society.[30]

The biggest shift, though, was prompted by a new political organization, the Liberty Party, born in the midst of the *Amistad* events in 1840 and a project intended to challenge the hegemony of the Democrats and Whigs in national and local Northern politics. The Liberty Party, led by Gerrit Smith, a wealthy upstate New Yorker; James G. Birney, a former Alabama slaveholder who experienced a transformation and moved north; and Joshua Leavitt, the Yale-educated minister, editor, and *Amistad* activist, sought legitimate abolitionist alternatives in electoral politics. They hoped at least to affect the balance of power between the two mainstream parties in key states like Massachusetts, New York, and Ohio. Some Liberty men, as they were known, adopted an antislavery interpretation of the Constitution, especially as they read works by the radical theorists Lysander Spooner and William Goodell.[31]

Despite its sensational publicity and duration, the *Amistad* case had little if any constitutional traction in the abolition movement over the following twenty turbulent years down to the Civil War. The crisis over slavery descended into secession and war in 1861, with almost no mention of the *Amistad* except as a marker of how a "Slave Power" in the United States had grown in influence and dominance, despite the legal liberation of thirty-five West Africans in 1841. The story has echoed in New Haven, at Yale, and beyond for more than 180 years. A prominent monument to its memory, with a quotation from Kale as part of the inscription ("Make Us Free"), sits proudly in front of the New Haven City Hall overlooking the Green today.[32]

And its legacy runs deeper: at least some among the early nineteenth-century graduates of Yale emerged as abolitionists, determined to fight and destroy slavery under law. In this sense the *Amistad* story inspired its veterans as it also educated them about the long and winding road ahead to emancipation; they were learning that the cause might demand reform and revolution. Cinqué and his comrades helped teach them that.

The *Amistad* Africans spent twenty-seven months in the United States, nineteen of them in jail. When the legal case finally ended, the only crimes committed were against them. After the verdict, they were wary of the decision; too many disappointments and betrayals, in court and otherwise, had made them cautious freemen. Shortly after the news reached Westville, Cinqué asked Kale to read aloud a newspaper account as the group gathered around. Soon they realized they were truly free and had to decide where to go. By late March, the group moved to Farmington, Connecticut, near Hartford, in the hope of escaping the constant gaze of journalists, tourists, and demanding well-wishers. While in Farmington, some of them worked on a fifteen-acre farm nearby, operated by an abolitionist, John Treadwell Norton.[33]

The return to Sierra Leone they had dreamed of for so long required money and planning. To raise funds, the Amistad Committee drew on antislavery networks to organize a series of tours for the rebels. In the late spring of 1841, they performed eight times in New York and Philadelphia; during a second, more extensive tour later in summer, they appeared sixteen times all over New England. Just as they had seized their own freedom on board the *Amistad*, so the former captives labored, on the road and onstage, to earn the money they needed to return home. Although supported by many allies and friends, their journey of self-emancipation continued. The Africans recited Bible verses, sang hymns, and some told their personal and collective stories, sometimes in English, often in their native languages with Tappan, Booth, or another American supporter offering some form of translation. Huge crowds turned out and paid twenty-five cents each at churches or in grand halls such as the Broadway Tabernacle in New York City. The famous former prisoners would march onto a stage, carrying copies of the Bible and dressed well in American clothing. This was abolitionist celebrity beyond anything seen before. The young Kale, Kinna, and Fuli were the best English speakers, and they were the stars of these shows. But Cinqué was almost always the final act and his appearance the moment everyone awaited. In Mende he would tell of his background and then act out scenes from the rebellion and its aftermath in what some described as captivating sermons or dazzling theater. Kinna would often provide a translation, but the language differences did not seem to matter to mesmerized American audiences.[34]

Cinqué did not disappoint the audiences, although he and others at times objected to the circus nature of their display as African revolutionaries transformed into Christian students delivering recitals. The Africans sang songs, both Christian hymns and some of their native songs. Cinqué's performances were often characterized as "perfectly electrifying," his presence as that of a "master spirit." Lydia Maria Child, who later introduced and brought to publication Harriet Jacobs's famous slave narrative, *Incidents in the Life of a Slave Girl*, attended the final Broadway Tabernacle event and came away impressed at the intelligence of Kinna in particular. Newspapers called Cinqué "the great man of the evening." Audiences often stood and wept or offered raucous cheers as they gave money not only for a voyage to Africa but for the creation of a "Mendi Mission" in Sierra Leone, an outpost for Christian education and conversion planned by the Amistad Committee.[35]

Black churches and relief organizations also plunged full force into helping the *Amistad* veterans in their quest to return home. Even while the *Amistad* case wound through the courts, James W. C. Pennington, who escaped slavery on Maryland's Eastern Shore in 1827 and became a distinguished Congregational minister at the Talcott Street Church in Hartford, led fundraising campaigns to promote the captives' return to Sierra Leone. Pennington was the first African American known to attend Yale; denied formal admission on account of his race, he was allowed to audit classes at the divinity school from 1834 to 1837. The Reverend Jehiel C. Beman, father of New Haven's Amos Beman and himself a prominent Black abolitionist, hosted a jam-packed fundraiser for the *Amistad* heroes at the African Methodist Episcopal Zion Church in Boston. The "Mende Exhibition" even played at the cotton mills in Lowell, Massachusetts, where they raised a remarkable $58.50 from workers there. And the New York African Society for Mutual Relief raised money and passed a series of resolutions, largely written by James McCune Smith, the Glasgow-trained Black physician, essayist, and scientist. Smith delivered a robust assertion of natural rights, declaring that the *Amistad* rebels had exercised a "natural resistance against tyrannical oppression." The *Amistad* rebellion and success in achieving freedom before the Supreme Court was nothing less than "the faint glimmering of a more auspicious morn, which will usher in that bright and glorious day" when men in high places in America will "declare that property in man cannot be held, whither by inheritance, purchase, or theft."[36] These ringing words about natural rights followed the *Amistad* veterans everywhere they traveled on their pecuniary quest to gain the means to achieve something far more important than their fame: the return home.

By late 1841, the wait had become a torment for some of the former prisoners. They tired of performing on tours; some fell into despair and believed they would never see their parents or families again. The ravages of this ordeal were too much for Foone, a short but strong, athletic, and much-admired member of the Mendi group. Foone went to the Farmington River ostensibly to swim but, by all accounts, drowned himself. His death devastated the collective spirit of the Mendi community, and the horrible incident forced the Amistad Committee to speed up preparations for a return voyage. Finally, on November 27, 1841, thirty-five surviving *Amistad* rebels, along with five missionaries hoping to create the Mendi Mission, boarded a ship, the *Gentleman*, in New York Harbor.[37]

The return voyage of the *Amistad* veterans was a highly unusual event: survivors of a "successful" slave insurrection sailed back to Sierra Leone. But when they arrived, their homecomings were anything but simple. Most shed their Western clothes, to the chagrin of the missionaries of the Mendi Mission. Many returned to Mende territory; some rejoined their parents and other family members in emotional reunions. They soon found themselves back in an African society ravaged by war and slave trading. The ordeal experienced by the "Mendi people" remains a story of tragedy and transcendence, of loss and some forms of renewal, of an African and an American crucible full of what Frederick Douglass called "sacrilegious irony."[38]

The ultimate fate of Cinqué, forever famous in images and words in American textbooks, on the streets of New Haven, and in the annals of antislavery heroism, is not precisely known. During the recrossing, he wrote to Tappan with a certain calm joy, "Captain good—no touch Mendi People."[39] After so much brutality, agony, loneliness, and fear, a peaceful voyage at sea must have felt like a special blessing, well earned. Gratefully, they had good food and plenty of water as they weighed their memories and sailed home.

CHAPTER 8

Antebellum Yale and Its Abolitionist Discontents

[Moderates] are politic men—they are cautious men—they are accommodating men; and they cherish a sacred horror of fanaticism, and do not like irritation, and love to sail beneath a cloudless sky upon an unruffled stream.

—WILLIAM LLOYD GARRISON, *Liberator*, January 17, 1835

The Reverend James W. C. Pennington, a former slave, possessed a passion for education as much as the religious faith in his life. He sought mentors and tutors wherever he roamed, including into lecture halls at Yale College's divinity school as an auditor. He would become a prominent religious leader, pastoring two famous churches for many years, as well as a key activist on behalf of the *Amistad* captives and the Black convention movement across the North. He also later traveled to England twice to attend abolitionist conventions and to do missionary work. Born James Pembroke in Queen Anne's County on Maryland's Eastern Shore in approximately 1807, Pennington escaped from slavery in 1827 through Pennsylvania, where he received the protection and friendship of White Quakers. He changed his name and spent some twenty-four years as a fugitive slave living in Northern communities such as New Haven, Hartford, and New York. While still living at risk himself as a fugitive in 1838, he officiated in the marriage of two other Eastern Shore people, another escaped slave and his fugitive free Black wife, Frederick Bailey and Anna Murray. The couple soon changed their name to Douglass.[1]

Pennington earned an international reputation as an abolitionist and the author of two books, including a first attempt to tell the story of Black people's history, culture, and achievements, *A Text Book of the Origin and History, &c. &c. of the Colored People*, published in 1841. But in the preface to his classic autobiography, *The Fugitive Blacksmith: Or, Events in the History of James W. C. Pennington*, he told a different, unforgettable story, exploiting the irony of slaveholders and their Northern defenders who repeatedly argued that many bondspeople lived and were "reared in the mildest form of slavery." Pennington wrote, "In the month of September 1848, there appeared in my study, one morning, in New York City, an aged coloured man of tall and slender form." He had "anxiety bordering on despair" on his face. The old man also hailed from Maryland, like Pennington. He laid out a batch of letters in front of the minister. The letters demonstrated that the desperate man had two daughters, age fourteen and sixteen, who were about to be sold South. Their slaveholder demanded large sums of money from their father to prevent the sale.[2] Pennington knew a great abolitionist story when he encountered one.

The Reverend James W. C. Pennington, 1848.
National Portrait Gallery, Smithsonian Institution.

On the following Sabbath, Pennington "threw the case before my people" (his congregation). They and other churches managed to raise some $2,250 to purchase the two girls' freedom. Pennington did not miss the opportunity to employ this story for antislavery propaganda against the "chattel principle," the idea that there can be property in humans. He made it clear that Black people were fed up with the notion of "property vested in their persons," and that they might have to purchase their own natural liberty. By the time he wrote his autobiography in 1849, Pennington declared on behalf of his fellow free Black people in Connecticut that they were also fed up with a certain kind of moderate, paternalistic racism. He was grateful for his Yale educational opening in the 1830s but wrote nonetheless, "I beg our Anglo-Saxon brethren to accustom themselves to think that we need something more than mere kindness. We ask for justice, truth, and honour as other men do."[3]

Pennington's experience in Yale classrooms provides a marker in the university's history, now commemorated with a portrait and a room named for him at the divinity school. But it also represents a historical moment—one that followed from the failure, in 1831, to establish a Black college in New Haven. From the fall of 1834 into at least the summer of 1836, Pennington attended theology lectures by professors Nathaniel William Taylor and Josiah Willard Gibbs. Both were among the four original faculty of the Yale Theological Department. Pennington later called this period his "visitorship," since he was never officially admitted. "My voice was not to be heard in the classroom," Pennington wrote in an 1851 article, "asking or answering a question. I could not get a book from the library and my name was never to appear on the catalogue." He boarded in quarters given or rented to him by Simeon Jocelyn, who, though he had moved away from New Haven after the debacle of the Black college a few years earlier, still owned property in the city. Indeed, Jocelyn smoothed Pennington's transition to Yale and likely helped him get part-time work at the Temple Street Church, of which Jocelyn had been a founder. The former slave and now student who sought training in order to be formally ordained helped pastor the African American congregants at that church while studying at Yale.[4]

After his Yale studies, Pennington took to the newly founded Black newspaper, the *Colored American*, in the late 1830s to argue organizationally and ideologically for revival of the Colored Convention movement as a crusade for African American rights and community self-elevation. It was as if Pennington took in his theology education at Yale and then put some of the Gospels as well as lessons from the Hebrew prophets to work fighting both the stilted inaction of his teachers and the inertia of his own congregations. The newly ordained minister not only preached on Sundays but wrote many articles under the name "the Reflector." From 1838 to 1840, Pennington called for both regional conventions and a "national assembly" that would represent the race. He hoped to create the political arm of Black activism. "The Greeks, the Romans, the Cathagenians [*sic*], the Egyptians," he said, "and as many people of antiquity . . . have had their national councils." He judged the Black community to be weak because of its lack of national organization. They were "without a seat in any political body in the land, and also without any such body among ourselves." He aimed high, imagining representatives and branches "in every city, town, village, or place . . . to take the oversight" of everything from agriculture, education, and economic planning to political and cultural affairs. "Political talents," Pennington declared, "are always drawn out by being exercised. . . . Let us try it!"[5] American governments, local and national, which disfranchised and ignored Black people generally, might take notice; or so sang some prophets of this Black American dream in a proslavery country.

Pennington's experience was unusual but not entirely unique. Although there are no official records of Alexander Crummell's time at Yale, the future pan-Africanist attended classes at the theological school under similar circumstances as Pennington. Born in 1819 to free parents in New York, Crummell spent his youth moving about the northeastern United States in search of educational opportunities. By 1840, he was living in New Haven, where Harry Croswell, the longtime White rector of Trinity Church, recorded in his diary a "call from Crummell, a black man who is a candidate in the church, and is pursuing his studies in the Yale Theo. Sem." While in New Haven, Crummell was a speaker at meetings held in the homes of Black residents, as recorded in papers passed down by Alexander Du Bois, the grandfather of W. E. B. Du Bois and an organizer, with Crummell, of St. Luke's, the first Black Episcopal Church in Connecticut. After leaving Yale, Crummell was denied admission to the General Theological Seminary on account of racism, but he was later ordained a deacon and a priest in the Episcopal Church. He eventually made his way to England, where he was finally able to enroll for his undergraduate degree. Scholar, priest, missionary, educator, and organizer, Crummell is today considered the first Black graduate of Cambridge University.[6]

In the 1830s and 1840s, free African American communities in the North lived and labored against the headwinds of a kind of racial caste system that denied them most civil and political rights. And they built communities in the face of economic discrimination and hardship. Black laborers in New Haven struggled mightily to overcome an economy that welcomed them only as menial workers at meager wages, yet some fought to acquire trades as blacksmiths, in the maritime crafts, or as artisan carpenters and masons. When the carriage-making industry boomed in the Elm City by the 1840s, Black workers tended to be closed out by newly arriving Scotch, English, Welsh, and German immigrants. As in most other cities, Black men did manage to control a major portion of the profession of barbers, some of whom also performed as personal valets at Yale College for faculty and students.[7] Indeed, William Grimes worked as a barber and a servant-valet next to and on campus. As a church leader and a spokesman of his communities, Pennington's words reflect these travails. But they also reflect determination, a demand that America fulfill its creeds and open its hearts and minds. Pennington took both doctrine and morality out into the mean and unforgiving environment of antebellum, ruggedly capitalist Northern society.

One of the most prominent professors at the Yale theology school during Pennington and Crummell's time was Nathaniel William Taylor. A Calvinist and an Edwardsean, he nonetheless allowed sinning Christians to try to find their own ways to faith. He believed people could practice repentance and conversion, which turned a key part of Jonathan Edwards's legacy on its head and led to new forms of revivals. Taylor was extraordinarily learned, an imposing lecturer with a vast reputation, and staunchly conservative, and he no doubt had some influence on Pennington. The Black theology student would never become a radical militant, advocating foreign emigration or violent revolution, although he wrote with great passion about equal civil and political rights. Taylor lectured in a room, according to Roland Bainton, where the "windows rattled and heat was supplied only by a gaseous stove." In the mid-1830s, Yale still consisted only of the seven primary buildings of the "brick row" in what is today Old Campus. So Pennington walked the same routes and pulled open the same heavy doors as all other Yale students. He trod the same worn paths Jethro Luke had followed a century earlier around Connecticut Hall. He did not complain of any particular ill-treatment by the Yale students with whom he daily brushed elbows, but clearly wished for more from his shortened encounter with a Yale divinity education. Some of the faculty may have been open to antislavery impulses, but none ever seemed to have taken the former fugitive slave under a mentoring wing. And although he was active in various reform causes, Taylor much preferred preserving the social order over the strategies and ideas of abolitionists. Like most of his colleagues, he embraced colonization as the best ultimate solution to easing rather than solving race problems in America.[8] Amid this kind of conservatism, Pennington studied the Bible, learned something of homiletics, and observed the Congregationalist and Presbyterian approach to moral reform. In the process, he became an abolitionist despite his teachers at the school he could never call his alma mater.

Leading members of the Yale faculty and the city's ministerial elite stood with Taylor in support of colonization schemes. Taylor's colleagues and friends, Benjamin Silliman and Leonard Bacon, advocated for severe prescriptions even as colonization fell in and out of favor over time. In a published address in 1828, the Connecticut colonizationists painted a bleak, dystopian picture of Black people's capacities and their prospects in America. They contended that free African Americans were "degraded and miserable" and called them "aliens and outcasts." Nothing could be done to uplift or improve their lot, which loomed "dark and deep and hopeless." Even worse, the South's vast enslaved population represented danger. The colonizationists described the South as a "sleeping volcano . . . we hear its stifled murmurings from afar."[9] Hopefully Pennington did not read such words before trying to enter the Yale divinity school; they illuminate the environment Taylor and his colleagues fostered. They believed racial prejudice and proslavery law and practice to be so intractable and Black people so backward that only separation and removal were viable options in the America they sought to build. Into the 1850s, with their support for Black removal from the United States, these leading Yale thinkers—among them Pennington's professors—were the embodiment of an anti-abolition imagination.

Taylor thrived on what he called "disputations." He served as president of a student debating group called the Rhetorical Society, which met in the 1840s and 1850s regularly on Wednesday nights. In the fall of 1842, the society took up the following question on multiple occasions: "Does the greatest good of the greatest number justify the continuance of slavery at the South?" Taylor voted yes, while the students initially did not vote, but under pressure from Taylor to reach a decision, they concluded that they simply did not know. On other occasions between 1845 and 1852, the society took up such questions as the morality of helping slaves escape and the constitutionality of the Fugitive Slave Act. Taylor repeatedly went on record in support of slavery and against emancipation, as on October 15, 1851, when the gathering faced the question of whether slavery "on the whole" had been for the country "an evil." And on January 12, 1853, with "ladies present," and some nine months after publication of the novel *Uncle Tom's Cabin*, both Taylor and students judged the book not "a valid argument against Slavery." It is difficult to judge how much this debating society reflected the ideas of all Yale students, but the views of the university's most famed professor of theology were quite clear. Slavery was a system to be endured, tolerated, mollified, and even morally or historically justified. It was not until 1854, in the wake of a Kansas Nebraska rally in New Haven, that Taylor spoke out publicly against the continuation of slavery.[10]

Taylor achieved wide influence across American society with this "New Haven theology." He had studied personally under the rigid scholar and Yale president Timothy Dwight for four years, but now the old eighteenth-century Calvinist Congregationalism underwent a refashioning for an expanding, more populist White society eager for freewill revivals and more democratic economic success. Taylor trained an estimated 815 ministers who spread across New England and to the western states. One of his most famous protégés was Charles Grandison Finney, who, although not a Yale graduate, became one of the greatest revivalist preachers of the Second Great Awakening. Finney closely followed and greatly advanced Taylor's freewill doctrine but left the elder adviser far behind to become a radical abolitionist and later president of the antislavery Oberlin College in Ohio. Pennington met and collaborated with Finney, even sharing the podium with him in 1839. But unlike Finney, the majority of Yale ministers and scholars much preferred to understand slavery than to condemn it. To the extent that moderation can be aggressive, that is what Taylorism fostered. Pennington had to forge a Black Protestantism within and against this world of Yale's studied theological and social moderation about slavery and racism. On slavery, adherents of the New Haven theology operated with a genteel sensibility; its practitioners sought conciliation with the South, believing that any process toward abolition would require the consent of slaveholders. They found a moral and intellectual retreat in moderation and colonization. To Pennington and most Black communities, this social and religious philosophy was largely repulsive, since it changed nothing in their political or economic lives and stood contrary to the teachings of Christ.[11]

From the 1820s to the eve of the Civil War, a wide variety of Yale personalities and thinkers left marks on the country's struggles over slavery, Indian Removal policies, and abolition in its many forms. Although moderation and colonization dominated in the approach of Yale's faculty and numerous famous graduates, the overall story is richly complex and often contradictory. There is no better epitome of what we might call Yale moderation than Taylor's close friend, the charismatic Leonard Bacon. An 1820 Yale graduate and the longtime minister of the Center Church in New Haven, Bacon plowed deep the dominant colonizationist worldview preached at Yale and on the Green. A prolific preacher and writer, Bacon built a kind of wall of restraint and anti-abolitionism. He feared and despised radical immediatists, especially the Garrisonians. In 1834, he maintained that their doctrines caused a myriad of problems: "misapprehension, misrepresentation, confusion, wrath, denunciation, hatred, violence, tumults," and perhaps even "convulsion, bloodshed, and revolution." Above all, Bacon remained a steadfast colonizationist in the 1830s and 1840s, with a particularly keen interest in the fate of Liberia. No wonder that radicals attacked Bacon openly, including his New Haven friends like Simeon Jocelyn. In 1836, Bacon wrote to Jocelyn playing the victim, complaining of his fate caught "between the opposing fires of two furiously contending parties." And William Lloyd Garrison himself captured the character and meaning of men such as Bacon, at least from a radical's point of view. Such moderates on slavery, said Garrison, "are politic men—they are cautious men—they are accommodating men; and they cherish a sacred horror of fanaticism, and do not like irritation, and love to sail beneath a cloudless sky upon an unruffled stream."[12] One of Garrison's primary aims, as for those he influenced such as Frederick Douglass and many others, was to foment social irritation, to stir social discontent. Although Garrison may or may not have intended this comment for Yale's hierarchy of ecclesiastical and educational leadership in 1835, the very moment Pennington sat in theology classes, the description is fitting.

Bacon even lectured Southern slaveholders with a certain paternal righteousness. Yes, he was antislavery in his own studied ways. His was an earnest brand of conservative antislavery; he said he would never banish a slaveholder from the church, especially if he "conscientiously" cared for the "welfare" of his slaves. He further suggested that the "legal power" of slaveholders to their property was "not necessarily a crime," particularly if the enslaved were "properly instructed, especially in the things of their everlasting peace." But regarding the institution of slavery, Bacon admonished that a slaveholder "ought to declare himself, fearlessly, the enemy of slavery."[13] Such sentiments are hardly the kind of antislavery views that gained respect in abolitionist societies, nor among Black activists, nor certainly over time in the ever-changing reputations of abolitionists. And his aims were all but unreachable from his pulpit in New Haven. But Bacon had many readers and admirers in his own domain of the Center Church and in the Connecticut branch of the American Colonization Society. And for those looking for middle ground on the increasingly frightening slavery question, he stood out as a hero.

In the Bacon tradition of moderation on slavery also stood the important theologian Moses Stuart, a 1799 graduate of Yale. Another student of President Timothy Dwight's conservative theology, Stuart was ordained in 1806, and for the next four years he was the minister of the First Church on the Green in New Haven. From 1810 to 1848, he was professor of sacred literature at Andover Theological Seminary in Massachusetts. Stuart published one of the first grammars of Hebrew in the English language. More than one hundred of Stuart's students became missionaries all over the world, working in languages from Burmese to Hawaiian, Cherokee to Chinese. Most of his writings were close biblical exegesis, but he also made a mark as an apologist for slavery and a fierce opponent of abolitionists.[14]

In 1850, in the fevered aftermath of the passage of the Fugitive Slave Act as part of the congressional compromise of that year, Stuart wrote a major treatise of proslavery literature, *Conscience and the Constitution*. This 120-page theological polemic was partially an extended analysis of slavery's presence in both the Old and New Testaments. It was also a strong endorsement of Senator Daniel Webster's famous defense of the Fugitive Slave Act, of unionism, and of moderation in the debates over passage of the compromise. Stuart especially admired Webster's calling out of abolitionists for their "noise and confusion and perpetual vituperation" on the slavery question. He admitted that slavery was "immeasurably the most difficult problem ever before this great nation" but believed that "universal and immediate emancipation would be little short of insanity. The blacks themselves would be the first and most miserable victims." Stuart went as far as to list some ten "principles of Christianity" that he believed slaveholding violated through the destruction of family relations, the forced ignorance of enslaved people, the sexual attacks on young Black women, and the rendering of humans as "*goods* and *chattels*," among others. But he still blamed the abolitionists for the national dilemma and for the risk of "war" when the "horrors of St. Domingo" might only be a "faint image." The real culprits of America's crisis over slavery were those who lumped slaveholders into a single image of "men-stealers, murderers, tyrants, villains, and every other reproachful name." In Stuart's kind of moderation, if only abolitionists would tone back their language, the country would find a way to peaceful gradual abolition and foreign removal of some Black people. Stuart, like Bacon, portrayed himself as a victim of terrible attacks from radicals, which he countered with stories of meeting "many a kind-hearted, well-instructed, moral, high-minded Southerner."[15] Stuart died in 1852, before he could witness the tragedy of his ideology as it blew up first in political and then violent conflict.

One of Bacon's and Stuart's admirers who later developed a deeper commitment to antislavery was Andrew Dickson White, a student at Yale from 1850 to 1853. White, a historian who went on to teach at the University of Michigan and later cofounded and became president of Cornell University in his native upstate New York, left some revealing commentary about how the slavery issue and abolitionism animated Yale's public and campus intellectual life in the early 1850s. "The general sentiment of that university in those days," White wrote in his autobiography, "favored almost any concession to save the Union. The venerable Silliman, and a great majority of older professors spoke at public meetings in favor of pro-slavery compromise measures which they fondly hoped would settle the difficulty between North and South." Most Yale faculty opposed the Fugitive Slave Act of 1850 but "as a rule, took ground against anti-slavery effort." Much was wrong about slavery, but these Yale faculty and students believed the abolitionists made matters worse. White portrayed himself as a brave dissident to this consensus, part of a "small minority of students who remained uncompromisingly anti-slavery." He proudly claimed that his friends would greet him upon return to campus with, "How are you Gerrit; how did you leave the Rev. Antoinette Brown and brother Fred Douglas?" These were all references to radical abolitionists: Gerrit Smith, philanthropist and radical political abolitionist; Brown, the first woman ordained in the Congregational church as a minister (and a founder of feminist theology); and Frederick Douglass (the use of "Fred" was a common racist insult to Douglass in this period of his emerging fame). White recalled a moment of revelation while walking across the New Haven Green to the door of North College: "I stopped a moment, ran through the whole subject in an instant, and then and there, on the stairway leading to my room, silently vowed that, come what might, I would never be an apologist for slavery or for its extension, and that what little I could do against both should be done," White wrote his memoir in 1905. Such recollections were common among former Yankee elites by the turn of the twentieth century as they claimed their places, sometimes with rosy self-righteousness, in the memory of the nation's destruction of slavery.[16]

Yale people in the antebellum era ranged from staunch proslavery and anti-abolitionist advocates to abolitionists of various degrees of commitment. Jeremiah Evarts (Yale 1802) fell on the latter end of that spectrum. He became a distinguished lawyer, editor, and missionary-activist, especially on behalf of American Indian nations in the South—the Cherokee, Choctaw, and Chickasaw. Evarts strongly opposed the displacement of Indigenous people from their lands and worked assiduously through his writing and speaking, and especially through the American Board of Commissioners for Foreign Missions, to prevent the 1830 Indian Removal Act by the Andrew Jackson administration. As editor of the *Panoplist* and its successors, he wrote prolifically, not only about

Indian affairs but also about slavery, especially about the moral culpability of slaveholders. But his fondness for colonization angered radicals such as William Lloyd Garrison. To his disappointment, Garrison discovered that "for all his sympathy for the outraged Indians," Evarts "would not speak or write a word in behalf of the slave, or countenance any effort for his emancipation." Evarts made many friends among slaveholders in his extensive travels in the South and sometimes wrote in vague, gradualist tones about slaveholding. "Let us here say," he declared, "to those of our southern brethren . . . that we would by no means countenance the habit of bringing local prejudices to bear upon discussions like the present. . . . On the contrary, the whole business ought to be conducted with an enlarged reference to the permanent good of the whole union, and with particular reference to the permanent security of the southern people, and the gradual improvement of the condition of the black population." Gradualist moderation and sympathy for the plight of slaveholders had rarely been expressed with more saccharine ambiguity.[17]

But Evarts, who died young in 1831 when abolitionism had only found its early institutional form, predicted dire consequences for the country if it did not face and end slavery by some staged process. If Americans did not begin now to plan for the end of slavery, "the issue," said Evarts, "will be more disastrous than has ever yet been imagined. Before the number of slaves in North America shall amount to twenty millions, how many plots, and murders, and massacres will have taken place? How much blood will have been shed to suppress embryo insurrections? . . . How many barbarous enactments will have found their place in the slave codes? How much cruel suffering is to be endured by the unhappy blacks; how much agonizing fear by the more unhappy whites?" He feared a "future Spartacus" or "Toussaint" who would lead violent rebellions. In Evarts's view, "miracles" would never solve the slavery question. "Wise, judicious, public-spirited measures" would. Such was the approach of gradualism in antislavery circles, and it would have a long shelf life in American reform thought. But Evarts left a trenchant, apocalyptic warning: "Black men will at last be free; and if they are not freed by kindness, under the direction of wisdom, they will gain their liberty by violence, at the instigation of revenge."[18] Some sober moderates understood slavery's future threats in similar ways to the early radicals.

In bold contrast to the moderate Evarts is the largest nineteenth-century donor to Yale and fierce anti-abolitionist Joseph Earl Sheffield. Born in Southport, Connecticut, in 1793, Sheffield became a wealthy cotton merchant, eventually headquartered in the port of Mobile, Alabama. He inherited some wealth and business acumen from his father, who was deeply invested in the

West Indian trade, particularly with sugar production and slavery in Cuba. By 1835, Sheffield moved his family back north to New Haven because he did not want his children to grow up in a slave society, even as he owned the people who worked in his house. He continued to spend winters in Mobile managing his lucrative trade interests. His fortune emerged from diversified businesses; by the 1840s, he was the owner of the Farmington Canal and a part owner of the New York and New Haven Railroad.[19]

With major donations, the merchant established the Sheffield Scientific School at Yale and helped put the college on the world map for science education. The key event in this process was the marriage of the Sheffields' daughter, Josephine Sheffield, to John Addison Porter (Yale 1842), a newly hired professor of chemistry. Joseph Sheffield purchased the old Medical Department building on College Street in 1858, added two wings, and remodeled the entire structure. With a supporting gift of $50,000 more for "the maintenance of Professorships of Engineering, Metallurgy, and Chemistry," Sheffield made Yale a university to train scientists. He lived in a handsome house on Hillhouse Avenue, behind the school that by 1861 carried his name. Starting in that historic year, and modeling German universities, Yale began awarding PhD degrees in psychology, classical languages and literature, philosophy, and physics. In the end Sheffield's financial gifts to Yale before his death in 1882 reached $1.1 million, a figure not matched by any Yale donor until well into the twentieth century.[20]

Sheffield despised abolitionists. He warmly defended his many friends among Southern planters and believed the enslavement of African Americans was a benevolent practice that could never be terminated suddenly without enormous social and economic upheaval. When the Civil War erupted in 1861 and caused great disruption at Yale, Sheffield was among those Northern merchants who blamed the radicalism of abolitionists for the entire crisis. When the transcontinental railroads emerged as a Republican Party initiative during the war, he hatched an elaborate proposal to use Black labor to build the railroads through the Pacific West. "By the employment of the emancipated slaves," Sheffield imagined, "they may be gradually withdrawn from our midst and ultimately diffused through the fertile region of the West . . . now inhabited by the Indian and the Buffalo; so that in the course of time when these regions shall have been peopled by the ever moving Anglo-Saxon, we shall find the negro so mixed and amalgamated, so improved by cultivation, precept and example, so *diluted* as a people, that their presence will hardly be noticed or detected in the mighty nation which is to inhabit these regions."[21] Even though his terrible scheme never materialized, Sheffield demonstrated the extent to which cunning and racist theory could be put to material ends in the nineteenth century.

Sheffield's political positions in the Civil War era provide a window into the worldviews of many others around Yale, as well as a stark contrast. In his "Personal Reminiscences," he wrote, "Of course, then although an *outspoken hater of slavery as such*, I was the defender of the slave holders from the foul aspersions of the abolitionists and often predicted the results which would be precipitated if the people of the North persisted in fanning the flames." When Abraham Lincoln was elected and secession exploded in the Deep South, Sheffield was "so certain of the consequences, that I sold, at great sacrifice, my remaining property in Mobile. I had always been an ardent *old-line Whig of the Clay and Webster School*, but when that party began to run after the abolitionists and other gods, for the sake of votes; when in fact they began to *run away* from *their principles*, I could not follow them." In 1860 Sheffield voted for John Bell, the Constitutional Union Party candidate, the embodiment of a failed moderate hope to save the Union. Disgruntled that history had seemed to surge beyond him, he recollected it as "the *last vote* I ever cast on any occasion."[22]

One of the most intriguing Yale graduates of the early nineteenth century was Cassius Marcellus Clay of Kentucky, a cousin of the famous Whig statesman Henry Clay. Born into a prominent slaveholding family, an inheritor of a major plantation just southeast of Lexington, Clay developed into a paradoxical, if legendary, figure in Southern politics. He was the youngest son in the large Clay family, and with his brother Brutus staying behind to manage the plantation, its agriculture, and its slaves, Cassius sought an education and a political career. He first attended Transylvania University in Lexington in 1828, the first such college founded west of the Allegheny Mountains. From there, Clay went to Washington, DC, and met many leading politicians, including President Andrew Jackson. The ambitious young Southerner, eager to get away for the time being from the region, next went to New England to choose a college that might have him. His family could certainly afford it. He elected to attend Yale in 1831, he claimed, because of the "beauty of the trees" and "its prime reputation for thoroughness in education."[23]

Clay entered Yale as a junior and quickly fit in, as there were "quite a number of Southerners then in Yale; so I soon felt at home," he later remembered. In 1832, he experienced what he judged a life-changing event: hearing William Lloyd Garrison speak in New Haven. In his memoir, Clay admitted he had "never known anything of Garrison" and had "never heard an Abolitionist." Although Garrison was "boisterously hissed" by the standing-room-only audience, the young Kentuckian sat in awe in a front pew of the church. Garrison spoke "so as to burn like a branding-iron into the most callous hide of the slaveholder and his defenders." Clay would have known. "My parents were slave-holders," he reminisced, "all my known kindred in Kentucky were slave-holders." Although he had considered slavery one of the "evils of humanity," Garrison's speech brought him to a new understanding, and he recalled that the Boston abolitionist had "dragged out the monster from all his citadels, and left him stabbed to the vitals, and dying at the feet of every logical and honest mind." In the years to come, Clay became himself a talented public speaker in this age of oratory as well as a vivid writer, and his recollections of Garrison's effect on his audience became part of how he told his own redemption story. As it happened, most of these Yale men of the antebellum era repeatedly shaped and revised a memory of themselves for posterity.[24]

Clay later contended that, "as water to a thirsty wayfarer," Garrison's speech and his time at Yale had put him on the path to abolition. After the speech, and the subsequent night when the same church hosted an anti-abolition meeting denouncing Garrison and all he stood for, Clay returned to his room, he said, "full of tumultuous emotions. . . . I then resolved . . . when I had the strength, if ever, I would give slavery a death struggle." Before leaving the elm trees behind, Clay was selected by students to deliver an address on February 22, 1832, in honor of George Washington's birthday. He remembered it as his "first antislavery speech," although it was, appropriately (for Yale in these years), vaguely moderate, employing Thomas Jefferson's famous declaration and telling his classmates, "I tremble for my country, when I reflect that God is just." The florid oration warned of potential disunion as "northern and southern champions stand in sullen defiance" of one another. Clay graduated from Yale and returned to Kentucky, to farming and slaveholding, but quickly entered the rough and tumble of Whig Party politics, which in his state were sometimes violent.[25]

Clay did become an abolitionist, albeit a gradualist within a slave state, trying to work within the law. He eventually denounced slaveholding fiercely but advocated long-term emancipation by the states themselves, not unlike the Northern states had accomplished in the late eighteenth and early nineteenth centuries. Yet, unlike many fellow leading White Southerners, he was quite serious about putting slavery on a course to extinction; in 1845, he founded and edited an antislavery newspaper in Lexington, the *True American*. Mobs attacked him and the paper, forcing him to relocate the project to Cincinnati for a period of time. Clay joined a Kentucky cavalry unit and fought in the War with Mexico in 1846–47, and in the 1850s he helped found the Republican Party in his state, no easy task in the face of violent opposition. In the midst of the Civil War, President Lincoln appointed Clay as U.S. ambassador to Russia, where he served for most of 1863–69. His colorful life included helping negotiate the purchase of Alaska as well as several marriages and quite a few personal scandals.[26] Above all, Clay is remembered as a unique political figure. He learned his initial abolitionism in New Haven in his early twenties and sustained a successful career in politics as a true believer in ending slavery, albeit slowly.

Antislavery sentiment took many forms among Yale graduates and in New Haven. William H. Russell, Yale class of 1833, came from a very different background from Clay. A direct descendant of two of Yale's founding ministers, Noadiah Russell and James Pierpont, Russell was the fourth generation in his extended family to attend Yale. He was valedictorian of his class and completed his MA and MD degrees at Yale. In 1833, he was the primary founder of the senior society Skull and Bones, established originally under what was known as the Russell Trust Association. From 1836, Russell led a military preparatory school for boys on Wooster Square. Over nearly fifty years, until it closed at Russell's death in 1885, the academy educated some four thousand boys, some of whom attended college nearby at Yale.[27] Russell entered politics with fervor as well, helping organize the Republican Party in the state in 1854 in the wake of the Kansas-Nebraska Act. In fact, his most important contribution as an abolitionist may have been his support of the antislavery crusader John Brown.

Russell established his firm antislavery credentials as a member of the National Kansas Committee, raising funds, arms, and supplies for Brown and other free-soil warriors in Kansas territory. Russell befriended Brown and hosted him at his house in New Haven likely several times, including at a fundraising gathering on March 9, 1857. Apparently, the Russell circle of activists did not produce the full $1,000 that Brown believed they had promised; the Panic of 1857 ruined financial well-being, even among the prosperous in New England, right when the secretive rebel Brown most needed their largesse for his schemes in Kansas as well as his plot to attack Harpers Ferry. In one letter to his wife, Brown alerted her to look out in the post for hefty contributions soon to arrive from "Russell of New Haven," as well as others. At one point, Brown tried to enroll his son Oliver in Russell's military academy to train him for what was to come. The son refused, went home to hardscrabble upstate New York, got married, and at age twenty died at Harpers Ferry fighting next to his father at the ill-fated raid in October 1859.[28]

Russell was among a small group of "trustees" given control of Brown's meager finances in case he died or never returned from his Kansas exploits.

The failure of Brown's raid on Harpers Ferry and his subsequent martyrdom on the gallows in Virginia did not mar Russell's reputation in Connecticut. When the Civil War came in 1861, Southern boys at the academy went home to serve the Confederacy, but nearly three hundred graduates fought as officers in the Union army. In 1861, Governor William Buckingham put Russell in charge of organizing the state's militia. And at Russell's encouragement, in 1864 the faculty voted to allow students to participate in rifle practice. Although he never went to the front to command a military unit, behind the scenes he administered the men and materiel for this massive conflict with great skill. At the 1865 Yale commencement, just after the end of the war, Russell served as chief marshal, leading the alumni procession.[29] For the Yale community, Russell symbolized a resolute commitment to the "Union," rooted in a life of antislavery sympathy.

No residential college is named for any of Yale's antislavery advocates of the antebellum era. But there is one for Samuel F. B. Morse, the famous inventor and artist, and one of Yale's most notorious proslavery advocates of the antebellum and Civil War eras. On June 10, 1871, a statue of Morse was unveiled with great fanfare in Central Park in New York City. The eighty-year-old, regarded everywhere as the inventor of the telegraph, which over more than two decades had conquered time and space and connected humankind across oceans all over the globe, sent out a "farewell" telegram to the entire world. When he died in April 1872, little was said of Morse's views of humankind.[30]

Born in 1791, Samuel was the son of Yale graduate Jedidiah Morse, the famous geographer and Calvinist preacher. Jedidiah joined Timothy Dwight and others in defending Calvinist strictures, helped spread the conspiracy theory of the Illuminati at the beginning of the nineteenth century, and politically became a Federalist, suspicious of all liberal or radical legacies of the French Revolution. Samuel Morse's rigid conservatism derives from this influence and background, but he forged his own worldview. Entering Yale College in 1805 at age fourteen, Morse cultivated his talent as an artist, painting portraits, and imbibed lectures by Benjamin Silliman on electricity and other scientific subjects. After graduating from Yale in 1810, the Anglophile studied painting in London, the first of many sojourns in Europe to forge an artistic career. Returning to America, Morse created a studio in Boston and later moved back to New Haven, where he painted portraits of eminent Yale "worthies" Eli Whitney, Noah Webster, and President Jeremiah Day. Morse struggled for commercial success as a painter, but the young artist always had an eye for business ventures, especially as he entered the competitive world of scientific invention.[31]

Numerous other scientists and inventors had been experimenting with electricity, especially the American Joseph Henry. Morse made a series of partnerships with some scientists and especially with investors, and by 1837, he managed to string ten miles of wire and test his first telegraph. Soon his patent wars and legal battles began over who would take ownership of the amazing new technology. Morse was hardly the first or the only person to perfect the telegraph, but he surely knew how to take and get credit. He demonstrated the telegraph in a university studio, and then in Congress and to President Martin Van Buren at the White House. By 1840, he obtained his U.S. patent and was on his way to almost unparalleled fame as an inventor. Simplifying messages into a system of signals soon known as "Morse code," the former painter was ready to cash in and transform how people passed information, did business, checked a credit rating, gambled their money, gained news of sporting events, and even fought wars.[32] The "news" itself now spread "on the wires."

Through strong political connections, Morse convinced Congress to appropriate $30,000 in 1843 for an experimental line from Washington to Baltimore. He had first tried running lines underground in lead pipes, but they failed; above-ground poles became the answer. On May 24, 1844, with great publicity and surrounded by coils of wires and national leaders, Morse tapped out the first message on his telegraph from the Supreme Court chamber to the B&O Railroad depot in Baltimore. He chose the passage from Numbers 23:23: "What hath God wrought?" Through many patent fights, Morse eventually won in the Supreme Court in 1854, and the burgeoning telegraph companies had to pay him royalties. By 1850, some twelve thousand miles of lines, with poles spreading across the landscape, run by twenty companies, made Morse rich. In this golden age of patents in the expanding early American industrial economy, few people benefited from patent laws more than the former art teacher Professor Morse. Electric telegraphy now meant that after more than two thousand years of using galloping horses as the fastest means of communication, humans could send all manner of information instantaneously over forty miles to Baltimore, or even much farther. By 1861, the first telegraph line successfully reached California, and by 1866, after many breaks and failures, the first transatlantic cable transmitted across the ocean. Morse's name and reputation held center stage in this oceanic achievement, a kind of "moon landing" of the nineteenth century. By the Reconstruction era, Morse possessed a significant interest in the Western Union Company, which dominated telegraphic communication across the nation.[33]

Morse and his associates had changed the world, but the inquisitive man had other keen interests, both political and ideological. His thought was a synthesis of science and religion, of Enlightenment and latter-day Calvinism. He was a technological revolutionary and an ideological counterrevolutionary. Above all, he seems to have despised the idea of America as a pluralistic nation dedicated to any goal of equality, whether in law or in morality. He did not believe in the natural rights tradition, nor in the nod to equality in the Declaration of Independence. Morse was an aggressive white supremacist in an era when that was often no special distinction; he was doggedly anti-Catholic and anti-abolition. He changed how humans used technology but rejected most social change and the principles of democracy. Morse sought elective office early in his career, running for mayor of New York twice, in 1836 and 1841, on an intensely nativist, anti-immigrant platform, and for Congress from New York in 1854, also as a nativist, losing decisively all three times. He did, however, develop many political connections, moving from his father's old Federalism to the proslavery Jacksonian Democrats, and eventually in and out of the Know-Nothing Party.[34]

In 1835, Morse published *Foreign Conspiracy against the Liberties of the United States*, a series of essays under the pen name "Brutus," first serialized in his brother's newspaper, the *New York Observer*. The anti-Catholic screed came from deep in the well of Protestant fears of the conspiracies alleged against "Popery" and the priesthood. Morse relished the paranoid style of anti-Catholic conspiracists. Particularly from the Austro-Hungarian Empire he expected the fiercest "attack," first as a "war of opinion," and then as a "grand scheme" to pollute and take over American institutions. "Jesuit missionaries" were deviously "travelling through the land" spreading the methods of "Popery," which was in Morse's view the antithesis of individual "liberty." Catholics owed allegiance to Rome, so the argument went, and not to the United States. His fears included a distrust in America's own tradition of separation of church and state, which he saw as a weakness exploited by Catholics. "The Catholic," wrote Morse, "is permitted to work in the light of Protestant toleration . . . to mature his plans, and to execute his designs to extinguish that light." Allegiance to the pope supposedly arrived in America on every ship holding the "unlettered Catholic emigrant," ready to exploit the country's far too open "laws *encouraging immigration*," the other legal "weakness" he severely denounced.[35] Morse's anti-Catholicism found eager audiences and knew few moral bounds.

Morse saved perhaps his most ferocious criticism of his own country for abolitionists, whom he blamed for the slavery crisis generally. In his early years as an aspiring painter, Morse had spent four years in Charleston, South Carolina, cultivating his skills. He made many friends among Carolina slaveholders. By the 1830s he was among the most prominent Northerners advancing a counterrevolutionary conservatism rooted in old Federalist loyalties but now also devoted to proslavery ideology. Along with such figures as Congressman Charles Jared Ingersoll of Pennsylvania, Morse joined a group vigorously opposed to the blossoming antislavery movement. They considered abolitionism an "unmerciful fanaticism" imported from abroad and a "conspiracy" against America and its foundations. Morse took many public positions essentially identical to the standard Southern defense of slavery and hatred of abolitionists. By the early 1850s he defended slavery as "a social condition ordained from the beginning of the world for the wisest purposes, benevolent and disciplinary, by Divine Wisdom." And he simply loathed abolitionists. Morse judged them, especially immediatists, as "demons in human shape." A more "wretched, disgusting, hypocritical crew, have not appeared on the face of the earth," he wrote his brother in 1847, "since the times of Robespierre." The more he considered the slavery issue, he wrote by 1857, "the more I feel compelled to declare myself on the Southern side of the question."[36] Proslavery Northerners of influence were a declining lot in the 1850s, but some, like Morse, exercised political clout and possessed access to the press out of proportion to their numbers.

To Morse, and other members of what the historian Larry Tise has called the Northern "proslavery center," abolitionists were a dire threat to the social order. As the 1860 election neared and secession loomed, Morse launched an intensive campaign of letter writing to the South, assuring friends there of his support. In February 1861, when seven states had seceded and formed the Confederacy, Morse called the country, with approval, the "*Untied* and no longer the *United* States." Morse acknowledged with glancing support the potential violence against abolitionists; they deserved it and had to be stopped. The "cause" of secession, he judged, "in all that relates to Slavery is intrinsically Sound." The Southern rebellion was to Morse an admirable revolution, a "demonstration" to "convince fanaticism that the south were in earnest." He liked the audacity and the ultimate aim of preserving slavery, while still claiming to be a unionist. As we shall see, Morse's fervor would prompt him to lead Northern efforts to thwart emancipation when it came in 1862–63. "There was very little to distinguish," according to Tise, between anti-abolition and proslavery when it came to the ultimate crisis of 1861 among Morse and his conservative comrades.[37]

African Americans in New Haven and around Connecticut and New England themselves strove for education, social impact, and meaningful lives. They struggled mightily to establish schools, churches, mutual aid societies, and temperance organizations in an environment hostile to their aspirations, as the 1831 Black college events in New Haven had demonstrated.

Free Black communities, mostly in cities across the Northern states, functioned in the face of political and social prescription. But they also operated, at least until the 1850s, by a philosophy of individual self-reliance and collective self-improvement. Local leaders in the 1830s–40s were active abolitionists; they aided and rescued fugitive slaves and tried to found newspapers to advocate their causes, but most pushed especially hard for community development. Free Black leaders contended that their own moral improvement—embracing work ethics, Christian virtue, sobriety, and economic self-development—would convince a wider swath of Americans to see the evils in slavery and abolish it. They first had to establish, so the argument went, their own visible moral and social "elevation" in the face of racist expectations of Black behavior and poverty. "Nothing will contribute more to break the bondman's fetters," resolved a women's antislavery convention in New York in 1837, "than an example of high moral worth, intellectual culture and religious attainments among the free people of color." William Whipper, a Black Philadelphia leader and Garrisonian abolitionist, argued at the 1835 national convention of the American Antislavery Society that "Education, Temperance, Economy, and Universal Liberty" went hand in hand with ending slavery itself. Nothing, Whipper contended, quite like sober and successful Black communities as models would "facilitate the cause of immediate and universal emancipation."[38] Such a self-improvement formula was both inspired by and in part doomed by this kind of idealism.

Antebellum Northern society was a laboratory for all manner of reform impulses, driven by evangelical Christianity, utopian theories about the perfectibility of humankind, and faith in republicanism. At times the most widespread of these crusades was temperance, the religious quest to induce people to take the "cold water pledge" and denounce "demon rum" and all other alcoholic spirits. Connecticut led the way among Northern Black communities; the Temperance Society of the People of Color of New Haven was founded as early as 1829, fighting the liquor trade and proliferation of grog shops, many within a short walk of the Yale campus. Temperance societies flourished in tandem with antislavery meetings across Connecticut and New England throughout the 1830s. In 1836, Jehiel C. Beman and his son, Amos Beman, organized a temperance society in

Middletown, and by 1836 the elder Beman had established a statewide temperance society.[39] Their resources never matched the zeal of these organizations, and sometimes they faced mob violence from immigrant groups at their parades and festivals.

The younger Beman, after tutoring and early education in Middletown, arrived in New Haven in 1838; within three years he was lead pastor at the Temple Street Congregational Church, a leading Black religious institution of New Haven. Beman served seventeen years in this crucial position, only a few blocks from the Yale campus where some of his parishioners worked as janitors, cooks, and domestic workers of various kinds. Beman's church also served as a haven for fugitive slaves passing through the city, and even more enduringly, the pastor founded a primary school for local children in the building's basement. A formative experience in Beman's own life had been an ugly racist rejection in Middletown in 1834. Beman's tutor, L. P. Dole, a White student at Wesleyan, took issue with the expulsion of Charles B. Ray, a Black student at the college, because of White student opposition and reported the incident to Garrison's *Liberator* in Boston. After six months, Beman received the following letter from a group of students calling themselves "*Twelve of us*": "To young Beman—A no. of the students of this university, deeming it derogatory to themselves, as well as to the university, to have you and other colord [*sic*] students recite here, do hereby warn you to desist from such a course, and if you fail to comply with this *peacable* [*sic*] request, we swear, by the *ETERNAL GODS!* that we will resort to *forcible* means to put a stop to it."[40] As a minister and community leader, Beman became a moderate and a survivor, but his commitments to education and all other modes of self-improvement remained fierce.

Beman became a leading Black clergyman-abolitionist. At the 1840 first meeting of the American and Foreign Anti-Slavery Society, he was among eight African American founders of this organization created as an alternative to William Lloyd Garrison's older society, which was dedicated solely to moral suasion. Beman attended most national Colored Conventions, chairing the one in Buffalo in 1843 at which Frederick Douglass and Henry Highland Garnet famously squared off over whether African Americans ought to consider violence as a protest strategy. And in 1847, he joined Pennington in leading the Connecticut State Temperance and Moral Reform Society and demanding a state constitutional amendment restoring the right to vote for Black men, which had been eliminated by the so-called Black Law in 1818. "You have an interest then whether you feel it or not, in our welfare; in our being intelligent, virtuous and good citizens," Beman declared "to the good People of the State of Connecticut": "We

The Reverend Amos Beman. Amos Gerry Beman Scrapbooks. Yale Collection of American Literature, Beinecke Rare Book and Manuscript Library, Yale University.

cannot be ignorant, vicious and degraded without an injury to yourselves. . . . We do not wish to be pointed at as a degraded class in the community. Neither do we believe that the color of the skin is any indication either of virtue, wisdom, or justice any more than it is of personal degradation; but we regard it as a physical manifestation for which an ALL WISE CREATOR is alone responsible."[41] Such language rings in similar tones as the petitions of Revolutionary War–era Black veterans demanding their freedom; but now these missives emanated from educated community leaders.

Self-improvement organizations often went by titles such as "mental and moral improvement" associations, and one in Hartford, Connecticut, called itself the Hartford Literary and Religious Institution. They charged fees for lectures and other entertainments. The Hartford group was led in 1834 by the Reverend Hosea Easton, who was free-born in Massachusetts and an interesting and sometimes controversial reform figure. In 1837 Easton published an early classic of this era of self-reliance, *A Treatise on the Intellectual Character, and Civil and Political Condition of the Colored People of the U. States; and the Prejudice Exercised towards Them*. This manifesto provided an exposé of the brutal racism Easton had experienced in both Massachusetts and Connecticut, but also delivered a rather modern diatribe against the idea of "race" as anything but a creation by humans of a set of stereotypes and theories to harm each other. He drew upon the Declaration of Independence, demanded rights of citizenship, and argued that radical abolitionists should reconsider immediate emancipation until the social uplift of free Black communities had been achieved.[42] Virtually all such leaders of self-improvement organizations, at least until the late 1850s, sternly resisted the temptations of colonization movements, which were so popular among White moderates around the North and certainly at Yale. These leaders were especially interested in scratching out livelihoods, helping their people rise above menial labor, and building their own institutions.

Nothing motivated this Black self-improvement formula quite like the quest for schools. The Colored Conventions tried at least three times over the 1840s and 1850s to create a national manual labor college with funding as high as $50,000, but such a dream was never achieved. At local levels in the North, wealthy White people tended to send their children to academies and private schools. Common schools, the beginnings of the American tradition of public-supported schooling, tended to be segregated during the antebellum era. But in some Northern states, Black children attended private schools financially supported by White donors, with both Black and White teachers. In some cities in Ohio, Pennsylvania, and New York, free Black communities mustered meager resources to create primary education. Sometimes they vigorously petitioned state legislatures for financial support but persisted whether they achieved success or not. In some towns and cities, Black school boards were established to run separate schools, touching off a constant antebellum debate over whether Black people should accept or denounce segregated learning.[43]

As early as the printings of the first two Black newspapers, *Freedom's Journal* in 1827 and the *Colored American* by 1837, the merits or denigrations implied by segregated schools emerged as a nearly constant topic of division. Samuel Cornish found segregated education demeaning, a "fatal practice" driven by the assumption that Black youth needed only a "smattering" of training for their future of menial work. Black schools faced the brutal practicalities of inferior buildings and facilities, as well as a limited supply of teachers. Henry Highland Garnet believed integrated schools were the only viable future in a world inspired now, he contended in 1848, by the sweep of republican revolutions in Europe. Lewis Woodson, however, the mentor of Martin Delany, saw quality Black schools as a source of "race pride" and a way to thwart half-hearted efforts in integrated settings. And James W. C. Pennington, in 1848, wholeheartedly endorsed separate schools for training a new generation of professional Black teachers. That same year, in his newly founded *North Star* in Rochester, New York, Frederick Douglass led in exposing the failures of segregated schools in that city. His own five children attended those schools as well as later an integrated one. The city supported a school in the cold and dank basement of a Zion Methodist church, with bad conditions and inferior learning materials. By the mid-1850s Rochester would integrate its schools in part because it quietly found separate racial systems untenable financially. More famously, in 1855 Boston and the state of Massachusetts became the first to establish integrated schools by law after court challenges.[44]

In New Haven, prospects throughout the 1830s for Black schooling tilted against the tide created by the infamous denial of the Black college at the beginning of the decade. Violence had ensued against Black residents in the wake of the college vote. Popular attitudes, not unlike around the North generally, swung against abolitionism, its sentiments, and its strategies. Some writers in the *Connecticut Herald* made the dominant view explicit: advancing the "right of education" for Black youth only "tended to amalgamation" of the races. Education, many White people seemed to contend, was just too dangerous to risk on inferior people destined only to labor. A letter in the *Connecticut Journal* in fall 1831 said Black people could not be educated without "kindling the torch of the incendiary and unsheathing the sword of rebellion and insurrection." The writer declared himself threatened on the streets of New Haven, where "daily" he met the "impudent and insolent bearing" of many African Americans.[45] The very meaning and presence of New Haven's greatest cultural, and increasingly economic, institution—Yale College—sat at the center of this defining controversy about the future of America itself: What was the purpose of education, private and elite or public and democratic, in an expanding republic increasingly riven over racial slavery? Was a college a symbol and a test of whether American democracy would endure?

The first primary school in New Haven for Black children existed as early as 1811; Yale president Timothy Dwight, no great champion of African Americans, called it an "apology" for a school. In 1824, there were twelve schools in the city, but only one that admitted Black students, and it was only open six months out of the year. In 1834, in the wake of the Black college defeat, Simeon Jocelyn and Isaac Thomson, a local builder, raised money for Black education, and the Mount Pleasant School, also called Spireworth, opened in what is now known as the Hill District. By 1850, there were three schools for Black children, and Black women did most of the teaching: Elizabeth Ann Price held forth at the Goffe Street School, Rosannah Cooke at Spireworth, and Sarah Wilson at the Artisan Street School, operated in one room with benches. Years later, Wilson would teach a star student, Edward Alexander Bouchet, future Yale graduate and the first African American to receive a PhD. Black pupils and their teachers learned and worked in poor, crowded facilities with few proper books and supplies.[46]

On October 21, 1846, Yale University inaugurated a new president, Theodore Dwight Woolsey. Woolsey had never been a minister, so on the same day as his installation as president he was ordained, since no one had ever led Yale in its near century and a half who had not been a Congregationalist clergyman. Woolsey, the valedictorian of the Yale College class of 1820, was a professor of Greek and had trained, among other places, extensively in German universities. As a young man, Woolsey helped found the New Haven Anti-Slavery Association with Leonard Bacon and other classmates, and the following year, in 1826, he joined Bacon, Simeon Jocelyn, William Lanson, and others in establishing the African Improvement Society of New Haven. Woolsey replaced President Jeremiah Day, who had reigned long at the helm of Yale from 1817 to 1846. Day was a staunch social and religious conservative, a somewhat quiet force under whose leadership the divinity and law schools had been founded while he defended the college's classical liberal curriculum and set it on a firmer financial footing.[47]

The Yale Woolsey inherited was no longer strictly a New England institution. By as early as 1815, fully 25 percent of students came from outside New England. From 1820 until 1860, over 10 percent of the students in Yale College hailed from the South; 1850 was the high-water mark of Southern enrollment in Yale College, with seventy-two students from thirteen Southern states. And the Southern contingent was a point of pride for at least some at Yale. The *Yale Literary Magazine* commented in 1852, "It will be observed that the number of students from the South has been increasing. . . . It is supposed that no northern College has as great a representation from the South." In fact, the College of New Jersey (Princeton) had far more Southern students. But the Southern presence loomed large. "Yale was the favorite college of the southern planters," wrote Julian Sturtevant, an 1826 graduate, in a later memoir. "From the days of John C. Calhoun, almost to the war of the rebellion, the number of southern students was large." These Southerners created their own organizations and clubs; some with great means from their wealthy families lived in New Haven in rented housing. White Southerners and their proslavery roots had carved out a distinctive place in Yale's life and learning.[48]

In 1845, the year before Woolsey's installation, the United States "annexed" Texas into the American Union, prompting Mexico to break off diplomatic relations with its northern neighbor. In the spring of 1846, on April 24, after a three-week standoff on the north side of the Rio Grande in Texas, U.S. troops, placed there in an aggressive move by the expansionist slaveholder president James K. Polk, were attacked; eleven Americans died and sixty-three were captured. On April 26, U.S. general Zachary Taylor sent a dispatch overland to Washington, DC (it took two weeks to arrive), claiming that "hostilities had commenced." Polk immediately drafted a message to Congress for a declaration of war with Mexico. On May 13, 1846, while Yale students continued their daily recitations from the Bible and the classics, as well as attending the lectures of Benjamin Silliman and Nathaniel Taylor, the House of Representatives voted for war 174–14, and the Senate 40–2, with many Northern abstentions. Moderate, conservative Yale University, with its traditions and its high intellectual aims, increasingly now lived in the same history as everyone else, described so aptly by the essayist Ralph Waldo Emerson in his journal in 1847: "The United States will conquer Mexico, but it will be as the man swallows arsenic, which brings him down in turn. Mexico will poison us!"[49]

Great war fever swept across the land as the country marched toward what many Americans called its "manifest destiny," and its first foreign war of conquest. From the first day it was a highly controversial and very bloody conflict, causing some thirteen thousand American and an estimated fifty thousand Mexican casualties. Many Northern communities and political leaders judged the war as a conquest for the expansion of slavery and a gigantic land grab in the guise of Christian mission. Because of the two-year war, American politics and the crisis over the existence and spread of slavery would never be the same again.[50] President Woolsey soon faced all manner of curricular and academic challenges: how to enliven recitations and other teaching, whether to create a history department or an engineering school or a formal graduate school. But he and his colleagues also now faced, slowly but surely, the existential crisis of whether the United States would remain forever a slaveholding nation. Indeed, the slavery crisis in its moral and political dimensions would soon come home to the Yale campus, forcing nearly everyone to position or reposition themselves in relation to its power.

In the summer of 1850, it looked as if students in Yale College's Phi Beta Kappa Society would select antislavery politician William H. Seward as the speaker for their commencement the following year. To stop that from happening, a student referred to in the press as a "Fillmore whig from New York" objected because of the senator's well-known "extreme opinions." Soon the sectional nature of the slavery question among students became clear, with another student, a Mr. Gould of Georgia, threatening "the withdrawal of Southern patronage from the College" if societies support or honor "such men." Seward was not chosen, but the story from Yale and what it seemed to augur about Northern "servility" in the face of Southern demands had enduring appeal. Newspapers, including the *Liberator*, continued to report on the Yale argument into late 1852. It was not long, however, before Seward had his say at Yale; he delivered the Phi Beta Kappa address in 1854.[51]

During the intervening years, the student body felt the winds of national change blowing. The Calliopean Society, founded in 1819, always had a Southern identity, as distinct from the two older literary societies. Beginning in 1851, however, Southerners began to leave Brothers in Unity and Linonia in protest over the rise of antislavery activity and opinion on campus. A lengthy denunciation of this new spirit on campus appeared in the *New Haven Register* in 1853. One "James Hamilton" began by pointing first to Yale's reputation as a "national" college—the only one in New England, he thought, to deserve the honor. In contrast to neighboring institutions, Yale had long stayed out of supposedly sectional debates. "No one has heard of public gatherings of students here to denounce, *ex cathedra*, Slavery and the Fugitive Slave Law." Thanks to Yale's moderation on such issues, Southern students had felt welcome there. But all that had changed. "Within the last few months, Yale has caught the infection, and now raises her official hue and cry against Slavery, as an 'unjust institution,' and does reverence to the supremacy of the 'higher law,'" Hamilton wrote. Across several newspaper columns, he detailed the outrages: President Woolsey was speaking out openly against slavery, and *Uncle Tom's Cabin* was taught in classes; faculty and students alike felt comfortable openly assailing slavery. In all, Yale faculty and leaders were now teaching the students "entrusted to her care, a detestation for the institution of Slavery, a contempt for those who sustain it, and a hostility to the Constitution which sanctions it." As a result, Hamilton reported that Southern students were considering withdrawing "in a body" in protest.[52]

The greatest test—at Yale and across the nation—came the following year. In January 1854, Stephen A. Douglas, the ambitious Democratic senator from Illinois long associated with the theory of popular sovereignty—the idea that settlers in western territories should themselves decide, through voting, whether a territory would allow slaveholding—introduced a bill "to organize the Territory of Nebraska." The Missouri Compromise of 1820 prohibited slavery north of the 36°30′ latitude line, but the slave states, along with their Northern allies, had long wished for its repeal. For his part, Douglas hoped to dodge the question, but under pressure from a contingent of Southern colleagues, he revised the bill to explicitly include the repeal of the 1820 boundary line; his legislation meant that slavery could be permitted anywhere in the western territories, if the White inhabitants so desired. The bill, auguring the end of the tenuous compromise that had long kept the national party system in place, passed the Senate on March 4, 1854, and with strong support from Northern Democrats; the House passed it on May 22, 1854. For many Northerners, fearing for the fate of free labor in the West, the repeal of the Missouri line was the violation of a sacred pledge.[53]

The Kansas-Nebraska Act was, for several older Yale luminaries, the straw that broke the back of their longtime moderation. On March 8, 1854, just days after the bill's passage in the Senate, a public meeting convened in the Common Council Chamber of Brewster's Hall, the city's largest meeting space. The capacity crowd heard speeches from city leaders and several Yale scholars and clergy, among them Nathaniel William Taylor, the Reverend Leonard Bacon, and Benjamin Silliman Sr. Taylor, by then in his late sixties, had spoken out many times *against* abolitionist agitation. But on this night, he insisted that the North stop conceding to the South. Admitting he had publicly supported the Compromise of 1850, the eminent theologian said compromises could no longer be trusted. And trouble was coming. Taylor pledged that "if worst comes to worst, I could lay off the garments of my profession and put on a soldier's coat in the cause of freedom." The crowd responded with "tremendous and long continued cheering and shouts of applause," and Taylor continued, "If I should be too old I don't think I am yet—I would bear my part in any way, in prayer and in worship, or amid the battle and the blood."[54] With such bravado, Taylor vividly demonstrated the dire rift that the Kansas crisis had caused in American political life.

Bacon, the onetime colonizationist, was the most zealous of old-line clergy, promising that he would do his "utmost" to resist the spread of slavery; he called it his "sacred vocation," vowing, "In speech, in sermon, and in prayer, I will do what I can for justice and for liberty." After repeated calls to speak, Silliman took the stage and looked back at a life that coincided with the nation's struggles around slavery. His father, he told the audience, had served in the revolutionary army. Now a new movement for liberty demanded his attention. "I have never meddled in political gatherings—never in my life attended a caucus, and never before this day have I addressed a public assembly upon a political question," the professor, nearly seventy-five years old, said. But he felt "*a real crisis has now come over us, and now for the first time, I tremble for my country.*" Speaking of "very many warm friends" he still had in the South, the science professor condemned the "northern dough-face" (a popular term applied by antislavery Northerners to proslavery people from their states) who had betrayed the country. "I have never been alarmed at the threats of dissolution; but I do say if this thing is continued, the dissolution of the Union is sure." These were astonishing remarks by the venerable Silliman.[55]

Two days later, Brewster's Hall was again overflowing with a second meeting to oppose the act; the *New Haven Palladium* reported that hundreds were turned away. The speakers included other eminent Yale graduates and clerical leaders, including Eleazer Kingsbury Foster (Yale 1834), a descendent of the Reverend James Pierpont, one of the ten ministers who founded the Collegiate School. The crowd loudly called for Foster, a judge and politician, to speak, interrupting him several times with applause. Like others, Foster admitted that he had supported previous compromises but had lived to regret it. The question was not whether slavery would be permitted in Nebraska but rather, "Shall the whole North be slaves?" News of the fiery rhetoric from distinguished clergy, scholars, and civic leaders over these two days spread beyond the city of New Haven. The *Rhode Island Freeman* said of the meeting that "the strongest denunciations of the Nebraska Bill were thundered forth by some of the austere and venerable, and Reverend professors in Yale College," mentioning in particular Taylor, whose position on slavery had long been ambivalent and who just four years earlier had condoned the Fugitive Slave Act. But his redemption had come at last. The *National Anti-slavery Standard* wrote that out of "all the clergy of New England no one has sinned more deeply in matters pertaining to Slavery than the Rev. Dr. Taylor, of New Haven; but at a public meeting recently held in that city, he was one of the chief denouncers of Douglas' bill." Yale's vaunted moderation had begun to crumble in the face of the country's apparent proslavery future.[56]

Taylor and his peers were not finished. Later that month, Woolsey, Horace Bushnell (Yale 1827), Lyman Beecher (Yale 1797), and some three thousand other New England clergy of all denominations composed a "Remonstrance" against the Kansas-Nebraska bill, which stated, in part, "We protest against it as a great moral wrong, as a breach of faith eminently unjust to the moral principles of the community, and subversive of all confidence in national engagements; as a measure full of danger to the peace, and even the existence of our beloved Union, and exposing us to the righteous judgments of the Almighty." They asked Edward Everett, a U.S. senator from Massachusetts and former president of Harvard, to deliver the statement to the Senate in hope of swaying the vote over the bill. Everett delivered it, but apparently without much feeling. Still, the *Liberator* praised their action as "manly and dignified" and described the "high moral tone" of their message. According to one report, faculty at Harvard, Yale, Dartmouth, Brown, Middlebury, Williams, Amherst, Bowdoin, and Trinity, as well as professors from the seminaries and theological schools in Andover, Cambridge, Bangor, New Haven, Concord, and East Windsor, had likewise signed the memorial. Nearly all the Protestant ministers of Boston were thought to have signed. "The clergy of New England have probably never before spoken with such unanimity and promptness on a political measure," one newspaper declared.[57] The future of slavery now seemed to occupy everyone's mind, even and especially in the previously safe precinct of Yale College. The good moderates of Yale no longer lived above the fray; they were both reading and making news.

Yet another anti-Nebraska meeting was held in late May 1854, with Silliman again at the helm. The resolutions drawn up at this well-attended gathering received unanimous support. And the threat of a Southern student exodus continued to percolate. After the anti-Nebraska meetings, the *Richmond Whig* asked if the South "*will longer submit to the degradation of patronizing Northern Colleges!*" It asserted, "*Better, in our judgment, that the children of the South should live and die in ignorance of even the letters of the alphabet, than be subjected to the contaminating influences of Northern instructors.*" A Savannah newspaper urged Southerners to attend law school in Tennessee rather than in "Cambridge and Yale," where they were likely to encounter antislavery views.[58] Although the number of Southern students enrolled in Yale College declined over the course of the antebellum period, there is no indication of such a wholesale exodus until the secession crisis.

In March 1856, the Connecticut Kansas Colony was formed in New Haven, led by Charles B. Lines and H. A. Wilcox. The company, intending to go to Kansas territory, included people from the nearby communities of Hamden, Cheshire, Guilford, East Haven, Milford, and Derby. The *New York Daily Tribune* left a stunning description of the group, composed of roughly one hundred men, women, and children: "They are mostly large, athletic men, with strong hands and strong hearts, and some of them are the flower of this, the metropolis of Connecticut Yankeedom. Among the Colony are two ex-Members of the Legislature, one clergyman, one physician, one or two theological students; and quite a number of the members of the Colony have their diplomas from Old Yale. In point of education, talent and ability, the Colony stands unrivaled, and may well challenge competition."[59]

New Haven residents and members of the Yale community rallied around the colonists. In March 1856, a fundraising meeting was held at the North Church (today's United Church on the Green). The people of New Haven, including many of those eminences whose political consciences were aroused two years earlier, showed up to provide the Kansas emigrants with "proper weapons of self-defense" against border ruffians and "something with lock, stock and barrel" for war. The company was leaving to "found a *free city*," the *New York Times* reported, and among the prominent citizens, many clergymen of different denominations and a "full quorum" of Yale faculty filled the pews. Silliman the elder again presided, and the famous antislavery preacher, the Reverend Henry Ward Beecher, gave a lengthy, spirited, and widely publicized address. Beecher stressed Yale's representation in this freedom movement out west, telling the audience that "*every sixth man in Leavenworth is a graduate from College*!"[60]

At the end of the service, Silliman pledged to give the colonists a Sharps rifle. He hoped, he said, that rifles would never be needed but felt that the colonists should have them just in case, for self-defense. Soon after Silliman made his announcement, several audience members shouted that they would supply guns as well. Beecher himself promised that if the audience gave twenty-five rifles that night, his congregation in Brooklyn (Plymouth Church) would match that. Moments later, a Yale junior, Moses Tyler, promised to "pledge" a rifle from his class, followed not long after by a Yale senior, Mr. Dunlap, who "pledged" the same from his. In all, twenty-seven rifles were promised that night. But the powerful symbolism of the meeting may have meant more than the money or arms raised. The press referred to the meeting for "Bibles and Rifles," and the *New Haven Register* linked the meeting to the organizing by the clergy over the previous years: "This turning of Christian churches into military rendezvous and preaching the efficacy of rifles over the gospel of peace, is of modern origin, having its origin in the famous 'three thousand priests' power protest against the Nebraska bill."[61]

Five nights later, on March 31, 1856, there was a large farewell gathering for the colonists at Brewster's Hall. It was a festive event, "one of the largest mass meetings ever held in this city," according to the *New York Daily Tribune*. Hundreds of people had to be turned away at the door. Silliman presided once again while Bacon gave the opening prayer. The crowd sang, to the tune of "Auld Lang Syne," "Song of the Kansas Emigrant" and sent up cheers of "Freedom in Kansas."

They listened to a farewell address by Charles Lines, the colony's president, and to speeches by Silliman, Bacon, and others. As promised, the Yale junior class presented Lines with a rifle, embossed with a silver plate that read, "Ultima Ratio Liberarum" (the Last Resort of Freemen). (Beecher, though not in the crowd that night, also fulfilled his promise to the colony. He sent a letter to Lines before the farewell gathering wishing the colonists well, along with a box of twenty-five Sharps rifles and twenty-five bibles, supplied by his Brooklyn congregants. Sharps rifles would soon be referred to as "Beecher's Bibles.") As the colonists made their way to their steamboat, hundreds joined them and others crowded along the route to Long Wharf. The *Tribune* reported there was singing and a band, and "several buildings and private dwellings were illuminated in honor of the occasion." The newspaper noted, "Nowhere in the whole country is there more sympathy for the freemen of Kansas than in New-Haven, and this meeting was proof of the fact."[62]

In 1857, when the Massachusetts senator Charles Sumner was invited but not able to give the Yale commencement address (he had been beaten violently on the floor of the Senate the previous year by South Carolinian congressman Preston Brooks), his friend and abolitionist Wendell Phillips did so in his place. The *Liberator* reported that President Woolsey had requested there be no applause, but during the second half of the day, "the silence of the pulpit on our question, the portentous wrong of Dred Scott decision, the fate of Kansas trembling in the balance, the dastard, compromising spirit of American public life" became the topics of the "most emphatic and spirited rebuke, rung forth in tones of youthful, irrepressible eloquence." The "enthusiasm of the crowd" overruled the president's instructions, and they welcomed speakers with "loud applause, marked each emphatic sentence with cheers, while flowers and plaudits dismissed the young agitator at the close." Covered widely in the Northern press, Phillips's speech at Yale also attracted the ire of Southern newspapers. A letter purporting to be from "a distressed slaveholder" complained about Yale and its recent invitations to both Sumner and Phillips. Yale should remain "national," not "sectional," in its politics, the letter contended, referencing a recent antislavery speech by Woolsey and the anti-Nebraska meetings in New Haven. But by then, calls that Yale remain "national" rather than "sectional," and desist from taking a stand on the slavery issue, no doubt seemed plucked from a bygone era.[63] Moderation at Yale, at least on the slavery expansion question, tilted nearly to oblivion.

In the midst of such bitter conflicts, Black people in communities across the North increasingly faced existential decisions: whether to stay in America and fight for citizenship, or join one of an array of emigration schemes roiling about and leave the United States for possible resettlement in West Africa, Haiti, or Central America. Was there a refuge in the Americas or across the Atlantic for the sons and daughters of slaves, or those born free, safe from racism, economic hardship, and violence? For African Americans the 1850s had become a crucible for their identity, their status under law, and their very freedom. The debate over whether to stay or leave, contemplated by people of few means, tore apart some communities. Some folks found attractive a plan led by Henry Highland Garnet, the African Civilization Society, a religious mission that combined forces with the old American Colonization Society (a movement many Black Americans viewed with great suspicion). Others felt intrigued by abolitionist Martin R. Delany's effort to establish a colony far inland up the Niger River valley in West Africa. Delany himself toured Nigeria and hoped to secure land, but the scheme never took hold despite its emigrationist "back to Africa" romance. Closer to the United States, and more realistic, a Haitian emigration plan and company emerged, led by the Scottish abolitionist James Redpath and an African American Episcopal minister in New Haven named James Theodore Holly.[64]

In New Haven, the Reverend Amos Beman remained a steadfast proponent of radical abolitionism, temperance, and missionary work within the Black community and the nation. Churches like his Temple Street congregation faced many financial troubles as well as conflicts over leadership; in 1857 Beman lost his job when his parishioners rejected his marriage to a White woman and threw him out. Only blocks away on Park Street at St. Luke's Episcopal Church, however, the Reverend Holly took the pulpit in 1856 and held it until the secession crisis of 1861. Born in Washington, DC, and raised as a Catholic, Holly had moved north and was ordained as an Episcopal priest. Holly first visited Haiti in 1855 and established a lifelong commitment to the island's people and its fate. By the late 1850s Holly used his base in New Haven to serve as an outspoken advocate of Black "nationality" and recruiter for Haitian emigration by African Americans.[65]

The emigration issue caused tremendous turmoil and bitter fights among Black Northern leadership. Free African American communities faced not only legal discrimination and humiliation but also a national political scene riven with party conflict rooted in both their fate and that of slavery itself in the country's future. They looked inward and tried desperately to establish secure identities as Americans, as Canadians, or as immigrants to foreign lands. Their leadership engaged in brutal factional fights over strategy, personal rivalry, and the fruits of powerlessness and diminishing economic and political prospects. The physician, scientist, and activist James McCune Smith wrote to his close friend Frederick Douglass as early as 1854 complaining that the struggles over assimilation or separatism, political action or violent revolution, resistance or collaboration with White abolitionists, group self-reliance or a quest for citizenship rights splintered Black abolitionists from one another. "Each man feels his peculiar wrong," said Smith, "but no hundred men together feel precisely the same oppression; and, while each would do fair work to remove his own, he feels differently in regard to his neighbor's oppression."[66] And thus the challenge faced by James Holly at St. Luke's Church in New Haven, which was just a short walk from Yale College but, in terms of life chances as well as angle of vision on the national crises, was worlds apart. Professors, students, and administrators at Yale had their own rigorous disputes over the Union and slavery; the Black community around them, some of whom worked at the college, conducted their own, quite different struggles over the same issues.

Holly felt his wrongs deeply and made emigration the singular obsession of his life and eventually his ministry. He was only twenty years old when his family moved out of Brooklyn up to Burlington, Vermont, in 1850. The following year, he published his first piece of writing, a missive in the *Voice of the Fugitive*, edited by Henry Bibb, who was a former fugitive slave in Windsor, Canada, just across the river from Detroit. Holly condemned the Fugitive Slave Act of 1850, pointed to its dangers to all free Black people in Northern communities, and embraced emigration to Canada. He had already expressed serious interest in migration to Liberia under the American Colonization Society, but now the young man believed that African Americans' only hope rested in a separate attempt at their own nationality, a place with land and a government of their own making. In his earliest writings Holly maintained that Black people were "taxed without representation, practically denied the electoral franchise, denied the right in many states of protecting their chastity, liberty, lives, or property."[67]

Holly eventually soured on emigration to Canada, and soon he turned to the idea of Haiti as his race's destiny for a separate republic, moving with a growing family and an elderly mother first to Buffalo and then to Detroit, where he finished his study for the Episcopal priesthood, and then back to New Haven. Holly's first personal goal with Haitian emigration was for himself as a missionary to the island. Between 1856 and 1859 he worked assiduously from his base in New Haven to uplift the town's Black community, especially the schools, as he also recruited people for Haiti. He created his own short-lived school, the Select

School for Young Colored Ladies and Gentlemen, which taught Episcopal doctrine and race pride. The intrepid minister led sixty Black families in petitioning the New Haven Board of Education to improve the community's schools. In the spring of 1859, Holly published a series of short articles in the *Anglo-African Magazine*, making the case for African American destiny in Haiti and condemning racism in the United States. He desperately tried to raise money for Haitian emigration from the White hierarchy of the Episcopal Church as well as from Congressman Francis P. Blair of Missouri, a longtime colonizationist and advocate of Black removal from America. These overtures did not result in an effective alliance, but the Haitian government itself hired James Redpath, who in turn hired Holly, to encourage emigration to that country.[68]

By 1859, intense disputes had broken out among Black leaders. In the wake of the *Dred Scott* decision and later John Brown's raid on Harpers Ferry, they fought for the loyalty of Northern free Black people as well as for the tiny spoils of antislavery philanthropy. Martin Delany slammed Holly for working with White men, and Holly condemned Delany's scheme in Nigeria as a "fetish trick" he may have learned "from some savage tribe in the jungles of Central Africa." James McCune Smith attacked Holly for taking a "salary" from the Haitians and for his association with Redpath, whom many accused of corruption. The language became ugly as Smith said Holly's quest for a "negro nationality" was really "negro rascality," since his recruits were never told of the desperate failures of the 1824 attempt at Haitian emigration. Holly defended every aspect of his crusade; with or without resources, he recruited New Haven Black folks, as well as some from as far away as Canada. He preached a "manly self-reliance" to his charges and claimed they would become the modern "industrial Civilizers" of a redeemed Haitian republic.[69]

Holly did have Black allies; in the spring of 1861, what he called his "New Haven Colony" was ready to depart. The outbreak of the Civil War at Fort Sumter delayed the departure by at least a week since sea travel had suddenly become precarious. But on May 2, after a farewell gathering, 101 members of Holly's "colony" boarded a British ship, the *Madeira*, joining another 52 from Boston, and sailed for Haiti from New Haven Harbor. The dream of a free Haitian future collapsed quickly for many immigrants in Holly's group. In their first weeks on the island, in the midst of the rainy season, they coped with disease, desertion, and death. By July some had already returned in despair to New Haven. Holly soldiered on, but by the end of 1861 his own wife, Charlotte, and an infant son, Joseph, had died of disease; his son was the forty-third member of the original colony to succumb to the conditions.[70]

Holly remained the rest of his life in Haiti, where he eventually was ordained an Episcopal bishop, while his native land underwent the revolution of the Civil War and Reconstruction. As the exodus from Yale College by Southern students ensued, and as Northern students contemplated whether to enlist in the army to preserve the Union (while even some joined the newly formed Confederacy), Holly's contingent of Black emigrants cast their uncertain fate in a foreign land.

CHAPTER 9

Yale and New Haven in the Civil War

And so a great revolution has begun in these United (?) States whose end cannot be seen.

—THEODORE DWIGHT WOOLSEY,
president, Yale University, November 10, 1860

If one strolled near the Yale buildings on a day in June 1861, the "sound of fife and drum," reported the *Yale Literary Magazine*, might be heard nearly all day long, as students and even some faculty joined military drill companies. By the end of that month only thirteen of the more than five hundred Yale students had actually enlisted in the Union army and been sent to duty near Washington, DC, but war fervor and patriotism could be witnessed everywhere. Those students who left their studies for the army were often given send-offs at the train station and swords inscribed with their names. But the campus was not united in its support for the Union cause. An incident back on January 20 of that year, after South Carolina and several other Deep South states had seceded from the Union, had set the stage for more serious events to come. On a Sunday morning, students walking to chapel noticed an unusual flag flying from a tower on Alumni Hall. A witness identified the emblem as the "genuine Palmetto flag," and based on the description of "a Palmetto tree, a crescent and fifteen stars"—representing the fifteen states where slavery remained legal—it was likely one of the flags that appeared at South Carolina's secession convention the previous December. Some among the offended scaled the tower, tore down the flag, and, according to the *Literary Magazine*, "riddled" it with "pen knives" and took pieces for souvenirs.[1] Whether a youthful caper or a serious demonstration, a secessionist flag had indeed appeared in a prominent perch in the middle of the Yale campus.

Feb. 2, 1861.] FRANK LESLIE'S ILLUSTRATED NEWSPAPER. 173

cent in the corner, as I have tried to represent.

Truly yours,

Charles Lee Foster.

ISABELLA HINKLEY,

The American Prima Donna.

This accomplished and beautiful young lady, who achieved so marked a success at the Academy of Music on the night of the 23d inst., is a daughter of the soil, an American girl beyond peradventure, having been born in Albany, New York, in the year 1840. Her parents were both musical in temperament, and, therefore, her education began early, and with a careful mother to superintend her practice, she soon began to make a decided headway in the divine art. At the age of ten years she began studying the piano with Mr. O. J. Shaw (now a teacher in Utica), but had previously attained remarkable excellence as a pianist and reader of music. A few years afterwards, she commenced her vocal lessons with Mrs. Electra Cone Page, then a popular teacher of singing in Albany, and soon was capable of taking the entire charge of the music in the Church of the Holy Innocents. It was there that her voice was heard by Mr. George W. Warren, a leading professor of music in Albany, who was so much impressed with its beauty and power, that he made immediate offers to Miss Hinkley to become the soprano of St. Paul's Church (where he was organist), and also a pupil.

From that time her success in Albany was quite remarkable. She made her debut at an annual concert given for the relief of the poor by Mr. Warren, and accomplished a vocal triumph rarely ever before witnessed in that ancient city. She became the pet of the public, and her beautiful voice, daily increasing in power and expression, was the town's talk.

At the end of another two years, during which period she occasionally favored the public, she displayed such remarkable talent that her father, Dr. J. W. Hinkley, one of the most respected

ALUMNI HALL, YALE COLLEGE, AS IT APPEARED ON THE MORNING OF SUNDAY, JAN 20TH, THE SECESSION FLAG, PLANTED THERE BY THE SOUTHERN STUDENTS, FLYING ON ONE OF ITS TURRETS.—FROM A SKETCH BY OUR CORRESPONDENT.

political troubles in Italy determined Miss Hinkley to leave that city of arts and return to America. She accordingly departed from Florence on the 22d September, 1860, intending to sail immediately for America; but arriving at Paris, she was dissuaded from this rather hasty resolution by several celebrated artists of that city, who advised her to remain in Europe, until, acquiring some artistic reputation and receiving great encouragement from all, she gave a grand concert, with Madame Lorini—formerly Miss Virginia Whiting, of Boston—with great success, on the 12th October, 1860. In the following month she received and accepted an offer for Amsterdam, Holland, where she made her debut on the night of December 24, 1860, in the rôle of Adalgisa in "Norma," with Madame Rosa De Vries, in which she met with the greatest success ever obtained by any débutante. She sang, during the season there, also the operas "Linda di Chamounix" and "Il Trovatore," and also in opera and concerts at Rotterdam, Utrecht, the Hague, Harlaam, Arnheim and Nimeguen. She sang twice at Court at the Hague, and received a most flattering mark of attention from Her Majesty the Queen of Holland, who took her by the hand, complimented her highly upon her voice, and thanked her for the pleasure she had afforded her, and shortly after she was presented by the Queen with an elegant bracelet. On the night of February 16th, 1860, on the occasion of her benefit at Amsterdam, she received from her manager a diamond bracelet.

Finishing her engagement in Holland she was immediately secured by M. Merelli, and made her debut at Brussels, May 19th, in the opera of "Lucia di Lammermoor." She sang also with immense success at Antwerp, Frankfort-on-the-Maine, Wiesbaden, Homburg, Cologne, Bonn, Crefeld, Dusseldorf, Aix la Chapelle, Maestricht, Hamburg and Berlin, in the operas "Norma," "Linda," "Lucia," "Il Trovatore" (both parts), in "Don Pasquale," "Il Barbiere," "Il Matrimonio Segreto," and Zerlina in "Don Giovanni."

SECESSION IN YALE COLLEGE—THE NORTHERN STUDENTS BREAKING IN THE DOOR OF THE TOWER IN ALUMNI HALL, TO TAKE DOWN THE SECESSION FLAG PLANTED THERE BY THE SOUTHERN STUDENTS.—FROM A SKETCH BY OUR CORRESPONDENT.

physicians of Albany, determined that his daughter should have the superlative advantages of the masters of Italy. It was a sad blow to the Albanians to lose Miss Hinkley, but they honored her, just prior to her departure, with a grand complimentary concert, which was given on the evening of the 16th of April, 1857, which netted her a clear one thousand dollars. She sailed for Europe on the 16th of May of the same year, and soon after her arrival in Florence began a course of study with the celebrated Signor Pietro Romani, and soon became the favorite pupil of this renowned master. She made her first appearance in Florence at the Philharmonic Concert, in presence of the Grand Duke of Tuscany, December 21st, 1859, and shortly afterwards was made honorary member of the Florentine Philharmonic Society and presented with a diploma. Soon after, she received an engagement with the celebrated composer, Pacini, to sing his new opera, called "Il Saltimbanco," but the unfortunate revolution in Italy, which broke out almost immediately, caused the cessation of all amusements, and she was, therefore, obliged to renounce that honor. The continuation of

TEARING DOWN THE SECESSION FLAG FROM THE TOWER OF ALUMNI HALL, YALE COLLEGE, BY THE NORTHERN STUDENTS.—FROM A SKETCH BY OUR CORRESPONDENT.

While at Cologne, Ullman was present at a representation of "Il Barbiere," and immediately offered Miss Hinkley an engagement for New York. She was already engaged for Milan, but by paying a sum of money the engagement was cancelled and that of Ullman accepted, and to fulfil which she sailed in November for New York, arriving here on the 17th, after an absence of three years and seven months.

A TOUCHING RELIC.

A torn sheet of paper, evidently hastily taken from a ship's log book, on which there was some writing in the Norwegian language has been found in a bottle picked up floating past Barth Head, in Pentland Frith. The paper is found to relate to the Norwegian schooner Albion, a missing ship; and from the contents of the writing it is inferred that the unfortunate ship must have foundered and that all on board met with a watery grave. The translation of the writing by the Swedish Consul is as follows:

"The Norwegian schooner Albion, of Christiana, sunk on the 4th of December, about abreast of Bockarees. The crew, consisting of Captain Frantz Holst, the mate (Robert Bockman), who, in the hour

Frank Leslie's Illustrated Newspaper, February 2, 1861.

Library of Congress, Prints and Photographs Division.

The numbers of Yale students from the Southern states remained relatively steady throughout the antebellum era until the mid-1850s when the national crisis over slavery decimated this long tradition at the college. In 1840–41, the percentage of Southern students was approximately 11 percent; thereafter the numbers tallied at about 13 percent in 1845–46, 11 percent in 1850–51, 9 percent in 1855–56, and only 3 percent in the year of secession, 1860–61. Total Yale undergraduate enrollment reached a high of 574 in 1840 and a low of 521 in 1860. By the summer of 1861, as the war raged and mobilization ensued across the country, virtually no Southerners remained enrolled in New Haven. Yale's actual participation in the Civil War on both sides has long been studied and debated by various statistical methods. The most authoritative account of Yale men who served the Confederacy, including soldiers and civil officials, counts 511, 55 of whom died in the war. In counting Yale men serving the Union cause, some studies include graduates, undergraduates who did not graduate, and civilian officials, including those who might have served in the private United States Sanitary Commission. William Evarts estimated that one-quarter of living graduates, or about 600 men, had served in some capacity. In 1865, the *Yale Literary Magazine* said 737 alumni had contributed to the war effort. Around the same time, Franklin Bowditch Dexter counted 758 serving in the Union cause. In 1879, James Hoppin advanced a new number of 836, and in Ellsworth Eliot's 1932 book, the number rose to 1,044 devoted to the Union cause. In 1996 a Yale undergraduate, Garry Reeder Jr., produced an exhibit at Sterling Memorial Library, "Elms and Magnolia," in which he counted 836 in service to the United States.[2] These disparate numbers leave us with the realization that the conflict had profound effects on the Civil War generations of Yale men, although, numerically, a good deal less than on other segments of American society.

Among the 511 Yale Confederates, a remarkable 68 were from Northern states. Connecticut contributed an astonishing 28 Yale men who served the Confederate cause. New Haven's own William Webster, grandson of the iconic figure Noah Webster, attended West Point military academy after graduating from Yale. He was related to the Robert E. Lee family of Virginia, cast his lot with the South in 1861, and was killed at the Battle of Gaines's Mill in the Seven Days' campaign, defending Richmond, on June 27, 1862. Many among the Yale Confederates had moved South as teachers or lawyers after graduation and chose to serve their new region or state. And many were staunch defenders of slavery and secession. George Thatcher of Bennington, Vermont, had moved to Louisiana, where he became a captain in Confederate artillery. After surviving in the war, he opened a school in Shreveport.[3]

Of course, the South produced the lion's share of Yale's Confederates. William Barry (Yale 1841) returned to his native Mississippi, where he became a successful lawyer, Speaker of the state legislature, and the presiding officer at the Mississippi secession convention. Joseph E. Brown took his law degree at Yale in 1846 and went home to Georgia, where he rose as a successful politician and fierce advocate of states' rights and slavery. Brown served as Georgia's governor from 1857 to 1865, loyally defending his state to the bitter end of defeat. John T. Taylor (Yale Law School 1840) was a Unionist but followed the path of his state, Alabama, into secession. These men hardly all agreed. Allen Caperton (Yale 1832) resisted secession in his native Virginia, survived opposing the Confederate war effort, and eventually became governor of West Virginia, a new free state formed during the war.[4]

Certainly one of the most famous Yale men in the Confederate cause was Judah P. Benjamin. Born on the Danish Virgin Island of Saint Croix, Benjamin immigrated with his Jewish family to the American South as a boy, eventually settling in Louisiana. He entered Yale at age fourteen in 1825, staying only two years. Stories vary as to why he withdrew or was expelled. One unauthenticated version is that he was thrown out for theft at the tender age of sixteen. Benjamin became a successful lawyer, a planter and slaveholder, and finally a U.S. senator from Louisiana who resigned his post to secede with his state and support the Confederacy in 1861. Appointed by Jefferson Davis, Benjamin served as the Confederacy's attorney general, secretary of war, and secretary of state to the very end of the conflict. Becoming the first Jewish person to serve in cabinet positions in North America has long been Benjamin's most distinctive legacy. But he was a diehard proslavery Confederate who barely survived capture at the end of the war. After the South's defeat, Benjamin fled clandestinely through Florida and the Caribbean to England, where, after establishing a new legal career, he died in Paris, an unrepentant rebel, in 1882.[5]

Other Yale graduates never saw the battlefield or served in a cabinet position, but they influenced the course of the war in other ways. The famous inventor and Yale graduate Samuel F. B. Morse made his major contribution as a propagandist. Long a critic of abolitionism, Morse was in disbelief when the war broke out, and he tried to use his considerable wealth and influence to personally broker a peace between North and South. But in September 1862, when Abraham Lincoln signed the preliminary Emancipation Proclamation, Morse was so disgusted with what he called an "abominable hallucination" that he shifted his energy from reconciliation to an all-out propaganda war against the Union plan. Joining together with other wealthy, well-connected New York business leaders, he helped form an organization called the New York Society for the Diffusion of Political Knowledge; the group soon chose Morse as their president. Their central aim was to achieve the repeal of the president's proclamation. In addition to a magazine, the society soon set about producing and printing twenty pamphlets. Morse and his fellow millionaires heavily subsidized the effort so their pamphlets could be cheaply distributed in the thousands.[6]

Morse had made a great name for himself, and an enormous fortune, as an inventor. He felt both would allow him to shape the terms of the debate over emancipation, and he dove headfirst into spreading his message: attempts to end slavery were unwise, immoral, and unbiblical. His anti-Black views were not new. As early as 1826, Morse wrote that Black people were by nature inferior: "Witness the negro, the ouran outan, the baboon, the monkey by gradual and downward steps blending the human face divine, with the unseemly visage of the brute." And he had called abolitionists "demons in human shape." In the pamphlet he personally authored for the society, *An Argument on the Ethical Position of Slavery in the Social System, and Its Relation to the Politics of the Day*, he suffused these proslavery, anti-Black arguments with a neo-Puritan theology and his interpretation of the Bible. Like Timothy Dwight decades before, Morse insisted that the ideals of the revolution had been horribly misguided. He blamed the revolution and its American leaders for misleading the country about "the miserable delusion of *negro freedom*." He argued, "*Slavery*, the subjection of one's will to the will of another, since the fall of man, is the rule, and not *liberty*." The idea of human equality, in fact, was the "*fundamental error*." For Black people, he wrote, "Slavery to them has been Salvation, and Freedom, ruin."[7]

Morse's ideas about the inherent inequality of the races—and the sin of abolitionism—traveled far and wide. In fact, he complained of the "constant demand upon me" for copies of his pamphlet. And in 1863, he published another treatise building on his earlier themes. The Connecticut-born, Yale-educated inventor explained that Alexander Stephens, vice president of the Confederate States of America, had not gone far enough in his famous "cornerstone speech." Contra Stephens, Morse insisted, "The corner-stone is the inequality of the two races." He condemned "THE GREAT ERROR OF THE WORLD ON SLAVERY," writing, "The great fallacy, so rife every where throughout the world, that *slavery is the cause of our national troubles*." But Morse insisted slavery was not the cause of the war but "a blind and mad resistance to a physical condition which God has ordained and which man is, in vain, attempting to subvert."[8] Although he deplored abolitionism, what Morse hated more was the idea that Black people could ever be equal to his race.

War enthusiasm and mobilization remained strong in New Haven in the first two years of the struggle, although Yale men seemed hardly willing in any significant numbers to make the ultimate patriotic sacrifice. They no doubt observed many reasons for caution in the press coverage and increasingly popular awareness of the scale of casualties in the unprecedented battles of 1862: the Battle of Shiloh in southwestern Tennessee, April 6–7, with 23,741 dead and wounded in the combined armies; the Seven Days' Battles in the Peninsula Campaign at Richmond, June 25–July 1, with roughly 20,000 Union and 16,000 Confederate casualties; the Battle of Second Manassas in northern Virginia, August 28–30, with 22,180 casualties; the Battle of Antietam in Maryland, September 17, with 23,100 casualties in eight hours of horrific fighting, the bloodiest single day in American military history; the Battle of Fredericksburg in central Virginia, December 13, with 17,929 dead and maimed on a snowy winter landscape of hell. The numbers become clinical on the page, but in families and communities the shuddering reality sank deep, and the following two years would be much worse. In 1862, the horror to come could not yet be known—that, before this war ended, 30,218 Union soldiers would die in prison camps in the South and 25,976 Confederates would die in Northern prisons.[9] This ghastly human cost gave those with choices a reason to find a path out of the slaughter.

Nothing had ever challenged the values of young men in the nineteenth century—about courage, valor, duty, honor, and male gender expectations generally—like the Civil War. Whether to volunteer, to serve, or to use one's class or racial privilege to avoid serving in this all-out war for the survival of the United States and eventually to destroy slavery were potent challenges alone. If a man did enlist and face combat in a war using modern weapons—the rifled musket, deadly at hundreds of yards, and artillery of ever-expanding capacities to inflict mass casualties—the old-fashioned notion of an individual's bravery as the measure of the best soldier became a dangerous, irrelevant idea. And disease in the largest armies ever assembled, in field hospitals and prison camps, killed twice as many men in this war as battlefield wounds. With massive exposure to combat and killing, and after burying large numbers of comrades because of disease, the idealism of 1861 could only wane. The ideologies and purposes of the war on the Northern side shifted markedly with the emancipation policies of 1862–63, and an astonishingly high number of Yankees sustained patriotic devotion to the fullest measure down to 1865. But as the older values of an individual's duty, honor, courage, and country ran headlong into modern war, a Yale man's vaunted aspirations for leadership faced impossible odds and the bleak reality of slaughter.[10] Most simply chose not to abandon their road to success and power that a Yale College education made possible.

In order to fill the ranks, both sides in the Civil War resorted to conscription. In March 1863, with the pivotal summer military campaigns on the immediate horizon in the eastern and western theaters of the war, Congress passed a conscription act, and by July districts across the country faced designated quotas, pro rata shares of the population in relation to the president's call for three hundred thousand men, with only fifty days to fill them. But there were ways to avoid the draft—hundreds of thousands fled to Canada or out west—particularly by hiring and paying a "substitute," if one could afford it or found the means from loans. Under the draft law, a man who passed the physical exam could hire a substitute to go in his place or pay an average $300 commutation fee to obtain an exemption. Some eighty-seven thousand men paid commutation fees and another seventy-four thousand furnished substitutes to fill the ranks of cannon fodder in the Union infantry. The pool of substitutes came largely from eighteen-to-nineteen-year-olds and immigrants, rather than from Yale College undergraduates. Roughly three-quarters of all men who reported to provosts' offices under the draft were able to buy their way out of the army. In the end only about 7 percent of all troops in the Union forces were draftees. The one success that might be attributed to the conscription policy was that it prompted a great deal of volunteering; during the two years of the draft's operation, some eight hundred thousand men enlisted and fought in the war.[11]

Many eventually famous Yale graduates of the immediate prewar and war years chose to ignore the national upheaval and pursue their studies. O. C. Marsh (Yale 1860), the future paleontologist, spent two years at Yale's Sheffield Scientific School and the remainder of the war years at German universities. Josiah W. Gibbs (Yale 1858), with a deep Yale pedigree, stayed on to become the country's first recipient of a doctorate in engineering in 1863 on his way to great fame as a scientist and mathematician. And William Graham Sumner (Yale 1863) paid a substitute to take his place in the draft during his graduation year and left for extended international study on his way to becoming the famed laissez-faire economist and sometimes notorious social Darwinist.[12] The war failed to kill off these and many more brilliant young men who followed inner intellectual callings rather than that of their country.

Yale president Theodore Woolsey was a cautious man, although in private letters and public expressions he declared himself solidly against secession. In November 1860, just after the presidential election, Woolsey wrote to his friend Francis Lieber, who had spent much time as a scholar and teacher in the South and who soon would be tasked by the Lincoln administration with writing a new code of war: "And so a great revolution has begun in these United (?) States whose end cannot be seen." Woolsey took a stand on disunion under any guise. "I put no faith in secession," he said, "or the will of the mass of the people of the south to live by themselves, but if, perchance, the hotheads should carry out their will, it would, amid the evils of disunion, be the greatest stab to slavery that could be received." Here Woolsey stood with many radical abolitionists, even if unwittingly, in hoping Southern secession would open a political chasm in which slavery might not survive. He preferred "a conciliatory course," which reflected his temperament, "but if they must secede, let slavery try its self-sustaining power for the next half century. It will be an experience for the world's good." Woolsey could hardly grasp at that point how nothing so gradual would be the outcome of this terrible war. On the day of South Carolina's secession (December 20, 1860), he wrote to Lieber again, declaring that he believed the "crisis will pass over," but demanding a strong federal stance against secession for national "self-preservation." The South's actions with secession were "treasonable designs" and, in the Yale leader's view, should "be roughly and decisively dealt with."[13]

After the initial enthusiasm at the outbreak of the war, Yale College resumed in 1861, by and large, a business-as-usual campus and academic life. Woolsey's biographer, George King, contends that Yale College "continued in an uninterrupted, fairly placid manner." As president, suggests King, Woolsey had to manage the institution in a relatively nonpartisan way because Yale men were serving on both sides of the war, and the university had a proud history of attracting Southern students. But if the campus remained relatively tranquil, the students played a major role in keeping it so. Enrollments declined only slightly, new professorships were created, donations rolled in, and students continued debate and rowing competitions as usual. Only a small percentage of Yale students enlisted after the early rush. "No rallies were held at any time to encourage enlistment," and most students "remained merely spectators throughout the entire conflict," according to the historian Ellsworth Eliot. Little evidence emerges that any faculty openly promoted enlistment among students, at least not publicly.[14]

The military drafts of 1862–64 certainly garnered the attention of Yale students, their parents, and faculty. In the first year, New Haven County met its enlistment quotas from the larger working-class community. As a result of the Conscription Act of 1863, however, some ninety students and three faculty were drafted, including Timothy Dwight V, a future Yale president. Of the students, thirty-four were exempted for various reasons, although ten of those ended up serving anyway in various capacities. The New York City draft riots of July 1863 frightened the New Haven and Yale community. More than thirty students, almost all undergraduates, volunteered to serve in defense of the city, should any

The Reverend Theodore Dwight Woolsey, circa 1858.
Manuscripts and Archives, Yale University Library.

violent attacks emerge in response to the draft. By August the *Yale Literary Magazine* reported rumors that New Haven's "laboring classes" were planning to storm the campus in protest of the draft's inequities. No such violence occurred, but the *Magazine* wrote with grandiose, farcical language about Yale men: "The sons of Alma Mater rushed to her [Yale College's] defense" and "gallantly held . . . advanced positions."[15]

During the war President Woolsey received reams of correspondence about the causes and purposes of the war and especially about the draft. Mason Brown, a former classmate of Woolsey's from Kentucky, who held fifty-one people in slavery on the eve of the war, wrote in July 1862 to remind the president "how devoted to the Union" he was, but also to express his belief that "we will soon be a separate people." Brown had several sons (John Mason Brown had graduated from Yale in 1856) and feared that his eighteen-year-old would never be able to attend the Sheffield Scientific School at Yale. "May providence prevent your blood & mine from ever meeting in . . . combat." The son, John, also wrote to Woolsey about his dilemma of whether to enlist in the Confederate army. He was so torn, he reported, that he "resolved to abstain from the fight." A former student of Woolsey's, Jacob Cooper (Yale 1852), had taken a professorship in Greek at Centre College in Danville, Kentucky. He enlisted as chaplain in the Third Kentucky Infantry of the Union army. Cooper sought Woolsey's counsel because his "views on slavery" were "rather too northern for this latitude." Despite its official "neutrality" status, Kentucky was a horribly divided society during the war. Cooper felt under constant threat of "public violence" in spring 1862. The Reverend Joseph Parrish Thompson (Yale 1838), pastor of Broadway Tabernacle Church in New York, wrote to Woolsey in 1862 in a quandary about his son, John H. Thompson, then a student in the class of 1865 at Yale. The father did not want his son to enlist in the army. The elder Thompson believed that "young men engaged in a course of education" should be allowed to opt out. The younger Thompson thought otherwise and in June 1862, he joined the 106th New York Infantry. Less than a year later in March 1863, Woolsey received the news that John Thompson had died of pneumonia at North Mountain, Virginia. Joseph Thompson wrote with heartfelt honesty to the Yale president, "His life was peculiarly intertwined with mine; and I will not disguise the fact that I am in bitterness for him, as one who is 'in bitterness for his first born.'"[16] Such sentiments were all too common across America by that spring.

Great pivots in the war brought important news from Yale graduates around the nation. From Philadelphia, Charles J. Stillé (Yale 1839) observed "significant signs of the times" in the new Black regiments appearing and training at Camp Penn in 1863. "The negro regiments are magnificent," said Stillé, "more resembling in appearance foreign troops than any other soldiers we have." White officers were stepping up to command Black regiments. "The world is evidently moving," Stillé concluded. The Reverend Henry S. DeForest (Yale 1857), chaplain of the Eleventh Connecticut Infantry, entered Richmond at its collapse in April 1865 and witnessed Confederate evacuation as Lincoln toured the city and its ruins. But "grandest of all," wrote DeForest, "was the President's retinue of jubilant Freedmen. . . . Even-handed justice is finding the scale-beam horizontal." DeForest would later serve as president of Talladega College in Alabama, founded by and for freedmen at the end of the war.[17] Woolsey's many correspondents provided him with a multiplicity of perspectives on the events and popular attitudes at the heart of the war. Still, he did his best to keep his political views and reactions to the terrible losses in the war to himself.

Perhaps most vexing to Woolsey were the letters from Yale graduates and their family members asking for guidance about the draft. In August 1862, Governor William Buckingham offered Woolsey a deal indicating that if the president would confirm the names of enrolled Yale students who had been drafted, he would exempt them from service and require New Haven Selectmen to find them substitutes. That same month a student, James Cowles (Yale 1866), wrote to the president at his mother's urging: "I am an only son & she is a widow. Please answer soon if convenient as Mother is quite anxious about the draft." So was young Cowles. Howard Kingsbury (Yale 1863), seeking similar guidance, claimed he was "not at all anxious to escape service," because he would "much prefer volunteering to being drafted." Pride goeth before the fall. There is no evidence that Kingsbury ever enlisted. Horace D. Paine (Yale 1964), from Woonsocket, Rhode Island, asked Woolsey to help him understand how conscription would be enforced for out-of-state students. Finally, and above all, parents wrote directly to Woolsey seeking information about the draft. In August 1862, W. E. Heisler of Christiana, Delaware, inquired of Woolsey how the draft would affect his two sons who were about the enroll as freshmen. In a remarkable understatement, Heisler said that "owing to the troubled condition of our country," his sons needed to know whether they would be "exempt from Military duty."[18] It is not clear how or how often Woolsey answered these queries, but most definitely, news of Governor Buckingham's pledge of exemptions had spread far and wide.

By the summer of 1864, Yale came under attack by the *New York Times* for its alleged "draft-shirking." On August 23–24, the *Times* accused Yale students and their faculty and administration of "plotting evasion and desertion." At the college, claimed the *Times* editorials, "how to escape the draft" was the issue of the day. "The gutters are dragged for substitutes. Traps are set in Europe. Negro slaves, who owe to the Republic nothing but curses, are driven to the rescue." By the summer of 1864, the recruitment of Black soldiers was in full course, albeit with brutal discriminations in pay and denial of commissioned officer status. The *Times*, which at this juncture did not support the Lincoln administration in the high drama of the presidential election of that year, exploited the class issue fully. This controversy emerged at a bitterly sensitive moment in the war, with a condition of bloody stalemate in both Virginia and Georgia. The educated class should be at the front as officers, the *Times* editors asserted. Instead, Yale represented "an outrage upon all decency to make a diploma of good stout Latin a signal for desertion and a rallying rag for cowards." Yale seems to have avoided an official response to these accusations, but William Walter Phelps (Yale 1860), a valedictorian who had hosted a meeting in New York to advise Yale men of their options in the face of the draft, counterattacked. In a letter to the editor the following day, he claimed the gathering was to help in their "plans of cooperation" with the draft law by offering "assistance to procure a substitute or to support their families in their absence." Both motives may have been true, but Phelps's assertion of a search for "substitutes for those whose conscience did not send them, whose health would not suffer them, whose family could not do without them" sugarcoated the reality of the response by Yale men to the conscription law. They only sought to "distribute the burden of a draft," Phelps wrote with unrestrained noblesse oblige.[19]

In March 1862, the *Yale Literary Magazine* reported the first Yale death in combat. Theodore Winthrop, an 1848 graduate, had been killed in eastern Virginia at the Battle of Big Bethel, June 10, 1861, an early and humiliating Union defeat. The campus publication waited nine months to eulogize the soldier and tell his story. Born in New Haven, an admired student and a poet, novelist, and travel writer, Winthrop was President Woolsey's nephew. After college, Winthrop went west as an explorer and an adventurer; he joined one expedition that trekked through the Isthmus of Panama. Only a few days after Fort Sumter, on April 17, 1861, Winthrop told his uncle Theodore that he had enlisted in the army "for the purpose of lending my aid to the great work of attempting to get rid of slavery in this country." He enlisted in the Seventh New York Regiment, one of the earliest units formed anywhere in the North, and full of college graduates and aristocratic New York boys. Since he was an officer, his body was turned over to Union troops and transported by train to New York, where a military funeral was held. When the casket arrived in New Haven, a military escort including Yale students led the procession to Grove Street Cemetery, where he was buried.[20] Winthrop seems to have represented a beau ideal to the other Yale students, at least at this early juncture of the war; before long, battlefield deaths would not prompt quite the same pomp and ceremony for the individual fallen.

In death Winthrop achieved, at least for fifteen years or so, the literary fame he had sought in life. He had left behind drawers full of his manuscripts. When the war broke out, Winthrop lived in Greenwich Village and shared an apartment with the painter Frederic Church. Soon after his death, his gothic novel with strong queer themes, *Cecil Dreeme*, was published. Telling the story of a young bohemian New Yorker living with a handsome young painter in an area

Theodore Winthrop, Yale College class of 1848 and the first Yale graduate killed in the Civil War. Images of Yale Individuals (RU 684). Manuscripts and Archives, Yale University Library.

thinly disguised as Washington Square, it gained wide acclaim. As he went to war, Winthrop wrote dispatches for the *Atlantic Monthly*. In his first, he described in vivid terms the spectacular march through Manhattan of the Seventh Regiment in April. "It was worth a life, that march," he wrote. "Only one who passed, as we did, through that tempest of cheers, two miles long, can know the terrible enthusiasm of the occasion. I could hardly hear the rattle of our own gun-carriages, and only once or twice the music of our band came to me muffled and quelled by the uproar. Handkerchiefs, of course, came floating down upon us from the windows, like a snow. Pretty little gloves pelted us with love-taps." When the regiment reached Washington, DC, no quarters existed, so they encamped inside the chamber of the House of Representatives in the Capitol. Winthrop exploited the irony of the moment in the *Atlantic.* "Our presence here was the inevitable sequel of past events," he said. "We appeared with bayonets and bullets because of the bosh uttered on this floor; because of the bills—with treasonable stump-speeches in their bellies—passed here; because of the cowardice of the poltroons . . . the arrogance of the bullies, who had here cooperated to blind and corrupt the minds of the people." These images of nearly a thousand men sleeping on their knapsacks in the House chamber would be unforgettable to his eager readers in those early months of the war, especially after they learned of the journey of his flag-draped coffin to New York City and to the honored burial in New Haven.[21]

Another Yale student, Uriah Parmelee, enlisted immediately when the war commenced in April 1861. Parmelee dropped out in his junior year and joined a New York regiment of cavalry as a private because no Connecticut unit was yet available. In 1863, he transferred to the First Connecticut Cavalry and was promoted to lieutenant for special bravery at the Battle of Chancellorsville in May, and then to captain for the same combat leadership at the Battle of Ashland on June 1, 1864, during the Wilderness Campaign. His letters, as well as his diary, which he kept in 1864 and 1865, provide glimpses of the war's brutality and one soldier's effort to make sense of the suffering.[22]

Parmelee had attended sermons by the famous antislavery preacher Henry Ward Beecher at the Plymouth Church in Brooklyn while a student at Yale, and he carried into the army as strong a commitment to abolitionism as one may find in such a young Union soldier. In early 1862 Parmelee declared his passion for the cause. "I am fighting for Liberty, for the slaves & for the white man alike," he wrote to his mother. He believed that Confederates had "forfeited" any property rights to slaves by their secession. In April 1862, he announced to his brother Sam, "I am more of an abolitionist than ever—right up to the handle—if I had money enough to raise a few hundred contrabands & arm them I'd get up an insurrection among them—told capt. I'd desert to do it." Such bravado subsided in Parmelee's letters as he matured into a hardened veteran of too much real war. But his commitment remained intact. He chafed at the slow pace of what appeared to be an indifferent or hostile approach to emancipation by the Lincoln administration, and therefore by the army. Parmelee believed the constitutional questions would surely be solved by the war, "but the great heart wound, Slavery, will not be reached," he told his mother, without an aggressive emancipation policy enacted by the Union forces. On

September 8, 1862, only a week and a half before the pivotal Battle of Antietam, with the Army of the Potomac in pursuit of Robert E. Lee's Confederate army invading Maryland, the young soldier lamented that this cruel struggle had not yet resulted in "universal Emancipation." But in the wake of President Lincoln's Preliminary Emancipation Proclamation on September 22, and then one hundred days later with the final proclamation, Parmelee changed his tune. By March 1863, anticipating the spring and summer campaigns in Virginia, the Guilford farm boy turned intellectual soldier refused to apply for a furlough to take a break back home. "I do not intend to shirk now there is really something to fight for—I mean freedom," he declared. "Since the First of January it has become more and more evident to my mind that the war is henceforth to be conducted upon a different basis.... So then I am willing to remain & endure whatever may fall to my share."[23]

With his patriotic commitment to emancipation and Union refurbished, and believing in a kind of redemption through bloodshed that became a relatively popular Northern attitude, Parmelee nevertheless betrayed his caustic, hardened sense of what soldiering and war had done to his psyche. "We are liable to become mere machines," he complained in that same spring of 1863, enduring endless camp life. "One can make no plans in the army, indulge no hopes in any particular direction, have no independence, no voice in anything." A soldier does his duty, Parmelee concluded, but he was no unthinking machine as he read his Shakespeare and begged his mother to send him more published essays by Henry Ward Beecher from the *Independent*. "If it were not for that spark of hope which lives with nothing to feed upon," he "would soon give up everything," concluded the lonely son to his frightened mother. By late September 1863, after the horrific battles of Chancellorsville and Gettysburg, the hard campaigning in between and massive casualties, the idealist had become the mature realist. "Things appear mixed in this world & motives & actions are not as clearly defined as we might wish them." As he watched comrades die around him for nearly four years, he wondered at times why he lived to tell of it. Fifty-six percent of the First Connecticut died before the war ended; he was increasingly a scribe to the bereaved back home.[24]

In the winter and spring of 1865, his cavalry unit moved southward through western Virginia in a combined operation with General Ulysses Grant's army, which had had Lee's forces under siege at Petersburg since late summer 1864. On August 1, 1864, he wrote kindly of a mate named Tuttle who "sings plaintive songs—he is a great deal of company to me.... Read Othello to him last night." On August 11, Captain Parmelee was bereft that he had loaned his tattered volume of Shakespeare to a comrade named Harrison who had promptly lost it. By early 1865 his First Connecticut was part of General George Armstrong Custer's division and the large cavalry contingents in General Philip Sheridan's army. In South Carolina and soon North Carolina, the huge columns of General William T. Sherman's army moved slowly northward in what would ultimately bring about the military collapse of the Confederacy that spring. The slaveholders' rebellion teetered on destruction with Federal forces moving simultaneously from the south, the west, and all around its capital at Richmond. As his unit passed through Charlottesville, Parmelee saw Thomas Jefferson's Monticello, and he complained that Union forces had burned part of the university town with "carelessness." On March 4, he noted that Lincoln would give his second inaugural address that day in Washington, and he remembered reading the first one four years earlier in a Yale classroom. In the next few weeks, Sheridan's forces moved eastward to help surround and trap Lee's army as it tried to escape westward. On March 25, Confederate troops desperately tried to break the siege in a bloody assault on Fort Stedman, part of the massive trench works around Petersburg, but failed. The next day Sheridan's army, and Parmelee's unit, crossed the James River and made a junction with Grant's forces. In his diary one can feel Parmelee trying to make sense of this vast geography of war. Petersburg and now Richmond, the Confederate capital, would have to be abandoned. Parmelee made his final entry in the diary on March 30, saying he "went out alone seeking intellectual clearness. What mightn't a man do with this state of mind habitually?"[25]

Lee gave orders to hold at all costs the area around Five Forks, southwest of Richmond, as he sought a corridor of escape. After two days of pelting rain, and with spring blossoms of red bud and dogwoods now in full bloom all over central Virginia, the last major battle of the war occurred at Five Forks on April 1. About midday, dismounted, the First Connecticut saw Confederates at a short distance in a peach orchard in full bloom. Parmelee, as was his way, stood up and led his men in a charge as cannon opened up from the orchard. He was struck in the chest by an artillery shell and fell dead on the field. Later that day amid the carnage, his body was recovered and buried in a temporary grave in the yard of a nearby large farmhouse.[26] Only eight days later, the end that everyone sought came as Lee surrendered some twenty-two thousand malnourished soldiers to Grant farther west at Appomattox Court House in one of the signal events of American history. Parmelee's unit and Custer's division were given the honor to accept the arms of their defeated foes. A stillness and a quiet for the moment fell over the armies and a flower-bedecked village in Virginia.[27]

Parmelee never finished his studies at Yale, and he never retrieved his copy of Shakespeare's plays during that final march. But he understood all sides of war's deadly attractions after four harrowing years. Perhaps the abolitionist Parmelee would have agreed with Shakespeare's courageous Hotspur in *Henry IV* that "the arms are fair / When the intent of bearing them is just." But he surely knew, by April 1865, the meaning of a soldier's words to his king in *Henry V*: "There are few die well that die in a battle."[28]

During the war, New Haven became a major gathering point for regiments of Connecticut soldiers. Troops camped at Oyster Point (today's City Point on the harbor), Grape Vine Point (today's Criscuolo Park), Brewster Park (later Hamilton Park, near what is today Edgewood Park), and East Rock Park (called Camp Russell at the time). All of these are regular sites of leisure or recreation today; in 1861–65, they bustled with thousands of soldiers and all the horses, wagons, supply vehicles, chaos, and pathogens that came with armies. In 1861, New Haven was the largest city in Connecticut, with nearly forty thousand people, some ten thousand more than Hartford. It was also a thriving early industrial city with a booming and diverse manufacturing base. The railroad depot, in the center of town with a north entrance right on Chapel Street, was only a five-minute walk from the Yale campus. More than five hundred Yale students watched the arrival and marching of the troops nearly every day, especially in the early years of the war, even as they could manage a certain seclusion inside the Brick Row. The New York and New Haven Railroad arrived and departed ten times a day from early morning until late at night. The majestic elm trees, planted under James Hillhouse's direction, lined Temple and Chapel Streets, but the rumblings of the railcars and their whistles could be heard from dormitories. Four steamboats also ran daily between New Haven and New York.[29]

Connecticut regiments that mustered and initially trained in and around New Haven held ceremonial parades and final send-offs on the Green, flag-draped events no witness could ever forget. On August 28, 1862, the day the Battle of Second Manassas commenced in northern Virginia, with Lee's army invading northward, the Fifteenth Connecticut Regiment marched from State Street to Chapel, and then to Church Street and onto the Green near the State House. According to the *New Haven Palladium*, an "immense crowd" cheered "amid sunshine, tears and hearty good-byes." Much of that regiment had been recruited in New Haven County, and their families and friends waved from the crowds. The regiment traveled to Washington, DC, on a train of thirty cars; some two hundred had purchased "'steel' armored vests" from the Atwater Armor

Soldiers assembled on the New Haven Green, circa 1865. Buildings, Grounds, and Landmarks in New Haven Photographs (RU 685). Manuscripts and Archives, Yale University Library.

Company on Chapel Street. With the bounties soldiers had been paid by both state and federal governments, they were good consumers for local businesses. Most of the vests, however, had been discarded as useless beside the railroads before the regiment ever reached the nation's capital.[30]

At its fullest strength the Fifteenth Regiment counted 1,040 men. Arriving too late in Maryland, they were spared the horror at Antietam on September 17. But they were part of the new invasion of Virginia later in the fall and suffered significant losses at the Battle of Fredericksburg on December 13. The regiment continued its campaigns throughout 1863–64 on both the Virginia and North Carolina fronts. Before the Fifteenth was mustered out back in New Haven on June 27, 1865, their ranks were ravaged. They had lost 185 men, 142 of those from disease, particularly a yellow fever outbreak in coastal North Carolina. Many of their dead had been left behind in New Bern in what became by 1867 a national cemetery. The unit's regimental history is full of harrowing and fascinating details of this collection of Connecticut men, their sufferings and triumphs. One former soldier remembered Fredericksburg in a simple exclamation: "O what a day of slaughter it had been!" Another recalled their own burial crews working in the dark of night on Marye's Heights, singing "John Brown's Body" in the terrible cold of December. The remnants of this and other Union regiments that came home to Connecticut and countless other communities across the North needed far more aid than they ever received. Men with the "empty sleeve," sitting around train stations or in front of stores and bars, became a common sight after the war. Suffering from mental and physical wounds, many veterans experienced what one historian of Union veterans calls "mental anguish," some suicidal even if they managed to get admitted to soldiers' asylum homes. Alcoholism ran rampant among veterans; in some cities laws prohibited former soldiers from gathering in public, and employers often shunned them.[31]

Returning New Haven veterans would have found a booming economy in a modernizing manufacturing town. Before the war New Haven proudly counted at least a dozen carriage-making establishments and fifty servicing shops for the vehicles. With the loss of the Southern market for carriages, that important industry, the largest in the country, waned fast. But the coastal trade out of New Haven Harbor thrived nonetheless because of other manufacturing; companies that produced clocks, locks, rubber products, wrought-iron fencing, paper boxes, flour, machine parts, shirts, year-round ice supplies, cigars, corsets, and pianos all were headquartered in the city and its environs. Along the Quinnipiac River, the commercial oyster fishery prospered. New Haven produced some portion of virtually every tool or product of the early American Industrial Revolution, including railroad locomotives. One of the largest firms in the city was the J. B. Sargent hardware manufacturing and distribution company, employing 160 workmen when it relocated to New Haven in 1864. Last but hardly least, New Haven held the beginnings of an important firearms industry. Oliver Winchester brought his gun business to New Haven in 1857, establishing it as the New Haven Arms Company and setting up a plant at Orange and Grove Streets. But it was close to bankruptcy in 1861 when the Civil War saved the business and made fortunes in government contracts for Winchester and other gun manufacturers. Eli Whitney Jr. was considering getting out of the gun business altogether, but then the Civil War began; instead, he bought new machinery, grew the workforce to roughly four hundred employees, and built new facilities on both sides of the Mill River. By 1865, the state of Connecticut had produced a significant share—43 percent, by one estimate—of all revolvers, breech-loading rifles, and muskets bought by the U.S. War Department for the Union army.[32]

The artisanal crafts tended to decline as machines dominated production in this economy. Black workers, therefore, since they were usually less educated and poorer to begin with, lost out on the best advantages of modernization in a city like New Haven. The service economy declined in relation to manufacturing jobs, for which employers generally hired European immigrants, especially the Irish and German workingmen, who tended to vote for Democrats and resisted competition from their Black neighbors.[33] As always, racism could be blunt and violent, or the result of cunning assumptions and economic practices.

The New Haven Black community proudly supported its few schools, six churches, a literary society, and a library and owned real estate valued at well over $200,000. But that did not get them the skilled jobs at most levels of the burgeoning industrial enterprises. Abolitionism, bolstered at least by 1863 and the emancipation policy of the federal government, did not penetrate to the daily realities of employment in the oyster fisheries or the hardware, shirt, or arms manufacturers. Nor did the abolition of slavery in the South open jobs in New Haven's first major department stores, such as the Edward Malley Company, which by 1865 employed one hundred people and sported a seventy-five-foot front, four show windows, and three stories on Chapel Street. Indeed, emancipation in the South made the prospect of new waves of Black laborers in a Northern city like New Haven all the more threatening to White workers who had themselves only arrived in the past decade. The industrial economy and the growth in inventions that characterized it led to the creation of banks and a vast field for patent lawyers; such financial and legal services may have accepted Black people as customers, but they could not yet enter those professions. The titans of New Haven industry built their beautiful houses around town; Black men and women worked for them in domestic service and other forms of daily labor. Similarly, Yale faculty and students employed local African Americans in various kinds of service labor at the college, continuing a tradition as old as the institution itself.[34]

African Americans may not have attained access to key parts of wartime employment, but when the chance arose, they went to war as soldiers. One of the most revolutionary aspects of the Civil War was the enlistment of Black men in the Union army and navy; before the war's end, nearly two hundred thousand Black men, formerly enslaved in the South as well as free in the North, served in both state and federal regiments. Official recruiting of Black soldiers began in the spring of 1863. Some Black men from Connecticut sought their chance in the famous Fifty-Fourth Massachusetts Infantry Regiment, recruited in the Bay State by summer of that year. Not until November 1863 did the Connecticut General Assembly authorize the organization of an African American regiment; Governor William A. Buckingham thereupon called for the recruitment of the Twenty-Ninth Regiment Connecticut Volunteers. These enactments were highly partisan in the state: Democratic Party representative William W. Eaton of Hartford called the legislation "the most disgraceful bill ever introduced" at the New Haven State House. Eaton declared he would rather "let loose the wild Camanchees [*sic*] than the ferocious negro." Black soldiers would only "spread lust and rapine all over the land." Against such racist perceptions, hundreds of men came forward immediately, and by early January 1864, the ranks of the Twenty-Ninth, eventually over 1,200 strong, were filled. The response was so robust that a second regiment, the Thirtieth Connecticut, was formed at the same time.[35]

Soldiers of the Twenty-Ninth Regiment came from several Northern states, but more than half hailed from Connecticut's cities, towns, and countryside. In civilian life, they had worked a variety of jobs and attained different levels of education, some signing their names and others using an *X*. For some, bounties no doubt served as an inducement: they were promised $310 from the state, $75 from the county where they enlisted, New Haven County, and $300 from the federal government. According to Isaac J. Hill, who wrote a narrative of his service in the Twenty-Ninth, the men received the Connecticut bounties but not the other two. Moreover, bitter disputes over soldiers' unequal or late pay haunted this regiment throughout its combat and garrison service. The regiment went into training at the huge encampment at Grapevine Point, today's Criscuolo Park, in Fair Haven at the corner of Chapel and James Streets on the bank of the Mill River before it empties into New Haven Harbor. Of all the regiments formed and passing through New Haven during the war, none left such an indelible mark on the city's Black community as this regiment of Black soldiers in blue uniforms, with a "US" on their belt buckles, cartridge cases on their belts, regulation Winchester muskets on their shoulders, their kepis tilted on their heads just as they pleased, drilling in the cold winter air of Grapevine Point. Crowds came to watch them over the more than three months they trained and practiced; the sounds of marching feet and officers' shouted commands, the smell of cook fires, and the sight of flags around an African American regiment were scenes that staid Connecticut had never witnessed. It took until March for the proper number of commissioned White officers (by regulation and law) to be secured to command the unit. Some were even transferred to serve as nurses; soldiering was hardly a path to glory alone. Skirmishes and fistfights broke out in the city, especially down by Long Wharf, between soldiers and White residents. And by mid-January the camp was a scene of sickness and disease; approximately one hundred men

Alexander Herritage Newton (*left*) and Daniel S. Lathrop, quartermaster sergeants, Twenty-Ninth Regiment Connecticut Volunteers, circa 1865. Randolph Linsly Simpson African-American Collection. James Weldon Johnson Memorial Collection in the Yale Collection of American Literature. Beinecke Rare Book and Manuscript Library, Yale University.

from the Twenty-Ninth and Thirtieth had to be moved to the Knight Hospital with fevers, measles, and other disorders.[36]

One of the most striking features of the Twenty-Ninth Connecticut is that its more than a thousand Black men either hailed from or enlisted with adjutants or clerks in some 119 towns and cities around the small state. At the stunning memorial designed by artist Ed Hamilton and dedicated in 2008 in Criscuolo Park, hard by the Mill River, eight pillars record the name and rank of each man by his town of origin. Seeing the names, counting the towns and numbers, one gains a sense of the deep social impact the recruitment of such a regiment had on communities. Seventeen towns sent one man each, while many produced seven or eight, with fifteen coming from Bridgeport, twenty from Greenwich, twenty-four from Danbury, twenty-five from North Stonington, twenty-seven from Norwich, and twenty-nine from Norwalk. Fairfield, in the county where slavery had once been most prominent, sent thirty-three Black soldiers to battle. From Connecticut's two largest cities emerged 71 soldiers from Hartford and 135 from New Haven.[37] In the homes, workplaces (including Yale College), and churches of African Americans in the Elm City, constant excited, if nervous, conversation ensued about whether young or even middle-aged men should enlist. That so many did is a testament to economic status, but especially to a widespread understanding of the meaning of the war.

On January 28, 1864, the great orator Frederick Douglass came to town for two extraordinary events. Touring the North at that point with a speech entitled "The Mission of the War," Douglass was the most famous and significant Black leader in the United States. He had recruited approximately one hundred members of the Fifty-Fourth Massachusetts Regiment during the first half of 1863, including two of his sons. He had met with President Abraham Lincoln at the White House in the previous August to protest discriminations against Black soldiers, especially unequal pay and the denial of commissions as officers. Douglass's current speaking tour was a crusade to convince White and Black audiences that they must grasp the meaning of the war in the idea of "national regeneration"—a painful rebirth and a struggle to first save and then remake the United States out of the great achievement of emancipation of the slaves. The *Palladium* advertised his speech as "Fred. Douglass To-night," at the Music Hall in New Haven on Crown Street, at twenty-five cents per person. Seventy additional recruits had just arrived at Grapevine Point that very day, January 28, but it is not known how many members of the Twenty-Ninth were given leave to attend the public lecture, nor do we know how many Yale faculty or students attended, though surely many did on that Thursday evening.[38]

The Music Hall, later known as the New Haven Opera House, was filled beyond its capacity for Douglass's speech. In this, one of the great orations of Douglass's life, which he delivered many times, he offered perhaps his clearest description of the war as an apocalyptic, purposeful collision in history, in which "Providence" (God, nature, or fate) entered human affairs and turned that history in a new direction. The results of the war would usher from human choices, and they would be either "national salvation" or "national ruin." The war, said Douglass, was a "potent teacher." He maintained, "The most hopeful fact of the hour is that we are now in a salutary school—the school of affliction. If sharp and signal retribution, long-protracted, wide-sweeping and overwhelming, can teach a great nation respect for the long-despised claims of justice, surely we shall be taught now and for all time to come." The "lessons" in such a school of history, pronounced the orator, were "written in characters of blood." The Confederacy represented evil of epic proportions, and in his customary way, he threw down lightning bolts from scripture to underline his point: the Confederacy represented "a rebellion which in the destruction of human life and property has rivalled the earthquake, the whirlwind and the pestilence that walketh in darkness, and wasteth at noonday."[39]

Partisan even as it described "divine forces" and "overpowering logic" at work in the war's character, Douglass's address soared with idealism as well as blood-stained patriotism. The "old Union" had already died in the war, he said, and a new Union had been born. In stirring terms, Douglass declared a new day possible with a Union victory: "What we now want is a country—a free country—a country nowhere saddened by the footprints of a single slave—and nowhere cursed by the presence of a slaveholder. We want a country . . . which shall not brand the Declaration of Independence as a lie." The war's result should be a re-imagined egalitarian country "transplanting the whole South with the higher civilization of the North." These were transcendent, high aims on a winter's night in a packed New Haven hall. Reaching for language all would know, although admitting he did not "go all the lengths to which such theories are pressed," Douglass declared it "the manifest destiny of this war to unify and reorganize the institutions of this country—and that herein is the secret of the strength, the fortitude, the persistent energy, in a word the sacred significance of this war."[40] Black New Haveners, and especially any of those soldiers who may have attended from their camp at Grapevine Point, left the Music Hall that night savoring an unforgettable experience.

The following day Douglass rode out to Grapevine Point and delivered a different kind of address to the assembled troops of the Twenty-Ninth and Thirtieth Connecticut. According to a report in the *Connecticut War Record*, the soldiers "were drawn up beneath the large garrison flag in front of the officers' headquarters. Mr. Douglass stood in full view upon a sort of rude balcony." A partial transcription of his speech demonstrates that the orator, who had two sons in the army, one still recuperating from terrible wounds at the Battle of Fort

Wagner in July 1863, called on the men to adhere to military discipline, duty, and obedience. "You are pioneers of the liberty of your race," Douglass announced. "With the United States cap on your head, the United States eagle on your belt, the United States musket on your shoulder, not all the powers of darkness can prevent you from becoming American citizens." He left no doubt of the heavy burden on these men. "On you depends the destiny of four millions of the colored race in this country."[41]

Then Douglass shifted tone, admitting that these men and other Black people were nowhere near "actual equality" yet. They possessed "natural equality," but not in practical "knowledge and skill." Douglass asked, "Who plans and builds yonder ships to balance perfectly in the water and stand the storms of the ocean? The white man. Who makes your caps? The whites. Who your coats? The whites. We have not had the advantages which they have had." The forty-five-year-old abolitionist and former slave challenged the soldiers to learn and perform, to salute and say "yes sir," and thus gain manly respect. Douglass penetrated the most sensitive issues. "Some of you complain that you are commanded by white officers," he remarked. "I should like to see you commanded by black officers. But the color makes little difference." He even suggested that at this moment in their training they might have more confidence in a White officer. At this juncture in the war, better to get to the front, to fight and to serve, he argued. In stern, perhaps surprising strictures, Douglass urged the assembled to "be content . . . for the present, and LEARN. Obey orders; be cleanly; guard your morals; take care of your health; do your duty always, at any cost, without a murmur. The future is yours." Any cost. In this military setting, in a war far from won, on a cold afternoon, the men from so many towns all over New England strained to hear the legendary speaker. They gave him three rousing cheers at the end of the address.[42] Douglass offered no easy road ahead; he preached a soldier's unquestioned duty as the means to freedom and ultimate equality by personal sacrifice. He also showered the men with a father's tough love. As always, rhetoric and reality in war strained against one another in tragic imbalance. In the blue uniforms and muskets rested the hopes of generations of African Americans.

Just over two miles away from the encampment of Black soldiers, Yale students stayed warm, went to class, and performed their recitations. The surge of enlistments among students early in the war had largely subsided by 1863–64. On March 8, the Twenty-Ninth Regiment broke camp and marched into the center of New Haven, down Chapel Street, right next to the Yale campus. The visual and auditory spectacle of the marching Black men in military step, rifles skyward, their officers shouting orders, drew large crowds of spectators, including Yale students as well as, according to Isaac Hill, a member of the regiment, "the first families in the city." Hill described the "weeping" among Black family members who came to see off their loved ones. "Strangers ministered unto me," wrote the emotionally moved Hill, as "white and colored ladies and gentlemen grasped me by the hand, with tears streaming down their cheeks." The regiment shipped out at Long Wharf the next morning for South Carolina. Some Yale students may have been stirred to at least a kind of action. Exactly one week later, March 16, a Yale faculty meeting took up a resolution about "the propriety of giving instruction in rifle practice to the students." They concluded "that if the students desire an organization for that purpose with proper regulation, the Faculty will not object." A few students did enlist later that summer, and by faculty vote they were excused from recitations.[43] In small gestures Yale College supported the war, but at only minimal cost or disruption. The thousands dying in Virginia that summer, many in unmarked graves while some returned in simple pine boxes to their hometowns, no longer needed the target practice sought by college boys in New Haven.

That spring and summer of 1864, the country faced not only the weariness of the bloodiest campaigns of the war in Virginia and Georgia but a presidential election in the midst of the Civil War. Federal contracts continued to flow into munitions and clothing manufacturers all up and down the Connecticut River valley from the Quartermaster Corps in Washington to support the most expensive and expansive war ever waged. The quiet confines of the Yale College Brick Row, however, did not remain without political conflict. In the presidential election campaign, a Union Club squared off against an active McClellan Club supporting the former general, George B. McClellan, as candidate of the Democratic Party. Democrats, often called Peace Democrats, promised a vaguely defined negotiated settlement of the war that might preserve the Union but also most elements of slavery. National Democrats pilloried Lincoln and the Republicans with a relentless array of racist accusations of race mixing and radicalism. Locally, they held a torchlight parade in October on campus and in New Haven streets. The majority of Yale students and faculty, to be sure, supported the Lincoln administration and the prosecution of the war. The Union Club held its first meeting on October 17 and, according to reports in the *Yale Literary Magazine*, "it was a proud night for Yale," bolstering the "New American Union, in which walks not a single slave!" The club solicited letters from numerous famous dignitaries and Yale graduates, including Edward Everett, William Cullen Bryant, Charles Sumner, the Reverend Dr. Joseph P. Thompson, William Evarts,

George W. Curtis, and Connecticut governor William A. Buckingham, all of which were read at the meeting and published. All the letters firmly supported the war and national unity, but none mentioned slavery.[44]

On October 19, some three hundred students and faculty, including apparently President Woolsey, marched in a "Union Convention" parade in the streets of New Haven. A student poll taken just before the election in November tallied 372 votes for Lincoln and 96 for McClellan. These numbers reflected similar figures in some, though not all, parts of the North in an election won by Lincoln with 55 percent of the vote, aided by battlefield successes at the fall of Atlanta and the taking of Mobile Bay in late August and early September. In all of New England, only a handful of counties voted for McClellan: a few rural ones in New Hampshire, one in coastal Maine, and one in Connecticut—New Haven. The margin was 900 for McClellan in New Haven County and 400 in the conservative city of New Haven. The carriage industry had collapsed, but other jobs had surged in the state's largest city. It is possible that the horror of war news that summer had soured many against the new draft and the Union cause generally. Moreover, the sheer virulence of the white supremacy campaign conducted by Democrats may have stuck with a sufficient number of working-class voters to produce the McClellan margins. And the public reluctance of "gown" to serve in any serious numbers late in the war (amplified in articles in the *New York Times*) no doubt increased the level of disdain from "town."[45]

As the war mercifully ended in April 1865, and much of the country faced the all but impossible logistical and emotional task of finding and burying the dead, the assassination of President Lincoln, and the unprecedented challenges of Reconstruction of the nation and society, Yale completed another year of education and planned a unique commencement ceremony. It was around midnight on April 9 when the people of New Haven learned of Robert E. Lee's surrender to Grant at Appomattox Court House. Ringing bells and gun salutes awakened residents as revelers gathered on Chapel Street and on the Green and built a bonfire. The astonishing news of Lincoln's murder less than a week later tempered all joy for the time being.[46]

During commencement week in late July 1865, moods revived; Yale held a celebration of itself as well as a major commemoration of the meaning of the war. On July 26, some 175 distinguished invited guests and another 400 alumni attended the festivities, which included an elaborate dinner at the Music Hall and a large event with many speakers. At the Center Church, a keynote address by the Reverend Horace Bushnell (Yale 1827), a longtime minister in Hartford and a prolific, sometimes controversial theologian, drew great attention. Bushnell vigorously acclaimed the war for Union and Black freedom. Slavery figured prominently in all the speeches that day, especially Bushnell's. The "madness and defiant wrong of slavery" had been vanquished, he said. He hoped that they would all live "to see that every vestige of slavery is swept clean." He further condemned the "black code" emerging in Southern states, enactments that constricted and destroyed all liberties and hopes of equality for the freedpeople. He demanded that his Yale audience remember the service and sacrifice of Black soldiers, even mentioning the "massacre of Fort Pillow," an especially horrible mass murder in Tennessee in April 1864 by Confederates of over three hundred Union soldiers, nearly two hundred of whom were Black, who had attempted to surrender.[47]

William M. Evarts (Yale 1837), a distinguished lawyer, served as toastmaster for the ceremony. He read aloud a telegram from President Andrew Johnson in Washington, DC. In his remarks, Evarts too rejoiced that the war had "rid the country of the institution of slavery, without the destruction of society." Numerous Yale graduates who had attained the rank of general also delivered speeches of varying lengths, as did Governor Buckingham. General Lewis B. Parsons (Yale 1840) spoke of his war experience in his home state of Missouri, which he believed had been redeemed "from the reproach and sin of slavery." General Henry B. Carrington (Yale 1845), a Connecticut native, reminisced about his youth when he witnessed a mob throwing rocks at the *Amistad* captives during their incarceration in Farmington. He now saw the divine hand in "destroying slavery and making this a free, Christian republic." When it came time for President Woolsey to speak, he began with an odd metaphor about Yale as the "good mother" Alma Mater, and his own role as the "headwaiter." Woolsey recovered his bearings and delivered a firm condemnation of "secession theory" as he also paid moving tribute to his nephew, Theodore Winthrop, who had fallen in battle so early in the war.[48]

At the dinner in the Music Hall, the room was draped in U.S. flags as well as the regimental battle flags of many Connecticut units. And at the front of the hall hung twenty-one white shields with the laurel-lettered names, the class, and the place of death in battle for select Yale graduates. The tone of the special commencement event was elegiac and, understandably, intensely patriotic. No "lower motive" had inspired the intentions of the fallen Yalies, contended Woolsey. They had all given their lives with "pure, disinterested patriotism." In such settings that first summer after the killing had ended, memory needed cleansing, performative half-knowing rituals that laid the groundwork for the gradual culture of reconciliation to follow. The ceremonial, self-congratulatory rhetoric aimed to express the transformations the war had wrought at Yale and in the nation. General Carrington, like the others, related many anecdotes, the most telling of which was his remembrance of the bitter hostility abolitionists faced on the campus during his college days in the 1840s. Now he could only marvel, he said, at how the end of slavery had gained such public acceptance. The triumphs, perils, and defeats of the Reconstruction period to follow were as yet unknown to Yale's gathered elite. They could not have, or chose not to have, any firm idea of the tenuous, contingent nature of the victory they celebrated that July day. Emotions of profound mourning, bitter revenge, and explosive hope all danced in the minds of Americans that summer. At the 1865 Yale ceremony commemorating the war and its dead, the chosen memory was one of success and comfort, a story of great providential change purchased with noble blood, and a narrative that would sustain a redeemed future, nurtured by education. The gathered Yale elite could have no idea of how fundamentally different the message would be on the university's war memorial a half century later. Bushnell at least broke momentarily from the mold. There would be no "debt of honor" paid, he maintained, unless Black men achieved the right to vote.[49]

James W. C. Pennington, likely the first African American to attend or audit courses at Yale, agreed wholeheartedly with Bushnell. Pennington, too, believed in providential change and never lost faith that the course of history might be profoundly altered by an interventionist God. He had achieved a remarkable career as a preacher, an abolitionist, and an activist in the Black convention movement, but he had endured enormous suffering and hardship as well. He had lost two wives to illness and struggled mightily to make a living and support his family. Pennington traveled the lecture circuit and wrote essays in many journals to keep a financial grip on life. He also spent considerable time abroad as an activist for Black freedom and rights, especially in Presbyterian Scotland. But he never gave up and seemed to possess an astonishing devotion to his faith.[50]

Down to his death at the age of sixty in 1870, the peripatetic Pennington worked as a sometime pastor in Portland, Maine, then as an intrepid minister and teacher for the freedmen in Natchez, Mississippi, and finally as a missionary, also among former slaves, in Jacksonville, Florida.[51] He never embraced emigration plans among his people and always condemned colonization schemes. This brilliant theological thinker, pastor, prolific writer, devoted reformer, and abolitionist had lived to see the same world as the Yale College assemblage in July 1865. Pennington shared many of their memories and hopes, and certainly their biblical faith. He shared now their country as the citizen he had always claimed to be. He also did his utmost to forge a bracing, sobering memory of this new American revolution.

In an essay he wrote just after the Yale commencement, to which he obviously was not invited, Pennington offered a different vision of the road ahead. He announced the historical turn of 1865 and the end of the war as "The New Evangel." He spoke for African Americans, formerly enslaved or free, down through time. "We have fulfilled the gospel of endurance," he declared, "thoroughly, completely, exhaustively, in such a way as gospel never was fulfilled before." The grace and patience in African American Christianity had, in great part, run its course and a new gospel had emerged with emancipation. "We have fulfilled it [endurance] as a race, through six generations," Pennington asserted, "in all the relations of life . . . through all the recesses of the soul, mind and body." Black folk, young and old, as well as their ancestors had been "saturated, crushed, from birth to death with this doom of endurance under slavery and caste." The endurance "game is 'played out,'" wrote the preacher. "There must be a new deal . . . we must exchange the gospel of endurance for the gospel of resistance. . . . Let this new gospel of resistance, or self-assertion, be clearly understood."[52] Pennington could hardly have grasped the headwinds his new evangel would soon face in the raw memory wars at the heart of Reconstruction.

INTERLUDE

A Yale Family in Slavery and Freedom

> Had not the slaves been emancipated and the freedmen been employed, the terms of peace might have been dictated from Richmond rather than at Appomattox Courthouse.
>
> —JOHN WESLEY MANNING, Yale College class of 1881

During the Civil War, a couple named Alfred and Eliza Manning boarded a steamship off the coast of North Carolina with their young son. They found an empty steamer drum, drilled holes in it, and placed their child, John, inside. Like the mother of Moses hiding her baby in a basket of bulrushes, they covered their own boy with clothes and told him to be quiet. The vessel belonged to the Union navy, part of a Northern blockade intended to prevent the Confederacy from transporting—and profiting from—plantation goods. Alfred and Eliza said goodbye to John and asked the Union sailors to take him to safety. The ship was bound for New Haven, Connecticut, and the Mannings, along with other family members, eventually joined the little boy there. Many years later, in 1881, John Wesley Manning graduated from Yale College. When his own wife gave birth to their first child, they christened her "Yale."[1]

Stories like this one—of separation and unification, daring and sacrifice, death and new life—played out in ways both spectacular and mundane during the Civil War. And in the years following Appomattox, the country had to reckon with the consequences of a conflict that had torn apart both families and a nation. African Americans searched for loved ones who had been sold away, sometimes many years earlier, or others who had escaped of their own volition when the timing was right. Others sought new opportunities away from those who had held them as chattel, sometimes in faraway cities like New Haven.

Alfred Manning and Eliza (Allston) Manning were born in the rich plantation country around Edenton, North Carolina. A preponderance of evidence suggests that Eliza, her brothers, and other family members were enslaved by James Cathcart Johnston, a Unionist landowner from a politically prominent family who owned thousands of acres and hundreds of people over the course of his lifetime. James's father, Samuel, graduated from Yale in the eighteenth century, his education financed in part by Thomas Clap, college rector and president. Samuel had served as a delegate from North Carolina to all four provincial congresses, then in the new state senate, in the Continental Congress, and later as governor of North Carolina and a U.S. senator. His brother-in-law, James Iredell, was one of the first justices of the Supreme Court, and his son James Johnston graduated from Princeton in 1799. James inherited hundreds of enslaved workers and several plantations from his father and continued to grow enormously wealthy off the profits of slave-produced cotton. At Hayes, one of his plantations, he hired a British-trained architect to design an immense neoclassical mansion featuring Greek Doric columns and a "massive portico." He ordered marble, walnut, mahogany, and gold-leaf paint to decorate and adorn his home, and enslaved people built and maintained the mansion and grounds.[2]

During the Civil War, Johnston's ornate and luxurious world came tumbling down. In February and March 1862, Union forces took control of the coastal waters around Roanoke Island and New Bern as part of the Burnside Expedition. As they did throughout the war, Black people abandoned farms and plantations and sought refuge, rations, and work with the Union army—part of the "General Strike," as W. E. B. Du Bois called it, an exodus of enslaved people that crippled the South and ultimately turned the tide of the war. Not long after the arrival of Union forces, it was clear that "all . . . the young efficient negroes" had left the Hayes plantation, as one close observer put it. But Alfred Manning, like many other enslaved people, was determined to take back some of what had been stolen from him and his family. On August 7, 1862, one of Johnston's relatives wrote to Colonel William A. Howard, First New York Marine Artillery, stationed near Edenton, to complain that the Union forces had given "a runaway negro called Alfred Manning a pass to plunder his plantation." Furthermore, the aggrieved Southerner reported that "the woman who is now, I understand, on board Capt. Gerard's Steamer is the property of Mr. J. If you wish to annoy Mr. Johnston, which I am satisfied cannot be the case as he is an old man & a great sufferer, you cannot do so more effectively than by sending the negroes to plunder his premises."[3]

Plundering was indeed widespread in the neighborhood. Allen Parker, enslaved on a plantation only a few miles from Edenton, recounted how he and his friends were inspired to escape after they discovered "that lots of the slaves from the neighboring plantation were running away [and] we concluded that we would take our chance, as soon as we could get any." When they heard gunfire, Parker and his compatriots fled to a Union vessel they saw docked on the river. Once on board, with the blessing and cooperation of the Union officers, they led the sailors back to their old plantation, where they "got quite a lot of chickens, ducks and geese," Parker recalled.[4] Very likely this is what Alfred Manning was doing, with a pass from Union soldiers and his wife, Eliza, waiting for him on board.

Some Union authorities wanted to stop the exodus of Black workers, but they found the task impossible. Edward Stanly, the military governor of North Carolina who opposed all efforts to help Black people in his midst, wrote an exasperated letter to Secretary of War Edwin Stanton from New Bern, North Carolina, that same season the Mannings escaped: "When steamers and vessels are almost daily leaving this State, and negroes, the property of loyal citizens, are taken on board, without the consent of their owners—who are sometimes widows and orphans—will authority be given to prevent their being removed?" Stanly soon resigned his position in protest over the Emancipation Proclamation, but not before writing to one of those "loyal citizens," James Johnston, to apologize for the "outrages" committed by his enslaved people. Stanly promised further that one of the men Johnston had complained about would be arrested.[5]

Johnston died childless in 1865, but before his death he made special arrangements for one of his older enslaved men, Eliza's father, Osborn. "I wish Osborne to be suffered to work for himself and support himself; he was formerly a faithful servant; I do not wish him to suffer for anything in his old age." Notes prepared for the 1860 census include two pages of names, ages, and in some cases the values of enslaved people living at Hayes. Osborn was fifty-nine years old; Isom, twenty-six; Eliza, thirty (noted as having four children); James, seventeen; and Lewis, thirty-five.[6] At some point, and probably not all at once, various members of this family made their way north.

Enslaved people made reconstituting their families a priority during the war and in the wake of emancipation, and the Allstons were no different. In 1866, Isom Allston placed a notice in a Philadelphia newspaper—one of hundreds of similar advertisements purchased by freedpeople in search of lost family members: "INFORMATION WANTED Of my three brothers, Osborn, Philip and James

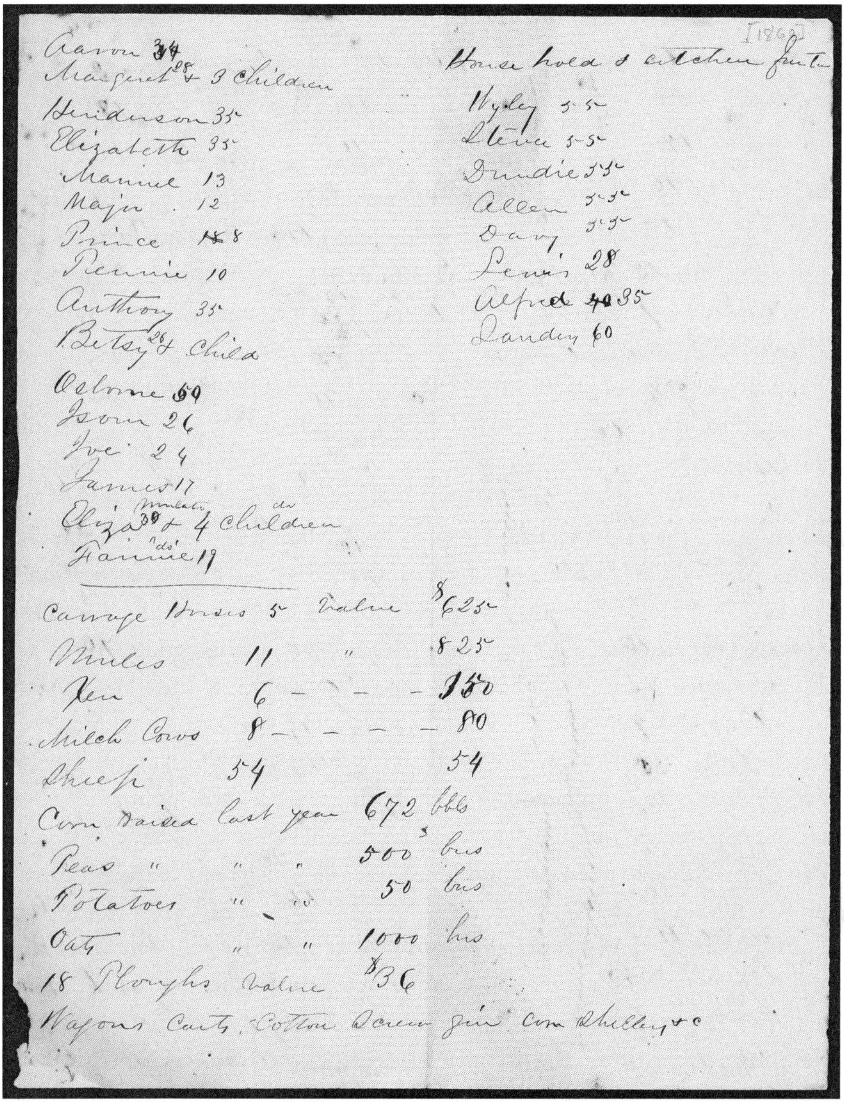

[1860]
Aaron 34
Margaret 28 & 3 Children
Henderson 35
Elizabeth 35
Mannie 13
Major 12
Prince 18 8
Pennie 10
Anthony 35
Betsy 26 & Child
Osborne 60
Isom 26
Joe 24
James 17
Eliza 30 (mulatto) & 4 children
Fannie "do" 19

House hold & kitchen furn.
Wyley 55
Steven 55
Dudie 55
Allen 55
Davy 55
Lewis 28
Alfred 40 35
Dandy 60

Carriage Horses	5	value	$625
Mules	11	"	825
Oxen	6		150
Milch Cows	8		80
Sheep	54		54

Corn raised last year 672 bbls
Peas " " " 500 bus
Potatoes " " 50 bus
Oats " " 1000 bus
18 Ploughs value $36
Wagons Carts, Cotton Screw gin, Corn Sheller &c

Partial list of enslaved people living on the Hayes plantation in 1860. Hayes Collection (00324), Southern Historical Collection, Wilson Special Collections Library, University of North Carolina at Chapel Hill.

Johnson. They were originally residents of Edenton, N.C., owned by Jas. C. Johnson, who sold them to a man named Jas Allston." Isom, who gave an address on Winter Street in New Haven, succeeded in reuniting with at least some of his family members: he, along with brothers Osborn and Lewis Allston, all found employment as janitors, or "sweeps," at Yale. James and Philip, their father Osborn, and other members of the extended Allston family also settled in New Haven.[7]

Meanwhile, Alfred Manning continued to practice and perfect his trade as a ship caulker and carpenter. Also in 1866, not long after moving to Connecticut, he registered a patent with the U.S. Patent Office for an invention relating to a ship. And although his daughter later reported that Alfred had "no literary education" and Eliza possessed only "a slight knowledge of reading and writing," they ensured that their children had greater educational opportunities. Their oldest, John Wesley Manning (1857–1922), attended the prestigious private Hopkins Grammar School in New Haven before entering Yale in 1877, where he was a member of Linonia, one of the most respected student literary societies, and lived with another Black student, Edward Enoch Reed, class of 1878, his first year. John Manning graduated in 1881, and like other academically gifted Black graduates, he spent his career at segregated schools. Moving to Tennessee, he taught Latin and served as the principal of a school in Knoxville. Active in church and civic affairs, Manning held leadership positions in the East Tennessee Association of Teachers in Colored Schools and the Tennessee Conference of Educational Workers and participated in the Southern Sociological Congress in 1915. His Yale obituary notice reported that he "had been recommended to President Harding for appointment as minister to Haiti." Other accomplishments included writing a history of the school where he spent his career, receiving a master's degree from Wilberforce University, and contributing articles for church journals—a full and rich life built in spite of prevailing winds of racism and segregation. John Manning would become an embodiment and a chronicler of the second American Revolution.[8]

His brother, Henry Edward Manning, attended the Yale School of Fine Arts from 1878 to 1883 and received the three-year certificate from the school in 1883. (The art school did not begin granting degrees until 1891.) Henry Manning may have been the first Black student to receive a certificate from the Yale art school. After graduation, he taught drawing at a school in Knoxville, Tennessee (perhaps the same school where his brother was principal), and at Allen University in Columbia, South Carolina, but he spent the majority of his career as a sign painter in New Haven. In the 1920 census, he was listed as self-employed, owning his own business and his own house. When their father, Alfred Manning, died in 1886, his obituary, which ran in the *New York Freeman*, a Black newspaper, mentioned his patent, his decades of service and leadership to his church, and his family. John's and Henry's Yale educations were prominently featured. And it made clear his pride in his family and their accomplishments: "He leaves his wife in comfortable circumstances, also seven children, three girls and four boys."[9]

Decades later, in 1902, John Wesley Manning returned to New Haven with a speech he had prepared called "The Cry of the Children of Slavery." The title was a reference to Elizabeth Barrett Browning's poem "The Cry of the Children," and it was peppered with references to Alexandre Dumas, other English poets, and the Bible. In it Manning recounted the history of Black people in the New World, from their capture in Africa to their years of forced labor and then to the Civil War. Although chiefly concerned with the present status of African Americans and their future prospects, Manning was deeply attuned to the ironies of the war—chiefly, the great unintended consequence of emancipation. "Little did the boys in blue think when they shouldered their arms to protect the Stars and Stripes and defend the union, that slavery would be abolished. Little did the men in gray think when they fired on Fort Sumpter [*sic*] that they had sounded the death knell of their fondest hopes," he wrote. "Had not the slaves been emancipated and the freedmen been employed, the terms of peace might have been dictated from Richmond rather than at Appomattox Courthouse."[10]

It was not only the roughly two hundred thousand African American men who shouldered muskets who had contributed to the Union effort. Manning's own family, with their determination to leave North Carolina and restart their lives in the North, also helped sound the Confederacy's "death knell." And in doing so, they had experienced *and* helped bring about one of the most spectacular transformations of the nineteenth century. Four million formerly enslaved people had helped turn a war to preserve the Union into a war to end human bondage—immediately and without compensation, a thing without precedent in modern times. Being able to raise a family, unburdened by the threat of sale or estrangement, was one of the great distinctions between slavery and freedom, and the Allstons and Mannings achieved it.[11]

In another turn, John Wesley Manning, Henry Edward Manning, and Samuel Johnston, their family's onetime enslaver, all came to share the same alma mater. In time, this family, along with many other wartime migrants, would leave their mark on both the university and the city of New Haven.

CHAPTER 10

Black Students at Yale

> In view of the record made by colored students in Yale, Harvard, Princeton, Cornell, Columbia, Dartmouth, Bowdoin, Amherst, Williams and Brown . . . it is indeed somewhat amusing to see Keane, the noted ethnologist, quoting Colonel Ruffin as authority in saying that it was impossible to educate the Negro.
>
> —WILLIAM H. FERRIS, Yale College class of 1895

As the postwar nation struggled over what "a new birth of freedom" might really mean, both Yale and its home city of New Haven were changing. A May 1871 headline in the *Connecticut Courant* promised "A Good Story from Yale." The article told of a Democratic politician from New York who was upset his son was forced to sit next to Edward Bouchet, a student in the Yale College class of 1874. The politician wrote to the professor on his son's behalf, asking for a new seat, "as it was for many reasons distasteful to sit so near a negro." But according to the article, "the professor wrote back that at present the students were ranged in alphabetical order, and it was not in his power to grant the favor, but 'next term the desired change will be brought about, for the scholarship then being the criterion, Mr. Bouchet will be in the *first* division, and your son in the *fourth*.'"[1]

This anecdote, highlighting young Edward Bouchet's academic prowess and the Yale professor's wit, originally appeared in the *New York Globe* and was then picked up by the Connecticut newspaper—a reflection of the story's broad appeal. Here was proof that a new age of opportunity had dawned for African Americans. Yet at the same time Bouchet was excelling at Yale, violence targeting Black people was sweeping across the South. Armed White vigilantes attacked newly freed African Americans and their allies at home and in school when they attempted to vote or attend a Union League meeting. This campaign of terrorism, built on the paramilitary foundation that had sustained the plantation class under slavery, was aimed at reinstating White rule anywhere Black people attempted to assert newfound rights and freedoms. Only a month before the Bouchet story appeared in print, Congress passed the Third Enforcement Act, also known as the Ku Klux Klan Act of 1871, in an effort to rein in what was beginning to seem like a second civil war. And as Bouchet and the politician's son sat beside each other in class, hundreds of witnesses, including African Americans, spoke to the Joint Select Committee, meeting in the seven Southern states that had experienced the most violence, to describe the atrocities the Klan and other White insurrectionaries had committed.[2]

In the North, the picture appeared to be different. Harvard College admitted its first Black student, Richard T. Greener, in 1865. Inman Page and George Washington Milford entered Brown University two years after Bouchet enrolled at Yale and became that university's first Black graduates. In 1879, James Brister, today recognized as the first Black student to earn a degree from the University of Pennsylvania, began dental school in Philadelphia. Black students were pushing open the doors to Yale and other Ivy League institutions, ever so slightly. Yet the broader American culture, even in Northern cities like New Haven, teemed with blatant, ubiquitous racism. In Yale's classrooms, lecture halls, and debating societies, the advances of Radical Reconstruction were questioned and often condemned, while the extralegal regime of terror was romanticized or condoned, as revealed in the pages of the *Yale Daily News*, the student newspaper founded in 1878. Even as small numbers of Black students gradually took their places in Yale classrooms, they continued to face limited professional opportunities after graduation. The "good story from Yale" was more complex than it seemed.[3]

Bouchet's arrival as a student at Yale was in many ways the product of decades of growth and organizing within the city's African American community. Born in 1852 on Bradley Street in New Haven, Edward was the youngest of four children. His mother, Susan Cooley Bouchet, was a native of Connecticut; his father, William Francis Bouchet, may have come to New Haven in 1824 as the "body servant" of a student from South Carolina. Their son Edward grew up in the Temple Street congregation, where he would have known other prominent Black families with strong ties to Yale, including Robert M. Park and John Creed. Like them, the elder Bouchet worked as a janitor and porter at Yale. He became the clerk of his church as well as a frequent participant in the reform and antislavery activities nurtured by his congregation. In 1845, William Bouchet was elected vice president of the Connecticut State Temperance and Moral Reform

Society, an organization that had been founded by Jehiel Beman, the father of Amos Beman, the abolitionist and longtime Black pastor of the Temple Street Church. In 1849, Bouchet and Park served as delegates to the Connecticut State Convention of Colored Men, held at Temple Street, "to consider our Political condition, and to devise measures for our elevation and advancement." Many years later, Bouchet was again a delegate to the convention, held in June 1865, this time at the African Methodist Episcopal church on Sperry Street in New Haven.[4]

Young Edward, a prodigy, first attended school at his church, where children were taught by Vashti Duplex Creed, the city's first Black schoolteacher. (Creed, the daughter of Prince Duplex, a Revolutionary War veteran, was married to John Creed. Their son, Cortlandt Van Rensselaer Creed, was the first Black graduate of Yale's medical school.) Edward later went to the Artisan Street Colored School and from there to the New Haven High School from 1866 to 1868. From 1868 to 1870, he attended the Hopkins School in New Haven. Bouchet was not the first Black student to enroll in the prestigious preparatory school—Amos Beman Jr. had graduated from Hopkins in 1856—but he flourished there, graduating as valedictorian in 1870. Bouchet was soon admitted to Yale College, where he excelled in mathematics, physics, and chemistry, graduating sixth in his class of 124 students, and was nominated to Phi Beta Kappa. Bouchet attracted the attention of philanthropist Alfred Cope, who encouraged him to return to Yale to pursue further study.[5]

In 1876, just two years after finishing his bachelor's degree, Bouchet earned his PhD in physics from Yale. He was the first African American to earn a PhD in any subject in the United States and only the sixth person of any background or race to earn a PhD in physics. His research delved into geometrical optics and refraction in glass. These singular achievements shine today in Yale's lore and in its modern celebration of Bouchet's brilliance as a "first." Yet despite his sterling academic credentials, the professional obstacles he faced throughout his adult life presaged the challenges to come for African Americans, even for those, like Bouchet, who had reached the highest tiers of educational achievement.[6]

The first Black students at Yale were supported by a working-class community invested in their success. On April 10, 1871, a Black New Haven woman, Mary A. Goodman, signed her last will and testament, leaving her entire estate, except a small annual bequest to her father, to the Theological Department to "be used in aiding young men in preparing for the Gospel ministry, preference being always given to young men of color." Goodman had worked her entire life in domestic service and as a washerwoman taking in laundry. But when she died

Edward Bouchet as a young man. Images of Yale Individuals (RU 684). Manuscripts and Archives, Yale University Library.

in 1872, her real and personal property was worth about $5,000. A church newspaper out of Boston, reporting on the gift, said that Goodman had been a member of the College Street Church and "felt that the time was coming, in the rapid progress of her race and people, when they would require a more highly educated ministry." The university had her buried in the Grove Street Cemetery, inscribing the tombstone, "Of African Descent, she gave the earnings of her life to educate men of her own color in Yale College for the gospel ministry."[7]

Two years later, in 1874, James W. Morris became the first Black student to graduate from the Yale Theological Seminary. His contemporary Solomon M. Coles, born enslaved in Virginia, matriculated before Morris but graduated the next year; Coles was the first African American student to complete the entire three-year course of study in theology. Other Black students were making inroads in the School of Medicine. Bayard Thomas Smith and George Robinson Henderson both transferred to Yale's medical school from Lincoln University, a Black institution in Oxford, Pennsylvania, when its medical department closed. They graduated in 1875 and 1876, respectively. Between 1876 and 1903, when Cleveland Ferris graduated, at least eight Black students received medical degrees from Yale. This number, while small, exceeds all the known Black graduates of the Yale School of Medicine for the forty years after Ferris's graduation.[8]

During Reconstruction, some observers believed that widening educational opportunity at Yale presaged hopeful trends in the country at large. In 1874, the *Connecticut Courant* reported that the U.S. Senate had passed an amended version of a civil rights bill. They noted that one of the senators, Orris S. Ferry of Connecticut (Yale 1844), opposed the bill "because the wisdom, expediency, and right of such legislation were doubted." The editors of the *Courant* were dismayed by Ferry's opposition, suggesting that much of the opposition to the bill centered on school integration. But, as a counterargument, they pointed to Yale. "The battle has been fought and won in New England, and the prejudice was effectually killed here when Yale opened its doors to the colored student. If the new bill shall in the end accomplish the same good for the country at large, it will prove the best piece of legislation of any congress since slavery was abolished."[9] Their optimism was premature.

For this first generation out of slavery, there was no single path to Yale, although common threads emerge. Like Henderson and Smith, a significant number of Black students attended, or even graduated from, Black colleges before enrolling at Yale. Religious background may have played a role, as several students came to Yale by way of Talladega College, a Congregationalist institution in Alabama. One Black graduate attributed the influence of his professors at Talladega, "who [were] all Yale men," with his decision to follow in their footsteps.[10]

Thomas Nelson Baker was born enslaved in Virginia in 1860. His path toward higher education was difficult and full of interruptions—he finished his secondary schooling at the age of twenty-nine. In 1896, Baker completed a second bachelor's degree from the Yale Divinity School and then went on to study for a PhD in philosophy while serving part of the time as an ordained minister at the Dixwell Avenue Congregational Church (formerly known as Temple Street, Bouchet's congregation). In 1903, Baker finished his second Yale degree, becoming the first African American in the United States to earn a PhD in philosophy.[11]

As they had since the days of James W. C. Pennington, who escaped the South and audited courses at the Yale Theological Department while still technically enslaved, some Black scholars took great risks in seeking an education. Henry Gamble worked as a "houseboy" on an estate belonging to John Staige Davis, a professor of medicine at the University of Virginia, where Davis's son taught him secretly. When his employer, who had served as a surgeon in the Confederate army, found out and put a stop to the lessons, Gamble paid a tutor to teach him at night. Gamble eventually attended Lincoln University, beginning his studies at the age of twenty and graduating six years later. The path through Yale was arduous; Gamble worked evenings and nights as a janitor and waiter to pay his way, but he graduated with honors in 1891.[12]

In fact, quite a number of early Black students, like some poor White students, had to work one or more jobs while in school. William Fletcher Penn (Yale MD 1897) and Isaac N. Porter (Yale MD 1893) waited tables and sweated in the city's kitchens when they were not studying or in class. Walter J. Scott, an 1881 graduate of Yale Law School, was trained as a printer, one of only two Black men in that trade in the state of Connecticut. He began his studies in Yale College but left without finishing to run the New Haven *Free Press*, an early Black newspaper. Scott continued studying with a Yale tutor while running the newspaper, and then enrolled in the law school. An orphan, he lived with his uncle in New Haven—who was variously listed in city records as a "hostler," as a "moulder," and at times as having "no occupation"—while Scott worked at the paper and completed his law degree. Although Scott died at the young age of twenty-nine, he achieved distinction during his short legal career; he is credited with being the first Black person to try a case before a Connecticut court.[13]

William Pickens—a 1904 graduate of Yale College who became a noted civil rights leader, scholar, educator, and leading member of the National Association for the Advancement of Colored People (NAACP)—recalled the financial insecurity that hounded him as a student. He arrived at Yale as a junior with a mere fifteen dollars to his name. In his autobiography, *The Heir of Slaves*, Pickens wrote, "I secured work in the roof garden and restaurant of the city Young Men's Christian Association, where I could assist the kitchen force in various sorts of work and wash the windows to earn my board. Board is a large and necessary item." In a surprising turn, Pickens received a check for fifty dollars from David Stuart Dodge, a son of the wealthy industrialist and magnate William Earl Dodge Sr., whom he had never met. After Pickens wrote to thank Dodge and inform him that he was earning his board and would save

William Pickens, circa 1904. Manuscripts and Archives, Yale University Library.

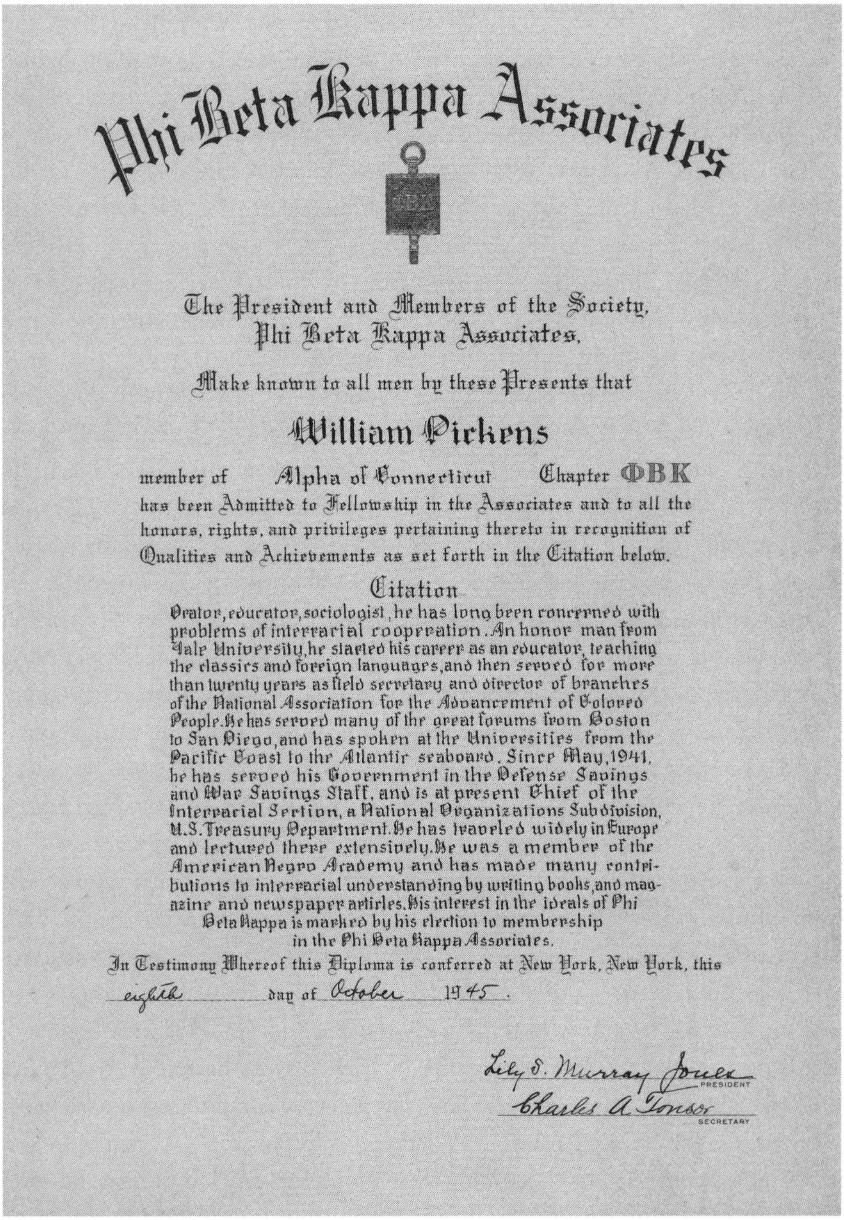

Phi Beta Kappa Associates

The President and Members of the Society,
Phi Beta Kappa Associates,

Make known to all men by these Presents that

William Pickens

member of Alpha of Connecticut Chapter ΦBK
has been Admitted to Fellowship in the Associates and to all the honors, rights, and privileges pertaining thereto in recognition of Qualities and Achievements as set forth in the Citation below.

Citation

Orator, educator, sociologist, he has long been concerned with problems of interracial cooperation. An honor man from Yale University, he started his career as an educator, teaching the classics and foreign languages, and then served for more than twenty years as field secretary and director of branches of the National Association for the Advancement of Colored People. He has served many of the great forums from Boston to San Diego, and has spoken at the Universities from the Pacific Coast to the Atlantic seaboard. Since May, 1941, he has served his Government in the Defense Savings and War Savings Staff, and is at present Chief of the Interracial Section, a National Organizations Subdivision, U.S. Treasury Department. He has traveled widely in Europe and lectured there extensively. He was a member of the American Negro Academy and has made many contributions to interracial understanding by writing books, and magazine and newspaper articles. His interest in the ideals of Phi Beta Kappa is marked by his election to membership in the Phi Beta Kappa Associates.

In Testimony Whereof this Diploma is conferred at New York, New York, this eighth day of October 1945.

Lily S. Murray Jones
PRESIDENT

Charles A. Tonsor
SECRETARY

Phi Beta Kappa certificate awarded to William Pickens. William Pickens Papers, James Weldon Johnson Collection in the Yale Collection of American Literature, Beinecke Rare Book and Manuscript Library, Yale University.

his check for future expenses, Dodge responded with another fifty dollars, and the promise of more, as well as twenty-five dollars from his mother, the heiress Melissa Phelps Dodge, "for winter clothes." Few early Black students enjoyed this kind of patronage, but even so, Pickens continued to hold a variety of jobs to pay his bills. As an undergraduate, he was known around the city for his "original readings from stories of Joel Chandler Harris' 'Uncle Remus'" and his "dialect readings at private entertainments," a way he apparently profited from the demand for such performances among White audiences. Pickens excelled at Yale, earning Phi Beta Kappa and attracting national attention when he won the prestigious Ten Eyck Prize for oratory.[14]

Black students sometimes found a welcome in the city's African American community. "A Well Known Society of Colored People to Have a Royal Entertainment," announced the *New Haven Evening Register* in 1891. Several Black students from the divinity, medical, and law schools, as well as the college, had been invited to a "grand soiree" given by this group, among them Isaac Porter, Henry Gamble, and the law student and future diplomat James Spurgeon. A few of these professional school graduates established themselves in New Haven after graduation. Porter stayed in the city and built a successful medical practice on Dixwell Avenue. An active Republican, he served on the New Haven City Council, representing the Ninth Ward, and was a member of the chamber of commerce and other civic organizations.[15]

For some educated Black scholars and professionals, political patronage helped smooth their journey through the turbulent waters of segregation. This helps explain why the history of early Black graduates at Yale is also, in part, the story of opportunity within the U.S. diplomatic service—one that begins with Ebenezer Don Carlos Bassett. Born in 1833, of mixed African, European, and Indigenous heritage, he studied at Yale and the University of Pennsylvania and was the first Black graduate of the State Normal School (now Central Connecticut State University). While teaching in New Haven, Bassett married Eliza Park, daughter of Robert M. Park. Bassett left Connecticut to take a position at the Institute for Colored Youth in Philadelphia. In 1869, he was appointed U.S. minister resident to Haiti, becoming the nation's first Black diplomat. Bassett's appointment was a milestone for African Americans and celebrated as such. In 1879, the law school invited him to speak, with the *Yale Daily News* identifying him as a "prominent colored citizen." Bassett would return to Haiti in 1889–91 as the personal assistant to Frederick Douglass when the famous abolitionist became U.S. minister to the Caribbean nation. Bassett's fluency in French made him indispensable to Douglass. Two of Ebenezer and Eliza's children attended

Yale, including a son named Ulysses S. Grant Bassett. That son earned "honors in all studies" and, as of his twenty-fifth reunion, had attended every reunion of his Yale College class.[16]

The tradition of Black alumni in the diplomatic service continued with John Edward Thompson, an 1883 graduate of the medical school. Thompson married Elizabeth Augusta McLinn, a daughter of the head carpenter at Yale, Charles McLinn, a leading African American citizen of the city. Thompson and McLinn's "fashionable" wedding, along with their plans to relocate to France, were reported in the *New Haven Evening Register*. Thompson practiced medicine for a while before his appointment as U.S. minister resident and consul general to Haiti, a position he held from 1885 to 1889. James Spurgeon, an 1892 graduate of the law school, held several diplomatic posts in Liberia, including as acting minister resident and consul general.[17]

One of the most distinguished Black members of the consular service was George Henry Jackson. Before coming to Yale, he had worked at a shoe factory, as a French interpreter, and as a Baptist preacher in New Haven. But with the goal of working in the mission field, he received degrees from both the Yale Divinity School and Yale Medical School before setting off for the Congo Free State. Jackson spent eighteen months as a medic and missionary, witnessing firsthand the horrors of King Leopold's brutal colonial regime. Back in New Haven, he gave lectures about his missionary work, donated "tribal weapons" he had acquired to the Yale Peabody Museum, and worked as an assistant instructor in clinical medicine at the Yale Medical School.[18]

Black Yale graduates entered the world of politics as well as diplomacy. Jackson made no secret of his wish for a consular appointment: "George H. Jackson Wants Place. New Haven Colored Man Applies for a Consulate," read the headline in the *New Haven Register*. Doing what was necessary to curry favor with the McKinley administration, he served as a census taker and presided over a rally in 1896 held by the Afro-American McKinley Club. When news of his eventual appointment became public, the Black community responded with a grand send-off. "A very elaborate farewell complimentary dinner," attended by one hundred guests, was given at Savin Rock, a popular local resort destination. T. Thomas Fortune, the influential editor of the Black newspaper the *New York Age*, played toastmaster, while politicians, the mayor, local celebrities, and other dignitaries gave speeches. From 1897 to 1914, Jackson served as the American consul to Cognac and La Rochelle, France. In these roles he made extensive reports on trade and took a special interest in the manufacture and understanding of cognac, later publishing a book, *The Medicinal Value of French Brandy*. He also promoted the sport of rugby, serving as club president of Stade Rochelais, the local rugby club in La Rochelle, from 1904 until 1911. When Jackson was dismissed from his post in 1914, the Black press laid the blame at the feet of the Taft administration, whose racial policies were widely seen as less liberal than those of McKinley. The *Crisis* reported, "This position is perhaps the best in the consular service ever held by a colored man and was supposed to be protected by the civil service." Jackson, seemingly undeterred, served as an organizer of W. E. B. Du Bois's Pan-African Congress of 1919, where his recommendations were informed by his experiences in the Congo.[19]

Africa as a place and an idea was central to another Yale graduate, the Black author and intellectual William H. Ferris. Born in New Haven, the son of a Civil War veteran, Ferris graduated from the college in 1895 and went on to receive master's degrees from both Yale and Harvard. Ferris's unfinished opus, a sprawling compendium, stands alongside the work of Jacob Oson and James W. C. Pennington, whose writings also highlighted the accomplishments, dignity, and humanity of the African diaspora. And Ferris drew from his own lessons at Yale, and the skepticism he learned there, to argue against the conception of the separate origins of the "races" popular at the dawn of the new century. "I remember that Professor [William Graham] Sumner warned us not to accept all that we read in books on sociology, anthropology and ethnology," Ferris wrote. "I remember, too, that Professor George Trumbull Ladd of Yale said, as we were reading Lotze's 'Microcosmus,' 'the origin of man is shrouded in mystery.' And I thank these two eminent scholars and thinkers for cautioning and warning us against believing that the science of anthropology had had its last say." Ferris found a mentor in Alexander Crummell, a distinguished pan-Africanist who attended Yale Theological Seminary in the 1840s. Ferris authored a book on Crummell and was one of the original members of his organization, the American Negro Academy, dedicated to Black uplift and self-improvement. But Ferris's most noteworthy professional achievement came as part of Marcus Garvey's Universal Negro Improvement Association, where he served as literary editor of the *Negro World*. Ferris followed and promoted Garvey's brand of pan-African Black nationalism, which was both inspirational and controversial to more than one generation of African Americans.[20]

Although Ferris associated with some of the leading Black intellectuals of the early twentieth century, the *Journal of Negro History* noted that when he died in 1941, he did so "in obscurity in his room . . . and his body was saved from the Potter's Field" by Yale treasurer George Parmly Day, who contributed $300 toward funeral expenses. Ferris's stature among his Yale classmates must have been high, however, because the *Journal* printed a glowing tribute from a committee of his White classmates. "A brilliant scholar, many of us will recall his penetrating comprehension of the course in psychology under Professor Ladd, and the latter's expression of delight at his understanding," wrote Lanier McKee, Roger S. Baldwin, and Allen Wardwell. "The recipient of many honors, his impressive work, 'The African Abroad,' is an outstanding encyclopedic study and presentation of the Negro and his achievements in all lands. With such a remarkable record of accomplishment, he was indeed a credit to his university and his country." Whatever his standing today in scholarly memory, Ferris was held in great esteem by his Yale peers.[21]

Like Bouchet, other promising African American scholars spent their careers teaching at Black schools and working within segregated institutions. After graduating in 1881, John Wesley Manning moved to Tennessee, where he served as principal of the Austin School in Knoxville. He also taught Latin, led institutes for teachers, and participated in the Southern Sociological Congress in 1915. Manning's Yale obituary noted his leadership positions in the East Tennessee Association of Teachers in Colored Schools and the Tennessee Conference of Educational Workers.[22]

Over a decade later, Charles Henry Boyer, class of 1896, followed a similar path. Born in Elkton, Maryland, Boyer graduated from the Institute for Colored Youth in Philadelphia while Edward Bouchet was on the faculty. They likely knew each other, which may explain why the young Boyer ended up enrolling in the Hopkins Grammar School and then at Yale. As a student, Boyer served as treasurer of the Freshman Union and a member of the Yale Union and distinguished himself academically, earning a "second dispute" at the junior exhibition, a showcase of scholarly talent in front of the president, faculty, and students. He then spent most of his career as a teacher of Greek and mathematics, a classics scholar, and then dean of Saint Augustine's School (later college), a Black institution in Raleigh, North Carolina; one of his children later served as its president. Boyer's own father had been a cook and butler and a Civil War veteran who served time in Libby, the infamous Confederate prison in Richmond, Virginia. Charles Boyer had come far, and yet many doors remained closed to him. Like Boyer, Manning, and Bouchet, the eminent William Pickens, class of 1904, also taught at Black institutions: Talladega, Wiley College in Texas, and Morgan State College in Baltimore, where he served as dean of academics, before working full time for the NAACP, which he helped build, for over two decades. Pickens was a close associate of James Weldon Johnson at the NAACP when Johnson served as its executive director in the 1920s.[23]

Edwin Archer Randolph, the first Black graduate of the law school, was also the first African American admitted to practice law in Connecticut, although he never did. Instead, after graduation he moved to Virginia, where he went into private practice, was elected to political office, and founded the *Richmond Planet*, a Black newspaper. Walter J. Scott had also moved South and set up his own legal practice, but he became ill and moved back home to New Haven, where he died in 1888. But perhaps no other early Black graduate traveled as far as Robert Bradford Williams. Born in Georgia in 1860, he graduated from Yale College in 1885, older than most of his peers. Not long after, Williams joined the Fisk Jubilee Singers on a world tour. One stop was New Zealand, where he decided to stay: Williams studied law, set up a practice, and held political office, becoming the longest-serving mayor of a town in Wellington.[24]

On the other hand, George W. Crawford, a contemporary of William Pickens, ascended the highest ranks of Black professional life in New Haven. Born in Tuscaloosa, Alabama, Crawford attended the Tuskegee Institute and received his undergraduate degree from Talladega College. In 1903, he graduated from the Yale Law School, where he was awarded the prestigious Townsend Prize for oratory. Crawford's achievement, which included an award of one hundred dollars and the honor of speaking at graduation, was covered in newspapers across the country. "Negro and Chinaman Divide Highest Commencement Honors," announced the *Philadelphia Record*. (Chung Hui Wang, a Chinese student, was also honored for academic achievement.) Crawford practiced law in New Haven for decades and served four terms as the city's corporation counsel. He was active in the Niagara Movement and the NAACP, establishing a branch in New Haven. Crawford, a longtime member of the Dixwell Church and a founder of the Dixwell Community House, served on the boards of Howard University and, for over fifty years, of Talladega College.[25]

The decades following the end of the Civil War were a time of new opportunity for Black male students at Yale. Some formed lifelong friendships with White students across a hardening color line. But they did so while navigating a broader campus culture steeped in cruel, unapologetic racism. The *Yale Daily News* routinely printed racist stories and jokes and used racist slurs in poems, letters to the editor, and advertisements. An 1879 story described a Yale student taking the arm of a young Black woman without realizing her identity; two fellow students, "though firm believers in the fifteenth Amendment," could not understand his behavior. When the young man noticed that his "new found friend was as black as the ace of spades," he "utter[ed] a piercing cry [and] fled most precipitately."

An 1883 poem published in the student daily similarly turned on a case of mistaken (racial) identity. It described a sophomore whose heart is "struck" by a dancer he sees across the room at a masquerade. At the end of the night when the masks are raised, however, the student is "paralyzed, / Dumbfounded, dazed, / When he beholds—a [n——]."[26]

Racist epithets, dialect, and imagery appeared not only in the *Yale Daily News* but in other student publications as well. In the *Yale Banner*, the college yearbook since 1841, extracurricular organizations listed their members, and those of the student eating clubs often included hand-drawn sketches of African Americans in the role of waiters, with exaggerated lips and other stereotypical features. Although most of the eating club depictions of African Americans showed them in the common role of waiter, a handful showed more sinister fantasies of "savage" violence. In an 1886 drawing, several Black figures surround a White figure being roasted alive over a pit. The Black figures are mostly unclothed—an indication of their supposedly uncivilized status—except for boots, pants, hats, and other items that they have taken from their victim. Their appropriation of their victim's Western clothing is meant to underline the grotesque inversion of power their crime has brought about. An 1889 drawing shows a White figure restrained with ropes while a Black figure in "tribal" clothing menaces him with spears. Images of African Americans in the *Banner* became less frequent over time. The exception, however, were pages devoted to the Southern Club, which was established at Yale in 1890. Into the twentieth century, its pages often included grossly caricatured figures playing the banjo, dancing in a minstrel style, or napping out of doors—a nod to the antebellum Old South that its members sought to glorify.[27]

More serious publications engaged in a different kind of racism. An author named only as "R. M. H." managed to fit a wide variety of racist tropes and stereotypes into a concise, one-page essay entitled "The Negro" in the *Yale Literary Magazine* in 1886: "The ancient 'uncle' has doubtless the common failings of his race, shiftlessness, and a more than scriptural carelessness for the morrow." He is superstitious, "happy, though poor," "happy-go-lucky," and "to him life is a continual holiday." In a conventional turn, the author concluded wistfully that "we are inclined to question whether we do not pay a high price for our superior opportunities and endowments, and to admit that there is perhaps, after all, a certain compensation in nature."[28]

Racist language was so commonplace that an especially popular game at Yale was called "n——baby," and it was played on campus at least from the 1880s through the early decades of the twentieth century. The Yale pastime was a version of a popular carnival amusement, called "hit the n——baby," "hit the coon," or "African dodger." Lewis Sheldon Welch and Walter Camp, in their 1900 book, *Yale, Her Campus, Class-Rooms, and Athletics*, described it in glowing terms as "the pastime of god-like Seniors," writing, "You must see it. . . . Cries of great joy fill the summer evening at every successful throw." Accounts of the game appeared frequently in the *Yale Daily News*. "Top-spinning, marbles and 'n——baby' were resumed by the Seniors yesterday," the paper reported. "The satisfaction which the denizens of South [a dormitory] take when they get a Durfee man up against the wall in the game of 'n——baby' is surprising," noted another piece a few days later. Harvey Cushing, the "pioneer and father of neurosurgery," who graduated from Yale in 1891, proudly told his mother that the game was played only at Yale. Cushing was mistaken; by that point it had traveled as far afield as Salt Lake City, Philadelphia, Washington State, and Oklahoma, and likely many other places. But the pastime was closely associated with Yale and, in its earliest years at least, unknown at sister Harvard. The *Crimson*, the Harvard student newspaper, noted in 1877 that their Yale peers had "forsaken 'hop-scotch' for the more fascinating game of 'n——baby.'" A few months later, the Harvard editors again smirked, "'N——baby' and 'foot-and-a-half'—whatever they may be—are popular pastimes." The uncensored name of the game appeared in the pages of the *Yale Daily News* dozens of times.[29]

Minstrel shows were another popular choice of entertainment. An unsigned editorial in the *Yale Courant* in 1866 bemoaned "what folly it is for us to waste time in card-playing and attending negro minstrels." Yet attend they did. An 1870 review gives a sense of the frequency of these performances: "Madame Rentz's Female Minstrels exhibited their stale legs; the next night Delehanty, Hengler and Bloodgood's Phunniegraphic Sensation made a stir; and on the twenty-fourth Dan Bryant's minstrels gave us the genuine Ethiopian in unadulterated blackness." One act in 1869 was described in the *Yale Literary Magazine* as "dulciflouously incanting nigrescent minstrels." From the 1870s onward, the *Yale Daily News* was full of advertisements, promotions, and reviews for shows such as "HAVERLY'S COLORED MINSTRELS," "CALLENDER'S COLOSSAL COLORED MINSTREL FESTIVAL," and similar fare. Downtown venues including the Grand Opera House, Carll's Opera House, and New Haven Opera House drew students to see performances like "Dockstader's Magnificent Minstrels," promising the "most realistic," "most legitimate" "Negro Minstrelsy in Existence." There were so many minstrel shows in 1884, in fact, that the *Yale Daily News* commented, "Judging by the play-bills, we are to have a kind of negro minstrel festival at the theaters for the next ten days." Students

Advertisement for a minstrel show, 1875. Randolph Linsly Simpson African-American Collection. James Weldon Johnson Memorial Collection in the Yale Collection of American Literature. Beinecke Rare Book and Manuscript Library, Yale University.

themselves performed in minstrels. "College fun by college boys," the *News* announced in 1884, "a characteristic college entertainment given wholly by undergraduates of Yale College." The Yale Glee Club and a group called Four End Men were to perform in a "negro minstrel." A student from the class of 1887 sang "Put on de Golden Shoes," "rendered in the genuine plantation manner." For an encore, Holmes and Bottsford, who had performed clog dancing earlier in the evening, ended the evening by "personifying an old negro couple," performing in blackface. As in other American communities, minstrelsy provided White Yale students with an entertaining distraction from real life as well as a real, if carnivalistic, expression of their racial attitudes.[30]

In the waning decades of the nineteenth century, White Northerners consumed all manner of supposedly authentic Southern entertainment. This was the age of Joel Chandler Harris's fabulously popular "Uncle Remus" stories, which first appeared in print in 1876, and Thomas Nelson Page's "Marse Chan," published in 1884. The *Yale Daily News* kept readers up to date on these authors, announcing, for example, in 1886 that Page had a new story coming out, entitled "Meh Lady: A Story of the War." The editors wrote, "The romantic and affecting narrative is put in the mouth of old Billy, an ex-slave." These authors and their rosy depictions of slavery and the antebellum South remained popular well into the twentieth century. When Page visited New Haven to give a lecture in 1898, the *Yale Daily News* anticipated it would be "one of the best lectures of the season." A review of Southern literature printed in the *Yale Literary Magazine* declared in 1894, "That musical negro dialect of Page's, by no other writer so skillfully handled, has made heroes seem more heroic, the stories only the more charming, and however rose-colored his view, this representative of the old aristocracy has made us feel that southern chivalry, fairest flower of the new world, is no idle myth." The writer praised another Yale favorite: "The folklore of the negroes is one of the most interesting productions of a distinct national trait. . . . The 'Uncle Remus' stories are certainly the best exposition of negro character, but they are also the translating into literature of some of the most poetic of conceptions. To Harris belongs the credit of establishing a literary landmark." Harris was a complicated writer, but he contributed to a growing body of literature that largely reduced, flattened, and degraded Black characters.[31]

It is not surprising, then, that the "soulful music of the Southern negro camp meetings, merry-makings, and slave cabins of the South" would attract a Yale audience. An advertisement in 1883 promised "a troupe of simon-pure old plantation ex-slaves." For added realism, the performers would even be "seated on genuine cotton bales." The event promised they would "be dressed in the varied and grotesque garb they wear in their Southern homes, and sing, as the procession moves."[32] Yale students, like so many White Americans in the late nineteenth century, consumed music, literature, and theater depicting a cheerful, sanitized version of Southern life under slavery. They lived in and contributed to the creation of a culture of romantic racial fantasy about the Old South—and thus an evolving national culture of reconciliation.

Despite the popularity of shows, theater, and schoolyard games, Yale was not an unserious place. From the 1880s into the early decades of the twentieth century, Yale students engaged with the most pressing issues of the day as they flocked to hear national figures speaking on their campus. A sampling of topics from these years reflects the urgency with which the college, and the nation, wrestled with the legacy of the Civil War and Reconstruction. Perhaps most striking is the extent to which the question of Black rights, political inclusion, and humanity were considered valid topics of debate.

No subject better highlights the way Yale students engaged with contemporary issues in the late nineteenth century than lynching. As a subject of national attention, it was difficult to ignore. In February 1893, the front page of the *New York Times* carried the headline, "Another Negro Burned . . . Drawn through the Streets on a Car—Tortured for Nearly an Hour with Hot Irons and Then Burned—Awful Vengeance of a Paris (Texas) Mob." The *Times* explained how a crowd of ten thousand people had gathered in Paris, Texas, to watch the torture and murder of Henry Smith, a Black man accused of raping and murdering a three-year-old White girl. White townspeople tied Smith to a scaffold, the word "JUSTICE" painted on its side. The sheriff, along with members of the dead girl's family, applied hot irons to Smith's body for an hour. They poked out his eyes and burned his tongue. Then they threw kerosene on his body and set him on fire.[33]

Smith was one of thousands of Black victims of lynching—and not only in the Deep South. Six months after his execution, a Black day laborer named Sam Bush was taken from a jail in Decatur, Illinois. Surrounded by a crowd of 1,500 White spectators, Bush was hanged on the courthouse lawn. That summer, the civil rights activist and antilynching crusader Ida B. Wells wrote, "Three human beings were burned alive in civilized America during the first six months of this year (1893). Over one hundred have been lynched in this half year. They were hanged, then cut, shot and burned." The previous year, Wells had spoken and written frequently on lynching, publishing what would become one of her best-known treatises on the subject, *Southern Horrors:*

Lynch Law in All Its Phases. Although they had been a feature of American life, particularly in the South and West, before the Civil War, lynchings became more frequent after the end of Reconstruction. An estimated 4,400 Black people were killed in lynchings between the end of Reconstruction and World War II. One scholar estimates that more than 80 percent of these violent acts took place in the South, and the vast majority of all lynching victims in the country—83 percent—were Black.[34]

The same year that Wells published an essay on "lynch law" for the opening of the 1893 Columbian Exposition in Chicago, Yale offered twelve-dollar prizes to six of the best essays written by seniors for the Townsend essay competition; one of the subjects was "The Revival of Lynch Law." Over the years, as Wells's antilynching campaign progressed, Yale students continued to consider the relative merits and drawbacks of extrajudicial mob killings. In 1897, the Sheffield Debating Club took as its topic, "Resolved: That lynching is justifiable." Two speakers argued in the affirmative and two in the negative; "The decision of the judges and the house was in favor of the affirmative." That year, over 120 Black people were lynched in the United States.[35]

The subjects for junior disputes and essays in the 1880s included, "Lynch law as now practiced in the United States," "Are the Southern Negroes Better Off than in the Days of Slavery?," and "The Future of the Negro in America." The Dwight Literary Society debated the resolution "that lynch law is sometimes justifiable." The sophomore composition topics in 1890 included the question, "Should the emancipated negro have received unconditional citizenship?" Colonization and disenfranchisement were floated as solutions to "the Negro Problem." In 1895, the first meeting of the Freshman Union attracted seventy-five students to consider the following: "Resolved: That the Southern States should take steps to disfranchise the negroes by means of state constitutions." The *Yale Daily News* reported that "the affirmative won the debate." In 1896, the Political Science Club considered the "Negro Problem from a Southern Standpoint." Debate topics followed closely from sensational news stories of the day. In 1891, mere days after eleven Italian immigrants were lynched—shot to death—in New Orleans, the law school invited students to choose sides on the resolution "that lynch law is sometimes justifiable in a civilized community," competing for substantial prizes of thirty and twenty dollars. Days later, the Yale Union took up a related resolution for its April debate—this time, "Resolved, that the people of New Orleans were justified in lynching the Italians connected with the Hennessy murder case." Prurient and sensationalistic, Yale debaters could not take their eyes and their minds off race and violence.[36]

Such debates were a focal point of university life. Judging from the coverage in the *Yale Daily News*, the 1890s represented a high point in terms of debate's centrality on campus: the intercollegiate debating team was covered like a sports team. The anti-Reconstruction, antiequality side did not always carry the day. Those arguing against the resolution "that the disfranchisement of the colored race in certain sections of this country is justifiable" won the argument at a meeting of the law school's Kent Club in 1900. Yet questions on campus about Black equality or African Americans' fitness for political participation were far from settled. The following year, the Yale Union took up "one of the most interesting and close debates in the year," in which the "Democratic side" held the day, resolving that a repeal of the first section of the Fourteenth Amendment and the Fifteenth Amendment to the Constitution should be "proposed" in several states.[37]

When Yale faced Princeton in 1901, the intercollegiate debate was featured in multiple front-page articles of the *Yale Daily News*. Princeton submitted the debate question—"Resolved, that the adoption of the fifteenth amendment to the Constitution of the United States has been justified"—giving Yale the choice of which side to argue. At the final trials, eighteen students vied for a spot on the Yale team; fourteen of these would-be orators chose to argue against the Fifteenth Amendment. All six of those who made the team took the position that the Fifteenth Amendment, giving African American men the right to vote, was not justified. In making their case, the Yale debaters repeated racist stereotypes of Black inferiority and laziness. The first speaker noted that the Fifteenth Amendment had "enfranchise[d] a race of utterly ignorant freedmen." Students insisted that even Ulysses S. Grant and William Tecumseh Sherman had seen the error of their ways. "The Republican party has since repudiated universal suffrage, and the whole country tacitly acquiesces in the practical nullification of the Fifteenth Amendment." Based on these and other arguments, the *News* deemed it an "Unusually Interesting Contest."[38]

Students clearly felt questions of Black rights and political inclusion to be relevant and worthy of their attention. In these years Yale students were the children of Reconstruction, and its enduring, unfinished legacy hung all over their debates. The Yale Union exhorted its members to take part in a debate on the topic of disenfranchisement. "The subject at the Yale Union this evening is one dealing with the attempt of North Carolina to solve the negro problem by the almost total disfranchisement of the colored man. It is an experiment which will probably be followed by many of the other Southern States and as a question of right and expediency is deserving of the attention and thought of all educated men." None of these debates settled the question, of course—for Yale students or the country. On the contrary, the fact that student clubs engaged with these issues through debate tells us that they were considered unresolved and worthy of discussion. And the longevity of such topics is notable. The repeal of the Fifteenth Amendment was still being debated by the Freshman Union in both 1909 and 1911, and John Brown's legacy was a topic for the Porter Prize as late as 1910, the year after the fiftieth anniversary of the raid on Harpers Ferry in 1859. Given debate's importance on campus, it is all the more noteworthy that Pickens and Crawford, two African American students, won the most prestigious awards for oratory in 1903 and 1904. Despite these accolades, Pickens was denied a spot on the university debating team, depriving Yale of one of its best speakers when the team competed against Princeton. One newspaper declared, "Reason Seems Obvious to Many Why Winner of Ten Eyck Prize is Not to Face the Tiger Debaters."[39]

Invited guests helped to ignite and shape campus discourse around these issues. In 1890, Daniel H. Chamberlain, a White Yale College graduate and Republican who had served as governor of South Carolina during Reconstruction, spoke to the Kent Club on "the race problem." Chamberlain, a formerly staunch Republican who now had changed his tune, told his law school audience that when African Americans were given the right to vote, they were "wholly unfitted for this great trust." They were now, he admitted, "in complete political subjection" in the South after the end of Reconstruction. Like so many Yale students of the era, Chamberlain considered it an open question whether Black Southerners should enjoy the right to vote. His answer was a version of Booker T. Washington's prescription for self-help: "They must be taught self-reliance, self-assertion and independence of the white race, in fine they must be taught those qualities of their white brethren which they do not naturally possess." Contra Washington, however, Chamberlain argued that Southern schools were as well funded as their Northern counterparts, and just as good. It would take time, Chamberlain admitted, for Black people to catch up to their White counterparts, but that was as it should be. "The negro has been assisted as no other race ever was—now let him assist himself," he asserted. The remarks were reviewed favorably by the *News*, particularly because, the editors said, the speaker approached his topic from "a purely non-political basis."[40] This perspective was a normative and popular view in Chamberlain's political class.

Yet not all the eminent visitors to Yale spoke with one voice. In 1892, the writer George W. Cable held forth on "the Southern Question" (another version of the ubiquitous "negro problem"). In direct contrast to Chamberlain, a

Northern man who spent most of his career in the South, Cable was a native of New Orleans whose critical depiction of Southern life had led to his self-exile in Massachusetts. Cable traced the roots of the "problem" to slavery. He did not pretend that the South's schools were up to the task of educating its people, White or Black. In keeping with many speakers from the South's Black colleges who visited Yale and New Haven during this era, Cable called for greater attention to "the education of the masses in the South."[41]

Among all the public figures who spoke on campus in these years, perhaps no one was as notable or visited as frequently as Booker T. Washington. Washington spoke at Yale no fewer than six times between 1895 and 1915, including not long after his influential 1895 speech at the opening of the Cotton States and International Exposition. It was there, in Atlanta, that Washington had encouraged African Americans to "cast down your bucket where you are," in front of a predominantly White audience, drawing the ire of W. E. B. Du Bois, who joined others in dubbing it the "Atlanta compromise speech." The *Yale Daily News* favorably reviewed Washington's remarks at Yale, also noting that "before and after the address a number of plantation hymns were sung by a colored quartet from the Tuskegee school." In December 1899 and again in March 1901, the Black leader and founder of the Tuskegee Institute in Alabama came to Yale to speak on "Some Results of Negro Education" and "Solving the Race Problem in the Black Belt of the South." The latter event was moved to Battell Chapel, a larger venue, "on account of the exceptionally large number of members of the University who . . . desired to attend." Afterward the *Yale Daily News* carried a substantial article on his remarks with lengthy excerpts.[42]

By the turn of the century, Washington had indeed become one of the nation's most powerful voices for sectional reconciliation. His prescriptions were rooted in a vision of African American self-help, industrial education, and racial peace forged without demands for enforcement of those very constitutional amendments that Yale students so eagerly debated. In that very year of 1901, Washington published his famous autobiography, *Up from Slavery*, in which he made his own distinctive, best-selling contribution to the image of the "loyal slave." Arguing that Black people had a "kindly and generous nature," along with a resistance to "feelings of bitterness against the whites" during and after the Civil War, Washington depicted a beneficent "school of slavery." Washington's widely read and controversial assertion that slavery had been a necessary stage on the path to human progress played exceedingly well in a culture of reconciliation, White racial solidarity, and violence. Hence did Yale students and their teachers broadly listen to Washington's claim that "notwithstanding the cruel wrongs . . .

the black man got nearly as much out of slavery as the white man did." In a typical argument out on the lecture circuit, which included New Haven, Washington contended that enslaved Africans had landed in America over two centuries ago devoid of culture and language, equipped only with "barbarous . . . 'fetishism' . . . a childish way of looking at and explaining the world." Out of enslavement they had emerged Christians on a long journey of "construction," Washington contended, requiring "patience, time, courage and toil."[43]

"Dignify and glorify common labour and put brains and skill into the common occupations of life"—with these words, Washington implored his fellow African Americans to settle for economic security, of a sort, when making "the great leap from slavery to freedom." Where, in such a world, did Edward Bouchet, scholar and physicist, belong? With a Yale doctorate in hand, Bouchet could not find a job in the universities or laboratories of Jim Crow America. Instead, he did what several of his fellow educated African Americans did in this period: he taught in segregated schools. After completing his PhD at Yale, Bouchet moved to Philadelphia and taught chemistry and physics at the Institute for Colored Youth, where his patron Cope served on the board. The only African American high school in the city, the institute did not have a library or laboratory facilities. In Philadelphia, Bouchet was a member of the country's oldest Black Episcopal church, Saint Thomas's, serving on the vestry and as church secretary and lay reader. He lectured on scientific topics and was a member of the Franklin Institute, which championed scientific education for the general public. After twenty-six years at the Institute for Colored Youth, Bouchet was fired, along with the rest of the faculty, when the all-White board embraced the industrial educational philosophy promoted by Booker T. Washington. Bouchet spent the next few years teaching and working various jobs in Saint Louis before returning to his family home on Bradley Street in New Haven.[44]

It was then that Bouchet, at the age of fifty-two, sought a teaching position at his alma mater. His Yale application, dated 1905, delineated his sterling qualifications—six years of Latin, six of Greek, ranked sixth in his Yale class—and described teaching as his "life work." Bouchet listed Arthur W. Wright, professor of experimental physics at Yale, as his reference. Wright was himself an alumnus twice over and a towering figure within the Yale scientific community. In a confidential questionnaire attesting to Bouchet's personality, scholarship, and "force of character and ability," Wright recommended Bouchet without reservation. In addition to his "excellent" scholarship, he possessed "agreeable personal qualities, gentlemanly manners, and good address." The distinguished professor thought Bouchet was "eminently well fitted for a professorship," and wrote of his one-time pupil, "I should have entire confidence in Mr. Bouchet's ability and character, and believe that with a successful experience as a teacher, such as he has had, he would not fail to be efficient and successful in any position he was called to occupy."[45]

Yale did not hire Bouchet. Over the next fourteen years he lived a peripatetic life, crisscrossing the country to hold teaching jobs in Missouri, Ohio, and Virginia. He became ill and eventually returned to New Haven, where he died in 1918, in a house on the same street where he had grown up. He was buried in an unmarked grave in Evergreen Cemetery. Bouchet's life and tragic end were a tale of intellectual success and social discrimination, an illustration of what a Yale education in the nineteenth century might have nurtured into being. But neither Yale nor the country at large was willing to recognize his gifts with job security or scholarly acclaim. Today, fellowships, awards, and societies at Yale and far beyond are named for the eager learner from the tiny Artisan Street School. His portrait hangs in the nave of Yale's Sterling Memorial Library; in it, Bouchet appears young, ready to smile and explain some portion of the physical universe most of us can hardly imagine.[46]

Despite the campus culture in these years, several early Black alumni, including Bouchet, remained connected to the university and their classmates. John Wesley Manning attended his triennial reunion and named his firstborn child "Yale." At a class dinner held in New York in 1903, classmates read a letter written by Charles Boyer, in absentia, and he "was given a long cheer." Boyer also sent a biographical update and several photographs to be included in the quarter-century record, published in 1924, including one of him with his large family. In the questionnaire for his thirty-fifth reunion, which he attended in 1909, Bouchet listed several classmates whom he saw "frequently," and he was among the handful of classmates who spoke at the reunion dinner. A White classmate, James Sellers, wrote Bouchet's obituary, which noted his participation in alumni affairs: "During his residence in Philadelphia Bouchet took much interest in the local Yale Alumni Association and was a faithful attendant at its meetings and annual dinners. He won and retained the regard and kindly interest of its other members and was always received by them with cordiality and respect." Sellers, a prominent Philadelphia lawyer, also gave a speech at the school where Bouchet had spent many years teaching, "in commemoration of" his friend, several months after he died—a record of which was included in the *Yale Alumni Weekly*. Bouchet remains, like many of his fellow Black graduates in the late nineteenth and early

Charles H. Boyer and his family, 1924. Manuscripts and Archives, Yale University Library.

twentieth centuries, a symbol both of the meaning of education and of the grace and courage it took to endure the humiliations of Jim Crow.[47]

African American scholars have called this era—bookended chronologically by the promises of Radical Reconstruction and the lynchings and violence of the early twentieth century—the "long dark night" and the "nadir" of American race relations.[48] So it was. At the same time, these were years of possibility for Black students at Yale. Some were born into slavery and others were just one generation removed. Yet they seized new educational opportunities at one of the country's best-regarded institutions of higher learning. Working on behalf of themselves, their families, and their communities, many went on to harness their knowledge, networks, and credentials to build new institutions both in the United States and around the world. These men enjoyed opportunities their parents had not known, but they were also surrounded by reminders of their second-class status and the knowledge that they could become victims of racist violence at the slightest provocation. From the pages of the student newspaper to the theater stage, in class and in lecture halls, Black people's intellectual abilities, their standing as citizens, and their very humanity were routinely questioned, debated, and derided.

John Wesley Manning, the 1881 Yale College graduate whose parents had risked their lives to escape slavery and bring their family north during the Civil War, was raised and educated in Connecticut but spent most of his life teaching in Tennessee. In a speech given in New Haven—preserved and passed down by his daughter named Yale—Manning covered five hundred years of history, from the origins of the slave trade in Africa to the dawn of the twentieth century. His assessment of the contemporary moment in 1902 was grim. "After freedom, lavishly were citizenship and civil rights proclaimed for the Negro, but grudgingly and stingingly were they accorded," Manning wrote. "State after state has re-enacted laws of proscription and the tidal wave of reaction is sweeping northward, in sentiment, if not by legislative enactment. It seems that the Negro, shorn of the essentials of freedom, citizenship, franchise, civil rights and the pursuit of happiness, must begin life anew at the bottom rung of the ladder where he was left by the Emancipation Proclamation." Chastened and in near despair, Manning said the Black man "would not complain at this were he left free to climb. At every effort put forth to rise, he is restricted by slights, thrusts, and jeers until it seems that Jehovah himself had deserted him."[49]

The Civil War had ended slavery. Four million men, women, and children had claimed their freedom in the throes of the bloody conflict. But the nation had not delivered on the full promise of emancipation or the unfathomable sacrifice it had required. By the early years of the twentieth century, so many of the advances of Reconstruction were either forgotten or, in a very real sense, debated, suppressed, and openly denounced. In the years to come, Yale University, in trying to look ahead to the future, would be forced to confront its own history and reflect on the war's unsettled legacy. But not, with occasional exceptions, for another two generations.

INTERLUDE

Black Employees at Yale

With fingers dirty and black,
From lower to upper room,
a COLLEGE SWEEP went dustily 'round,
Playing his yellow broom.
Dust! dust! dust!—
And with voice not loud but deep,
He sang this song in a mournful way,
This dolorous song of the sweep.

"Sweep! sweep! sweep!
From morning to evening prayers!
And sweep! sweep! sweep!
From the ground to the garret stairs!
It's oh! to be a slave
Equal to negro or Turk,—
This sweeping and dusting and making of beds,
This worse than slaving work!

—From "Song of the Sweep" in *Songs of Yale* (1853)

In the decades after the Civil War, despite inroads made by early pioneers like Edward Bouchet, John Wesley Manning, and others, it was still far more likely to find African Americans cleaning rooms or selling their wares on campus than it was to see them sitting in those rooms as students. The war changed much about New Haven, but employment opportunities for Black men and women remained limited. A small number of educated Black men entered the ranks of the professional class and opened offices as doctors and lawyers by the end of the nineteenth century. But the majority, largely excluded from the trades and the city's nascent industrial sector, continued to work as barbers, porters, waiters, laborers, laundresses, and the like. Given these constraints, a job at Yale as a custodian or a "sweep," as they were known, was desirable.[1]

Sweeps made students' beds, swept the dormitory rooms weekly, and were responsible for keeping campus buildings clean. For many years, there were both private sweeps, paid by individual students, and "regular sweeps" employed by the university. Lyman Hotchkiss Bagg, a member of the class of 1869, identified a private sweep as "a negro who, besides making the beds and doing the ordinary chamber work, builds the fires, draws the water, blacks boots, buys the oil, fills and trims the lamps, and runs on miscellaneous errands." They were paid about a dollar a week. Bagg noted that since his own student days, there had been a ban on students hiring private sweeps or paying or tipping the regular sweeps, but, he wrote, "of course the former prohibition is evaded."[2]

Quite a number of men who worked as regular sweeps were prominent in New Haven's Black community, where they were active in church and civic affairs. William Bouchet, father of Edward, was born in South Carolina and brought to New Haven as the "body servant" of a Yale student named John Brownlee Robertson. After Robertson graduated (he went on to hold various

Yale custodians, known as "sweeps," circa 1879. *Left to right:* Osborn Allston, Isom Allston, James Jackson, and George Livingston. Custodial and Administrative Services, Yale University, Photographs (RU 763). Manuscripts and Archives, Yale University Library.

political offices, including serving as mayor of New Haven), William Bouchet worked at Yale as a custodian, served as a deacon of the Temple Street Congregational Church, and was active in the temperance and abolitionist movements. George T. Livingston was also a church deacon. A Civil War veteran and an active Republican, Livingston served on the vestry of Saint Luke's Episcopal Church. Luke Lathrop, another Yale sweep, served as a delegate to the National Colored Conventions. Charles McLinn was employed as the head carpenter at Yale for decades and was described by the *Yale Banner* as a "key-fitter, and handy man generally . . . ready at all times to repair furniture, locks, pack furniture, and box goods for shipment as students may require." Beyond Yale, McLinn was a trustee and longtime parishioner of the Temple Street Church, and in 1874, he was elected to the city council. Two of his daughters married Black Yale graduates, and another, Nellie McLinn, was a public school teacher at the Dixwell Avenue Grade School. William H. Ferris wrote that President Arthur Twining Hadley and other eminent faculty members attended McLinn's funeral.[3]

The men who held these jobs occupied an unusually visible place at Yale. In issues of the *Yale Banner* yearbook from roughly 1870 to 1880, they were listed by full name, along with the buildings for which they were responsible and their home addresses. They show up by name in the handwritten financial records of the university from that era, as their pay was carefully recorded. The Yale archives contain formal portraits of many of them. But the attention they received from White students was not always laudatory. On the contrary, in several student publications and memoirs, they were also the focus of scorn, derision, and racist epithets. A student writing in the *Yale Courant* in 1866 complained, "not only do sweeps not sweep the dirt away" but the "private sweeps" "steal your coal." One writer found "heaps of dust—long lost treasures!" under his sofa. "Books, sleeve-buttons, letters, books, collars, tooth-picks, and other mementoes of past life. He thanks the gods of laziness that sweeps (how do they endure the cutting name?) never sweep under articles of furniture." In a lengthier diatribe, the *Courant* claimed it was not asking for a "golden spoon," but insisted that the sweeps system required significant reform. "How would you like to have half an inch of dust on your books, on your writing-desk, your water pitcher, your bed, your pictures, your tables, chairs, lamps and bureau? How, furthermore, would you like to have from two to three inches of dust under all the above and in your slippers and tobacco-box? . . . So we eat dust and drink it and breathe it. We should not be surprised to find ourself [*sic*] metamorphosed into a Dead Sea apple some of these days." That spring, various writers discussed the rumor that the system of sweeps was to be replaced by female custodians. One student, characteristically, blamed "the great indolence of the sweeps themselves" and said they would prefer "a pied cat" to "the best sweep that we have seen in Colleges."[4]

Memoirs by Yale alumni include perhaps the most disparaging and caricatured accounts, full of racist slurs, dialect, and stereotypes. Henry Beers, an 1869 graduate and a longtime professor of English at Yale, included many references to various African Americans in his memoir, *The Ways of Yale in the Consulship of Plancus*, which he published in 1895 while he was on the faculty. There was Epaphroditus, "the negro costermonger" (a fruit and vegetable vendor), whom students paid five dollars to perform "an epileptic fit in the gallery of Music Hall during a temperance lecture, and was carried out howling and foaming at the mouth." Then there was Beers's own "aged sweep," whom he remembered as a "smooth old swindler, with a molasses-candy complexion and great elasticity of conscience." Beers's conscience seems to have been questionable: he persuaded the man to steal chairs for him and his friends. But this bit of fun, Beers wrote, kept them "in thraldom to our aged sweep."[5]

Beers's stories about the sweep turned on the humor of an inverted order—of Yale students supposedly taken advantage of by a foolish yet cunning trickster. Beers recounted the following story about his roommate, quoting his roommate as saying, "'That blasted n——woke me up, and it's only a quarter of seven.' 'Well, you left a notice for him to wake you, didn't you?' 'Yes; but I thought he couldn't read.'" The humor was premised on the sweep's supposed illiteracy, but the students were made the fools. In his telling, Beers was often duped by a deceitful Black man. Unpredictable and capricious, Beers's sweep would disappear for a week or more at a time, but they were too afraid of their "coffee-colored tyrant" to object. Beers and his friends later discovered that the same man was "an energetic exhorter at 'n——union.'" The revelation was made by Yale students visiting a Black church, "not, it must be confessed, in an entirely devotional spirit," but in the spirit of mockery. Beers recalled, "On one such occasion, our sweep having been absent from his duties several days, presumably tossing upon a bed of pain, we were surprised to see him in the pulpit, sustained on either side by a sturdy deacon, while he called sinners to repentance with an expenditure of horsepower that would have sufficed, if applied along the line of his work, to black our boots for a week and to carry a hogshead of water from the south pump to our bedroom. Whether he recognized us in the congregation we never knew. He certainly did not change color."[6]

Other recollections range from violently scornful to condescending, or in some cases a combination of both. Pontificating on the advantages of living in the dormitories as opposed to lodging in town, one alumnus wrote that in the dorm he "is his own master. His room is his castle. And if he can't 'wallop his own n——,' he can at least swear at his private sweep." Other students appreciated the way sweeps offered a window onto a bygone era of servility. In an 1886 essay, a student described his relationship with Jackson, a "queer, good-humored old darkey," and remarked on his "likeness to a class of persons whom I never thought to have found outside of half a dozen Southern States, the real old-fashioned household negro servants." Although Jackson had been born enslaved, he hailed from New Jersey, not the Deep South. Nevertheless, he seemed to have fulfilled this student's wish for a glimpse of the Black people he had encountered only in romantic Southern literature. Jackson, to this young man, was a "traditional character . . . so common in fiction, and so rare but real in life." This student believed that Jackson, like the happy-go-lucky slaves of the Old South, was "by nature lazy" but loyal to those he served, possessing a "perfectly childish love of mischief and of laughter." The student praised Jackson's "faithful heart" and the ease with which one could capture "its affection and its service."[7] No wonder these generations of Yale students were so primed to join the choruses of reunion and reconciliation, joining arms with a defeated, but romanticized, South.

White students' views of slavery and its aftermath were shaped by minstrel shows and the Brer Rabbit stories so beloved on campus in the decades after the war. Uncle Remus's creator, the author Joel Chandler Harris, said he wanted to imbue Remus with "quaint and homely humor" but also "a certain picturesque sensitiveness—a curious exaltation of mind and temperament."[8] These authors were wildly popular among Yale students—and the nation at large—so it should come as no surprise that memoirs and student accounts of the Black people they encountered in service roles were shaped by the tropes with which they were familiar from literature and the minstrel stage. Perhaps, too, the men who held these positions understood what was expected of them—and what types of behaviors would be rewarded. The Yale student certainly appreciated Jackson's habit of calling him "my gentleman," allowing him to experience a small fantasy of bygone mastery.

Not long after that essay was published, the *Yale Daily News* reported on its front page that John Jackson, "the former janitor of D.K.E," had died. Jackson, the article explained, had been enslaved in New Jersey. "At the abolition of slavery in that state, he escaped with the assistance of his master's brother, who . . .

slipped some money in his hand and told him not to take the train with the others." Three members of the fraternity attended Jackson's funeral and sent "a handsome floral emblem" as well.[9]

In addition to the sweeps, a cast of so-called campus characters, nearly all African American, were part of Yale life and lore in these years. "Apple Boy," "Candy Sam," "Old Clothes' Man," "Fine Day," and "Free Bill" were among the itinerant

Theodore and Mary Ferris. Student Life at Yale Photographs (RU 736). Manuscripts and Archives, Yale University Library.

salespeople, known also as "nondescript purveyors, vendors, beggars, ragamuffins, and other nuisances," mentioned in the *Yale Banner* and included as "itinerant licentiates," along with the college sweeps, in the *Banner* and *Yale Pot-Pourri.* Members of the class of 1868 remembered them as part of their first initiation into college life: "We made an early acquaintance with Candy Sam, who was always to be found, just before recitation, in his place leaning against the wall of the old Atheneum, and, with his dejected smile, trying to persuade us to part with our fractional currency." Candy Sam, whose real name was Theodore Ferris, was blind, and he was often accompanied by his wife, Mary, whom the students called Mrs. Candy Sam. A lengthy profile of Ferris in the *Yale Literary Magazine* reflected students' affection for and interest in him, declaring his "life more adventurous than many of us imagined. We hope it may long be preserved, for if the Candy Man were removed, college life would lose much of its sweetness."[10]

Another Black confectioner was George Joseph Hannibal, L. W. Silliman (no relation to the prominent Silliman family of Yale). Known around Yale as Hannibal, he was distinguished by his speeches, which were as long as his full name. "Notwithstanding, even under the most superlative temptation, to interrupt the gentlemen in their studies, I beg to ask whether they are not moved to purchase a package of my old-fashioned, home-made molasses candy," quoted Clarence Demming in his 1915 book *Yale Yesterdays*. Demming said "every graduate of Yale since the later sixties" would be able to recall this speech and remember Hannibal, whom Demming deemed the "alpha" of the "original Campus characters." Around him others like Candy Sam and Fine Day "twinkled as minor stars."[11]

Other observers were less generous than Demming and the alumni whose memories were steeped in nostalgia. One anonymous member of the class of 1868 complained about "the uninvited and usually unwelcome guests who knock at the college doors." These included Ferris (a.k.a. Candy Sam), "the blind negro who for the past dozen years has 'helped hold up the Athenaeum tower,' and exhorted the Freshmen to patronize the only legitimate candy seller recognized by the institution. Each day he finds his way to every college room, with his apples and confectionery, and soon learns to recognize by their voices, his individual patrons." With a less than charitable attitude, this author remembered that freshmen would take up a collection for Ferris at Thanksgiving and that he would receive donations of old clothes from the students. He recalled his "chief rival," Silliman, as a "crafty black man" and another salesperson named "Trade Wind" who sold sweets.[12]

Hannibal Silliman, circa 1875. Student Life at Yale Photographs (RU 736). Manuscripts and Archives, Yale University Library.

The students knew little about the lives of these men. A native of New Haven, Silliman had served with the Black Twenty-Ninth Infantry in the Civil War. When he enlisted on December 8, 1863, at the advanced age of twenty-five, he gave his occupation as "confectioner." Silliman served for the duration of the war, mustering out on October 4, 1865, and returning to his work making and selling sweets. It is unknown whether many students knew about Silliman's wartime service or considered his life outside campus, but it was reported in the newspapers when he died in 1907. The *Boston Herald* mourned the loss of Yale's "famous old candy man and boxing professor," explaining that Silliman had taught boxing to Yale students for many years and introduced himself at Yale athletic events where he hawked his wares as "professor of the manly art of self-defense at Yale University." The tribute also noted that Silliman was one of the marshals of the procession at Noah Porter's inauguration as Yale president. A few weeks later, the *Yale Alumni Weekly* devoted a three-page spread to Silliman, Ferris, and others among the "extinct human curios of the campus." It was a fond remembrance. Although some might consider Silliman "a freak," the *Weekly* said that "those who knew him longer and better saw the actor; and with these the satiric smile, which now and then broke his crust of gravity, betrayed the underlying man of trade and of profit to be coined by eccentricity."[13] In other words, Silliman had had a schtick, speech and all. In this business of selling to Yale students, humor, drama, and an air of mystery were as important as confections; Silliman, Ferris, and their competitors sold theater as well as sweets. And though they could never have known it, they worked in the tradition established by none other than William Grimes, who had worked amid so many Yale students, written his story, and found his final resting place across the street in Grove Street Cemetery.

Osborn Allston, whose nephews John and Henry graduated from Yale, was another working-class African American who entered the pages of college lore by capturing the hearts and imaginations of Yale students. Allston worked as a regular sweep, employed by the university, from at least 1870 until his death in 1884. When he died, the *Yale Daily News* remarked that "Old Allston" was only fifty-five years old, but "a life of poverty, and heavy sorrows and hard toil, had aged him before his time." A few days later, the student daily printed a long remembrance of "honest and faithful old Allston" on its front page. "The announcement of the death of Allston will cause more than passing regret to the many graduates of Yale who at some time during their course in old South college or Psi Upsilon enjoyed his faithful services, and came into the sunshine of his cheerful disposition," the eulogy read.[14]

Allston was born into slavery and had migrated to Connecticut during or after the Civil War, as had his sister's family and several brothers. His former life had become part of Yale lore and the romance surrounding him. "Many a time do I remember when we gathered about the glorious open fires of South college hearing Allston tell, as he rested for a few moments on his broom, of old slavery days. He himself had been a slave, but fortunately had a kind-hearted 'massa' of whom Allston always spoke in grateful terms." They remembered Allston as "always cheerful." Even with all the sadness in his life and in his past, he mustered courage and happiness for the students. "There were times when Allston confided his troubles to us boys. And then those eyes grew dim with tears, but his smile grew only more tender," the writer recalled. Thus these elite Yale boys received just what they desired from Black people—sentiment, pathos, and entertainment that made no real demands on them, except perhaps a dollar a week.[15]

The students also were aware of Allston's financial troubles—his "family was large, his pay small"—and he talked to them about the mortgage he owed on his house. Every Christmas, students "made up a purse and sent him down South" to see friends and family. He repaid them with stories for their entertainment and expressions of gratitude for their patronage. "For months afterwards he interested and amused us with the tale of his travels, and it seemed as though he could never thank us enough for our trifling remembrance." The writer went on to remind readers that the "college holds the mortgage and there may be an opportunity for our benevolence in rewarding a faithful servant." Whether or not students helped with his mortgage, we know that they formed a committee to raise money for his funeral expenses. Allston had done "his duty," and he was rewarded with a grave marker in Grove Street Cemetery that recorded the donors' benevolence toward their "faithful janitor."[16]

Osborn Allston was not alone. Other hardworking, ambitious African American men received homage in death if not in life as a tribute to their labors. One such man was Robert M. Park, who witnessed tremendous changes in New Haven and at Yale over the course of his long and active life. A founding member of the Temple Street Church, Park was active in several movements for social and political rights for African Americans, and he watched as promising young Black men and women, including Edward Bouchet, came out of his congregation and achieved distinction as scholars, teachers, and professionals. He would live to witness his son-in-law, Ebenezer Bassett, appointed as the nation's first Black diplomat to the hemisphere's first Black republic, Haiti, and see some of his grandchildren attend Yale. Before the war, Park had worked in the laboratories of both Benjamin Sillimans, where he carried out experiments and earned a reputation for scientific knowledge. In his later life, Park spent over twenty years as the janitor of Skull and Bones, and he was known to wear the secret society's badge on his lapel.[17]

When Park died in 1895, a veritable who's who of Yale came to pay their respects to a person the *New Haven Register* called "one of the oldest and best known colored citizens of this City." The *Register* reported that "a great many Yale men" attended the funeral, among them Winthrop E. Dwight, a recent Yale graduate and the son and great-grandson of two Yale presidents; two prominent judges; the editor of the *Hartford Courant*; political appointees; and eminent professors. The newspaper reported that Park had been initiated as a member of Skull and Bones, the only nongraduate to be so honored. His tombstone in the Grove Street Cemetery is inscribed with the initials "S. B. T."[18]

Jackson, McLinn, Bouchet, Park, Allston: in their time, being a "faithful servant" or "faithful janitor" could lead to literary eulogies, great displays of appreciation, and even the presence of dignitaries at one's funeral. Several lived to see their children or grandchildren enrolled as Yale students, glimpsing how future generations might be able to move away from the strain and precarity of manual labor and into the small but growing ranks of Black professionals. Yet these men lived and worked within a world of circumscribed possibilities, and jokes and caricatures written by Yale students, alumni, and faculty members reflect the hostility of a community that did not take seriously Black people's abilities, integrity, or humanity. In spite of the indignities they experienced, however, these Black employees and their families left their own imprint on the historical record: in the families they reared and supported; in the religious and community institutions they built; and in the movements for political and social equality they nurtured and sustained—a different legacy of "faithful service," but one that remains inscribed on the city and the university.

CHAPTER 11

Embracing the White South

> Though Yale does not have, as far as we know it, in its academic halls today a man who shall represent the greatest and most disinterested and noble southern ideals as once did Calhoun, we have not forgotten that we need such men.
>
> —ARTHUR TWINING HADLEY, Yale College class of 1876, president of Yale, 1899–1921

"For God, for country, and for Yale." These were the pillars of the Reverend Joseph Twichell's life. An 1859 graduate of Yale College and a longtime member of the Yale Corporation, Twichell was the pastor of Asylum Hill Congregational Church, a prominent White parish in Hartford, Connecticut. Beyond the pulpit, he was known widely as Mark Twain's closest friend, and he traveled in distinguished literary and social circles. Yale was a central feature of Twichell's Gilded Age life. He organized reunions, gave toasts at alumni dinners, and said the benediction at commencement. But above all, the pastor and writer considered the Civil War a defining experience for himself, his generation, and the nation at large. The pages of his journal, kept for over forty years, document his dogged determination to honor those who had served—and died—for the Union cause.[1]

Not long after his college graduation, Twichell enlisted as a chaplain in the Excelsior Brigade, a largely working-class, Irish Catholic brigade raised in New York. At some of the most important engagements of the war, Twichell moved bodies off the battlefield, ministered to the wounded and dying, and witnessed the dreadful cost of war up close. In the years following, he wrestled with the war's meaning and searched for ways to honor the sacrifices of his brothers-in-arms. From the 1870s until his death in 1918, Twichell was involved in an array of efforts to memorialize the war: he organized reunions of the Third Army Corps, served on the committee to erect the Soldiers and Sailors Memorial Arch in Hartford, spoke at the laying of the cornerstone of the Excelsior Brigade monument at Gettysburg, advocated for a monument in Georgia to Connecticut soldiers who died in Andersonville prison, and eulogized Ulysses S. Grant from his pulpit.[2]

And so it was fitting that Twichell was invited to speak at the dedication of a new statue of Theodore Dwight Woolsey during the commencement festivities in June 1896. Later that afternoon, the senior class, in keeping with tradition, would plant its "class ivy." But just before ascending the platform to give his speech, Twichell learned that the senior class had chosen to plant a sprig of ivy from the grave of Robert E. Lee. The very idea of it—honoring the "Confederate chief," as Twichell called him, on the same day as they gathered to remember Union stalwart Woolsey—horrified Twichell. How could such a thing be happening at his beloved Yale? "I disliked the thing so much that I could not forbear an open protest against it," he later wrote.[3]

Over the preceding years, Twichell had indeed watched as the country moved toward honoring Confederate and Union soldiers together. And he participated in these efforts of national reconciliation himself, despite his Union loyalty. In 1886, for example, he was on hand to dedicate the memorial arch in Hartford, where participants sang, "Blue and gray united at one altar kneel and pray,—/ Union and Freedom forever!" oddly set to the old Union ballad "Marching through Georgia." In 1888, Twichell took a leading part in organizing the twenty-fifth anniversary of the Battle of Gettysburg, a grand event in which both Union and Confederate veterans were invited to participate. There, in addition to speaking at the dedication of the Excelsior monument, Twichell served as the chaplain at the "Blue and Gray" meeting. Such meetings of White Union and Confederate veterans were becoming more common in the 1880s. The *New York Times* underlined the "unusual importance" of the Gettysburg Blue and Gray reunion, but also noted that "twenty-four such exchanges of friendly courtesies" had taken place over the previous seven years. Not everyone embraced this approach: fewer Confederates participated in the silver anniversary than organizers had expected, and some Union army veterans criticized as "bosh" the idea that both sides had been in the right. Twichell, however, praised the attempt to unite the Blue and Gray at Gettysburg, writing in his journal, "There never was a grander occasion of its kind than this Reunion, nor was there ever *such* an occasion in the world before. It was certainly historic. . . . It was a time to praise and worship God, and believe in Him anew."[4]

In his own public remarks, however, Twichell tended to keep the focus on the Union army, its soldiers, and its cause. Also in 1888, the same year as the "historic" Gettysburg reunion, the editor of the *Meriden Journal* said, approvingly, that Twichell's Memorial Day speech was given "entirely in honor of the men who wore the Blue" and did not "divide[] the honors with the men who wore the Gray."[5] And Twichell was not afraid to mention slavery, which he believed was the central issue that had led to war in the first place. Speaking at the Hartford memorial service for former president and Union army general Ulysses S. Grant, Twichell intoned, "How many men and women that were born slaves, would if they might, kiss the sword that lies above your still bosom, and rain drops of gratitude upon it, as the sword that made them free." Despite the growing mood of reconciliation between White Northerners and Southerners, Twichell believed that, through the sacrifices of his friends and fellow soldiers in the Union army, God had carried out his divine plan to free the slaves. As he told his congregants, Grant, like the biblical David, was a "Providential Man."[6]

Even as Twichell venerated the Union cause, he demonstrated a remarkable commitment to personal reconciliation, as his relationship with classmate Robert "Bob" Stiles reveals. Twichell and Stiles had been close friends at Yale, spending vacations and school breaks together and living in the same New York boarding house after graduation. But Stiles, although raised in New Haven, identified with the South, enlisted in the Confederate army early in the war, and was captured at Sailor's Creek in April 1865. It was around this time, only days before Lee and Grant's meeting at Appomattox Court House, that Twichell was traveling through Virginia when he encountered a group of Confederate prisoners of war. One called his name, and he realized it was his old friend Bob Stiles. But when Twichell approached him, Stiles refused to shake his hand. It was a stinging rebuke, but in 1868, Twichell tried again to rekindle the relationship. This time he received a hostile letter in return. "We had *better not see each other*," Stiles wrote. "My whole past life is a grave which yawns upon me with wretchedness, relieved only by a conscience *absolutely clear and pure* as regards all the *main issues & decisions* of it. . . . For while I trust I have only kind feelings toward & wishes for you personally; yet there cannot be any *pleasant easy sympathy* or *communion* between me and a man who sympathized with the North in the late war; most *especially* is this true with regard to one who was formerly my intimate friend."[7]

In 1877, twelve years after their wartime encounter, Twichell tried yet again, sending him a picture of his children, and this time, Stiles responded warmly. From then until Stiles's death in 1905, the two men visited each other and exchanged affectionate letters. Stiles, most likely at Twichell's encouragement, gave a speech at their twentieth Yale reunion in 1879. When they met that year, Twichell was pleased they had "much to talk of both in the old times and in later years . . . though there were some delicate themes which we avoided." And still nearly a decade later, when Twichell stayed with Stiles in Richmond, he rejoiced in their reconciliation. The "words and acts of kindness by which I was surrounded in his house, made that day in 1865 when I met him a prisoner of war, and he refused to take my offered hand seem a great way off. Truly times are changed. Yet he is a 'Southerner' still." Indeed, Stiles remained not only a Southerner but deeply convinced of the righteousness of the Confederate cause. Just before his death, Stiles published a memoir of his wartime service entitled *Four Years under Marse Robert* ("marse" being slang for "master" and Robert referring to Robert E. Lee). The book's dedication read, "To that great captain to whom the world to-day attributes more of the loftiest virtues and powers of humanity, with less of its grossness and littleness, than to any other military hero in history; and to my comrades living and dead—who composed that immortal army which fought out for him his magnificent campaigns."[8]

This is how a Yale alumnus, one of many who served as Confederate officers, honored Lee. How would the university itself remember him?

On that day in June 1896, Twichell ascended the platform and began delivering his prepared remarks about Woolsey. "His patriotism was passionate in its intensity," he told the audience of faculty, trustees, graduating seniors, and their families. A particular memory from the war years stood out: Twichell, passing through New Haven on leave during the summer of 1863, had seen the college president as they both walked to morning prayers. Woolsey stopped and asked him for news from the front, and peppered the young soldier with "eager questions about the battle of Gettysburg, which had just been fought, and the Yale men who had borne part in it." Twichell realized from "his whole tone and manner . . . that [Woolsey] loved his country with all his hopes and fears."[9]

Up to this point, Twichell had largely followed his notes. But going forward, he spoke extemporaneously. The *Yale Alumni Weekly* reported that Twichell paused, turned, and looked "into the face of the statue . . . showing the intensest feeling in his voice and manner" and then spoke: "And if I may be pardoned, I must say that if it were possible that face would be averted from the scene, when it shall happen this afternoon . . . that an ivy from the grave of Robert Lee, a good man, but the historic representative of an infamous cause, shall be planted on this campus to climb the walls of ever loyal Yale."[10]

"Like a clap of thunder from a clear sky," the *New Haven Evening Register* declared, his words were "the surprise of the commencement exercises." When the ceremony was over, everyone began to talk over what Twichell had said. Members of the senior class ivy committee gathered around the new statue and began an "animated discussion." Would they go forward with planting the Lee ivy, or change course? One senior insisted they had to stick to their plan or risk insulting Southern students. Another rejoined that planting the ivy would insult the majority of students who were from the North. Still another, presciently, worried that the newspapers would get wind of the controversy. (In fact, the story made the front page of the *New York Times*.) Ultimately, it was one of the more "prominent" members of the senior class who charted the path forward. The *Evening Register* quoted him at length: "We were offered the ivy and accepted it with the best of feeling. It was offered with a spirit of reconciliation and accepted in the same spirit. Hundreds of Southern men have come to Yale, especially before the war, and certainly the act accepting the ivy was one taken by all parties concerned in the kindliest spirit."[11]

"The ivy was planted nevertheless," Twichell wrote in his journal, "but I had the satisfaction of speaking my mind." What is more, his opinion still held some sway. "Had the condemnatory words come from almost any other man they would not have received the same attention," the city newspaper noted. And Twichell learned he was not alone in his feelings. After his remarks, Charles Lane Fitzhugh, a brevet brigadier general in the Union army and a fellow Yale graduate, "heartily embraced" Twichell. It was an intentionally public gesture. Another alumnus informed the ivy committee members that Twichell spoke for the older generation. Rumors spread that alumni who graduated during the war years "had expressed the intention of tearing up the ivy tonight," so the seniors posted a guard to protect it. And in the weeks following, Twichell received many letters supporting his public declaration—and others, "chiefly from the South," he said, "condemning it."[12]

Not long afterward, the original ivy was, in fact, removed, and in the fall, the class of 1896 planted *another* sprig from Lee's grave—but this time along with an additional sprig. The second ivy came from the grave of Theodore Winthrop, class of 1848, Woolsey's nephew, and the first Yale casualty in the war. Wallace Bruce, alumnus, poet, and Union army veteran, who suggested the Winthrop ivy, said, "Let the two entwine in loving embrace, as this nation will do in all centuries to come." Chauncey W. Wells, chair of the ivy committee, told the newspaper that "as the vines grow together, they will typify the wish of every loyal Yale man for a union in spirit of the North and South, and a blow at any attempt to create sectionalism in any form among Yale alumni and undergraduates."[13]

Twichell's rebuke made headlines and elicited support from older alumni, but it did not alter the trajectory of how Yale, or the nation as a whole, would remember the Civil War. Instead, the planting of the Lee ivy was more of an olive branch, and the university would extend several more to Southern students and alumni in the coming decades. Major university celebrations, including the bicentennial in 1901 and the university pageant in 1916, provided special opportunities to embrace the White South and make room for it in the Yale pantheon—especially for that Southerner par excellence, John C. Calhoun. For as the university celebrated, and refashioned, its own history to suit the national mood of reconciliation, it also undertook a deliberate campaign to attract Southern alumni and students back to New Haven. Questions remained, of course; not all alumni were willing to forgive and forget when it came to the memory of slavery and secession.

The university's bicentennial in 1901 was a grand celebration of Yale. Over the course of several days in October, nearly five thousand alumni, students, and distinguished guests enjoyed speeches, athletic competitions, and even "a great torchlight parade" through campus, complete with costumes, to portray the institution's history. Each event presented an opportunity to tell a story about Yale's past, present, and future. And out of a cacophony of voices—there were many speakers—one message was clear: Yale aspired to national greatness. And being a truly national university meant welcoming White Southerners back to New Haven.

This embrace of the South was articulated explicitly throughout the bicentennial. President Arthur Twining Hadley, still relatively new in his role (he served from 1899 to 1921), established the theme in his welcoming remarks in Battell Chapel. "On this two hundredth birthday of Yale University, it is our chief pride to have with us representatives of that brotherhood of learning which knows no bounds of time or place, of profession or creed." The theme was quickly taken up by the next speaker, Anthony Higgins, who gave the "Response for the Alumni." Higgins, a member of the class of 1861 and a former Republican officeholder, was explicit about the importance they attached to Southern alumni on this occasion. Speaking "on behalf of the Alumni of the North," Higgins gave "a heartfelt welcome" to Southern alumni who attended Yale before the Civil War. He said moreover that the college had "ever been proud" of these Southern alumni of the antebellum era, and praised them as "eminent as statesmen, as soldiers, as scholars, and as divines." In addition to Calhoun of South Carolina and John M. Clayton of Delaware, he named eight other Southerners, the first seven of whom were officers in the Confederate army. (The sole exception in this list was John T. Croxton, who supported emancipation and fought for the Union army.)[14]

The South's intellectual leaders also had their say at the bicentennial. Charles William Dabney, president of the University of Tennessee, was invited to speak on behalf of "the Universities of the South." Dabney (who received an honorary degree at the bicentennial) praised Yale, saying, "Southern institutions rejoice especially that there is no sectionalism at Yale; that Yale is first of all an American university, with plans as broad as our continent and a spirit as free as the air that blows over it." He declared, too, "The South produced but Yale educated that greatest of Southern statesmen, John Calvin [*sic*] Calhoun." And Dabney was far from the only speaker who heaped praise on the South's great nullifier during the bicentennial.[15]

The unusually large number of honorary degrees presented at the bicentennial offered further opportunities to express Yale's values. President Theodore Roosevelt and the writer Mark Twain were among over sixty honorees, as were a number of well-known Southerners—all of whom were recognized for accomplishments related to the Civil War or its aftermath. Dabney received an honorary doctor of laws "as an honored representative of university education in the South." And Hollis Burke Frissell, principal of Hampton Institute, was commended for his efforts to solve "one of our greatest national problems, and the performance of one of our profoundest national duties,—the education of the Indian and the Negro." No African Americans or Native Americans shared the stage or the honors with these distinguished guests. It was already clear, however, that cultural attitudes and historical interpretations of the war were the primary tools of any reconciliation between North and South. The industrialist-turned-historian James Ford Rhodes was praised for his scholarship on "a most difficult period of American history"; at the time, Rhodes was in the midst of publishing his multivolume work, *History of the United States from the Compromise of 1850 to the McKinley-Bryan Campaign of 1896*. Although Rhodes saw slavery as the cause of the war, he was sympathetic toward Southern leaders, particularly military greats like Lee. He absolved both sections of any real responsibility for slavery; it had been a force no one could truly control. The ex-Confederate soldier George Washington Cable, the popular writer of *Old Creole Days* and other works of Southern fiction, was heralded for his "distinguished success in depicting and judging a civilization which is fast becoming extinct."

Despite his prior sympathies, however, he began to write critically of racism, discrimination, and other problems in the South.[16]

Another writer, Thomas Nelson Page, the Virginia-born author of popular sentimental fiction about the Confederate Lost Cause and of supposedly loyal, happy enslaved people, was singled out by President Hadley in his extensive remarks. Not only did Hadley refer to Page's "magic power" as a writer about the Old South, but in honoring him Yale acknowledged the Southerner's enormous Northern readership. For many years by then, Page had been one of the most popular speakers on the Northern lecture circuit, reciting his stories, often in dialect, to huge and delighted audiences. As an entertaining national voice of white supremacy, he had visited New Haven on occasion as well. In May 1898, for example, Page had been an invited speaker at Yale and appeared at the College Street Hall, where he delivered "dialect stories" and poems.[17]

In the 1880s and 1890s, Page was extraordinarily popular, and he played a key role in a literary calculus by which a sentimental vision of the Old South and the Civil War took hold of the American imagination. The characters he created were figments of an imaginary antebellum and wartime Virginia—White Southern gentlemen like "Marse Chan," White Southern ladies, and unwavering loyal Black servants. Enslaved Black women or "mammies" and older Black men looked back on slavery and times "befo' de war" with longing and reverence. In "Marse Chan: A Tale of Old Virginia," his most popular story, the old man Sam went to war with his owner and then brought his body home to bury it with honor. In these and other stories, freedom is rendered not as an achievement or even a gift; it is a curse that leaves Black characters lonely and lost. Page invented a language; indeed, it was the voices of fictional faithful slaves that echoed in the minds of millions of American readers as they embraced the romance of reunion and reconciliation between North and South, rooted in soldierly virtues. How better to forget a fratricidal war about slavery than to have faithful Black characters play the mediators of White folks' reunion? Smiles beamed all around. Page had so many admirers that every major American magazine published in New York vied for his creative pen. He played as well in New Haven as he did in Richmond. Indeed, a direct line may be drawn between those racist parodies of the sweeps and candy salesmen by Yale students and Page's popular stories. The lead characters were one and the same.[18]

At the end of 1903, the Yale Graduate Club hosted Page to speak on the topic of the "Old Plantation Negro and His Successor." Page was so popular as a writer and speaker because he delivered an almost retrievable utopian world of agrarian virtue and racial harmony. The plantation legend and the "faithful slave" were among the lies on which the Lost Cause ideology built its foundation. And what a pleasing escape it was in fictional short stories or in a Northern lecture hall with an audience primed to burst with laughter at Page's minstrelsy. He gave them alternatives to an age of teeming cities, smoke-puffing factories, and political skullduggery. Most of Page's White characters had opposed secession, which made them easier to admire as noble victims. But Page also plied his readers with a vicious image of Reconstruction, especially in widely read essays. What "fell upon the South" after the war, he argued, was "destruction under the euphemism of reconstruction. She was crucified; bound hand and foot . . . laid away in the sepulchre . . . sealed with the seal of government, and a watch was set. The South was dead, and buried, but yet she rose again."[19] The South had been sacrificed on the cross of slavery, and only in the refurbishing of white supremacy for a new age could it and the nation achieve redemption. Yale did its part in that cultural and political reunion.

Another honoree, Mark Twain, developed a new language as well—a Western-Southern, ironic, wry idiom through which race and slavery might be seen differently, if through the eyes and troubled imagination of a frontier scamp and sinner named Huck Finn. *The Adventures of Huckleberry Finn* was published in 1885 to some initial literary popularity and criticism. It eventually became controversial for the nature of its satire, its uses of racial language, and judgments about whether it was "good" for young readers, all of which made the book a massive best seller in the twentieth century.[20] At the 1901 Yale bicentennial, for those who were avid readers, one wonders how many inwardly smiled at this contrast between old Confederate, racially charged sentimental sap and biting Yankee satire. Or was it merely intended to establish harmonious feelings between the sections—two kinds of fame rendered equal and unthreatening—that would eventually become the explicit, earnest purpose of the Yale Civil War Memorial? Had the quest for national reunion become so normative, even all but unthinking, that such stark contrasts would simply dissolve in pomp and ceremony?

Samuel L. Clemens (Mark Twain) had once written that he could detect "the secret sigh behind the public smile." Exactly what Twain said about his honorary degree on the day he received it in 1901 is not recorded. But in his posthumously published autobiography he left no doubt. "To me university degrees are unearned finds, and they bring the joy that belongs with property acquired in that way," he wrote. The irreverent Twain always walked the thin line between his famous humor and life and history's undersides of tragedy. "It pleased me beyond measure when Yale made me a Master of Arts, because I didn't know anything about art; I had another convulsion of pleasure when Yale made me a Doctor of Literature, because I was not competent to doctor anybody's literature but my own, and couldn't even keep my own in a healthy condition." He was further thrilled when Missouri University "made me a Doctor of Laws, because it was all clear profit, I not knowing anything about laws except how to evade them and not get caught." Perhaps in retrospect it is perfectly appropriate that Yale found a way to recognize the sardonic, absurdist Twain at this moment of preparing the ground for national reconciliation by also honoring the earnestly racist and, to so many readers, equally funny Page.[21]

It was one thing to make speeches and bestow honorary degrees on Southern exemplars. But as the university embarked on its third century, it needed more than symbolic expressions of affection or unity: it needed money. Not long before leaving office, Hadley's predecessor, Timothy Dwight V, estimated that the university needed to bring in $3–$4 million in the following six to seven years. Hadley's outreach to alumni was part of broader fundraising and reform measures intended to make the institution both national and modern.[22] From speeches made on campus to his trips around the country, Hadley and other administrators made it a priority to bring Southerners—along with their tuition dollars and donations—back to Yale.

The revival of Southern feeling on campus may have started among the students. Established in 1890, the Southern Club was a student organization open to "all men whose homes are or were south of the old Mason and Dixon line." At the initial meeting, the founders decided "no party lines [would] be drawn so long as a man comes from the South and is in full sympathy with the Southern people and their best interests." Although only about fifteen students attended the club's first meeting, the *Yale Daily News* estimated that about one hundred students hailed from the South. The club was modeled on one at Harvard, established in 1888, although there was discussion in New Haven as early as 1884 about forming such a group. Both Southern clubs aimed not only to provide a social space but also to bolster the number of Southern students in attendance. In 1890, the club at Harvard invited the president of the newly formed Yale Southern Club to their annual dinner, held at the fashionable Parker House hotel in Boston. The flavor of the gathering is conveyed by the toasts to "the South and the Constitution" and "Jefferson Davis." Other highlights included a reading of an "Ode on 'The New South'" and a speech by a law professor, "in which he offered a solution of the race problem," according to a report in the *Harvard Crimson*.[23] Although fledgling at first, the Yale Southern Club had come

Mastheads of the Southern Club in the *Yale Banner*, 1895 and 1901. Manuscripts and Archives, Yale University Library.

into its own only five years later. In 1895, the club occupied an entire page in the *Yale Banner*, the yearbook, with a long list of members and a cartoon featuring a buffoonish, stereotypical Black figure. And in 1901, the club took up *two* full pages and featured a new image—a White female figure as well as two cartoons of Black figures.[24]

Trends on campus aligned with the university's broader plans for courting the South. The same year that the *Yale Daily News* "joked" that the Southern Club was planning to "lynch" "a n—— . . . on the Green," President Hadley began announcing plans for a Southern tour. The *Yale Alumni Weekly* reported in 1904 that before the Civil War, about 11 percent of students "came from the Slave states," whereas that figure stood at about 6 percent in the 1903–4 academic year. However, the organization of alumni groups in Texas, Alabama, New Orleans, and Savannah, and soon Charleston, heralded "a revival of Yale interests at the South." The alumni magazine looked favorably on the president's plans to visit "for the first time" "Yale's far away children." The tour of Southern clubs would, it was hoped, bring about a "closer union" and "the forging of fresh links of sympathy and of interest." It was important, they believed, that Hadley was making "a definite and official expression of the fact that the University, as a national seat of learning, tolerates no sectional divisions."[25]

Hadley and his wife, Anne, visited alumni clubs in Baltimore, Charleston, Savannah, Dallas, and New Orleans. The president spoke of the university's needs—new dormitories, a new library, and "sufficient money to help the University out of her difficulties"—but he also invoked Yale's broader ambitions. Bringing the South back to Yale, he suggested, meant recapturing some of the honor and grandeur that Southern students had once brought to the college. In front of the new Yale Alumni Association of South Carolina, Hadley said, "Though Yale does not have, as far as we know it, in its academic halls today a man who shall represent the greatest and most disinterested and noble southern ideals as once did Calhoun, we have not forgotten that we need such men." Calhoun held a place not only in Yale lore but now again in its living, indispensable institutional memory. In Charleston, in a great gesture of reconciliation, the Hadleys visited Fort Sumter and the Magnolia Gardens.[26]

Yale needed the South—not only to fill its coffers but to reignite that sense of national purpose that Southerners like Calhoun seemed uniquely qualified to bring. To be a "national university," Hadley said it was essential for students to mingle with peers from other backgrounds and geographies. The ideal student is one "who has seen all kinds of men, known their thoughts, and learned thereby to be neither Northern nor Southern, but, in the largest sense, an American, a gentleman, a Christian." In Savannah, where the toastmaster was former Confederate army officer William W. Gordon, he expounded on this theme: "Every man from the South helps twenty northern men to understand those questions which require the consideration of men from all parts of the country." Hadley's tour continued with stops in New Orleans and Dallas, where he likewise told audiences of the unique and necessary gifts (White) Southern students brought to a Northern college.[27] In the years to come, other university administrators reached out to Southern alumni, too, including alumni registrar and Yale graduate Edwin R. Embree, who made his own Southern tour in 1913.[28]

Delivering the baccalaureate address in Woolsey Hall, named for Yale's antislavery president, Hadley encouraged members of the class of 1906 to consult the "pages of history" for examples of strong leadership. "In the great drama of slavery and secession," he told them, "we draw our largest inspiration, not from the brilliant arguments of the orators nor the brilliant strategy of the generals, but from the patient endurance of two great, heavy-hearted men on opposite sides, unlike in all else but alike in unselfish devotion to principle as they understood it—Lee and Lincoln."[29] Several years later, in his matriculation sermon at the beginning of the 1912–13 academic year, Hadley called Lee a "gallant gentleman" and praised his "unfaltering resolution" and "courtesy of demeanor." This time he compared Lee to Ulysses S. Grant, finding commonalities between them and encouraging Yale students to emulate them both. "I have chosen these two instances from the lives of the two great leaders on opposite sides, Grant and Lee, because they show the essential reason why those men were leaders," Hadley declared. "The quality that lifted these men above their fellows, and gave them the loyal confidence of the soldiers under them and the people behind them, was a moral one." The man Joseph Twichell had called "the historic representative of an infamous cause" had become, for Hadley, a model of morality for Yale students to emulate.[30]

Whether due to the university's outreach campaign or for other reasons, the composition of Yale's alumni body began to change. In 1908, the *Yale Daily News* rejoiced that the number of alumni living in the South Atlantic and the South Central divisions of the country had increased by 20 percent and 21 percent, respectively, over the previous four years. "The increase in the South, where her graduates were very prominent before the Civil War, is most gratifying, as is also the Western growth in spite of the rising state universities," the *Yale Daily News* remarked. The writers interpreted these trends to mean that "Yale is more than maintaining her position as a national institution." The next report, in 1912, showed an even more substantial increase of 45 percent in the number of Southern alumni. The economic opportunities presented by the New South probably attracted more Yale graduates than the university's outreach, but at times these went hand in hand. Chauncey M. Depew, the railroad president, Yale alumnus and trustee, and founding member of the Yale Alumni Association of New York, told a gathering of alumni, "The South is the bonanza of the future." Praising this "vast country," with its promising climate, mineral deposits, and soil, Depew told his audience—in words reported and reprinted in several Southern newspapers—"Go South, Young Man."[31] Depew's sentiments betrayed no interest in or awareness of the racial apartheid system of Jim Crow that formed the essential fabric of Southern society.

For some, Northern interest in the South was recreational. And so in 1913, a group of alumni from the Yale College class of 1885 embarked on a weeklong tour, traveling by train from New York to South Carolina. They believed it was the first alumni trip of its kind, writing in their commemorative book, *A Sentimental Journey through South Carolina*, "In all the history of Yale, no reunion of the men of any class that graduated there had ever before been celebrated in the South. Men from the South, distinguished in the annals of our country, had gone to Yale; but never before had Yale, save by the influences that radiate from every great seat of learning, come to the South." They enjoyed the "full-blown flower of 'Southern hospitality,'" visiting Magnolia Gardens in Charleston and enjoying the "still redolent . . . charm of the old South." Other stops included a cotton mill in Columbia, where they posed for pictures with young Black and White boys in work clothes, apparently part of the child labor force that underpinned economic activity in the New South. One of the highlights of the graduates' "sentimental journey" was "an old-fashioned Southern barbecue," which included a humorous "monologue of an old-time negro mammy." For these White members of the class of 1885, themselves born in the waning days of the Civil War, the home state of secession and Fort Sumter, of nullification and John C. Calhoun, had become a place to enjoy "royal entertainment" and relax under "the blooms of azaleas and magnolias."[32]

Yale's efforts to court Southern students and alumni yielded a public and tangible result in 1915, with the establishment of the John C. Calhoun Memorial Scholarships. Founded and funded by the Southern Club of Yale and the Yale Southern Alumni Association, with the blessing and praise from university leaders, the Calhoun scholarships were to be awarded to two Southern students each year. The *Yale Daily News* reported that the dean of Yale College, the alumni registrar, the Southern Club president, and "two Southern Yale graduates," yet to be named, would form a committee to raise the requisite $15,000. "The Southern Club has long felt the need of establishing a memorial of some sort to J. C. Calhoun, and it seems most fitting that the scholarships for general excellence in athletics and scholarship should be dedicated to this eminent Yale graduate and national statesman," the Southern Club president declared. Stewart L. Mims, an assistant professor in the history department and a native of Arkansas, was "delighted" with the new Calhoun scholarships. In language with some loud future echoes, he told the *Yale Daily News*, "Certainly we have very few more distinguished names upon our roll of honor—a fact which will be more and more appreciated as historians get the proper perspective and are enabled to write the story of his career. It is to be hoped that the scholarships will become monuments worthy of his memory."[33]

Not long after the Calhoun scholarships were announced, the Southern Club held its annual banquet in the grand President's Room in Woolsey Hall. One hundred twenty-five members of the Southern Club—"the largest gathering of the Club ever held at Yale"—listened as Professor Mims praised Calhoun as a national, rather than sectional, hero. Embree, the alumni registrar who had done so much to nurture the university's relationship with Southern alumni, played toastmaster. The crowning event was President Arthur Hadley's lengthy speech on "Yale in the South." Expounding on a theme he had been developing at least since the bicentennial, Hadley explained what it meant for Yale to be a "national university": "Not simply that she gets students from all parts of the country, though this helps to make her atmosphere national. Not simply that she sends graduates to all points of the country, though this helps to make her influence national." Rather, Hadley believed that a university was national by dint of the people one met and mingled with as students. Southerners were vital because they brought distinctive worldviews and experiences to Yale's campus and classrooms. Hadley continued, "The men who come under [Yale's] influence must learn to see public questions from all sides, instead of from one side only. They must understand the thought and feeling and conscience which inspire the different parts of our country." Calhoun's importance thus extended not only to his college friends but far beyond to his political career. "Who shall measure the influence of the fact that Calhoun of South Carolina and [Jabez W.] Huntington of Connecticut met on the floor of the United States Senate as old friends who understood one another's thoughts and purposes, and even when they differed were in the habit of differing like honorable gentlemen?" In these sentiments, no Civil War had occurred, except the one that fostered unity. Looking through the pages of national history, Hadley argued that the antebellum Southerners shaped not only their classmates while at Yale but also their perspectives long after graduation. Calhoun's legacy, he argued, along with those of other Yale Southerners, had been truly national in scope.[34]

In 1902, speaking in New Haven, John Wesley Manning—a Black educator and 1881 graduate of Yale College—described the disturbing trends he had noticed in his own lifetime. The old abolitionist fervor had all but disappeared. The changes in the North, in both attitude and behavior toward African Americans, troubled him. Raised and educated in Connecticut, Manning had lived in Tennessee since graduation. Speaking from personal experience, Manning said, "To one who has traveled from one to the other sections for the past twenty-five years, the change of sentiment is plainly apparent. Restrictions in accommodations, offensive remarks, an utter disregard of humanitarian considerations and a tendency to minimize the race questions Northern and to magnify the conditions Southern are characteristic revelations." He noted grimly, "The North became as it were Southernized."[35]

This process of "Southernization" only intensified in the years following Manning's remarks—both nationally and at Yale. At the same time that the university was making its official overtures to White Southerners, a small number of African American students were making their own way through the institution. Later in the same year that Calhoun was feted and honored with a scholarship in his name, a Black student played football in the newly built Yale Bowl for the first time—but not for the Blue. Frederick Douglass "Fritz" Pollard, a halfback for Brown University, had to enter the field separately from the rest of his team to avoid the hostile crowds. William M. Ashby, a student in the divinity school, went to the game with a handful of other Black students. As Ashby recalled later, they had heard of Pollard, who was rumored to be an exceptional player. Yet they, like Pollard, expected to face insults and perhaps injury—even from their fellow Yale students. Ashby wrote, "We went to the Brown side of the field, wanting to give Pollard as much moral support as possible, but also because we knew that there would be animosity toward us in the Yale stands. We would be baited with the foulest and vilest epithets hurled right into our teeth, and we could do nothing about it." Over the course of an outstanding career on and off the field, Pollard would distinguish himself as the first African American player to appear in the Rose Bowl and the first African American quarterback and the first African American head coach in the National Football League, among many other barrier-breaking achievements. On that November day in 1915, however, he was something else to the White Yale fans. When Pollard had the ball, Ashby remembered, "the Yale stands arose, 'Catch that n——. Kill that n——,' they screamed." Brown's win against Yale that day was one stop on the team's—and Pollard's—journey to the Rose Bowl. But the victory was not sweet for Pollard. "For all the glory he achieved in New Haven, Pollard later expressed bitterness about his playing in the Yale Bowl. He had never felt so 'n—ized,' as he put it," said one historian of the game.[36]

As for Ashby, he carried with him another little-known piece of Yale and New Haven history. In late 1915, it became known that Booker T. Washington was scheduled to visit Yale and speak in Woolsey Hall. To support his studies, Ashby worked in the dining hall, and one day, Holland, the African American head waiter in the Student Union, approached him, concerned that Black people who wanted to hear Washington would not be able to get into Woolsey. Holland wanted Ashby, as a student, to invite him to speak separately to a Black audience. Ashby agreed to draft a letter to Washington, and Holland and his fellow church leaders signed it; Washington accepted their invitation. Ashby recalled, "When Dr. Washington came out of Woolsey Hall by a side door, Mr. Holland and I were waiting for him in a horse and carriage." They drove him to Varick Memorial African Methodist Episcopal Zion Church on Dixwell Avenue. Given how inhospitable both Yale and the North had become to African Americans—how "Southernized"—it is fitting that the Great Accommodator gave separate speeches that day: one to a White audience in Woolsey Hall and another at a Black church just one mile, but also a world, away from the Yale

Black waiters in the newly constructed Commons, 1906.
Buildings Constructed for Yale University's Bicentennial Photographs (RU 697).
Manuscripts and Archives, Yale University Library.

Booker T. Washington, founder and president of Tuskegee Normal and Industrial Institute, was among the delegates to Yale's bicentennial celebration in 1901. Manuscripts and Archives, Yale University Library.

campus. "All records claim that the last public appearance made by Dr. Washington was before that select audience in Woolsey Hall," wrote Ashby. "But I know that his last public appearance was before a Negro audience in the Dixwell Avenue A. M. E. Church. I was there."[37]

Washington died three weeks after his visit to New Haven. Among the many tributes was one from "the Waiters of the Yale Dining Club." In the pages of the *New York Age*, they called Washington "our leading educator and advocate." Offering "these resolutions as an expression of our esteem for the deceased," the waiters lamented the death particularly "when we as a race are in need of such great characters."[38] For decades following the end of the Civil War and the violent suppression of Radical Reconstruction, Booker T. Washington had represented "the race" to so many Americans, White and Black. Although he acquiesced to the Lost Cause mythology and preached accommodation to segregation and White rule, many African Americans revered Washington and respected his national prominence and leadership. Whatever he had represented in life, his death heralded the end of an era.

In October 1916, Yale held an elaborate pageant in the Yale Bowl to celebrate its two hundredth year of residence in New Haven. At least seven thousand people, many of them women and children, members of the Yale community and residents of the city and surrounding neighborhoods, participated by re-creating key "scenes" from the history that "town and gown" shared. These living tableaux portrayed moments of community and national importance, such as the British invasion of New Haven and Eli Whitney's invention of the cotton gin. One of the first scenes representing "modern Yale," however, was the class of 1896 planting its ivy from the grave of Robert E. Lee. The book of the Yale pageant described the panel's significance: "Prior to the Civil War, Yale drew a large percentage of her students from the South, but many years elapsed before she was again well represented in that section of the country. The honor thus paid by the Class of '96 to the distinguished General of the Confederacy, who is slowly but surely coming to be recognized as one of the really great Americans, was highly significant. It demonstrated how completely sectional feeling has died out in this country and emphasized the position of Yale as a national rather than a local university."[39]

Yale made good on its commitment to become a truly national university. It did so in part by welcoming back living White Southerners—students and alumni—but also by burnishing the reputations of men like Calhoun and Lee, paragons of the Old South. But there were dissenting voices along the way. John

Window fragments from the Calhoun College Dining Room. Original design by Nicola d'Ascenzo, 1932. Yale University Art Gallery, lent by Grace Hopper College.
On June 13, 2016, Corey Menafee, a Yale employee working in what was then the Calhoun College dining hall, used a broom to knock out this window representing enslaved Black figures working in a cotton field. Menafee initially resigned and was charged with a felony. Yale subsequently dropped the charges against him and rehired him. In July 2016, Yale announced that other windows depicting a romanticized view of antebellum Southern life would be removed. In 2022, a new set of windows by artist Barbara Earl Thomas was installed in the Hopper College dining hall.

Wesley Manning spoke out about how the North was becoming more like the South, and the price paid by Black people. And Yale stalwart Joseph Twichell took his stand in 1896, insisting there was a difference—one that mattered—between the traitor Lee and the abolitionist Woolsey. But if Lee could inspire such different interpretations, within Yale and the nation at large, then the task of remembering Yale's Civil War dead would inspire even more fierce disagreement on campus in these years of "reconciliation."

CHAPTER 12

Yale's Civil War Memorial

> Monuments to the "lost cause" will prove monuments of folly, both in the memories of a wicked rebellion which they must necessarily perpetuate, and with failure to accomplish the particular purpose had in view by those who build them. It is a needless record of stupidity and wrong.
>
> —FREDERICK DOUGLASS, December 1, 1870

A 2021 study of memorials in America counted 5,917 monuments of various kinds that memorialize the Civil War. In that total, only 1 percent include the word "slavery"; Yale's striking Civil War Memorial, carefully and artfully designed, located in a very public setting, and dedicated in 1915, is not among that 1 percent.[1] Most students, faculty, and staff members, and thousands of tourists and prospective undergraduates, have at some point walked through the corridor leading to either the vast dining commons or the large performance space in Woolsey Hall. Or they simply hurry by the many names on the walls in their trek from one part of campus to another, from Hewitt University Quadrangle to the intersection of Prospect and Grove Streets, perhaps the most traversed location of the entire landscape of Yale University. Most never stop to examine the character and meaning of the memorial. For more than a century, Yale's Civil War Memorial has stood guard over the honored sacrifice of Yale men on both sides in the struggle of 1861–65, as well as over the deliberate forgetting of the deepest meanings of that event.

On the floor of the slightly sloped hallway, some verses of the reconciliationist poem "The Blue and the Gray" were etched into stone as part of the 1915 memorial. By then the poem, by 1849 Yale graduate Francis Miles Finch, was a national classic that had already appeared and still does on monuments and wayside markers at national cemeteries and Civil War battlefield sites. While at

Yale, Finch was valedictorian and a sometime poet and song writer. His songs included student favorites, perhaps for smoking and drinking rituals, such as "Gather Ye Smiles," "Linonia" (for the club by that name), and "The Last Cigar." Born and raised in Ithaca, New York, after graduation, Finch returned to his hometown and became a successful lawyer and later judge on the New York Court of Appeals. He also played key roles at Cornell University, including as dean of the Cornell Law School. Finch never stopped writing poetry, sometimes about his own courtroom dramas, including a couple of murder cases.[2]

As the story goes, Finch was deeply moved by an incident he read about in spring 1866, when White Southern women in Columbus, Mississippi, had gone to a Civil War cemetery and adorned with flowers the graves of both Confederate and Union dead buried there. In September 1867 in the *Atlantic Monthly*, he published his nine-verse poem that soon became the sentimental symbol of national reconciliation of North and South around the elegiac memory of the mutual valor of soldiers on both sides of the conflict. In 1868 when an "official" beginning to Memorial Day was announced by the Grand Army of the Republic, the growing Union veterans' organization, Finch's poem suddenly soared in significance as people who wished to believe in a reunion devoid of cause and conflict, but steeped in the solemnity of soldierly virtue and sacrifice, now had lovely, well-timed verses through which to advance their cause.[3] No one need be blamed for all the bloodshed; everyone who fought with courage and died for devotion to a cause, whichever they believed in, was equal and heroic in death. Finch's sweet mutuality intones,

> No more shall the war-cry sever,
> Or the winding rivers be red;
> They banish our anger forever,
> When they laurel the graves of our dead!
> Under the sod and the dew,
> Waiting the judgment day;—
> Love and tears for the Blue;
> Tears and love for the Gray.[4]

That single verse is carved into the floor of the corridor of Memorial Hall near the following inscription, which precedes it on the path from the rotunda to the quadrangle:

TO THE MEN OF YALE
WHO GAVE THEIR LIVES IN THE CIVIL WAR

THE UNIVERSITY HAS DEDICATED THIS MEMORIAL
THAT THEIR HIGH DEVOTION
MAY LIVE IN ALL HER SONS AND THAT THE BONDS
WHICH NOW UNITE THE LAND MAY ENDURE
MCMXV

The inscriptions, which are badly faded and worn by foot traffic, with some of Finch's words unrecognizable, are today hidden beneath industrial-strength removable carpets protecting the floor; the burgundy-colored rugs have a special effect in afternoon sunlight from the doors. Any casual visitor to the Memorial Hall will note the sounds of thuds and clicks of shoes on the uncarpeted sections of the rotunda and the larger spaces commemorating the Yale dead of the twentieth-century world wars and other conflicts. Voices echo in this hallowed space, depending on how crowded it is. One will also witness an endless array of people hurrying by, faces leaning into cell phones, unaware of anything hallowed around them. Indeed, as scholars working in a range of disciplines, cultures, and time periods have shown, no monument means anything without knowledge of its conception and purpose, of its significance at its unveiling and then over time.[5] The Yale memorial masks the deep meanings of the Civil War as it also almost perfectly reveals the solemn tragedy of the national culture of reunion and reconciliation that came to dominate American society after the beginning of the twentieth century.

Yale's Civil War Memorial has a long lineage. In 1865–67, at commencements and in early planning for the construction of a new memorial chapel, Yale considered how to honor its war dead. At first the university contemplated only those of its sons on the Union side, as stated at the July 1865 Soldiers' Festival, naming those who fought for "maintenance of national sovereignty and constitutional liberty," although that language would later be adopted by ex-Confederates as well. In 1866 and 1867 the Yale Corporation began to solicit money for a future Yale memorial chapel (what would eventually become Battell Chapel) as a means of commemorating the Civil War dead. A committee established to raise as much as $150,000 to build the chapel sent out letters of appeal in 1867 about a memorial "for those of our associates who have sacrificed their lives for the life of the Nation, and also a fitting thank-offering for the preservation of the Union and the deliverance of the slave."[6] Construction of Battell Chapel, now Yale's official church, began in 1874 and was completed in the centennial year of American independence, 1876, a delicate and conflicted political moment in the history of Reconstruction. It was not then, nor has it ever been, a Civil War memorial.

For nearly thirty years little public discussion ensued at Yale about the construction of a memorial to the Civil War dead. The city of New Haven, however, did not lack for a stunning monument to the Union warriors from their town and county during those decades. In 1887, after some years of planning, the 110-foot-high Soldiers' and Sailors' Monument was delivered to the summit of East Rock in several wagons and dedicated in June. The dedication ceremony, attended by the famous Union generals William T. Sherman and Philip H. Sheridan, drew an estimated 100,000 to 175,000 people to the city, perhaps the largest crowd ever assembled in New Haven, with 20,000 participating in the parade itself. That obelisk, fully lighted at night, is still one of the most visible landmarks in the New Haven area, identifiable from out in Long Island Sound and any second- or third-story building in the middle or on the east side of the city. The Grand Army of the Republic played a major role in the conception and erection of the Soldiers' and Sailors' Monument (one of a genre of monuments that exists in several Northern cities).[7]

In January and February 1895, the *Yale Daily News* ran editorials calling out the university to create a memorial to the "heroes" of both the American Revolution and the Civil War. The student paper provided a list of the dead among Yale alumni on its front page and announced it "humiliating" that these men had not been properly commemorated as their comrades had been at other universities. The paper made frequent reference to the huge Memorial Hall at Harvard, constructed in the 1870s to honor its Union dead, as a contrast to Yale's lack of any memorial. Such memorialization, said the paper's editors, should be created as "inspiration to student life." In 1896, Yale celebrated the tangling of ivies from the graves of Confederate general Robert E. Lee and Theodore Winthrop, the first Yale student to die in the war. And by 1901 the university officially declared Memorial Day on May 30 a permanent feature of the college calendar. The day was to be set aside for "patriotic exercises" of various kinds, and as May of that year arrived, the *Yale Daily News* sought and received official determination that the "sons of veterans who fought on the Southern side" would be warmly welcomed at the commemoration. Less than two weeks before the Memorial Day event, all alumni were sent the following appeal: "All sons of men who served in the Union and Confederate armies in the Civil War are urged to send their names, with the names of their fathers and the regiments in which they served." A special box number was set aside at the Yale Station of the U.S. Post Office.[8] Both the intent and form for the future memorial took hold in these appeals.

In October 1901, at the commemoration of Yale's two hundredth anniversary, the university hosted thousands of people for ceremonies and awarded over sixty honorary degrees, among them to former president Theodore Roosevelt and the writer Mark Twain. The architectural structures built to commemorate the bicentennial would give rise to the Civil War Memorial, although in their original design that was not quite their intent. A special "Bi-centennial Building Issue" of the *Yale Alumni Weekly*, January 31, 1900, announced an architectural design called "the New Yale." The winning design came from John M. Carrère and Thomas Hastings, who both had been educated at the École des Beaux-Arts in Paris and had established their fame in part as the winning artists for the design of the magnificent New York Public Library at Forty-Second Street and Fifth Avenue in 1897. The five-member competition committee hoped that in size and scope—in the reach for "dignity" and "grandeur," in the words of one adviser to the project—these buildings would surpass anything ever imagined on Yale's growing campus.[9]

The commemorative buildings, constructed in 1901–2, were three structures connected by a dome modeled in part on the Roman Pantheon: Woolsey Hall to the east, a grand performance space and the first secular one at the university, soon to be graced with a great organ; Commons, the huge student dining hall to the west; and a vestibule that would become Memorial Hall and the corridor that connects the other two large rooms with the rotunda. The exterior was built of luminous light limestone; the grand dimensions and the classical style were unlike any other architecture at Yale, a fact of both delight and some criticism. Just south of Woolsey Hall is Woodbridge Hall, named for Timothy Woodbridge, one of the ten founding ministers of Yale and the largest slaveholder among them. The names of the ten are inscribed around the top of the building. Built around the same time as the Bicentennial Buildings, but as a distinct project, Woodbridge Hall for more than a century housed the Yale president's offices and the Corporation Room, where the university's governing body formally meets. The donors for Woodbridge Hall, Olivia and Caroline Phelps Stokes, were descendants of the namesake; the building's designer, Isaac Newton Phelps Stokes, was also a Woodbridge descendant and the nephew of the donors. At the dedication of the building in December 1901, the extended Stokes family attended, as did the majority of corporation members. But tellingly, so did luminaries including William Dean Howells (father of the hall's architect, John Mead Howells), Thomas Nelson Page, George Washington Cable, and Booker T. Washington, whose Tuskegee Institute the Stokes family supported philanthropically.[10]

Architectural drawing of Woodbridge Hall, 1900.
Manuscripts and Archives, Yale University Library.

Sectional reconciliation from the Civil War hovered over the dedication of Woodbridge Hall—indeed it could hardly have been more conspicuous—even as it had at the earlier bicentennial celebration. Anywhere Page appeared, a veneer of polite white supremacy arrived with him. He was by far the most prominent writer of the plantation legend. His stories were not, though, merely tales of lost unity and comity of White and Black in the Old South; they flowed with cleverness, pathos, and vicious racism, depicting the humor but especially the depravity of Black people, centering their utter inability to become modern citizens, or to even function outside the structure of slavery. Page and his publishers became especially adept at appealing to White Northern sensibilities; it was the Yankee literary market that he cultivated with themes of race and gender. Page wrote to Richard Gilder, editor of the *Century*, pitching one of his stories, in 1885: "A Virginia girl is the heroine and a young Union Captain the hero. The scene is laid during the war, and the story is told by an old negro after the war. It deals with the female rebel element, but I think will not wound anyone, and I will vouch for its fidelity." The intersectional marriage, pretty Southern women delivering a softer, more attractive femininity than allegedly found now in the hard-driving industrial North, and elderly former slaves telling the tales provided a formula for reunion.[11] It would not "wound" anyone; neither would Page's prominence at Yale commemorative events, according to the university's leadership.

Page's wounds on the American psyche, on the national imagination about race, were palpable everywhere one looked, even as they remained unrecognized and unspoken at Yale University.

The large courtyard leading up to Woolsey and Commons was known as Quadrangle Court until 1914, when it became Hewitt University Quadrangle. Since the completion of the magnificent Beinecke Rare Book and Manuscript Library in 1963, the entire open space, no longer green, has been called, informally, Beinecke Plaza. At a total cost of $1,047,386, the bicentennial structures were imagined as a way to link all of Yale's older campus to the Sheffield science buildings on Hillhouse Avenue to the north and east.[12] In this most central, highly commemorative, and grand space Yale now planned to create its memorial to the Civil War dead. The corridor through what is today named the Schwarzman Center was initially conceived for many purposes—a main walking route through campus, a place of social gathering, artistic performance, and in time memorialization. For those who stop to notice and investigate, it has always told a story of solemnity, honor, and sentimental deception.

All monuments tell a story, some more precisely and purposefully than others. Monuments and memorials carry meaning from the moment and purpose of their unveiling; they can retain that meaning or greatly change in public interpretation over time. All across America common soldier monuments appeared in town squares, intersections, and parks from the 1880s into the era of World War I. They tended to represent the experience of the individual private soldier of both sides, and sometimes of specific regiments. The stone soldiers "doze over muskets / and muse through their sideburns," as the poet Robert Lowell wrote in his immortal "For the Union Dead." The key was the generic nature of such monuments; each standing soldier looked off in the distance, equal in undescribed, heroic endurance, unnamed but alive in memory for their sacrifice of self. They may have fallen or may have survived. They represented whichever sense of cause—either blind to politics or fiercely partisan—local viewers chose to attribute to them. There were also many monuments across the South and some in the North dedicated in these years explicitly to the Lost Cause ideology. The Lost Cause had many animating elements: it became a series of explanations that helped defeated Southerners cope with loss; it was a set of popular assumptions searching for a history, however fabricated. The Lost Cause took root in a Southern culture of the 1870s and 1880s awash in physical destruction, the psychological trauma of defeat, a revived Democratic Party resisting Reconstruction, racial violence, and, with time, an abiding sentimentalism. On the broadest level it represented a mood, or an attitude toward the past. Like all mythologies, the Lost Cause changed with succeeding generations and shifting political circumstances.[13]

During the spread of Lost Cause ideology, several forces planted it deep in American culture: the movement's efforts to write and control the history of the war and its aftermath; its use of white supremacy as both means and ends; and the role of women in its development through organizations such as the Ladies Memorial Associations and especially the United Daughters of the Confederacy, the leaders of which raised money, commissioned monuments, and managed textbook campaigns to forge an emerging memory on neo-Confederate terms. By the 1890s, and especially in the wake of the war with Spain in 1898, the goal of the Lost Cause was national reconciliation on White Southern racial terms. Indeed, by then the Lost Cause in popular culture, in monuments, and even in policy was not about loss at all; instead, it became a victory narrative about the South's and the nation's triumph over the alleged mistakes and "failure" of Reconstruction. "No! No!" announced S. A. Cunningham, the editor of the *Confederate Veteran*, the popular magazine of the United Confederate Veterans. "Our cause was not lost, because it was not wrong." Reconstruction had colonized and oppressed the noble South, and its overthrow—even, and for some especially, with the terror and violence enacted by the Ku Klux Klan and its imitators—had provided one of the most heroic stories of American history. In endless refrains about true and false history, claims of nonpartisanship, worship of Robert E. Lee as a national hero, disclaimers that the war had anything to do with slavery, and endless tales of faithful slaves, depicted regularly in the *Confederate Veteran* as well as by Page and many other local-color writers, the Lost Cause tradition grew as one of the most enduring partisan mythologies in American experience. Above all, it was a racial ideology, using history explicitly to forge a Jim Crow society in law and habit.[14] Black humiliation became the building material for a White Southern rehabilitation, aided potently by a Blue-Gray reunion culture forged in the story of soldier sacrifice on both sides, and with considerable Northern complicity.

Yale's Civil War Memorial is one prominent Northern outpost in this evolving national Lost Cause tradition. It is Yale's tribute to its own, but it is also very much part of America's tragedy of Civil War memory that exalted the martial virtues of soldiers but did not face the reasons and consequences for which they fought. In naming the performance hall for Theodore Woolsey, Yale's president of antislavery sentiments during the era of the Civil War, the university acknowledged that story, although it did not explicitly represent it. Woolsey is also commemorated with a monument in Old Campus, although it does not contain any direct mention of his opposition to secession and strong support of the Union cause. The statue of Woolsey, by the sculptor John Ferguson Weir, unveiled in 1896, shows the former president and professor of Greek sitting as a symbol of learning on a Greek Revival klismos chair. The only inscription, in Greek, is the succinct, "The most excellent, the most wise, the most just."[15] Had Yale wished to stress any feature of its moderate abolitionist past, with the statue or in Woolsey Hall, opportunities arose to do so. Such were not the institutional imperatives, however, nor would they serve the cause of sectional reconciliation that the university advanced.

On September 28, 1903, Yale hosted a special event in the newly opened Woolsey Hall for veterans of the Spanish-American War. The mayor of New Haven as well as the Connecticut governor participated. President Arthur Twining Hadley delivered the main address, in which he praised the former soldiers of "North and South fighting shoulder to shoulder" in 1898. Hadley celebrated a new "blending together" of the sections and reflected back on the Civil War era as a time of "misunderstandings" that had now "lost their danger on account of common feeling" in the country. A terrible past had been rendered safe. Three years later at commencement time in 1906, Hadley gave a baccalaureate address in which he again drew on the Civil War to project generalized notions of sectional harmony, praising both Lee and Lincoln for being men of "principle." For those seeking to forge sectional reunion in these years, even among some Northern writers and orators, folding Lincoln and Lee into the same glorious harmony born of strife was a common move. It allowed a kind of depoliticized reconciliation that tended to please power brokers, potential donors, and racial conservatives who needed official respect. W. E. B. Du Bois, one of the greatest thinkers of the early twentieth century, later delivered a ferocious rebuke to this kind of historical forgetting. "One thing—one terrible fact—," he wrote, "militates against" such honoring of Lee. "And that is the inescapable truth that Robert E. Lee led a bloody war to perpetuate human slavery." The legacies of the South's "Robert Lees and Jefferson Davises," Du Bois continued, forever meant that "their courage will be physical and not moral." In Du Bois's view, Lee "surrendered not to Grant, but to Negro Emancipation," and represented the "most formidable agency this nation ever raised to make 4 million human beings goods instead of men." As the concept for the war memorial emerged over time at Yale, a growing, militant countermemory developed among African American writers and their allies across the country.[16]

In January 1907 the College Street Hall hosted a lecture for the Yale community by a popular writer-orator, Guy Carleton Lee. Lee (no relation to the general), a staunch apologist for the South and a proponent of Lost Cause ideology, delivered an address, "The True Jefferson Davis." Lee was a prolific author of such books as *Principles of Public Speaking* (1900), *The World's Great Orators* (1899), and *The True History of the Civil War* (1903), the last of which was a decidedly pro-Confederate version of the meaning of the conflict. A review in the *American Historical Review* in 1904 called the book a "searching criticism of the northern side" and referred to his treatment of abolitionists as nothing but "frothing fanatics." The speech on Davis, as represented in the *Yale Daily News*, glorified the Confederate president as a genuine American patriot who led his side with "marvelous skill" and, as always acknowledged in this kind of rhetoric, devotion to the cause as he saw it. Davis, according to Lee, "suffered outrage and insult from his enemies" but "never hated" in return. Lee had apparently never read Davis's more than 1,200-page memoir, the most turgid and partisan defense of secession and slavery perhaps ever written. One of Lee's most popular lectures in that season was entitled "The Reunion of the States."[17] Yale students and faculty did not have to go far to breathe in some Lost Cause contagion.

At Yale's 1909 commencement, the effort for the new war memorial finally commenced. A *Yale Daily News* editorial anticipated the gathering as a "beautiful thought—this unprejudiced appreciation of men" regardless of what cause they supported. Time had "tempered the passions" of the Civil War. Yale's own William Howard Taft, recently inaugurated president of the United States, presided at the meeting, and Henry E. Howland and William W. Gordon, both of the class of 1854 and who had served on opposite sides in the war, were named cochairs of the newly formed war memorial committee. The remainder of the committee included Simeon Eben Baldwin (Yale 1861); Henry P. Wright (Yale 1868); secretary Talcott Russell (Yale 1869), the son of William Huntington Russell; Charles H. Strong (Yale 1870); Frank L. Polk (Yale 1894), who later served as assistant treasurer; Anson Phelps Stokes Jr. (Yale 1896); treasurer Lee McClung (Yale 1892); Henry V. Freeman (Yale 1869); chairman of the finance committee Allen W. Evarts (Yale 1869); William W. Gordon Jr. (Yale 1886), son of the elder Gordon; and Thomas West (Yale 1896).[18]

Howland, the elder Gordon, and McClung would all die before the memorial was installed in 1915, but not before representing the intersectional reunion spirit of the war memorial. McClung, known as "Bum," was a Southerner from Knoxville, Tennessee, a star football player at Yale, and later an executive for two railroads, including the Southern Railway Company; he served as treasurer of Yale before Taft appointed him treasurer of the United States from 1909 to 1912. Gordon was from Savannah, Georgia, the son of a cotton merchant. Gordon attended the Hopkins School in New Haven as preparation for Yale, and after graduation went home to Savannah, where he worked as a clerk for a cotton and rice company. He enlisted on May 1, 1861, in the Confederate forces and served as a captain and adjutant on the staffs of two Confederate generals. He was wounded once in August 1864. In postwar Savannah Gordon rose to prominence as head of the Cotton Exchange, a bank vice president, director of a railroad, a member of the Georgia state legislature, and the operator of a plantation near Louisville, Georgia. He served in the war with Spain with the rank of brigadier general. Howland hailed from Walpole, New Hampshire, and graduated from Yale at age nineteen. He became a distinguished lawyer after taking a law degree at Harvard. Howland served a mere three months in the war as part of the New York National Guard. After the war he became a judge and president of the Yale Alumni Association; his wealthy family gave a $15,000 endowment to his alma mater at his death in 1913 for a student prize in his name.[19]

Howland set a tone for the memorial in 1909, admitting that, immediately after the war, "it would have been ill-timed to have suggested that sons of the South should have been remembered in such a memorial." But now, he said, "when the passions of that time have died away . . . it seems an appropriate moment to bring . . . the propriety of commemorating the men of both sides who gave their lives in the great struggle." "Both sides" became a clarion call of the planning committee for several years. In January 1910, Simeon Baldwin, a longtime law professor at Yale and soon to be elected, as a Democrat, the governor of Connecticut in 1911, wrote to Talcott Russell urging some purging of those Northern names lacking adequate data from their lists of soldiers to be recognized in order to more "equalize the numbers of the Union and Confederate dead." In March 1910 Russell gave an interview to the *Yale Daily News* in which he said that the "archway" between Woolsey and Commons would be used as a war memorial. He further declared it a "fitting tribute to both the Blue and the Gray," and a demonstration that the "Union, which at the close of the war was one of force, is now a union of hearts." Like their Lost Cause counterparts in the South, Northern reunionists also advanced bold assumptions in search of an elusive history. Russell received much advice from other alumni about the language of any future inscriptions. One urged "avoid[ing] express mention of North and South" and suggested calling the conflict "the War between the States," long the preferred label of former Confederates.[20]

That same year, the committee sent out press notices in the South to solicit names of fallen Confederates educated at Yale. Gordon himself wrote and published such a call in the *Savannah News* in February 1910. He claimed it was relatively easy to compile Northern names for the memorial but feared that "the names of some Southern soldiers have been overlooked." Russell maintained a steady correspondence with former Confederate officers, as well as representatives of the United Daughters of the Confederacy, to determine an accurate list of the Confederate dead. Russell also tried to get the list of Union soldiers verified by the War Department. Then committee members argued in correspondence for two years over the language of inscriptions and whether to include military titles and units. Russell assembled many voices inside and outside the committee. Stokes suggested that all ranks and titles be avoided because some former Union soldiers might object to seeing Southerners so recognized. Frank Polk worried somewhat that Union veterans might also oppose using the phrase "their high devotion" for Confederates who had seceded, yet he also chastised anyone who would still "clamor" for any bitterness from the war. The whole idea of the memorial was to cause no one any offense. But Southerners were offended. Charles H. Strong, a Southern member of the committee, objected forcefully, accusing those who rejected military titles on the monument of waving the "bloody shirt." Such a decision "came like a blow to us," wrote Strong, speaking for his fellow Southerners. Strong came from a very wealthy family and his colleagues listened to him. His family eventually left a huge amount of money to Yale on his death in 1936. Gordon objected the most strenuously, telling Russell, "The soldiers of the South were Confederates; they believed in their cause and died in defence [*sic*] of the faith that was in them. If this fact is to be ignored, their names upon a Yale memorial tablet will be a mockery—if not an insult." Southerners, insisted Gordon, deserved fully "*equal tribute*," and the memorial should declare to the world "that the mingled dust of both armies created a solid foundation for the future of the nation."[21]

The committee conducted a mostly civil argument among elite White men deciding how they should commemorate themselves and how Yale University should remember the most embittered and divisive event in its nation's history by fashioning elaborate ways of forgetting. In April 1910, Russell delivered a lecture, soon printed as a pamphlet, to the New Haven County Historical Society in which he laid out in detail an explicit neo-Confederate, reconciliationist case for the war memorial. Russell—whose father ran the well-known military academy that had trained so many future Union army officers—chose to call the conflict the "war between the states" and notably not the "War of the Rebellion" or

"Civil War." Much of the pamphlet reads like a speech at a Confederate reunion to which some Northern veterans might have been invited out of courtesy. Russell made much of the strong historical ties of White Southerners to Yale, even stressing that New Haven had been a "summer resort" for planters who came north for respite at the old Pavilion Hotel. Russell attributed the nearly half century it had taken for Yale to construct its war memorial to how "close socially and commercially" Southerners had been to New Haven and the university. Those ties and the passage of time, he argued tellingly, meant that "no memorial now erected will breathe any spirit of exultation in the victory of one portion of a common country, or the defeat of another." Only the "heroic sacrifices of the sons of Yale" ought to be remembered.[22] Thus, Yale in its official wisdom of 1910–15, at the war's fiftieth anniversary, could not and would not create a memorial to Union *victory* nor the end of slavery. All causes and consequences of a war that had freed four million people from bondage, slaughtered as many as seven hundred thousand people, laid to waste large swaths of the South, saved and reinvented the American Constitution and nation, and made possible the freedom of the mind that a university celebrated in its very essence had to be dissolved into misty sentiments about unity and the strained image of "mingled dust."

Yale's memorial committee did not stumble unthinkingly into this kind of commemoration; it was fully intentional. Russell did not just lay out the story of a need to "worthily honor the valor of . . . opponents"; he tried to efface slavery and antislavery from memory altogether. He took his ideology straight from the Lost Cause mental manual of approved concepts. "Both sides . . . were animated by the high sense of devotion to principle as they saw it." Slavery was a "cause" for why the war came about, but not the reason it was fought. Some of these Yale men may have even known they were pleading with themselves with such splintered and lame logic. "The armies of the North did not fight for its [slavery's] extinction," Russell contended, nor should any Southerner's memory be sullied with the claim that "they died for the perpetuation of human slavery." The real issue in the war, Russell said, imbibing the drug Lost Causers have always taken when needed, was states' rights, or a "narrow" versus "broad" view of the Constitution. Surely, in this corner of the American highly educated class, the Civil War had nothing to do with race, especially if one just said so or utterly ignored it often enough. But Russell was not finished taking sides where there were to be no sides. "We of the North have much of error to confess," he sprightly announced in what became an official Yale document. "It is fair that we should ask forgiveness of our Southern brethren for the disasters and needless humiliation caused them by many of our acts during the so-called 'reconstruction' period."[23] Indeed, the ultimate memorial, in its content and form, served as an institutional Yankee apology for Reconstruction.

The impact of these ideas became even more insidious as Russell droned on. Robert E. Lee and Stonewall Jackson represented "types of the best manhood," and they should be symbols of a "common country." It was as if violent, divided Jim Crow America could be nicely stitched up and mended by merely saying so and using the honor of ex-Confederates as the thread. Even more, Russell wanted Yale and its extended collective memorial community to believe that all "the issues were settled" from the war by a memorial to mutual martial glory. He declared himself "grateful that the war happened" so that a greater unity of Americans could result, a common refrain by 1910 in the culture of reconciliation. To some degree this document fits a time and a culture of sentimental reunion; but from a famous institution of higher learning it is also astounding. Russell had purified the savagery of the Civil War, rendered its causes gone like bad weather, and prepared the ideological ground for a memorial utterly devoid of politics or any mention of slavery and its legacies. If, as secretary Russell claimed, the war had been "conducted in a spirit of humanity," someone might have asked him why there had been so much martial valor and death.[24] The Yale war memorial is a highly political creation, steeped in a politics of race and forgetting.

Southerners on the committee should have been overwhelmingly pleased with Russell's pamphlet, but debates over the details of the memorial ensued nonetheless as artists and designers had to be chosen. Charles Strong, who was president of the Yale Southern Association of Alumni, urged Russell to hold firm to a "both sides" approach to the inscriptions. Strong wanted Southerners to embrace a new American nationalism even as he demanded that Yale exhibit its proud "Southern ancestry." And Gordon, from Savannah, weighed in frequently demanding equal presence for former Confederates, asking that a line be added after "Their High Devotion," saying, "(each to the cause in which he believed)." Gordon seemed to struggle with trusting his Northern colleagues to keep the pledge of blended North-South honor in the project. He fought vehemently for use of the label "War between the States" on the memorial, a battle he would ultimately lose to the term "Civil War" by what appears to have been a seven-to-four vote. Stokes had taken up the labeling question with intensity. To him "the great War of the Sixties" could only accurately be called the "Civil War" because only a portion of the states had seceded. But he was certain that "Southern friends" must be placated by dropping any use of "War of the Rebellion." Not satisfied, Gordon kept warning of any hint of discrimination "between Federal and Confederate" motives or sacrifice. "Both sides believed their view was right," he wrote to Russell in November 1910, and then described the essence of the Yale memorial. "The monument is not to commemorate victory or defeat"; he declared, "it is to perpetuate the memory of men who died 'for the faith that was in them.'"[25] With unspoken power, Gordon did not have to name his faith.

The need for fundraising slowed the work of the committee; Gordon particularly complained of the pace of the project. He eventually admitted defeat and relented in 1912 to the use of "Civil War" just before he died. The committee engaged in a vigorous courtship of the famous sculptor Daniel Chester French to design the memorial. French did create a design and had strong supporters within the committee, but in the end the artist found the interior archway too restricting. French wanted to build the memorial in the upper story of Woolsey Hall, and the majority of the committee voted it down. Through 1911, the majority, led by Stokes, admired the "beauty" of French's design but thought it invoked "death rather than life" and would be more appropriate for a "mortuary." They wanted the archway on the first floor to be used so as to create a "daily inspiration" for "the majority of Yale students." French was greatly disappointed to lose the commission and requested a face-to-face meeting, which eventually occurred. At an October 1911 meeting the committee arrived at a plan that resulted in the memorial's ultimate form. The tablets in the archway would list all the Yale men who died in the war in chronological order of their classes, with a line indicating the date of his death and name of the battlefield if killed in action.[26]

By early 1912, the committee engaged Henry Bacon of New York, at French's recommendation, as the designer of the full memorial and Henry Hering as the artist. Early the following year, they authorized Bacon and Hering to choose four out of five bas relief subjects: devotion, peace, memory, courage, and vision. Unlike the grand Soldiers' and Sailors' Monument on top of East Rock, there would be no theme of "victory." Bacon soon became the architect and oversaw the construction of the Lincoln Memorial in Washington, DC, and Hering had been a student of the great American sculptor Augustus Saint-Gaudens. As for the inscription, committee members argued persistently right up until final decisions were voted. One suggestion, made by Frank Polk, was to consult English professors at Yale to edit their work, but that idea met fierce opposition from Gordon in one of his final acts. Professor of English and longtime editor of the *Yale Review* Wilbur L. Cross weighed in to Stokes and urged simplicity in the inscription. Do not allow it to become "poor burlesque verse," Cross advised, "the effect of the mock sublime." Bacon seemed to comprehend fully the intent of the committee for the nature of the figures in relief. The designer assured them that he would create "four figures . . . one at each end of the tablets signifying qualities in common to participants in both sides of the Civil War." In the spring and summer of 1912 the committee announced to alumni that they had reached a definitive plan with artists in place.[27]

In late September, President Hadley gave a "matriculation sermon" for incoming students on the theme of "Grant and Lee." Civil War anniversaries were receiving notice and commemoration all over the country, but just why Hadley would choose to stress this theme with freshmen is hard to discern. The impending war memorial may have been one reason, but likely an even more compelling one was that there were increasing numbers of Southern students coming to Yale, and many hailed from wealthy families. Hadley's reading about the two generals may have been thin, but even if not, at that moment in time Lee was widely considered the greater strategist and the most "moral" of heroic men, according to the Yale president. "Both were calm men," he assured the students. They were "not unduly exalted by victory nor unduly depressed by defeat."[28] With such saccharine rhetoric, Hadley set the stage for the memorialization to follow. War, mass violence, and savagery just faded away if couched in a collective narrative in which no one was ever wrong, and devotion alone made everyone noble. Had Grant survived to hear such rhetoric, he would have spit out his cigar in laughter.

In 1913, the Yale Corporation approved the plans and announced a campaign to raise an additional $20,000 to build the memorial. The circular sent to all alumni to raise money included the official inscription that would go on the floor in the archway. The letter concluded with the university's assurance that "the North and South find themselves thoroughly united in spirit." The institution thus exuded confidence that the "bonds" of North and South, a reconciled White America, though such racialized words were never used, stood permanently triumphant in such a memorial. But this was 1913, the fiftieth anniversary of the Emancipation Proclamation, commemorated in a host of complicated ways all over Black America. The "bonds" supposedly holding Americans together were breaking everywhere. Across the South and occasionally in the North and the Far West, mobs continued to commit lynchings at terrifying rates. The Tuskegee Institute's archive records sixty-four lynchings in 1912, sixty-two of them African Americans; in 1913, fifty-two and fifty-one, respectively; in 1914, fifty-five and fifty-one; and in 1915, sixty-nine and fifty-six.[29]

This horrific record of racial murder had long been part of sensational journalistic headlines and the subject of protest by Black people and their allies in public demonstrations, fiction, essays, and public oratory. In her courageous and prolific writing about lynching, Ida B. Wells-Barnett had explained the practice and challenged America's elites for years to face it legally and morally. In a lecture at a National Negro Conference in New York in 1909, she called lynching "the gruesome tribute the nation pays to the color line" and the most violent method "to suppress the colored vote." Wells-Barnett, as always, aimed her arguments at America's power brokers. "Thousands of American citizens have been put to death," she declared, "and no American president has yet raised his hand in effective protest." Yale's own President Taft, just then, helped lead the effort for the "both sides" monument at his alma mater but steered carefully around racial issues. When speaking in the South, Taft openly employed a mantra of Blue-Gray comity friendly to former Confederates and their sons and daughters. At a gathering of Confederate veterans in New Orleans in 1909, Taft assured the old men that "we've got beyond the time . . . when we discuss the war. . . . All who were in the bloody four years contest are proud of the courage and fortitude of both sides." And at a Blue-Gray reunion in Virginia a year later, he declared the sections united by a "confession that all that was done was well done, that the battle had to be fought." In these messages of settled history and national unity, where did the story of lynching fit? It did not fit, but that never stopped artists and essayists from exposing this darkest corner of American racism and violence. Taft's party, the Republicans, expressed tepid opposition to segregation in the South, but not until his reelection campaign in 1912 did he openly condemn lynching by calling it "cowardly murder."[30]

If the members of Yale's war memorial committee were paying attention at all to coverage of the hundreds of emancipation exhibitions and celebrations held all over America in 1913, they likely misinterpreted them. Most probably, they were unaware and did not read the Black press where coverage was extensive. They might have seen the great commemorative poem "Fifty Years," by James Weldon Johnson, published in the *New York Times* on January 1, 1913. The poem, itself a jewel of a literary monument, brims with Johnson's customary darkness and hope about African American history. Some six verses in, he struck his central theme:

> Then let us here erect a stone,
> To mark the place, to mark the time;
> A witness to God's mercies shown,
> A pledge to hold this day sublime.

And let that stone an altar be
Whereon thanksgivings we may lay—
Where we, in deep humility,
For faith and strength renewed may pray,

With open hearts ask from above
New zeal, new courage, and new pow'rs,
That we may grow more worthy of
This country and this land of ours.

For never let the thought arise
That we are here on sufferance bare:
Outcasts, asylumed 'neath these skies,
And aliens without part or share.

This land is ours by right of birth,
This land is ours by right of toil;
We helped to turn its virgin earth,
Our sweat is in its fruitful soil.

Johnson claims the center of America's historical memory, demands an African American birthright by the right of soldiering, of "blood" and devotion to the "flag": "We've bought a rightful sonship here, / And we have more than paid the price." Then, in a subtle jab at ex-Confederates, Johnson calls out the Lost Cause:

And never yet—O haughty Land,—
Let us, at least, for this be praised—
Has one black, treason-guided hand
Ever against that flag been raised.[31]

The tragedy of American Civil War memory is that it is impossible to imagine that sublime poem etched into the floor of the Yale memorial in 1915. Intentionally, the memorial had nothing to do with emancipation. In the twenty-first century, Johnson's humble "stone" might yet find a place in Yale's identity and elsewhere, as did his voluminous papers at the Beinecke Library in the middle of the twentieth century.

As the Yale war memorial moved toward completion, with continuing fundraising, the committee expressed pride that so little criticism of the purpose and design came their way. By December, the new secretary, Stokes, reported that they had received "less than half a dozen" critical letters but "hundreds" of approving

A view of Yale's Civil War Memorial, looking toward Grove Street. Photograph by Daniel Vieira.

One of four allegorical figures on Yale's Civil War Memorial. "Memory here guards ennobled names." Photograph by Daniel Vieira.

"Devotion gives a sanctity to strife." Photograph by Daniel Vieira.

notices from alumni for the memorial's message of healing. In December 1913, the New York Commandery of the Loyal Legion, a Union veterans' organization, protested that Southerners would be honored along with Northerners who had given their lives. They argued that the "loyalty" implied was hardly equal. A *Yale Daily News* editorial strongly supported the memorial in all dimensions, pitifully contending that there should be no distinction between "treason and patriotism" because all who fought did so with "devotion" and "sincerity." Another person, D. E. Burton, wrote to Frank Polk in early 1915 vehemently rejecting the entire premise of the memorial. Burton found "high devotion" to "perpetuate human slavery" appalling and not worthy of honor. He also did not believe "all distinctions between right and wrong, treason and loyalty, should be ignored in the interest of a sentimental good will . . . in the North."[32] Burton effectively named the argument banished from the Yale memorial process. If others objected to the reconciliationist Lost Cause memorial, they seemed to keep silent.

On June 20, 1915, in an elaborate ceremony, Yale's Civil War Memorial was dedicated. Among three official speeches, the first, called the "Historical Statement," came from William W. Gordon Jr. who had received a PhD from Yale. As the Southerner on the program, and son of the former cochair of the effort, Gordon kept his remarks descriptive, including that the final cost had reached

$24,000, although he pointed proudly to the "broader scope" and the "soldiers of each section," compared with the earliest consideration in 1865. Former Connecticut governor Simeon Baldwin made the second address, called the "presentation," in which he too stressed that "each side" in the war had "good men" who fought with "a spirit of devotion." Then Baldwin, oddly, addressed at some length the Tenth Amendment to the Constitution and its key role in states' rights. Finally, President Hadley gave an "acceptance" address with repetitive language about how the "devotion of Yale men in the last century" had led to the "common allegiance" of all Yale men in 1915.[33] No one uttered a word of what the Civil War had been fought about, with the exception of Baldwin's discussion of states' rights. It was a Sunday, a day of rest, except for the Black waiters who served at the reception to follow; their families and neighbors in New Haven may have enjoyed a June afternoon in one of the city's new parks. On Monday they would be back to work as clerks, as janitors, and in other largely working-class jobs.

And so Yale finally had its war memorial nearly one full year into the unfathomable collapse of civilization in Europe and the most horrid war ever fought. The day after the Yale memorial was dedicated, on June 16, 1915, the French Tenth Army launched an attack at Vimy Ridge that would cost them one hundred thousand casualties and the Germans sixty thousand. Those numbers paled in comparison to the slaughter to come; more than twenty million soldiers died in the Great War, and the notions of sentimentality and comity on the tablets in Woolsey Hall would eventually seem quaint. One year earlier, on June 3, 1914, the *Yale Alumni Weekly* had run an article touting the impending war memorial as a lesson that, in the new twentieth century, "man's power to think things through increases as the generations unfold. His tendency to physical settlement of quarrels decreases as he learns the potency of the brain."[34] Such was only one fond dream that died in the trenches and in every disease-ridden hospital from the Somme to Gallipoli to Sydney, from Qingdao to East Africa, to hundreds of villages on the vast Russian front, to every town in England, and to many training camps in the Jim Crow South.

Yale's war memorial, commemorating its own sons who had died in the Civil War, needs to be viewed in these larger contexts: first, the American culture of reunion forged in mutual soldiers' sacrifice, in racism and the refusal to face the role of slavery and its destruction in its own now sentimentalized Armageddon of fifty years past; and second, the explosion of modernity engulfing societies across the globe and the shattering end of innocence drenched in the blood of

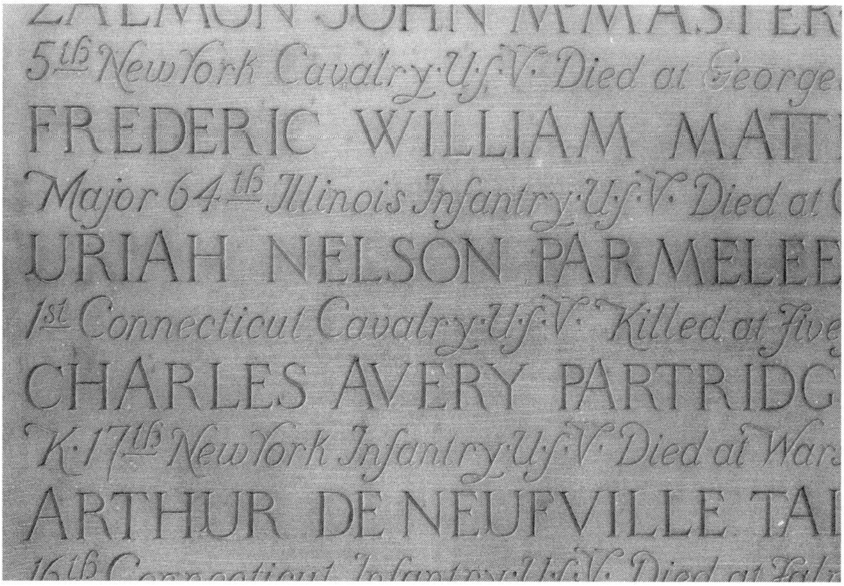

Name of Uriah Nelson Parmelee, engraved on Yale's Civil War Memorial. Photograph by Daniel Vieira.

the Great War. Perhaps it was a never-to-be-admitted *anxiety* of the highly educated Yale men who fashioned the war memorial, honored Thomas Nelson Page and Booker Washington, and above all honored themselves and their vaunted moral certainties, that made such a quest for sectional and White racial reconciliation necessary. And Uriah Parmelee and his fellow Yale Union dead on those tablets never had a vote about honoring their foes.

Donor dollars were at stake, but far more important, a regime, even a creed of nineteenth-century ideas about education, social order, power, and white supremacy was at stake. The Yale men needed to convince themselves that if they could make history itself calm, unifying, and permanent on walls, on floors, and in marble, they could surely do the same with their university and their country. But history never stands still for us to really control it. The Yale memorial is a remarkable, even beautiful, act of remembrance forged through an elaborate process of forgetting. Never again through the twentieth century, the most violent in human history, would they be able to so comfortably think of war and warriors as above and beyond victory or defeat.

INTERLUDE

The Birth of a Nation *in New Haven, 1915*

On October 26, 1915, Booker T. Washington gave a lecture to a huge audience in Woolsey Hall, immediately next to Yale's new memorial to the Civil War. The Tuskegee Institute and Negro Business League head, and most famous African American leader, delivered an address on Black education and the need for uplift and self-reliance. Washington had become the socially accepted spokesman of Black America. But his grip on such a position had faded in recent years. It would be one of the last public addresses of his life; he died on November 14 in Tuskegee at the age of fifty-nine. As an educational leader Washington had achieved considerable social and political power in the Jim Crow era, although by then he encountered many Black leaders who fiercely defied his leadership.[1]

At the same moment Washington appeared at Yale, the extraordinary and infamous new motion picture *The Birth of a Nation*, made by D. W. Griffith, was under injunction in New Haven; but soon it would open at the Hyperion Theater with both massive publicity and local resistance. As Washington left town, local Black residents led by George W. Crawford, a Yale Law School graduate and an official in the National Association for the Advancement of Colored People (NAACP), were in court to try to stop the screening of the notorious white supremacist film. The movie had been shown all across the nation since the previous February, when it opened in Los Angeles.[2] These instances of local resistance to *The Birth of a Nation* and racist actions and policies represented a new era in Black protest, especially centered in the rising influence of the interracial NAACP.

So far as we know, Washington did not weigh in on the film dispute in New Haven, but by this juncture he remained an important voice of both Black economic self-assertion and sectional reconciliation over the Civil War. If he had stopped to examine Yale's Civil War Memorial, its meaning and content, he likely would have approved. And had he seen the memorial, the filmmaker Griffith would have approved as well, especially the features honoring Yale Confederates.

Despite the persistence of lynchings across the country and race riots in Atlanta, Fort Worth, and other cities during these years, as World War I exploded in Europe, African Americans forged a new confidence and professional advancement beyond what W. E. B. Du Bois called the "vast veil" of segregation. They were building communities and their own thriving institutions—colleges, churches, and newspapers. Some five hundred thousand Black people lived now in approximately eighteen cities west of the Mississippi River, and even more were beginning the decades-long Great Migration from the Deep South to midwestern and northeastern cities in search of jobs and in the hope of equality. Into these roiling contexts of racial unrest, foreign war, migrations, and the semicentennial of the Civil War, Griffith injected his viciously racist epic film, complete with all the irresistible powers of the new medium of the silent movies. Griffith began his filmmaking collaboration with Thomas Dixon, author of the best-selling novel *The Clansman*, in 1913. *The Clansman* was adapted for the stage with sensational success within a year of its publication in 1905. As a rousing tale of the victimized White South and the heroism of the Ku Klux Klan as a necessary force to save America, the book and play found an audience plied for years by Thomas Nelson Page and a legion of Lost Cause and plantation school writers, cartoonists, and other caricaturists. These works promoted aggressive action, within and outside the law, to achieve social order and white supremacy.[3]

Born in North Carolina, Dixon went to college at Wake Forest and then on to Johns Hopkins University in Baltimore for a short time, where he met and befriended the future president Woodrow Wilson. Dixon briefly practiced law but found his true calling as a lecturer and a Baptist preacher in pulpits in Boston and New York City, as well as back home in North Carolina. His trilogy of white supremacist novels—*The Leopard's Spots* (1902), *The Clansman* (1905), and *The Traitor* (1907)—made him a kind of white supremacist celebrity in both North and South. Dixon possessed a boundless desire, he said, to "teach the north, the young north, what it has never known—the awful suffering of the white man during the dreadful reconstruction period. I believe that God . . . anointed the white men of the south . . . to demonstrate to the world that the white man must and shall be supreme." Dixon's was no casual racism; it formed his worldview, his belief system, and his artistic subject. The races were different in capacities by nature and no form of equality ought to ever be attempted, nor any method spared in suppressing it. Griffith, who grew up in Louisville, Kentucky, came of age during the rise of the Lost Cause, and he loved melodrama and the Southern martial tradition. He and Dixon shared a quest to be actors, but by 1908 the Kentuckian was in New York making short films, many of which had stock Civil War scenes and characters: rebel soldiers going off to war with Black field hands cheering; gentle but sturdy White Southern women; Confederate and Union soldiers, sometimes brothers, shaking hands while wrapped in the folds of their flags; and loyal slaves saving or dying for their owners in a war to save Southern civilization. Griffith thus established a hardening stereotype for Black characters that would stand for decades as essentially the only image allowed in the movies. Some of Griffith's Black characters would go to any extent to avoid having to become free, including hiding their owner's will so as not to face the manumission clause.[4]

In the spectacle of *The Birth of a Nation*, Griffith and Dixon combined their visions and their methods to produce the message not only that former slaves did not desire their freedom but also that emancipation had been America's most fundamental and dangerous disaster. With its stunning battle scenes filmed on desert land north of Los Angeles, suspenseful chases, and hundreds of hooded Klansmen on horses galloping to the rescue, the movie made technical cinematic history. But it was the racial dramas, the depiction of the sexual desires of Black men, the sinister corruption of Yankee carpetbaggers, and the disaster of Reconstruction political policies that injected a lethal racism into the bloodstream of American popular culture. The war had been noble, the film argued, but Reconstruction in the South, directed by deranged radicals and sex-crazed Black people, especially those of mixed racial background given unwarranted power, required a violent crusade of redemption. The South not only wins in the end in *The Birth of a Nation*, it transforms the misbegotten history of emancipation into an alternative story of the dawning of a new age of white supremacy. In the film, which reached millions, history became a tool, a weapon of racial theory in the age of advertising. Publicity for the movie made excited claims that it presented history as real and authentic as no one had ever seen before in a moving picture.[5] The new medium represented a new reality for those who could employ it.

The NAACP and other civil rights organizations, as well as some prominent White dissenters (Northern and Southern) protested and condemned *The Birth of a Nation*. In many cities, NAACP chapters, armed with pamphlets and organizing their first large-scale direct-action protests, sought to achieve local bans or at least to get portions of its content censored. Almost nothing stopped the Griffith company's promotions, including a parade by hooded cavalry outside a theater in New York City; Griffith and Dixon staged screenings in Woodrow Wilson's White House and in Congress. Violence and brawls broke out at theaters in Boston, where William Monroe Trotter, editor of the *Guardian* newspaper, did achieve at least a partial mayoral ban on the film for reasons of public safety. Censorship was then, as always, a tricky First Amendment issue; Booker T. Washington supported Griffith's right to show the film, however repugnant he found its content.[6]

Some Black artists launched their own efforts to make counter films, while other intellectuals took unequivocal stands against the work's physical threat to African Americans. In the *New York Age*, James Weldon Johnson, the poet, novelist, musical lyricist, and soon-to-be field secretary of the NAACP, published two editorials denouncing *The Birth of a Nation*. Johnson argued that it was a dangerous adaptation of Dixon's *The Clansman* and as a "moving picture it can do . . . incalculable harm" to Black people. Johnson cut to the heart of the matter: "A big, degraded looking Negro is shown chasing a little golden-haired white girl for the purpose of outraging her; she, to escape him, goes to her death by hurling herself over a cliff." Johnson stepped beyond the issue of censorship as a legal question into the realm of social safety, collective self-defense, and national security. "Can you imagine," he asked, "the effect of such a scene upon the millions who seldom read a book, who seldom witness a drama, but who constantly go to the 'movies'?" Johnson felt especially offended by Griffith and Dixon's attempt to soften the impact of their racism by adding to the beginning of the film something about Black education at Hampton Institute. They were merely "laying a trap" with their "hell-inspired production," said the often circumspect Johnson. He favored bans on the film. "If the picture can be killed, let it die, from first scene to last. . . . The whole representation was conceived only in hatred for the North and contempt for the Negro; so let it die! Kill it!" It was no small step for such a sublime artist and writer to advocate so strict a use of censorship. But Johnson saw the highest stakes for the entire country. The "sole purpose" of the film, he maintained, was to "convince the North that it made a mistake in fighting to free the slaves" and to keep Black people "down."[7]

S. Z. Poli, an Italian immigrant, owned the Hyperion Theater in New Haven. An adept promoter himself, he draped the entry hall to the theater with American flags and portrayed the film as a supreme "patriotic" experience with "great educational appeal." In late October, articles appeared on the front pages of all four of the city's daily newspapers: the *New Haven Register*, *New Haven Journal-Courier*, *New Haven Times-Leader*, and *New Haven Union*. Initially, George W. Crawford and his legal team managed to get the New Haven mayor and chief of police to refuse a license to show the film. Crawford argued that the film "threatened" the safety and livelihoods of Black citizens. He also used an indecency claim, contending that *The Birth of a Nation* was "lascivious, sacrilegious, indecent" in its depiction of Black people as "murderous . . . moral perverts." Finally, the Black resisters made an economic case that the film would lead to so much White "hostility" that it foreshadowed the "loss of business and trades and professions" for African American New Haveners. Poli countered with publicity. "See War as It Really Is," ran one newspaper advertisement. And in another, the Ku Klux Klan rose as "the price that has been paid to make us the great nation today."[8]

The injunction did not last long. In court in the final week of October, Judge James Henry Webb heard testimony from three Black businessmen and one physician fearing the loss of his practice, which was composed of 98 percent White people. Other witnesses opposed specific scenes in the film, such as all those pertaining to the character Gus, as well as the presentation of Black men holding office in Reconstruction Southern state legislatures, with their feet on desks, throwing objects, and chewing on chicken bones. Webb held a private screening of the film to see for himself. He sympathized with the plaintiffs, calling the movie "pernicious," but found no legal grounds for economic harm. So in this case a judge condemned the film but allowed it to go forward in the interest of free expression. A deal was struck with Griffith's company to cut certain scenes, but the show proceeded. On October 30, Webb issued his order, and *The Birth of a Nation* played to packed audiences, selling 24,000 tickets over the next two weeks in a city with 150,000 people.[9] No one recorded how many Yale students went to see the film, but undoubtedly many could not have resisted such a phenomenon in the autumn of 1915.

Racism can take many forms, some blunt and others more subtle. So conditioned were many Yale students to appreciate the arguments of *The Birth of a Nation* that a review in the *Yale Daily News* called it a "wonderful film" and admired all the melodramatic elements of a "typical 'movie.'" The reviewer especially appreciated the "unforgettable reality, the stirring events of the Civil War and Reconstruction." He also lamented the local "negroid opposition" and the "absurd sentimentality of the local clergy" in forcing the censoring of some scenes. But the reviewer reserved the highest praise for Griffith for "the production of

Schoolchildren waiting to enter the Hyperion Theater in New Haven to see *The Birth of a Nation,* 1915. Photograph by Thomas S. Bronson. Courtesy of New Haven Museum.

the first American epic . . . marvelous battle scenes, and in the gathering of the Ku Klux Klan, the pathway to a new art."[10] For this Yale student journalist, the film had completely succeeded as both history and social philosophy. It reinforced well-honed historical memory and laid the artistic, visual, and narrative foundations of future social policy.

In the nineteenth century, Frederick Douglass had probed the meaning of what he called "long-standing prejudice" (that is, racism) more than most Americans. In season and out for fifty years, he performed as the nation's prose poet of democracy and antiracism. In 1881, Douglass called racism "a moral disorder, which creates the conditions necessary for its own existence, and fortifies itself by refusing all contradiction." All but anticipating the later reactions to *The Birth of a Nation*, the old abolitionist said racism "paints a hateful picture according to its own diseased imagination." Such an imagination, ever ready if so educated, "distorts the features of the fancied original to suit the portrait." Racists, Douglass argued, must be primed, educated, and equipped for their task. Similarly, for the twentieth century, W. E. B. Du Bois led a new generation in probing the deepest meanings of the racism at the root of Jim Crow. In 1903, Du Bois characterized so vast a "strange prejudice" as "that personal disrespect and mockery, the ridicule and systematic humiliation, the distortion of fact and wanton license of fancy" that produced "the all-pervading desire to inculcate disdain for everything black."[11] *The Birth of a Nation* harvested generations of racism and fifty years of fanciful history to the very ends that Douglass and Du Bois so brilliantly exposed: diseased imaginations and systematic humiliation. More than a century later, Americans still grapple with, defeat, and reinforce these contagions from our past.

Epilogue

> Nations reel and stagger on their way; they make hideous mistakes; they commit frightful wrongs; they do great and beautiful things. And shall we not best guide humanity by telling the truth about all of this, so far as the truth is ascertainable?
>
> —W. E. B. DU BOIS, *Black Reconstruction* (1935)

Universities are communities of memory, either loosely or firmly held together by collective values, rituals, habits, or precepts that can change over time. Somehow bonds develop or fray between the generations of these communities and their divergent members. Administrations, faculty, students, and alumni often, by definition, do not share the same aspirations or duties. They do all hope to achieve that ideal of the wondrous terrain that can happen between teacher and student, what the Puritans called "grace," and what secular moderns might call "mystery," the magic moments of inspiration, illumination, and endless reflection that happen in classrooms or laboratories, on a stroll through the quad, or during a precious reading moment in a corner of the library. And all parts of these conglomerate institutions, riddled with conflict, vanity, and pretense, also, hopefully, share a common quest for the free pursuit of knowledge of all kinds, even when we disagree on what constitutes legitimate knowledge from one discipline to the next. What may hold this chaotic, beautiful, indispensable creation—the university—together is a shared memory of purpose, rituals, and rules upon which learning directly depends.[1] As for a nation, so too a university: our purpose may often be more unconsciously assumed or performed than it is examined or probed, composed of the powerful myths that exist as though no one ever made them up. But our memory has a history made by people; it is always prelude to the sovereign present. But it will not just come to us in our habits; we have to go find it.

Yale University's current mission statement reads as follows: "Yale is committed to improving the world today and for future generations through outstanding research and scholarship, education, preservation, and practice. Yale educates aspiring leaders worldwide who serve all sectors of society. We carry out this mission through the free exchange of ideas in an ethical, interdependent, and diverse community of faculty, staff, students, and alumni."[2] This simple, carefully crafted, twenty-first-century institutional self-definition is at its heart an ethical, outward-looking statement rooted in the long American tradition of pluralism, as well as in a modern, democratic conception of a global university. An essentially moral mission must, however, live in a world of donor-driven imperatives for institutional growth, faculty autonomy over curriculum and hiring, rising costs and family debt, and students who build their cases for admission from childhood in a frightfully competitive, multibillion-dollar preparation industry. The mission must also ultimately achieve goals that are highly contested, the old aims of classical humanistic education struggling with the imperatives of practical, professional training, options that are never the same for less endowed institutions (which make up the majority). And such a mission is now also complicated by some of its very strengths—the rich diversity of a changing university community strives to educate itself about identity and cultural pluralism as it also struggles to think beyond those priorities to surviving universals about the good, the true, and the beautiful, as well as the survival of the planet and the geopolitics of war and peace. We study our species as well as the physical universe in all of its parts.

The Yale mission statement does not say that it intends to face, research, and tell its own history wherever that inquiry may take us. Such a project would be too specific for the statement's general purposes. But perhaps it is implied in its devotion to teaching, although that word is also not used. "Whatever the style or technique, teaching at its best can be a generative act," writes Andrew Delbanco in his probing study of "what college is for." Teaching, he says, is "one of the ways by which human beings try to cheat death—by giving witness to the next generation so that what we have learned in our own lives won't die with us." Mission statements these days tend to read as the written equivalents of the gloriously colorful pamphlets sent to prospective students, which depict smiling youth from every background on bucolic campuses. Such expressions of both "faith and dread," as Delbanco writes about teaching, though, "have always been at the heart of the college idea."[3] Not many of us go to the classroom each day with the notion that we are cheating death of what we have spent our lives learning. But unthinkingly, in our pretentious assumptions as well as our ideals, we may be doing just that. Thus, good teachers are always anxious about their performance. What if the history of ancient Mesopotamia or French and Italian literature can never keep pace with Economics 101 or computer science in student interest? What if no one comes? What if our PowerPoints are old-fashioned already, or nonexistent? We gather up our notes, keeping an ancient faith, and march to class in a ritual we love and justifiably fear.

Can it not be the same for whole institutions of higher learning? Are they not cheating death of their own essential ideal, of their reason to be, if they too do not engage in a search for collective self-knowledge and memory and then teach all that they find? Is that not what generations that hardly know one another owe to each other, as well as to dozens of generations long gone and those to come? And might the impulse to historically explore institutional involvement in slavery and other past practices that our own age deems unequivocally evil not also derive from similar fears and imperatives? What, indeed, might we be doing today that will be judged in similar ways a century from now? A university may sponsor studies of its own past for utilitarian reasons—to forge positive publicity and meet demands for repair before they land at the trustees' door. Or they might engage the past freely and openly, dare we say, from the ethical impulses of their own mission statements and the ancient notion of universities as places of reflection and action on the most compelling questions facing humankind. Might we do this history simply because, in our best traditions and however painful its lessons, it is both good and true? Are we not, therefore, whatever the consequences of facing our institutional collective memories, doing exactly what universities ought to do?

In any given present, especially among the young with limited memories, the past can be quite alien. Why did people live like that, or how could they do such things to each other? a child might ask in a museum or at a historical site. Many freshmen arrive at college in the early twenty-first century with a good deal of formal, if swirling and unchronological, history in their heads; many arrive with little at all. Those essential elements of curiosity—*why* and *how*—are at the root of why we have the historical disciplines in libraries, museums, and classrooms. As a community we have to find, know, and translate our past; otherwise, like the unknowing individual, an institution too may wander aimlessly into a future that will always challenge or shock us. The past is waiting for us. This is why all societies, all institutions, practice commemorations, memorialization, and monument building. We would like to slow down and control that past before it finds us in unexpected ways. A university is itself a landscape of monuments, some inert, like classroom buildings awaiting the opening of term or athletic fields and gymnasiums awaiting their own recurring and ancient rituals, or living and breathing, like libraries, brimming with the infinity of knowledge. In today's world of hyperactive and omnipresent information overload emanating from ever-changing technologies, the past can seem only more remote, distant, irretrievable, unreal, artificial, or even unnecessary. Digitization has made more history accessible, but do we yet know who goes there and why and how they may take it out into their public lives?

"The past is a foreign country: they do things differently there," the English novelist L. P. Hartley famously wrote in the opening line of *The Go-Between* in 1953. The past *is* foreign; we are obviously not there. But humans possess something uniquely our own: imagination, developed beyond that of any other animal as far as we know. Our imaginations, when trained and cultivated, can almost get us there, if by "there" we mean understanding with some empathy the glories and horrors of the past from some kind of verifiable sources. Imaginations are forged, though, by a myriad of forces, some conscious and some not. The past of any institution and memory community as old as Yale University traverses immense changes over time in mores, political philosophies, conceptions of human possibilities, constituencies, and systems of learning. Depending on how one defines the illusive idea of a generation, there have been between at least fifteen and twenty generations of Yalies. Indeed, a college or university generation, given the traditional four-year residence of undergraduates, may be much shorter in its cohorts of experience than the time span we commonly associate with family generations.[4] In cultural and intellectual terms, Yale has existed as an eighteenth-century theology college, a nineteenth-century college that became a university exploring the sciences and creating professional schools, and a twentieth- and twenty-first-century American and international hub of learning and teaching in every field of knowledge. To study the story of Yale's connections to slavery and abolition is to try to make sense of these many different contexts, these foreign environments, their vast complexity, and their distant and often alien actions and perceptions that may not be our own. A solidarity among all these generations is a utopian goal, out of the reach of our poor human abilities or the reach of even the most persistent and resourceful alumni associations. But institutional and individual ancestors are there awaiting our pilgrimage, our communion. The documents in the archives, their compelling tactile nature, their vastness and their specificity, their elusiveness, their silence until we search and breathe on them, open their power to our imaginations as though they have been waiting all this time for us to show up.

Humility and awe for what we can know or not know about our predecessors are the best attitudes with which to approach this search for truth and an effort to narrate its twisting story. The joy is in the search. In one of the most courageous works of history ever written, *The Historian's Craft*, Marc Bloch, a French scholar of feudalism and medieval peasantry, reminded us that past and present are always intertwined. He called this connection the "solidarity of the ages," in a book he began writing while fighting in the French resistance against the Nazis in 1940–41. Bloch was eventually captured and executed by a firing squad in a field, but not before finishing approximately two-thirds of a draft of this now-classic book. Past and present entangled with one another? How well and tragically Bloch understood that reality as he fled and then was consumed by the Holocaust. Calmly and heroically, he could declare that "misunderstanding of the present is the inevitable consequence of ignorance of the past." Bloch would not leave us self-satisfied, though, with such a perennial complaint. "But a man may wear himself out," he continued, "just as fruitlessly in seeking to understand the past, if he is totally ignorant of the present." Ignorance of the dead or the living was for Bloch not a moral option.[5] It is not a moral option for us either.

What is at stake in doing history, Bloch made explicit, "is nothing less than the passing down of memory from one generation to another." The past can be a "tyrant," Bloch said, as it forces us to never stray far from our sources, and it frequently does not reveal itself easily. But we also worship the "goddess Catastrophe." Events shape how we do research and write; they sometimes shock us into action in the streets, at lecterns, and on the page. "A good cataclysm suits our business," Bloch astutely admitted.[6] And thus, we might return to understanding that what prompted President Peter Salovey to call on the Yale community to engage the question of John C. Calhoun's legacy for the university was the mass murder of African Americans in an African Methodist Episcopal church in Charleston in 2015; he further responded to the murder of George Floyd in 2020 by launching this inquiry into Yale's ties to slavery and abolition. The present breathes into the past, sometimes steadily as in a normal breeze, and at other times like a howling storm. And the past, especially after the storm, rises anew, however horrible the ruins, reshaped and in need of reasoned reconstruction.

Colleges and universities are among the "slowest-changing institutions in American life," writes Andrew Delbanco. They are "slower, even, than the post office."[7]

Our study of Yale and slavery may only reinforce that perception, but as we have seen with so many universities and colleges looking seriously into their pasts with race, slavery, and beyond, perhaps a fruitful crossroad has been reached in how institutions of higher learning now approach the construction or reconstruction of their own institutional memory. Even more so, we are experiencing a reckoning with the very idea of the changing mission or purpose of colleges, as well as primary and secondary schools and curriculums, and the value of the freedom to read and learn without religiously or politically driven censorship. The *free* university, inside and outside its gates, its pursuit of diversity, its attempted meritocracy, its curriculums, and its business models, is undergoing scrutiny and pressure in ways the Puritan founders of Yale would not recognize. The American college or university is a profoundly important American reinvention of an ancient idea, remade in medieval times in Italy, Germany, and Britain, and then re-created again in colonial America. Education has always been a laboratory of both social mobility and economic and racial inequality. Among Americans' most treasured values is that a "higher" education can remake one's life. As endangered as such a great ideal may be, who involved in education, or aspiring to it, does not want to believe in this gospel?

Much work remains to be done. Another century and more remains of Yale's history with slavery's legacies, as well as with abolition, racism, and racial ideas. That final century deserves its own volume, and it will face challenges at least as difficult as those confronted in this work. A second volume will need to tackle many huge subjects and turning points in Yale's modern development: its emergence as the international center for the study of and advocacy for eugenics in the 1920s, including its racist concepts, sterilization programs, and broad influence on social policy and the sciences generally; the rebuilding of Yale's central campus and the naming of its residential colleges in the 1930s, most for slaveholders; the transformations of World War II and Yale's place in the global struggles with fascism and eventually communism; the opening of old Yale to the integration of Black students in the 1960s and 1970s; the integration of undergraduate women at Yale in the 1970s; the role of Yale historians (and their legions of former doctoral students) in forging the modern field of slavery studies from U. B. Phillips to David Potter, C. Vann Woodward, John Blassingame, David Montgomery, David Brion Davis, and many more still living and at work at Yale and across the world of higher education; the transformations in curriculum, including the emergence of area studies on race, gender, ethnicity, and international relations in the late twentieth and early twenty-first centuries; the tremendous growth and prestige of its professional schools; the presence of generations of world-class faculty in so many disciplines; and a variety of national crises of modern times that challenged and changed the mission of the university.

Evelyn Brooks Higginbotham, who teaches history and African American studies at Harvard, has marveled at how, after so many decades of explosive and transformative scholarship on slavery, the subject of the universities' role in the story could itself become a surprising "new field." In a 2019 essay, she names four ways the field had found so much traction: first, through the study of the "presence" of enslaved people on eighteenth- and nineteenth-century campuses, sometimes owned by the institutions, sometimes not; second, through the contributions of earlier eras of scholarship in many disciplines, for better and for worse, to the creation of knowledge about race and the so-called racial sciences; third, through the discoveries of student ideas and attitudes about race and slavery in American colleges over the ages, a story that, once again, leaves one educated about if not aghast by the depths of popular racism in the history of higher education; and fourth, through the forging—prompted by the look inward and the quest for institutional self-examination—of new kinds of pedagogy across many disciplines, in the humanities and the natural sciences. All four of these trends have certainly emerged in our study of Yale. Higginbotham concludes with a calm, but poignant, historiographical point: "For those who thought that nothing new could be written [in slavery studies], slavery's haunting legacy in the academy has yet more stories to tell."[8]

To these perceptive observations we might add another by way of the writings of two distinguished Yale graduates, both of unusual origins and from the early twentieth-century period when this book concludes. The field of universities and slavery may offer new angles of vision on the old themes of *irony* and *tragedy* as lenses through which to see this experience. Both concepts have always informed, even driven, slavery studies around the world, although Americans are rarely fond of the notion of tragedy as a way of explaining or understanding their history.

Few Americans, and likely no theologian, had more to say about the role of tragedy and irony in American spiritual life and history than Reinhold Niebuhr. Born in Wright City, Missouri, in 1892, Niebuhr was the son of German immigrants and his father was a German evangelical pastor. His first language was German, which was spoken through his youth at home and in his church community. He attended Elmhurst College in Illinois, graduating in 1910, and then Eden Theological Seminary in Webster Grove, Missouri. Niebuhr's father died shockingly in 1913, and for nearly six months, the twenty-three-year-old took over as pastor of the elder's church in Lincoln, Illinois. Then, with help and hope, but great trepidation, he landed at the Yale Divinity School in the fall of that year. Niebuhr was a fish out of water in New Haven, or what he aptly called a "mongrel among the thoroughbreds." He felt intimidated by so many young men who emphasized their middle names as much as their last. An outsider, always in debt, Niebuhr nevertheless bore down on his reading and his preparation for the life of a pastor and eventually an enormously influential theologian. He took a bachelor's in divinity in 1914 and, with uncertain funding, a master's in divinity in 1915. While at Yale, Niebuhr almost always felt unprepared, uneducated, a misfit who did not even speak good English when he arrived. But no graduate in divinity, or perhaps any other field, in 1915, as Yale was about to unveil its Civil War Memorial, went on to change the world quite like Niebuhr.[9]

His English had improved, both spoken and written. His bachelor of divinity thesis was inspired by William James's *The Will to Believe* and his famous 1910 essay, "The Moral Equivalent of War." For his master of divinity, Niebuhr wrote a thesis titled "The Contribution of Christianity to the Doctrine of Immortality." At heart, Niebuhr was deeply Christian but a practicing philosopher. At one point while at Yale, though, he declared himself "bored" with "schools of epistemology." He sought and soon practiced a social gospel in the real world. Immediately after graduating in 1915, he moved to Detroit, where he would pastor the Bethel Evangelical Church for the next thirteen years, transforming a congregation of only sixty-six into a vibrant one with seven hundred members. In these years Niebuhr became deeply involved with Detroit auto workers and in racial and class issues. The Ku Klux Klan was active in the city, even running a candidate for mayor, and the young pastor fought them in every way he publicly could. He mastered preaching and soon the craft of persuasive, religious, and socially engaged writing that would inspire presidents, activists, and thousands of academics, especially historians, as well as ordinary people who fell under his intellectual spell after his move to Union Theological Seminary in New York. Among his most prominent works are *Moral Man in an Immoral Society* (1932), *The Nature and Destiny of Man* (1941), and *Faith and History* (1949), as well as many others. But in our context of understanding how institutions, much less individuals or nations, might face their pasts, no book informs as it challenges us quite like *The Irony of American History* (1952).

Irony was Niebuhr's take on America's predicament in the Cold War and its struggle to conceive of a foreign policy in the wake of victory in World War II. But above all it was the theologian's brilliant analysis of human pretension, of resistance by people to the inherent tragedy in their nature, their behavior and experience, and the utter necessity to recognize how the use of irony is an indispensable method of comprehension and survival. Niebuhr did not make it easy for triumphal Americans. Human pride and evil knew no borders. "Pure tragedy elicits tears of admiration and pity," wrote Niebuhr, "for the hero who is willing to brave death or incur guilt for the sake of some great good." But irony was the more powerful force. And Niebuhr detested melodrama. "Irony . . . prompts some laughter and a nod of comprehension beyond the laughter; for irony involves comic absurdities which cease to be altogether absurd when fully understood. Our age is involved in irony because so many dreams of our nation have been so cruelly refuted by history."[10]

"The pretensions of virtue," Niebuhr insisted, "are as offensive to God as the pretensions of power." In Christian teachings, at least to Niebuhr, humans are destined for "ironic failure." Born in sin, the human is living while headed toward death. He was certain, despite all our claims to great knowledge and material prowess, that "human limitations catch up to human pretensions." He saw no greater examples of this in his own time than the making and use of the atomic bomb and the ever-recurring American struggle with racism. Banish your "humorless idealism," Niebuhr urged Americans; try to achieve "contrition" as well as historical and self-knowledge as means of using irony—the kind that causes a wink of recognition or bitter sorrow—as a kind of "abatement" to "pretensions."[11] All who wish to face the past, as individuals or as organizations and institutions, and who seek forms of repair for past wrongs would do well to see their task through Niebuhr's ironic conception of our collective human complicity in the evils we have committed. Niebuhr was much less interested in winners or losers in history and much more interested in knowing human nature and its potential for both evil and good.

In 1915, the same year Niebuhr left Yale for the world, another Yale graduate, William Pickens, published a compelling essay, "The Constitutional Status of the Negro from 1860 to 1870." Born in Anderson County, South Carolina, in 1881, Pickens was the son of freed slaves. With his mother he moved to Arkansas, where he grew up, attending the Black schools of the town of Argenta. He worked in cotton fields and in a sawmill. His mother died when he was only thirteen, but he made education the quest of his life and his escape from loneliness and poverty. At first Pickens was self-taught as a writer before attending Talladega College in Alabama, graduating in 1902. Then, with what must have been insecurities the sons of plutocrats and other Yale students may not have felt, Pickens came to Yale, admitted as a junior. He achieved his BA in 1904, earning Phi Beta Kappa.

As chapter 10 describes, Pickens worked several jobs, including performing in dialect, to pay his expenses at Yale, despite receiving some financial support from a wealthy patron. He especially embraced languages, and eventually taught Greek, Latin, and German. After graduation, Pickens completed a master's degree at Fisk University in Nashville and held teaching jobs at Talladega, Wiley College in East Texas, and Morgan State in Baltimore, where he also became a dean. He wrote a remarkable autobiography that helped launch the more modern, twentieth-century phase of that genre—*The Heir of Slaves* (1911), later expanded and published as *Bursting Bonds: The Autobiography of a "New Negro"* (1923). By 1918, Pickens's essays and especially his oratorical skills brought him to the NAACP in New York, where he served as a special assistant to James Weldon Johnson in organizing local branches of the protest organization, as well as on the effort for a federal antilynching law. By 1923, Pickens was appointed field secretary; he would serve the organization all the way to the 1940s in many capacities.[12]

Pickens read his 1915 essay at the nineteenth annual meeting of the American Negro Academy in December of that year, just as Niebuhr arrived in Detroit. Meanwhile, the film *The Birth of a Nation* played all across the nation, the world exploded in unspeakable war, and Yale engaged in its elaborate self-congratulation ceremonies commemorating the reconciliation of the Civil War at its Lost Cause memorial. In his essay, Pickens sought first to refute the popular notions spreading across the country that the Reconstruction era had been a colossal failure and its achievements buried in racist notions of Black incapacity for democracy. Indeed, his essay is a manifesto for American democracy, as reborn in Reconstruction and since, which in too many ways seemed crushed by the Jim Crow world. Pickens wrote with wit and a deep sense of irony. The Fourteenth and Fifteenth Amendments, he maintained, had been "great products of statesmanship." There was no "spirit of revenge" at work in the measures enacted by the radical Republicans. Never mind their "motives," Pickens insisted. The two later amendments were passed "to keep the Thirteenth Amendment from being a mere farce." And if they contained "compromises," such is a reality of politics, said the wry Latin professor. "It does not lessen the beauty of the rose if the plant was sprouted in manure."[13]

Pickens saved his most biting wit for the absurdities of the Jim Crow legal and social system that followed Reconstruction and against which he now devoted his life of resistance and organizing. He lampooned the "one drop" rule for race in America. "What is a Negro?" he asked. "It takes only one drop 'to make you whole,'" Pickens laughed. "If the pattern is left to the eyes, millions of American 'Negroes' will have to be taken into the Caucasian race." State legislatures had resorted to the manifold madness of using percentages of "blood" to determine race, or what Pickens called "the finer discriminations of mathematics." And then there were all the attempts to banish interracial marriage, which Pickens termed the "queer laws." He called these queer, he said, because "in spirit and in effect" they "tend to make the honorable relation of marriage a worse crime than the naturally dishonorable practice of illicit intercourse." The American Negro Academy was an earnest, august group; one wonders if Pickens prompted even them to laugh along with him. Was the idea of tragedy and its irony expressed any better in this era than when Pickens concluded that the entire Jim Crow enterprise sought to put "honor under the foot of dishonor"?[14]

The primary cause at the root of the American apartheid system, to Pickens, was the "advance in education" by African Americans. He embodied such advances. All those new laws, that new Constitution, all that freedom born of emancipation and the Civil War had to be thwarted. It was nothing less than an effort by White people to defeat the new "democracy" by "indirection and duplicity" when violence had not alone been a sufficient weapon. Like Niebuhr, Pickens insisted on rejecting earnestness and good intentions, as well as all manner of both-siderism. The problem was in human beings and their absurd desperation to sustain power and control. "All the humiliation, wrong and robbery possible against a free people, the devil and the Sicilian tyrants working together could never have devised a more ingenious scheme than the 'Jim Crow' car." Pickens left his audience with the bracing assertion to never forget that the Fourteenth and Fifteenth Amendments were "for the benefit of all races, at all times, in all America."[15] And as he so poignantly implied, so was all that educational advance.

And so it is for us and all peoples and institutions that believe in the impulses of those amendments and the natural rights tradition and sacrifices from which they were born, as we face, explain, and commemorate our pasts—not merely for ourselves, not for our own "vainglory," as Niebuhr called it, but for the generations past, present, and, especially, those to come.[16]

Notes

INTRODUCTION

1. Avishai Margalit, *The Ethics of Memory* (Cambridge, MA: Harvard University Press, 2002), 82–83.
2. For the full schedule of the Yale and Slavery conference in October 2021, see "2021 Annual Conference: Yale and Slavery in Historical Perspective," Gilder Lehrman Center for the Study of Slavery, Resistance, and Abolition, MacMillan Center at Yale University, accessed August 31, 2023, https://glc.yale.edu/events/past-events/conferences/2021-annual-conference. Videos of the entire conference proceedings are also available at the website.
3. Peter Salovey, "Launching a Difficult Conversation," Freshman Address, Office of the President, Yale University, August 29, 2015, https://president.yale.edu/president/speeches/launching-difficult-conversation. The Charleston massacre led to a massive outpouring of journalism, protests over Confederate flags and monuments, and new teaching curriculums; and it forms a tragic straight line to the white supremacy march, and other backlashes, in Charlottesville, Virginia, in August 2017. See Chad Williams, Kidada E. Williams, and Keisha N. Blain, *The Charleston Syllabus: Readings on Race, Racism, and Racial Violence* (Athens: University of Georgia Press, 2016). And see David W. Blight, "Clementa Pinckney, a Martyr of Reconciliation," *Atlantic*, June 22, 2015.
4. Antony Dugdale, J. J. Fueser, and J. Celso de Castro Alves, "Yale, Slavery and Abolition," 2001, http://www.yaleslavery.org. Over time, the 2001 report has served future researchers as a valuable resource. At publication, amid the university's tercentennial celebrations and during a labor dispute between Yale and graduate students organizing a union, it was criticized by the university and a few scholars at Yale. The report was defended by other scholars and New Haven community members. For a sample of contemporary

commentary, see Jia Lynn Yang, "Yale Slavery Report Questioned by Experts," *Yale Daily News*, December 12, 2001.

5. For the Gilder Lehrman Center and its many programs, see the center's website, https://glc.yale.edu. Since it was founded in 1998—around the work of David Brion Davis and rooted in the philanthropy initially of Yale graduates Richard Gilder and Lewis Lehrman—several other such centers have emerged around the world at the University of Toronto, Brown University, the University of Hull (UK), the University of Nottingham (UK), the University of Sheffield (UK), and the University of Vancouver (Canada).
6. See R. Owen Williams, "Forgetting Slavery at Yale and Transylvania," in *Slavery and the University: Histories and Legacies*, ed. Leslie M. Harris, James T. Campbell, and Alfred L. Brophy (Athens: University of Georgia Press, 2019), 315–37; and Ayla Besemer and David Yaffe-Bellany, "Community Skeptical of Renaming Committee," *Yale Daily News*, October 27, 2016.
7. "Report of the Committee to Establish Principles on Renaming," Committee to Establish Principles on Renaming, Yale University, November 21, 2016, https://president.yale.edu/sites/default/files/files/CEPR_FINAL_12-2-16.pdf. The committee surveyed opinion on campus and among alumni, did a good deal of research in Yale archives, sought comparisons with other universities, and filmed interviews with committee members. On Grace Murray Hopper, see "Biography of Grace Murray Hopper," Office of the President, Yale University, accessed August 31, 2023, https://president.yale.edu/biography-grace-murray-hopper. The choice of Hopper as the new namesake for the residential college was, by and large, a popular decision in the various Yale communities. At the formal dedication in the college's dining hall in spring 2017, the United States Navy Band came to Yale and played "Anchors Away."
8. For the Yale-Brown conference of 2005, see "2005 Conference Overview: Repairing the Past: Confronting the Legacies of Slavery, Genocide, and Caste," Yale MacMillan Center, accessed August 31, 2023, https://glc.yale.edu/justice. On the beginning of Brown's reckoning and the Simmons quotation, see James T. Campbell, Leslie M. Harris, and Alfred L. Brophy, introduction to Harris, Campbell, and Brophy, *Slavery and the University*, 12–13. And see Mary Frances Berry, *My Face Is Black Is True: Callie House and the Struggle for Ex-Slave Reparations* (New York: Knopf, 2005).
9. Craig Steven Wilder, *Ebony and Ivy: Race, Slavery, and the Troubled History of America's Universities* (New York: Bloomsbury, 2013); Alfred L. Brophy, *University, Court, and Slave: Pro-Slavery Thought in Southern Colleges and Courts and the Coming of the Civil War* (New York: Oxford University Press, 2016). Those Yale historians would include, though hardly exclusively, David Potter, C. Vann Woodward, John W. Blassingame, David Brion Davis, Edmund S. Morgan, David Montgomery, and the legions of younger scholars they trained from the 1960s until the current day. In conjunction with scholars at the University of Wisconsin working on the Atlantic slave trade, as well as those at Johns Hopkins University and the University of Rochester who worked on colonial and antebellum America, these historians helped to build the field of slavery and abolition studies. The field then grew quickly at many other American and British universities.

10. Leslie M. Harris, "Higher Education's Reckoning with Slavery," *Academe*, Winter 2020, https://www.aaup.org/article/higher-education%E2%80%99s-reckoning-slavery. For Universities Studying Slavery, see the consortium's website, https://slavery.virginia.edu/universities-studying-slavery/. Its coordinating website is operated by Kirt von Daacke at the University of Virginia. See Rachel L. Swarns, *The 272: The Families Who Were Enslaved and Sold to Build the American Catholic Church* (New York: Random House, 2023); and Rachel L. Swarns, "My Church Was Part of the Slave Trade: This Has Not Shaken My Faith," *New York Times*, June 19, 2023.
11. Martha A. Sandweiss and Craig B. Hollander, "Princeton and Slavery: Holding the Center"; and Sven Beckert et al., "Harvard and Slavery: A Short History," in Harris, Campbell, and Brophy, *Slavery and the University*, 46–47, 227–29, 231. For the Princeton and Slavery Project, see its website, https://slavery.princeton.edu/. For the Harvard report, see Presidential Committee on Harvard and the Legacy of Slavery, *Harvard and the Legacy of Slavery* (President and Fellows of Harvard College, 2022), https://legacyofslavery.harvard.edu/report. The Harvard report provides a good deal of historical narrative and background from their recent study. Harris, Campbell, and Brophy declare in their fine introduction to *Slavery and the University* that slavery was not only for Americans of the nineteenth century the "central political, intellectual and moral question of their age" (14). They imply that it still is today for those studying universities and their pasts.
12. Deuteronomy 27:1–8; Joshua 4:9; Saint Augustine, *Confessions*, trans. Edward Bouverie Pusey (New York: Book-of-the-Month Club, 1996), 240.
13. Maurice Halbwachs, *The Collective Memory* (1925; repr., New York: Harper and Row, 1950). Histories of memory in its many mediums have appeared in waves of scholarly literature in the past few decades. Among my own favorites as most influential have been Jay Winter, *Sites of Memory, Sites of Mourning: The Great War in European Cultural History* (Cambridge: Cambridge University Press, 1995); Michael Kammen, *Mystic Chords of Memory: The Transformation of Tradition in American Culture* (New York: Knopf, 1991); Pierre Nora, "Between Memory and History: Les Lieux de Memoire," *Representations* 26 (Spring 1989): 7–25; Andreas Huyssen, *Twilight Memories: Marking Time in a Culture of Amnesia* (London: Routledge, 1995); Edward T. Linenthal, *Sacred Ground: Americans and Their Battlefields*, 2nd ed. (Urbana: University of Illinois Press, 1993); David Lowenthal, *The Past Is a Foreign Country* (New York: Cambridge University Press, 1985); and Paul Connerton, *How Societies Remember* (Cambridge: Cambridge University Press, 1990). Winter, Kammen, and Linenthal have been, over time, personal mentors to me in the field of memory studies.
14. John Lukacs, *Historical Consciousness and the Remembered Past* (1968; repr., New York: Schocken Books, 1985), 33.
15. See David W. Blight, "The Memory Boom: Why and Why Now?," in *Memory in Mind and Culture*, ed. Pascal Boyer and James V. Wertsch (Cambridge: Cambridge University Press, 2009), 240. On memory booms, see Jeffrey K. Olick, Vered Vinitzky-Seroussi, and Daniel Levy, introduction to *The Collective Memory Reader*, ed. Jeffrey K. Olick, Vered Vinitzky-Seroussi, and Daniel Levy (New York: Oxford University Press, 2011), 3–6. In 1993, while teaching on a Fulbright fellowship at the University of Munich, I visited many

Holocaust sites around Germany. On a visit to Weimar I saw that sign in the Bahnoff and spent considerable time seeing the contrasts between Goethe's magnificently preserved Garten Haus and the former Nazi concentration camp at Buchenwald, up on the heights overlooking the city.

16. Toni Morrison, "A Bench by the Road," *The World: Journal of the Unitarian Universalist Association* 3, no. 1 (January–February 1989), https://www.uuworld.org/articles/bench-road. The remarks, which the journal reproduced, were given in 1988.
17. Daniel T. Rodgers, *Age of Fracture* (Cambridge, MA: Harvard University Press, 2011), 3–6, 111–43. On the first memory boom, roughly 1890–1920, see Jay Winter, "The Memory Boom in Contemporary Historical Studies," *Raritan* 21, no. 1 (Summer 2001): 52–66.
18. William L. Kingsley, ed., *Yale College: A Sketch of Its History, with Notices of Its Several Departments, Instructors, and Benefactors, Together with Some Account of Student Life and Amusements* (New York: Holt, 1879); Lewis Sheldon Welch and Walter Camp, *Yale, Her Campus, Class-Rooms, and Athletics* (Boston: L. C. Page, 1900); Anson Phelps Stokes, *Memorials of Eminent Yale Men: A Biographical Study of Student Life and University Influences during the Eighteenth and Nineteenth Centuries*, 2 vols. (New Haven, CT: Yale University Press, 1914); Robert Dudley French, *The Memorial Quadrangle: A Book about Yale . . . Including Biographies of Forty-Three Eminent Yale Men, Written by Various Hands* (New Haven, CT: Yale University Press, 1929); Rollin G. Osterweis, *Three Centuries of New Haven, 1638–1938* (New Haven, CT: Yale University Press, 1953); Roland H. Bainton, *Yale and the Ministry: A History of Education for the Christian Ministry at Yale from the Founding in 1701* (New York: Harper and Brothers, 1957); Richard Warch, *School of the Prophets: Yale College, 1701–1740* (New Haven, CT: Yale University Press, 1973); Brooks Mather Kelley, *Yale: A History* (New Haven, CT: Yale University Press, 1974); George Wilson Pierson, *Yale: A Short History* (New Haven, CT: Yale University Libraries, 1976). A notable exception is Edwin Oviatt, *The Beginnings of Yale (1701–1726)* (New Haven, CT: Yale University Press, 1916), which notes the likely presence of the founding trustees' enslaved people at their early meetings. We sincerely hope that our own work will, along with a new Yale and Slavery website, form merely the beginning for future scholarship on this university or others.

CHAPTER 1. WAR, SLAVERY, AND CHRISTIANITY

Epigraph: John Underhill, *News from America, or a Late and Experimental Discovery of New England*, in *Collections of the Massachusetts Historical Society*, vol. 6, 3rd ser. (Boston: American Stationers' Company, 1837), 25. For readability, quotations have been modernized from the original.

1. James Noyes to John Allyn, October 1676, Yale Indian Papers Project, https://findit.library.yale.edu/yipp/catalog/digcoll:1018040.
2. Willie James Jennings, *The Christian Imagination: Theology and the Origins of Race* (New Haven, CT: Yale University Press, 2010), 61–62, 233, 241.
3. Lisa Brooks, *Our Beloved Kin: A New History of King Philip's War* (New Haven, CT: Yale University Press, 2018), 8.
4. William A. Starna, "The Pequots in the Early Seventeenth Century," in *The Pequots in Southern New England: The Fall and Rise of an American Indian Nation*, ed. Laurence M.

Hauptman and James D. Wherry (Norman: University of Oklahoma Press, 1990), 33–39; Jenny Hale Pulsipher, *Subjects unto the Same King: Indians, English and the Contest for Authority in Colonial New England* (Philadelphia: University of Pennsylvania Press, 2005), 21–23; Michael Leroy Oberg, *Dominion and Civility: English Imperialism and Native America, 1586–1685* (Ithaca, NY: Cornell University Press, 1999), 96–97, 99–102.

5. Ned Blackhawk, *The Rediscovery of America: Native Peoples and the Unmaking of U.S. History* (New Haven, CT: Yale University Press, 2023), 61–62; Pulsipher, *Subjects unto the Same King*, 12–14, 269–71.
6. On wampum, see Blackhawk, *Rediscovery of America*, 64–68; and Andrew Lipman, *The Saltwater Frontier: Indians and the Contest for the American Coast* (New Haven, CT: Yale University Press, 2015), 106–7, 110–11.
7. On disease and epidemics, see David S. Jones, *Rationalizing Epidemics: Meanings and Uses of American Indian Mortality since 1600* (Cambridge, MA: Harvard University Press, 2004), 22–25; and Blackhawk, *Rediscovery of America*, 51–52, 55–56, 62–63, 66–67.
8. Jones, *Rationalizing Epidemics*, 59–67; Brooks, *Our Beloved Kin*, 76–79; Cotton Mather, "Of Providence," in *Magnalia Christi Americana* (1702; repr., Hartford, CT: Silas Andrus and Son, 1853), 1:85; Francis Jennings, *The Invasion of America: Indians, Colonialism, and the Cant of Conquest* (Chapel Hill: University of North Carolina Press, 1975), 15.
9. Starna, "Pequots," 46; Laurence M. Hauptman, "The Pequot War and Its Legacies," in Hauptman and Wherry, *Pequots in Southern New England*, 69–75; Blackhawk, *Rediscovery of America*, 70; Underhill, *News from America*, 25, quotation also in Charles Orr, *History of the Pequot War: The Contemporary Accounts of Mason, Underhill, Vincent and Gardener* (Cleveland: Helman-Taylor, 1897), 80–81.
10. Hauptman, "Pequot War," 76; Benjamin Trumbull, *A Compendium of the Indian Wars in New England, More Particularly Such as the Colony of Connecticut Have Been Concerned* (Hartford, CT: Edwin Valentine Mitchell, 1926), 25–26, 55–56; Treaty of Hartford (Copy), September 21, 1638, 1638.09.21.00, Yale Indian Papers Project, Yale University, https://hdl.handle.net/10079/digcoll/2389. On the outbreak and character of the Pequot War, see especially Blackhawk, *Rediscovery of America*, 68–72.
11. Brooks, *Our Beloved Kin*, 1–6, 10–12; Increase Mather, *The day of trouble is near* [. . .] (Cambridge, MA: printed by Marmaduke Johnson, 1674), quoted in Jill Lepore, *The Name of War: King Philip's War and the Origins of American Identity* (New York: Knopf, 1998), 7. For the list of Indigenous peoples in this region, see Christine M. DeLucia, *Memory Lands: King Philip's War and the Place of Violence in the Northeast* (New Haven, CT: Yale University Press, 2018), 8.
12. Lipman, *Saltwater Frontier*, 200–202.
13. Lipman, 220; Lepore, *Name of War*, 173–75.
14. Lipman, *Saltwater Frontier*, 220–22; DeLucia, *Memory Lands*, 303, 320.
15. Trumbull, *Compendium of the Indian Wars*, 28–29, 50.
16. Wendy Warren, *New England Bound: Slavery and Colonization in Early America* (New York: Liveright, 2016), 6–7; Edgar J. McManus, *Black Bondage in the North* (Syracuse, NY: Syracuse University Press, 2001), 6; Chauncey W. Fowler, *The Historical Status of*

the Negro in Connecticut [...] (Charleston, SC: Walker, Evans and Cogswell, 1901), 4. On Lucretia, see Charles J. Hoadly, ed., *Records of the Colony and Plantation of New-Haven, from 1638 to 1649* (Hartford, CT: Case, Tiffany, 1857), 296.

17. See David Hackett Fischer, *African Founders: How Enslaved People Expanded American Freedom* (New York: Simon and Schuster, 2022), 41–45; and Christopher R. DeCorse, *An Archaeology of Elmina: Africans and Europeans on the Gold Coast, 1400–1900* (Washington, DC: Smithsonian Institution Press, 2001), 7.
18. Robert Hayden, "Middle Passage," from *Collected Poems of Robert Hayden*, ed. Frederick Glaysher (New York: Liveright Publishing Corporation, 1962). Used by permission of Liveright Publishing Corporation.
19. See Fischer, *African Founders*, 33–34, 51–52, 11–14.
20. Elizabeth J. Normen, ed., *African American Connecticut Explored*, with Katherine J. Harris, Stacey K. Close, and William Frank Mitchell (Middletown, CT: Wesleyan University Press, 2013), 4–7.
21. Jackson Turner Main, *Society and Economy in Colonial Connecticut* (Princeton, NJ: Princeton University Press, 2014), 177. Main has done the most extensive work on the utility of probate inventories in Connecticut, finding that they provide remarkable coverage of households across demographic groups.
22. Lorenzo Johnston Greene, *The Negro in Colonial New England* (New York: Columbia University Press, 1942), 89–93; Katherine J. Harris, "Freedom and Slavery," in Normen, *African American Connecticut Explored*, 9.
23. On Ambo, Desire, and their mother, see chapter 3. I thank Kenneth Minkema, executive editor of *The Works of Jonathan Edwards* and the Edwards Online Archive and director of the Jonathan Edwards Center at Yale Divinity School, for the story of onions from Wethersfield.
24. George Marsden, "Biography," in *The Cambridge Companion to Jonathan Edwards*, ed. Stephen J. Stein (Cambridge: Cambridge University Press, 2006), 20.
25. George Marsden, *Jonathan Edwards: A Life* (New Haven, CT: Yale University Press, 2003), 14–17.
26. Marsden, "Biography," 20–23.
27. Jonathan Edwards, *A History of the Work of Redemption*, sermon 27, in *The Works of Jonathan Edwards*, ed. Perry Miller, John E. Smith, and Harry S. Stout (New Haven, CT: Yale University Press, 1957), 9:472, 480. Also see Marsden, *Jonathan Edwards*, 258.
28. Jonathan Edwards, "To the Mohawks at the Treaty, August 16, 1751," in *The Sermons of Jonathan Edwards: A Reader*, ed. Wilson H. Kimnach, Kenneth P. Minkema, and Douglas A. Sweeney (New Haven, CT: Yale University Press, 1999), 108. Also see Marsden, *Jonathan Edwards*, 385, 452.
29. Edwards, quoted in Harry S. Stout, "Edwards the Revivalist," in Stein, *Cambridge Companion to Jonathan Edwards*, 134, 140–41; Jonathan Edwards, "Sinners in the Hands of an Angry God," in *The Sermons of Jonathan Edwards*, 57–58.
30. See Fischer, *African Founders*, 55–60.
31. William Richard Cutter, comp., *New England Families, Genealogical and Memorial: A Record of the Achievements of Her People in the Making of Commonwealths and the Founding of a Nation* (New York: Lewis Historical, 1913), 3:1366. On the people they enslaved,

see Marsden, *Jonathan Edwards*, 255; Kenneth P. Minkema, "Jonathan Edwards's Defense of Slavery," *Massachusetts Historical Review* 4 (2002): 43–44; Kenneth P. Minkema and Harry S. Stout, "The Edwardsean Tradition and the Antislavery Debate, 1740–1865," *Journal of American History* 92, no. 1 (2005): 49n6; and Marsden, *Jonathan Edwards*, 555n5. See also Kenneth P. Minkema, "Jonathan Edwards on Slavery and the Slave Trade," *William and Mary Quarterly* 54, no. 4 (1997): 823–34. For the deed of conveyance of Joseph and Sue (the sale was executed by Timothy Edwards and Timothy Dwight Jr.), see Fowler, *Historical Status*, 13–14.

32. Edwards, quoted in Minkema, "Jonathan Edwards's Defense," 40; and Minkema, "Jonathan Edwards on Slavery," 823–30.
33. Jonathan Edwards, "Personal Narrative," in Miller, Smith, and Stout, *Works of Jonathan Edwards*, 16:791.
34. *Report of the Treasurer and Associate Treasurer and Comptroller of Yale University* (New Haven, CT: Yale University, 1923), 216; Benjamin Trumbull, *A Complete History of Connecticut Civil and Ecclesiastical* (New Haven, CT: Maltby, Goldsmith, 1818), 2:301.
35. Roland H. Bainton, *Yale and the Ministry: A History of Education for the Christian Ministry at Yale from the Founding in 1701* (New York: Harper and Brothers, 1957), 1–2.

CHAPTER 2. FOUNDERS

1. All quoted in Lorenzo Johnston Greene, *The Negro in Colonial New England* (New York: Columbia University Press, 1942), 36–38, 40.
2. On the Gold Coast's transformation into a "slave coast," see Stephanie Smallwood, *Saltwater Slavery: A Middle Passage from Africa to American Diaspora* (Cambridge, MA: Harvard University Press), 9–32; and David Eltis and David Richardson, eds., *Atlas of the Transatlantic Slave Trade* (New Haven, CT: Yale University Press, 2010), 215.
3. Smallwood, *Saltwater Slavery*, 33–58; Eltis and Richardson, *Atlas*, 167.
4. Nathan Irvin Huggins, *Black Odyssey: The African American Ordeal in Slavery* (1977; repr., New York: Vintage Books, 1990), 24.
5. Ira Berlin, *Many Thousands Gone: The First Two Centuries of Slavery in North America* (Cambridge, MA: Harvard University Press, 1998). For over two hundred enslaved people identified by the Yale and Slavery Research Project, see Interlude: Names of the Enslaved in the present book.
6. Edwin Oviatt, *The Beginnings of Yale (1701–1726)* (New Haven, CT: Yale University Press, 1916), 3–20.
7. Oviatt, 24–26, 28, 35–40, 57, 71, 86–101, 144; Charles J. Hoadly, ed., *Records of the Colony and Plantation of New-Haven, from 1638 to 1649* (Hartford, CT: Case, Tiffany, 1857), 40, 210.
8. See Nancy Finlay, "A Separate Place: The New Haven Colony, 1638–1665," ConnecticutHistory.org, November 4, 2020, https://connecticuthistory.org/a-separate-place-the-new-haven-colony-1638-1665; and Leonard Bacon, *Thirteen Historical Discourses, on the Completion of Two Hundred Years, from the Beginning of the First Church in New Haven: With an Appendix* (New Haven, CT: Durrie and Peck, 1839), 388.
9. Oviatt, *Beginnings of Yale*, 31.

10. Richard Warch, *School of the Prophets: Yale College, 1701–1740* (New Haven, CT: Yale University Press, 1973), 16–31; Brooks Mather Kelley, *Yale: A History* (New Haven, CT: Yale University Press, 1974), 5–10. Chauncey is also spelled "Chauncy" in the sources.
11. Oviatt, *Beginnings of Yale*, 196.
12. Oviatt, 196. On Buckingham, see F. W. Chapman, *The Buckingham Family; or the Descendants of Thomas Buckingham, One of the First Settlers of Milford, Conn., Etc.* (Hartford, CT: Case, Lockwood and Brainard, 1872), 338; and will of Thomas Buckingham, Connecticut, U.S., Wills and Probate Records, 1609–1999, Ancestry.com. On Chauncy, see will of Israel Chauncy, Connecticut, U.S., Wills and Probate Records, 1609–1999, Ancestry.com. On Noyes, see will of James Noyes and James Noyes to John Allyn, October 1676, Yale Indian Papers Project. On Pierpont, see Craig Steven Wilder, *Ebony and Ivy: Race, Slavery, and the Troubled History of America's Universities* (New York: Bloomsbury, 2013), 121; and Connecticut, U.S., Church Record Abstracts, 1630–1920, vol. 78, pt. 2, New Haven, 499, Ancestry.com. On Pierson, see Wilder, *Ebony and Ivy*, 120.
13. On Russell, see estate of Noadiah Russell, Connecticut, U.S., Wills and Probate Records, 1609–1999, Ancestry.com. On Webb, see estate of Joseph Webb of Fairfield, October 31, 1732, Probate Records, vols. 6–8, 1717–1750, Image 639, FamilySearch.org.
14. Oviatt, *Beginnings of Yale*, 333; George Leon Walker, *History of the First Church in Hartford, 1633–1883* (Hartford, CT: Brown and Gross, 1884), 255n33; *Historical Catalogue of the First Church in Hartford, 1633–1885* (Hartford, CT: published by the Church, 1885), 242, 194, 196, 195, 188, 204, 206, 207, 191; probate records of Timothy Woodbridge and Abigail Woodbridge, Connecticut, U.S., Wills and Probate Records, 1609–1999, Ancestry.com. Also see Barbara J. Beeching, "African Americans and Native Americans in Hartford 1636–1800: Antecedents of Hartford's Nineteenth Century Black Community" (Hartford Studies Collection: Papers by Students and Faculty, 1993), 7, https://digitalrepository.trincoll.edu/hartford_papers/7; Katherine A. Hermes, "Uncovering Their History: African, African-American and Native-American Burials in Hartford's Ancient Burying Ground, 1640–1815," https://www.africannativeburialsct.org/methodology-and-process. For the enslaved people, with their values, included in the estate inventory of Abigail's first husband, Richard Lord, see Charles William Manwaring, *A Digest of the Early Connecticut Probate Records* (Hartford, CT: R. S. Peck, 1904), 2:254–55. More information about Sessions and his indenture can be found in the probate records of his parents: probate of Philip Moore Sr. in Manwaring, *Digest*, 1:488–89; probate of Ruth More in Manwaring, *Digest*, 1:574.
15. See Warch, *School of the Prophets*, 28–29, especially n45, 18–19, 24–25.
16. Samuel Sewall, *The Selling of Joseph: A Memorial*, in *The Diary of Samuel Sewall*, ed. M. Halsey Thomas (New York: Farrar, Straus and Giroux, 1973), 2:1117–21; David. W. Blight, "Samuel Sewall Writes the Selling of Joseph," in *A New Literary History of America*, ed. Greil Marcus and Werner Sollors (Cambridge, MA: Harvard University Press, 2009), 69–74.
17. Sewall, *Selling of Joseph*, 2:1118; Lawrence Towner, "The Sewall-Saffin Dialogue on Slavery," *William and Mary Quarterly* 21 (1964): 40–52; Mark A. Peterson, "The Selling of Joseph: Bostonians, Antislavery, and the Protestant International, 1689–1733," *Massachu-*

setts Historical Review 4 (2002): iv, 1–22; Wendy Warren, *New England Bound: Slavery and Colonization in Early America* (New York: Norton, 2016), 221–31.

18. Sewall, *Selling of Joseph*, 2:1119; Peterson, "The Selling of Joseph."
19. Diana Scarisbrick and Benjamin Zucker, *Elihu Yale: Merchant, Collector, and Patron* (London: Thames and Hudson, 2014), 10; Warch, *School of the Prophets*, 84–85.
20. Franklin Bowditch Dexter, *A Selection from the Miscellaneous Historical Papers of Fifty Years* (New Haven, CT: Tuttle, Morehouse and Taylor, 1918), 89–91. Also see Robert Harms, "Introduction: Indian Ocean Slavery in the Age of Abolition," 1–22, and Gwyn Campbell, "Servitude and the Changing Face of Demand for Labor in the Indian Ocean World, c. 1800–1900," 32, in *Indian Ocean Slavery in the Age of Abolition*, ed. Robert Harms, Bernard K. Freamon, and David W. Blight (New Haven, CT: Yale University Press, 2013).
21. Records of Fort St. George, Diary and Consultation Books, MS 566, Elihu Yale Collection, Manuscripts and Archives, Yale University Library; for "peon," see Box 1, Folder 4, Diary and Consultation Book, 1679–1680, 50; for "ten Slaves" to Saint Helena, see Box 1, Folder 7, Diary and Consultation Book, 1687, January 17, 1687, 8; for "famine" and "one hundred Slaves," see Box 1, Folder 7, Diary and Consultation Book, 1687, August 8, 1687, 108; for "for well secureing the slaves," see Diary and Consultation Book for 1689, October 21, 1689, 88; for "Three people were punished," see Box 1, Folder 7, Diary and Consultation Book, 1687, September 24, 1687, 149–50; for two convicted of robbery, see Box 1, Folder 8, Diary and Consultation Book, 1688, August 28, 1688, 137; for Francisco, see Box 1, Folder 9, Diary and Consultation Book for 1689, October 18, 1689, 99. Information from 1688 and 1689 are from the HathiTrust editions. For Elihu Yale's collections and wealth in so many other commodities, see Scarisbrick and Zucker, *Elihu Yale*, 57–81.
22. Joseph Yannielli, "Elihu Yale Was a Slave Trader," Digital Histories @ Yale, November 1, 2014, https://digitalhistories.yctl.org/2014/11/01/elihu-yale-was-a-slave-trader/. And see Gauri Viswanathan, "The Naming of Yale College: British Imperialism and American Higher Education," in *Cultures of United States Imperialism*, ed. Amy Kaplan and Donald E. Pease (Durham, NC: Duke University Press, 1993), 85–108. Unfortunately, even twenty-first-century scholars have repeated the inaccuracy that Yale opposed the slave trade while in Madras; see Scarisbrick and Zucker, *Elihu Yale*, 30.
23. Warch, *School of the Prophets*, 62–63, 65–67; Scarisbrick and Zucker, *Elihu Yale*, 57–80, 104; Dexter, *Selection*, 91, 93. On Ellea, see February 23, 1699, in *Records of Fort St. George Diary and Consultation Book of 1697* (Madras: printed by the Superintendent, Government Press, 1921), 16, via HathiTrust.
24. Scarisbrick and Zucker, *Elihu Yale*, 34–35. This work on Yale as collector is hagiographic, and in its lavish use of paintings of the college's namesake, the publisher crops out the image of the young African boy with a metal collar on the right side of portraits.
25. Jeremiah Dummer, "A List of Books Given to Yale College," 1712–1713, Box 4, Folder 1, RU 1154, Early Yale Documents Collection, Manuscripts and Archives, Yale University Library; "Catalogue of the Books Sent by Elihu Yale," circa 1718, Box 4, Folder 46, Early Yale Documents Collection; "An Account of Sale of Sundry Goods and Merchandizes," June 28, 1721, Box 4, Folder 9, Early Yale Documents Collection; "Donations List and

Donations from the State of Connecticut, 1700–1765," Box 370, Folder 1, Treasurer, Yale University, Records, Manuscripts and Archives, Yale University Library; Hiram Bingham, *Elihu Yale: The American Nabob of Queen Square* (New York: Dodd, Mead, 1939), 300–306, 316–35; Dummer to Pierpont quoted on 318. Scholars have often miscalculated the value of the gift, citing numbers as various as £500 and £800. Although Yale left £500 to the college in his will, it was never received, as the will was deemed invalid.

26. For research on cloth from India, see Bhasha Chakrabarti, "The Warp and the Weft of the Wealth of Yale" (unpublished paper for Slavery, Race and Yale seminar, Fall 2021, Yale University).
27. Thomas Clap, *The annals or history of Yale-College, in New-Haven, in the colony of Connecticut, from the first founding thereof, in the year 1700, to the year 1766* [. . .] (New Haven, CT: John Hotchkiss and B. Mecom, 1766), 29–30; John Steele Gordon, "Most Overrated Philanthropist," *American Heritage* 50, no. 3 (May/June 1999): 68.

INTERLUDE: NAMES OF THE ENSLAVED

1. The names included here were found in probate records, wills, baptismal and church records, town records, censuses, and, in some cases, diaries and court cases. A fuller account of sources, biographical information, relationships to enslavers, and more can be found on the Yale and Slavery Research Project website.

CHAPTER 3. WEST INDIAN TRADE, CONNECTICUT, AND THE COLLEGE

Epigraph: John Stuart Mill, *Principles of Political Economy: With Some of Their Applications to Social Philosophy* (London: John W. Parker, 1848), 2:229.

1. Thomas Tryon, *Friendly Advice to Gentlemen Planters of the East and West Indies* (London, 1700), quoted in Sidney W. Mintz, *Sweetness and Power: The Place of Sugar in Modern History* (New York: Viking, 1985), 47–48.
2. Eric Kimball, "An Essential Link in a Vast Chain: New England and the West Indies, 1700–1775" (PhD diss., University of Pittsburgh, 2009), 71–112. On the example of Boston, see Mark Peterson, *The City-State of Boston: The Rise and Fall of an Atlantic Power, 1630–1865* (Princeton, NJ: Princeton University Press, 2019), 55–81.
3. The literature on the relationship between slavery and the emergence of the Atlantic world is rich, vast, and complex, but a defining work remains that of Trinidadian scholar Eric Williams, *Capitalism and Slavery* (Chapel Hill: University of North Carolina Press, 1944).
4. James Walvin, *Sugar: The World Corrupted from Slavery to Obesity* (London: Pegasus, 2018), 101–13, 43.
5. Kimball, "Essential Link," 8, 80–81, 110–11, 98–99, 88, 92–93; Edwin Oviatt, *The Beginnings of Yale (1701–1726)* (New Haven, CT: Yale University Press, 1916), 387.
6. Philip D. Morgan, "Slavery in the British Caribbean," in *The Cambridge World History of Slavery*, vol. 3, *AD 1420–AD 1804*, ed. David Eltis and Stanley L. Engerman (New York: Cambridge University Press, 2011), 381–82.
7. "An Act for the Better Regulating the Duty of Impost upon Rhum," in *The Public Records of the Colony of Connecticut* [. . .] (Hartford, CT: Case, Lockwood and Brainard, 1872), 6:282–84.

8. On Saltonstall's involvement in Yale and Collegiate School affairs, see J. M. Poteet, "The Lordly Prelate: Gurdon Saltonstall against His Times," *New England Quarterly* 53, no. 4 (1980): 496–99; will of Gurdon Saltonstall Sr., Probate Records, 1675–1916, Connecticut, Probate Court (New London District), Probate Place: New London, Connecticut, Ancestry.com; Eliphalet Adams, *A Funeral Discourse occasioned by the* [. . .] *death of the Honourable Gurdon Saltonstall, Esq., Governour of Connecticut, etc. (Addenda from the Boston News-Letter, No. 1079, Thursday October 1. 1724.)* (New London, CT: T. Green, 1724), 39 (emphasis in original).
9. Robert P. Forbes, "Grating the Nutmeg: Slavery and Racism in Connecticut from the Colonial Era to the Civil War," *Connecticut History Review* 52, no. 2 (2013): 175. On the Abda case, see the Saltonstall quotation in Frederick Calvin Norton, "Negro Slavery in Connecticut," *Connecticut Magazine* 5 (January–December 1899): 321; Catherine Adams and Elizabeth H. Pleck, *Love of Freedom: Black Women in Colonial and Revolutionary New England* (New York: Oxford University Press, 2010), 46–49; Guocun Yang, "From Slavery to Emancipation: The African Americans of Connecticut, 1650s–1820s" (PhD diss., University of Connecticut, 1999), 235–242; and Lorenzo Johnston Greene, *The Negro in Colonial New England* (New York: Columbia University Press, 1942), 183.
10. Gurdon Saltonstall to Thomas Allen, October 6, 1755, and Thomas Allen Account Book, 1755–1758, quoted in Joseph Avitable, "The Atlantic World Economy and Colonial Connecticut" (PhD diss., University of Rochester, 2009), 167, 165.
11. Gabrielle Sevillano, "Yale, Transatlantic Trade, and Connecticut's Colonial Aristocracy" (unpublished paper for Slavery, Race and Yale seminar, Fall 2021, Yale University); Barbara W. Brown and James M. Rose, *Black Roots in Southeastern Connecticut, 1650–1900* (Detroit: Gale Research, 1980), 486, 495, 501, 532. For an exploration of slavery and the slave trade through logbooks kept by Dudley Saltonstall, grandson of the governor, see Anne Farrow, *The Logbooks: Connecticut's Slave Ships and Human Memory* (Middletown, CT: Wesleyan University Press, 2014).
12. Ebenezer Baldwin, *Annals of Yale College, from Its Foundation, to the Year 1831*, 2nd ed. (New Haven, CT: B. and W. Noyes, 1838), 307; Thomas Clap, "Account of the Cost of the New College 1748–52," Thomas Clap, President of Yale College, Records, Box 1, Folder 7, Manuscripts and Archives, Yale University Library; First Census of the United States, New Haven County, Connecticut County, 1790; Franklin Bowditch Dexter, *Biographical Sketches of the Graduates of Yale College*, vol. 2, *May, 1745–May, 1763* (New York: Henry Holt, 1896), 311–13; Franklin Bowditch Dexter, *Biographical Sketches of the Graduates of Yale College*, vol. 4, pt. 1, *July, 1778–June, 1792* (New York: Henry Holt, 1907), 151–53. For the names of some people enslaved by the Munsons, see Connecticut, U.S., Church Record Abstracts, vol. 78, pt. 2, New Haven, Ancestry.com. Aeneas or Eneas Jr. recorded the death of "his negro child," six weeks of age, on January 29, 1804; Sabina, "negro servant woman of Dr. Munson," was married on January 20, 1774, at the First Congregational Church, New Haven.
13. Dexter, *Biographical Sketches*, 2:74–75; Eben Edwards Beardsley, *The History of the Episcopal Church in Connecticut: From the Settlement of the Colony to the Death of Bishop Seabury* (New York: Hurd and Houghton, 1865), 171; estate of Enos Alling, Connecticut, U.S., Wills and Probate Records, 1609–1999, Ancestry.com; *Connecticut Gazette*,

September 3, 1760; "Honor Roll: Biographies of Notable Trinity Parishioners," Trinity on the Green, accessed June 17, 2023, https://www.trinitynewhaven.org/biographies-extended.

14. Cynthia A. Kierner, *Traders and Gentlefolk: The Livingstons of New York, 1675–1790* (Ithaca, NY: Cornell University Press, 1992), 65; Craig Steven Wilder, *Ebony and Ivy: Race, Slavery and the Troubled History of American Universities* (New York: Bloomsbury, 2013), 52.
15. "Trans-Atlantic Slave Trade Database," SlaveVoyages, accessed September 6, 2023, https://www.slavevoyages.org/voyage/database; Cathy Matson, *Merchants and Empire: Trading in Colonial New York* (Baltimore: Johns Hopkins University Press, 1998), 202–3; Kierner, *Traders and Gentlefolk*, 71–72; James G. Lydon, "New York and the Slave Trade, 1700 to 1774," *William and Mary Quarterly* 35 (1978): 388–89; Eric Foner, "Columbia and Slavery: A Preliminary Report" (Columbia University, 2016), 11, https://columbiaandslavery.columbia.edu/content/dam/cuandslavery/about/Eric-Foner-Preliminary-Report.pdf; will of Robert Livingston, New York, U.S., Wills and Probate Records, 1659–1999, Ancestry.com; will of Philip Livingston, New York, U.S., Wills and Probate Records, 1659–1999, Ancestry.com; Graham Russell Gao Hodges and Alan Edward Brown, eds., *"Pretends to Be Free": Runaway Slave Advertisements from Colonial and Revolutionary New York and New Jersey* (New York: Fordham University Press, 2019), 44.
16. Matson, *Merchants and Empire*, 191, 184; Kierner, *Traders and Gentlefolk*, 65–66; Wilder, *Ebony and Ivory*, 60–68.
17. Quoted in Matson, *Merchants and Empire*, 174; on the "paradox," see Edmund Morgan, *American Slavery, American Freedom: The Ordeal of Colonial Virginia* (New York: Norton, 1975), 375–87.
18. Robert Dudley French, comp., *The Memorial Quadrangle: A Book about Yale* (New Haven, CT: Yale University Press, 1929), 32, 398–99; Brooks Mather Kelley, *Yale: A History* (New Haven, CT: Yale University Press, 1974), 63–64; *Yale Endowments: A Description of the Various Gifts and Bequests Establishing Permanent University Funds* (New Haven, CT: Tuttle, Morehouse and Taylor, 1917), 34.
19. Wilder, *Ebony and Ivy*, 76.
20. Thomas Clap, *The annals or history of Yale-college, 1700 to 1766* (New Haven, CT: John Hotchkiss and B. Mecom, 1766), 38; George Berkeley, *A proposal for the better supplying of churches in our foreign plantations, and for converting the savage Americans to Christianity* (London: H. Woodfall, 1724), 6; Wilder, *Ebony and Ivy*, 93–95.
21. Henry M. Fuller, "Bishop Berkeley as a Benefactor of Yale," *Yale University Library Gazette* 28, no. 1 (July 1953): 16; Richard H. Popkin, "Berkeley's Influence on American Philosophy," *Hermathena* 82 (1953): 128.
22. On the people Berkeley enslaved, see Edwin Gaustad, *George Berkeley in America* (New Haven, CT: Yale University Press, 1979), 94; Alice Brayton, *George Berkeley in Newport* (Portland, ME: Anthoensen, 1954), 113. For his views on slavery, see George Berkeley, "Anniversary Sermon before the Society for the Propagation of the Gospel," in *The Works of George Berkeley, Bishop of Cloyne*, electronic ed. (Charlottesville: InteLex, 1999), 7:122; George Berkeley, "A Proposal for the Better Supplying of Churches in Our

Foreign Plantations and Berkeley's Petition," in *Works*, 7:346; and George Berkeley, "The Querist and Other Writings on Economics," in *Works*, 6:136–37. See also Michael J. Rozbicki, "To Save Them from Themselves: Proposals to Enslave the British Poor, 1698–1755," *Slavery and Abolition* 22, no. 2 (2001): 29–50; David Berman, *Berkeley: Idealism and the Man* (Oxford: Oxford University Press, 1994), 130; and Travis Glasson, "'Baptism Doth Not Bestow Freedom': Missionary Anglicanism, Slavery, and the Yorke-Talbot Opinion, 1701–30," *William and Mary Quarterly* 67, no. 2 (2010): 279–318. On the philosophical influences on proslavery thought, see, for example, Michael O'Brien, *Conjectures of Order: Intellectual Life and the American South, 1810–1860* (Chapel Hill: University of North Carolina Press, 2004).

23. Robert E. Desrochers, "Slave-for-Sale Advertisements and Slavery in Massachusetts, 1704–1781," *William and Mary Quarterly* 59, no. 3 (2002): 630. Sarah Whipple was a daughter of Abraham Redwood, a major enslaver, human trafficker, and sugar merchant with significant interests in Antigua; see Collection of Redwood Family Papers, Redwood Library and Athenaeum, Newport, RI. On Handy and Cooke, see Elaine F. Crane, "'The First Wheel of Commerce': Newport, Rhode Island and the Slave Trade, 1760–1776," *Slavery and Abolition* 1, no. 2 (1980): 178–98. For a reference to a person enslaved by McWhorter, see Robert Treat Paine to Eunice Paine, June 13, 1763, Robert Treat Paine Papers, Volume 2, Massachusetts Historical Society, https://www.masshist.org/publications/rtpp/index.php/view/RTP2d261. On Cooke's dealings with fugitives and his own financial troubles, see Wilder, *Ebony and Ivy*, 118; Susan Stanton Brayton, "Silas Cooke—a Victim of the Revolution," *Rhode Island Historical Society Collections* 31 (1938): 110–16; and S. Cooke to Aaron Lopez, October 25, 1776, Newport Historical Society. On the condition of Whitehall and other properties, see Fuller, "Bishop Berkeley," 13–14. On the income derived from the farms, see Reports on Memorial of President and Fellows to the General Assembly, October 2, 1795, Box 370, Folder 2, Treasurer, Yale University, Records (RU 151), Manuscripts and Archives, Yale University Library, with gratitude for notes provided by Harold Rose.

24. Richard Warch, *School of the Prophets: Yale College, 1701–1740* (New Haven, CT: Yale University Press, 1973), 130–36; Glenn Weaver, "Elisha Williams: The Versatile Puritan," *Connecticut Historical Society Bulletin* 53 (1988): 119–233.

25. On the Native American woman and her two children, see Oviatt, *Beginnings of Yale*, 333; and Mary H. Mitchell, "Slavery in Connecticut and Especially in New Haven," *Papers of the New Haven Colony Historical Society* 10 (1951): 288; on Ambo in the muster rolls and church records, see Henry R. Stiles, *The History of Ancient Wethersfield, Connecticut: Comprising the Present Towns of Wethersfield, Rocky Hill, and Newington, and of Glastonbury Prior to Its Incorporation in 1693: From Date of Earliest Settlement until the Present Time* (New York: Grafton, 1904), 1:404; and see their baptisms in Connecticut, U.S., Church Record Abstracts, vol. 122, pt. 3, West Hartford, Ancestry.com.

26. On Elisha Williams's business and other activities beyond Yale, see Weaver, "Elisha Williams." On enslaved people, see Elisha Williams Account Book, and transcription by Diane Cameron, Wethersfield Historical Society, Wethersfield, CT; Stiles, *History of Ancient Wethersfield*, 700–701; draft codicil of will of Elisha Williams, 1749, Box 1, Folder

11, and will of Elizabeth Williams Smith, 1776, Box 2, Folder 57, Williams Family Papers, Beinecke Rare Book and Manuscript Library, Yale University; and will of Elisha Williams, Connecticut, U.S., Wills and Probate Records, 1609–1999, Ancestry.com. And see Diane Cameron, "Circumstances of Their Lives: Enslaved and Free Women of Color Wethersfield, Connecticut, 1648–1832," *Connecticut History Review* 44, no. 2 (2005): 248–61. Research into the Williams family's slaveholding is ongoing at the Wethersfield Historical Society; we are grateful to Gillie Johnson and Diane Cameron for sharing their 2023 findings with us.

27. George M. Marsden, *Jonathan Edwards: A Life* (New Haven, CT: Yale University Press, 2003), 255, 93, 87, 146. For extensive research on the Luke family, we are indebted to Michael Morand; see also Morand's talk, "Revisiting Jethro Luke and Race and Slavery in 18th Century New Haven and Yale with Michael Morand," Mondays at Beinecke, April 25, 2022, YouTube video, 30:20, https://youtu.be/bpsJkeEAXtI.
28. Wadsworth Map, 1748, Beinecke Rare Book and Manuscript Library, Yale University; Thomas Clap, "Sundry Accounts, etc. of Pres. Clap, 1749–54," Thomas Clap Papers, Box 1, Folder 8, Yale University; Franklin Bowditch Dexter, *Historical Catalogue of the Members of the First Church of Christ in New Haven, Connecticut (Center Church) A. D. 1639–1914* (New Haven, CT, 1914), 65.
29. Louis Leonard Tucker, *Puritan Protagonist: Thomas Clap, First President of Yale College* (New York: Xlibris, 2006), 83–90, 70–72. And on Clap's presidency, described as the "tumultuous years," see Kelley, *Yale*, 49–72.
30. *The New England Historical and Genealogical Register* (Boston: Samuel G. Drake, 1853), 7:271; Vol. 129, Windham Congregational, 128, Connecticut, U.S., Church Record Abstracts, 1630–1920, Ancestry.com; runaway ad, *Connecticut Gazette*, October 7, 1758. We do not know whether the George in the advertisement is the same person listed as "Mr. President's Negro" in the accounts of Connecticut Hall. See Clap, "Account of the Cost." On George's dramatic escape, see David Waldstreicher, *Runaway America: Benjamin Franklin, Slavery, and the American Revolution* (New York: Hill and Wang, 2004), 12–17.
31. Clap, "Sundry Accounts"; Clap, "Account of the Cost." On Connecticut slaveholders, see Mitchell, "Slavery in Connecticut."
32. Clap, "Account of the Cost"; Kelley, *Yale*, 59–60.
33. Clap, "Account of the Cost."

CHAPTER 4. SLAVERY AND THE AMERICAN REVOLUTION

1. Quoted in Cedrick May, introduction to *The Collected Works of Jupiter Hammon*, ed. Cedrick May (Knoxville: University of Tennessee Press, 2017), xxiv–xxv.
2. Vincent J. Rosivach, "Three Petitions by Connecticut Negros for the Abolition of Slavery in Connecticut," *Connecticut Review* 17, no. 2 (Fall 1995): 79–92. For "Laws of Nature and of Nature's God," see the Declaration of Independence, lines 3–4, July 4, 1776. And see Edmund S. Morgan, *The Challenge of the American Revolution* (New York: Norton, 1976), 88–138.
3. On the slavery metaphor, see especially the famous quotation by the Virginian Patrick Henry: "There is no retreat but in submission and slavery! . . . Is life so dear, or peace so

sweet, as to be purchased at the price of chains and slavery? . . . As for me, give me liberty or give me death!" Patrick Henry, "Give Me Liberty or Give Me Death," March 23, 1775, Yale Law School, Avalon Project: Documents in Law, History and Diplomacy, https://avalon.law.yale.edu/18th_century/patrick.asp. Massachusetts 1774 petition quoted in Albert J. Raboteau, "The Slave Church in the Era of the American Revolution," in *Slavery and Freedom in the Age of the American Revolution*, ed. Ira Berlin and Ronald Hoffman (Urbana: University of Illinois Press, 1983), 193; J. Franklin Jameson, *The American Revolution Considered as a Social Movement* (Princeton, NJ: Princeton University Press, 1926), 9.

4. On Native Americans' varied roles and allegiances during the Seven Years' War, see Ned Blackhawk, *The Rediscovery of America: Native Peoples and the Unmaking of U.S. History* (New Haven, CT: Yale University Press, 2023), 123–38; Colin G. Calloway, *The Scratch of a Pen: 1763 and the Transformation of North America* (New York: Oxford University Press, 2006), 3–18. On slave insurrections, see, for example, Vincent Brown, *Tacky's Revolt: The Story of an Atlantic Slave War* (Cambridge, MA: Harvard University Press, 2020); and Marjoleine Kars, *Blood on the River: The Untold Story of the Berbice Slave Rebellion* (New York: New Press, 2020). The literature on the global revolutionary era, especially Haiti's pivotal role, is rich; an excellent starting place is Robin Blackburn, *The American Crucible: Slavery, Emancipation and Human Rights* (London: Verso, 2011).
5. Jane Kamensky et al., *A People and a Nation: A History of the United States*, 11th ed. (Boston: Cengage, 2019), 157–58, 160. On the myriad responses of different Indigenous peoples during this period, see Colin G. Calloway, *The American Revolution in Indian Country: Crisis and Diversity in Native American Communities* (Cambridge: Cambridge University Press, 1995); and Blackhawk, *Rediscovery of America*, 139–75.
6. Edmund S. Morgan, *The Gentle Puritan: A Life of Ezra Stiles, 1727–1795* (New York: Norton, 1962), 328.
7. Guocun Yang, "From Slavery to Emancipation: The African Americans of Connecticut, 1650s–1820s" (PhD diss., University of Connecticut, 1999), 83, 87, 197; *Connecticut Gazette*, June 15, 1763, January 5, 1764, May 9, 1779, in John Warner Barber, *Connecticut Historical Collections, Containing a General Collection of Interesting Facts, Traditions, Biographical Sketches, Anecdotes, &c. Relating to the History and Antiquities of Every Town in Connecticut, with Geographical Descriptions* (New Haven, CT: Durrie & Peck and J. W. Barber, 1836), 165–66, 178. Yang's meticulous and thoughtful work has been a valuable resource for our understanding of slavery in Connecticut.
8. Yang, "From Slavery to Emancipation," 21, 94, 98, 89.
9. Benjamin Huntington to Jabez Huntington, March 19, 1777, in "Huntington Papers: Correspondence of the Brothers Joshua and Jeremiah Huntington during the Period of the American Revolution," in *Connecticut Historical Society Collections* (Hartford, CT, 1923), 20:58, quoted in Yang, "From Slavery to Emancipation," 99. For his political offices, see Olga Tsapina, "Ebenezer Huntington Papers: Finding Aid," Huntington Library, Online Archive of California, 2002, https://oac.cdlib.org/findaid/ark:/13030/kt096n97hs/entire_text/.
10. "A Specimen Bill of Indenture," in Yang, "From Slavery to Emancipation," appendix 2B, 273.

11. Yang, "From Slavery to Emancipation," 120, 277, 319–22.
12. Yang, 299, 315, 312, 306, 302, 303, 304, 302, 309–10, 312.
13. See Morgan, *Gentle Puritan*, 22.
14. Massachusetts 1774 petition quoted in Raboteau, "Slave Church," 193; Bristol Lambee, petition, "To the Sons of Liberty in Connecticut," *Providence Gazette*, October 22, 1774 (emphasis in original).
15. Lambee, "To the Sons."
16. Kenneth P. Minkema and Harry S. Stout, "The Edwardsean Tradition and the Antislavery Debate, 1740–1865," *Journal of American History* 92, no. 1 (2005): 47–74, especially 51–52; Jonathan D. Sassi, "'This Whole Country Have Their Hands Full of Blood This Day': Transcription and Introduction of an Antislavery Sermon Manuscript Attributed to the Reverend Samuel Hopkins," *Proceedings of the American Antiquarian Society* 112, no. 1 (2004): 29–92; Sheryl A. Kujawa, "'The Path of Duty Plain': Samuel Hopkins, Sarah Osborn, and Revolutionary Newport," *Rhode Island History* 58, no. 3 (August 2000): 75–90. On "visible saints," see, for example, Edmund S. Morgan, *Visible Saints: The History of a Puritan Idea* (Ithaca, NY: Cornell University Press, 1963).
17. George E. Brooks Jr., "The Providence African Society's Sierra Leone Emigration Scheme, 1794–1795: Prologue to the African Colonization Movement," *International Journal of African Historical Studies* 7, no. 2 (1974): 185; Samuel Hopkins, *The Works of Samuel Hopkins: With a Memoir of His Life and Character* (Boston: Doctrinal Tract and Book Society, 1854), 1:138, 28, 110; Roland H. Bainton, *Yale and the Ministry: A History of Education for the Christian Ministry at Yale from the Founding in 1701* (New York: Harper and Brothers, 1957), 143.
18. Transcription of the Hopkins sermon in Sassi, "'This Whole Country,'" 91–92, 71 (emphasis in the original). Minkema and Stout dubbed this work the "independence sermon": see their "Edwardsean Tradition," 56.
19. Samuel Hopkins, *Dialogue Concerning the Slavery of Africans* (Norwich, CT: J. P. Spooner, 1776), 26, 39, 41. See David Lovejoy, "Samuel Hopkins: Religion, Slavery, and the Revolution," *New England Quarterly* 40 (June 1967): 233–34.
20. "Some Observations upon the Slavery of Negroes," *Connecticut Journal and the New-Haven Post Boy*, October 8, 15, December 17, 24, 31, 1773; Minkema and Stout, "Edwardsean Tradition," 50, 57–58; John Ericson, "When God Ceased Winking: Jonathan Edwards the Younger's Evolution on the Problem of Slavery," *Connecticut History Review* 57, no. 1 (Spring 2018): 7–32. On Jonathan Edwards Jr.'s life, see James McLachlan, *Princetonians, 1748–1768: A Biographical Dictionary* (Princeton, NJ: Princeton University Press, 1976), 492–96; and Robert L. Ferm, *Jonathan Edwards the Younger, 1745–1801: A Colonial Pastor* (Grand Rapids, MI: William B. Eerdmans, 1976). See also James D. Essig, *The Bonds of Wickedness: American Evangelicals against Slavery, 1770–1808* (Philadelphia: Temple University Press, 1982), 16, 171n40; and James Essig, "Connecticut Ministers and Slavery, 1790–1795," *Journal of American Studies* 15 (April 1981): 27–44.
21. Charles J. Hoadly, ed., *The Public Records of the Colony of Connecticut, from October, 1772, to April, 1775, Inclusive* (Hartford, CT: Case, Lockwood and Brainard Company, 1887), 329. On Rhode Island, see "An Act Prohibiting the Importation of Negroes into This Colony," reprinted in W. E. B. Du Bois, *The Suppression of the African Slave-Trade to the*

United States of America (New York: Oxford University Press, 2007), 154. Petitions in Benjamin Quarles, *The Negro in the American Revolution* (Chapel Hill: University of North Carolina Press, 1961), 44; and Alan Gilbert, *Black Patriots and Loyalists: Fighting for Emancipation in the War for Independence* (Chicago: University of Chicago Press, 2012), 107.

22. Morgan, *Gentle Puritan*, 307–10, 271–72.
23. Ezra Stiles, *The Literary Diary of Ezra Stiles, D. D., LL. D., President of Yale College*, ed. Franklin Bowditch Dexter (New York: C. Scribner's Sons, 1901), 2:272; Morgan, *Gentle Puritan*, 309.
24. Edmund Morgan, "Slavery and Freedom: The American Paradox," in *The Challenge of the American Revolution* (New York: Norton, 1976), 139–73 (originally published in *Journal of American History* 59, no. 1 [June 1972]: 5–29).
25. Morgan, *Gentle Puritan*, 124–25, 309, 51; Stiles, *Literary Diary*, 2:269, 271–72, 395, 3:50–51, 104, 327. See Leonard Bacon's handwritten notes in *Catalogue of the Members of the First Church in New Haven, from March 1, 1758, to May 1, 1847: To Which Are Prefixed the Profession of Faith, Covenant and Standing Rules of the Church* (New Haven, CT: B.L. Hamlen, 1847). Bacon wrote that Newport had been purchased at Cape Mount in present-day Liberia, had been a member of the church, and had died in 1830.
26. Brooks, "Providence African Society's"; Ezra Stiles and Samuel Hopkins, "To the Public" (Newport, RI: [printed by Solomon Southwick], 1776); Stiles, *Literary Diary*, 1:363–67, 486, 489, 2:378, 3:59, 210, 327, 400, 402, 431, 449, 494, 504; James T. Campbell, *Songs of Zion: The African Methodist Episcopal Church in the United States and South Africa* (New York: Oxford University Press, 1995), 65–66; David Brion Davis, *The Problem of Slavery in the Age of Revolution* (Ithaca, NY: Cornell University Press, 1975), 218n6.
27. Kelley, *Yale*, 73–74; Judith Ann Schiff, "Naphtali Daggett: Pastor, Yale President, Sniper," *Yale Alumni Magazine*, July–August 2006; estate of Naphtali Daggett, Connecticut, U.S., Wills and Probate Records, 1609–1999, Ancestry.com.
28. Kelley, *Yale*, 83–89.
29. Amy Athey McDonald, "American Revolution History Made Tangible in Yale Collections," YaleNews, June 30, 2015, https://news.yale.edu/2015/06/30/american-revolution-history-made-tangible-yale-collections.
30. *Connecticut Journal*, February 3, 1779, quoted in Morgan, *Gentle Puritan*, 293, 331.
31. Stiles, *Literary Diary*, 2:351–53; Schiff, "Naphtali Daggett."
32. Stiles, *Literary Diary*, 2:353–57.
33. Stiles, 2:353–54; Naphtali Daggett, "Account of Treatment He Received from the Enemy," sworn July 26, 1779, reprinted in Barber, *Connecticut Historical Collections*, 174–75; Schiff, "Naphtali Daggett."
34. Stiles, *Literary Diary*, 2:356–57.
35. Quarles, *Negro*, 68–93, 19–20; Woody Holton, *Liberty Is Sweet: The Hidden History of the American Revolution* (New York: Simon and Schuster, 2021), 426; Maya Jasanoff, *Liberty's Exiles: American Loyalists in the Revolutionary World* (New York: Alfred A. Knopf, 2011); Kamensky et al., *People and a Nation*, 158, 161.
36. Kamensky et al., *People and a Nation*, 165–66; Quarles, *Negro*, 73; John Trumbull, *The Battle of Bunker's Hill, June 17, 1775*, 1786, oil on canvas, Yale University Art Gallery, New

Haven; Emanuel Leutze, *Washington Crossing the Delaware*, 1851, oil on canvas, Metropolitan Museum of Art, New York.

37. Quarles, *Negro*, 71–72; "Muster Roll of African Americans in the 6CR," 6th Connecticut Regiment, last updated 2020, https://www.6thconnecticut.org/blank-c1bxl, compiled from *Connecticut's Black Solders, 1775–1783*, by David O. White (Chester, CT: Pequot, 1973), 17–19.
38. White, *Connecticut's Black Soldiers*, 22, 27; Trumbull, *Battle of Bunker's Hill*; "Asaba (Grosvenor)," National Park Service, last updated August 11, 2021, https://www.nps.gov/people/tg-asaba.htm. Although the Black man in the painting was previously identified as being, potentially, Peter Salem, David O. White and the National Park Service both claim that this is unlikely; see "Asaba (Grosvenor)"; and "*Lieutenant Thomas Grosvenor (1744–1825) and His Negro Servant*, c. 1797, John Trumbull," Slavery and Portraiture in 18th-Century Atlantic Britain, Yale Center for British Art, accessed September 6, 2023, https://interactive.britishart.yale.edu/slavery-and-portraiture/299/lieutenant-thomas-grosvenor-1744-1825-and-his-negro-servant. On Hemingway, see Judith Ann Schiff, "Yale's First Student," *Yale Alumni Magazine*, May–June 2004, http://archives.yalealumnimagazine.com/issues/2004_05/old_yale.html.
39. Robert Ewell Greene, *Black Courage, 1775–1783: Documentation of Black Participation in the American Revolution* (Washington, DC: National Society of the Daughters of the American Revolution, 1984), 29, 37, 41, 47–48, 59, 69, 73, 79; Gilbert, *Black Patriots and Loyalists*, 106–7. And see Duplex's pension and extensive documentary research related to the extended Duplex family here: "Duplex Family Genealogy," Tompkins County NYGenWeb Site, accessed June 29, 2023, http://tompkins.nygenweb.net/Genie/duplex/index.htm.
40. Curtis Patton, "Leadership and Race at Yale, 1854–1954," reported in "Talk Recounts Experience of Yale's First Black Graduates," *YaleNews*, April 24, 2009; Ronald E. Mickens, ed., *Edward Bouchet: The First African-American Doctorate* (Hackensack, NJ: World Scientific, 2002), 6, 8; White, *Connecticut's Black Soldiers*, 4; Daryl Keith Daniels, "African-Americans at the Yale University School of Medicine: 1810–1960" (master's thesis, Yale University, 1991), 25–36; Ariel Kaminer, "Discovery Leads Yale to Revise Chapter of Its Black History," *New York Times*, February 28, 2014.
41. Mark David Hall, *Roger Sherman and the American Republic* (New York: Oxford University Press, 2010), 82–83, 91; White, *Connecticut's Black Soldiers*, 21. And see Quarles, *Negro*, 184; and Arabas v. Ivers, 1 Root 92 (Conn. Super. Ct. 1784), in *Connecticut Superior Court Records*, Connecticut State Library, 24:7, 11–12.
42. Benjamin Quarles, "The American Revolution as a Black Declaration of Independence," in Berlin and Hoffman, *Slavery and Freedom*, 301.
43. David Menschel, "Abolition without Deliverance: The Law of Connecticut Slavery 1784–1848," *Yale Law Journal* 111, no. 1 (2001): 183–84, 187–91, 220; Peter P. Hinks, "Gradual Emancipation Reflected the Struggle of Some to Envision Black Freedom," ConnecticutHistory.org, January 2, 2020, https://connecticuthistory.org/gradual-emancipation-reflected-the-struggle-of-some-to-envision-black-freedom.
44. Rosivach, "Three Petitions."
45. Jonathan Edwards Jr., *The Injustice and Impolicy of the Slave Trade and Slavery of Africans: Illustrated in a Sermon Preached before the Connecticut Society for the Promotion of*

Freedom, and for the Relief of Persons Unlawfully Holden in Bondage (New Haven, CT: Thomas and Samuel Green, 1791), 4, 8–10, 13–15, 23, 27, 29.

46. Edwards, 33–36. Also see Minkema and Stout, "Edwardsean Tradition," 57–58.
47. On what one historian calls "a revolution in favor of government" following the war's end, see Holton, *Liberty Is Sweet*, 517–37.
48. Morgan, *Gentle Puritan*, 252–61, 456–60; and see Ezra Stiles, *A History of Three of the Judges of King Charles I . . .* (Hartford, CT: Printed by Elisha Babcock, 1794).
49. Morgan, *Gentle Puritan*, 377–78, 420–23.
50. Cedrick May and Julie McCown, "'An Essay on Slavery': An Unpublished Poem by Jupiter Hammon," *Early American Literature* 48, no. 2 (2013): 457–71. Also see Jupiter Hammon, *America's First Negro Poet: The Complete Works of Jupiter Hammon of Long Island*, ed. Stanley Austin Ransom (Port Washington, NY: Associated Faculty Press, 1983); and Sondra A. O'Neale, *Jupiter Hammon and the Biblical Beginnings of African American Literature* (Metuchen, NJ: Scarecrow, 1993). Neither of the authors of these latter works could have known about the discovery in 2011 of "An Essay on Slavery."
51. May and McCown, "'Essay on Slavery,'" 457–58.
52. May and McCown, 465–71.

INTERLUDE: GRADUAL EMANCIPATION IN CONNECTICUT

Epigraph: Jupiter Hammon, "A Dialogue, intitled, The Kind Master and the Dutiful Servant," in *An evening's improvement. Shewing, the necessity of beholding the Lamb of God.: To which is added, a dialogue, entitled, The kind master and dutiful servant* (ca. 1778), Evans Early Imprint Collection, https://quod.lib.umich.edu/e/evans/N35063.0001.001/1:3?rgn=div1;view=fulltext.

1. Patricia Grandjean, "City on a Hillhouse," *Daily Nutmeg*, August 22, 2014, https://dailynutmeg.com/2014/08/22/james-hillhouse-city; Judith Ann Schiff, "James Hillhouse: For New Haven, for Country, and for Yale," *Yale Alumni Magazine*, October 2001, http://archives.yalealumnimagazine.com/issues/01_10/old_yale.html. On William Lanson, see Katherine J. Harris, *William Lanson: Triumph and Tragedy: Entrepreneur, Political and Social Activist, Black King (Governor), Contractor on Long Wharf and the Farmington Canal Projects* (New Haven, CT: Amistad Committee, 2010).
2. Leonard Bacon, *Sketch of the Life and Public Services of Hon. James Hillhouse of New Haven: With a Notice of His Son, Augustus Lucas Hillhouse* (New Haven, 1860), 16–17; Don Edward Fehrenbacher, *Slavery, Law, and Politics: The Dred Scott Case in Historical Perspective* (New York: Oxford University Press, 1981), 47–48. For a more detailed explanation of the various "Hillhouse amendments" and their fate in Congress, see Sean Wilentz, *No Property in Man: Slavery and Antislavery at the Nation's Founding* (Cambridge, MA: Harvard University Press, 2008), 175–81.
3. On the Lloyd family slaveholding, including transcriptions of these wills, see "1687–1787. Slave Life at Lloyd Manor," Papers of the Lloyd Family of the Manor of Queens Village, Lloyd's Neck, Long Island, NY, 1654–1826, New York Historical Society, Collections 1927, https://robcanobbio.files.wordpress.com/2020/01/1687-1787.lloyd-manor.pdf; and James Hillhouse to Abigail [Lloyd Cogswell], March 3, 1779, Box 1, Folder 4, Hillhouse Family Papers, Manuscripts and Archives, Yale University Library.

4. For mentions of other enslaved and free laborers working for the Hillhouses, see James Hillhouse to Rebecca Hillhouse, February 4, 1795, Box 1, Folder 10; Rebeca Hillhouse to James Hillhouse, February 9, 1795, Box 1, Folder 10; Rebecca Hillhouse to James Hillhouse, January 12, 1800, Box 1, Folder 12; and Rebecca Hillhouse to James Hillhouse, April 27, 1800, Box 1, Folder 13, Hillhouse Family Papers.
5. Karen Kauffman, "James and Rebecca Hillhouse: Public and Private Commitments in the Early Republic," *Connecticut History* 38, no. 1 (Fall 1997–Spring 1999): 106; *Woolsey Papers: Letters of Rebecca Woolsey, 1783–1785* (Champlain, NY: Moorsfield, 1929), 9–10.
6. *Vital Records of New Haven, 1649–1850, Part I* (Hartford: Connecticut Society of the Order of the Founders and Patriots of America, 1917), 420; "1687–1787. Slave Life at Lloyd Manor."
7. David Menschel, "Abolition without Deliverance: The Law of Connecticut Slavery 1784–1848," *Yale Law Journal* 111, no. 1 (2001): 186–87 passim; Peter P. Hinks, "Gradual Emancipation Reflected the Struggle of Some to Envision Black Freedom," ConnecticutHistory.org, January 2, 2020, https://connecticuthistory.org/gradual-emancipation-reflected-the-struggle-of-some-to-envision-black-freedom; Connecticut, U.S., Church Record Abstracts, 1630–1920, vol. 78, pt. 2, New Haven, Ancestry.com; Thomas Day, Enoch Perkins, and John Treadwell, eds., *The Public Statute Laws [of] the [State of] Connecticut* (Hartford, CT: Hudson and Goodwin, 1808), bk. 1, 625.
8. Judith Cocks to James Hillhouse, March 8, 1795, Box 1, Folder 10, Hillhouse Family Papers. On the Woodbridges, see Meg Hixon, Dudley Woodbridge Papers finding aid, Clements Library, University of Michigan, November 2011, https://quod.lib.umich.edu/c/clementsead/umich-wcl-M-2662a25woo?id=navbarbrowselink;view=text; and Louise Rau, "Lucy Backus Woodbridge, Pioneer Mother: January 31, 1757–October 6, 1817," *Ohio History Journal* 44, no. 4 (October 1935): 405–42.
9. Rau, "Lucy Backus Woodbridge," 434.

CHAPTER 5. YALE IN THE EARLY REPUBLIC

Epigraph: William Grimes, *Life of William Grimes, the Runaway Slave*, ed. William L. Andrews and Regina E. Mason (New York: Oxford University Press, 2008), 103.
1. Robert Ewell Greene, *Black Courage, 1775–1783: Documentation of Black Participation in the American Revolution* (Washington, DC: National Society of the Daughters of the American Revolution, 1984), 14, 22, 30–31, 32, 37, 38, 41, 59–60, 65, 73, 75, 79–82, 101, 105. Also see Alan Gilbert, *Black Patriots and Loyalists: Fighting for Emancipation in the War for Independence* (Chicago: University of Chicago Press, 2012), 106–9.
2. Brian Baaki, "Circulating the Black Rapist," *New England Quarterly* 90, no. 1 (March 2017): 37, 40–41, 44; Richard Slotkin, "Narratives of Negro Crime in New England, 1675–1800," *American Quarterly* 25, no. 1 (1973): 20, 22.
3. Lawrence B. Goodheart, *The Solemn Sentence of Death: Capital Punishment in Connecticut* (Amherst: University of Massachusetts Press, 2011), 80, 91–96.
4. Ezra Stiles, *The Literary Diary of Ezra Stiles, D. D., LL. D., President of Yale College*, ed. Franklin Bowditch Dexter (New York: C. Scribner's Sons, 1901), 3:516–17;

Edmund S. Morgan, *Gentle Puritan: A Life of Ezra Stiles, 1727–1795* (New York: Norton, 1962), 461.

5. Chad D. Lower, "The Political Ideology of Connecticut's Standing Order" (PhD diss., Kent State University, 2013), 84–94; Kenneth Silverman, *Timothy Dwight* (New York: Twayne, 1969), 81–114; Charles E. Cunningham, *Timothy Dwight, 1752–1817* (New York: Macmillan, 1942), 173–76.
6. Dwight to Hillhouse quoted in Robert J. Imholt, "Timothy Dwight, Federalist Pope of Connecticut," *New England Quarterly* 73, no. 3 (September 2000): 405.
7. Lower, "Political Ideology," 84–94. Also see Stephen E. Berk, *Calvinism versus Democracy: Timothy Dwight and the Origins of Evangelical Orthodoxy* (Hamden, CT: Archon, 1974).
8. Ralph Henry Gabriel, *Religion and Learning at Yale: The Church of Christ in the College and University, 1757–1957* (New Haven, CT: Yale University Press, 1958), 57; Timothy Dwight to his son, March 31, 1800, Box 1, Folder 2, Dwight Family Papers, Manuscripts and Archives, Yale University Library.
9. Bond for Naomi (1788), Box 1, Folder 1, Dwight Family Papers, Manuscripts and Archives, Yale University Library. The Fairfield registrations are reproduced in Lorraine Cook White and Nancy E. Schott, eds., *The Barbour Collection of Connecticut Town Vital Records*, vol. 12, *Fairfield 1639–1850, Farmington 1645–1850* (Baltimore: Genealogical Publishing, 1998), 47.
10. Timothy Dwight, *Greenfield Hill: a poem in seven parts* (New York: Childs and Swaine, 1794), 36–37. See James Essig, "Connecticut Ministers and Slavery 1790–1795," *Journal of American Studies* 15, no. 1 (1981): 30–32. And see Larry Tise, *Proslavery: A History of the Defense of Slavery in America, 1701–1840* (Athens: University of Georgia Press, 1987), 210–11.
11. Tise, *Proslavery*, 211–12; Timothy Dwight, *The Duty of Americans, at the Present Crisis, Illustrated in a Discourse, Preached on the Fourth of July, 1798* (New Haven, CT: Thomas and Samuel Green, 1798), 18.
12. Timothy Dwight, *A Discourse, in Two Parts, Delivered August 20, 1812, on the National Fast, in the Chapel of Yale College* (New Haven, CT: Howe and Deforest, 1812), 4; Brooks Mather Kelley, *Yale: A History* (New Haven, CT: Yale University Press, 1974), 138–39; Vernon Louis Parrington, ed., *The Connecticut Wits* (New York: Harcourt, Brace, 1926), xl.
13. Timothy Dwight, *Statistical Account of the City of New-Haven* (New Haven, CT: printed and sold by Walter and Steele, 1811), 44.
14. Timothy Dwight, *Remarks on the Review of Inchiquin's Letters* (1815), quoted in Tise, *Proslavery*, 217.
15. Angela Lakwete, *Inventing the Cotton Gin: Machine and Myth in Antebellum America* (Baltimore: Johns Hopkins University Press, 2003), 47–71; Eric Herschthal, *The Science of Abolition: How Slaveholders Became the Enemies of Progress* (New Haven, CT: Yale University Press, 2021), 137–39.
16. For this, the traditional narrative of Whitney's invention, see James A. B. Scherer, *Cotton as a World Power: A Study in the Economic Interpretation of History* (New York: Frederick A. Stokes, 1916), 158–67. Others are skeptical of Whitney's account; see Lakwete, *Inventing the Cotton Gin*, 54–60.

17. Lakwete, *Inventing the Cotton Gin*, 40–41, 48–49, 57–58, 64–65, 76, viii; Herschthal, *Science of Abolition*, 137–38; Sven Beckert, *Empire of Cotton: A Global History* (New York: Vintage Books, 2014), 104.
18. For the numbers of slavery's expansion, see J. David Hacker, "From '20. and Odd' to 10 Million: The Growth of the Slave Population in the United States," *Slavery and Abolition* 41, no. 4 (2020): 840–55.
19. Chandos Michael Brown, *Benjamin Silliman: A Life in the Young Republic* (Princeton, NJ: Princeton University Press, 1990), 89, 266–68, xiv, 305–7, xiii.
20. Brown, 32, 34, 36, 88, and, for the Silliman quotation about Ely, 120. Poem quoted in Herschthal, *Science of Abolition*, 134.
21. George Park Fisher, *Life of Benjamin Silliman, M D., LL., D., Late Professor of Chemistry, Mineralogy, and Geology in Yale College, Chiefly from His Manuscript Reminiscences, Diaries, and Correspondence* (New York: Charles Scribner, 1866), 1:22, quoted in Brown, *Benjamin Silliman*, 164.
22. Fisher, *Life of Benjamin Silliman*, 2:296, 1:22.
23. Kelley, *Yale*, 136; Herschthal, *Science of Abolition*, 135–37; Wilmarth S. Lewis, *The Yale Collections* (New Haven, CT: Yale University Press, 1946), 27–28; some donations recorded in Ebenezer Baldwin, *Annals of Yale College, from Its Foundation, to the Year 1831*, 2nd ed. (New Haven, CT: B. and W. Noyes, 1838), 319. On John Elliott or Elliot, see 1790 Census, Guilford, New Haven, Connecticut, Series M637, Roll 1, p. 108, image 202, Family History Library Film 0568141.
24. Herschthal, *Science of Abolition*, 139–40. And see Robert Elder, *Calhoun: American Heretic* (New York: Basic Books, 2021), 33, 41–43.
25. See Herschthal, *Science of Abolition*, 140–42.
26. Quoted in Herschthal, 141–42. Herschthal's analysis and research have provided this fascinating new angle on Silliman's ambivalent but forthright work with enslavers.
27. See the City Directories for New Haven, Ancestry.com. Park was listed variously as a caterer or janitor in the 1860s and 1870s. In 1853 and 1854, he was listed as "col'd, sexton, chem. lecture room." In 1885, he was listed as "caterer and janitor, Hopkins Grammar School." See Robert Austin Warner, *New Haven Negroes: A Social History* (New Haven, CT: Yale University Press, 1940), 185. When Park died in 1895, the newspaper stated that, in addition to working for the Sillimans, he had served as the janitor for Skull and Bones for over twenty years. See "Funeral of Robert Park," *New Haven Register*, September 21, 1895. In contrast to his absence from scholarship on Silliman, the Black scholar (and Yale graduate) William H. Ferris included Park among his "history-makers," writing, "Mr. Parks [*sic*] . . . was a mathematician and an astronomer." Ferris was a native of New Haven and included many local figures in his book. See William Henry Ferris, *The African Abroad, or, His Evolution in Western Civilization: Tracing His Development under Caucasian Milieu* (New Haven, CT: Tuttle, Morehouse and Taylor, 1913), 2:699.
28. On Silliman's reputation, see Margaret W. Rossiter, "Benjamin Silliman and the Lowell Institute: The Popularization of Science in Nineteenth-Century America," *New England Quarterly* 44, no. 4 (1971): 603.
29. Fisher, *Life of Benjamin Silliman*, 1:343–47.

30. Fisher, 1:359.
31. Rossiter, "Benjamin Silliman," 603, 605. Ralph Waldo Emerson believed that Silliman had received more than $3,000 for giving fifteen or sixteen lectures in Boston in 1835. Ralph Waldo Emerson, *The Journals and Miscellaneous Notebooks of Ralph Waldo Emerson* (Cambridge, MA: Harvard University Press, 1966), 6:242n19. These are significant sums. By one estimate, the gift of $1,000 to Silliman's daughter in 1835 would be the equivalent of over $34,000 today. See "CPI Inflation Calculator," Alioth Finance, accessed December 14, 2022, https://www.officialdata.org; "Guide to the Silliman Family Papers," May 1973, Manuscripts and Archives, Yale University Library.
32. Andrew Dickson White, *An Address Delivered at the Unveiling of the Statue of Benjamin Silliman at Yale College, June 24, 1884* (Ithaca, NY: Andrus and Church, 1885), 15; "The Late Mrs. Bassett," *New Haven Evening Register*, August 24, 1895; Amos Gerry Beman Scrapbooks, vol. 3, 93, 240, Yale Collection of American Literature, Beinecke Rare Book and Manuscript Library. And see chapter 10.
33. Kelley, *Yale*, 138; White, *Address*, 13–14.
34. Elder, *Calhoun*, 35–36; on concurrent majority theory, see 482–90.
35. Elder, 61–82, 290, 443; David M. Potter, *The Impending Crisis, 1848–1861* (New York: Harper, 1963), 98. Elder's recent biography is an important contribution to our understanding of Calhoun in his own time and his ongoing legacy in our own.
36. Elder, *Calhoun*, 335–43, 546. On "Calhoundom," see "Is the Constitution Pro-slavery: A Debate between Frederick Douglass, Charles C. Burleigh, Gerrit Smith, Parker Pillsbury, Samuel Ringgold Ward, and Stephen S. Foster, Syracuse, NY, Jan. 17, 1850," in *The Frederick Douglass Papers*, ed. John W. Blassingame et al. (New Haven, CT: Yale University Press, 1982), ser. 1, vol. 2, p. 228.
37. Joanne Pope Melish, *Disowning Slavery: Gradual Emancipation and "Race" in New England, 1780–1860* (Ithaca, NY: Cornell University Press, 1998), 189–93; Nicholas Guyatt, *Providence and the Invention of the United States, 1707–1876* (Cambridge: Cambridge University Press, 2007), 183–94.
38. Melish, *Disowning Slavery*, 192. On the formation of the ACS, see Paul J. Polgar, *Standard-Bearers of Equality: America's First Abolition Movement* (Chapel Hill: University of North Carolina Press, 2019), 214–36.
39. Jedidiah Morse, *A Report to the Secretary of War of the United States, on Indian Affairs* (New Haven, CT: S. Converse, 1822), 11–13, 65–66, 82; Guyatt, *Providence and the Invention*, 174–77. On Morse's antislavery beliefs, see Joseph W. Phillips, *Jedidiah Morse and New England Congregationalism* (New Brunswick, NJ: Rutgers University Press, 1983), 182–86.
40. Anson Phelps Stokes, *Memorials of Eminent Yale Men*, vol. 1, *Religion and Letters* (New Haven, CT: Yale University Press, 1914), 69; Peter Vroom, "Address to the New Jersey Colonization Society" (1827) and Gurley quoted in Guyatt, *Providence and the Invention*, 184, 193. On Gurley, also see Polgar, *Standard-Bearers of Equality*, 250–51; and Hugh Davis, *Leonard Bacon: New England Reformer and Antislavery Moderate* (Baton Rouge: Louisiana State University Press, 1998), 1–5, 56.
41. David Brion Davis, *The Problem of Slavery in the Age of Emancipation* (New York: Alfred A. Knopf, 2014), 160; Hugh Davis, *Leonard Bacon*, x; Benjamin Silliman, "Some

Causes of the National Anxiety. An Address Delivered in the Centre Church in New Haven, July 4th, 1832," *The African Repository, and Colonial Journal* VIII (August 1832): 172–73; Fisher, *Life of Benjamin Silliman*, 2:45, 47.

42. Leonard Bacon, *A Plea for Africa, Delivered in New Haven, July 4, 1825* (New Haven, CT: T. G. Woodward, 1825), 10–18; Bacon, "Anti-colonizationism in Old Times," quoted in Guyatt, *Providence and the Invention*, 188.
43. Resolutions reprinted in William Lloyd Garrison, *Thoughts on African Colonization* [...] (Boston: Garrison and Knapp, 1832), pt. 2, 30–31.
44. David Brion Davis, *Problem of Slavery*, 162.
45. Petition quoted in Warner, *New Haven Negroes*, 51. Also see Guyatt, *Providence and the Invention*, 203–7. On Cuffe, see Henry Louis Gates Jr. and Evelyn Brooks Higginbotham, eds., *African American Lives* (New York: Oxford University Press, 2004), 200–202.
46. Frederick Douglass, "The Colonizationist Revival: An Address Delivered in Boston, MA, on 31 May 1849"; Frederick Douglass, "Henry Clay and Colonization Cant, Sophistry, and Falsehood: An Address Delivered in Rochester, New York on 2 February 1851"; and Frederick Douglass, "Persecution on Account of Faith, Persecution on Account of Color: An Address Delivered in Rochester, New York, on 26 January 1861," in *Douglass Papers*, ser. 1, vol. 2, pp. 205–6, 309, 311, 313, 318, 322.
47. Grimes, *Life of William Grimes*, 30, 30n3, 33, 34–36, 50, 73, 114. Andrews has written the most careful and trenchant literary critique of the Grimes narrative: William L. Andrews, introduction to *Life of William Grimes*, 3–26.
48. Grimes, *Life of William Grimes*, 82–86.
49. Grimes, 85–91, 94, 97, 138, and chronology, 113–17.
50. Grimes, 95–98.
51. See the correspondence for the self-purchase agreement, all reprinted in the photos and images section of Grimes, 112–28; and Andrews, introduction to *Life of William Grimes*, 5.
52. Grimes, *Life of William Grimes*, 41, 55, 65, 67, 80–81; Andrews, introduction to *Life of William Grimes*, 13–14.
53. Andrews, introduction to *Life of William Grimes*, 20, 22–23; Grimes, *Life of William Grimes*, 103.
54. William Grimes, conclusion to 1855 edition, in *Life of William Grimes*, 104–8.
55. Obituary in *Palladium* (New Haven), August 21, 1865, quoted in Grimes, *Life of William Grimes*, 105, 116.
56. Henry Taylor Blake, *Chronicles of New Haven Green from 1638 to 1862: A Series of Papers Read before the New Haven Colony Historical Society* (New Haven, CT: Tuttle, Morehouse and Taylor, 1898), 33; "The Final Sale of Slaves," online exhibit, New Haven Museum, June 19, 2020, https://www.newhavenmuseum.org/museumcollections/online-exhibitions/micro-histories/the-final-sale-of-slaves; Adrienne Joy Burns in "A Reckoning with Our Past," *Yale Alumni Magazine*, January–February 2022, https://yalealumnimagazine.com/articles/5450-a-reckoning-with-our-past?page=6.
57. Neil Hogan, "A Black Journalist Views Early 19th Century Connecticut," *Journal of the New Haven Colony Historical Society* 35, no. 1 (Fall 1988): 29–46.

58. Quoted in Hogan, 34–36. On "self-improvement" and Northern free Black communities, see James Oliver Horton and Lois E. Horton, *In Hope of Liberty: Culture, Community and Protest among Northern Free Blacks, 1700–1860* (New York: Oxford University Press, 1997), chaps. 4–6.
59. Quoted in Hogan, "Black Journalist," 36–37.

CHAPTER 6. THE 1831 BLACK COLLEGE

Epigraph: Minutes and Proceedings of the First Annual Convention of the People of Colour, Held by Adjournments in the City of Philadelphia, from the Sixth to the Eleventh of June, Inclusive, 1831 (Philadelphia: published by order of the Committee of Arrangements, 1831), 15, https://omeka.coloredconventions.org/items/show/72.

1. "Act for Liberty to Erect a Collegiate School, 1701," reproduced in *The Yale Corporation Charter and Legislation* (New Haven, CT: printed for the president and fellows, Yale University, 1976), 4–5, https://www.yale.edu/sites/default/files/files/University-Charter.pdf.
2. Henry Peck, *The New Haven State House with Some Account of the Green: And Various Matters of Historical and Local Interest, Gathered from Many Sources* (New Haven, CT: H. Peck and G. H. Coe, 1889), 15.
3. The documentary evidence surrounding the proposed Black college is rich, and the story has been known to historians. See Robert A. Gibson, "A Deferred Dream: The Proposal for a Negro College in New Haven, 1831," *Journal of the New Haven Colony Historical Society* 37, no. 2 (1991): 22–29; Hilary J. Moss, "'Cast Down on Every Side': The Ill-Fated Campaign to Found an 'African College' in New Haven," *Connecticut Explored*, Summer 2017, https://www.ctexplored.org/cast-down-on-every-side-the-ill-fated-campaign-to-found-an-african-college-in-new-haven/; Hilary J. Moss, "Education's Inequity: Opposition to Black Higher Education in Antebellum Connecticut," *History of Education Quarterly* 46, no. 1 (Spring 2006): 16–35; and James Brewer Stewart, "The New Haven Negro College and the Meanings of Race in New England, 1776–1870," *New England Quarterly* 76, no. 3 (September 2003): 323–55.
4. Moss, "Education's Inequity," 26; "Table 6. Population of the 90 Urban Places: 1830," U.S. Bureau of the Census, June 15, 1998, https://www2.census.gov/library/working-papers/1998/demographics/pop-twps0027/tab06.txt; Kathy Leonard Czepiel, "Wooded Path," *Daily Nutmeg*, June 8, 2020, https://dailynutmeg.com/2020/06/08/sachems-wood-science-hill-wooded-path.
5. Robert Austin Warner, *New Haven Negroes: A Social History* (New Haven, CT: Yale University Press, 1940), 301. On suffrage restrictions and the Stanley and Lanson petition, see Katherine J. Harris, "'No Taxation without Representation': Black Voting in Connecticut," *Connecticut Explored*, Spring 2016, https://www.ctexplored.org/no-taxation-without-representation-voting-petitions-in-connecticut. On social and political organizing within New Haven's Black community, see Warner, *New Haven Negroes*. On Bias and Margaret Stanley, who left a substantial estate to support church and community efforts when they died, see Mike Cummings, "Archive illuminates New Haven's Bias Stanley, a 19th-Century Civil Rights Advocate," YaleNews, April 18, 2023, https://news.yale.edu/2023/04/18/illuminating-new-havens-bias-stanley-19th-century-civil-rights-advocate-1.

6. George W. Pierson, *A Yale Book of Numbers: Historical Statistics of the College and University 1701–1976* ([New Haven, CT]: Yale University, 1983), 4; Johann N. Neem, "Liberal Education Confronts the Rise of Democracy: Yale's *Reports* of 1828," *History of Humanities* 4, no. 2 (2019): 401–22. See also Michael S. Pak, "The Yale Report of 1828: A New Reading and New Implications," *History of Education Quarterly* 48, no. 1 (2008): 30–57; A. L. Chapin, "Yale the Mother of Colleges," in *Yale College, a Sketch of Its History, with Notices of Its Several Departments, Instructors, and Benefactors, Together with Some Account of Student Life and Amusements, by Various Authors*, ed. William L. Kingsley (New York: Holt, 1879), 1:411–14.
7. "The Meeting That Launched a Movement: The First National Convention," Colored Conventions Project, accessed November 19, 2022, https://coloredconventions.org/first-convention.
8. Kurt Schmoke, "The Dixwell Avenue Congregational Church, 1829–1899," *New Haven Colony Historical Society* 20 (May–June 1971): 3, 5; Hilary J. Moss, *Schooling Citizens: The Struggle for African American Education in Antebellum America* (Chicago: University of Chicago Press, 2009), 31.
9. Kabria Baumgartner, "Towers of Intellect: The Struggle for African American Higher Education in Antebellum New England," in *Slavery and the University: Histories and Legacies*, ed. Leslie M. Harris, James T. Campbell, and Alfred L. Brophy (Athens: University of Georgia Press, 2019), 182; Moss, *Schooling Citizens*, 37–38, 48.
10. Simeon Smith Jocelyn to William Lloyd Garrison, May 28, 1831, Anti-slavery Collection, Boston Public Library Rare Books Department, https://ark.digitalcommonwealth.org/ark:/50959/2z10zf581.
11. Jocelyn to Garrison; "Nomination of Mr. Wirt," *Vermont Advocate and State Paper*, November 24, 1831, 3, America's Historical Newspapers database. The site was originally a hotel and then, briefly, a gymnasium, or boarding school, operated by Henry and Sereno Edwards Dwight, sons of Timothy Dwight IV, eighth president of Yale, and great-grandsons of Jonathan Edwards.
12. Kabria Baumgartner, "Gender Politics and the Manual Labor College Initiative at National Colored Conventions in Antebellum America," in *The Colored Conventions Movement: Black Organizing in the Nineteenth Century*, ed. Sarah Lynn Patterson, Jim Casey, and P. Gabrielle Foreman (Chapel Hill: University of North Carolina Press, 2021), 231, 232.
13. *Minutes and Proceedings*, 6; Lewis Tappan, *The Life of Arthur Tappan* (New York: Hurd and Houghton, 1870), 148.
14. James Brewer Stewart, "The New Haven Negro College and the Meanings of Race in New England, 1776–1870," *New England Quarterly* 76, no. 3 (September 2003): 330; *Minutes and Proceedings*, 7; *Liberator* (Boston), June 18, 1831.
15. *New York Evangelist*, July 30, 1831, 4; "Education—An Appeal to the Benevolent," September 5, 1831, *Philadelphia Chronicle*, reprinted in notice reprinted in *College for Colored Youth: An Account of the New-Haven City Meeting and Resolutions: With Recommendations of the College, and Strictures upon the Doings of New-Haven* (New York: published by the committee, 1831), 3; *Connecticut Journal* (New Haven), September 6, 1831. Simeon Jocelyn compiled the *College for Colored Youth* pamphlet

at the request of the superintending committee of free Black New York leaders, including the Reverend Peter Williams, Thomas Downing, Peter Vogelsang, Boston Cromwell, and Philip A. Bell.

16. *Connecticut Journal* (New Haven), September 6, 1831. See Moss, "Education's Inequity"; and Julia Bernier, "'Chains of a Stronger Kind': The Trials of Prudence Crandall and the Limits of African-American Freedom in Antebellum New England" (MA thesis, City College of the City University of New York, 2011).
17. "To either of the Sherifs [*sic*] of the city of New-Haven—Greeting," and "Preliminary Meeting of the Alumni of Yale College," *New Haven Daily Advertiser*, September 9, 1831, and see *College for Colored Youth*, 4.
18. *New Haven Advertiser*, September 13, 1831 (reprinted in the *Columbian Sentinel*).
19. *College for Colored Youth*, 4. There are no known official records of the vote count, but see Tappan, *Life of Arthur Tappan*, 149–50; and the obituary of John Warner Barber in John Warner Barber Papers, MSS 107, New Haven Museum. Both Warner and Roger Sherman Baldwin would go on to play prominent roles in the *Amistad* affair. On the speakers opposed to the college and their backgrounds, see *New Haven Advertiser*, September 13, 1831; Judith Ann Schiff, "The First Female Students at Yale," *Yale Alumni Magazine*, September/October 2009, http://archives.yalealumnimagazine.com/issues/2009_09/oldyale024.html; and "Guide to the David Daggett Papers," MS 162, Manuscripts and Archives, Yale University Library.
20. *New Haven Advertiser*, September 13, 1831 (reprinted in the *Columbian Sentinel*).
21. *College for Colored Youth*, 5.
22. *Middlesex Gazette* (Middletown), September 28, 1831; question for November 9, 1831, Yale clubs and organizations, circa 1768–1973, Box 10, Folder 48, Manuscripts and Archives, Yale University Library.
23. *American Mercury* (Hartford, CT), September 12, 1831, quoting earlier New Haven papers; *Connecticut Journal* (New Haven), October 11, 1831. Timothy Dwight wrote of the free Black population, "Their vices are of all the kinds, usually intended by the phrase 'low vice.' Uneducated to principles of morality, or to habits of industry and economy . . . many of them are thieves, liars, profane, drunkards, sabbath-breakers, quarrelsome, idle, and prodigal, the last in the extreme." Yet he supported educational opportunities for Black children and believed they would "furnish the first rational hope of a reformation among the people." Timothy Dwight, *Statistical Account of the City of New-Haven* (New Haven, CT: Printed and sold by Walter and Steele, 1811), 57–58.
24. *Commercial Advertiser* (New York), September 17, 1831.
25. *Commercial Advertiser* (New York), September 16, 1831. The article also shared the contemporaneous announcement that Colonel John Trumbull's paintings were to be transferred to Yale, another sign of the college's growth and development at the time.
26. Stonington Phenix, "Yale Commencement," *Liberator* (Boston), October 1, 1831; "Sonnet," *Liberator* (Boston), October 8, 1831. Garrison's metaphor may have carried particularly powerful meaning in 1831, given the great eclipse earlier that year on February 12.
27. *New Haven Daily Advertiser*, October 21, 1831; "Riots at New Haven!," *Liberator* (Boston), October 22, 1831; *Philadelphia Inquirer*, October 18, 1831; Arthur Tappan to William Lloyd Garrison, October 18, 1831, Anti-slavery Collection, Boston Public Library

Rare Books Department, https://ark.digitalcommonwealth.org/ark:/50959/2z10zf88r. Garrison's *Liberator* reported on this incident on October 22, 1831, and observed, "New Haven has almost irretrievably lost the high reputation which it lately sustained." These actions in New Haven occurred at a time of race riots in many Northern communities, such as Cincinnati in 1828 and Providence in 1831. For more context, see Leonard L. Richards, *Gentlemen of Property and Standing: Anti-abolition Mobs in Jacksonian America* (New York: Oxford University Press, 1970).

28. *Georgian* (Savannah, Georgia), September 24, 1831; *Richmond (VA) Enquirer*, September 27, 1831, https://www.natturnerproject.org/richmond-enquirer-sept-27; "Negro College," *Southern Clarion* (Natchez, MS), October 21, 1831.
29. "The Canterbury Seminary," *Norwich Republican*, April 24, 1833; *Baltimore Gazette and Daily Advertiser* quoted in Donald E. Williams Jr., *Prudence Crandall's Legacy: The Fight for Equality in the 1830s, "Dred Scott," and "Brown v. Board of Education"* (Middletown, CT: Wesleyan University Press, 2014), 260.
30. Crandall v. State, 10 Day 347 (1834), quoted in Williams, *Prudence Crandall's Legacy*, 145 (emphasis in original). And see "The Black Law of Connecticut (1833)," Citizens ALL: Africans Americans in Connecticut, Gilder Lehrman Center for the Study of Slavery, Resistance, and Abolition, Yale University, https://glc.yale.edu/sites/default/files/files/The%20Black%20Law%20of%20Connecticut(1).pdf.
31. Dred Scott v. Sandford, 60 U.S. 393, 415, 407 (1856), https://supreme.justia.com/cases/federal/us/60/393. See also Edmund Fuller, *Prudence Crandall: An Incident of Racism in Nineteenth Century Connecticut* (Middletown, CT: Wesleyan University Press, 1971); Philip S. Foner, "Prudence Crandall," in *Three Who Dared: Prudence Crandall, Margaret Douglass, Myrtilla Miner—Champions of Antebellum Black Education*, ed. Philip S. Foner and Josephine F. Pacheco (Westport, CT: Greenwood, 1984), 5–40; Susan Strane, *A Whole-Souled Woman: Prudence Crandall and the Education of Black Women* (New York: W. W. Norton, 1990), 34–65, 73–90; and "Prudence Crandall—State Heroine," State of Connecticut Judicial Branch Law Library Services, accessed September 7, 2023, https://www.jud.ct.gov/lawlib/history/crandall.htm. On antislavery constitutionalism, see James Oakes, *The Crooked Path to Abolition: Abraham Lincoln and the Antislavery Constitution* (New York: Norton, 2021).
32. Hilary J. Moss, "Opportunity and Opposition: The African American Struggle for Education in New Haven, Baltimore and Boston, 1825–1855" (PhD diss., Brandeis University, 2004), 67.

CHAPTER 7. LA AMISTAD

1. See Marcus Rediker, *The "Amistad" Rebellion: An Atlantic Odyssey of Slavery and Freedom* (New York: Viking, 2012), 11–63, 104, 127; and Howard Jones, *Mutiny on the "Amistad": The Saga of a Slave Revolt and Its Impact on American Abolition, Law, and Diplomacy* (New York: Oxford University Press, 1987), 35, 37, 42–43, 77, 122, 125, 203. We have gratefully drawn from Rediker's and Jones's authoritative works throughout this chapter. There is rich scholarship on nearly every aspect of the *Amistad*; see also "The Amistad," ConnecticutHistory.org, July 1, 2022, https://connecticuthistory.org/the-amistad; and "The Amistad Case," National Archives, accessed September 8, 2023, https://www.archives.gov/education/lessons/amistad.

2. We follow Rediker in referring to the rebellion's leader as Cinqué, as he was known during the *Amistad* ordeal, rather than Sengbe Pieh, the name he was likely given at birth. See Rediker, *"Amistad" Rebellion*, 246n1.
3. Rediker, *"Amistad" Rebellion*, 27–28.
4. Rediker, 44–45, 51–63; Jones, *Mutiny on the "Amistad,"* 14–15, 123–24 (emphasis in original).
5. Rediker, *"Amistad" Rebellion*, 58–64.
6. Rediker, 65–68; "Amistad Case," National Archives; Michael Zeuske and Orlando García Martinez, "*La Amistad* de Cuba: Ramon Ferrer, contrabando de esclavos, captividad y modernidad atlantica," *Caribbean Studies* 37 (2009): 97–170. I commented on an early version of this paper at an annual meeting of the Organization of American Historians, 2007. On a sunny Sunday in August 2022, I visited the famous replica of the *Amistad* as it docked at Long Wharf in New Haven Harbor. The ship now has some modern, required amenities, such as a motor, of course, but also four hatchways. The three beautiful arched masts and the length and width of the ship are identical to those of the original schooner.
7. Eleven people provided eyewitness testimony of the rebellion aboard the *Amistad*. These accounts emerged in written documents, court testimony, and interviews in newspapers. The witnesses included six of the *Amistad* rebels. For a detailed account, see Rediker, *"Amistad" Rebellion*, 73–79, 81; and for the beginnings of testimonies, see the large compilation by the New Haven writer and sketch artist John Warner Barber, *A History of the Amistad Captives: Being a Circumstantial Account of the Capture of the Spanish Schooner Amistad, by the Africans on Board* [. . .] (New Haven, CT: E. L. and J. W. Barber, 1840). For a brief but robust, if romanticized, source on the rebellion, see "The Long, Low Black Schooner," *New York Sun*, August 31, 1839.
8. Jones, *Mutiny on the "Amistad,"* 26–28; Rediker, *"Amistad" Rebellion*, 82–94.
9. Such sensational depictions of Cinqué and the other captives appeared in the *New London Gazette*, August 28, 1839; the *New York Sun*, September 7, 1839; and the unsympathetic but robust *New York Morning Herald*, September 4, 1839, which sold out a first run of one issue at four thousand copies.
10. Rediker, *"Amistad" Rebellion*, 108–9.
11. Rediker, *"Amistad" Rebellion*, 111; Joseph Yannielli, "The Mendi Mission: Africa and the American Abolition Movement" (PhD diss., Yale University, 2015), 57–60, 63–64.
12. William H. Townsend, "Sketches of the Amistad Captives," ca. 1839–40, Beinecke Rare Book and Manuscript Library, Yale University, https://beinecke.library.yale.edu/AmistadPortraits. And see Charles Allen Dinsmore, "Interesting Sketches of the Amistad Captives," *Yale University Library Gazette* 9 (1935): 51–55.
13. Rediker, *"Amistad" Rebellion*, 104–5, 119–20, 135–40; *New London Gazette*, October 16, 1839. The remarkable zeal and speed with which Gibbs and others worked to find translators and begin to assemble the story is noteworthy. See Barber, *History*, 24–31.
14. Barber, *History*, 16; *The African Captives: Trial of the Prisoners of the Amistad on the Writ of Habeas Corpus before the Circuit Court of the United States for the District of Connecticut, at Hartford: Judges Thompson and Judson, September Term, 1839* (New York: American Antislavery Society, 1839), 9–15; Jones, *Mutiny on the "Amistad,"* 64, 66, 68–74.

15. Barber, *History*, 16. For diplomatic correspondence, see the sixteen-page special issue of *American and Foreign Antislavery Reporter*, December 1840, http://morris.law.yale.edu/record=b482937.
16. *African Captives*, 44–47; Rediker, *"Amistad" Rebellion*, 130, 133–34; Yannielli, "Mendi Mission," 56–57, 60–63, 68; George E. Day to editors, *New York Journal of Commerce*, October 8, 15, 1839, in *African Captives*, iv–vi.
17. For the "Connecticut Black Law," see "The Connecticut Black Law of 1833," and for Prudence Crandall, see "A Canterbury Tale," both in "Citizens ALL," Gilder Lehrman Center for the Study of Slavery, Resistance, and Abolition, Yale University, accessed September 8, 2023, https://glc.yale.edu/citizens/stories. And see James B. Stewart, *Holy Warriors: The Abolitionists and American Slavery* (New York: Hill and Wang, 1976), 63–64; Judson quoted in Jones, *Mutiny on the "Amistad,"* 96–98 (emphasis in original).
18. Rediker, *"Amistad" Rebellion*, 143–44.
19. Jones, *Mutiny on the "Amistad,"* 119, 111–16.
20. See Jones, 121–25, 242n28, 242n32–33.
21. For the legal decisions, see Bruce A. Ragsdale, "'Incited by the Love of Liberty': The *Amistad* Captives and the Federal Courts," *Prologue Magazine* 35, no. 1 (Spring 2003), https://www.archives.gov/publications/prologue/2003/spring/amistad-1.html.
22. Yannielli, "Mendi Mission," 67–71; Rediker, *"Amistad" Rebellion*, 179–82. See "The Mendi People," *Emancipator*, September 23, 1841. This was Leavitt's newspaper.
23. Kale to John Quincy Adams, January 4, 1841, in Simeon Baldwin, "The Captives of the Amistad," reprinted in *Papers of the New Haven-Colony Historical Society* 4 (1888): 354–55, transcribed at https://glc.yale.edu/kale-john-quincy-adams-141841; Rediker, *"Amistad" Rebellion*, 181–83.
24. Rediker, 189.
25. Rediker, 186–87; Jones, *Mutiny on the "Amistad,"* 185–86.
26. *Argument of Roger Baldwin of New Haven before the Supreme Court of the United States in the Case of the United States, Appellants, vs. Cinque and Others, Africans of the Amistad* (New York: S. W. Benedict, 1841), 3, 5, 15, 17–23.
27. *Argument of John Quincy Adams before the Supreme Court of the United States in the Case of the United States, Appellants vs. Cinque, and Others, Africans, Captured in the Schooner Amistad* (New York: S. W. Benedict, 1841), February 24, March 1, 1841, 8–9, 17, 19, 21–23, 42, 8–9, 17, 19, 83–87; Jones, *Mutiny on the "Amistad,"* 170–71, 196, 182.
28. Jones, 188–94.
29. Stewart, *Holy Warriors*, 71–72, 75–77, 82, 88–91, 50, 130; Henry Mayer, *All on Fire: William Lloyd Garrison and the Abolition of Slavery* (New York: St. Martin's, 1998), 200–208, 312. On the *Creole* case and Douglass, see David Blight, *Frederick Douglass: Prophet of Freedom* (New York: Simon and Schuster, 2018), 295–96.
30. Stewart, *Holy Warriors*, 95, 88–89, 137.
31. Stewart, 97–105.
32. The *Amistad Memorial*, by the artist Ed Hamilton, was dedicated on September 26, 1992. It is a three-sided relief depicting three images of Cinqué in different clothing and with accoutrements appropriate to each: one in Africa, one as the shipboard rebel leader, the third as a citizen in court.

33. Rediker, *"Amistad" Rebellion*, 190–93.
34. Rediker, 196–204.
35. Rediker, 201, 203, 204.
36. "Meetings of Liberated Africans," *Colored American*, May 22, 1841; "The Amistad Africans, Farewell Meetings and Embarkation," *New York Tribune*, December 25, 1841 (reprinted in *Connecticut Courant*). On the public performances, see Rediker, *"Amistad" Rebellion*, 196–208. This would have marked one of the early efforts of James McCune Smith in the abolition movement as a writer and thinker. He later became a prolific contributor to Frederick Douglass's newspapers and an essayist in his own right.
37. Rediker, *"Amistad" Rebellion*, 211–15; Yannielli, "Mendi Mission," 86.
38. Rediker, *"Amistad" Rebellion*, 217–23. In language that easily could have been a description of Cinqué's many command performances in the "Mendi exhibitions," Douglass declared, "This Fourth of July is yours, not mine. You may rejoice, I must mourn. To drag a man in fetters into the grand illuminated temple of liberty, and call upon him to join you in joyous anthems, were inhuman mockery and sacrilegious irony." Frederick Douglass, "What to the Slave Is the Fourth of July? An Address Delivered in Rochester, New York, on 5 July 1852," in *The Frederick Douglass Papers*, ed. John W. Blassingame et al. (New Haven, CT: Yale University Press, 1982), vol. 2, ser. 1, p. 368.
39. Quoted in Rediker, *"Amistad" Rebellion*, 217.

CHAPTER 8. ANTEBELLUM YALE AND ITS ABOLITIONIST DISCONTENTS

Epigraph: William Lloyd Garrison, "American Union," *Liberator*, January 17, 1835, 11.

1. Christopher L. Webber, *American to the Backbone: The Life of James W. C. Pennington, the Fugitive Slave Who Became One of the First Black Abolitionists* (New York: Pegasus, 2011), 34–35, 98–99. On the Douglass marriage, see David W. Blight, *Frederick Douglass: Prophet of Freedom* (New York: Simon and Schuster, 2018), 173. Yale's divinity school was established in 1822, but its official name was the Theological Department until 1888. See Ray Waddle, *"This Grand Errand": A Bicentennial History of Yale Divinity School* (New Haven, CT: Yale University Press, 2022), 29.
2. James W. C. Pennington, *A Text Book of the Origin and History, &c. &c. of the Colored People* (Hartford, CT: L. Skinner, 1841); James W. C. Pennington, *The Fugitive Blacksmith: Or, Events in the History of James W. C. Pennington, Pastor of a Presbyterian Church, New York, Formerly a Slave in the State of Maryland, United States* (London: Charles Gilpin, 1849), vii–x. Also see Webber, *American to the Backbone*, 149–56.
3. Pennington, *Fugitive Blacksmith*, ix, xii–xiii.
4. "Rev. Dr. Pennington," *Frederick Douglass' Paper*, August 14, 1851. This article is Pennington's own account of his time at Yale. And see Webber, *American to the Backbone*, 97–101; Kurt Schmoke, "The Dixwell Avenue Congregational Church, 1829–1899," *New Haven Colony Historical Society* 20 (May–June 1971): 6; and Robert Austin Warner, *New Haven Negroes: A Social History* (New Haven, CT: Yale University Press, 1940), 83. Warner's volume—the only book-length history of Black New Haven—is an indispensable resource for local history and is cited frequently in this work.

5. *Colored American*, June 2, 16, July 21, 1838. And see Webber, *American to the Backbone*, 111–13, 116–17.
6. Randall K. Burkett, "The Reverend Harry Croswell and Black Episcopalians in New Haven, 1820–1860," *North Star: A Journal of African American Religious History* 7, no. 1 (Fall 2003): 7; Wilson Jeremiah Moses, *Alexander Crummell: A Study of Civilization and Discontent* (New York: Oxford University Press, 1989), especially 30–31, 310n91; "Rev. Alexander Crummell, A.B.," *Harper's Weekly*, April 16, 1866; Alexander Du Bois, *Account of Moneys Contributed for the Benefit of Mr. Alexander Crummel* [*sic*], December 1840, W. E. B. Du Bois Papers (MS 312), Special Collections and University Archives, University of Massachusetts Amherst Libraries; Stephen Bates, "Alexander Crummell, Cambridge's First Black Graduate," *Guardian*, October 19, 2011. W. E. B. DuBois devoted an entire chapter to Crummell, with whom he helped found the American Negro Academy; see W. E. B. Du Bois, *The Souls of Black Folk*, ed. Henry Louis Gates Jr. (New York: Oxford University Press, 2007), 103–10. And see the Harry Croswell Papers, Special Collections, Yale Divinity School Library; research into Crummell's time in New Haven is ongoing. Yale University awarded M.A. privatim degrees to Pennington and Crummell in 2023; Mike Cummings, "'They Were Men of Yale': Two Black Scholars Honored Posthumously," YaleNews, September 15, 2023, accessed October 3, 2023, https://news.yale.edu/2023/09/15/they-were-men-yale-two-black-scholars-honored-posthumously.
7. See Warner, *New Haven Negroes*, 13–26.
8. Douglas A. Sweeney, *Nathaniel Taylor, New Haven Theology, and the Legacy of Jonathan Edwards* (New York: Oxford University Press, 2003), 63, 58; Roland H. Bainton, *Yale and the Ministry: A History of Education for the Christian Ministry at Yale from the Founding in 1701* (New York: Harper and Brothers, 1957), 83. Also see Kenneth P. Minkema and Harry S. Stout, "The Edwardsean Tradition and the Antislavery Debate, 1740–1865," *Journal of American History* 92, no. 1 (2005): 66–67.
9. Sweeney, *Nathaniel Taylor*, 63; *An Address to the Public by the Managers of the Colonization Society of Connecticut, with an Appendix* (New Haven, CT: Treadway and Adams, 1828), 3–4.
10. The Rhetorical Society debates, in John Terrill Wayland, *The Theological Department in Yale College, 1822–1858* (New York: Garland, 1957), 298–300; Waddle, *"This Grant Errand,"* 47.
11. Sweeney, *Nathaniel Taylor*, 3–4, and on his influence, 144–54. On Finney, see James David Essig, "The Lord's Free Man: Charles G. Finney and His Abolitionism," *Civil War History* 24, no. 1 (March 1978): 25–45; Bainton, *Yale and the Ministry*, 145–47; and Webber, *American to the Backbone*, 114.
12. Leonard Bacon, *Journal of Freedom*, December 8, 1834; Leonard Bacon, *Religious Intelligencer*, September 10, 1836; and Garrison, "American Union," all quoted in Hugh Davis, *Leonard Bacon: New England Reformer and Antislavery Moderate* (Baton Rouge: Louisiana State University Press, 1998), 83, 86.
13. Leonard Bacon, *Quarterly Christian Spectator*, 1833, in "Leonard Bacon Pleads for Moderation," in *The Antislavery Argument*, ed. William H. Pease and Jane E. Pease (Indianapolis: Bobbs-Merrill, 1965), 111–14.

14. Bainton, *Yale and the Ministry*, 90–93. On Stuart's influence, see also Shalom Goldman, *God's Sacred Tongue: Hebrew and the American Imagination* (Chapel Hill: University of North Carolina Press, 2004), 116.
15. Moses Stuart, *Conscience and the Constitution* (Boston: Crocker and Brewster, 1850), 112, 101, 117, 108, 107. Stuart portrayed himself as a victim of abolitionist scorn for his support of Webster (see Stuart, 2–10).
16. Andrew Dickson White, *The Autobiography of Andrew Dickson White*, 2 vols. (New York: Century, 1905), 1:66–69.
17. Quoted in Natalie Joy, "The Indian's Cause: Abolitionists and Native American Rights," *Journal of the Civil War Era* 8, no. 2 (2018): 221–22, 237n27. Evarts's admiring biographer in 1845, E. C. Tracy, suggested that the missionary forcefully opposed slavery. Other modern historians, such as Natalie Joy, dispute this and argue that the anti-removalist was at best only a moderate gradualist on slavery and sympathetic to colonization for Black Americans. See E. C. Tracy, *Memoir of the Life of Jeremiah Evarts, Esq.* (Boston: Crocker and Brewster, 1845), 80.
18. Quoted in Tracy, *Life of Jeremiah Evarts*, 84.
19. Henry W. Farnam, "Joseph Earl Sheffield: The Father of the Sheffield Scientific School," October 9, 1901, in *Papers of the New Haven Colony Historical Society* (New Haven, CT: printed for the society, 1908), 7:65–119; "Joseph E. Sheffield and Yale Scientific School: A Memoir," *American Journal of Education* 3 (1878): 325. And see Joseph Earl Sheffield Letters and Writings, General Collection, Beinecke Rare Book and Manuscript Library, Yale University.
20. Brooks Mather Kelley, *Yale: A History* (New Haven, CT: Yale University Press, 1974), 184–85, 262–64; Russell Chittenden, *History of the Sheffield Scientific School of Yale University* (New Haven, CT: Yale University Press, 1928), 1:213.
21. Sheffield, *Morning Journal and Courier* (New Haven, CT), January 24, 1863, quoted in Farnam, "Joseph Earl Sheffield," 102 (emphasis in original).
22. Farnam, "Joseph Earl Sheffield," 117–18 (emphasis in original).
23. Quoted in H. Edward Richardson, *Cassius Marcellus Clay: Firebrand of Freedom* (Lexington: University of Kentucky Press, 2014), 15–18; Cassius Marcellus Clay, *The Life of Cassius Marcellus Clay: Memoirs, Writings, and Speeches* (Cincinnati: J. Fletcher Brennan, 1886), 1:54.
24. Clay, *Life*, 54–57; David L. Smiley, *Lion of White Hall: The Life of Cassius Marcellus Clay* (Madison: University of Wisconsin Press, 1962), 20–25.
25. Clay, *Life*, 56–58; Cassius Clay, "Address before the Senior Class of Yale, Feb. 22, 1832, Centennial Birth-Day of Washington," in *The Writings of Cassius Marcellus Clay: Including Speeches and Addresses*, ed. Horace Greeley (New York: Harper and Brothers, 1848), 42–43.
26. Smiley, *Lion of White Hall*, chaps. 9–16.
27. Norris Galpin Osborne, *Men of Mark in Connecticut: Ideals of American Life Told in Biographies and Autobiographies of Eminent Americans* (Hartford, CT: W. R. Goodspeed, 1906), 416; *Obituary Record of Graduates of Yale College, Deceased during the Academical Year Ending in June, 1885 . . .* (Presented at the meeting of the Alumni, June 23d, 1885),

241–42; William Richard Cutter, *New England Families, Genealogical and Memorial: A Record of the Achievements of Her People in the Making of Commonwealths and the Founding of a Nation* (New York: Lewis Historical, 1913), 3:1430; Joshua L. Chamberlain, *Universities and Their Sons, Yale University: Its History, Influence, Equipment and Characteristics, with Biographical Sketches and Portraits of Founders, Benefactors, Officers, and Alumni* (Boston: R. Herndon, 1900), 242–43.

28. John Brown, letter, April 14, 1857, naming George Luther Stearns, Samuel Caleb Jr., and William H. Russell "trustees" of his finances should he not return from Kansas, in Gilder Lehrman Collection, New York Historical Society, doc. no. 00502. We rely here on the private research and generosity of David Alan Richards.
29. *Obituary Record*, 241; Osborne, *Men of Mark*, 421–23; Ellsworth Eliot, *Yale in the Civil War* (New Haven, CT: Yale University Press, 1932), 19–20; *Addresses and Proceedings, Including the Oration Pronounced by Rev. Dr. Bushnell, at the Commemorative Celebration, Held July 26th, 1865, in Honor of the Alumni of Yale College Who Were in the Military or Naval Service of the United States during the Recent War; Together with the Names Comprised in the Roll of Honor* (New Haven, CT: Tuttle, Morehouse, and Taylor, 1866), 8.
30. See "Timeline of Samuel F. B. Morse's Life and Career," Samuel F. B. Morse Papers at the Library of Congress, accessed September 11, 2023, https://www.loc.gov/collections/samuel-morse-papers/articles-and-essays/timeline/.
31. Kenneth Silverman, *Lightning Man: The Accursed Life of Samuel F. B. Morse* (New York: Da Capo, 2004), 4, 9, 12–66.
32. Silverman, 192–246, 167.
33. See Daniel Walker Howe, *What Hath God Wrought: The Transformation of America, 1815–1848* (New York: Oxford University Press, 2007), 1–4, 691; Silverman, *Lightning Man*, 323–24, 300, 240, 404–5, 417, 326, 406; "Timeline, 1840–1872," Samuel F. B. Morse Papers at the Library of Congress, accessed May 31, 2023, https://www.loc.gov/collections/samuel-morse-papers/articles-and-essays/timeline/1840-1872. Howe makes the communication revolution the central theme of his distinguished synthesis of early antebellum America. Silverman develops the story of Morse's extraordinary entrepreneurial marketing skills.
34. See Silverman, *Lightning Man*, 141–42, 335–38; and "Timeline, 1840–1872."
35. Samuel F. B. Morse, *Foreign Conspiracy against the Liberties of the United States: The Numbers of Brutus, Originally Published in the New York Observer* (New York: Leavitt, Lord, 1835), 21, 35, 40, 52, 55–58 (emphasis in original).
36. Samuel Morse to his brother, Sydney Morse, September 1846 (no day), and Samuel Morse to Sydney Morse, October 12, 1847, Morse Papers, New York Historical Society, quoted in Silverman, *Lightning Man*, 256, 468; quotations in Larry E. Tise, *Proslavery: A History of the Defense of Slavery in America* (Athens: University of Georgia Press, 1987), 251, 254.
37. Background and quotations in Tise, *Proslavery*, 250–60 (emphasis in original). And see Silverman, *Lightning Man*, 400–401.
38. Women's convention quoted in Benjamin Quarles, *Black Abolitionists* (New York: Oxford University Press, 1969), 91, and "elevation," 92; Whipper quoted in James Oliver Horton and Lois E. Horton, *In Hope of Liberty: Culture, Community and Protest among*

Northern Free Blacks, 1700–1860 (New York: Oxford University Press, 1997), 221. On growth of the self-improvement community impulse, see Horton and Horton, *Hope of Liberty*, 125–54; and Jane Pease and William Pease, *They Who Would Be Free: Blacks' Search for Freedom, 1830–1861* (New York: Atheneum, 1974), 124–43.

39. See Quarles, *Black Abolitionists*, 93–94; and on Amos Beman generally, see Robert A. Warner, "Amos Gerry Beman: 1812–1874, a Memoir on a Forgotten Leader," *Journal of Negro History* 22, no. 2 (April 1937): 200–221.

40. "Another Specimen!!," signed "Truth," Middletown, CT, *Liberator*, September 1833 (emphasis in original), Amos Beman Scrapbooks, vol. 2, 126, Beinecke Rare Book and Manuscript Library, Yale University.

41. Quarles, *Black Abolitionists*, 68; Warner, "Amos Gerry Beman," 210.

42. Hosea Easton, *A Treatise on the Intellectual Character, and Civil and Political Condition of the Colored People of the U. States; and the Prejudice Exercised towards Them; with a Sermon on the Duty of the Church to Them* (Boston: I. Knapp, 1837); James Brewer Stewart, "The New Haven Negro College and the Meanings of Race in New England, 1776–1870," *New England Quarterly* 76, no. 3 (September 2003): 342–46.

43. Background in Pease and Pease, *They Who Would Be Free*, 282, 154–56; on common schools, 147, 282.

44. Cornish, Garnet, Woodson, Pennington, and Douglass, quoted or discussed in Pease and Pease, 148–49, 152–56.

45. *Connecticut Journal*, September 13, 1831, and *Connecticut Herald*, October 4, 1831, quoted in Warner, *New Haven Negroes*, 56–57. And on New Haven Black schools generally, see Warner, 69–77.

46. Warner, 72–74; Gardner Morse, "Recollections of New Haven between 1825 and 1837," Papers of the New Haven Historical Society (New Haven, CT: Printed for the Society, 1894), 5:103.

47. Kelley, *Yale*, 171–73, on Day's achievements, 140–70; Leonard Woolsey Bacon, *The Services of Leonard Bacon to African Colonization* (Washington, DC: Judd and Detweiler, 1900), 6–7; George A. King, *Theodore Dwight Woolsey: His Political and Social Ideas* (Chicago: Loyola University Press, 1956), 46; Judith Ann Schiff, "Yale's First Global President," *Yale Alumni Magazine*, September/October 2020; Peter Hinks, "'This Beautiful and Rapidly Improving Section of Our City': Race, Labor, and Colonizationists in Early Industrializing New Haven, 1800–1830," *Labor: Studies in the Working-Class History of the Americas* 13, no. 1 (February 2016): 73. Kelley challenges Day's conservative reputation.

48. Kelley, *Yale*, 138; Charles Franklin Thwing, *A History of Higher Education in America* (New York: D. Appleton, 1906), 254–55; *Yale Literary Magazine* 17 (1852): 30–31; Julian Monson Sturtevant, *Julian M. Sturtevant: An Autobiography* (New York: F. H. Revell, 1896), 99. David Alan Richards calls Yale "the nation's most genuinely national educational institution in terms of the origins of its students and the ultimate destinations of its graduates" between 1820 and 1860; Richards, *Skulls and Keys: The Hidden History of Yale's Secret Societies* (New York: Pegasus, 2017), 46.

49. On changes under Woolsey, see Kelley, *Yale*, 171–208; and Ralph Waldo Emerson, *Journals of Ralph Waldo Emerson: With Annotations*, ed. Edward Waldo Emerson and Waldo Emerson Forbes (Boston: Houghton Mifflin, 1912), 7:206.

50. On the U.S.-Mexico War, see, for example, Amy S. Greenberg, *A Wicked War: Polk, Clay, Lincoln, and the 1846 U.S. Invasion of Mexico* (New York: Vintage, 2012); and Peter Guardino, *Dead March: A History of the Mexican-American War* (Cambridge, MA: Harvard University Press, 2017).
51. "Yale College Influence of Slavery," *Emancipator and Republican*, August 29, 1850; "Northern Servility," *Liberator*, October 1, 1852; "Address before the Phi Beta Kappa of Yale College, July 26, 1854 by William H. Seward," *National Era*, August 10, 1854. On Fillmore, see Elizabeth R. Varon, *Disunion: The Coming of the American Civil War, 1789–1859* (Chapel Hill: University of North Carolina Press, 2008), 225–26.
52. Kelley, *Yale*, 222; "Abolitionism at Yale College," *National Anti-slavery Standard*, March 23, 1853, reprinted from *New Haven Register*, February 22, 1853. "Higher law" doctrine represented the idea that biblical or moral principles took precedence over human laws. Both sides in the slavery crisis made rhetorical use of this idea, proslavery advocates as an epithet, antislavery advocates as a doctrine.
53. William W. Freehling, *The Road to Disunion: Secessionists at Bay, 1776–1854* (New York: Oxford University Press, 1990), 1:536–65.
54. Bainton, *Yale and the Ministry*, 157; *Speeches and Other Proceedings at the Anti-Nebraska Meetings Held in New Haven, Connecticut, March 8th and 10th, 1854* (New Haven, CT: J. H. Austin, 1854), 13.
55. *Speeches and Other Proceedings*, 17–18 (emphasis in original).
56. *Speeches and Other Proceedings*, 19; John Hooker, "Obituary Notice of Eleazer K. Foster," in *Connecticut Reports: Proceedings in the Supreme Court of the State of Connecticut* (Hartford, CT: Case, Lockwood, and Brainard, 1878), 44:606–9; "The Divinity of Yale College Aroused against Slavery," *Rhode Island Freeman*, March 17, 1854; "Clerical Remonstrance," *National Anti-slavery Standard*, March 18, 1854.
57. Paul Revere Frothingham, *Edward Everett: Orator and Statesman* (Boston: Houghton Mifflin, 1925), 356–57; King, *Theodore Dwight Woolsey*, 49–51; "The Voice of the Religious Community," *Liberator*, March 17, 1854; "Anti-Nebraska Movements," *New England Farmer*, March 18, 1854.
58. Rollin G. Osterweis, *Three Centuries of New Haven, 1638–1938* (New Haven, CT: Yale University Press, 1953), 302–7; "Withdrawal of Patronage," reprinted in *Liberator*, April 7, 1854 (emphasis in original); "A Dangerous Southern Man," *Savannah News*, July 10, 1858, reprinted in *National Era*, August 19, 1858.
59. "Departure of the Connecticut Colony for Kansas," *New York Daily Tribune*, April 1, 1856.
60. "Kansas. Sharp's Rifles in New Haven. Meeting in the North Church. Speech of Henry Ward Beecher. Weapons from the Church and Yale College. Prof. Silliman Bidding for Rifles," *New York Times*, March 22, 1856 (emphasis in original).
61. "Bibles and Rifles—Kansas Meeting in New Haven," *Liberator*, March 28, 1856; Judith Ann Schiff, "Praise the Lord and Pass the Ammunition," *Yale Alumni Magazine*, May/June 2022; Henry Peck, *The New Haven State House with Some Account of the Green; and Various Matters of Historical and Local Interest, Gathered from Many Sources* (New Haven, CT: Henry Peck and George H. Coe, 1889), 83.
62. "Departure of the Connecticut Colony"; "Bibles and Rifles in Kansas: Interesting and Instructive Correspondence," *New York Daily Tribune*, April 4, 1856; Osterweis, *Three*

Centuries of New Haven, 302–7; Schiff, "Praise the Lord." Not long after the Connecticut Kansas Colony arrived in Kansas, proslavery vigilantes attacked Lawrence, followed by a counterattack by John Brown and his sons. Despite the violence, some of the Connecticut colonists remained and built the Beecher Bible and Rifle Church in Wabaunsee, which is still in existence.

63. "Speech of Wendell Phillips," *Liberator*, August 14, 1857; "A Distressed Slaveholder," *Anti-slavery Bugle*, August 29, 1857.
64. On early Haitian emigration ideas, and on the larger late 1850s conflicts among Black people over whether to stay or leave the United States, see Horton and Horton, *In Hope of Liberty*, 91–96, 237–68.
65. See David M. Dean, *Defender of the Race: James Theodore Holly, Black Nationalist Bishop* (Boston: Lambeth, 1979), 2–3, 9–22, 25; Manisha Sinha, *The Slave's Cause: A History of Abolition* (New Haven, CT: Yale University Press, 2016), 563–65; and Warner, *New Haven Negroes*, 97.
66. "From Our New York; Correspondent," *Frederick Douglass' Paper*, May 12, 1854. On the fundamental powerlessness of late antebellum Black leaders, see Pease and Pease, *They Who Would Be Free*, 281–99.
67. Dean, *Defender of the Race*, 5–11.
68. Dean, 18–21, 28–38.
69. Dean, 35–37.
70. Dean, 40–44.

CHAPTER 9. YALE AND NEW HAVEN IN THE CIVIL WAR

1. *Yale Literary Magazine*, June 1861, 292; *Yale Literary Magazine*, February 1861, 162–63; *Frank Leslie's Illustrated Newspaper*, February 2, 1861, 172. And also see Ellsworth Eliot, *Yale in the Civil War* (New Haven, CT: Yale University Press, 1932), 17–18. On the South Carolina flag, see John M. Coski, *The Confederate Battle Flag: America's Most Embattled Emblem* (Cambridge, MA: Belknap Press of Harvard University Press, 2005), 5.
2. George W. Pierson, *A Yale Book of Numbers: Historical Statistics of the College and University, 1701–1976* (New Haven, CT: Yale University Press, 1983), 69; *Addresses and Proceedings, Including the Oration Pronounced by Rev. Dr. Bushnell, at the Commemorative Celebration, Held July 26th, 1865, in Honor of the Alumni of Yale College Who Were in the Military or Naval Service of the United States during the Recent War; Together with the Names Comprised in the Roll of Honor* (New Haven, CT: Tuttle, Morehouse, and Taylor, 1866), 48, 100; *Yale Literary Magazine*, October 1865, 30; James M. Hoppin, "The College in the Civil War," in *Yale College: A Sketch of Its History with Notices of Its Several Departments, Instructors and Benefactors Together with Some Account of Student Life and Amusements by Various Authors*, ed. William L. Kingsley, 2 vols. (New York: Henry Holt, 1879), 2:256; Eliot, *Yale in the Civil War*, 27–28; Garry Reeder, "Southern Exposure," *Yale News*, April 24, 1996.
3. James Edward Greenleaf, *Genealogy of the Greenleaf Family* (Boston: Frank Wood, 1896), 220; Nathaniel Cheairs Hughes Jr., *Yale's Confederates: A Biographical Dictionary* (Knoxville: University of Tennessee Press, 2008), xv–xvi, 11–12, 206–7.
4. Hughes, *Yale's Confederates*, 30, 204–5, 36.

5. On Benjamin, see James Traub, *Judah Benjamin: Counselor of the Confederacy* (New Haven, CT: Yale University Press, 2021); Eli N. Evans, *Judah P. Benjamin: The Jewish Confederate* (New York: Free Press, 1988); and Hughes, *Yale's Confederates*, 21–22.
6. Kenneth Silverman, *Lightning Man: The Accursed Life of Samuel F. B. Morse* (New York: Da Capo, 2004), 392–402.
7. Samuel F. B. Morse, *An Argument on the Ethical Position of Slavery in the Social System, and Its Relation to the Politics of the Day* (New York, 1863), quoted in Silverman, 256, 401, and debt to Puritanism, 402 (emphasis in original). On Morse's lineage connecting him not only to his father, Jedidiah, but also to Timothy Dwight, see Larry E. Tise, *Proslavery: A History of the Defense of Slavery in America, 1701–1840* (Athens: University of Georgia Press, 1987), 239, 255–60.
8. *The Letter of a Republican, Edward N. Crosby, Esq., of Poughkeepsie, to Prof. S.F.B. Morse, Feb. 25, 1863; and, Prof. Morse's Reply, March 2d, 1863* (New York: [Society for the Diffusion of Political Knowledge], [1863]) (emphasis in original).
9. "Death and the Civil War | Timeline: Significant Civil War Battles," American Experience, PBS, accessed September 11, 2023, https://www.pbs.org/wgbh/americanexperience/features/timeline-death.
10. See Gerald F. Linderman, *Embattled Courage: The Experience of Combat in the Civil War* (New York: Free Press, 1987); Reid Mitchell, *Civil War Soldiers: Their Expectations and Their Experiences* (New York: Viking, 1990), 56–89; and James M. McPherson, *What They Fought For, 1861–1865* (Baton Rouge: Louisiana State University Press, 1994), 41–46.
11. James McPherson, *Battle Cry of Freedom: The Civil War Era* (New York: Oxford University Press, 1988), 601–6.
12. Brooks Mather Kelley, *Yale: A History* (New Haven, CT: Yale University Press, 1974), 197; on Marsh, Charles Schuchert, "Biographical Memoir of Othniel Charles Marsh, 1831–1899," *National Academy of Sciences of the United States of America Biographical Memoirs* 20 (1938): 6–8; on Gibbs, Richard Panek, "The Greatest Mind in American History," *Yale Alumni Magazine*, May/June 2017, https://yalealumnimagazine.org/articles/4496-josiah-willard-gibbs; on Sumner, Robert Bierstedt, *American Sociological Theory: A Critical History* (New York: Academic Press, 1981), 1n1. Also see Richard Hofstadter, "William Graham Sumner, Social Darwinist," *New England Quarterly* 14, no. 3 (September 1941): 457–77. Part of Sumner's theory was that the wealthy provided a service to society by passing on their naturally attained wealth to their children.
13. Theodore Woolsey to Francis Lieber, November 10, December 20, 1860, quoted in George A. King, *Theodore Dwight Woolsey: His Political and Social Ideas* (Chicago: Loyola University Press, 1956), 57–58.
14. King, *Theodore Dwight Woolsey*, 70; Eliot, *Yale in the Civil War*, 19, 8.
15. Eliot, *Yale in the Civil War*, 13–16; *Yale Literary Magazine*, August 1863, 342.
16. Meredith Mason Brown, "John Mason Brown during the Civil War: Indian Country and Fighting Morgan's Raiders," *Register of the Kentucky Historical Society* 111, no. 1 (2013): 53; *Obituary Record of Graduates of Yale University Deceased during the Academical Year Ending June, 1904* [. . .] (presented at the meeting of the alumni, June 28, 1904), 321; Mason Brown to Woolsey, January 4, 1861, Box 17, Folder 285; March 1, Box 17, Folder

300; July 27, 1862, Box 18, Folder 305; John Mason Brown to Woolsey, April 30, 1861, Box 17, Folder 288; Jacob Cooper to Woolsey, June 11, 1861, Box 17, Folder 290; March 22, 1862, Box 17, Folder 300; Joseph P. Thompson to Woolsey, June 2, 1862, Box 17, Folder 303; March 26, 1863, Box 18, Folder 315, Woolsey Family Papers, Manuscripts and Archives, Yale University Library.

17. Charles J. Stillé to Woolsey, September 26, 1863, Box 18, Folder 322; Henry Swift DeForest to Woolsey, April 4, 1865, Box 19, Folder 34, Woolsey Family Papers.
18. Gov. William A. Buckingham to Woolsey, August 11, 1862; James L. Cowles to Woolsey, August 13, 1862; Howard Kingsbury to Woolsey, August 13, 1862, Box 18, Folder 306; Horace D. Paine to Woolsey, August 25, 1862, and W. E. Heisler to Woolsey, August 20, 1862, Box 18, Folder 307, Woolsey Family Papers.
19. "Evading Public Service—A Bad Example," *New York Times*, August 23, 1864; "The Insurance Against the Draft—The Yale College Alumni," *New York Times*, August 24, 1864.
20. Judith Schiff, "Two Months in the Civil War," *Yale Alumni Magazine*, July/August, 2011; "The Late Major Winthrop-Arrival of His Remains in This City," *New York Tribune*, June 20, 1861.
21. Winthrop, quoted in Adam Goodheart, "In Death a Young Author Is Born," *New York Times*, "Disunion" series, June 19, 2011. The novel is republished in a modern edition. See Theodore Winthrop, *Cecil Dreeme* (New York: New York University Press, 2016). For the manuscript of the novel, see Theodore Winthrop Collection, Beinecke Rare Book and Manuscript Library, Yale University.
22. For the details of Parmelee's background, I am grateful to the research and correspondence of Dennis Culliton of Guilford, Connecticut; Norman McLeod of Woodstock, Vermont; and Katherine Bartlett of Durham, North Carolina, a law professor emeritus, Duke University. And see Randall Jimerson, *The Private Civil War: Popular Thought during the Sectional Conflict* (Baton Rouge: Louisiana State University Press, 1988), 38–39; and Eliot, *Yale in the Civil War*, 47, 50, 176.
23. Uriah Parmelee to his mother, November 11, 1861, January 10, September 8, 25, 1862; Parmelee to his brother Samuel, April 23, 1862; Parmelee to his father, March 29, 1863, Samuel Spencer Parmelee Papers, Duke University.
24. Parmelee to his mother, March 7, September 28, 1863, Parmelee Papers; Katherine Bartlett, email to author, January 28, 2013.
25. Uriah Nelson Parmelee, *The Civil War Diary of Uriah Nelson Parmelee*, ed. Charles Lewis Biggs (1940; repr., Yale University Library, 1991), microfilm, 5–11.
26. Dennis Culliton, email to author, February 26, 2016; Katherine Bartlett, email to author, January 23, 2013; Norman McLeod, emails to author, September 15, 28, 2009, February 20, 2013.
27. At least one of the many local researchers and scholars who have taken a deep interest in Parmelee's story, Dennis Culliton, has suggested that his tale is an American version of that of the character Paul Baumer in Erich Maria Remarque's *All Quiet on the Western Front*, published in Germany in 1928, a massive best seller until banned by the Nazis. Baumer, his psyche utterly ravaged by trench warfare and his savage experience of killing, and with only one soul left with whom he could really connect, his mother (most of Parmelee's letters were also to his mother), is himself bayoneted and dies on Armistice Day

in a final assault after Germany and France had finally made a settlement to end the slaughter of World War I. Another writer with keen interest in Parmelee, Katherine Bartlett, who grew up in Guilford, Connecticut, and became a law professor at Duke University, is writing an epistolary novel based on the young soldier's trove of letters from the front. Thousands of Yale students, faculty, staff, and visitors of all kinds have passed through the War Memorial in Woolsey Hall for more than a century and unknowingly hurried past Parmelee's name, etched in stone about shoulder high on a tall man, and those of many more. His story reveals one small measure of the larger meanings of the Civil War and its costs, at Yale and far beyond.

28. William Shakespeare, *Henry IV, Part I*, ed. Barbara Mowat et al. (Washington, DC: Folger Shakespeare Library, n.d.), 5.2.91–92, https://www.folger.edu/explore/shakespeares-works/henry-iv-part-1/read; William Shakespeare, *Henry V*, ed. Barbara Mowat et al. (Washington, DC: Folger Shakespeare Library, n.d.), 4.1.146, https://www.folger.edu/explore/shakespeares-works/henry-v/read/.
29. For this portrait of New Haven, see Ira Spar, *New Haven's Civil War Hospital: A History of Knight U.S. General Hospital, 1862–1865* (Jefferson, NC: McFarland, 2014), 87.
30. "The Fifteenth," *New Haven Palladium*, August 28, 1862, quoted in Spar, *New Haven's Civil War Hospital*, 89–90. Also see "15th Regiment, Connecticut Infantry," National Park Service, accessed May 25, 2023, https://www.nps.gov/civilwar/search-battle-units-detail.htm?battleUnitCode=UCT0015RI.
31. Sheldon Brainerd Thorpe, *The History of the Fifteenth Connecticut Volunteers in the War of Defense of the Union, 1861–1865* (New Haven, CT: Price, Lee and Adkins, 1893), 13–16, 35, 39, 265, 259, 76–79. On Union veterans, see Brian Matthew Jordan, *Marching Home: Union Veterans and Their Unending Civil War* (New York: Liveright, 2014), 43–44, 186–91.
32. Rollin G. Osterweis, *Three Centuries of New Haven, 1638–1938* (New Haven, CT: Yale University Press, 1953), 251–61; Edward E. Atwater, ed., *History of the City of New Haven to the Present Time* (New York: W. W. Munsell, 1887), 589; Karyl Lee Kibler Hall and Carolyn Cooper, *Windows on the Works: Industry on the Eli Whitney Site, 1798–1979* (Hamden, CT: Eli Whitney Museum, 1979), 29, 54–56; Pamela Haag, *The Gunning of America: Business and the Making of American Gun Culture* (New York: Basic Books, 2016), 53–55, 65–69, 94–102; Dean E. Nelson, "Connecticut Arms the Union," *Connecticut Explored*, Spring 2011, https://www.ctexplored.org/civil-war-connecticut-arms-the-union.
33. Robert Austin Warner, *New Haven Negroes: A Social History* (New Haven, CT: Yale University Press, 1940), 114.
34. Warner, 112; Osterweis, *Three Centuries of New Haven*, 356.
35. Charles (Ben) Hawley, "The Twenty-Ninth Regiment Colored Volunteers," in *African American Connecticut Explored*, ed. Elizabeth J. Normen, with Katherine J. Harris, Stacey K. Close, and William Frank Mitchell (Middletown, CT: Wesleyan University Press, 2013), 177–80; Diana Ross McCain, *Connecticut's African American Soldiers in the Civil War, 1861–1865* (Hartford, CT: Connecticut Historical Commission, 2000), http://www.ctfreedomtrail.org/data/files/resource-library/reports/CT-African-American-Soldiers-in-the-Civil-War.pdf; Eaton quoted in Matthew Warshauer, *Connecticut in the American Civil War: Slavery, Sacrifice, and Survival* (Middletown, CT: Wesleyan University

Press, 2011), 134–35. With gratitude to Ry Walker for "Monument Dedicated to the 29th Regiment Colored Volunteers," research on behalf of the Gilder Lehrman Center for the Study of Slavery and Abolition, 2017.

36. David Drury, "Called to Arms in Civil War, Connecticut's Black Soldiers Respond," *Hartford Courant*, January 18, 2014; Walker, "Monument"; Isaac J. Hill, *A Sketch of the 29th Regiment of Colored Troops* (Baltimore: Daugherty, Maguire, 1867), 7.
37. Visit by author to the monument for the Twenty-Ninth Connecticut Regiment and counting of names, Criscuolo Park, March 26, 2023.
38. *Daily Palladium* (New Haven, CT), January 28, 29, 1864; research and transcriptions by Thalia Pitt, Gilder Lehrman Center, 2019; Osterweis, *Three Centuries of New Haven*, 346–47. Also see David W. Blight, *Frederick Douglass: Prophet of Freedom* (New York: Simon and Schuster, 2018), 478–84. The day after Douglass's visit, the *Palladium* reported on "a head-of-the-wharf row," in which "Colored and white folks were inextricably mixed up for a time. High words, blows, and then a pistol shot, was the order of the Programme" (January 30, 1864).
39. Frederick Douglass, "The Mission of the War," address delivered many times from December 1863 through the summer of 1864, in *Frederick Douglass Papers*, ed. John W. Blassingame and John R. McKivigan (New Haven, CT: Yale University Press, 1991), ser. 1, vol. 4, pp. 4–7.
40. Douglass, 13–15, 19.
41. *Connecticut War Record* 1, no. 7 (February 1864): 147.
42. *Connecticut War Record*, 147; Walker, "Monument."
43. Hill, *Sketch of the 29th*, 8–9; Eliot, *Yale in the Civil War*, 19–20.
44. *Yale Literary Magazine*, November 1864, 45–49, 82–83; Eliot, *Yale in the Civil War*, 17.
45. *Yale Literary Magazine*, November 1864, 84; *New York Times*, August 24, October 24, 1864. On vote counts, see William W. Ginsberg, "'The Most Undignified, Unstatesmanlike, Unfeeling, Incompetent Man That Ever Occupied the Presidential Chair': New Haven's Rejection of Abraham Lincoln in 1864," remarks to the Social Science Club, New Haven, CT, April 14, 2008.
46. Atwater, *History of the City*, 80; Eliot, *Yale in the Civil War*, 17.
47. *Addresses and Proceedings*, 3–8, 20, 36–37. On Bushnell, see Bainton, *Yale and the Ministry*, 113–26. Also see King, *Theodore Dwight Woolsey*, 76.
48. *Addresses and Proceedings*, 42–43, 50, 59, 61–62; Eliot, *Yale in the Civil War*, 58–60.
49. *Addresses and Proceedings*, 37, 51, 59–62.
50. Christopher L. Webber, *American to the Backbone: The Life of James W. C. Pennington, the Fugitive Slave Who Became One of the First Black Abolitionists* (New York: Pegasus, 2011), 403–9, 427.
51. Webber, 424–33.
52. James Pennington, "The New Evangel," *Anglo-African*, October 7, 1865, and quoted in Webber, *American to the Backbone*, 420–21.

INTERLUDE: A YALE FAMILY IN SLAVERY AND FREEDOM

Epigraph: J. W. Manning Sr., "The Cry of the Children of Slavery," August 21, 1902, handwritten manuscript in possession of Walter B. Sanderson III and Darlene Sanderson. And for one of the landmark works about Black families before and after the Civil War, to which the chapter title nods, see Herbert G. Gutman, *The Black Family in Slavery and Freedom, 1750–1925* (New York: Pantheon Books, 1976).

1. Walter Sanderson, Jr., interviewed by Larry Crowe, March 9, 2012, HistoryMakers Digital Archive, A2012.068, session 1, tape 1, story 3, Walter Sanderson, Jr. talks about his maternal grandfather. Sanderson suggests that his grandfather's extraordinary journey took place in 1861; however, the Union blockade did not extend to the Port of Wilmington until 1865. It is also unlikely that John Wesley Manning's parents, who were enslaved in Edenton, would have been hired out in Wilmington, nearly two hundred miles away. However, such an escape may have been made in 1862, when, as a result of the Burnside Expedition, Union forces succeeded in controlling the coastal waters around Edenton (and beyond). Yale Manning Sanderson provided a slightly different account, relating that Alfred and Eliza Manning hid John in a trunk and mailed it to an address in New Haven; both family oral histories suggest that the Mannings had relatives or friends already living in New Haven. See Yale Manning Sanderson, "How I Got My Name," in possession of Walter B. Sanderson III and Darlene Sanderson. Robert Austin Warner found that a number of African American migrants to New Haven hailed from coastal North Carolina; he writes, "Early arrivals served as advance agents for relatives and friends." Warner, *New Haven Negroes: A Social History* (New Haven, CT: Yale University Press, 1940), 124–25.

    Based on biographical information provided by John Wesley Manning for his Yale class reunion book, his parents were Alfred Manning, identified as a ship carpenter and caulker, born in Edenton, North Carolina, and Eliza Manning, daughter of Osborn and Lucy (Iredell) Allston. James C. Johnston's family was closely connected to the Iredells and Allstons. See John G. Zehmer Jr., *Hayes: The Plantation, Its People, and Their Papers* (Raleigh: North Carolina Office of Archives and History, 2007), 48, 86, 108; "North Carolina as a Civil War Battlefield," North Carolina Historic Sites, accessed January 19, 2023, https://historicsites.nc.gov/resources/north-carolina-civil-war/north-carolina-civil-war-battlefield; and *A History of the Class of 'Eighty-One Yale College, Covering Thirty Years from Its Admission into the Academic Department, 1877–1907* (New York: Trow, 1909), 415–16.

2. Zehmer, *Hayes*, 1, 4, 26, 48. The maiden name of Eliza's mother, Lucy, was Iredell, suggesting the ways enslaved people were sold or gifted among family members.
3. "North Carolina as a Civil War Battlefield"; W. E. B. Du Bois, *Black Reconstruction in America* (New York: Atheneum, 1992), 55–83; Zehmer, *Hayes*, 98–99. Gerard is likely Lieutenant George Gerard, who attended Yale Law School before enlisting in the Union army. See "Report of Col. William A. Howard, First New York Marine Artillery," April 20, 1862, in *The War of the Rebellion: A Compilation of the Official Records of the Union and Confederate Armies*, by U.S. War Department (Washington, DC: Government Printing Office, 1883), series 1, vol. 9, pp. 308–9; and Mary Jo Ignoffo, *Captive of the Labyrinth: Sarah L. Winchester, Heiress to the Rifle Fortune* (Columbia: University of Missouri Press, 2022), 37–38.
4. Allen Parker, *Recollections of Slavery Times* (Worcester, MA: Chas. W. Burbank, 1895), chap. 8.

5. Edward Stanly to Edwin Stanton, June 12, 1862, in *A Military Governor among Abolitionists: A Letter from Edward Stanly to Charles Sumner* (New York, 1865), 29, North Carolina Collection, Wilson Library, University of North Carolina at Chapel Hill; Zehmer, *Hayes*, 99–101.
6. Zehmer, *Hayes*, 108, 86. Although Johnston and subsequent Yale publications spelled Osborn with a final "e," we have retained the spelling used by the family, including the younger Osborn Allston. See, for example, Allston's signature on receipts for Aug. 14, 1876, and Sept. 4, 1883, in Records of the Treasurer (RU 151), Box 34, folders 308 and 312, Manuscripts and Archives, Yale University Library.
7. "Information Wanted," *Christian Recorder* (Philadelphia), April 28, 1866. On families after emancipation, see the magnificent work of the Freedmen and Southern Society Project in, for example, Ira Berlin and Leslie S. Rowland, eds., *Families and Freedom: A Documentary History of African-American Kinship in the Civil War Era* (New York: New Press, 1997). The Osborn Allston employed by Yale was the son of the elder man of the same name living at Hayes, for whom James Johnston made provisions before he died. Three members of the Allston family were listed as Yale custodians in the *Yale Banner*, the yearbook, in the following years: Isom Allston, 1871–80; Lewis Allston, 1869; Osborn Allston, 1870–80. James Allston, identified as a cook, is listed in a New Haven city directory of 1881; see Ancestry.com. U.S., City Directories, 1822–1995 [database on-line]. Lehi, UT, USA: Ancestry.com Operations, Inc., 2011. Philip Allston, identified as a laborer, is listed at the same address years later; see Ancestry.com. U.S., City Directories, 1822–1995 [database on-line]. Lehi, UT, USA: Ancestry.com Operations, Inc., 2011. James Allston's birth year in the 1870 federal census aligns with the age given in the Hayes census notes; see Year: 1900; Census Place: New Haven, New Haven, Connecticut; Roll: 146; Page: 8; Enumeration District: 0383. Henderson Allston, also listed on the Hayes census notes and most likely a brother to Eliza, was living in New Haven with his family and working as a carpenter in 1870; see Year: 1870; Census Place: New Haven Ward 1, New Haven, Connecticut; Roll: M593_109; Page: 89A. The elder Osborn Allston died October 8, 1872, and is buried in plot 38, in an unmarked grave in Evergreen Cemetery in New Haven along with a son and daughter-in-law, Henderson and Ann Allston; visit by the research team on September 22, 2023.
8. U.S. Patent Office, *Annual Report of the Commissioner of Patents for the Year 1867* (Washington, DC: Government Printing Office, 1867), 685; *Obituary Record of Yale Graduates, 1921–1922* (New Haven, CT: Published by the University, 1922), 415–16; Henry Edward Manning alumni record, Alumni Records Office, Yale University, Records of Alumni from the Classes of 1701–1978 (RU 830), Box 1174, Manuscripts and Archives, Yale University Library. The patent was for "Jaws for Booms and Gaffs for Vessels."
9. Henry Manning alumni record; Edward Manning, 1920 United States Federal Census, Ancestry.com; "New Haven Letter," *New York Freeman*, May 22, 1886.
10. Manning, "Cry of the Children."
11. Ira Berlin, Joseph Patrick Reidy, and Leslie S. Rowland, eds., *Freedom's Soldiers: The Black Military Experience in the Civil War* (Cambridge: Cambridge University Press, 1998), i.

CHAPTER 10. BLACK STUDENTS AT YALE

Epigraph: William Henry Ferris, *The African Abroad, or, His Evolution in Western Civilization: Tracing His Development under Caucasian Milieu* (New Haven, CT: Tuttle, Morehouse and Taylor, 1913), 2:594. The ethnologist Augustus Henry Keane quoted Ruffin as saying, "The Negro is incapable of receiving what white men call religion and education, and he is worse after professing to have received them than he was before," in A. H. Keane, *Africa* (London: Edward Stanford, 1895), 2:125.

1. "A Good Story from Yale," *Connecticut Courant*, May 27, 1871.
2. See, for example, Steven Hahn, *A Nation under Our Feet: Black Political Struggles in the Rural South from Slavery to the Great Migration* (Cambridge, MA: Harvard University Press, 2003), 265–95. The historiography of Reconstruction-era violence is rich and expansive. For a recent work that centers African Americans' first-person accounts of the horrors they witnessed and experienced, see Kidada E. Williams, *I Saw Death Coming: A History of Terror and Survival in the War against Reconstruction* (London: Bloomsbury, 2023). See also "Reconstruction in America: Racial Violence after the Civil War, 1865–1876," Equal Justice Initiative, 2020, https://eji.org/report/reconstruction-in-america. For testimony, see U.S. Congress Joint Select Committee, *Report of the Joint Select Committee to Inquire into the Condition of Affairs in the Late Insurrectionary States*, 13 vols. (Washington, DC: Government Printing Office, 1872). These hearings were conducted by tribunals of congressmen in seven Southern states.
3. Black students did graduate from Yale before the Civil War: Richard Henry Greene, class of 1857, is now remembered as the first Black graduate of Yale College; Cortlandt Van Rensselaer Creed graduated from the medical school the same year. See Judith Ann Schiff, "The Life of Richard Henry Green," *Yale Alumni Magazine*, May/June 2014, https://yalealumnimagazine.org/articles/3875; Mark Alden Branch, "History, found," *Yale Alumni Magazine*, March/April 2023, https://yalealumnimagazine.org/articles/5622-history-found; and Richard Henry Green Papers (MS 2005), Manuscripts and Archives, Yale University Library. Branch notes that Greene started spelling his name with an "e" at the end after 1861, as did his wife and daughter. On Richard T. Greener of Harvard, see Katherine Reynolds Chaddock, *Uncompromising Activist: Richard Greener, First Black Graduate of Harvard College* (Baltimore: Johns Hopkins University Press, 2017). And see Stefan M. Bradley, *Upending the Ivory Tower: Civil Rights, Black Power, and the Ivy League* (New York: New York University Press, 2018), 23–45.
4. Thomas Rodd Jr., "Edward A. Bouchet—the Years at Hopkins Grammar School: 1868–1870," 24; H. Kenneth Bechtel, "Edward Alexander Bouchet—the Master Teacher and Educator," 46–47; and on the Bouchets, Creeds, and their community, Curtis L. Patton, "Early African American Presence in New Haven and Yale University," 1–18, all in *Edward Bouchet: The First African-American Doctorate*, ed. Ronald E. Mickens (Hackensack, NJ: World Scientific, 2002). The essays in this volume are invaluable for understanding not only Bouchet and his significance but also his broader social and political worlds. Also see *Christian Freeman*, letter to the editors, signed Joseph Browne, September 6, 1845, Amos Gerry Beman Scrapbooks, vol. 1, Yale Collection of American Literature, Beinecke Rare Book and Manuscript Library, Yale University; Liz Warner, "A Family of

Reformers: The Middletown Bemans," *Connecticut Explored*, Winter 2008/9, https://www.ctexplored.org/a-family-of-reformers-the-middletown-bemans; and "Proceedings of the Connecticut State Convention of Colored Men, Held at New Haven on September 12th and 13th, 1849" and "Proceedings of the Conn. State Convention of Colored Men," New Haven, June 6 and 7, 1865, Beman Scrapbooks, vol. 3.

5. Patton, "Early African American Presence," 6–8, 18; Rodd, "Edward A. Bouchet," 24; Bechtel, "Edward Alexander Bouchet," 47. On the Creed family, see chapter 4. Bouchet was the first African American person to be nominated to Phi Beta Kappa; however, Yale's chapter was inactive at the time so he is considered the second African American person to be elected; see "Edward A. Bouchet Graduate Honor Society Charter," last updated April 1, 2019, https://gsas.yale.edu/sites/default/files/page-files/bghs_charter_0_0.pdf.
6. On his dissertation, see Bechtel, "Edward Alexander Bouchet," 45–46.
7. Will papers of Mary A. Goodman, Connecticut, U.S., Wills and Probate Records, 1609–1999, Ancestry.com; "Interesting Gift to Yale Divinity School," *Congregationalist*, February 1, 1872; Mary Goodman's (1804–1872) Headstone in Grove Street Cemetery, New Haven, Yale University Library Online Exhibitions, https://onlineexhibits.library.yale.edu/s/treasures-of-the-area-studies-collections-reconsidering-primary-sources-and-collections/item/13741#?c=&m=&s=&cv=&xywh=-1363%2C-1%2C4551%2C2555.
8. On Morris, see *Obituary Record of Graduates of Yale College, Deceased during the Academical Year Ending in June, 1876, Including the Record of a Few Who Died a Short Time Previous, Hitherto Unreported, Presented at the Meeting of the Alumni, June 28, 1876* (New Haven, CT: Tuttle, Morehouse & Taylor, 1880), 233. On Coles, see Moses N. Moore Jr. and Yolanda Y. Smith, "Solomon M. Coles: Preacher, Teacher, and Former Slave—the First Black Student Officially Enrolled in Yale Divinity School," revised May 1, 2007, https://storm.yale.edu/sites/default/files/pages/coles_5_1_07.pdf; and Gerard N. Burrow, *A History of Yale's School of Medicine: Passing Torches to Others* (New Haven, CT: Yale University Press, 2002), 206. Many of the achievements of these Black graduates were noted in the *Connecticut Courant*. See "News of the State," *Connecticut Courant*, May 16, 1874; and "News of the State," *Connecticut Courant*, February 24, 1876. On medical students, see Daryl Keith Daniels, "African-Americans at the Yale University School of Medicine: 1810–1960" (master's thesis, Yale University, 1991), 51, 53–54, 69–70.
9. "The Civil Rights Bill," *Connecticut Courant*, May 30, 1874.
10. Henry L. Foote, ed., *Yale College Class Book 1904* (New Haven, CT: Yale University, 1904), 18.
11. "Baker, Thomas Nelson, Sr.," in *African American National Biography*, ed. Henry Louis Gates Jr. and Evelyn Brooks Higginbotham (New York: Oxford University Press, 2008), 1:237–38.
12. Daniels, "African-Americans," 55; Emily Matson, "John Staige Davis (1824–1885)," Encyclopedia Virginia, last updated December 22, 2021, https://encyclopediavirginia.org/entries/davis-john-staige-1824-1885; R. L. Gamble, "Henry Floyd Gamble, M.D., 1862–1932," *Journal of the National Medical Association* 64, no. 1 (January 1972): 85–86. The Yale Theological Department was founded in 1822; it officially became the Yale Divinity School in 1888; see Ray Waddle, *This Grand Errand: A Bicentennial History of Yale Divinity School* (New Haven, CT: Yale University Press, 2022), 29n1.

13. Frederick Pierce, "Working One's Way," in *Life at Yale*, ed. Edwin Rogers Embree (New Haven, CT: Yale University Press, 1912), 53–56; Robert Austin Warner, *New Haven Negroes: A Social History* (New Haven, CT: Yale University Press, 1940), 175–76; Daniels, "African-Americans," 60–66; "Walter J. Scott of Virginia," *New York Freeman*, December 13, 1884; J. Clay Smith Jr., *Emancipation: The Making of the Black Lawyer, 1844–1944* (Philadelphia: University of Pennsylvania Press, 1993), 126; *Biographies of Graduates of the Yale Law School, 1824–1899* (New Haven, CT: Tuttle, Morehouse and Taylor, 1911), 433–34. The *New York Freeman* identified the *New Haven Free Press* as the first Black newspaper in New England; see *Boston Daily Advertiser*, September 26, 1877. It was still listed as a newspaper in the *Boston Herald*, November 4, 1888. On Scott's uncle, Oscar Jarvis, see *Benham's New Haven Directory* for 1869, 260; *Benham's New Haven Directory* for 1873, 269; and 1880 Federal Census, all via Ancestry.com.
14. William Pickens Papers Finding Aid, James Weldon Johnson Collection, Yale Collection of American Literature, Beinecke Rare Book and Manuscript Library. David Stuart Dodge further put Pickens in touch with his cousin, Anson Phelps Stokes, secretary of the university. See William Pickens, *The Heir of Slaves: An Autobiography* (Boston: Pilgrim, 1911), 116–18; "William Pickens. A Short Sketch of This Brilliant Colored Man. History of His Struggle for an Education," *Evening Leader, New Haven*, [date unclear, 1903], and "The Story of Pickens of Yale," *Cleveland Leader*, August 23, 1903, Box 2, Pickens Papers; and Robert Austin Warner, *New Haven Negroes*, 175–76. Pickens's winning speech argued against self-rule for Haiti. His award was covered in the national press, where he was hailed as "a promising youth" and "a negro worth mentioning." See "A Promising Youth," [handwriting unclear], April 4, 1903; and "A Negro Worth Mentioning," *Washington Post*, April 1903. Other papers saw his award as a reflection of Yale, writing "Yale Is Democratic: Winning of Ten Eyck Prize by a Negro Conclusive Proof" (*Chicago Evening*, unclear date), "An Illustration of the Democratic Spirit at Yale" (*New Haven Palladium* [?], unclear date), and "No Color Line Drawn at Yale." Former president Grover Cleveland wrote to Pickens to ask for a copy of his speech, and his letter was reprinted in "Cleveland to a Negro," *New York Sun*, April 6, 1903. See Pickens Papers, Box 2, for clippings. For a reprinting of his prize-winning speech, see William Pickens, "Hayti," *Yale Literary Magazine*, April 1903, 232–38.
15. "Soiree of the A. O. S.," *New Haven Evening Register*, April 29, 1891; Daniels, "African-Americans," 61–62.
16. Brandon R. Byrd, "Emancipation, Reconstruction, and the Quandary of Haiti," in *The Black Republic: African Americans and the Fate of Haiti* (Philadelphia: University of Pennsylvania Press, 2020), 37, 39; Amy J. Barry, "Another First for Ebenezer Bassett," *Courier: News from Central Connecticut State University*, accessed July 14, 2023, https://www2.ccsu.edu/courier/?article=382; "The Late Mrs. Bassett," *New Haven Register*, August 24, 1895; *Quarter Century Record of the Class of Ninety-Five, Yale College* (New Haven, CT: Tuttle, Morehouse and Taylor, 1922), 105–6; Henry N. Hyde, Emerson G. Taylor, and Roger W. Tuttle, eds., *Quindecennial Record of the Class of Ninety-Five, Yale College* (New Haven, CT: Tuttle, Morehouse and Taylor, 1911), 11, 30; "Yale Log," *Yale Daily News*, February 5, 1879; David W. Blight, *Frederick Douglass: Prophet of Freedom* (New York: Simon and Schuster, 2018), 778–802. In his entry for his class's twenty-fifth reunion, Ulysses

Simpson Grant Bassett provided details about his siblings, including an older brother, Ebenezer Jr., who was a member of the Yale College class of 1885 (he did not graduate); see *Yale Banner* 53 (1894): 144.

17. *The National Cyclopedia of American Biography* [. . .] (New York: J. T. White, 1906), 13:477–78; "Wedded To-morrow," *New Haven Evening Register*, August 1, 1883; *Biographies of Graduates of the Yale Law School, 1824–1899* (New Haven, CT: Tuttle, Morehouse and Taylor, 1911), 679–82.
18. "Work in Mission Fields. Foreign and Home Service Methods Discussed Today," *New Haven Register*, November 8, 1895; Marcus Bruce, "The Making of a Pan-Africanist: George Henry Jackson and the Lukunga Mission in the Congo Free State," in *In Search of Liberty: African American Internationalism in the Nineteenth-Century Atlantic World*, ed. Ronald Angelo Johnson and Ousmane K. Power-Greene (Athens: University of Georgia Press, 2021), 146, 142, 152–53; *Message from the President* [. . .] *Transmitting, in Response to the Resolution of the Senate of March 2, 1901, a Communication from the Secretary of State Submitting Reports from Consular Officers* [. . .] (Washington, DC: U.S. Government Printing Office, 1902), 128; George H. Jackson's outline for the Alumni Record (1902), Box 47, Divinity School, Yale University, Student Records (RU 913), Manuscripts and Archives, Yale University Library.
19. "George H. Jackson Wants Place. New Haven Colored Man Applies for a Consulate," *New Haven Register*, May 15, 1897; "The Enumeration Begun. McCarthy's Assistants at Work," *New Haven Register*, June 2, 1890; "Two Ward Rallies," *New Haven Register*, October 17, 1896; "Dinner to Consul G. H. Jackson," *Springfield Republican*, August 31, 1897. On Jackson's work, see "Brandy Making in France," in *Consular Reports* (Washington, DC: Government Printing Office, 1899), 255–56; "George H. Jackson," FranceAndUS, accessed July 11, 2023, https://www.franceussports.com/voices/005-george-h-jackson; *Crisis* 7, no. 4 (February 1914): 170; and *Bulletin of Yale University, Obituary Record of Graduates Deceased during the Year Ending July 1, 1944* (New Haven, CT: Yale University, 1945), 307–8. For the argument that his experiences in the Congo shaped his work as a pan-Africanist, see Bruce, "Making of a Pan-Africanist," 159. Bruce's work is the most comprehensive secondary source to date concerning Jackson.
20. Ferris, *African Abroad*, 2:525. On Crummell, see chapter 8. And on Garvey, see Robin D. G. Kelley, *Freedom Dreams: The Black Radical Imagination* (Boston: Beacon, 2002).
21. "William Henry Ferris," *Journal of Negro History* 26, no. 4 (October 1941): 549–50; Cary D. Wintz and Paul Finkelman, eds., *Encyclopedia of the Harlem Renaissance* (London: Taylor and Francis, 2004), 1:369–70.
22. *Obituary Record of Yale Graduates, 1921–1922* (New Haven, CT: Published by the University, 1922), 415–16.
23. Brooks Mather Kelley, *Yale: A History* (New Haven, CT: Yale University Press, 1974), 221. The junior exhibition was discussed frequently in the *Yale Daily News*; see "Junior Appointments," *Yale Daily News*, January 19, 1893, for the grading system. On Boyer, see Robert Austin Warner, *New Haven Negroes*, 175; A. B. Caldwell, ed., *History of the American Negro, North Carolina Edition* (Atlanta: A. B. Caldwell, 1921), 4:249–52; Clarence S. Day Jr., *Decennial Record of the Class of 1896, Yale College* (New York: printed for the class at the De Vinne Press, 1907), 67, 227–28; and James Alexander Boyer Papers,

1893–2000, Finding Aid, Southern Historical Collection, Wilson Library, University of North Carolina at Chapel Hill. On Pickens, see Sheldon Avery, *Up from Washington: William Pickens and the Negro Struggle for Equality, 1900–1954* (Newark: University of Delaware Press, 1989), 9–11, 35, 54–57, and passim.

24. Smith, *Emancipation*, 126–27, 225–26; "Alumni Notes," *Yale Daily News*, February 9, 1888; *Quarter-Centenary Record of the Class of 1885 Yale University* (Boston: Fort Hill, 1913), 339; "Robert Bradford Williams," in *Obituary Record of Yale Graduates, 1942–1943* (New Haven, CT: Published by the University, 1944), 287. Also see the Kent A. Leslie Collection on Robert Bradford Williams, MS 2098, Manuscripts and Archives, Yale University Library.
25. "Win Yale Law Prizes: Negro and Chinaman Divide Highest Commencement Honors," *Philadelphia Record*, June 23, 1903; Smith, *Emancipation*, 127, 162; "George Crawford Dead at 94; Held State and City Offices," *New Haven Register*, August 2, 1972. Also see "George W. Crawford," *New York Times*, August 3, 1972.
26. "Yale Log," *Yale Daily News*, March 28, 1879; "Verses," *Yale Daily News*, October 23, 1883. For instances of racist slurs and dialect, see the *Yale Daily News*, October 30, 1882, December 12, 1882, February 1, 1883, October 4, 1883, June 21, 1893. This is not a comprehensive list.
27. *Yale Banner* 45 (1886): 146; *Yale Banner* 48 (1889): 191. For other stereotypical depictions, all in the *Yale Banner*, see 32 (1875): 81; 35 (1878): 82; 36 (1879): 85, 89; 41 (1882): 113, 120; 45 (1886): 153, 160; 34 (1887): 156; 47 (1888): 205; 59 (1900): 283; 60 (1901): 387; 65 (1906): 289.
28. R. M. H., "The Negro," in "Portfolio," *Yale Literary Magazine*, October 1886, 27.
29. "The African Dodger," Jim Crow Museum, October 2012, https://jimcrowmuseum.ferris.edu/question/2012/october.htm; Lewis Sheldon Welch and Walter Camp, *Yale, Her Campus, Class-Rooms, and Athletics* (Boston: L. C. Page, 1900), 147–48; "Yale Log," *Yale Daily News*, April 3, 1879; "Yale Log," *Yale Daily News*, April 8, 1879; "Tomorrow," *Yale Daily News*, April 9, 1879; "Yale Log," *Yale Daily News*, May 28, 1879; "Communication," *Yale Daily News*, May 13, 1885. For "the pioneer and father of neurosurgery," see "Dr. Harvey Cushing," Harvey Cushing / John Hay Whitney Medical Library, accessed September 12, 2023, https://library.medicine.yale.edu/cushingcenter/harvey-cushing; and Michael Bliss, *Harvey Cushing: A Life in Surgery* (New York: Oxford University Press, 2007), 52, 529n34. For mentions of the game beyond New Haven, see "Pacific Coast News—Nevada," *Salt Lake Tribune*, April 8, 1874; "Charity and Blood," *Tacoma Daily News*, June 4, 1894; "No 'Willie's' Game," *Cherokee Advocate*, February 6, 1897; "At Other Colleges," *Harvard Crimson*, May 18, 1877; and "At Other Colleges," *Harvard Crimson*, December 20, 1877.
30. Unsigned editorial, *Yale Courant*, January 27, 1866; *Yale Literary Magazine*, December 1869; *Yale Literary Magazine*, October 1870; "Amusements This Week," *Yale Daily News*, February 21, 1881; "Callender's Colossal Colored Minstrel Festival," *Yale Daily News*, January 16, 1884; advertisement, *Yale Daily News*, March 26, 1888; "Yale Log," *Yale Daily News*, January 15, 1884; "Amusements," *Yale Daily News*, March 18, 1884; "The Navy Benefit," *Yale Daily News*, March 24, 1884.
31. "Yale Log," *Yale Daily News*, May 12, 1886; "Lecture by Thomas Nelson Page," *Yale Daily News*, May 18, 1898; *Yale Literary Magazine*, December 1894, 121–25. A contemporary

scholar credits Page with the "invention of the 'plantation tradition,' which overtly romanticized slavery"; see Amy Kaplan, "Nation, Region, and Empire," in *The Columbia History of the American Novel*, ed. Emory Elliott et al. (New York: Columbia University Press, 1991), 244.

32. "Old Plantation Southern Slaves," *Yale Daily News*, May 14, 1883.
33. "Another Negro Burned," *New York Times*, February 2, 1893; Manfred Berg, *Popular Justice: A History of Lynching in America* (Chicago: Ivan R. Dee, 2011), 90–91.
34. "On This Day—June 3, 1893," A History of Racial Injustice, Equal Justice Initiative, accessed September 12, 2023, https://calendar.eji.org/racial-injustice/jun/3; Ida B. Wells, *The Reason Why the Colored American Is Not in the World's Columbian Exposition* (Chicago: privately published, 1893), 26–27; Equal Justice Initiative, *Lynching in America: Confronting the Legacy of Racial Terror*, 3rd ed. (Equal Justice Initiative, 2017), https://eji.org/reports/lynching-in-america; Berg, *Popular Justice*, 92.
35. "Subjects for the Townsend Essays," *Yale Daily News*, November 20, 1893; "Sheffield Debating News," *Yale Daily News*, November 27, 1897. These were not isolated cases. In 1901, the John A. Porter Prize in American History invited juniors and seniors to write original essays on topics including "the History of the Lynchings of Negroes in the South." See "John A. Porter Prize," *Yale Daily News*, November 4, 1901; and "Lynchings by Year and Race," University of Missouri Kansas City Law School, accessed September 12, 2023, http://law2.umkc.edu/faculty/projects/ftrials/shipp/lynchingyear.html.
36. "Junior Disputes," November 8, 1882; "Junior Dispute Subjects," October 12, 1883; "Junior Compositions," January 21, 1887; "Notices," February 16, 1887; "Sophomore Compositions," March 6, 1890; on colonization, "Kent Club," March 12, 1895; on disenfranchisement, "Freshman Union," October 26, 1895; "Yale Log," December 3, 1896; "Law School Prize Debate," March 24, 1891; "Yale Union," April 4, 1891, all in *Yale Daily News*. On New Orleans, see Matthew Frye Jacobson, *Whiteness of a Different Color: European Immigrants and the Alchemy of Race* (Cambridge, MA: Harvard University Press, 1999), 56–62.
37. "Kent Club," December 11, 1900; "Sophomore Wigwam," January 12, 1901; "Sophomore Wranglers," January 24, 1901; "Yale Union," February 9, 1901, all in *Yale Daily News*. The Wigwam was organized in 1898; see Welch and Camp, *Yale, Her Campus*, 191.
38. "Princeton Debate," October 26, 1901; "Princeton Debating Team," November 5, 1901; "Yale-Princeton Debate," December 6, 1901; "Yale Wins Debate," December 7, 1901, all in *Yale Daily News*.
39. "Yale Union," December 7, 1900; "Freshman Union Debate," February 25, 1909; "University Prizes," November 23, 1910; "Freshman Debating Union," January 7, 1911, all in *Yale Daily News*. On Pickens's exclusion from the Yale debating team, see unattributed clipping in scrapbook, Box 2, Pickens Papers, Beinecke Rare Book and Manuscript Library. For Reconstruction as "unfinished," see Eric Foner, *Reconstruction: America's Unfinished Revolution, 1863–1877* (New York, NY: Harper & Row, 1988).
40. "Kent Club Lecture," *Yale Daily News*, March 27, 1890.
41. "George W. Cable," in *The Literature of the American South: A Norton Anthology*, ed. William L. Andrews (New York: W. W. Norton, 1998), 275–77; "Phi Beta Kappa Lecture," *Yale Daily News*, April 23, 1892. Also see David W. Blight, *Race and Reunion: The Civil War in American Memory* (Cambridge, MA: Harvard University Press, 2001), 294–95.

Representatives from the Hampton Institute spoke at Yale in 1887, 1889, and 1895; E. T. Ware, class of 1897, spoke about his work at Atlanta University in 1897. See "Hampton Institute," December 2, 1887; "Gen. Armstrong's Lecture," February 15, 1889; "Lecture on Hampton School," March 25, 1895; and "Sunday Services," November 6, 1897, all in *Yale Daily News*.

42. "Lectures of the Week," *Yale Daily News*, March 11, 1901; "Lectures of the Week," *Yale Daily News*, March 15, 1901; "Mr. Washington's Address," *Yale Daily News*, March 16, 1901; "Booker Washington's Address," *Yale Daily News*, November 25, 1895; "Booker T. Washington," *Yale Daily News*, November 30, 1896, December 2, 1899, March 11, 1901; W. E. B. Du Bois, *The Souls of Black Folk* (Oxford: Oxford University Press, 2007), 22. The last *published* speech in New Haven was "Address before the American Missionary Association and National Council of Congregational Churches," October 25, 1915, reprinted in Booker T. Washington, *The Booker T. Washington Papers Collection*, 14 vols., ed. Louis R. Harlan and Raymond W. Smock (Urbana: University of Illinois Press, 1972–80), 13:410–14. See also B. T. W. to Margaret James Murray Washington, October 26, 1915, in *Booker T. Washington Papers Collection*, 414. Washington's very last speech, however, took place at the Varick Memorial African Methodist Episcopal Zion Church; see chapter 11.

43. Booker T. Washington, *Up from Slavery: An Autobiography* (1901; repr., Williamstown, MA: Corner House, 1978), 13–14, 16, 17, 247; Booker T. Washington, "Address before Brooklyn Institute of Science," February 2, 1903; Booker T. Washington, "Religious Life of the Negro," *North American Review*, July 1905; and *Boston Globe*, October 4, 1904, in *Booker T. Washington Papers Collection*, 8:333, 84. And see Blight, *Race and Reunion*, 319–20.

44. Booker T. Washington, "The Atlanta Exposition Address," in *Up from Slavery: An Autobiography* (New York: Doubleday, 1901), 220; Bechtel, "Edward Alexander Bouchet," 47–54.

45. "Yale University Application for Position as a Teacher," June 8, 1905, Yale Alumni Records Office, RU 830, Series VI, Box 1042, Manuscripts and Archives, Yale University Library.

46. Bechtel, "Edward Alexander Bouchet," 45; Bouchet obituary in *Bulletin of Yale University, Obituary Record of Yale Graduates, 1918–1919*, no. 11 (New Haven, CT: Yale University, 1919), 919–20. Information on Bouchet's years at the Institute for Colored Youth can be found in Linda M. Perkins, *Fanny Jackson Coppin and the Institute for Colored Youth, 1865–1902* (New York: Garland, 1987). On the portrait, see "Architectural History of Sterling Memorial Library," Yale University Library Online Exhibitions, accessed July 13, 2023, https://onlineexhibits.library.yale.edu/s/architecturalhistorysml/page/almamater. Awards and events honoring Bouchet at Yale include the Edward A. Bouchet Conference and Edward Alexander Bouchet Graduate Honor Society: "Edward A. Bouchet Conference," Yale Graduate School of Arts and Sciences, accessed September 12, 2023, https://gsas.yale.edu/diversity/office-graduate-student-development-diversity/edward-bouchet-conference. On past and continuing efforts to understand and elevate Bouchet's contributions, see Ainissa Ramirez, "On Henry, Trailblazer Gets His Due," *New Haven Independent*, August 30, 2021.

47. *Yale College Obituary Record, 1921–1922*, 415–16; *A History of the Class of 'Eighty-One Yale College, Covering Thirty Years from Its Admission into the Academic Department, 1877–1907* (New York: Trow, 1909), 243–45; Henry Walcott Farnam, ed., *Biographical Record of the Class of 1874 in Yale College: Part Fourth, 1874–1909* (New Haven, CT: Tuttle, Morehouse and Taylor, 1912), xxii; obituary quoted in John A. Wilkinson, "In Search of Edward Bouchet," in Mickens, *Edward Bouchet*, 77; *Yale Alumni Weekly* 28 (1918): 1036.
48. Scholars have debated when this period ended and a new, more promising era for Black Americans began. John Hope Franklin believed the "long dark night" continued into the 1920s. See Rayford W. Logan, *The Negro in American Life and Thought: The Nadir, 1877–1901* (1965; New York: Collier Books, 1972), 11.
49. J. W. Manning Sr., "The Cry of the Children of Slavery," August 21, 1902, handwritten manuscript in possession of Walter B. Sanderson III and Darlene Sanderson and generously shared with the Yale and Slavery Research Project.

INTERLUDE: BLACK EMPLOYEES AT YALE

Epigraph: N. W. T. Root, "Song of the Sweep," in *Songs of Yale* (New Haven, CT: E. Richardson, 1853), 12–13.

1. See Robert Austin Warner, *New Haven Negroes: A Social History* (New Haven, CT: Yale University Press, 1940), 246–47. Warner writes, "In the Negro community, Yale employment carried an aura of prestige." The term "sweep" may derive from "chimney sweep."
2. A Graduate of '69 [Lyman Hotchkiss Bagg], *Four Years at Yale* (New Haven, CT: Charles C. Chatfield, 1871), 293–94.
3. On John Brownlee Robertson, see *Obituary Record of Graduates of Yale University, Deceased during the Academical Year Ending in June, 1893* [. . .] (New Haven, CT: Tuttle, Morehouse & and Taylor, 1893), 146; and on William Bouchet, see chapter 10. The names of sweeps and other service employees were culled from issues of the *Yale Banner*, 1869–80. On McLinn, see *Yale Banner* 37 (1880): 136; Warner, *New Haven Negroes*, 176–78; and William Henry Ferris, *The African Abroad, or, His Evolution in Western Civilization: Tracing His Development under Caucasian Milieu* (New Haven, CT: Tuttle, Morehouse and Taylor, 1913), 2:700.
4. Custodial and Administrative Services, Yale University, Photographs, RU 763, Manuscripts and Archives, Yale University Library; *Yale Courant*, January 6, 1866, 20; *Yale Courant*, February 10, 1866, 38; *Yale Courant*, January 16, 1867, 139; *Yale Courant*, March 10, 1866, 55; *Yale Courant*, May 19, 1866, 81.
5. "Prof. Henry A. Beers of Yale Dead at 79," *New York Times*, September 8, 1926; Henry A. Beers, *The Ways of Yale in the Consulship of Plancus* (New York: Henry Holt, 1895), 183–84, 50–51.
6. Beers, *Ways of Yale*, 79–80, 48–55.
7. [Bagg], *Four Years at Yale*, 297; John Addison Porter, ed., *Sketches of Yale Life: Being Selections, Humorous and Descriptive, from the College Magazines and Newspapers* (Washington, DC: T. Arlington, 1886), 99–104.
8. Quoted in Joseph Boskin, *Sambo: The Rise and Demise of an American Jester* (New York: Oxford University Press, 1988), 103–4.

9. "Funeral of John Jackson," *Yale Daily News*, March 3, 1887.
10. *Yale Banner* 27 (1870): 68; *Yale Courant*, October 17, 1866, 51; Henry P. Wright, ed., *History of the Class of 1868, Yale College, 1864–1914* (New Haven, CT: Tuttle, Morehouse and Taylor, 1914), 5; *Yale Literary Magazine* 34, no. 4 (February 1869): 165–68.
11. Clarence Deming, *Yale Yesterdays* (New Haven, CT: Yale University Press, 1915), 95.
12. [Bagg], *Four Years at Yale*, 294–95.
13. *Compiled Military Service Records of Volunteer Union Soldiers Who Served with the United States Colored Troops: Infantry Organizations, 26th through 30th, Including the 29th Connecticut (Colored)* (Washington, DC: National Archives), microfilm, Serial M1824, Roll 66, Ancestry.com; "Hannibal Is Dead," *Boston Herald*, November 11, 1907; *Yale Alumni Weekly*, November 20, 1907, 196–98.
14. "Osborne Allston," *Yale Daily News*, November 10, 1884; "A Tribute of a Member of '84 to Allston," *Yale Daily News*, November 14, 1884.
15. "Tribute"; see also Interlude: A Yale Family in Slavery and Freedom, on the Manning and Allston family.
16. "Tribute"; on the gravestone, see "Notices," *Yale Daily News*, December 8, 1884.
17. On Park's earlier life, see chapter 5.
18. "Was Janitor of Skull and Bones," *New Haven Register*, September 18, 1895; "Mortuary Notice," *New Haven Register*, September 21, 1895; David Alan Richards, *Skulls and Keys: The Hidden History of Yale's Secret Societies* (New York: Pegasus Books, 2017), 386.

CHAPTER 11. EMBRACING THE WHITE SOUTH

Epigraph: "Pres. Hadley in Charleston," *Yale Alumni Weekly*, April 12, 1905, 556–57.

1. Joseph Hopkins Twichell Papers, Yale Collection of American Literature, Beinecke Rare Book and Manuscript Library. On Twichell's life, see Steve Courtney, *Joseph Hopkins Twichell: The Life and Times of Mark Twain's Closest Friend* (Athens: University of Georgia Press, 2008).
2. Joseph Hopkins Twichell, *The Civil War Letters of Joseph Hopkins Twichell: A Chaplain's Story*, ed. Peter Messent and Steve Courtney (Athens: University of Georgia Press, 2006), 1. See, for example, May 6–11, 1878, Journal 3; June 4–5, 1878, Journal 3; June 28–July 3, 1886, Journal 5; "Dedication of Arch Erected by the Town of Hartford in Memory of Its Soldiers and Sailors in the War for the Union, 1861–1865," program, Journal 5; June 29–July 5, 1888, Journal 6; October 21–26, 1907, Journal 9; and July 26, 1885, Journal 5, all in Twichell Papers.
3. June 22, 1896, Journal 6, Twichell Papers.
4. "Dedication of Arch"; "The Blue and the Gray," *New York Times*, July 2, 1888; June 29–July 5, 1888, Journal 6, Twichell Papers (emphasis in the original). On Blue and Gray reunions, see David W. Blight, *Race and Reunion: The Civil War in American Memory* (Cambridge, MA: Harvard University Press, 2001), 198–210.
5. May 30, 1888, Journal 6, Twichell Papers.
6. July 26, 1885, Journal 5, Twichell Papers; Grant memorial service program, Journal 5, Twichell Papers.
7. Robert Stiles to Joseph Twichell, May 8, 1868, Box 9, Twichell Papers (emphasis in original); on their college friendship, see Courtney, *Joseph Hopkins Twichell*, 28–39, and on their wartime encounter, 109–10.

8. June 27–30, 1879, Journal 3, and March 14–29, 1888, Journal 5, Twichell Papers; Robert Stiles, *Four Years under Marse Robert* (New York: Neale, 1904), vii. See also Courtney, *Joseph Hopkins Twichell*, 54–55.
9. June 22, 1896, Journal 6, Twichell Papers.
10. *Yale Alumni Weekly*, June 10, 1896; June 22, 1896, Journal 6, Twichell Papers. Twichell wrote in his journal that the Associated Press coverage of his remarks was less accurate. He pasted into his journal the *Yale Alumni Weekly* article.
11. "Rev. Twichell Condemns Class Ivy," *New Haven Evening Register*, June 22, 1896; "Yale Class Day Gayety," *New York Times*, June 23, 1896.
12. June 22, 1896, Journal 6, Twichell Papers; "Rev. Twichell Condemns"; John H. Eicher and David J. Eicher, *Civil War High Commands* (Stanford, CA: Stanford University Press, 2001), 236. In an ironic turn, Twichell recalled that he had last seen Fitzhugh the night after Lee's surrender.
13. On Winthrop, see Judith Schiff, "Two Months in the Civil War," *Yale Alumni Magazine*, July/August 2011; Wallace quoted in "Yale Men Applauded," *Daily Charlotte Observer*, June 27, 1896; Wells quoted in "Yale's Ivy Union. Proposition to Plant a Slip from Theodore Winthrop's Grave with That from the Tomb of General Lee," *Boston Daily Journal*, October 2, 1896.
14. *The Report of the Celebration of the Two Hundredth Anniversary of the Founding of Yale College, Held at Yale University, in New Haven, Connecticut, October the Twentieth to October the Twenty-Third, A.D. Nineteen Hundred and One* (New Haven, CT: published by the university, 1902), 250–55. On the first seven, in the order they are named, see Nathaniel Cheairs Hughes Jr., *Yale's Confederates: A Biographical Dictionary* (Knoxville: University of Tennessee Press, 2008), 82–83, 205–6, 112–13, 107, 194–95, 170, 106. On Croxton, see "The Obituary Record of Graduates of Yale College, Deceased during the Academical Year Ending in June, 1874, Including the Record of a Few Who Died a Short Time Previous, Hitherto Unreported. Presented at the Meeting of the Alumni, June 24th, 1874," June 24, 1974, http://mssa.library.yale.edu/obituary_record/1859_1924/1893-94.pdf, 147–48, 254; and Rex Miller, "John Thomas Croxton: Scholar, Lawyer, Soldiers, Military Governor, Newspaperman, Diplomat and Mason," *Register of the Kentucky Historical Society* 74, no. 4 (1976): 281–99.
15. *Report of the Celebration*, 273, 276, 187–88. Thomas Thatcher, in his lecture "Yale in Its Relation to Law," described Calhoun as "strong and keen in intellect, upright in character, determined, tenacious, and indefatigable," and as "the apostle of a lost cause."
16. On Rhodes, see Blight, *Race and Reunion*, 357–59. On Cable, see "George W. Cable," in *The Literature of the American South: A Norton Anthology*, ed. William L. Andrews (New York: W. W. Norton, 1998), 275–77. For honorary degree recipients, see *Report of the Celebration*: Roosevelt, 414; Clemens, 406; Dabney, 397; Frissell, 43, 397–98; Rhodes, 404; Cable, 405–6; Page, 406–7. On Page and his "invention of the 'plantation tradition,'" see Amy Kaplan, "Nation, Region, and Empire," in *The Columbia History of the American Novel*, ed. Emory Elliott et al. (New York: Columbia University Press, 1991), 244.
17. *Report of the Celebration*, 406–7; "Lecture by Thomas Nelson Page," *Yale Daily News*, May 18, 1898.
18. Thomas Nelson Page, "Marse Chan," in *In Ole Virginia, or Marse Chan and Other Stories* (1887; repr., New York: Scribner's, 1920), 4, 10. "Marse Chan" first appeared in the *Century*

Magazine, April 1884, 932–42. For different readings of Page, see Fred Hobson, *Tell about the South: The Southern Rage to Explain* (Baton Rouge: Louisiana State University Press, 1983), 132–44; and Edmund Wilson, *Patriotic Gore: Studies in the Literature of the American Civil War* (1962; Boston: Northeastern University Press, 1984), 604–16. And on Page, also see Blight, *Race and Reunion*, 222–27.

19. "Yale Log," *Yale Daily News*, December 1, 1903; Thomas Nelson Page, *The Old South: Essays Social and Political* (New York: Scribner's, 1892), 4. Also see Blight, *Race and Reunion*, 227.
20. On how *Huckleberry Finn* was treated by critics in its early years and the role of William Dean Howells in reviving widespread interest in Twain, see Henry F. May, *The End of American Innocence: The First Years of Our Own Time, 1912–1917* (New York: Oxford University Press, 1959), 46–47.
21. Twain's "secret sigh" quotation in Sarah B. Daugherty, "William Dean Howells and Mark Twain: The Realism War as a Campaign That Failed," *American Literary Realism* 29, no. 1 (Fall 1996): 24; Mark Twain, *The Autobiography of Mark Twain*, ed. Charles Neider (1917; repr., New York: Perennial Classics, 1966), 456; Mark Twain, *The Adventures of Huckleberry Finn* (1885; repr., Boston: Houghton Mifflin, 1958), 268.
22. Brooks Mather Kelley, *Yale: A History* (New Haven, CT: Yale University Press, 1974), 318. Kelley dubs the period of Hadley's presidency "revival."
23. "Southern Club Organized," *Yale Daily News*, February 5, 1890; "Southern Club," *Yale Daily News*, February 10, 1890. The possibility of forming a Southern club was mentioned as early as December 3, 12, 1884, and June 12, 1885, in the *Yale Daily News*. On Harvard, see "Yale Log," *Yale Daily News*, March 12, 1888; and "Southern Club Dinner," *Harvard Crimson*, February 24, 1890.
24. See *Yale Banner* 54 (1895): 283; 55 (1896): 299; 60 (1901): 387–88.
25. "Yale Stick," *Yale Daily News*, May 30, 1904; "Yale and the South," *Yale Alumni Weekly*, December 21, 1904, 236.
26. "Pres. Hadley in Charleston," *Yale Alumni Weekly*, April 12, 1905, 556–57.
27. "Pres. Hadley in the South," *Yale Alumni Weekly*, April 19, 1905, 573; "The Dallas Meeting," *Yale Alumni Weekly*, April 26, 1905, 591; "New Orleans Meeting," *Yale Alumni Weekly*, May 10, 1905, 624.
28. "Yale Spirit in the South," *Yale Daily News*, April 19, 1913; "Pres. Hadley in Charleston."
29. "Yale Baccalaureate Address," *Yale Daily News*, June 27, 1906.
30. "Matriculation Sermon Delivered," *Yale Daily News*, September 30, 1912.
31. "Graduate Statistics," *Yale Daily News*, November 6, 1908; "Directory of Living Graduates," *Yale Daily News*, October 25, 1912; Depew quoted in James Charles Cobb, *Away Down South: A History of Southern Identity* (New York: Oxford University Press, 2005), 76.
32. *A Sentimental Journey through South Carolina via Robertson's Special* [. . .] *"Yale '85," April Sixth to Twelfth, 1913* (New York: American Bank Note, 1913), 7, 25–26, 33. For Northern tourism in the postwar South, see Nina Silber, *The Romance of Reunion: Northerners and the South, 1865–1900* (Chapel Hill: University of North Carolina Press, 1993), 66–92.
33. "Calhoun Memorial," *Yale Daily News*, April 20, 1915.

34. "Yale and the South," *Yale Daily News*, May 4, 1915. Hadley referred to Jabez W. Huntington, an 1806 graduate of Yale College who served in the U.S. Senate from 1840 until his death in 1847. Calhoun served in the Senate during some of the same years (1832–43 and 1845–50); "Senators (1789–Present)," United States Senate, accessed September 13, 2023, https://www.senate.gov/senators/Senators1789toPresent.htm. And see Franklin Bowditch Dexter, *Biographical Sketches of the Graduates of Yale College* [. . .] (New Haven, CT: Yale University Press, 1912), 6:38–40.
35. J. W. Manning Sr., "The Cry of the Children of Slavery," August 21, 1902, handwritten manuscript in possession of Walter B. Sanderson III and Darlene Sanderson.
36. William M. Ashby, "Black Yale, circa 1915," *Yale Alumni Magazine*, January 1970, 26–28; Pollard quotation in Julie Des Jardins, *Walter Camp: Football and the Modern Man* (New York: Oxford University Press, 2015), 241. Ashby graduated from the Yale Divinity School in 1916 and went on to become the first African American social worker in New Jersey and a distinguished community leader. See William Ashby, *Tales without Hate* (Newark, NJ: Newark Preservation and Landmarks Committee, 1980); and Dennis Hevesi, "William Ashby, Longtime Worker for Civil Rights, Is Dead at 101," *New York Times*, May 19, 1991. On Pollard, see "Remembering Fritz Pollard," Brown University Library, accessed July 24, 2023, https://library.brown.edu/cds/pollard/frames.html; and John M. Carroll, *Fritz Pollard: Pioneer in Racial Advancement* (Urbana: University of Illinois Press, 1998).
37. Ashby, "Black Yale, circa 1915," 29. Mr. Holland was likely Morris K. Holland, listed as "head waiter, dining hall" in the 1920 federal census. See 1920 Census, Ward 9, New Haven, Connecticut, Roll T625_191, p. 8B, Enumeration District 362, Ancestry.com.
38. "Yale Dining Club Waiters on Washington," *New York Age*, November 25, 1915.
39. "1916 Bicentennial Plans," *Yale Alumni Weekly*, September 22, 1916, 10; George Henry Nettleton, ed., *The Book of the Yale Pageant, 21 October 1916, in Commemoration of the Two Hundredth Anniversary of the Removal of Yale College to New Haven* (New Haven, CT: Yale University Press, 1916), 46–53, 201–5, 94–100.

CHAPTER 12. YALE'S CIVIL WAR MEMORIAL

Epigraph: Frederick Douglass, "Monuments of Folly," *New National Era*, December 1, 1870.

1. "National Monument Audit," Monument Lab and Andrew W. Mellon Foundation, accessed September 14, 2023, https://monumentlab.com/audit. The Monument Lab Audit was first published on September 21, 2021, but has been updated since. And see Jillian McManemin, Toppled Monuments Archive, accessed September 14, 2023, https://www.toppledmonumentsarchive.org/. And also see Nora McGreevy, "Scholars Spent a Year Scrutinizing America's Monuments. Here's What They Learned," *Smithsonian Magazine*, October 1, 2021; and "Whose Heritage? Public Symbols of the Confederacy (Third Edition)," Southern Poverty Law Center, February 1, 2022, https://www.splcenter.org/20220201/whose-heritage-public-symbols-confederacy-third-edition. Of some 2,089 Confederate monuments of varying kinds counted by the Southern Poverty Law Center, the vast majority are in former Confederate states; the Union states and the District of Columbia contain 44; the nonseceded border states, 102; and states admitted to the

Union since the war, 30. One Confederate monument exists in Puerto Rico. This means that the Yale memorial, which openly honors the Confederate dead, is in a tiny minority of such memorials on Northern soil.

2. Albert M. Rosenblatt, ed., *The Judges of the New York Court of Appeals: A Biographical History* (New York: Fordham University Press, 2007), https://history.nycourts.gov/biography/francis-miles-finch/. And on Finch, see David W. Blight, *Race and Reunion: The Civil War in American Memory* (Cambridge, MA: Harvard University Press, 2001), 84–85.
3. The first "Decoration Day" was observed by African American former slaves in Charleston, South Carolina, on May 1, 1865. On the origins of Memorial Day generally, see Blight, *Race and Reunion*, 64–97; and David W. Blight, "Forgetting Why We Remember," *New York Times*, May 30, 2011.
4. Francis Miles Finch, "The Blue and the Gray," *Atlantic Monthly*, September 1867, 369–70.
5. Scholarship on Civil War memory and monuments has seen major growth for more than two decades. Among other important works, see Caroline Janney, *Remembering the Civil War: Reunion and the Limits of Reconciliation* (Chapel Hill: University of North Carolina Press, 2013); W. Fitzhugh Brundage, *The Southern Past: A Clash of Race and Memory* (Cambridge, MA: Harvard University Press, 2008); Gaines M. Foster, *Ghost of the Confederacy: Defeat, the Lost Cause, and the Emergence of the New South, 1865–1913* (New York: Oxford University Press, 1987); Thomas J. Brown, *Civil War Monuments and the Militarization of America* (Chapel Hill: University of North Carolina Press, 2019); Kevin M. Levin, *Searching for Black Confederates: The Civil War's Most Persistent Myth* (Chapel Hill: University of North Carolina Press, 2019); Kevin M. Levin, *Civil War Memory* (blog), https://kevinmlevin.substack.com/; and Blight, *Race and Reunion*. This is only a sampling and reflects some of the author's favorites.
6. "*Cogite Concilium, et Pacem laudate sedentes*," July 4, 1865, report of a committee to advise the alumni on a "permanent memorial in honor of those who have given up their lives in the good cause"; "Yale College Soldiers' Festival," July 16, 1865; "Patriotic Commemoration," July 26, 1865; letter from subcommittee appointed to "mature some plan for a Permanent Memorial, in honor of the sons of Yale," April 30, 1866; letter titled "Yale College Memorial Chapel," January 20, 1867, that includes the hiring of New York architects Vaux, Withers, & Co., all in "Material Relating to Yale University and the Civil War," Manuscripts and Archives, Yale University Library.
7. "Soldiers' and Sailors' Monument," Connecticut's Civil War Monuments, accessed September 14, 2023, https://chs.org/finding_aides/ransom/074.htm. Extensive planning of several years went into the design and construction of the Soldiers' and Sailors' Monument. It was originally conceived for the town green, but plans shifted. The artists were John M. Moffit and Alexander Doyle; the granite was brought from Hallowell, Maine, and cut at the firm of Smith and Sperry of New Haven.
8. *Yale Daily News*, January 12, 1895, February 27, October 3, 1896, May 7, 8, 18, 1901.
9. Catherine Lynn, "Building Yale and Razing It from the Civil War to the Great Depression," in *Yale in New Haven: Architecture and Urbanism*, by Vincent Scully et al. (New Haven, CT: Yale University, 2004), 176, 178.

10. Lynn, 176, 179–81, 373n251. The Phelps Stokeses were longtime supporters and promoters of colonization, Tuskegee, Booker T. Washington, and his vision of industrial-style education and uplift. In 1929, the Phelps-Stokes Fund, established with a bequest from Caroline Phelps Stokes, founded the Booker Washington Institute in Liberia, in cooperation with the American Colonization Society. See Angela Elisabeth Zimmerman, *Alabama in Africa: Booker T. Washington, the German Empire, and the Globalization of the New South* (Princeton, NJ: Princeton University Press, 2010), 202–4. The first flag of Liberia was created in one of the Phelps Stokes homes. See Eric S. Yellin, "The (White) Search for (Black) Order: The Phelps-Stokes Fund's First Twenty Years, 1911–1931," *Historian* 65, no. 2 (Winter 2002): 328–29, 321n3.
11. Thomas Nelson Page to Richard Gilder, March 31, 1885, quoted in Nina Silber, *The Romance of Reunion: Northerners and the South, 1865–1900* (Chapel Hill: University of North Carolina Press, 1993), 113; and for Silber's astute analysis of how much Southern writers like Page appealed to Northern readers and consumers of popular culture, see 93–123.
12. Lynn, "Building Yale," 176, 179.
13. Robert Lowell, "For the Union Dead," in *For the Union Dead* (New York: Farrar, Straus and Giroux, 1967), 72; Blight, *Race and Reunion*, 258.
14. Blight, *Race and Reunion*, 258–59, 264–65, 272, 277–78; "Terms as to Who Was 'Right,' Etc.," *Confederate Veteran* 17 (July 1909): 313.
15. "Theodore Dwight Woolsey, 1896," Visitor Center, Yale University, accessed June 26, 2023, https://visitorcenter.yale.edu/tours/public-art-yale; Patrick L. Pinnell, *The Campus Guide: Yale University, an Architectural Tour* (Princeton, NJ: Princeton Architectural Press, 1999), 14.
16. *Yale Daily News*, September 29, 1903; "Yale Baccalaureate Address," *Yale Daily News*, June 27, 1906; W. E. B. Du Bois, "Robert E. Lee," *Crisis*, March 1928, 97.
17. Guy Carleton Lee, *The True History of the Civil War* (Philadelphia: Lippincott, 1903); Theodore Clark Smith, review of *The True History of the Civil War*, by Guy Carleton Lee, *American Historical Review* 9, no. 4 (July 1904): 839–42; *Yale Daily News*, January 23, 1907. On Jefferson Davis's memoir, see Blight, *Race and Reunion*, 259–61.
18. *Yale Daily News*, June 17, 1909; Ellsworth Eliot, *Yale in the Civil War* (New Haven, CT: Yale University Press, 1932), 60–61.
19. Nathaniel Cheairs Hughes Jr., *Yale's Confederates: A Biographical Dictionary* (Knoxville: University of Tennessee Press, 2008), 87–88; *Obituary Record of Graduates of Yale University Deceased from June, 1910, to July, 1915* (New Haven, CT: Published by the University, 1915), 545–47, 835–37; Anson Phelps Stokes, *Yale Endowments: A Description of the Various Gifts and Bequests Establishing Permanent University Funds* (Yale University, 1917), 98–99; "Howland Prize Awarded," *New York Times*, January 20, 1937, 18.
20. Howland quoted in Ali Frick, "The Mingled Dust of Both Armies Yale's Compromised Civil War Memorial" (unpublished essay), April 9, 2007; Simeon E. Baldwin to Talcott H. Russell, January 12, 1910, Box 1, Folder 2, Committee on the Civil War Memorial (RU 529), Manuscripts and Archives, Yale University Library; *Yale Daily News*, March 16, 1910; H. A. Beers to Russell, March 17, 1910, Box 1, Folder 13, Committee on Civil War Memorial.

21. "Monument to the Yale Men Who Died in the War," *Savannah News*, February 17, 1910, Box 1, Folder 16; Henry P. Wright to Talcott Russell, January 30, 1912, March 26, 1912, April 2, 1912, and March 15, 1912, Box 1, Folder 12; Lee McClung to Russell, Jan. 12, 1910, Box 1, Folder 7; Anson Phelps Stokes Jr. to Russell, March 30, 1910, Box 1, Folder 10; Frank L. Polk to Russell, April 1, 1910, Box 1, Folder 8; Charles H. Strong to Russell, April 7, 1910, Box 1, Folder 11; W. W. Gordon to Russell, April 12, April 18, 1910, Box 1, Folder 5, Committee on the Civil War Memorial (emphasis in the original).
22. Talcott H. Russell, "Movement to Establish a Memorial to Yale Men Who Lost Their Lives in the War between the States, Read before the New Haven County Historical Society," April 18, 1910, 3, 7–9, Material relating to Yale University and the Civil War, Manuscripts and Archives, Yale University Library.
23. Russell, "Movement," 9–12.
24. Russell, "Movement," 12–16.
25. Charles H. Strong to Russell, April 20, July 29, 1910, Box 1, Folder 11; W. W. Gordon to Russell, May 6, November 14, 1910, January 12, 1911, June 6, 1912, Box 1, Folder 5; Anson Stokes to Russell, October 27, 1910, Box 1, Folder 10, Committee on the Civil War Memorial.
26. Daniel Chester French to Russell, January 10, July 3, July 23, August 7, 1911, Box 1, Folder 4; Stokes to Henry Howland, August 4, 1911, Box 1, Folder 10; and Stokes Jr. to Talcott Russell, "A meeting of the Executive Committee on the Civil War Memorial was held in New York, Monday, October 9, 1911. There were present Mr. Polk and Mr. Stokes," undated, Box 1, Folder 14, Committee on the Civil War Memorial.
27. French to Russell, August 7, 1911; "Fall Corporation Meeting," *Yale Daily News*, September 24, 1913; Henry Bacon to Frank L. Polk, February 13, 1912, Box 1, Folder 1; Frank L. Polk to Russell, July 19, 1912, Box 1, Folder 8; W. L. Cross to Stokes Jr., October 12, 1912, Box 1, Folder 10; Talcott Russell, "To the Alumni of Yale University," June 18, 1912, Box 1, Folder 14; minutes from January 28, 1913, meeting, Box 1, Folder 10, Committee on the Civil War Memorial.
28. Arthur Twining Hadley, "Matriculation Sermon," *Yale Daily News*, September 30, 1912.
29. *Yale Daily News*, September 24, October 11, 1913; Committee on the Civil War Memorial, circular sent to Yale graduates soliciting donations for the Civil War Memorial, drafted October 1, 1913, Box 22, Folder 287, Office of the Secretary (RU 49); C. W. Johnson, "Lynching Information," Tuskegee University, November 16, 2020, http://archive.tuskegee.edu/repository/digital-collection/lynching-information/.
30. Ida Wells-Barnett, "Lynching Our National Crime," in *Proceedings of the National Negro Conference, New York, May 31–June 1, 1909*, https://librarycollections.law.umn.edu/documents/darrow/Proceedings%20of%20the%20National%20Negro%20Conference%201909_%20New%20York_%20May%2031%20and%20June_1.pdf, 174–79; Taft address to the National League of Negroes, May 2, 1912, pamphlet, https://www.gilderlehrman.org/collection/glc09588; Blight, *Race and Reunion*, 357.
31. For Johnson's poem, see "Fifty Years: To-day Is the Fiftieth Anniversary of Lincoln's Emancipation Proclamation," *New York Times*, January 1, 1913. On African American commemorations and exhibitions, see Blight, *Race and Reunion*, 303–37, 368–80; and Mitch Kachun, *Festivals of Freedom: Meaning and Memory in African American Emancipation Celebrations, 1808–1915* (Amherst: University of Massachusetts Press, 2003).

32. *Yale Daily News*, December 5, 6, 1913; D. E. Burton to Frank Polk, March 3, 1915, Box 22, Folder 287, Office of the Secretary.
33. "Civil War Memorial Dedication Memorial Hall, Yale University," June 20, 1915, Box 270, Folder 5, Office of the Secretary; speeches in *Yale Daily News*, October 2, 1915.
34. *Yale Alumni Weekly*, June 3, 1914.

INTERLUDE: THE BIRTH OF A NATION *IN NEW HAVEN, 1915*

1. On Washington's last public appearances in New Haven, see chapter 11.
2. Nicholas Forster, "'A Most Serious Loss in Business': Race, Citizenship and Protest in New Haven, Connecticut," in *In the Shadow of "The Birth of a Nation": Racism, Reception, and Resistance*, ed. Melvyn Stokes and Paul McEwan (New York: Palgrave Macmillan, 2023), 148–49.
3. For westward migrations of Black Americans, see *Crisis*, July 1913, 130–32; Thomas Cripps, *Slow Fade to Black: The Negro in American Film, 1900–1942* (New York: Oxford University Press, 1993), 26–32; and Raymond A. Cook, *Thomas Dixon* (New York: Twayne, 1974).
4. Dixon quoted in Cripps, *Slow Fade to Black*, 44. On Griffith, see Michael Rogin, "'The Sword Became a Flashing Vision': D. W. Griffith's *The Birth of a Nation*," *Representations* 9 (Winter 1985): 150–94; and John Hope Franklin, "'Birth of a Nation'—Propaganda as History," *Massachusetts Review* 20 (Autumn 1979): 417–24.
5. See David W. Blight, *Race and Reunion: The Civil War in American Memory* (Cambridge, MA: Harvard University Press, 2001), 394–95.
6. Charles Flint Kellogg, *A History of the National Association for the Advancement of Colored People* (Baltimore: Johns Hopkins University Press, 1967), 142; *Crisis*, May 1915, 40–42; *Crisis*, June 1915, 87; Thomas R. Cripps, "The Reaction of the Negro to the Motion Picture Birth of a Nation," *Historian* 25, no. 3 (May 1963): 344–62; Cripps, *Slow Fade to Black*, 53–65.
7. James Weldon Johnson, "Uncle Tom's Cabin and the Clansman," *New York Age*, March 4, 1915; James Weldon Johnson, "A Trap," *New York Age*, May 6, 1915.
8. Forster, "'Most Serious Loss,'" 149–51.
9. Forster, 152–56.
10. "At the Theaters," *Yale Daily News*, November 2, 1915.
11. Frederick Douglass, "The Color Line," *North American Review*, June 1881, in *Frederick Douglass: Speeches and Writings*, ed. David W. Blight (New York: Library of America, 2022), 647; W. E. B. Du Bois, *The Souls of Black Folk*, ed. Henry Louis Gates Jr. (New York: Oxford University Press, 2007), 6.

EPILOGUE

Epigraph: W. E. B. Du Bois, *Black Reconstruction in America, 1860–1880* (1935; repr., New York: Atheneum, 1972), 714.

1. See Andrew Delbanco, *College: What It Was, Is, and Should Be* (Princeton, NJ: Princeton University Press, 2012), 47–51; and Paul Connerton, *How Societies Remember* (Cambridge: Cambridge University Press, 1989), 1–40. I rely here on Delbanco's use of the terms "grace" and "mystery."
2. "Mission Statement," Yale, accessed August 17, 2023, https://www.yale.edu/about-yale/mission-statement.

3. Delbanco, *College*, 10–11.
4. L. P. Hartley, *The Go-Between* (1953; repr., New York: Penguin Books, 1979), 3; on generations, see Amy Corning and Howard Schuman, *Generations and Collective Memory* (Chicago: University of Chicago Press, 2015), 1–17, 207–9.
5. Marc Bloch, *The Historian's Craft: Reflections on the Nature and Uses of History and the Techniques and Methods of the Men Who Write It* (New York: Knopf, 1953), 43.
6. Bloch, 71, 73–75.
7. Delbanco, *College*, 21–22.
8. Evelyn Brooks Higginbotham, afterword to *Slavery and the University: Histories and Legacies*, ed. Leslie M. Harris, James T. Campbell, and Alfred L. Brophy (Athens: University of Georgia Press, 2019), 338–42.
9. Richard Wightman Fox, *Reinhold Niebuhr: A Biography* (Ithaca, NY: Cornell University Press, 1985), 23–40.
10. Reinhold Niebuhr, *The Irony of American History* (1952; repr., Chicago: University of Chicago Press, 2008), 2.
11. Niebuhr, 158–62, 169.
12. On Pickens, see chapter 10; William Pickens Papers Finding Aid, James Weldon Johnson Collection, Yale Collection of American Literature, Beinecke Rare Book and Manuscript Library; and William Pickens, *Bursting Bonds, and the Heir of Slaves* (Boston: Jordan and More, 1923).
13. William Pickens, "The Constitutional Status of the Negro from 1860–1870," *Papers of the American Negro Academy*, read at the nineteenth annual meeting, December 28–29, 1915 (Washington, DC, 1916), 63–64.
14. Pickens, 67–69.
15. Pickens, 69–72.
16. Niebuhr, *Irony of American History*, 174.

Acknowledgments

This book has been uniquely collaborative, built on the labors of generations of scholars, archivists, descendants, staff, and community members. Just since the inception of the Yale and Slavery Research Project in late 2020, we have amassed a long list of debts. It is a pleasure to thank some of our key contributors and colleagues here.

Much research for this project was undertaken by Yale students. Kate Kushner, then a student at Yale College, was one of our first researchers. With tremendous perseverance, Kate navigated the obstacles of conducting archival research in the midst of the COVID-19 pandemic, doing valuable work in early American newspapers, the Amos Beman scrapbooks, and Ezra Stiles's diary, among other collections. Teanu Reid, a PhD candidate in history, served as one of our team leaders when we were first conceptualizing and starting the research. Teanu's work on Connecticut Hall and the West Indies trade was foundational for our early chapters, and the project as a whole benefited greatly from her intellectual leadership and her deep knowledge of the seventeenth and eighteenth centuries. Steven Rome, then a student at Yale College, mined decades' worth of *Yale Daily News* issues, along with other sources, tracing and synthesizing some of the most significant and revelatory stories in this volume. His superb research guides on topics such as campus culture, intellectual discourse, Confederate memory, and Black education will serve as indispensable resources for future scholars. Emily Yankowitz, a PhD candidate, brought her considerable talents as a researcher and editor to this project while she was researching and writing her own dissertation. Her scholarly acumen and careful eye have made this a much better book, and we are especially grateful for her assistance with fact-checking the manuscript.

Our team benefited tremendously from the contributions of Daniel Lanpher and Jane Coppock; as veteran historians in their own right, they were stalwarts of this project. Daniel conducted deep archival research, producing meticulous dossiers. His talents as a researcher are legendary among many Yale faculty. Jane, who retired from the School of the Environment at Yale, has been a special asset to our team. Her willingness to take on any research topic, track down any lead, and think creatively about so many issues has strengthened the book and the project as a whole. She is also a marvelous editor. We are grateful for the many months of work Jane devoted to our shared endeavor.

We lost two research partners when other institutions gained them as faculty members. Bennett Parten, PhD, was a core member of our team early on, convening our nineteenth-century experts and helping us identify topics and turning points within a complex timeline. Ben, along with Teanu and Steven, also delivered special online talks about our research. James Shinn, PhD, contributed helpful dossiers on early donors and leaders before moving on to his new job. Students leave, as they should and must; this project makes me miss them more than usual.

A number of other Yale students conducted various kinds of research for this project, and we thank them for their time and efforts: Fisayo Akinlude, Miguel Ceballo-Countryman, Bhasha Chakrabarti, Christy Charnel, Ambre Dromgoole, Sami Elrazky, Sydney Green, Nithya Krishnamurthy, Chaka Laguerre, Kenya Loudd, Matthew Quallen, Wyatt Reynolds, Mariko Rooks, and Charlie Tran. We are also grateful to Ry Walker and Thalia Pitti, whose research conducted on behalf of the Gilder Lehrman Center before the start of this project was valuable here as well. Tarel Dennie (Yale class of 2024), a community engagement intern at the Beinecke Rare Book and Manuscript Library, generously shared his transcriptions of documents related to Margaret and Bias Stanley. And we are grateful to faculty colleagues Crystal Feimster and Edward Rugemer, as well as all the students in their fall 2021 seminar, Slavery, Race and Yale.

Harold Rose and Susan Sawyer in the Office of the General Counsel volunteered as researchers. We thank them both and would like to particularly acknowledge Harold's painstaking research in the New Haven Custom House records. The volunteer spirit on the part of these distinguished attorneys is especially endearing.

Early on in this project, we benefited from hearing about the experiences of scholars engaged in similar work at peer institutions; we warmly thank Sven Beckert, Daina Ramey Berry, James Campbell, Marcia Chatelain, Tiffany Momon, Woody Register, Martha Sandweiss, and Kirt von Daacke. In the summer of 2021, we learned much from scholars who joined us for online seminars to help frame and inform the research: Anne Farrow, coauthor of *Complicity*, on Connecticut and the West Indies trade; Eric Herschthal, University of Utah, on the history of natural sciences at Yale; Kenneth Minkema, Jonathan Edwards Center, and distinguished Edwards scholar, on religion and slavery in colonial and early national New England and Connecticut; Frank Mitchell, historian and curator, coeditor of *African American Connecticut Explored*, on the history of slavery in Connecticut, relevant sources and organizations, and local reckonings; and Deborah Shapiro, former director of Middlesex Historical Society.

This project builds on the contributions of many others who have labored to illuminate Yale's history. Judith Ann Schiff, Yale's longtime chief research archivist, Yale University Library, devoted her career to preserving and sharing Yale and New Haven history. We benefited from the vast expertise and great enthusiasm she brought as a member of the working group before her death in 2022. Judy's memory is a blessing to all who knew her, and her writings endure in the research and the notes for this book.

Curtis Patton, PhD, professor emeritus at the Yale School of Public Health, and Ronald Mickens, PhD, Distinguished Fuller E. Callaway Professor of Physics at Clark Atlanta University, worked for many years to make Edward Bouchet's name and accomplishments better known. This book is in some measure a recognition of their perseverance, and we thank them for their faith and commitment to uplifting Black history at Yale, long before it received broad institutional support. We build on and acknowledge our debt to Antony Dugdale, J. J. Fueser, and J. Celso de Castro Alves, who as graduate students researched and authored the 2001 report "Yale, Slavery and Abolition."

Since its founding in 1969, the Afro-American Cultural Center at Yale has been a site of historical memory, recovery, and action. Through the work of the History Keepers Program and other initiatives, the House has helped preserve, reclaim, and share Black history. The Dixwell Community House (known as the Q House), founded in 1924, is a center for Black community life and historical memory in New Haven, as are the city's many historic Black churches. We also thank Dennis Culliton, Adrienne Joy Burns, and all those associated with the Witness Stones Project and the Amistad Committee for bringing forward the rich history of African Americans in New Haven and in Connecticut. Our work builds on, and we acknowledge our debts to, these and other efforts of recovery and remembrance at Yale and in New Haven.

We are grateful to David Alan Richards, writer and historian, for sharing his Yale-related research with us. Joseph Yannielli, a former PhD advisee and a gifted historian, graciously shared his research on the *Amistad* story and the Mendi mission. We also benefited from early conversations about slavery in Old Saybrook, Connecticut, with the Reverend David W. Good, the Reverend Steven R. Jungkeit, Tedd Levy, and Don Perreault.

This book cites scores of books and articles by generations of scholars past and present. Among the key works related to New Haven, Connecticut, and New England Black history, we acknowledge our reliance on and inspiration from works such as Robert Austin Warner, *New Haven Negroes: A Social History*; Elizabeth J. Normen, ed., *African American Connecticut Explored*, with Katherine J. Harris, Stacey K. Close, and William Frank Mitchell; David O. White, *Connecticut's Black Soldiers*; Ronald E. Mickens, ed., *Edward Bouchet: The First African-American Doctorate*; Kurt Schmoke, "The Dixwell Avenue Congregational Church, 1829–1896" (1971); Craig Steven Wilder, *Ebony and Ivy: Race, Slavery, and the Troubled History of America's Universities*; Alfred L. Brophy, *University, Court, and Slave: Proslavery Thought in Southern Colleges and Courts and the Coming of the Civil War*; and many more.

We could not have done this project without the Yale Library—its vast and marvelous collections as well as its wonderful staff. Michael Lotstein, university archivist, and staff throughout Beinecke Library and other special collections have helped us locate, retrieve, and access countless resources for this project. Among many others, we thank Melissa Barton, Jessica Becker, Mary Ellen Budney, Jennifer Coggins, Tubyez Cropper, Joan Duffy, Moira Fitzgerald, Stephen Goeman, Melissa Grafe, Kathryn James, Scott Libson, Jonathan Manton, George Miles, Anu Paul, and Stephen Ross. Thanks to their enthusiasm and commitment, we know that the work of elevating and sharing Yale's complex history will continue to grow. Tubyez also served as filmmaker and media expert for many of our events.

Individuals at many other institutions provided valuable assistance, and we thank the following organizations and their staffs: the New Haven Museum and Whitney Library; Fairfield Slavery Project: The Vincent J. Rosivach Register of Slaves, especially Alec Lurie; Wethersfield Historical Society, especially Gillie

Johnson; Rhode Island Historical Society; Newport Historical Society; Westport Museum for History and Culture; and Wilson Special Collections Library, University of North Carolina at Chapel Hill. And we thank Walter B. Sanderson III and Darlene Sanderson for graciously sharing cherished family documents from their private collection with us. Leslie Frost at the University of North Carolina at Chapel Hill read portions of the manuscript and made valuable suggestions, especially for the introduction.

Conversations with the Yale and Slavery Working Group, convened by President Peter Salovey in fall 2020, helped launch this project and this book. Every member deserves special thanks for helping put this project on sure footing and sharing their ideas and insights: Adrienne Joy Burns, Deborah R. Coen, Crystal Feimster, James Forman Jr., Jay Gitlin, John Stuart Gordon, Gerald Jaynes, Willie James Jennings, Michael Lotstein, Kenneth Minkema, Michael Morand, Risë Nelson, Stephen Pitti, Carolyn Roberts, Edward Rugemer, Judith Schiff (dearly departed), Edward Town, and Charles Warner Jr. I am personally very thankful to all of these colleagues for their selfless devotion to this effort.

From the outset, we wanted to share our work as broadly and with as many communities as possible. The pivot to online events during the pandemic allowed us to reach even larger audiences, especially through the Yale and Slavery in Historical Perspective Conference, held over Zoom on October 28–30, 2021. We are grateful to all participants: Elizabeth Alexander, Daina Berry, Paola Bertucci, Catherine Brekus, Adrienne Joy Burns, Deborah Coen, Christine DeLucia, Sami Elrazky, Anne Farrow, Crystal Feimster, Cheryl Finley, James Forman Jr., John Stuart Gordon, Dora Guo, Jonathan Holloway, Daniel Martinez HoSang, Willie Jennings, Nithya Krishnamurthy, Michael Lotstein, Courtney J. Martin, Kenneth Minkema, Frank Mitchell, Louis P. Nelson, Bennett Parten, Kymberly Pinder, Romita Ray, Marcus Rediker (presenting for Eric Kimball), Teanu Reid, Carolyn Roberts, Dorothy Roberts, Steven Rome, Mariko Rooks, Edward Rugemer, Peter Salovey, Barbara Earl Thomas, Edward Town, Charlie Tran, Kirt von Daacke, Charles Warner Jr., Deborah Gray White, and Craig Wilder. On behalf of all involved, I personally thank Dan HoSang for his intrepid pedagogical and intellectual leadership of the student group studying eugenics. Their presentations and writings have a life of their own, especially for a future second volume.

We gratefully acknowledge the following individuals who participated in virtual events organized by the Gilder Lehrman Center for the Yale and Slavery Research Project: Rebecca Amonor, Kahlil Greene, Henry Jacob, Matthew Quallen, Eden Senay, and Nina Todd in the "Student Perspectives" presentation on

February 25, 2021; Newman Baker, Jamie Weems, Charles Warner Jr., Rebecca Motley, and Valerie Rooks in "Gleaming in the Shadow of Slavery: A Conversation with Descendants of African Americans of Old Yale" on September 16, 2021; and Christy Charnel, Deborah Coen, Daniel Martinez HoSang, Nithya Krishnamurthy, Mariko Rooks, Angela Saini, and Charlie Tran in "From Slavery to Eugenics: Confronting Legacies of Racism in Medicine and across the Disciplines" on April 20, 2022. We also thank those who participated in the Mondays at Beinecke online presentations organized by the library: Michael Morand in the "Reckoning with History: 1748 Map of New Haven" on February 15, 2021, "1831 Proposal for a Black College in New Haven" on September 13, 2021, "Revisiting Jethro Luke and Race and Slavery in 18th Century New Haven and Yale" on April 27, 2022, and "W. E. B. Du Bois in New Haven and in the Archives at Yale" on February 13, 2023; Adrienne Joy Burns and George Miles in "Sketches of the Amistad Captives and Contemporary Commemoration" on March 29, 2021; Kenneth Minkema in "Jonathan Edwards and Slavery" on June 14, 2021; Regina Mason in "Life of William Grimes" on September 27, 2021; Ben Parten in "Yale and the Politics of Slavery in the 19th Century" on October 4, 2021; Steven Rome in "Reconciliation and Race at Yale's Civil War Memorial" on October 10, 2021; Jason Mancini in "Ezra Stiles, Census Making, and Indian Erasure in New England" on November 1, 2021; Eric Herschthal on "Science and Slavery at Yale" on November 15, 2021; Alvin Ashiatey, Tubyez Cropper, and Charles Warner Jr. in "What Could Have Been" on April 21, 2022; Tarel Dennie and Michael Morand in "Grove Street Cemetery, Bias and Margaret Stanley" on October 17, 2022; and Hope McGrath in "Finding Robert M. Park in the Archives and in New Haven" on April 24, 2023; as well as Edward Town in "at Home: Art in Context | New Light on a Portrait of Elihu Yale, His Family, and an Enslaved Child," online from the Yale Center for British Art on April 27, 2021.

One of the most compelling events in this book is that of the aborted attempt to establish the nation's first Black college in New Haven. Many people already know this story thanks to the magnificent short documentary film *What Could Have Been: America's First HBCU*, created by Tubyez Cropper with Alvin Ashiatey, Michel Morand, and Charles Warner Jr. Here we express our gratitude to them for uplifting this crucial history.

Many people helped make this book stronger. We are especially grateful to Christine DeLucia, Ken Minkema, Mark Petersen, and Ed Rugemer for reading early chapters and providing valuable feedback. For reading the full manuscript and offering insightful comments, we thank the three anonymous readers for Yale University Press and John Fabian Witt, Allen H. Duffy Class of 1960 Professor of Law and professor of history at Yale. They caught mistakes and prodded us on to deeper thinking, insights, and precision with prose. The talented people at Yale University Press made it possible for us to share our work with the world in record time. For their heroic efforts, we especially thank Adina Popescu, our editor; John Donatich; and Eva Skewes.

Many friends and organizations bolstered this book project simply through extended conversations and by inviting me to speak on the subject. I especially thank John Pepper and Owen Williams on this account. Both love Yale and want its history told well. Luis C. deBaca and Lorena Chambers also discussed this project with me more than they may have wished. Dean Heather Gerken of Yale Law School invited Michael Morand and me to address a meeting of her faculty. The Association of Board Secretaries for the Ivy League universities and several others, the good residents of Bay View in Michigan, numerous Yale alumni groups, and the Legacies of American Slavery project at the Gilder Lehrman Center, done in conjunction with the Council of Independent Colleges, all afforded me opportunities to lecture on this research in progress.

President Peter Salovey, Chief of Staff Susan Gibbons, and their staff deserve special and deep thanks for supporting this endeavor. In our many conversations, and in several presentations to trustees, deans, vice presidents, and other university administrators, we have discovered how fully and seriously Yale and its leadership support this work. I am personally grateful for the confidence Peter and Susan extended to me and to all in the project.

Some of my greatest debts go to the staff of the Gilder Lehrman Center. Associate Director Michelle Zacks has served as an administrative one-person headquarters for this book, as well as an expert reader and organizer of our webinars and our major conference. Michelle made communication between all zones of this project—the president's office, Beinecke Library, researchers and authors, and countless participants in events—operate smoothly. She gave countless hours and days and nights to the cause, and it could not have been finished without her. Melissa McGrath held our office in order, helped me organize my work life and schedule, did all logistics for conferences and gatherings, and processed all payments and communications to our researchers. They and I thank her endlessly. Daniel Vieira, our technology and media expert, planned and executed more events, online and in person, than any of us can calculate. He took several striking photographs, four of which we include in chapter 12. Tom Thurston helped steady our ship with his incomparable knowledge of the field and of the world of teaching. Lisa Monroe managed our Legacies of American Slavery project and supported the cause of this book.

Finally, my deepest thanks of all are to Michael Morand and Hope McGrath. Early in the project, Michael and I in effect cochaired the working group and coplanned each tentative step in our work. His place in the Beinecke Library as director of community engagement made his leadership crucial to this book ever seeing the light of day. His connections in town and around the university made my job possible. Michael's knowledge of the collections, his enthusiastic assembly of documents in Beinecke classrooms, and his toastmaster's ability in presenting them have carried the story we tell to many at Yale and in the communities beyond. Yale has countless people who make it such a special place of learning; none are more important to so many different constituencies than Michael Morand. Thanks for the two and a half years of joy and battle and argument over lemon chicken soup at Yorkside. And thanks for calling me when I wanted to quit.

I thank God and Peter Salovey for the wisdom of sending us Hope from his own staff. A very talented historian with a PhD in American history from the University of Pennsylvania, Hope had been working as a writer and researcher in the president's office until assigned to us. She expertly led our research team, kept them all on task, and assembled dossiers of documents that in turn were sent to me. Hope further wrote two full chapters of the book, chapters 10 and 11, and four of the five interludes. Michael wrote chapter 6. We all edited each other, again and again. Hope's enormous skills, her lucid writing, editing chops, and savvy grasp of Yale's mores, guided me as a writer and the book into existence.

—DAVID W. BLIGHT, August 18, 2023, New Haven, Connecticut

Index

Italicized page numbers indicate figures, illustrations, and photographs.